MULTIMEDIA TECHNOLOGY FOR APPLICATIONS

Also of Interest from IEEE Press ...

THE CIRCUITS AND FILTERS HANDBOOK
Copublished with CRC Press
Edited by Wai-Kai Chen
1995   Cloth   2896 pp   IEEE Product No. PC5631   ISBN 0-8493-8341-2

RANDOM PROCESSES FOR IMAGE AND SIGNAL PROCESSING
Copublished with SPIE Optical Engineering Press
Edited by Edward R. Dougherty
1998   Cloth   IEEE Product No. PC5732   ISBN 0-7803-3495-7

MICROSYSTEMS TECHNOLOGY FOR MULTIMEDIA APPLICATIONS: An Introduction
Edited by Bing J. Sheu
1995   Paper   752 pp   IEEE Product No. PP5370   ISBN 0-7803-1157-4

MULTIMEDIA TECHNOLOGY FOR APPLICATIONS

Edited by

Bing J. Sheu
University of Southern California

Mohammed Ismail
Ohio State University

Assistant Editors

Michelle Y. Wang
University of Southern California

Richard H. Tsai
University of Southern California

**IEEE
PRESS**

IEEE Circuits and Systems Society, *Sponsor*

IEEE Solid-State Circuits Society, *Sponsor*

The Institute of Electrical and Electronics Engineers, Inc., New York

This book and other books may be purchased at a discount
from the publisher when ordered in bulk quantities. Contact:

IEEE Press Marketing
Attn: Special Sales
445 Hoes Lane, P.O. Box 1331
Piscataway, NJ 08855-1331
Fax: (732) 981-9334

For more information about IEEE PRESS products,
visit the IEEE Home Page: http://www.ieee.org/

Printed in the United States of America

10   9   8   7   6   5   4   3   2   1

ISBN 0-7803-1174-4
IEEE Order Number: PC5645

Library of Congress Cataloging-in-Publication Data

Multimedia technology for applications / edited by Bing J. Sheu,
  Mohammed Ismail; assistant editors, Michelle Y. Wang, Richard H.
  Tsai.
     p.   cm.
  Includes bibliographical references and index.
  ISBN 0-7803-1174-4 (cloth)
  1. Multimedia systems.   I. Sheu, Bing J.   II. Ismail, Mohammed.
QA76.575.M85225   1998
006.7—dc21
                                         97-44804
                                           CIP

CONTENTS

Contents

LIST OF CONTRIBUTORS

CHAPTER 1

Dr. Atul Puri and Dr. Tsuhan Chen AT&T Laboratories—Research, Visual Communications Research Dept., 101 Crawfords Corner Road, Holmdel, NJ 07733-3030, U.S.A.

Professor Hsueh-Ming Hang Dept. of Electronics Engineering, National Chiao Tung University, Hsinchu City 300, Taiwan

CHAPTER 2

Dr. Horng-Dar Lin (NEC America) HolonTech Corp., 2039 Samaritan Dr., San Jose, CA 95124, U.S.A.

CHAPTER 3

Dr. I-Chang Jou Telecommunication Laboratories, P.O. Box 71, Chung-Li, 320, Taiwan

CHAPTER 4

Mr. Yoichi Oshima Semiconductor Devices Section, 4th Dept., Japanese Patent Office, 3-4-3 Kasumigaseki, Chiyoda-ku, Tokyo 100, JAPAN

Professor Bing Sheu and Steve H. Jen Powell Hall, Room 604, Dept. of Electrical Engineering, University of Southern California, Los Angeles, CA 90089-0271, U.S.A.

CHAPTER 5

Dr. Bryan Ackland and Dr. Alex Dickinson AT&T Laboratories—Research, 101 Crawfords Corner Road, Holmdel, NJ 07733-3030, U.S.A.

Dr. Eric R. Fossum Photobit LLC, 2529 Foothill Blvd., La Crescenta, CA 91214, U.S.A.

CHAPTER 6

Professors Abeer Alwan, Rajeev Jain, Greg Pottie, John Villasenor, Charles Chien, Etan Cohen*, and Leader Ho** Dept. of Electrical Engineering, University of California Los Angeles, CA 90024, U.S.A. (*Also with Angeles Design Systems) (**Also with LSI Logic Corp.)

CHAPTER 7

Dr. William O'Connell Lucent Technologies Inc., Bell Laboratories, 600 Mountain Avenue, Murray Hill, NJ 07974, U.S.A.

Dr. David Schrader NCR Corporation, 100 N. Sepulveda Blvd., El Segundo, CA 90245, U.S.A.

Dr. Homer Chen Rockwell International Science Center, 1049 Camino Dos Rios, Thousand Oaks, CA 91360, U.S.A.

CHAPTER 8

Professors S.-Y. Kung, Yin Chan, and Shang-Hung Lin Dept. of Electrical Engineering, Princeton University, Princeton, NJ 08544, U.S.A.

CHAPTER 9

Dr. Harold S. Stone NEC Research Institute, 4 Independence Way, Princeton, NJ 08540, U.S.A.

CHAPTER 10

Professor Ming-Syan Chen Dept. of Electrical Engineering, National Taiwan University, Taipei City 107, Taiwan

CHAPTER 11

Professor W. Melody Moh Dept. of Mathematics & Computer Science, San Jose State University, San Jose, CA 95192-0103, U.S.A.

CHAPTER 12

Dr. Chung-Sheng Li IBM T. J. Watson Research Center, P.O. Box 704, Room H4-B33, Yorktown Heights, NY 10598, U.S.A.

CHAPTER 13

Dr. B. J. Sano* and Professor A. F. J. Levi Dept. of Electrical Engineering, DRB-118, University of Southern California, Los Angeles, CA 90089-1111, U.S.A. (*Currently with Digital Equipment Corporation)

CHAPTER 14

Professor Oscal T.-C. Chen Dept. of Electrical Engineering, National Chung-Cheng University, Chia-Yi 621, Taiwan

CHAPTER 15

Professors Jhing-Fa Wang and Chung-Hsien Wu Institute of Information Engineering, National Cheng Kung University, Tainan City 701, Taiwan

CHAPTER 16

Professor Hsin-Chia Fu, Mou-Yen Chen*, and Cheng-Chin Chiang* Dept. of Computer Engineering, National Chiao-Tung University, Hsinchu City 300, Taiwan (*Currently with ITRI/ Computer & Communication Research Lab.)

CHAPTER 17

Professors Chein-Wei Jen and Bor-Sung Liang Dept. of Electronics Engineering, National Chiao-Tung University, Hsinchu City 300, Taiwan

CHAPTER 18

Professor Julie A. Dickerson Electrical & Computer Engineering Dept., Iowa State University, Ames, IA 50011, U.S.A.

Professor Bart Kosko Signal & Image Processing Institute, EEB-400, University of Southern California, Los Angeles, CA 90089-2564, U.S.A.

CHAPTER 19

Professors Liang-Gee Chen and Chung-Wei Ku Dept. of Electrical Engineering, National Taiwan University, Taipei City 107, Taiwan

CHAPTER 20

Dr. Ram Rao School of Electrical Engineering, Georgia Institute of Technology, Atlanta, GA 30332, U.S.A.

Dr. Tsuhan Chen See Chapter 1.

PREFACE

Multimedia is formed through the merger of the computer, communication, and entertainment industries. It has the potential of becoming one of the most powerful forms of searching for information, communicating ideas, and experiencing new concepts of any form of communication or networking. It is connecting the world through what we now call the "Information Superhighway." As microelectronic technologies continue to advance, system algorithms and software tools are gaining yet more sophistication. Moreover, as the hardware becomes cheaper to construct, the potential for multimedia systems and machines to be commonly used is becoming tremendous. Therefore, the computer, telecommunication, entertainment, cable, and other consumer electronics industries are racing to this emerging market. Knowledge and results achieved by researchers/engineers in the Circuits and Systems Society and Signal Processing Society of IEEE have been making a significant impact on the development of multimedia machines. This book is a culmination of these efforts.

Multimedia pervades our lives. It has forever changed the way we live, work, entertain, and learn. With wide access to the Internet, kids can spend more time online experimenting with and learning from computers through the Information Superhighway than on the TV. Once the power of image, video, and graphics through high-speed fiber-optics transmission or wireless communication is enjoyed, the old-fashioned approach of using plain text as a main source of information will be a thing of the past.

This book is written by experts in the multimedia industry and leading academic institutions who share their thoughts and experience with readers on the multimedia technologies for practical applications. Chapters are written in a tutorial style so that they will be easy to understand by the readers; yet state-of-the-art technological breakthroughs are also reported to bring the readers to the very forefront of the multimedia revolution. This book is suitable for advanced undergraduate and beginning graduate students from several disciplines: electrical and computer engineering, computer science, information science, and communication. Engineers and managers will also find this book to be a valuable source of information on leading technologies in multimedia and multimedia applications.

Bing J. Sheu
University of Southern California

Mohammed Ismail
Ohio State University

ACKNOWLEDGMENTS

The great support given by the IEEE Press and the Integrated Media Systems Center (IMSC) at the University of Southern California, which is an NSF/Engineering Research Center in the multimedia field, is greatly appreciated. We would like to thank members of the Multimedia Technical Committees in the IEEE Circuits and Systems Society, the Signal Processing Society, the Computer Society, and the Communication Society for their active participation, contribution, and promotion of this extremely fast-growing field. Assistant Editors Michelle Y. Wang and Richard H. Tsai have helped us by converting numerous manuscripts to the LATEXform and proofreading the results. Interactions with faculty in IMSC, especially Dean Len Silverman, Director C. L. Max Nikias, Deputy Director Alexander Sawchuck, and Associate Director for Education Jerry Mendel, have been most beneficial and have given us numerous inspirations in software and hardware technologies for multimedia applications. Input from Drs. Eric Fossum and Sabrina Kemeny of Photobit LLC, who are pioneers and leaders in the camera-on-CMOS chip business, helped us to better appreciate the multimedia opportunities. Interactions with international researchers, Professor/Dean Chung-Yu Wu, Professor/Dean Che-Ho Wei of National Chiao Tung University, Professor/Director Lin-Shan Lee, Professor/Chairman Soo-Chang Pei of National Taiwan University, and Professor/Chairman Jhing-Fa Wang of National Cheng-Kung University, all of them in Taiwan, have been highly beneficial. We would also like to thank the authors for contributing fascinating chapters. Reviews and comments provided by many of our colleagues were very useful and are greatly appreciated. During the publication process, we have benefited from the kind assistance of the IEEE Press staff and would like especially to thank Production Editor Denise Phillip, Assistant Editor Marilyn Giannakouros, Senior Acquisitions Editor John Griffin, and Director Ken Moore for all their efforts.

Bing J. Sheu
University of Southern California

Mohammed Ismail
Ohio State University

INTRODUCTION

The IEEE community is actively involved in research and development efforts in various areas of theory, algorithms, components design, and system integration technologies for multimedia applications. This book is a collection of 20 chapters contributed by leading experts in those areas. It covers selected topics of critical importance to the multimedia field and should be useful as a reference book for engineers, scientists, professionals, and managers as well as graduate students. Each chapter is prepared for the nonspecialist and covers both basic concepts and recent advances. Multimedia is an emerging multidisciplinary field that takes advantage of the rapid developments in signal and information processing, telecommunications, computer engineering, silicon, very large-scale integration (VLSI), microelectronics, and consumer electronics. It has been widely used in business as it provides timely information to clients, and therefore helps companies maintain a competitive edge, especially in marketing, public relations, and training.

Multimedia will significantly enhance standard educational techniques. With a large-screen projector and multimedia playback system, the teacher can use multimedia titles to enhance classroom presentation and stimulate questions. The students can further explore topics at home using a multimedia platform. In the home entertainment area, a high-definition television (HDTV) monitor serves as the system display. It offers good image resolution and a wide screen aspect ratio. New services like home shopping, remote electronic banking, medical diagnosing, and video-on-demand can be easily supported. Customized information, which is tailored to one's interests and tastes, can be available through the interactive network.

The biggest challenge we face is to make multimedia technologies compact, lightweight, and cost-effective, with advanced features for the general public. The price of sophisticated multimedia equipment is still too high for most people and in many cases is beyond the reach of many schools, particularly in rural areas where such equipment is most needed. However, the future of multimedia looks very bright indeed, and it is expected that multimedia products will eventually become affordable with rapid advances in microelectronic and packaging technologies and with increased efforts in research and development. With the ability of the consumer electronics industry to mass-produce sophisticated electronic equipment, the price of multimedia systems will become cheaper for both schools and the home in the future.

Significant advances in hardware and software codesign technologies have occurred over the past 10 years. The microprocessing power has been increased from 10 million to 1200 million instructions per second (MIPS). Continued progress toward more than 10 billion instructions per second can be available in the early twenty-first century. With the new packaging technologies, tens of millions of transistors can be compactly integrated for very low-power operation in advanced multimedia applications.

Figure FM1   Image of George Washington from a US $1 bill taken with the CMOS APS chip.

Video technology has made explosive progress during the past 10 years. Various image and video coding standards for still image compression (JPEG), video conferencing (CCITT H.261 and H.263), and motion video for storage media applications (MPEG-1/2) have been established, and many more (such as MPEG-4 and digital HDTV) are under intensive development. Significant progress in the use of wavelet transform to realize high-compression ratios and fast search in digital library have been made. It is widely recognized that a new era of global visual communication has arrived.

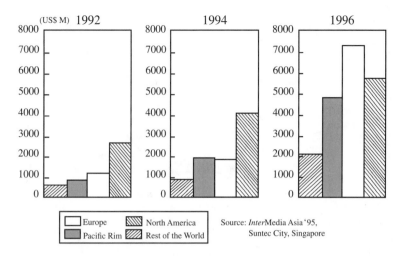

Figure FM2   Total multimedia hardware and software market: revenue by geographic region [2].

According to a recent projection [1], multimedia will represent a new total market of $40 billion by the year 2000 and $65 billion by the year 2010. Another key market survey [2] illustrates dramatic near-term market expansion from 1992 to 1996, as shown in Fig. FM2. Europe is expected to surpass the United States in total multimedia hardware and software expenditures, while Pacific Rim countries are quickly closing the gap.

This book has been arranged into five major parts: *Multimedia Systems, Standards, and Trends; Submicron Electronic Technologies; Digital Library and Servers; Networking;* and *Multimedia Signal Processing and Applications* as shown in Fig. FM3. Part 1 is strongly related to the activities of the Consumer Electronics Society; Part 2 is a contribution from the Circuits and Systems Society and the Electron Devices Society; Part 3 represents the efforts of the Computer Society; Part 4 presents ongoing research of the Communication Society; while Part 5 comes from the Signal Processing Society and Neural Networks Council. The ultimate goal is to build multimedia systems with desirable performance and features at a reasonably low cost.

Part 1 includes three chapters. *Chapter 1* addresses different compression standards and covers three portions: the MPEG-4 standard, the Digital Audio-Visual Council (DAVIC) specification, and various standards for network applications. The MPEG-4 standard was originally intended for coding limited-complexity audiovisual scenes at low bit rates. Its expanded scope is to include advanced features not supported by other standards. It will provide solutions for audio coding, video coding, and system multiplexing of coded audiovisual data in a truly flexible and extensible manner. This chapter clearly describes three standards for network applications: the Virtual Reality Modeling Language (VRML), Java from Sun Microsystems, and the Multimedia and Hypermedia Expert Group (MHEG) standard.

Chapter 2 is devoted to VLSI systems technology for multimedia. The VLSI technology not only implements but also bridges what is theoretically optimal and what is economically desirable. It involves application-oriented algorithm design, algorithm to architecture mapping, architecture

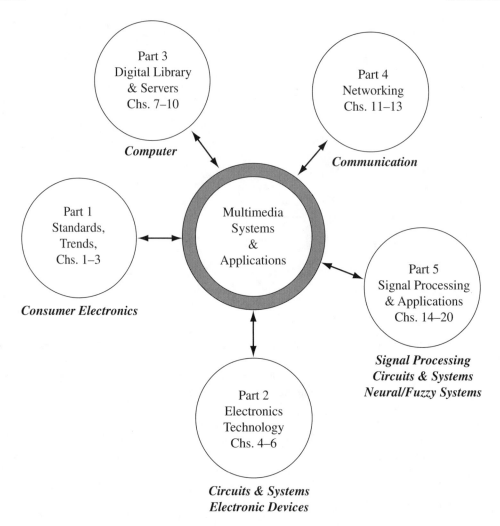

Figure FM3   Organization of this book.

design, architecture to circuits on silicon, circuits techniques, and VLSI design methodology and tools. Regardless of whether the communications are micro, local, or remote, VLSI systems are important in three main application areas: the physical, the link, and the protocol and application levels. VLSI systems for processing multimedia information focus on sampling, regeneration, filtering, signal enhancement, format conversion, data compression/decompression, and composition. Use of coarse-grain MIMD architecture, fine-grain MIMD architecture, and high-level/low-level multiprocessor architecture is appropriate.

Chapter 3 describes the research and development activities of the Telecommunication Laboratories in Taiwan. Such activities support the ISDN distance learning system, teleshopping system, asynchronous transfer mode (ATM), broadband networks, and video-on-demand and interactive video services. The intelligent human–machine interface systems include the pen-based input technique, written recognition technique, automatic office document processing system, computer speech synthesis system, and trademark and commercial logo database system. Several advanced devices are also described, including the PC-based ISDN terminal, PC-based ISDN videophone system, and 384 Kbps videoconference system.

Part 2 covers the use of submicron silicon technologies for the cheaper, better multimedia systems. It includes three chapters. *Chapter 4* focuses on advanced memory architectures for multimedia systems. Semiconductor memories play an increasingly important role in information processing. A variety of multimedia applications require advanced storage methods which permit storage of a huge quantity of data, achievement of a high-processing throughput rate, and operability with battery power for a long period of time. Memory chips with higher density, low-power consumption, and a high throughput rate are in strong demand. The synchronous DRAM improves throughput performance by introducing the synchronous operation. The Rambus DRAM provides an optimized solution for transfer between the central processing unit (CPU) and memory. It is based on the system-on-a-chip architecture without dedicated address bus. The number of pins and the chip size of Rambus DRAM are much smaller than those of conventional DRAMs. The Indigo2 IMPACT 3D graphics workstation by Silicon Graphics Corporation, Visual-Media accelerators by Cirrus Logic Inc., and Ultra-64 3D home video games by Nintendo Inc. are examples of Rambus DRAM applications. The cache DRAM (CDRAM) and enhanced DRAM (EDRAM) combine the advantages of SRAM speed with DRAM density and cost. The video RAM is an application-specific memory for high-quality display. However, its cost per bit is very high.

Chapter 5 describes a breakthrough technology for image/video processing and computer vision: camera-on-a-chip. The advanced pixel system (APS) architecture supports the integration of sensor array with analog-to-digital converter, timing, control, video signal processing, and even microlenses on a single silicon die. The architecture and operation of the CMOS image sensors are reviewed first. Design issues such as fixed-pattern noise, exposure control, readout techniques, packaging, and microlenses are carefully discussed.

Use of advanced computer-aided design (CAD) tools for multimedia system construction is addressed by a group of researchers at the University of California at Los Angeles in detail in *Chapter 6*. The tools allow for rapid algorithm simulations using a functional model library and scripting procedures that automate iterative optimization of algorithm parameters. Implementation examples for image, video, speech, and channel coding are included.

Part 3 brings us the knowledge and design information of the exciting digital library and servers field where search can be conducted though the images, video, in addition to the text scripts. *Chapter 7* describes a multimedia database system from NCR Corporation. An efficient multimedia database is to address several important issues such as ease of use, integrated languages, scalability of both coded and multimedia data, optimization options for storage costs, great communication channels among clients and servers, extending call level interface for large objects, and enhanced security definitions. Subjects related to object-oriented database management and relational database are discussed. The Teradata multimedia database architecture is described in detail. A key component is the multimedia object manager, which is a general-purpose content-based server designed for symmetric multiprocessor and massively parallel processor environments. The system supports content-based retrieval and multimodal integration. Application examples with feature extraction and spatial indices, and with use of speech, image, and video, are included.

Chapter 8 is devoted to video indexing and retrieval and is a contribution by a team of researchers at Princeton University. It includes valuable tutorial materials on the computation of different image and video features to characterize the content of images/video for efficient indexing and retrieval. Use of low-level features such as color, texture, shape, and motion, and high-level features such as faces is carefully described. Formulas and practical examples are given to guide readers in implementing real-world application systems.

Chapter 9 addresses issues on image retrieval of the extremely large database. The Fourier transform and the wavelet transform are briefly reviewed and compared. The wavelet transform has the clear advantage that features in wavelet representation of an image correspond directly to features in the original image at corresponding coordinates. Thus, discriminant functions can be analyzed in the wavelet domain. Important architectural supports are also described. The goal is to reduce access-time delays to near zero on critical paths within the memory hierarchy because all accesses are known in advance. Access time, rather than bandwidth, is the main source of performance degradation in the memory hierarchy. *Chapter 10* addresses the use of disk-array-based video servers, especially in video-on-demand applications. Data storage and disk scheduling schemes are described in detail. Methods to support interactive viewing functions, such as pause/resume and fast browsing operations, are considered. Downloading is an alternative approach for real-time play.

Part 4 is dedicated to networking and contains three chapters. *Chapter 11* gives extensive reviews on the local area networks, metropolitan area networks, wide area networks, and the asynchronous transfer mode networking. The collision rate, delay, and throughput in supporting messages for different priorities among different networking schemes are compared. For the ATM protocol, results on the available bit-rate congestion control mechanisms and performance in supporting messages of different burstiness are presented. Extensive simulation results are included in figures and tables.

Chapter 12 describes the use of optical interconnect technology to reduce the input/output bottleneck at the board and the backplane levels. Packaging levels of microelectronic systems include chip-to-package interconnection, ceramic and plastic chip modules, package-to-board interconnections, and printed-circuit boards. Metallic wires suffer severe performance degradation at high speed due to reflections, ground-loop noise, crosstalk, and frequency-dependent signal distortion. Optical interconnect using free space, optical waveguides, or optical fiber becomes a viable and attractive alternative to increase the system throughput. Potential advantages of optical interconnect include support of sophisticated interconnection patterns, electrical reflection reduction, higher bandwidth, and higher spatial density. Challenges associated with the use of optical interconnect are also described, and detailed architecture of optical interconnection is presented.

Chapter 13 describes the efficient use of distributed resources in the professional campus environment. A new network technology for such a unique environment consists of fiber-optic interconnects, high throughput, low-latency data transfer protocols, and visualization server-based clusters of high-end workstations. An industrial-university cooperative research example to deploy multi-Gbps parallel fiber-optic link technology is described in detail.

Part 5 covers signal processing techniques and various application domains of multimedia systems. *Chapter 14* reviews the speech and audio processing techniques. Various industrial standards in this field are carefully described. Text-to-speech synthesis, automatic speech recognition, and speaker recognition are covered. Use of speech in advanced multimedia computers and workstations is reported. Music processing is another important subject of this chapter, and application-specific silicon solutions for speech processing are described. *Chapter 15* also focuses on speech recognition

systems. The neural network is used as the underlying technology for the application-specific speech recognition system. A commercial-strength product, VenusDictate, is used extensively for illustration purposes. This chapter can be further strengthened by the inclusion of speech recognition of Western languages such as English.

Chapter 16 focuses on handwritten recognition for the human–machine interface in advanced multimedia systems. The recognition methods for English, numeric, and Chinese handwritings are first introduced. Handwritten recognition can be classified as on-line and off-line applications. Five stages are involved in the recognition process: boxed discrete characters, spaced discrete characters, run-on discretely written characters, pure cursive scriptwriting, and mixed cursive/discrete/run-on discrete. Various steps in recognition include preprocessing, feature extraction, classification, hidden Markov models, postprocessing, and use of language models.

Chapter 17 is devoted to hardware design for 3-D graphics. The 3-D graphics is one of the most important subjects in multimedia systems. Customers are fascinated by the effects of 3-D graphics as compared to the conventional 2-D display. This chapter reviews technical issues in computer graphics, including real-time rendering, image quality, cost, and system integration. It gives detailed review on the hardware modules. Advanced techniques for 3-D graphics hardware are described, including parallelism, and advanced memory I/O. Many 3-D graphics engines are reported, including Pixel-Plabe 5 and SGI machines.

The virtual worlds as fuzzy dynamical systems are described in *Chapter 18*. The fuzzy cognitive maps can structure virtual worlds that change with time. These maps guide actors in a virtual world as the actors move through a web of cause and effect and react to events and other actors. Complex fuzzy cognitive maps can give virtual worlds with new or chaotic equilibrium behavior. Application of an adaptive fuzzy cognitive map to model the undersea virtual world of dolphins, fish, and sharks is presented.

Use of compression standards such as MPEG-4 and H.324 in visual telephony is reported in *Chapter 19*. First, the related standards are reviewed. The architecture for an H.263 coder/decoder and a G.723 coder/decoder is described. For lossless compression purposes, Huffman coding and Arithmetic coding are discussed. An advanced prediction mode is supported to achieve a high-compression ratio.

Audiovisual synchronization or interaction is an interesting and important area for multimedia systems. It is especially critical for the person-to-person conversation environment. *Chapter 20* covers audiovisual bimodality in speech production and perception, automatic lipreading, face animation, and lip synchronization. Computer tools for image analysis and synthesis that enable these technologies are also reported. Examples of audiovisual interaction to process talking-head sequences are described.

Multimedia is an extremely fast-growing field. The number of multimedia publications has doubled every year since 1994. The materials presented in this book are intended to serve as a foundation. References listed at the end of each chapter can provide further information.

With rapid development of Internet technology, multimedia will have significant impact on religion. Religions have been associated with people from the very beginning of civilization and will continue to exist in human societies as long as our understanding of the Universe remains incomplete and there is more for people to learn from Nature. Both the media technology and religion are facets of our society; they are interrelated and mutually influencing. Development of the Internet and use of the World Wide Web approach tremendously affect our languages and lifestyles because people communicate a lot through the Internet, transcending the limitations of physical location and time-zone difference. Electronic business, electronic entertainment, electronic education, and electronic religion have started to emerge and will become very popular among the new generations of the Information Age. We shall pay good attention to this development and explore the use of the multimedia Internet to enrich our lives with ''religions through electronic means,'' or even a new variant of religion as nurtured by the Internet.

References

[1] *Project California Update*, 1994.
[2] *InterMedia Asia* 95, Suntec City, Singapore.

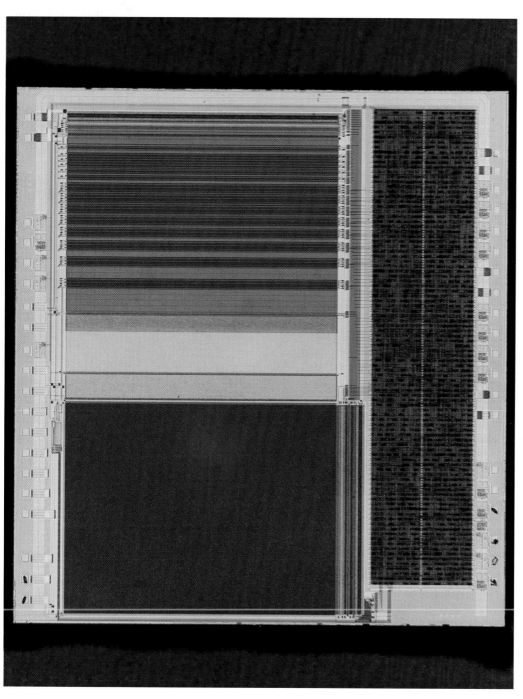

A 256 × 256 element CMOS active pixel sensor (APS) with on-chip timing and control electronics and on-chip analog signal processing electronics. Total power dissipation is under 10 mW. (Courtesy R. Nixon, Photobit).

MULTIMEDIA IN THE VIEW OF THE YOUNGER GENERATION

Technological advances have constantly turned luxuries into the essentials of life, as when cars replaced horses as the major transportation medium, electric bulbs replaced gas lamps for lighting, and dreams became reality with innovations such as the telephone, television set, airplane, and computer. Many new devices have become inseparable parts of our daily lives; more precisely, they have become part of ourselves, because we were born with them.

Multimedia will also go through this process. It is a technology destined to change the lives of the next many generations. Our life has never been more vivid!

Development of multimedia technology to date has made the human–machine interaction easy, simple, and colorful. It transforms the output of computers from being hard, cold numbers into pictures, images, and videos that are easy to grasp and manipulate. Now even little kids in kindergarten can play with computers, clicking the mouse to look at their favorite cartoon figures, and they can also edit new adventurous events for them and add voice to them, which is to give these figures new lives. Who knows how many future artists will come from these kids knitting stories with computers, through the quickly growing multimedia technology?

The future of the development will focus on the other way of human–machine communication—that is, letting machines understand human beings more easily through natural language, smell, and touch—and give us virtual or augmented reality. In the near future, one may be able to sit on the beach enjoying the bright sunshine and in the meantime be using the personal computer to participate in a teleconference with colleagues in the company through a personal communication system. Several sensors in the computer detect how that person feels during the conversation from his or her voice, facial expression, body temperature, and even blood pressure. Then the computer will adjust its volume of audio/speech and brightness of the video to fit the person's needs. When he or she is found to be sick, the computer will automatically send current data to the doctor and download the relevant references from the medical databases. Many more new services can be provided to make our lives more enjoyable.

Multimedia technology can be used in any possible situation we can imagine. The problems for us now are not only in making progress in the technology itself, but also in finding out the most suitable use of them. By doing so, we can guarantee a more brilliant life in the future.

I am thankful to my research adviser, Professor Bing Sheu, for allowing me to assist in editing this creative book. I wholly embrace the opportunities of the multimedia era with no fear, but joy.

Michelle Y. Wang
University of Southern California

PART

I

MULTIMEDIA SYSTEMS, STANDARDS, AND TRENDS

<table>
<tr><td>Chapter
1</td><td># CURRENT AND FUTURE TRENDS IN MULTIMEDIA STANDARDS</td></tr>
</table>

CURRENT AND FUTURE TRENDS IN MULTIMEDIA STANDARDS

Atul Puri, Hsueh-Ming Hang, Tsuhan Chen

1.1 PART I: MPEG-4[1]

Atul Puri

Abstract

The ISO MPEG committee, after successful completion of the MPEG-1 and the MPEG-2 standards, is currently working on the next-generation standard called MPEG-4. Originally, MPEG-4 was conceived as a standard for coding limited-complexity audiovisual scenes at very low bit rates. However, in July 1994, its scope was expanded to include the coding of generic audiovisual scenes at low bit rates, while supporting a range of advanced functionalities that are not supported by other standards. Furthermore, the MPEG-4 standard is being designed not only to provide solutions for audio coding, video coding, and systems multiplexing of coded audiovisual data but also to do it in a truly flexible and extensible manner.

This part of the chapter provides an overview of the current status of the MPEG-4 standard. First, we briefly describe the ITU-T H.263 standard, which forms the starting basis for the video part of the MPEG-4 standard. We then present the background of MPEG-4 and the requirements it is expected to satisfy. In the following four sections, we discuss the status of the four important parts of the MPEG-4 standard: MPEG-4 Video, MPEG-4 Audio, MPEG-4 Syntax Description Language (MSDL), and MPEG-4 Synthetic and Natural Hybrid Coding (SNHC). Finally, we summarize the current status of MPEG-4 and discuss the direction it is expected to take in the future.

1.1.1 Introduction

The MPEG-1 and MPEG-2 standards are two remarkable milestones whose overwhelming impact, in defining the next generation of digital multimedia, products, equipment, and services is already being felt. MPEG-1 decoders/players are becoming commonplace for multimedia on computers. MPEG-1 decoder plug-in hardware boards have been around for a few years, and now, software MPEG decoders are already available with the release of new operating systems or multimedia extensions for PC and Mac platforms. MPEG-2 is well on its way to making a significant impact in a range of applications such as Digital VCRs, Digital Satelite TV, Digital Cable TV, HDTV, and others. So, you may wonder, what is next?

[1] The description of MPEG-4 included here was completed in early 1996. Unfortunately we are unable to update this description at the time of publication, although there have been major evolutionary changes in the MPEG-4 standard.

MPEG-1 was optimized for applications requiring noninterlaced video at 30 (25 in the European format) frames/s at bit rates in the range of 1.2 to 1.5 Mbit/s, although it can certainly be used at higher bit rates and resolutions. MPEG-2 is more generic in the sense of picture resolutions and bit rates, although it is mainly optimized for interlaced video of TV quality in the bit-rate range of 4 to 9 Mbit/s. It also includes MPEG-1 such as noninterlaced video coding, and furthermore, it supports scalable coding. With regard to the question of what's next, a possible reply may be made in the form of yet another question—what about coding of video at lower (than 1 Mbit/s) bit rates?

Yet another question arises: Is it possible for a standard to be even more generic than MPEG-2 and still be efficient, flexible, and extendable in the future? If so, can it also be compatible with the previous standards such as MPEG-1, MPEG-2, or other related standards? Furthermore, can it efficiently represent multi-viewpoint scenes, graphics, and synthetic models, and can it allow functions such as interactivity and manipulation of scene content? Indeed, we seem to have very high expectations from a new MPEG standard! To what extent this wish list may eventually be fullfilled is difficult to predict. However, it appears that ongoing work in MPEG-4 (the next MPEG standard) is addressing these issues. We will discuss this matter in more detail a little later; for now we will explore the relationship of MPEG-4 with other low bit-rate video standards.

During the early 1980s, it was believed that for videoconferencing applications, reasonable quality was possible only at 384 Kbit/s or higher and that good quality was possible only at significantly higher bit rates, around 1 Mbit/s. Around 1984, the ITU-T) (formerly, CCITT) started a program to standardize video coding primarily for videophone and video conferencing applications. This effort, though originally directed at video coding at 384 Kbit/s and multiples of 384 Kbit/s to about 2 Mbit/s, was refocused after a few years to address bit rates of 64 Kbit/s and multiples of 64 Kbit/s ($p \times 64$ Kbit/s, where p can take values from 1 to 30). That standard was completed in late 1988 and is officially called the H.261 standard. (The coding method is often referred to as $p \times 64$.) The H.261 standard, like the MPEG-1 and MPEG-2 standards, is a decoder standard. In fact, the basic framework of the H.261 standard was used as a starting point in design of the MPEG-1 standard.

A few years ago, due to a new generation of modems allowing bit rates of 28 Kbit/s or so over PSTN, a new possibility of acceptable quality videophones at these bit rates arose. In early 1994, ITU-T launched a short-term effort to optimize and refine H.261 for videophone applications over PSTN. This effort is nearly complete and has resulted in a standard called H.263 [5]. Although, in this standard, video coding is optimized for the 10 to 24 Kbit/s range, as is usual, the same coding methods have also been found to be quite efficient over a wider range of bit rates. Within ITU-T, an effort is also in progress to come up with a version of this standard with more error resilience that would be robust for mobile applications as well. The ITU-T also has a plan for a long-term standard by 1998, capable of providing even higher coding efficiency. Joint work is in progress with MPEG, and it is expected that a subset of ongoing MPEG-4 standard will satisfy this goal.

Besides videophone applications, at very low to low bit rates, several new applications have recently arisen. The requirements of such applications appear to be fairly diverse and are not satisfactorily met by the H.263, MPEG-1, MPEG-2, or any other standard. To address such potential applications, in 1993, ISO started work toward the MPEG-4 standard, which is expected to reach the mature stage of Committee Draft (CD) by November 1997 and the final stage of International Standard (IS) by November 1998. Much of this chapter is an evaluation of the current status of MPEG-4 and what is foreseen beyond MPEG-4. However, before discussing MPEG-4, it is useful to focus on the coding methods and syntax of H.263 since H.263 has been found to offer a starting basis for MPEG-4 (history repeats itself!). MPEG-4, as we will see, is not only about increased coding efficiency but also about content-based functionalities, higher error resilience, and more additional features.

1.1.2 H.263: The ITU-T Low Bit-Rate Video Standard

The H.263 standard, since it is derived from the H.261 standard, is based on the framework of block motion-compensated DCT coding. Both the ITU-T H.261 and the H.263 standards, like the MPEG-1 and MPEG-2 standards, specify bit-stream syntax and decoding semantics. However, unlike the MPEG-1 and MPEG-2 standards, these standards are video coding standards only and thus do not specify audio coding or systems multiplex, which can be chosen from a related family of ITU-T standards to develop applications requiring full systems for audiovisual coding. Also, unlike the MPEG standards, the ITU-T standards are primarily intended for conversational applications (low bit rates and low delay) and thus usually do not include the coding tools needed for fully supporting applications that require interactivity with stored data.

The H.263 standard [5] specifies decoding with the assumption of block motion-compensated DCT structure for encoding. This is similar to H.261, which also assumes a block motion-compensated DCT structure for encoding. However, the H.263 decoding process differs quite significantly from the H.261 decoding process, and these differences allow encoding to be performed with higher coding efficiency. For developing the H.263 standard, an encoding specification called the Test Model Near-term (TMN) was used for optimizations. TMNs progressed through various iterative refinements, and the final test model was referred to as TMN5. Earlier, during the 1980s when H.261 was developed, a similar encoder specification referred to as the Reference Model (RM) was used and went through iterative refinement leading to the final reference model, which became known as RM8. The H.263 standard, although it is based on the H.261 standard, supports a structure that is significantly optimized for coding at lower bit rates such as several tens of Kbit/s, while maintaining good subjective picture quality at higher bit rates as well. We now discuss the syntax and semantics of the H.263 standard as well as how TMN5 encoding works.

1.1.2.1 Overview

The H.263 standard [5], although intended for low bit-rate video coding, does not specify a constraint on video bit rate; such constraints are given by the terminal or the network. The video coder generates a self-contained bit stream. The decoder performs the reverse operation. The codec can be used for either bidirectional or unidirectional visual communication.

The video coding algorithm is based on H.261, with refinements/modifications to enhance coding efficiency. Four negotiable options are supported to allow improved performance. The video coding algorithm, as in H.261, is designed to exploit both spatial and temporal redundancies. The temporal redundancies are exploited by interpicture prediction, whereas the spatial redundancies are exploited by DCT coding. Again as in H.261, although the decoder supports motion compensation, the encoder may or may not use it.

One difference with respect to H.261 is that instead of full-pixel motion compensation and the loop filter, H.263 supports half-pixel motion compensation (as per MPEG-1/2), providing improved prediction. Another difference is in the Group-of-Block (GOB) structure, the header for which is now optional. Furthermore, to allow improved performance, H.263 also supports four negotiable options that can be used either together or separately:

- Unrestricted Motion Vector mode This mode allows motion vectors to point outside a picture, with edge pixels used for prediction of nonexisting pixels.
- Syntax-based Arithmetic Coding mode This mode allows use of Arithmetic coding instead of variable-length (Huffman) coding.
- Advanced Prediction mode This mode allows use of overlapped block motion compensation (OBMC) with four 8×8 motion vectors instead of 16×16 vectors per macroblock.
- PB-frames mode In this mode, two pictures, one a P-picture and the other a B-picture, are coded together as a single PB-picture unit.

The details of the H.263 standard are not discussed here. Now, we are ready to introduce MPEG-4 and its various parts.

1.1.3 MPEG-4 Background

The MPEG-4 standard is the next-generation MPEG standard, which was started in 1993 and is currently in progress. It was originally intended for coding audiovisual information with very high compression at very low bit rates of 64 Kbit/s or under. When MPEG-4 video was begun, it was anticipated that with continuing progress in advanced (nonblock-based) coding schemes, for example, in region-based and model-based coding, a scheme capable of achieving very high compression, maturity for standardization would emerge. By mid-1994, two things became clear. First, video coding schemes that were likely to be mature within the timeframe of MPEG were likely to offer only moderate increases in compression (say, up to 2 compression ratio at the most) over existing methods as compared to the original goal of MPEG-4. Second, a new class of multimedia applications was emerging that required greater levels of functionality than those provided by any other video standard at bit rates in the range of 10 Kbit/s to 1024 Kbit/s. This led to broadening the original scope of MPEG-4 to a larger range of bit rates and important new functionalities [3].

1.1.3.1 The Focus of MPEG-4

The mission and focus statement of MPEG-4 explain the trends leading up to MPEG-4 and what can be expected in the future. They are directly stated here from the MPEG-4 Proposal Package Description (PPD) document [1].

The traditional boundaries between the telecommmunications, computer, and TV/film industries are blurring. Video, sound, and communications are being added to computers; interactivity is being added to television; and video and interactivity are being added to telecommunications. Yet, what seems to be convergence in reality is not. Each of the indus-

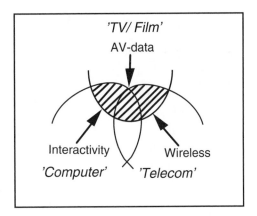

Figure 1.1 Applications area addressed by MPEG-4 (shaded region).

tries approaches audiovisual applications from different technological perspectives, with each industry providing its own, often incompatible solutions for similar applications.

Three important trends can be identified:

- The trend toward wireless communications
- The trend toward interactive computer applications
- The trend toward integration of audiovisual data into a number of applications

At the intersection of the traditionally separate industries, these trends must be considered in combination; new expectations and requirements arise that are not adequately addressed by current or emerging standards.

Therein lies the focus of MPEG-4: the convergence of common applications of the three industries. MPEG- 4 will address these new expectations and requirements by providing audiovisual coding solutions to allow interactivity, high compression, or universal accessibility.

Figure 1.1 shows the applications of interest to MPEG-4 arising at the intersection of different industries.

1.1.3.2 MPEG-4 Applications

We now provide a few concrete examples of applications or application classes for which the MPEG-4 Video standard may be most suitable.

- Video on LANs, Internet video
- Wireless video
- Video databases
- Interactive home shopping
- Video e-mail, home movies
- Virtual reality games, flight simulation, multi-viewpoint training

1.1.3.3   Functionality Classes

Now that we have some idea of the potential applications of MPEG-4, we will clarify the three basic functionality classes [1] that the MPEG-4 standard is addressing.

- Content-Based Interactivity allows interaction with important objects in a scene. Currently, such interaction is only possible for synthetic objects. Extending such interaction to natural and hybrid synthetic/natural objects is important to enable new audiovisual applications.
- High Compression is needed to increase efficiency in transmission or the amount of storage required. For low bit-rate applications, high compression is very important to enable new applications.
- Universal Accessibility means the ability to access audiovisual data over a diverse range of storage and transmission media. Due to an increasing trend toward mobile communications, it is important that access be available to applications via wireless networks. This acceptable performance is needed in error-prone environments and at low bit rates.

1.1.3.4   MPEG-4 Work Reorganization

Currently, the MPEG-4 work is subdivided into five parts.

- Video
- Audio
- Integration
  —Requirements
  —MPEG-4 Syntax Description Language (MSDL)
  —Synthetic and Natural Hybrid Coding (SNHC)
- Implementation Studies
- Test

Each part of MPEG-4 is handled by a separate subgroup. Furthermore, some parts are divided into a number of subparts; for example, Integration work consists of Requirements, MSDL, and SNHC. Each subgroup, depending on the number of technical issues that need to be addressed, forms a number of ad hoc groups, which by definition are temporary in nature to ensure maximum flexibility.

1.1.4   MPEG-4 Requirements

The process of collecting requirements for MPEG-4 began in late 1993 and is continuing [8] parallel with other work items. The process of development of an MPEG standard is intricate, tedious, thorough, and thus time intensive (about three to five years per standard with overlap between standards). To keep up with marketplace needs for practical standards at the right time and also to follow evolving trends, the requirements collection process is kept flexible. This ensures the ability to modify requirements as they develop over time as well as to add new ones when absolutely necessary. The work for various parts (or subparts) of MPEG-4, Video, Audio, MSDL, and SNHC is synchronized with the requirements collected at any given point in time, to the maximum extent possible. The major restructuring of the MPEG-4 effort in July 1994 to expand its scope to a number of useful functionalities and not be limited to very low bit rates only was in part due to an exhaustive effort in requirements analysis, which indicated a changing marketplace and new trends.

Before we specify the new functionalities of MPEG-4, the standard functionalities it must support, and some general requirements, we need to clarify the terminology used in MPEG-4. Some of the terms used have evolved from MPEG-1 and MPEG-2, while other terms are new.

1.1.4.1 MPEG-4 Terminology

Tool. A tool is a technique that is accessible or described by the MSDL. Tools may themselves consist of other tools. Motion compensation, transform filters, and audiovisual synchronization are some examples of tools.

Algorithm. An algorithm is an organized collection of tools that provide one or more functionalities. An algorithm may be composed of a number of tools, or even other algorithms. DCT image coding, Code Excited Linear Prediction, and speech-driven image coding are some examples of algorithms.

Flexibility. Flexibility is the degree of programmability provided in an MPEG-4 implementation. Three degrees of flexibility can be defined: fixed set of tools and algorithms (Flex_0), configurable but fixed tools (Flex_1), and downloadable tools, algorithms, and configuration (Flex_2).

Profile. A profile addresses a cluster of functionalities that can allow one or more applications. At each flexibility, one or more profiles can be defined. Thus, at Flex_0, a profile is a set of tools for configuring into an algorithm, at Flex_1, a profile is a set of tools, and at Flex_2, a profile enables the ability to download and configure tools and algorithms. MPEG-1 audio layer 3, MPEG-2 Video Profile, MPEG-2 System, and H.263 are all examples of profiles at Flex_0.

Level. A level is a specification of the constraints and performance criteria needed to satisfy one or more applications. Each profile is classified by a degree of flexibility and a value of level. At Flex_0, for a profile, a level simply indicates performance achieved. At Flex_1, for a profile, a level is the capability of a system to configure a set of tools and execute the resulting algorithms. At Flex_2, for a profile, a level specifies system capability relative to downloading, configuration of tools, and execution of resulting algorithms.

Conformance Points. Conformance points are specifications of particular Flexibility/ Profile/Level combinations at which conformance may be tested. Like MPEG-2, MPEG-4 expects to standardize a set of conformance points.

1.1.4.2 MPEG-4 Functionalities

Earlier, we discussed the various classes of functionalities that are addressed by MPEG-4. Eight key functionalities [1,2,8] can be clustered into three functionality classes as described below. These functionalities are supported through definition of a set of coding tools and a mechanism (MSDL) to access, download, combine, and execute these coding tools.

Content-Based Interactivity.   Content-Based Multimedia Data Access Tools: The access of multimedia data with tools such as indexing, hyperlinking, browsing, uploading, and downloading.
Content-Based Manipulation and Bit-Stream Editing: The ability to provide manipulation of content and editing of audiovisual bit streams without the requirement for transcoding.
Hybrid Natural and Synthetic Data Coding: The ability to code and manipulate natural and synthetic objects in a scene, including decoder-controllable methods of compositing of synthetic data with ordinary video and audio, allowing for interactivity.
Improved Temporal Random Access: The ability to efficiently access randomly in a limited time and with fine resolution parts (frames or objects) within an audiovisual sequence. This also includes the requirement for conventional random access.

Compression.   Improved Coding Efficiency: The ability to provide subjectively better audiovisual quality at bit rates compared to existing or emerging video coding standards.
Coding of Multiple Concurrent Data Streams: The ability to code multiple views/soundtracks of a scene efficiently and provide sufficient synchronization between the elementary streams.To obtain high coding efficiency, techniques for exploiting redundancies that exist between multi-viewpoint scenes are required.

Universal Access.   Robustness in Error Prone Environments: The capability to allow robust access to applications over a variety of wireless and wired networks and storage media. Sufficient robustness is required, especially for low bit-rate applications under severe error conditions.
Content-Based Scalability: The ability to achieve scalability with fine granularity in spatial, temporal or amplitude resolution, quality, or complexity. Content-based scaling of audiovisual information requires these scalabilities.

1.1.4.3 Basic Functionalities

Besides the new functionalities that the ongoing work in MPEG-4 expects to support, a set of basic functionalities are also required and can be listed as follows.

Synchronization.   The ability to synchronize audio, video, and other content for presentation.
Auxiliary Data Capability.   The ability to allocate channels for auxiliary data streams.
Virtual Channel Allocation.   The ability to dynamically partition video, audio, and system channels.
Low-Delay Mode.   The ability of system, audio, and video codecs to operate with low delay.
User Controls.   The ability to support user control for interactive operation.
Transmission Media Adaptability.   The ability to operate in a number of different media.
Interoperability with Other Systems.   The ability to interoperate with other audiovisual systems.

Security.   The ability to provide encryption, authentication, and key management.

Multipoint Capability.   The ability to have multiple sources or destinations.

Coding of Audio Types.   The ability to deal with a range of audio and speech data such as wideband, narrowband, intelligible, synthetic speech, and synthetic audio.

Quality.   The ability to provide audiovisual services at sufficient quality level.

Bit Rates.   The ability to operate efficiently over a range of bit rates from 9.6 to 1024 Kbit/s.

Low Complexity Mode.   The ability to operate with low complexity (in hardware, software or firmware).

1.1.4.4 Evolving Requirements

These various advanced as well basic functionalities give rise to certain requirements that an MPEG-4 coding system must satisfy. Furthermore, it is not surprising that several functionalities sometimes have common requirements, and often, one or more such functionalities is simultaneously needed in an application. One way to derive specific requirements is to choose a number of representative applications and provide numerical bounds or characteristics for every single parameter. However, such an exercise is feasible for applications that are already in use and are sufficiently well understood to allow full characterization. Another solution is to look for functional commonalities between applications to generate several clusters and specify parameter ranges for these clusters. Generating requirements for MPEG-4 is an ongoing exercise and is using a little bit of both approaches.

The requirements process is further complicated by the fact that requirements for MPEG-4 coding need to be translated into a set of requirements for video, audio, MSDL, and SNHC. The current approach is to specify requirements for flexibility/profile/level combinations. In this manner, for each degree of flexibility, the requirements for one or more profiles is being described. Furthermore, for each profile, requirements for one or more levels is also being specified.

1.1.5 MPEG-4 Video

MPEG-4 video was originally intended for very high-compression coding at bit rates of under 64 Kbit/s. As mentioned earlier, in July 1994, the scope of MPEG-4 was modified to include a new set of functionalities, as a consequence of which, it was no longer meaningful to restrict bit rates to 64 Kbit/s. Consistent with the functionalities it intends to support, the MPEG-4 video effort is now aimed at very efficient coding optimized at (but not limited to) the bit-rate range of 10 Kbit/s to about 1 Mbit/s, while seeking a number of content-based and other functionalities.

Following the tradition of previous MPEG video standards, the MPEG-4 video effort is currently in its collaborative phase after undergoing a competitive phase. The competitive phase consisted of issuing an open call for proposals in November 1994 to invite candidate schemes for testing in October/November 1995. A proposal package description (PPD) was developed describing the focus of MPEG-4, the functionalities being addressed, general applications at which MPEG-4 was aimed, the expected workplan, planned phases of testing, how verification models (VM) would be used, and the time itinerary of MPEG-4 development. The MPEG-4 PPD, which was started in November 1994, underwent successive refinements until July 1995. Parallel to the PPD development effort, a document describing the MPEG-4 Test/Evaluation Procedures started in March 1995 underwent several iterations and was subsequently finalized by July 1995.

1.1.5.1 Test Conditions for First Evaluation

For the first evaluation tests [2], proposers were required to submit algorithm proposals for formal subjective testing or tools proposals. Since not all functionalities were tested in the first evaluation, for the untested functionalities, tools submissions were invited. As it turned out, some tools submissions were made by proposers who were unable to complete the entire coding algorithm due to limited time/resources. In a few cases, proposers also used tools submissions as an opportunity to identify and separately submit the most promising components of their coding proposals. Since tools were not formally tested, they were evaluated by a panel of experts, who referred to this process as evaluation. The framework of the first evaluation involved standardizing test material to be used in the first evaluation. Toward that end, video scenes are classified from relatively simple to more complex by categorizing them into three classes: Class A, Class B, and Class C. Two other classes of scenes, Class D and Class E, were defined; Class D contained stereoscopic video scenes, and Class E contained hybrids of natural and synthetic scenes.

Since MPEG-4 is addressing many types of functionalities and different classes of scenes, it was found necessary to devise three types of test methods. The first type was called the Single Stimulus Method (SS) and involved rating the quality of coded scene on a 11-point scale from 0 to 10. The second type of test method was called the Double Stimulus Impairment Scale (DSIS) and involved presenting a reference scene (coded by a known standard) to assessors and after a 2-second gap, a scene coded by a candidate algorithm, with impairment of candidate algorithm compared to reference using a five-level impairment scale. The third test method was called the Double Stimulus Continuous Quality Scale (DSCQS) and involved presenting two sequences with a gap of 2 seconds in between. One of the two sequences was coded reference, and the other was coded by the candidate algorithm. However, the assessors were not informed of the order in which the reference scene and the coded scene under test was presented to them. In the DSCQS method, a graphical continuous quality scale was used and was later mapped to a discrete representation on a scale of 0 to 100.

1.1.5.2 First Evaluation and Results

The list of informal tests, an explanation of each test, and the type of method employed for each test are described below.

Compression. Class A sequences at 10, 24, and 48 Kbit/s: Coding to achieve the highest compression efficiency. Input video resolution is CCIR-601, and although any spatial and temporal resolution can be used for coding, the display format is CIF on a windowed display. The test method employed is SS.

Class B sequences at 24, 48, and 112 Kbit/s: Coding to achieve the highest compression efficiency. Input video resolution is CCIR-601, and although any combination of spatial and temporal resolutions can be used for coding, the display format is CIF on a windowed display. The test method employed is SS.

Class C sequences at 320, 512, and 1024 Kbit/s: Coding to achieve the highest compression efficiency. Input video resolution is CCIR-601, and although any combination of spatial and temporal resolution can be used for coding, the display format is CCIR-601 on a full display. The test method employed is DSCQS.

Scalability.   Object Scalability at 48 Kbit/s for Class A, 320 Kbit/s for Class E, and 1024 Kbit/s for Class B/C sequences: Coding to permit dropping of specified objects, resulting in the remaining scene at lower then the total bit rate; each object and the remaining scene are evaluated separately by experts. The display format for Class A is CIF on a windowed display, and for Class B/C and Class E it is CCIR-601 on a full display. The test method employed for Class A is SS, for Class B/C, DSCQS, and for Class E, DSIS.

Spatial Scalability at 48 Kbit/s for Class A and 1024 Kbit/s for Class B/C/E sequences: Coding of a scene as two spatial layers with each layer using half of the total bit rate. However, full flexibility in choice of spatial resolution of objects in each layer is allowed. The display format for Class A is Common Intermediate Format (CIF) on a windowed display, and that for Class B/C/E is CCIR-601 on a full display. The test method employed for Class A is SS, and that for Class B/C/E is DSCQS.

Temporal Scalability at 48 Kbit/s for Class A and 1024 Kbit/s for Class B/C/E sequences: Coding of a scene as two temporal layers, with each layer using half of the total bit rate. However, full flexibility in choice of temporal resolution of objects in each layer is allowed. The display format for Class A is CIF on a windowed display, and that for Class B/C/E is CCIR-601 on a full display.

Error Robustness.   Error Resilience at 24 Kbit/s for Class A, 48 Kbit/s for Class B, and 512 Kbit/s for Class C: Test with high random bit-error rate (BER) of 10–3, multiple burst errors with 3 bursts of errors with 50 within a burst, and a combination of high random bit errors and multiple burst errors. The display format for Class A and Class B sequences is CIF on a windowed display, and for Class C sequences it is CCIR-601 on full display. The test method employed for Class A and Class B is SS, and that for Class C is DSCQS.

Error Recovery at 24 Kbit/s for Class A, 48 Kbit/s for Class B, and 512 Kbit/s for Class C: Test with long burst errors of 50% in a burst with the length of 1 to 2 seconds. Display format for Class A and Class B is CIF on a windowed display, and Class C is CCIR-601 on full display. The test method employed for Class A and Class B is SS, and that for Class C is DSCQS.

To ensure that the MPEG-4 video subjective testing process will provide a means of comparison of performance of new proposals to known standards, it was decided to use existing standards as anchors. In tests involving Class A and B sequences, it was decided to use the H.263 standard (with TMN5-based encoding results generated by a volunteer organization) as the anchor. The anchors for Class A and B used test sequences downsampled for coding and upsampled for display using filters that were standardized. Similarly, in tests involving Class C sequences, it was decided to use the MPEG-1 standard (with encoding results generated by a volunteer organization) as the anchor. The anchor for Class C, however, used test sequences downsampled for coding and upsampled for display using proprietary nonstandardized filters. To facilitate scalability tests (object scalability, spatial scalability, and temporal scalability), standardized segmentation masks were generated so that all proposers could use the same segmentation, with the expectation of making the comparison of results easier.

The proposers were allowed to address one or more of the tests listed in the table. By the registration deadline of mid-September 1995, more than 34 proposers had registered. By the end of the first week of October, for the proposals being subjectively tested, proposers submitted D1 tapes with their results, the description of their proposals, coded bit streams, and executable code of their software decoders. By the third week of October, proposers of tools had also submitted demonstration D1 tapes and descriptions of their tool submissions. About 40 video tools submissions were received. The formal subjective tests of algorithm proposals as well as informal evaluation by experts of tools were started by the end of October 1995. The results of the individual tests and a thorough analysis of the trends were made available [14] during the November MPEG meeting.

The results [14] of compression tests in various categories revealed that the anchors performed quite well, in many cases among the top three or four proposals. In some cases, the differences between many top-performing proposals were found to be statistically insignificant. In some categories, however, there were innovative proposals that beat the anchors or provided as good a picture quality as the anchors, while providing additional (untested) functionalities. It was also found that since spatial and temporal resolutions were not prefixed, there was some difficulty in comparing subjective and objective (SNR) results, due to differences in the choices made by each proposer. It seemed that subjective viewers had preferred very low temporal resolutions, as long as the spatial quality looked good, over a more balanced tradeoff of spatial quality and temporal resolution. Besides compression, the proposers had also managed to achieve other functionalities.

Besides the results from subjective tests, the tools evaluation experts presented their results [15]; 16 tools or so were judged as promising for further study.

1.1.5.3 *Core Experiments Formulation*

In the period from November 1995 through January 1996, the process of definition of core experiments was initiated. A total of 36 core experiments were defined prior to the January 1996 MPEG meeting [7]; another 5 experiments were added at the meeting, bringing the total number of experiments to about 41. Experiments were classified into a number of topics.

1. Prediction
2. Frame Texture Coding
3. Quantization and Rate Control
4. Shape and Alpha Channel Coding
5. Object/Region Texture Coding
6. Error Resilience and Error Correction

7. Bandwidth and Complexity Scalability

8. Multiview and Model Manipulation

9. Pre-, Mid- and Postprocessing

A set of common experimental conditions were also agreed to, and a number of ad hoc groups were initiated, each focusing on one or more topics as follows.

- Coding Efficiency: topics, 1, 2, and 3
- Content-Based Coding: topics 4, 5
- Robust Coding: topic 6
- Multifunctional Coding: topics 7, 8, and 9

Between the January and March 1996 MPEG meetings, these ad hoc groups set out to produce an improved description of each core experiment consistent with the VM 1.0, seeking volunteer organizations to perform core experiments and finalize experimental conditions. In the meantime, a few new experiments were also proposed. At the MPEG meeting in March 1996, the ad hoc group on content-based coding was subdivided into two groups. At the same meeting, minor changes were made in rearrangement of experiments and three to four experiments were added.

1.1.5.4 Verification Model (VM)

It was agreed that MPEG-4 would have only a single verification model for development of the standard to address the various functionalities [6]. The first MPEG-4 Video VM (VM 1.0) was released on January 24, 1996. It supports the following features.

- Video Object Plane Structure
- Motion/Texture Coding derived from H.263
- Separate Motion/Texture Syntax as an alternative for error resilience
- Binary and Greyscale Shape Coding
- Padding

The second MPEG-4 Video VM (VM 2.0) [9] was released on March 29, 1996. It refines some existing features of VM 1.0 and adds a few new features, as follows.

- B-VOPs derived from H.263 B-pictures and MPEG-1/2 B-pictures
- DC coefficients prediction for Intra Macroblocks as per MPEG-1/2
- Extended Motion Vector Range
- Quantization Visibility Matrices as per MPEG-1/2

We now describe the important elements of the latest MPEG-4 Video VM [9].

An input video sequence consists of a sequence of related pictures separated in time. Each picture can be considered as consisting of a set of flexible objects, which from one

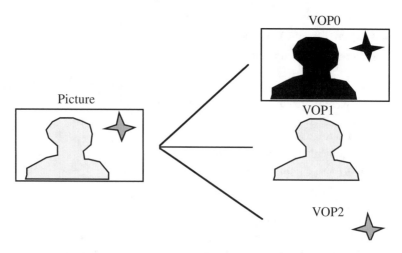

Figure 1.2   Semantic segmentation of a picture into VOPs.

picture to the next undergo a variety of changes such as translations, rotations, scaling, brightness, and color variations. New objects enter a scene and existing objects depart, leading to the presence of certain objects only in certain pictures. Sometimes scene changes occur, and thus the entire scene may either get reorganized or initialized.

Many MPEG-4 functionalities require access not only to individual pictures but also to regions or objects within a picture. On a very coarse level, access to individual objects may be thought of as generalization of the slice structure of MPEG-1/2 or that of the GOB structure of H.263, although such structures do not have a semantic meaning in these standards. Although potentially there is a way of accessing them, they are not intended for individual access or display. MPEG-4, in order to allow access to a picture's contents, introduced the concept of Video Object Planes.

A Video Object Plane (VOP) can be a semantic object that is represented by texture variations (a set of luminance and chrominance values) and (explicit or implicit) shape information. In natural scenes, VOPs are obtained by semiautomatic or automatic segmentation, and the resulting shape information can be represented as a binary mask. On the other hand, for hybrid (of natural and synthetic) scenes generated by blue screen composition, shape information is represented by an 8-bit component.

In Fig. 1.2, we show the decomposition of a natural scene into a number of VOPs. The scene consists of two objects (head and shoulders view of a human and a logo) and the background. The objects are segmented by semiautomatic or automatic means and are referred to as VOP1 and VOP2, while the background without these objects is referred to as VOP0. Each picture of interest is segmented into VOPs in this manner. The same object in a different picture is referred to by the VOP number assigned to it when it first appeared in the scene. The number of VOPs selected in a scene is dependent on the total available bit rate for coding, the degree of interactivity desired, and, of course, the number and size of unique objects in the scene.

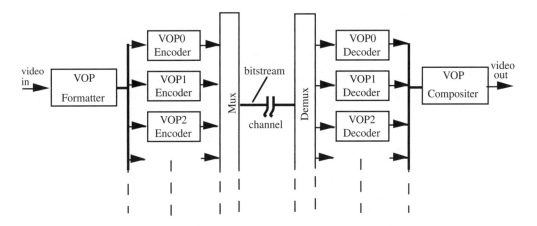

Figure 1.3   Structure of VOP-based codec for MPEG-4 Video.

The VOPs are encoded separately and multiplexed to form a bit stream that users can access and manipulate (cut, paste, and so on). The encoder sends together with VOPs, information about scene composition to indicate where and when VOPs are to be displayed. This information is optional, however, and may be ignored at the decoder, which may use user-specified information about composition.

In Fig. 1.3, we show a high-level structure of a VOP-based codec. Its main components are VOP Formatter, VOP Encoders, Mux, Demux and VOP Decoders, and VOP Compositor. VOP Formatter segments input scenes into VOPs and outputs formatted VOPs for encoding. Although separate encoders (and decoders) are shown for each VOP, this separation is more logical than physical. In principle, even though different VOPs can use different methods of coding, it is anticipated that this will mainly be the case when VOPs contain different data types such as natural and synthetic data. Thus, although many VOPs are possible, there may be only a few (typically, one or two) coders. The multiplexer, Mux, multiplexes coded data from different VOPs into a single bit stream for transmission or storage; the demultiplexer, DeMux, performs the inverse operation. After decoding, individual VOPs are fed to a VOP compositor, which either utilizes the composition information in the bit stream or composes VOPs under user control.

In Fig. 1.4, we show a block diagram structure of a VOP coder; this coder is meant for coding of natural video data. Its main components are Texture Coder, Motion Coder, and Shape Coder.

The Texture Coder codes the luminance and chrominance variations of the region bounded by the VOP. This region may be subdivided either into macroblocks and blocks and coded by DCT coding, or other nonblock-based techniques such as region-oriented DCT, or wavelet coding may be used. The coded signal may in fact be either intra- or motion-compensated interframe signal. The Texture Coder is currently assumed to be block-based DCT coder involving block DCT, quantizer, scan (and complementary operations of inverse DCT, inverse quantizer, and inverse scan) as per H.263, MPEG-1, and MPEG-2 standards. Since VOPs can be of irregular shape, padding of VOPs is needed.

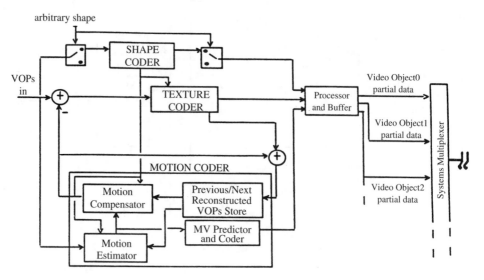

Figure 1.4   Detailed structure of VOP Encoder.

The Motion Coder consists of a Motion Estimator, Motion Compensator, Previous VOPs Store, and Motion Vector (MV) Predictor and Coder. The *Motion Estimator* computes motion vectors using the current VOP and temporally previous reconstructed version of the same VOP available from the *Previous Reconstructed VOPs Store*. The *Motion Compensator* uses these motion vectors to compute motion-compensated prediction signal using the temporally previous reconstructed version of the same VOP (reference VOP). The *MV Predictor and Coder* generates prediction for the MV to be coded using H.263 like median prediction of MVs. Currently, the motion estimation and compensation in the VM is block based and is basically quite similar to that in H.263. The current MPEG-4 VM employs not only default motion mode but also the Unrestricted Motion Vector mode and Advanced Prediction modes of H.263. These modes are not options, however. In the current VM, at the VOP borders, due to the irregular shape of VOPs, polygon matching is employed instead of block matching. This requires use of repetitive padding on the reference VOP for performing motion compensation and for texture coding when using block DCT.

In repetitive padding, each pixel outside the object boundary is considered a zero pixel, each line is scanned horizontally for zero pixel segments, and if the zero pixels occur between nonzero pixel segments, they are filled by the average of pixels at endpoints. Otherwise they are filled by pixels at endpoints of nonzero segment. Each line is then scanned vertically, repeating the filling operation as for horizontal scanning. If zero pixels can be filled by both horizontal and vertical scanning, an average of the two values is used. Finally, the remaining zero pixels are filled by the average of horizontally and vertically closest nonzero pixels.

While we are still on the subject of motion estimation and compensation, we should emphasize that the MPEG-4 VM now supports B-pictures. B-pictures currently in VM are derived by combining B-picture modes from H.263 and MPEG-1/2. Thus, motion estimation and compensation also have to be performed for B-pictures. In the current MPEG-4 B-pictures, a choice of one out of four modes is allowed on a macroblock basis and mainly differ in the type of motion compensation. The motion compensation modes allowed are Direct, Forward, Backward, and Interpolated. The Direct mode is derived from H.263 and uses scaled motion vectors and a delta update vector. The Forward, Backward, and Interpolated modes are from MPEG-1/2, with one vector each in Forward and Backward modes and two vectors in Interpolated mode.

The Shape Coder codes the shape information of a VOP and may involve a quadtree, chain, polygonal, or some other representation. If a VOP is of the size of a full picture, no shape information is sent. Thus, inclusion of the shape information is optional depending on the value of binary signal, binary_shape_VOP, which controls the associated switches. The Shape Coder in the current version of the VM is assumed to be quadtree based. Efforts are in progress to replace it by a chain or a polygon approximation-based technique.

The complete VOP Coder just described allows either combined coding of motion and texture data as in H.263, MPEG-1/2, or separate coding of motion and texture data for increased error resilience. The main difference is whether different types of data can be combined for entropy coding; this is not possible for separate motion and texture coding, which assumes that separate entropy coding belongs to individual Motion, Texture, and Shape coders rather than to a single entropy coder. Furthermore, since in our discussion we have assumed VOPs derived from natural image or video data, all VOPs are coded by the same VOP Coder and the coded data of each VOP are output (by Processor and Buffer) for multiplexing to Mux which generates the bit stream for storage or transmission.

Although earlier we mentioned the quadtree-based shape coding method currently in the MPEG-4 VM, a few words of explanation are in order. The shape information may be either binary or greyscale and is correspondingly referred to as binary alpha plane or grey scale alpha plane. Currently in VM, binary alpha planes are coded with quadtree (without vector quantization), and greyscale alpha planes are coded by quadtree with vector quantization. An alpha plane is bounded by the tightest rectangle that includes the shape of a VOP. The bounding rectangle is extended on the right-bottom side to multiples of 16×16 samples, extended alpha samples are set to zero, the extended alpha plane is partitioned into blocks of 16×16 samples, and encoding/decoding is done per a 16×16 block. We now briefly explain binary alpha plane coding.

Figure 1.5 shows the quadtree structure employed for binary alpha plane coding. At the bottom level (level 3) of the quadtree, a 16×16 alpha block is partitioned into 64 sub-blocks of 2×2 samples. Each higher level of quadtree is then formed by grouping 4 sub-blocks at the lower level as shown. The following sequence of steps is then employed.

1. Rounding process for bit-rate control
2. Indexing of sub-blocks at level 3
3. Grouping process for higher levels
   - grouping of sub-blocks from level 3 to level 2
   - grouping of sub-blocks from level 2 to level 1
   - grouping of sub-blocks from level 1 to level 0
4. Encoding process

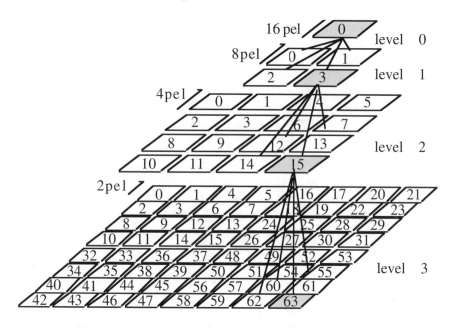

Figure 1.5 Quadtree structure for binary shape (alpha-plane) coding.

The rounding process is needed only for lossy coding of binary alpha planes and can be ignored for lossless coding.

The indexing of sub-blocks at level 3 consists of assigning an index to each 2×2 sub-block by first performing a swapping operation on alpha-pixels of the sub-block, comparing their values to values of upper-block alpha-pixels and left-block alpha-pixels, except for sub-blocks belonging to the uppermost row of 2×2 sub-blocks or the leftmost column of 2×2 sub-blocks in the level 3 block comprised of an 8×8 array of sub-blocks (each of size 2×2). After swapping, a numerical index is calculated for the 2×2 sub-block as follows.

$$\text{index} = 27 \times b[0] + 9 \times b[1] + 3 \times b[2] + b[3]$$

where $b[i] = 2$ if sample value $= 255$;
   $b[i] = 0$ if sample value $= 0$.

The current sub-block is then reconstructed and used as reference when processing subsequent sub-blocks.

The grouping process of blocks at a higher level first starts at level 2 where four sub-blocks from level 3 are grouped to form a new sub-block. The grouping process involves swapping and indexing similar to that discussed for level 3. The current sub-block is then reconstructed and used as reference when processing subsequent sub-blocks. At the decoder, swapping is done following a reverse sequence of steps as at the encoder. The grouping process is also performed similarly for level 1 where four sub-blocks from level 2 are grouped to form a new sub-block. The swapping, indexing, and reconstruction of sub-block follows the grouping, similar to that for other levels.

The encoding process involves use of results from the grouping process, which produces a total of 85 ($= 1 + 4 + 16 + 64$) indices for a 16×16 alpha block. Each index is encoded from the topmost level (level 0). At each level, the order for encoding and transmission of indices is shown by numbers in Fig. 1.5. Indices are encoded by variable-length codes.

As a final note on the current Video VM, it now supports a larger range of motion vectors (the H.263 range was too limited even when using the Unrestricted Motion Vector mode), MPEG-1/2 style quantization visibility matrices for intra- and inter-macroblocks, MPEG-1/2 style DC prediction for intra-macroblocks, and, of course, B-VOPs. The MPEG-4 Video VM is currently undergoing an iterative process, which is eventually expected to lead to convergence as core experiments get resolved and the successful techniques are adopted.

1.1.5.5 *Video Directions*

From our discussion of the MPEG-4 Video VM development process, it may appear that the only goal of VM is to address all functionalities via a single coding algorithm, the various parts of which are selected based on the best results of core experiments. In reality, the goal of MPEG-4 is to select a set of coding tools (and thus the resulting algorithms) in order to address the specified functionalities, in the best possible way. The tools selected are expected to minimize redundancy in the problems they solve. At times, however, a tool may be selected if it significantly outperforms another tool that was originally selected to solve a different problem.

Although it is difficult to completely predict which tools will eventually be selected in the MPEG-4 Video standard, the trends are quite clear. Block motion-compensation and DCT-based schemes still remain fairly competitive and in many cases outperform any other alternative scheme. The continuing core experiments will most likely be able to achieve about 30 to 40% improvement in specific bit-rate ranges of interest. A number of useful tools on content-based scalability, error-resilient coding, synthetic model-based coding, multi-viewpoint coding, and others will offer functionalities that are not offered by any other standard in an integrated manner.

The MPEG-4 Video effort is expected to contribute to tools and algorithms for part 2 of the MPEG-4 Working Draft-1 scheduled for November 1996. After the first revision, Working Draft-2 is scheduled for release in March 1997, and after a second revision, Working Draft Version-3 is scheduled for release in July 1997. Both revisions will involve refinements in tools and algorithms contributed to part 2. Also, in July 1997, the final MPEG-4 Video VM will undergo Verification Tests for its validation; any new candidate proposals at that time are also allowed to participate in those tests. The MPEG-4 effort (MSDL, Video, and Audio) is expected to lead to a stable stage of Committee Draft by November 1997 and be finally approved as the International Standard in November 1998.

1.1.6 MPEG-4 Audio

The MPEG-4 Audio coding effort is also in progress in parallel with the MPEG-2 NBC Audio coding effort that is now reaching a mature stage. The MPEG-4 Audio effort is targeting bit rates of 64 Kbit/s or under. Besides coding efficiency, content-based coding of audio objects and scalability are being investigated.

The MPEG-4 Audio effort also underwent subjective testing recently. Three classes of test sequences, Class A, B, and C, were identified. Class A sequences were single-source sequences consisting of a clean recording of a solo instrument. Class B sequences were single source, with background sequences consisting of a person speaking with background noise. Class C sequences were complex sequences consisting of an orchestral recording. All sequences were originally sampled at 48 kHz with 16 bits/sample and were monophonic in nature. For generating reference formats, filters were specified to downsample them to 24, 16, and 8 kHz. A number of bit rates such as 2, 6, 16, 24, 40, and 64 Kbit/s were selected to test audio/speech. Obviously, the first three bit rates are suitable only for speech material. The audio test procedures used were as defined in ITU-R Recommendation 814.

The submissions to tests included variants of MPEG-2 NBC Audio coding, improvements on MPEG-1 coding, and new coding schemes. For specific bit rates, improvements over existing coding solutions were found. The collaborative work has been started, and an initial MPEG-4 Audio VM has been developed. MPEG-4 Audio development is expected to undergo a core experiments process similar to the MPEG-4 Video development process. The MPEG-4 Audio effort is expected to contribute to tools and algorithms for part 3 of the MPEG-4 standard. The schedule of various versions of the Working Draft, the Committee Draft, and the International Standard is the same as that mentioned in the discussion of MPEG-4 Video.

1.1.7 MPEG-4 Syntax Description Language (MSDL)

Because of the diverse nature of the various functionalities to be supported by MPEG-4 and because of the flexibilities offered by software-based processing, it was envisaged that the MPEG-4 standard would be basically different from traditional audiovisual coding standards such as MPEG-1, MPEG-2, or others. While the traditional standards are fairly fixed in the sense of the bit-stream syntax and the decoding process they support, the MPEG-4 standard expects to relax these constraints and offer more flexibility and extensibility.

The MPEG-4 Syntax Description Language (MSDL) was originally conceived to deliver flexibility and extensibility by providing a flexible means to describe algorithms (including new ones in the future) and related syntax. With time, however, the MSDL [10] is evolving into the role of systems layer, addressing system capabilities needed to support MPEG-4 functionality classes such as content-based manipulation, efficient compression, universal accessibility, and basic functionalities, in addition to its original role.

1.1.7.1 MSDL Scope

To support flexibility and extensibility, MSDL [10] defines three types of decoder programmability as follows.

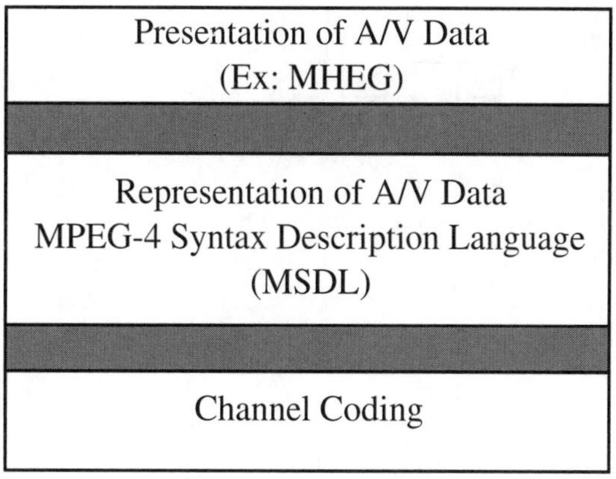

Presentation of A/V Data (Ex: MHEG)
Representation of A/V Data MPEG-4 Syntax Description Language (MSDL)
Channel Coding

Figure 1.6 Position of MSDL in a vertical stack of protocols.

- Level 0 (nonprogrammable) decoder incorporates a prespecified set of standardized algorithms that must be agreed upon by the decoder during the negotiation phase.
- Level 1 (flexible) decoder incorporates a prespecified set of standardized tools that can be flexibly configured into an algorithm by the encoder during the scripting phase.
- Level 2 (extensible) decoder provides a mechanism for the encoder to download new tools as well as algorithms.

The aforementioned definitions of various levels are nested; that is, Level 2 programmability assumes Level 1 capabilities, and Level 1 programmability assumes Level 0 capabilities. Currently, MPEG-4 is planning to address Level 0 and Level 1 capabilities only, and Level 2 may be addressed later.

To support MPEG-4 functionalities to the fullest, MSDL deals with presentable audiovisual objects (audio frames, video frames, sprites, 3-D objects, natural or synthetic objects, etc.) and their representation methods (waveform, splines, models, etc.). The decoder decodes each object, and either based on prespecified format or under user control composes and renders the scene. All audiovisual objects are assumed to have the necessary interfaces.

Figure 1.6 shows the position of MSDL in a vertical stack of protocols as was envisaged earlier. Then, the MSDL was considered as being in between the channel coding protocols and the presentation protocols, with some overlap with these protocols.

Because MSDL recently took over the role of systems layer also, the overlap with presentation protocols is expected to be even more significant.

Earlier, while discussing MPEG-4 requirements, we mentioned that one role of MSDL is to serve as the glue between tools, algorithms, and profiles. Since MSDL uses object-oriented methodology, we can represent tools, algorithms, and profiles as objects, each with a clearly defined interface for input/output. In the context of MPEG-4, a number of Tools when connected together in a meaningful manner result in an algorithm, and a profile contains a number of related algorithms. Figure 1.7 more clearly illustrates the role of MSDL as the glue between tools, algorithms, and profiles.

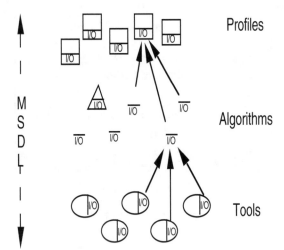

Figure 1.7 Role of MSDL in binding tools, algorithms, and profiles.

1.1.7.2 MSDL Requirements

Our discussion of the scope of MSDL, though quite helpful in clarifying the range of functions that MSDL addresses, is still not specific enough. We now list various categories of requirements [10] that MSDL is expected to satisfy and present detailed requirements in each category.

- General Requirements
- Structural Requirements
- Interface Requirements
- Construction Requirements
- Downloading Requirements

General Requirements

1. The MSDL should allow for genericity up to Level 2.
2. The MSDL should provide rules for parsing the bit stream. This will define the procedure for understanding the ensuing data.
3. The MSDL should define a Structure Module, the Interface Description Module, an Object Construction Module, a Downloading Description Module, and a Configuration Module.
4. The MSDL should provide solutions for a configuration phase, a learning phase, and a transmission phase.
5. The MSDL should provide the means for synchronization.

6. The MSDL should provide a means for error-free transmission of its data files (which contain setup information between encoder and decoder, downloading of new tools/algorithms, etc.).

Structural Requirements

1. The MSDL should provide a structural library for the objects (tools, algorithms, and profiles).
2. The MSDL should provide different ranges of programmability for different applications.
3. The MSDL objects should be extensible with a mechanism to add in future, ISO standardized data.
4. The MSDL structure shall use constructs, notations, and formats in a consistent manner.
5. The MSDL should provide for efficient coding of object identifiers.

Interface Requirements

1. The MSDL should provide ways to describe objects; this means describing their interfaces, what information fields exist, which fields have to be set up each time the object is used, and which ones have not.
2. The MSDL should use constructs, notations, and formats in a consistent manner.
3. The MSDL should code data with maximum efficiency. This means that dynamic and static parameters should be coded with maximum efficiency. Furthermore, there should be an efficient mechanism to default such parameters when coding them becomes necessary.

Construction Requirements

1. The MSDL should provide language to link elementary objects or already built complex objects to create new complex objects.
2. The MSDL via OCM should allow for easy mapping from the description of the objects used and connections among these objects to a real coding/decoding processor.

Downloading Requirements

1. The MSDL should be a language that has flexibility and expressiveness similar to those of other general-purpose programming languages.
2. The MSDL should have as a goal the construction of a machine-independent downloading language.
3. The MSDL should support dynamic binding of objects during runtime to allow adaptation and adjustment during communication.
4. The MSDL should provide for mechanisms to ensure security and preservation of intellectual property rights.

1.1.7.3 MSDL Parts

Having reviewed the requirements that the MSDL must satisfy, it is clear that the MSDL effort needs to be clearly partitioned into a number of areas [10]. Currently, the ongoing MSDL work expects to address the following areas.

- Architecture (MSDL-A): It specifies the global architecture of the MPEG-4 system. This includes the role of the MPEG-4 system to support complete audiovisual applications as well as conceptual objects and their data content exchanged between encoder and decoder.
- Class Hierarchy Definition (MSDL-O): It specifies particular classes of objects that are useful for specific audiovisual applications. It includes the definition of class libraries of MSDL.
- Readable Language Specification (MSDL-R): It describes a readable format for transmission of decoder scripts.
- Binary Language Specification (MSDL-B): It specifies a binary executable format for scripts or descriptions. This is the executable binary language understood by the decoder.
- Syntactic Description Language (MSDL-S): It specifies a language that can be used to describe the bit-stream syntax. It is expected to be an extension of the MPEG-2 syntax description method into a formal well-defined language that can be interpreted by machines.
- Multiplex specification (MSDL-M): It describes a procedure for multiplexing encoded information.

Work on all the aforementioned parts of MSDL is currently in progress, and thus it is best to discuss just the basic concepts behind these methods rather than give any details.

MSDL-A. The MSDL-A specifies the global architecture of an MPEG-4 system; an MPEG-4 system is a system for communicating audiovisual objects. An audiovisual (AV) object may be aural or visual, 2-D or 3-D, static or time varying, natural or synthetic, or combinations of these types. The architecture for communicating these objects is as follows. The coded AV objects and their spatial-temporal relationships, if any, are transmitted by an MPEG-4 encoder to an MPEG-4 decoder. At the encoder, the AV objects are compressed, error protected, multiplexed, and transmitted (downstream) to the decoder. Actual transmission may take place over multiple channels, each with different service qualities. At the decoder, AV objects are demultiplexed, error corrected, decompressed, composited, and presented to the user. The user may interact with the presentation; the user interaction information may be used locally at the decoder or transmitted back (upstream) to the encoder. Figure 1.8 shows the architecture of the MPEG-4 system from the MSDL point of view.

The encoder and the decoder exchange configuration information prior to the encoder transmitting AV objects. The encoder determines the classes of algorithms, tools, and other objects that the decoder must have to process coded AV objects it intends to send to the

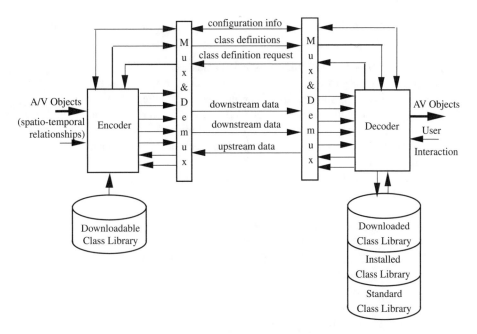

Figure 1.8   Overall system architecture from the MSDL viewpoint.

decoder. Each class of objects can be defined by a data structure and the executable code. The definitions of missing classes are downloaded to the decoder, where they supplement or override existing or predefined classes at the decoder. If the decoder needs new class definitions in response to the user interaction, it can request so from the encoder to download additional class definitions, in parallel with transmitted data. Figure 1.8 clarifies these various aspects.

For the new classes that the encoder communicates to the decoder, class definition can be considered as the header and the data component as the body of transmitted A/V objects. The class definition specifies the data structure and the methods that are used to process the data component. The specification of an AV object is illustrated in Fig. 1.9.

Not all AV objects need to transmit their class definition along with the data. For example, in the case of an MPEG-1 movie, its class definition can be found in a standard library. Similarly, if an AV object uses the same class definition as one already sent, it does not need to be sent again. Data are used to control the behavior of objects. For some AV objects, there may be no data component, for the behavior of the object may be predetermined.

Figure 1.9   Audiovisual objects specification.

Class Definition	Data
Header	Body

It is expected that all class definitions may be transmitted lumped separate from the data components.

MSDL-O. The MSDL-O specifies classes of MPEG-4 objects needed in specific applications. In particular, it addresses classes of objects that may need to be constructed during decoding in order to render and manipulate the audiovisual scene.

Audiovisual objects correspond to data structures that can actually be rendered by the compositor. In a coded bit stream, audiovisual objects are represented as a sequence of content objects of various types. Process objects correspond to a process that will be applied to content or presentable objects and will return a new presentable object. Hence, each process object contains an Apply() method. A partial class hierarchy for MSDL-O is as follows.

- Audiovisual and Content Objects
  —Audiovisual Scene Model
  —Hierarchical Model for Spatiotemporal Scene
  —Modeling 2-D Objects
  —Texture Information
  —Shape Information
  —Motion Information
  —Depth and Opacity Information
  —Location Information
- Process Objects
  —Quantizer Object
  —Transformer Object
  —Compensator Object

MSDL-R. The MSDL-R specifies a readable format for textual representation of the algorithm. It uses a subset of (C and) C++ as the starting point. However, it is envisaged that new capabilities not present in C++ such as multithreading and message passing will need to be added at some point. The MSDL-R features include the following.

- C variable names, expressions, and function calls
- C constructs: if–else, for, while, for which conditions are limited to constants, variables, and function calls
- Return statements

The MSDL-R excludes the following.

- Definition of functions, procedures, and global variables
- Preprocessor directives
- Statements such as goto, break, and continue
- Virtual functions

- Structures or classes and acess to them
- Type casts

Overall, for security reasons, the MSDL-R is strongly typed; that is, it involves no casts, function parameter type checking, no implicit type change. An MSDL-R program is a procedure. It has local parameters, local variables, global variables, and instructions. No new data structure can be defined in MSDL-R; only the standard elementary types and decoder known types are allowed.

MSDL-B. The MSDL-B is the specification of the binary executable format and can be generated from MSDL-R. Two approaches have been identified. In the first approach, MSDL-B is a coded version of the high-level language MSDL-R, for example, using Huffman coding of MSDL-R keywords. The second approach involves compilation of MSDL-R to a platform-independent low-level representation. Currently, both approaches are being evaluated, and there are concrete proposals for each.

In the first approach, MSDL-B is obtained by direct compression of MSDL-R code. MSDL-R keywords, arithmetic operators, and variables are mapped to predefined codewords. The decoder can reconstruct the original MSDL-R code but without the symbolic names used for class instances, variables, and methods. MSDL-B can be executed directly or translated to native machine code.

In the second approach, MSDL-B is obtained by compilation at the encoder. Compilation can be done based on ''lex'' or ''yacc,'' which are textual syntax analysis tools. Initially, the resulting MSDL-B code may be suboptimal in terms of efficiency, but its efficiency can be improved. Instructions are 32 bits long and are interpreted by Forth (programming language) like stack-based interpreters. The interpreter and tools are written in C++ and linked together. If required, a direct compilation to native machine language is also possible.

1.1.7.4 MSDL-S

The goal of MSDL-S is to provide a language that can be used to describe the bit-stream syntax. It is intended to separate the definition of bit-stream syntax from the decoding/rendering process. Since MPEG-4 seeks to provide flexibility and programmability, it becomes necessary to separate syntax from processing in order to allow content developers to disclose only the bit-stream structures they may use but not the details of any processing methods. Another advantage of this separation is that the task of the bit-stream architect is greatly simplified, allowing focus on decoding and preparing it for display rather than the mundane task of extracting bits from the bit stream. Furthermore, this separation also eases the process of compliance with the overall bit-stream architecture.

Some explanation is in order regarding the relationship of MSDL-S and MSDL-R. The MSDL-R, as discussed earlier, addresses the general programming facilities of MSDL and is the language in which decoding and generic processing operations are described. On the other hand, MSDL-S is an orthogonal subset of MSDL-R; orthogonality implies that the two are independent. The specification of MSDL-S does not affect the specification of

MSDL-R. There is, however, an assumption of commonality at the level of their capability to define object hierarchies. Currently, MSDL-S assumes a C++ or Java-like approach to be employed for MSDL-R. For example, MSDL-S can be thought of as generalizing the concept of declaring constants with hard coded values to declaring constants that derive values from the bit stream. An MSDL-R programmer can assume that a constant is parsed from the bit stream before it is accessed, similar to the way a programmer is not concerned about how the initialization of a constant occurs, as long as it does. We now briefly introduce the main elements of Syntax Description Language, on which work is currently in progress.

- Elementary Data Types
  - —Constant-length direct representation bit fields
  - —Variable-length direct representation bit fields
  - —Constant-length indirect representation bit fields
  - —Variable-length indirect representation bit fields
- Composite Data Types
- Arrays
- Arithmetic and Logical Expressions
- Temporary Variables
- Control Flow Structures
- Parsing Modes

MSDL-M. The goal of MSDL-M is to specify multiplexing and demultiplexing procedures for coded audiovisual information. In particular, this goal can be broken down into a number of functions such as interleaving of multiple compressed streams into a single stream, recovery of a system time base, managing of decoder buffer, synchronization of multiple compressed data streams on decoding and others. Because of the large variety of anticipated MPEG-4 applications such as broadcast, real-time bidirectional communication, database retrieval, and others, substantial flexibility needs to be provided.

The starting point for MSDL-M is the MPEG-2 systems specification (13818-1), the ITU-T multiplex specification H.223, and the evolving ITU-T multiplex specification H.22M. This approach is intended to maintain commonality with various current and evolving standards. To proceed further with design of MSDL-M, a number of categories of requirements, each with its own list of requirements, are taken into account. The main categories of requirements are as follows.

- General Requirements
- Application-dependent Requirements
- Timing/Synchronization Requirements
- Error Resilience Requirements
- Network Adaptation Requirements
- Compatibility Requirements

The specification of MSDL-M is currently being developed, taking into consideration the detailed requirements in each category and the system functionalities already in existence in other standards. A partial list of specific issues that are being addressed is as follows.

- Clock Synchronization
- Stream Synchronization
- Error Resilience
- Configuration
- Periodic Retransmission
- Buffer Management Models

1.1.8 MPEG-4 Synthetic and Natural Hybrid Coding (SNHC)

In recent years, with advances in digital video technology and fueled by ever-increasing demand for sophisticated multimedia, traditionally separate fields of natural images/video and synthetic images/animations have been merging at a breathtaking speed. For example, several recent movies have included composites of natural and quite realistic looking, synthetically generated scenes, with composition performed using chroma keying. The key to even more sophisticated multimedia is not only to produce more sophisticated composites but also to provide the ability to interact with audiovisual objects in these scenes. This ability is severely limited at the present time. Traditionally, audiovisual presentations have simply consisted of displaying the video frame and playing with it accompanying audio soundtrack/s. The increasing popularity of World Wide Web, which offers the opportunity to interact with and thus control the presentation of data in a highly nonlinear fashion, implies that increasingly, in the future, multimedia data will also be interacted with and presented in the same way. Thus, the coding of natural and synthetic image data, the ability to interact with and manipulate objects in coded domain, and the ability to control the order of presentation are related important functionalities that MPEG-4 is addressing via the Synthetic and Natural Hybrid Coding (SNHC) [12] effort.

The most obvious way to provide access to individual objects in coded domain is to code each object individually. In addition, it is anticipated that by coding objects separately some gain in overall compression efficiency may also be obtained as different coding strategies can be more easily used for different objects, as appropriate. A normal way to proceed would then simply appear to be to separately encode segmented or pre-rendered objects. However, in some applications, such as video games, CAD, medical, and geographical applications where many different types of image data are employed and no universal standards exist, the volume of data generated is usually too high, and user interactivity imposes additional synchronization requirements. In such cases, a different coding paradigm is better suited and involves sending a coded representation of parameters to the decoder, followed by rendering at the decoder prior to display. In general, when dealing with both natural and synthetic data, a combination of the two paradigms appears to offer a practical solution.

The MPEG-4 SNHC effort is aimed at addressing the needs of sophisticated multimedia applications involving synthetic and natural, audio and video data in an efficient, yet practical, way. The SNHC effort is expected to consist of two major phases—a competitive phase followed by a collaborative phase, much like the ongoing effort in MPEG-4 Video and Audio. MPEG-4 is currently seeking candidate proposals for consideration for standardization and is currently in its competitive phase.

1.1.8.1 SNHC Goal and Motivation

A more precise goal of MPEG-4 SNHC [12] work is to establish a standard for efficient coding, representation, and integration of 2-D/3-D, synthetic-natural hybrid data of an audiovisual nature. This standard is intended to support a wide variety of multimedia experiences on a range of current and future platforms. SNHC is expected to be employed in a variety of applications such as video games, multimedia entertainment, educational, medical surgery, industrial design and operations, geographical visualizations, and so on.

1.1.8.2 SNHC Architecture and Requirements

The functional architecture for the SNHC Decoding System [12] is shown in Fig. 1.10. It consists of a System Layer Decoder, a Video Decoder, an Image Synthesizer, an Audio Decoder, an Audio Synthesizer, a Cache, and a Display Processor. The Display Processor enables the user to control compositing of audio, video, and graphics objects for presentation. A Cache is used to store objects in repeated use such as 3-D geometry, texture, audio clips, and segmentation masks.

The SNHC effort, by defining what is referred to as a media model, is expected to focus on providing building blocks for efficient coding and rendering in interactive environments, which synchronize 3-D embedding of various objects such as images, real-time video, audio, and static or animated shapes. These objects may be either natural or synthetic. We now list the various issues that need to be resolved in completely defining a media model.

- Basic visual and audio primitives (polygons, sprites, textures, wave-tables)
- 2-D and 3-D spatial models, including geometric and structural properties
- Surface and material properties relative to scene illuminants
- Texture-mapping attributes for still and moving images
- Combination of natural and synthetic, static and moving images and audio
- Combination of synthetic spatial structures with traditional audio and video
- Structures for compositing scenes from objects
- Conventions for coordinate systems
- Parameterized models and free-form deformations
- Compressed and uncompressed data storage formats
- Static and dynamic behavior of objects
- Representation of viewers, cameras, and sound sources for rendering
- Naming and hyperlinking conventions for servers and libraries
- Modeling for different classes of terminal resources and scene degradation

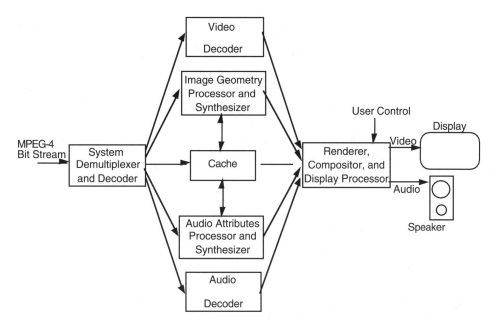

Figure 1.10   Overall decoding system architecture from the SNHC viewpoint.

1.1.8.3   SNHC Test Conditions

Currently, SNHC is in the process of establishing a standardized digital 2-D/3-D data
set referred to as the Virtual Playground (VP). The VP will include critical data sets needed to
discern performance differences between various competing approaches that are expected
to be submitted to MPEG-4 for SNHC evaluation. The VP is a collection of data sets
representing agreed-upon objects. These objects will be stored in popular formats such
as VRML 1.0 for geometric objects, JPEG for image textures, and AIFF for audio clips.
These objects, when selected, will be downloadable from the MPEG World Wide Web home
page. Various compositions of these VP objects will be used to demonstrate applications of
MPEG-4, as well as uncover areas for study and standardization.

The VP is expected to include objects with features such as animations, complex geometry, texture mapping, and various sound sources to test complexity and synchronization
issues. CAD models of various items such as furniture and vehicles may be used to represent complex geometry; talking synthetic characters may exercise the use of parametrized
models, audio synchronization, and 3-D localization.

1.1.8.4   SNHC Evaluation

SNHC focuses on coding for storage and communication of 2-D and 3-D scenes
involving synthetic-natural images, sounds, and animated geometry. Furthermore, the coded

representation should facilitate various forms of interactions. The SNHC group is seeking algorithm and tool proposals for efficient coding and interactivity in the coded domain. The following is a partial list of topics of potential interest [11].

- Compression and simplification of synthetic data representations—synthetic and natural texture, panoramic views, mapping geometry, mapping photometry, animation, and deformation
- Parameterized animated models—encoding of parameterized models and of parameter streams
- New primitive operations for compositing of natural and hybrid objects
- Scalability—extraction of subsets of data for time critical use and time critical rendering
- Real-time interactivity with hybrid environments
- Modeling of timing and synchronization
- Synthetic audio

In the competitive phase, the MPEG-4 SNHC effort, similar to the MPEG-4 video effort, made an official call for proposal evaluation. These proposals were evaluated by a group of experts in 1996. The evaluation criteria were based on functionality addressed, coding efficiency, quality of decoded model, real-time interactivity, anticipated performance in the future, and implementation cost. Each proposer was required to submit the following items [11,12].

- Technical description detailing scope, advantages, description, and statistics
- Coded bit stream of test data set and an executable decoder capable of decoding submitted streams
- A D1 tape showing the results of compression/decompression, simplification, or any other process that modifies the data

1.1.8.5 SNHC Directions

The SNHC proposers are expected to provide algorithms and tools to address certain functionalities, and to provide associated media models and bit-stream format. After the evaluation of SNHC proposals, the selected proposals will undergo further testing by core experiments, similar to those being used for MPEG-4 video. These experiments are expected to cover many categories such as compression, scalability, new media primitives, timing and synchronization, and real-time interactivity. A collection of algorithms, tools, and associated media models and bit-stream formats are expected to result from the SNHC standardization effort. It is also expected that during the convergence phase there will be a need to harmonize SNHC, MSDL, MPEG-4 Video, and MPEG-4 Audio.

In response to the recent SNHC Call for Proposals [11], the evaluation of proposals took place in September 1996.

The MPEG-4 SNHC effort is expected to contribute to tools and algorithms for part 2 and part 3 of the MPEG-4 Working Draft-1. Part 2 of MPEG-4 deals with synthetic and natural, visual representation and coding tools and algorithms, while part 3 of MPEG-4 deals with synthetic and natural, aural representation and coding tools and algorithms. The MSDL is expected to provide the framework and glue for uniformly addressing natural and synthetic representations.

1.1.9 Summary and the Future

In this chapter, we have gone a step beyond MPEG-2 and have introduced the next MPEG (MPEG-4) standard currently in progress. The necessary background information leading up to the MPEG-4 standard and the multiple facets of this standard are introduced, showing relationships to the MPEG-1 and MPEG-2 standards. In particular, we have presented the following.

- A brief review of the low-bit-rate ITU-T H.263 standard, which is the starting basis for the MPEG-4 standard.

- The basics of MPEG-4, including discussion of its focus, applications, functionality classes, and how it is organized.

- The requirements for MPEG-4, including terminology, advanced functionalities, basic functionalities, and analysis of evolving requirements

- The MPEG4 Video development process, including test conditions, first evaluation, results of evaluation, formulation of core experiments, definition of the Verification Model, and directions of ongoing work.

- A brief introduction to the MPEG-4 Audio development process.

- Discussion of the MPEG-4 Syntax Description Language, including its scope, requirements, its various parts, architecture, details of its parts, and directions of ongoing work.

- The MPEG-4 Synthetic and Natural Hybrid Coding effort, its goals, architecture, and requirements, test conditions, evaluation process, and directions of ongoing work.

- The Future, what are the implications of MPEG-4, and what lies beyond. Example applications involve audiovisual coding that seem promising for the short, medium, and long term.

Because of its flexibility and extensibility, the MPEG-4 standard is expected to remain a very useful standard for many years to come. Although this standard, when completed, is expected to support many functionalities, only the very basic functionalities may initially be applied for specific applications. This may occur on next-generation video signal processors or on custom VLSI chips. The more advanced functionalities are only likely to be deployed at a much later stage when powerful and flexible video processors that can take full benefit of the MSDL capabilities become possible.

1.2 PART II: SUMMARY OF DAVIC 1.0 SPECIFICATION

Hsueh-Ming Hang

Abstract

This part contains a summary of DAVIC 1.0 Specification[1] (released in January 1996) [16]. This summary provides a brief introduction of the lengthy DAVIC document. In order to be accurate, in many places it adopts the statements directly from the original document without modification. Therefore, even in this narrow sense, we are indebted to the numerous contributors of the DAVIC Specifications. In order to help readers grasp the key concepts of this rather huge and complicated set of specifications, simplified examples are used for illustration in this short article. However, we may lose the generalization and accuracy that the original document intends to convey. Therefore, readers are referred to the original document for complete and accurate descriptions.

1.2.1 What Is DAVIC?

The Digital Audio-Visual Council (DAVIC) is a nonprofit association registered in Geneva, Switzerland. It was organized by Dr. L. Chiariglione, the originator of ISO MPEG standards activity [17,18], and the first formal DAVIC meeting was held in June 1994 at San Jose, California [22]. As stated in the foreword of the DAVIC document: "the purpose of DAVIC is to advance the success of emerging digital audiovisual applications and services, initially of the broadcast and interactive type, by the timely availability of internationally-agreed specifications of open interfaces and protocols that maximize interoperability across countries and applications and services" (Foreword, [16]).

There are several interesting points in this statement. First, DAVIC tries to define a set of standards that a complete digital audiovisual (multimedia) communication system can build on. Although there exist many audio/video and communication standards such as MPEG and ATM, these standards were developed independently, and they are merely individual elements of a complete multimedia communication system. It takes additional and nontrivial effort to put them together and harmonize them to form a consistent and workable set of specifications. Second, this Council started with a rather ambitious plan and aggressive schedule. A multimedia communication system is a multidiscipline product. It consists of elements from computer server and terminal, digital modulation and coding, communication networking, data compression/processing, multimedia representation, consumer electronics, and so on. However, DAVIC reached its first goal of releasing the first set of specifications, DAVIC 1.0, by December 1995, roughly 16 months from the Paris meeting, for preparing the first call for proposals (CFP1) in September 1994 [22]. Third, the DAVIC specification defines only the *interfaces* and *protocols* of a multimedia communication system. It does not pose rigid specifications for the entire system and subsystem structures and implementations.

By December 1995, DAVIC had about 200 corporation members, including all the major players in this area. There have regularly been more than two hundred people attending the DAVIC meetings once every three months in the past year and a half. Standards are

[1] This work was partially supported by Computer and Communication Research Laboratories, Industrial Technology Research Institute (Hsinchu, TAIWAN, ROC).

drafted by the attendees split into six or so technical groups. The DAVIC 1.0 specification was released in December 1995 (an edited version was released in January 1996). It contains 12 parts and 700 or so pages. As one can imagine, there are loopholes in this massive document prepared by a large group of people in such a short period of time. And because it tries to accommodate all the relevant applications (e.g., TV over satellite, over public telephone network, over coaxial cable, etc.) and the existing international standards, its protocol stacks may be clumsy and less efficient for a specific application. This is an unavoidable tradeoff due to the interoperability requirement emphasized by the DAVIC. Nonetheless, the DAVIC 1.0 specification is by far the most complete and general set of standards in this area. Its wide acceptance and popularity remains to be seen; however, it is a reasonable starting point for establishing an international standard, if such a standard is eventually adopted by the community, for multimedia communication systems.

1.2.2 DAVIC Specification 1.0

The DAVIC 1.0 Specification is essentially a collection of existing standards, together with some glue made up by the DAVIC group to bridge the gaps. These standards are, in large percentages, communication interfaces and protocols (such as ATM and TCP/IP) and data compression and representation formats (such as MPEG [17,18] and MHEG [19]). The most significant work done by DAVIC is to identify and select appropriate established standards and smooth out the inconsistencies among various standards. Also, the DAVIC group chooses proper parameters of the existing interfaces and protocols and creates new ones only when necessary (such as graphics representation and modulation techniques). In terms of the vocabulary of Dr. Chiariglione, the founder of DAVIC, these interfaces and protocols are *tools*. A realistic system would most likely implement only a portion of these tools.

1.2.2.1 Document Organization

The entire DAVIC 1.0 is divided into 12 parts as shown in Table 1.1 [20]. The parts in Group 1 are the basic tools—interfaces and protocols of DAVIC subsystems. The parts in Group 2 describe the architectures of the three main subsystems in multimedia communications—service provider (server), service consumer (client), and delivery system (network), and how the DAVIC tools in Group 3 are assembled to form these subsystems. The parts in Group 3 are dealing with issues related to the entire system.

Parts 6 and 10 of the document are missing because the organization of DAVIC 1.0 has gone through a few major changes and the old numbering system has not been altered. The original Part 6 is the high layer protocols, which is now merged with Part 7, and thus Part 6 is unassigned now. Part 10 is the security (or access control) system, but there were too many unresolved security system issues when DAVIC 1.0 was frozen in June 1995. Hence, it is not included in Specification 1.0.

One may also note that each item in Table 1.1 is marked with either *Spec* (technical specification) or *Report* (technical report). The *Specs* are normative. They are the elements that a DAVIC-compliant system must comply with, whereas the *Reports* are informative— they are provided for understanding the background of the DAVIC Specs. Because the Reports give concrete examples of DAVIC systems and subsystems, it would be much

Table 1.1   Classification of DAVIC 1.0 Parts

	Part No.	Title	*Spec/Report*
Group 1		**DAVIC Tools**	
	7	High and midlayer protocols	*Spec*
	8	Lower-layer protocols and physical interfaces	*Spec*
	9	Information representation	*Spec*
	11	Usage information protocols	*Report*
Group 2		**DAVIC Subsystems**	
	3	Service Provider System architecture and interfaces	*Report*
	4	Delivery System architecture and interfaces	*Report*
	5	Service Consumer System architecture and high-level API	*Spec*
Group 3		**Systemwide Issues**	
	1	Description of DAVIC functionalities	*Report*
	2	System Reference Models and scenarios	*Report*
	12	Reference points, interfaces, and dynamics	*Spec*

easier to understand the DAVIC Specs through them. Therefore, our description below is based on both the Specs and the Reports.

1.2.2.2   DAVIC Applications

DAVIC identifies 19 applications that are relevant to this standard. They are prioritized into two groups: *core* applications and *other* applications. Priority was assigned through discussions and informal voting. They are summarized in Table 1.2. Most readers are probably familiar with these applications, and the detailed description of each item is found in Part 1 of DAVIC 1.0 [16]. Also described in Part 1 of DAVIC 1.0 are the various functionalities needed in implementing these applications. They are the rationales behind defining the subsequent DAVIC tools.

1.2.2.3   DAVIC-Compliant Systems

DAVIC-compliant systems must use the set of tools (interfaces and protocols) and follow the procedure defined in the DAVIC specifications (Clause 6, Part 12, [16]). An abridged version of these requirements is as follows:

- The system must be built based on the DAVIC 1.0 tools.
- The system must reflect one of the allowable *Physical Instances* defined in Part 12.

Table 1.2   DAVIC 1.0 Applications

Core	Movies on Demand (MOD), Teleshopping, Broadcast
Applications	Near Video on Demand, Delayed Broadcast
	Games, Telework, Karaoke on Demand
Other	News on Demand, TV Listings (schedule of TV programs)
Applications	Distance Learning, Videotelephony, Home Banking,
	Telemedicine, Content Production, Transaction Services,
	Videoconferencing, Internet Access, Virtual CD-ROM

- The system must illustrate DAVIC compliance at the *Reference Points*.
- The system must perform functionalities outlined in Part 1.
- The system dynamic behavior must be in accordance with the *dynamic flow scenarios* defined in Part 12.

A DAVIC *Physical Instance* is roughly a concrete DAVIC system realization. Further explanation of Reference Points, Physical Instances, and dynamic flows will be given in the following subsections.

In addition, an implementation procedure is suggested for a DAVIC system instance (condensed from Clause 7, Part 12):

1. Define the instance in terms of the static DAVIC Reference Model and one of the allowable Physical Instances.
2. Identify the to-be-used protocol tools from the DAVIC Physical Instance and the protocol network architectures.
3. Define the identified points using the DAVIC tools.
4. Identify the required DAVIC functionalities and demonstrate the implementation of these functions through the network instance, following the DAVIC dynamic flows.
5. Repeat steps 2 through 4 for the various network types to which the instance applies.

According to these requirements and procedures, a DAVIC-compliant system should have a *communication structure* (physical instance and dynamic flow) allowed in DAVIC, and at various Reference Points (defined below) it must comply with the DAVIC interfaces specifications. And, of course, it has to use DAVIC protocols and data representations. However, a subsystem located between two external Reference Points may be considered as a black box and can often be flexible in internal implementation.

1.2.2.4   The DAVIC Reference Model

A general DAVIC Reference Model is shown in Fig. 1.11. It consists of five system entities: a Service Consumer System (client, set-top box), a Service Provider System (server), a Content Provider System, and two Delivery Systems (networks) connecting them. Also shown in this figure are the four *Reference Points*: A1, A4, A10, and A11. The Content

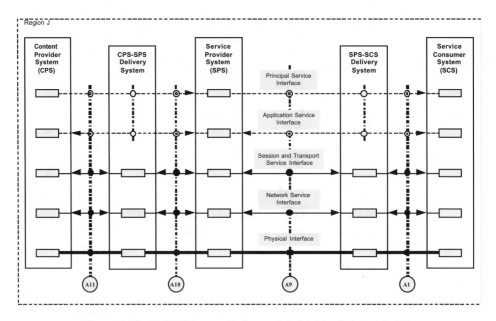

Figure 1.11   DAVIC System Reference Model (Fig. 7-2, Part 2, [1]).

Provider System and the interfaces at Reference Points A10 and A11 are not specified in DAVIC 1.0. There are other Reference Points inside the Delivery System (DS) and the Service Consumer System (SCS), as will be pointed out later.

The DAVIC specifications are built around the concepts of *information flows*, *service layers*, and *interface planes*. Some of these concepts overlap and are similar but not identical. These concepts are general and can be applied to all three system entities, but some of them may be more meaningful for a particular system entity and structure, for example, the interface planes for Service Provider System (SPS).

Logical Interface Planes (Clause 6.2, Part 2). Objects in a system are classified into user, control, and management categories. In the (abstract) reference model, peer-to-peer information exchanges can occur only between objects in the same category (plane). A logical interface category may be null if no objects in the system are assigned to that category.

- **User Plane (UP) interface**: Provides for transparent user information (flow) transfer between objects. The transfer of information is significant only to the sender and receiver objects. An example of user information is user-to-user content such as a movie.
- **Control Plane (CP) interface**: Provides for the flow of information between control objects in any protocol layer. For example, in the network layer, it performs the call control and connection control.

- **Management Plane (MP) interface**: Provides for the flow of information between management objects in any protocol layer. It performs management functions such as fault, configuration, accounting, and security.

Another interface category is **Physical interface**, which represents the physical description of the interfaces.

Service Layers (Clause 6.3, Part 2). A service layer contains a set of objects that interact with peers (in the same or in another system) to perform certain specific functions. There are four layers in DAVIC 1.0.

- **SL0: Principal Service Layer**—These objects interact with peers to use or provide principal services, for example, sending or receiving content information such as movies and music. SL0 objects are local SL1 service clients.
- **SL1: Application Service Layer**—These resources support the needs of the principal service consumers and service providers. They use SL2 services to communicate.
- **SL2: Session and Transport Service Layer**—They establish and maintain end-to-end communications for SL1 clients.
- **SL3: Network Service Layer**—This is the only layer that has physical communication links to other systems. All logical peer–service interaction information is carried in physical channels that interconnect SL3 service objects.

The aforementioned layers in the Reference Model are shown in Fig. 1.11. The layer classification can be viewed as the second dimension of partitioning objects in a system, whereas the plane classification is the first dimension. In other words, the User Plane of the server, for example, can be further partitioned into SL0, SL1, SL2, and SL3 layers as illustrated by Fig. 1.12.

Information Flows (Clause 7.2.2, Part 2). By far the most important concepts in DAVIC 1.0 are information flows.

- **S1 Information Flow**—S1 is content-information flow, normally in the User Plane of any service layer, from a source object to a destination object. The flow is transparent to any intermediate object through which the flow passes. Examples are audio and video.
- **S2 Information Flow**—S2 is control-information flow, normally in the Delivery System User Plane, from an Application Service Layer (SL1) source object to a peer destination object. It may often be viewed as the Control Plane data for the end-to-end information. The behavior of the source and destination object may change as a result of the flow. S2 messages often affect S1 information flows such as messages to *play* or *stop* a movie.
- **S3 Information Flow**—S3 is control-information flow, normally in the Control Plane, from a Session and Transport Service Layer (SL2) source object to a peer destination object. Other than the change of service layer, S3 is similar to S2. Examples are messages to establish, modify, or terminate a session.

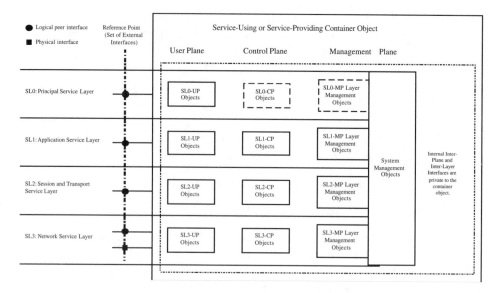

Figure 1.12   Service layers and planes (Fig. 6-5, Part 2, [1]).

- **S4 Information Flow**—S4 is control-information flow, normally in the Control Plane, from a Network Service Layer (SL3) source object to a peer destination object. Other than the change of service layer, S4 is similar to S3 and S2. Examples are messages to establish or release connections.

- **S5 Information Flow**—S5 is management-information flow from a source object to a peer destination object on the Management Plane.

Communication Protocol stacks are defined to facilitate information flows at various levels as described later.

1.2.2.5 Service Provider System

DAVIC adopted an object-oriented, distributed server model for the Service Provider System (SPS) using the concept of *Common Object Request Broker Architecture* (CORBA) [21]. Its high-layer protocols come from MPEG2 DSM-CC (Digital Storage Media Command and Control) [18] and OMG (Object Management Group) IDL (Interface Definition Language) [21]. A brief review of the key concepts in CORBA may help us to understand the DAVIC SPS. An object in CORBA is an identifiable, encapsulated entity that provides one or more services requested by a client. Objects can be created and destroyed. Their creation and destruction is an outcome of issuing requests. An *interface* of an object is a description of a set of operations that a client can ask the object to perform. In other words, the operations of an object are defined by its interfaces, and in CORBA, interfaces are specified in IDL. In a computing machine, requested service is performed by executing code that operates upon some data. One step further, CORBA defines a concrete system

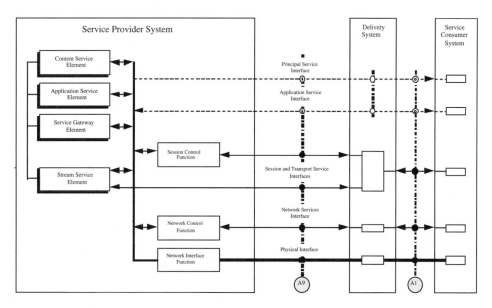

Figure 1.13   DAVIC Service Provider System model (Fig. 7-3, Part 2, [1]).

architecture. However, since DAVIC only specifies interfaces (in a sense broader than the interface in CORBA) and protocols, concrete architectures in implementation are outside its scope.

Figure 1.13 models a general Service Provider System (SPS) in DAVIC 1.0 (Clause 7.3, Part 2). SPS (Clause 1.2, Part 3) provides four core services (as shown in the figure):

- **Service Gateway**: It is a broker where services register to make their existence known to the clients. A client can thus activate or deactivate an instance of service.
- **Application Service**: A general-purpose service allows the invocation of specific applications. It provides these applications with a core set of functions for dealing with application objects.
- **Stream Service**: It is a repository and source for streams such as video and audio.
- **Content Service**: It supports the functions of content loading to and unloading from the server.

There are other important services, such as Session Gateway Service (add and delete resources using user-to-network messages), File Service (file access), Download Service (download operational or application code to the client), and Client Profile Service.

The aforementioned services are carried out by the *Service Elements*. Specialized Service Elements are derived from the abstract **Standard Service Element** and inherit all its protocols and interfaces (Clause 7.2, Part 3). A Standard Service Element is shown by Fig. 1.14. It has a Control Plane for session and connection control-related functions and interfaces, a User Plane for communication between Service Elements and between clients

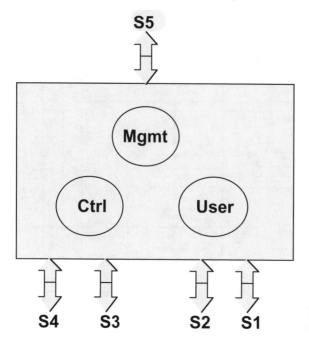

Figure 1.14 The Standard Service Element (Fig. 5, Part 3, [1]).

and Service Elements (such as VCR commands), and a Management Plane for configuration, accounting, security, and so on. The Standard Service Elements have interfaces to interact with the five information flows. Detailed protocols of these information flows are described in Section 1.2.2.9.

1.2.2.6 Delivery System

The DAVIC Delivery System (DS) includes a Core Network, an Access Network, Network and Service-Related Control, and Network Management. A Control Plane reference model of DS is shown in Fig. 1.15 (Clause 7.4, Part 2). This model demonstrates a DS configuration of transferring audio or video information from SPS to SCS. The (SL0, SL1, and SL2) Service-Related Control provides all control for the services that are offered by the DS. The Network-Related Control entity provides control functions for network configuration, connection establishment and termination, and information routing. In addition to system entities and information flows, several Reference Points, where the DAVIC compliance is checked, are indicated in this figure. One may note that the Reference Points are denoted by different shapes. The A1 and A9 Reference Points belong to the P1 partition level, the highest level partition. Reference Points A4 to A8 are inside DS and thus at the P2 (the second) partition level. Finally, Reference Points A2 and A3 are inside the Access Network and at P3 (the third) partition level.

The potential communication networks for multimedia applications can be rather broad, but DAVIC 1.0 only considers two types of networks: (1) Hertzian networks such

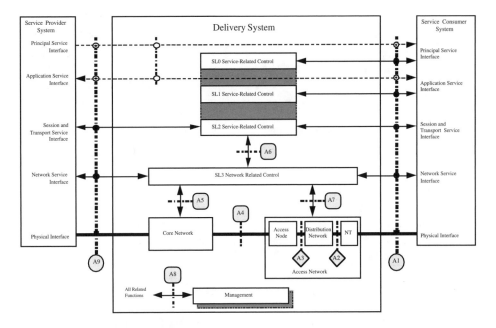

Figure 1.15   DAVIC Delivery System Control Plane model (Fig. 7-4, Part 2, [1])

as broadcast satellite and terrestrial broadcast, and (2) cabled networks such as telephone network and cable TV network. The other types of communication media such as disks, tape, and multipoint distribution system may be considered in the future (Clause 6.1, Part 4).

The Hybrid Fiber Coax (HFC) is one of the most popular network structures in current VOD trials. Figure 1.16 shows an example of an HFC Access Network with a passive Network Termination (NT) (Clause 7.2.2.4, Part 4). The HFC Access Network typically contains a fiber part and a coaxial part. The fiber extends from the Access Node to a "neighborhood node," to which 100 to 500 subscribers are connected via a common coaxial cable (bus topology). The neighborhood node performs optical to electrical conversion and makes the signals suited for transporting across the coaxial network. In this example, the client (Set-Top Box) is attached to the coaxial cable through a passive NT. Other cable network configurations such as FTTC (Fiber to the Curb), and ADSL (Asymmetric Digital Subscriber Line) are described in Clause 7.2, Part 4.

A realistic communication network needs detailed specifications on network architectures, physical interfaces, communication protocols, and network management systems. DAVIC tries to accommodate as much as possible the existing communication network standards. The choice on communication protocols is slightly easier, and they are mainly ATM, IP, and their extensions. Physical interfaces are associated with particular media and network architectures. Hence, they become *many* as described in Section 1.2.2.8. Finally,

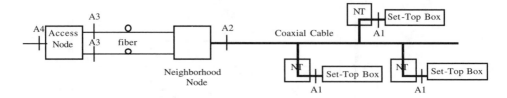

Figure 1.16   Example of an HFC Access Network (Fig. 7-6, Part 4, [1]).

the choices of Network Management Protocols are (1) Common Management Information Protocol (CMIP) defined by ITU-T X.711 and (2) Simple Network Management Protocol (SNMP) defined by RFC 1157 (Internet Society). In general, it is said that CMIP is more suited for public networks, while SNMP is more appropriate for server and STU equipment (Clause 10.4, Part 4).

1.2.2.7 Service Consumer System

There is a general Service Consumer System (SCS) reference model in DAVIC 1.0 (Clause 7.5, Part 2). However, it may be more constructive to show a realistic example, Fig. 1.17, whose modules can be found in commercial SCSs. The so-called Set-Top Box (STB) contains two main components: Network Interface Unit (NIU) and Set-Top Unit (STU). Several new Reference Points appear in this diagram. RP2 is the Reference Point located, at P1 partition level, between STU and Human Machine Service Consumer (HMSC, i.e., the "end user": peripheral, human, or machine such as TV and VCR). For example, the video interface at RP2 defines various video formats that it can handle. A0 is internal to STB and thus a P2 Reference Point. It is the interface between NIU and the rest of STB. There are other Reference Points such as RP3 and RP5. They may be important for the manufacturer to produce compatible STUs. Note that PR3, PR5, and PR7 are not specified in DAVIC 1.0.

The A0 interface in Fig. 1.17 handles the physical layer signals coming from the Access Network. There are different types of Access Network signals at the A1 interface. Hence, the purpose of NIU is to process signal based on the specific network type, whereas the A0 interface is network independent. The *Connectivity Entity* in STU deals with the low-level connection between STU and the server as well as the communication between STU and HMSC. It contains the DSM-CC User to Network (DSM-CC UN) communication module, the MPEG Stream module, the Device Driver module sending display information to the HMSC, and the Security module that performs various security functions such as authentication and data descrambling. The Session Manager in the *Environment Entity* sets up and manages the session. The *Application Entity* is the most versatile entity in STU. It contains several modules. The Media Decoding module decodes and manipulates all the media (MPEG streams, bit map, text, etc.) transferred to the STU. The DSM-CC User to User (DSM-CC UU) module translates the Runtime Engine (RTE, see below) requests to DSM-CC UU messages. The Input Device Driver handles the events from the user input

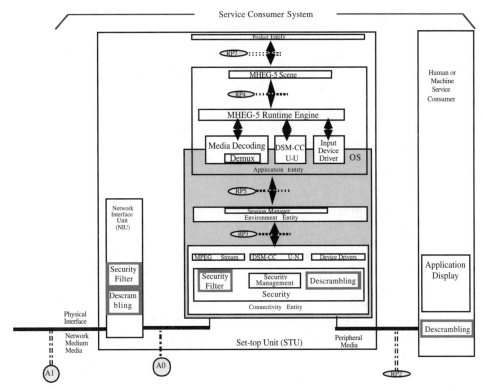

Figure 1.17   Example of DAVIC Service Consumer System (Fig. 6-1, Part 5, [1]).

devices. A key element in the STU is the MHEG-5 Runtime Engine that interprets the MHEG-5 data to run an application (producing an MHEG scene).

An overly simplified picture of an STU is a box that can show MHEG presentation. MPEG video and audio can be parts of an MHEG scene presentation. MPEG standards [17,18] have been covered elsewhere in this chapter. We now try to give a nutshell description of MHEG to those readers who are not familiar with it. The ISO/IEC JTC1/SC29/WG12 committee known as MHEG (Multimedia and Hypermedia Information Coding Expert Group) works on the exchange and presentation format for multimedia systems. The entire document (ISO/IEC 13522) is divided into five parts [19]:

- MHEG-1 (13522-1): MHEG object representation and base notation (ASN.1)
- MHEG-2 (13522-2): Alternate notation (SGML)
- MHEG-3 (13522-3): MHEG extensions for scripting language support and script object interchange
- MHEG-4 (13522-4): Registration procedure for MHEG format identifiers
- MHEG-5 (13522-5): MHEG subset for base-level implementation

Table 1.3 MHEG Inheritance Tree

MH-Object							
Behavior			Component		Descriptor	Container	Result
Action	Link	Script	Content	Container			

MHEG-1 gives the abstract definitions for the structures of MHEG objects, and MHEG-5 provides detailed implementation of a subset of MHEG-1. MHEG is also based on the object-oriented approach. An interactive multimedia presentation (an MHEG scene) is produced by creating MHEG objects, runtime instances of MHEG classes. The basic information unit in multimedia is thus encapsulated in the MHEG object. The lowest level building block is the *MH (Multimedia-Hypermedia)-Object*, which contains mainly two types of data structures: *(MHEG) Identifier* and *Description*. It is the root of the MHEG object hierarchy as shown in Table 1.3. A lower level node (object class) inherits the data structure and attributes of the node above it. Note that only the leaves of the tree denoted by boldface letters can be interchanged; they are the eight *object classes* defined in detail in MHEG-1.

One essential element in a multimedia terminal is the *Runtime Engine* that runs the presentation. An example of an MHEG engine is shown in Fig. 1.18 (Clause 7.1, Part 1, [19]). It consists of the following modules:

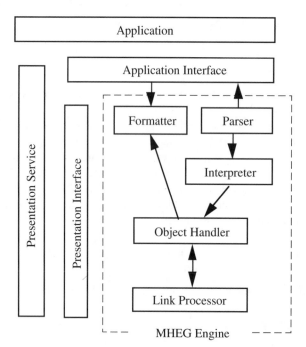

Figure 1.18 Example of MHEG engine (Fig. 4, Part 1, [4]).

- **MHEG Parser**: decodes ASN.1 (Abstract Syntax Notation One, ISO/IEC 8824-1) data

- **MHEG Interpreter**: converts MHEG object data in ASN.1 to the internal format of STU

- **MHEG Formatter**: converts internal MHEG objects into ASN.1 data

- **MHEG Object Handler**: allocates MHEG objects and controls the memory management

- **MHEG Link Processor**: evaluates the condition of MHEG objects or its element values and generates actions described in link.

The Presentation Interface in STU handles the communication between MHEG engine and Presentation services, which display images or receive input from users. DAVIC 1.0 adopts the MHEG-5 Runtime Engine (RTE) with the exclusion of certain functions (Clause 8, Part 5 [16]).

Here may be the place to say a few words about the information representation in DAVIC 1.0 (Part 9). This part is normative. It is outlined in Table 1.4. As shown in this table, other than the graphics, DAVIC 1.0 adopts the existing standards for text, audio, and video. DAVIC 1.0 defines its own formats for 16-bit RGB image and 8-bit, 4-bit, and 2-bit lookup-table graphics.

Table 1.4 DAVIC 1.0 Information Representation

Data	Coding Options
Characters	Subset of ISO 8859-1 as defined in HTML 2.0
Text	HTML 2.0
Language Information	ISO 639, Part 2
Compressed Audio	MPEG-1 audio
Linear Audio	AIFF-C
Compressed Video	MPEG-2 (MPEG-1) video
Still Picture	MPEG-2 video intra picture
Graphics	Defined in DAVIC 1.0, Part 9

ISO 8859-1: Information Technology—8-bit single-byte coded graphics character sets

HTML 2.0: HyperText Markup Language specification of the Internet Engineering Task Force (IETF)

ISO 639: Terminology—Codes for the representation of names of language

AIFF-C: Audio Interchange File Format, version C, allowing for Compression (Apple Computer, Inc.)

Table 1.5 S1 Flow High and Midlayer Protocol Stacks

ATM-based Transmission	non-ATM-based Transmission
MPEG Video/Audio Elementary Stream	MPEG Video/Audio Elementary Stream
MPEG-2 Packetized Elementary Stream	MPEG-2 Packetized Elementary Stream
MPEG-2 Transport Stream	MPEG-2 Transport Stream
AAL5	
ATM	(Lower layers)
(Lower layers)	

1.2.2.8 High, Mid-, and Low Layer Protocols and Physical Interfaces

Parts 7 (High and Midlayer protocols) and 8 (Lower Layer protocols and physical interfaces) are the two thickest volumes in DAVIC 1.0, and it is clear why. These two parts together with the Physical Instance and dynamic flow described in the next subsection are the most distinctive portion of DAVIC 1.0. They form the basis of checking a DAVIC-compliant system. The high and midlayer protocols are organized around five information flows, whereas the low and physical layers are divided according to different types of Access Network.

We first look at the high and midlayer protocols. They are essentially built around the existing standards, particularly MPEG2 DSM-CC, IP, ATM, CMIP, and SNMP. Tables 1.5–1.8 demonstrate some examples of these protocol stacks. However, these are simplified and

Table 1.6 S2 Flow High and Midlayer Protocol Stacks

User to User	Download (ATM)	Download (non-ATM)
DSM-CC UU		
OMG-CDR	DSM-CC Download Control	DSM-CC Download Control
OMG-UNO		
TCP	TCP	TCP
IP	IP	IP
	MPEG-2 Private Section	MPEG-2 Private Section
	MPEG-2 TS	MPEG-2 TS
AAL5	AAL5	
ATM	ATM	(Lower layers)
(Lower layers)	(Lower layers)	

OMG-CDR: Object Management Group—Common Data Representation
OMG-UNO: Object Management Group—Universal Network Object

Table 1.7 S3 Flow Protocol Stacks
(ATM)

DSM-CC UN
TCP/IP
AAL5
ATM
(Lower layers)

thus sometimes incomplete cases. For example, what is shown in Table 1.5 are for regular S1 data transmission. The *download* cases use different upper level MPEG2 data structures. The S2 Flow in the separate ATM VC (Virtual Channel) case can skip the MPEG2 Private Section and Transport Stream (TS) protocols. In many situations, DAVIC 1.0 supports only a subset of the existing protocols. Details are referred to Part 7, DAVIC 1.0. Also defined in this part are the Service Gateway functions (Clause 7.3.5, Part 7) and the initialization process at A0 (Clause 12, Part 7).

As for the low layer protocols and physical layer interfaces (PHY), DAVIC 1.0 adopts SDH (ITU-T Synchronous Digital Hierarchy), SONET (ANSI Synchronous Optical Network), and PDH (ITU-T Plesiochronous Digital Hierarchy) for the Core Network (Clause 6, Part 8). So this part is easy. There are many different types of Access Network, and some of them have not been completely standardized. Hence, this part becomes tedious. Several systems are described in detail, including the modulation techniques, error control codes, data frame structures, and spectrum allocation:

- *Short-range Baseband Asymmetrical PHY on copper and coax:* 16-CAP (Carrierless Amplitude/Phase Modulation) for downstream and QPSK (Quadrature Phase Shift Keying) for upstream (Clause 7.5, Part 8).
- *Passband Unidirectional PHY on coax:* 16, 64, and 256-QAM (Clause 7.6, Part 8).
- *Passband Bidirectional PHY on coax:* QPSK (Clause 7.7, Part 8).

Table 1.8 S4 Flow Protocol Stacks
(B-ISDN)

ITU-T Q.2931
ITU-T Q.2130
ITU-T Q.2110
AAL5
ATM
(Lower layers)

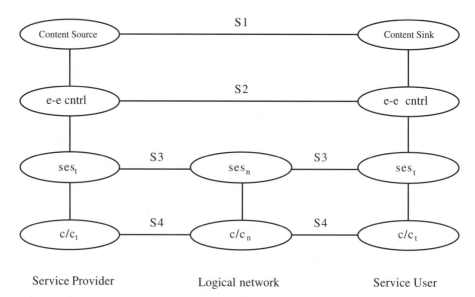

Figure 1.19 Functional entities and relationships in DAVIC dynamic modeling (Fig. 9-1, Part 12, [1]).

Other Access Networks mentioned in DAVIC 1.0 are (1) Long-range Baseband Asymmetrical PHY on copper (Clause 7.3, Part 8)—ANSI T1.413: Asymmetrical Digital Subscriber Line (ADSL), and (2) Passband Unidirectional PHY on satellite (Clause 7.8, Part 8)—ETS 300 421: Digital Broadcasting Systems (DBS). Also defined in this part is the A0 interface. Two levels are included: Level A is less than 2 Mbits/s, and Level B less than 51.8 Mbits/s (Clause 8, Part 8).

1.2.2.9 Physical Instances and Dynamic Flows

In addition to the static system reference points and interfaces specifications, a complete communication system needs to include the dynamic modeling for information flow. The functional entities involved in the DAVIC dynamic modeling are shown in Fig. 1.19. The definitions of these functional entities are as follows (Clause 9.1, Part 12).

- **Content Source**: e.g., MPEG Video Pump
- **Content Sink**: e.g., MPEG Video decoder at STU
- **e-e cntl**: terminates the S2 Flow and performs end-to-end control, e.g., VCR-like control.
- **ses**: session control entity that terminates the S3 Flow and coordinates the manipulation of resources, for example, request or clear sessions. It may be located at terminal, **ses$_t$**, or at network, **ses$_n$**

- **c/c**: call/connection control entity which terminates the S4 Flow and sets up conventional network connections. It could be at terminal side, c/c_t, or at network side, c/c_n.

In implementation, the previous dynamic model is mapped to a physical system, and thus a *Physical Instance* or *Physical Scenario* is created. Five Physical Scenarios are described in DAVIC 1.0 (Clause 9.2, Part 12), and the first three are shown in Fig. 1.20. All three scenarios are supported by ATM end-to-end. The differences among them are the locations of **ses** and **c/c**. When the STU c/c_t is located at either the Core or the Access Networks, it is called *proxy signaling*. In Physical Scenario 1, both the network ses_n and the STU c/c_t are located at the Access Network. This scenario may be used by the HFC network. Physical Scenario 2 represents the general and flexible case that matches the standard B-ISDN view: An (ATM) terminal (STB) contains a call/connection control entity, and the network session control entity resides in the Core Network. Physical Scenario 3 may be used for the non-ATM end-to-end networks, where the STU c/c_t resides in the Core Network. Hence, it relieves some of the DAVIC communication protocol requirements between the Core Network and STU. There are other cases in which the terminal connections are pre-provisioned, and therefore **c/c** entities can be eliminated. Depending on the location of network ses_n, two more scenarios are defined: Physical Scenario 4a, ses_n located at the Access Network, and Physical Scenario 4b, ses_n at the Core Network.

The final piece of specification is on the system dynamic flows. It is the dynamic behavior of a DAVIC system that is characterized by the sequence of information flows between control functional entities. Once a physical scenario is decided, we can then start a session. It is often initiated by an STU session setup request sent to the network session entity. Then, the network session entity sends a session setup request to the server. If the server session entity accepts this request, it instructs the server call/connection entity to set up S1 and S2 connections from the server to the STU. Then, the network c/c signals are transmitted among server, network, and STU to establish proper connections. Next, the session confirmation messages follow through. Depending on the physical scenarios, similar but somewhat different session setup sequences may be invoked. Another important element in the dynamic modeling is the appropriate communication protocols used at each step. It may thus be called protocol network architectures, or network instance so to speak (Clause 12, Part 12). There is no easy way to convey this portion in a paragraph or two. Hence, for details the original document should be consulted.

1.2.3 The Latest DAVIC[2]

The multimedia communication system that DAVIC is targeting is sophisticated and huge. After DAVIC 1.0 specification was completed in January 1996, it has gone through several revisions in the past 20 months and more importantly, many new items have been

---

[2]The manuscript of this chapter was completed in early 1996. Unfortunately, at the time of publication, we were unable to revise this DAVIC portion thoroughly based on the latest DAVIC Specification. Only a brief section describing the latest DAVIC progress is appended here. Readers can download DAVIC documents and learn about the latest DAVIC development through their Web site: http://www.davic.org.

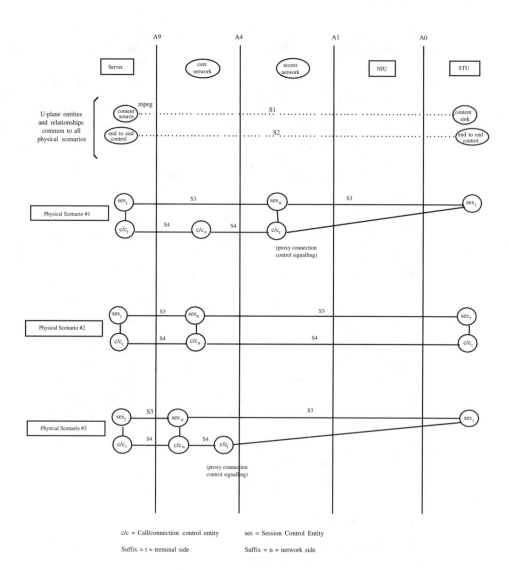

Figure 1.20 The first three Physical Scenarios in DAVIC 1.0 (Fig. 9-3, Part 12, [1]).

added into it. The so-called DAVIC 1.1 was finalized in September 1996, DAVIC 1.2 in December 1996, and DAVIC 1.3 in September 1997. Although a number of new tools have been included in these new versions, the basic structure defined in DAVIC 1.0 remains unchanged.

A partial list of the added and/or modified items in DAVIC 1.1 to DAVIC 1.3 is attached below.

- *Part 3:* Architecture for distributed server; A10 defined
- *Part 5:* Java virtual machine included in STB
- *Part 6:* Management architecture and protocol (new part)
- *Part 7:* Internet tools; protocols for A0 and STU data port
- *Part 8:* Physical interfaces for A0 and STU data port; MMDS (Multi-channel Multipoint Distribution System), LMDS (Local Multipoint Distribution System), cable modem.
- *Part 9:* Java API, reference decoder model
- *Part 10:* Basic security tools (new)
- *Part 11:* Usage information protocols (becomes a part of the normative specification)
- *Part 12:* Dynamic models for return channels, Internet access, etc.
- *Part 13:* Conformance and interoperability (new)
- *Part 14:* Contours: technology domain (new)

As the DAVIC activity progresses, an influential multimedia communication standard may eventually emerge and as we all know, an unambiguous standard is a precondition to the success of any ubiquitous communication system and service.

1.3 PART III: MULTIMEDIA STANDARDS FOR NETWORK APPLICATIONS

Tsuhan Chen

Abstract

In multimedia research and development, standards play a very important role, especially when multimedia content is to be sent over the networks. In this part, we introduce a number of important standards for network applications. These include: VRML, Java,[1] and MHEG. Some of them have been developed by international standards organizations, and others by consortiums of companies.

1.3.1 VRML

VRML, sometimes pronounced ''vermel,'' stands for Virtual Reality Modeling Language [23,24,25]. It is a language designed for multi-user interactive simulations. VRML

---

[1]Java, HotJava, JavaScript, and Java Developer's Kit (JDK) are trademarks of Sun Microsystems, Inc.

has gradually become the standard language for designing 3-D virtual worlds that can be networked together via hyperlinks over the Internet, similar to World Wide Web (WWW). It specifies the display of virtual worlds, the interaction, and the networking. Compared to the well-known Hypertext Markup Language (HTML) which is used to design text/image-based World Wide Web (WWW), VRML extends WWW to a 3-D interactive world. In other words, it defines the infrastructure and conventions of "cyberspace."

The current version of VRML that is widely used is Version 1.0, published in May 1995. VRML 1.0 defines virtual worlds with objects hyperlinked to other worlds, to HTML documents, or to other valid Multi-purpose Internet Mail Extensions (MIME) types. Future versions of VRML promise to provide more functionalities, including animation, motion physics, and real-time multi-user interaction. The development of VRML 2.0 is currently in progress.

VRML 1.0 is based on an existing specification Open Inventor, with some additions to allow linking out to the web, that is, to other universal resource locators (URL). Essentially, a subset of the Open Inventor ASCII File Format was adapted, together with some extensions to support networking, to form VRML. VRML 1.0 is designed to meet three requirements: platform independence, extensibility and ability to work well over low-bandwidth connections.

1.3.1.1 3-D Graphics

VRML is based on the Inventor File Format that supports complete descriptions of 3-D scenes with polygonally rendered objects, lighting, materials, ambient properties, camera angles, and other effects. Geometry, transformations, attributes, lighting, shading, and textures are the fundamentals of 3-D graphics.

Geometry is defined by XYZ coordinates and some semantics. VRML 1.0 has a few simple shapes: Cube, Cone, Cylinder and Sphere, and the IndexedFaceSet. Geometry has properties—specifically, "material" properties describe how light is reflected off the surface of an object. Transformations (scale, rotate, translate) can be used to position and scale objects in relation to others.

Lighting is the process of determining how much light strikes an object and how much should be reflected. There are spot lights, light bulbs (points), and sun (directional) light. There are also ambient light, to simulate what we call diffuse light, and diffuse reflection, which is conceptually similar in that it is independent of the viewing angle.

Shading determines how the colors (determined in the lighting step) are spread across the surface. The choices are flat shading, in which each facet can be seen to have the same color, and Gouraud shading. In Gouraud shading, the reflected color is calculated at each vertex and then smoothly interpolated between them.

1.3.1.2 Basic Nodes in VRML

Theoretically, VRML allows us to define objects that can contain anything—3-D geometry, musical instrument digital interface (MIDI) data, JPEG images, anything. In particular, VRML defines a set of objects useful for doing 3-D graphics. These objects are called "nodes."

Nodes are arranged in hierarchical structures called scene graphs. Scene graphs are more than just a collection of nodes; the scene graph defines an ordering for the nodes. The scene graph has a notion of state—nodes earlier in the scene can affect nodes that appear later in the scene. For example, a Rotation or Material node will affect all the following nodes in the scene. A mechanism is defined to limit the effects of properties (separator nodes), allowing parts of the scene graph to be functionally isolated from other parts.

A node has the following characteristics:

- *What kind of object it is:* A node might be a cube, a sphere, a texture map, a transformation, and so on.

- *The parameters that distinguish this node from other nodes of the same type:* For example, each Sphere node might have a different radius, and different texture map nodes will certainly contain different images to use as the texture maps. These parameters are called fields. A node can have zero or more fields.

- *A name to identify this node:* Being able to name nodes and refer to them elsewhere is very powerful; it allows a scene's author to give hints to applications using the scene about what is in the scene, and it creates possibilities for very powerful scripting extensions. Nodes do not have to be named, but if they are named, they can have only one name. However, names do not have to be unique; several different nodes may be given the same name.

- *Child nodes:* Object hierarchy is implemented by allowing some types of nodes to contain other nodes. Parent nodes traverse their children in order during rendering. Nodes that may have children are referred to as group nodes. Group nodes can have zero or more children.

The syntax chosen to represent these pieces of information is as follows:

```
DEF objectname objecttype { fields  children }
```

Only the object type and curly braces are required; nodes may or may not have a name, fields, and children. Node names cannot begin with a digit and cannot contain spaces or control characters, single or double quote characters, backslashes, curly braces, the plus character, or the period character.

For easy identification of VRML files, every VRML file must begin with the characters:

```
#VRML V1.0 ascii
```

Any characters after these on the same line are ignored. The line is terminated by either the ASCII newline or carriage-return characters. The # character begins a comment; all characters until the next newline or carriage return are ignored. Note that comments and whitespace may not be preserved; in particular, a VRML document server may strip comments and extraneous whitespace from a VRML file before transmitting it. Info nodes should be used for persistent information like copyrights or author information. Info nodes could also be used for object descriptions. After the required header, a VRML file contains exactly one VRML node. That node may of course be a group node, containing any number of other nodes.

VRML uses a cartesian, right-handed, three-dimensional coordinate system. By default, objects are projected onto a two-dimensional device by projecting them in the direction of the positive Z-axis, with the positive X-axis to the right and the positive Y-axis up. A camera or modeling transformation may be used to alter this default projection. The standard unit for lengths and distances specified is meters. The standard unit for angles is radians.

There are two general classes of fields: fields that contain a single value (where a value may be a single number, a vector, or even an image) and fields that contain multiple values. Each field type defines the format for the values it writes. Multiple-valued fields are written as a series of values separated by commas, all enclosed in square brackets.

1.3.1.3 An Example

Here we give a simple example of a VRML file named `test.wrl`.

```
#VRML V1.0 ascii

Separator {

        Material {
                diffuseColor 1 1 1
                shininess 0.2
                transparency 0
        } #Material

        AsciiText {
                string  "This is a test!"
                spacing 1
                justification CENTER
                width 0
        } #AsciiText

        DEF Cube1 Separator {
                Texture2 {
                        filename "test.gif"
                }
                Translation {
                        translation -20 30 0
                } #Translation
                Cube {
                        width  30
                        height 30
                        depth  30
                } #Cube
```

```
                } #Cube1 Separator

        DEF Cylinder1 Separator {
                Translation {
                        translation 20 30 0
                } #Translation
                WWWAnchor {
                        name "http://www.att.com"
                        map NONE
                } #WWWAnchor
                Cylinder {
                        parts ALL
                        radius 15
                        height 30
                } #Cylinder
        } #Cylinder1 Separator

    } #Separator
```

Most of the nodes defined in the above VRML program are easy to understand. The whole file test.wrl is a group node, enclosed in the Separator node. This group node contains four nodes: a Material node, an AsciiText node, a node called Cube1, and a node called Cylinder1. The Material node specifies surface material properties for the objects. The AsciiText node defines a text string. The node Cube1 contains three nodes. The Texture2 node specifies the mapping of an image file to the object. In this case, a GIF file test.gif is used as the texture of the cube. A translation node specifies where an object is. The cube node defines a cube of certain sizes as defined in its fields. The node Cylinder1 defines a cylinder. Note that a WWWAnchor link is attached to this node, so the user can "navigate" to the designated web site by clicking on the cylinder. A WWWAnchor node provides the same feature that HREF anchors provide in HTML. If we view this file with a VRML browser, we can get a 3-D world as shown in Fig. 1.21.

1.3.1.4 VRML 2.0

As mentioned earlier, except for the hyperlinking feature, VRML 1.0 does not support enough interactive behavior. This was intentionally left to be covered by later versions. Many things can be added to VRML 1.0 in order to create a full multi-user 3-D environment, such as a new protocol for registering presence and a mechanism for getting updates.

The VRML Architecture Group (VAG) put out a Request-for-Proposals (RFP) in January 1996 for VRML 2.0. Six proposals were received. One proposal, Moving Worlds, designed by the Silicon Graphics' VRML 1.0 team with Sony Research and Mitra, was eventually selected by the VRML community in a poll. At the time of this writing, it has also become an ISO standard, referred to as ISO/IEC CD 14772, Version 2.0. For more information, please see http://www.vrml.org.

Figure 1.21   An example 3-D world defined by VRML.

1.3.1.5   Further Information

For more information, the readers are encouraged to look into the VRML Repository (`http://www.sdsc.edu/vrml`) and visit the following web sites:

```
http://vrml.wired.com
http://www.oki.com/vrml/VRML_FAQ.html
http://www.vrml.org
```

1.3.2   Java

Java is a general-purpose object-oriented programming language that programmers can use to develop almost any applications. However, several important features of Java make it extremely suitable for networked-based applications, especially for WWW. Java has gradually become the standard programming language for the Internet. Many people believe Java to be the choice for adding multimedia programs and interactivity to web pages. In principle, interactive web pages can be constructed without Java. For example, data-entry forms and Common Gateway Interface (CGI) programming are also capable of providing interactivity to web pages. However, one main difference is that CGI scripts have to run on the server, which slows down the server when many clients attempt to run the CGI scripts. With Java, the applications can run on the client machine.

1.3.2.1   Features of Java

Many features of Java make it the choice of multimedia programming for network-based applications. Here are some of these important features:

Architecture Neutral It is often the dream of programmers that if they could develop an application and compile the code only once, then it would run on any number of platforms without modification. This is indeed one important feature of Java. A Java program, once compiled into an architecture neutral object file, called "bytecode," can be executed on any platform. More specifically, any platform that supports the

Java runtime environment, that is, Java interpreter, can execute bytecodes. It is called ''bytecode'' since most of the opcodes are 8 bits in length. The bytecode instruction set is designed to be both easy to interpret on any machine and easily translated into native machine code on the fly.

The other way to look at this is that the Java runtime is some kind of universal ''software microprocessor,'' or ''virtual machine,'' that makes arbitrary platforms, different architectures, and operating systems look the same to Java programs after they have been compiled into bytecode.

This feature is important for supporting applications on networks. In general, networks are composed of a variety of systems with a variety of CPU architectures and operating systems. With Java, the software developers do not need to worry about the platforms and operation systems that the users have. Also, the users do not need to worry about the software versions and compatibility. Distributing commercial or educational programs over the Internet is therefore much easier. In fact, development and distribution of software, not necessarily via networks, also become much easier.[2]

Simple For C and C++ programmers, the learning curve for Java is very smooth, because Java was designed to have a C look. The object-oriented nature is very similar to C++ with some extensions from Objective C for more dynamic method resolution. Also, Java avoids much complexity by doing away with many confusing features that C++ has. Another aspect of being simple is being small. One of Java's goals is to enable the construction of software that can run stand-alone in small machines. The size of the basic interpreter and class support is only about 40K bytes.

Distributed Java is designed for the concept of ''downloadable software.'' That is, applications are downloaded from the network server to the local machine only when necessary. Such applications are often called ''applets.'' (See Section 1.3.2.3 for details.) With Java, software version control is easy because every time a user runs a program, the most current version is automatically loaded for use. Java has an extensive library of routines for coping with TCP/IP protocols like HTTP and FTP. Java applications can open and access objects across the net via URLs with the same ease that programmers are used to when accessing a local file system.

For example, suppose you wanted to download a compressed postscript document from somewhere on the web. Currently, you would need to make sure that you had the correct version of the latest decompression and conversion utilities, word processor, and the like, all carefully integrated into the correct version of your operating system. But if all the needed applications were installed on the web site, the user could just click on the web page document link. The right applet could transparently load and display the requested document on your Java-capable browser, correctly and automatically.

Security For distribution of data and applications over a variety of unknown networks, security is, of course, the biggest concern. Toward that end, by default, applets are assumed to be hostile and untrusted (in the security sense) by a Java-capable browser. Before a Java interpreter executes a java bytecode, the bytecode is first authenticated by a bytecode verifier, based on public-key encryption. Even when a Java interpreter executes a bytecode, many restrictions are applied to keep the applets from doing harm

---

[2]It is understandable that some of the companies who have a monopoly based on their operating systems or microprocessor architecture may be made uncomfortable by this.

to the client machine. For example, writing on the local disk, accessing other local files, and saving what takes place at the client (such as keystrokes and mouse clicking) are not allowed. For the same reason, pointers that are common in C programming are removed from Java because the use of pointers would make it possible for an applet to access private data or to manipulate certain forbidden areas in the memory of the local machine.

Portable Unlike C and C++, there are no "implementation-dependent" aspects of the specification, which makes Java programs more portable. For example, int always means a signed two's complement 32-bit integer, and float always means a 32-bit IEEE 754 floating-point number. Also, the libraries that are part of the system define many portable interfaces, including window handling and other graphic user interfaces (GUI).

Performance Since Java is interpreted, the performance of interpreted bytecodes may not always be enough. When that happens, the bytecodes can be translated on the fly (at runtime) into machine code for the particular CPU the application is running on. The bytecode format was designed with generating machine codes in mind, so the actual process of generating machine code is generally simple.

Robust Java is intended for writing programs that must be reliable in a variety of ways. Java puts a lot of emphasis on early checking for possible problems, later dynamic (runtime) checking, and eliminating situations that are error prone. For example, Java requires declarations and does not support C-style implicit declarations. The linker understands the type system and repeats many of the type checks done by the compiler to guard against version mismatch problems. Dynamic languages like Lisp, TCL, and Smalltalk are often used for prototyping. One reason for their success in this area is their robustness: you don't have to worry about freeing or corrupting memory. Programmers can be relatively fearless about dealing with memory because they don't have to worry about it getting corrupted. Java has this property, and it has been found to be very liberating.

Dynamic The same principle can be extended to more complex Java software packages. Since Java supports dynamic binding, the data of interest can be loaded up front, and then the rest of the computer program can be cobbled together according to the user's choices "on-the-fly," without re-compiling the whole program. Applications of this function may include financial analysis and transaction tools, multi-user games and gaming, virtual worlds, audiovisual chat, telephony, wireless, Internet "shopping," and auctions. In short, since applets require no "advance purchase," applets are uniquely suited for application domains that may be linked to a web site and visited spontaneously. By making interconnections between modules later, Java completely avoids these problems and makes use of the object-oriented paradigm much more straightforward. Libraries can freely add new methods and instance variables without any effect on their clients.

Multithreading Programming Java provides multithreading programming so that multitasking is possible, which is an important feature especially for interactive multimedia applications. Java has a sophisticated set of synchronization primitives that are based on the widely used monitor and condition variable paradigm.

1.3.2.2   Java versus C++ and C

In addition to the above features through which Java distinguishes itself from other object-oriented program languages, here we describe a few other differences between Java and C/C++.

Java omits many rarely used, poorly understood, confusing features of C++. Many of these features have been omitted because they promote programming errors, security risks, or add unnecessary complexity to the language. These omitted features consist primarily of operator overloading, multiple inheritance, extensive automatic coercions, and C pointers. Memory management, such as the allocation and freeing of memory, is automatic; a garbage collection algorithm runs as a low-priority thread in the background. More details can be found in [26].

The biggest difference between Java and C/C++ is that Java has a pointer model that eliminates the possibility of overwriting memory and corrupting data. Instead of pointer arithmetic, Java has true arrays. This allows subscript checking to be performed. In addition, it is not possible to turn an arbitrary integer into a pointer by casting.

1.3.2.3   Java-Capable Web Browsers,
Applets, and JavaScript

Two web browsers are capable of running the Java program to incorporate audio, video, and animation into a web page: Hot-Java and Netscape Navigator 2.0.[3]

Since Java is a programming language, it can be used to program any stand-alone applications like any other programming language. However, Java is designed especially for network-based applications, so it is most often used as "applets." An applet is a Java program that executes in the context of a web browser. Java applets typically reside at the server and are downloaded to the client by the web browser only when activated.

Here is an example of a Java applet, named `Test.java`:

```
import java.applet.Applet;
import java.awt.Graphics;

public class Test extends Applets {
   public void paint(graphics g) {
      g.drawString("This is a test.", 40, 20);
   }
}
```

Here the `java.awt.Graphics` is part of a set of platform-independent GUI classes called Abstract Windows Toolkit (AWT). We compile `Test.java` to get the bytecode named `Test.class`. When an HTML page that refers to this applet using the following command line

```
<applet code="Test.class" width=300 height=100></applet>
```

[3]Netscape Navigator is a trademark of Netscape Communications Corporation.

is loaded by a web browser, the applet executes, and in this example, a window with the message `This is a test.` is displayed.

Of course, the most powerful feature of Java is that the Java bytecode may reside in a remote site. In this case, it can be activated by the following command line in an HTML page:

```
<applet codebase="home URL of the applet"
        code="Test.class" width=300 height=100>
```

Applets can also accept parameters from the web page, such as in the following example:

```
<applet>
   code="applet_name.class" width=300 height=100>
   <param name=parameter_name value=parameter_value>
</applet>
```

A stand-alone Java application that performs the same task (except for the window interface) would look as follows:

```
public class Test {
   public static void man (String[] args) {
      System.out.println("This is a test.");
   }
}
```

Of course, most Java applets do much more than this simple example. Java applets can be anything from animation to embedded spreadsheets to games. Compared to applets, a Java application does not require a browser or bytecode verification, and it may perform file I/O operations and other things that are not allowed for applets.

Another form of Java programming is called JavaScript. JavaScript is only available with Netscape Navigator 2.0 beta 3 and later. JavaScript is a scripting language that allows a Java code to be included in the HTML page. For example, if we want to include the above-mentioned Java application inside the HTML page, we can do

```
<SCRIPT LANGUAGE="JavaScript">
      document.write("This is a test.");
</SCRIPT>
```

JavaScript can also be used to define functions (or ''methods'' as they are called in Java), work with forms, and respond to other user-initiated events.

1.3.2.4 Summary

The Java language provides a powerful addition to the tools that programmers have at their disposal. Java makes programming for multiple platforms easier because the compiled

Java code is architecture-neutral. Hence, Java applications are ideal for a diverse environment like the Internet. For more information, the readers should visit the Java home site at `http://www/javasoft.com`. If you are interested in developing software in Java, you should download the Java Developer's Kit (JDK) from the web site.

1.3.3 MHEG

MHEG—the Multimedia and Hypermedia Expert Group—is part of the ISO's standard committee SC29. While the term *multimedia* is widely used and well understood, the term *hypermedia* refers to the ability of navigating multimedia objects across links, often referred to as hyperlinking [27,28].

While the JPEG working group, WG 1, deals with the coding of still pictures and the MPEG working group, WG 11, develops standards for motion pictures and the associated audio, the MHEG working group WG 12 works on the multimedia and hypermedia aspect. This group, formally known as ISO/IEC JTC 1 / SC 29 / WG 12, is developing a standard for coding, representation, and interchange of multimedia and hypermedia information. The standard itself is often referred to as MHEG as well, and sometimes MHEG is also used to refer to the objects defined in the standard.

The MHEG standard document has been assigned the number 13522 by ISO. The standard document has been approved to the Draft International Standards (DIS) stage, and the official title is ''ISO/IEC DIS 13522-1 Information technology—Coding of multimedia and hypermedia information.'' Currently, there are three parts:

- ISO/IEC DIS 13522-1 MHEG object representation—Base notation (ASN.1)
- ISO/IEC DIS 13522-3 MHEG script interchange representation
- ISO/IEC DIS 13522-4 Registration procedure for MHEG format identifier

Parts 1 and 3 cover representation, conversion, coding, communication processing, and information interchange of audio, graphics, image, and video data. Part 4 also covers formats, identification methods, organizations for code assignment, procedure, and registration of data. We will discuss these in more detail in the following sections.

The MHEG group also works closely with an ITU-T study group. The ITU-T identifies MHEG as Recommendation T.171, which is part of the T.17x series for audiovisual interactive services.

MHEG tries to provide a standard for the representation of multimedia and hypermedia objects that can be interchanged among a wide range of applications, from broadcast networks and telecommunications to storage devices. These multimedia and hypermedia objects are to be represented in the ''final form,'' which means there is no need to restructure/parse these objects before they can be used. These objects are intended for interactive and real-time use on equipment with minimal resources. Therefore, a system that decodes and presents MHEG objects is expected to be simpler than a typical graphics-based workstation. An MHEG implementation, sometimes referred to as MHEG runtime, typically has complexity in the range of a set-top box for interactive TV.

In MHEG, the objects are encoded using the syntax defined in the Abstract Syntax Notation One (ASN.1), Part 1 of the MHEG standard. This is also called Basic Encoding

Rules (BER). ASN.1 allows the specification of data structure to be system independent. Hence, the coding and representation are object-oriented. A minimal MHEG runtime environment should therefore provide an entity for decoding the ASN.1 data structures and an entity called MHEG engine, which parses and interprets the MHEG objects. The engine makes interactive presentation of the objects to the user. It communicates with the local presentation environment and the MHEG objects. It is even-driven in that it responds to the events initiated by the using application or the user, for example, a button press.

For the content representation, MHEG relies on other standards like JPEG or MPEG. No new content data model is introduced, but it is possible to integrate proprietary formats. For the description of the relation in time and space between the content data portions, a few basic mechanisms are introduced, which fulfill the needs of most multimedia and hypermedia objects and documents. More complex mechanisms can be added by the using applications.

MHEG is aimed at interactive hypermedia applications such as on-line textbooks and encyclopaedias. It is also suited for many of the interactive multimedia applications currently available (in platform-specific form) on CD-ROM. MHEG could, for instance, be used as the data structuring standard for a future home entertainment interactive multimedia appliance. To address such markets, MHEG represents objects in a nonrevisable form and is therefore unsuitable as an input format for hypermedia authoring applications: its place is perhaps more as an output format for such tools. Thus, MHEG is not a multimedia document processing format; instead it provides rules for the structure of multimedia objects, which permits the objects to be represented in a convenient form (e.g., video objects could be MPEG-encoded). It uses ASN.1 as a base syntax to represent object structure, but it allows for the use of other syntax notations. An SGML syntax is also specified.

1.3.3.1 Classes

As mentioned earlier, MHEG is object-oriented. MHEG objects belong to a number of classes. Three main classes are the content class, the action class, which defines actions happening to the content, and the link class, which links actions to the content.

Content. The content class describes the presentation objects. It contains several fields. The field `Classification` specifies the data type, for example, `Text` or `Video`. The field `Content-Hook` defines the encoding scheme, for example, ASCII or MHEG. The field `Content-Data.Data-Inclusion` specifies the data to be included, such as the text `"HELLO"`. The field `Content-Data.Data-Reference.System-Indentifier` defines the reference for the material, for example, filenames like `"c:\test.mpg"`. Here are two examples:

```
Content-Class {
   MHEG-Identifier.Object-Number : 1,
   Classification : Text,
   Content-Hook {
      Encoding-Identification : ASCII},
      Content-Data.Data-Inclusion : "HELLO"
```

```
    }

Content-Class {
    MHEG-Identifier.Object-Number : 2,
    Classification : Video,
    Content-Hook {
        Encoding-Identification : ISO-11172-MPEG-Video,
        Encoding-Description : video rate in kbs},
    Content-Data.Data-Reference.System-Indentifier :
            "c:\test.mpg",
    Original-Perception {
        Original-Size : 256 pt, 240 pt, null,
        Original-Duration : 15 min}
}
```

MHEG objects can also be combined into more complex objects. This is called composition. For MHEG 5, objects are combined into pages.

Action. The action class is used for user interaction. There are two kinds of interaction:

- Selection: user choice from alternatives (e.g., push buttons)
- Modification: typing text

The action class is used to define the behavior of MHEG objects—an action object is a message sent to a MHEG object. Some actions trigger a state change in the MHEG object; this state change may then be used to alter the behavior of another MHEG object.

Link. The link class provides the synchronization mechanism that links an action object with a content object. The links are triggered by events within the system. A link is between one source and one or more targets. The link is executed by the triggering of a trigger condition. This condition is expressed by a state change in the source objects. It is possible to combine trigger conditions with a constraint condition.

MHEG Objects. There are four main types of MHEG objects (which may be textual information, graphics, video, audio, etc.):

Input object. A user input such as a button press or modification

Output object. The content: graphics, audiovisual display, text

Interactive object. A ''composite'' object containing both input and output objects

Hyper object. A ''composite'' object containing both input and output objects, with links between them.

MHEG supports various synchronization modes for presenting output objects in these relationships. It will be some time before MHEG reaches IS status. Its future will then depend on market requirements and trends. At the time of this writing, there are no MHEG products, but British Telecom has developed a demonstration application called MADE. For more information, please see http://www.demon.co.uk/tcasey/wg12.html.

References

[1] AOE Group, ''MPEG-4 Proposal Package Description (PPD)—Rev. 3,'' ISO/IEC JTC1/SC29/WG11 N0998, Tokyo, July 1995.

[2] AOE Group, ''MPEG-4 Testing and Evaluation Procedures Document,'' ISO/IEC JTC1/SC29/WG11 N0999, Tokyo, July 1995.

[3] L. Chiariglione, ''MPEG-4 Call for Proposals,'' ISO/IEC JTC1/ SC29/WG11 N0997, Tokyo, July 1995.

[4] A. Puri, ''Status and Direction of the MPEG-4 Standard,'' International Symposium on Multimedia and Video Coding, New York, October 1995.

[5] ITU-T, ''Draft ITU-T Recommendation H.263: Video Coding for Low Bitrate Communication,'' Dec. 1995.

[6] T. Ebrahimi, ''Report of Ad hoc Group on Definition of VMs for Content Based Video Representation,'' ISO/IEC JTC1/SC29/WG11 MPEG 96/0642, Munich, Jan. 1996.

[7] A. Puri, ''Report of Ad hoc Group on Coordination of Future Core Experiments in MPEG-4 Video,'' ISO/IEC JTC1/SC29/WG11 MPEG 96/0669, Munich, Jan. 1996.

[8] MPEG-4 Requirements Ad hoc Group, ''Draft of MPEG-4 Requirements,'' ISO/IEC JTC1/SC29/WG11 N1238, Florence, Mar. 1996.

[9] MPEG-4 Video Group, ''MPEG-4 Video Verification Model Version 2.0,'' ISO/IEC JTC1/SC29/WG11 N1260, Florence, Mar. 1996.

[10] MSDL Ad hoc Group, ''MSDL Specification V1.1,'' ISO/IEC JTC1/SC29/WG11 N1246, Florence, Mar. 1996.

[11] MPEG-4 Integration Group,''MPEG-4 SNHC Call for Proposals,'' ISO/IEC JTC1/ SC29/WG11 N1195, Florence, Mar. 1996.

[12] MPEG-4 Integration Group, ''MPEG-4 SNHC Proposal Package Description,'' ISO/ IEC JTC1/SC29/WG11 N1199, Florence, Mar. 1996.

[13] L. Chiariglione, ''Resolutions of 34th WG11 Meeting,'' ISO/IEC JTC1/SC29/WG11, N1186, Florence, Mar. 1996.

[14] H. Peterson, ''Report of the Ad Hoc group on MPEG-4 Video Testing Logistics,'' ISO/IEC JTC1/SC29/WG11 Doc. MPEG95/0532, Nov. 1995.

[15] J. Osterman, ''Report of the Ad Hoc group on Evaluation of Tools for Nontested Functionalities of Video submissions,'' ISO/IEC JTC1/SC29/WG11 Doc. MPEG95/0488, Nov. 1995.

[16] Digital Audio-Visual Council, *DAVIC 1.0 Specification*, Jan. 1996.

[17] MPEG (Motion Picture Experts Group, ISO-IEC JTC1/SC29/WG11), 11172 *Information Technology—Coding of Moving Pictures and Associated Audio for Digital Storage Media at up to about 1.5 Mbits/s*, 1993.

[18] MPEG (Motion Picture Experts Group, ISO-IEC JTC1/ SC29/WG11), 13818 *Information Technology—Generic Coding of Moving Pictures and Associated Audio Information*, 1995.

[19] MHEG (Multimedia and Hypermedia Information Coding Expert Group, ISO-IEC JTC1/SC29/WG12), 13522 *Information Technology—Coding of Multimedia and Hypermedia Information*, drafts in 1995.

[20] L. Chiariglione, ''DAVIC—Preparing technology for end-to-end interoperability,'' *IEEE Multimedia Newsletter*, pp. 5–8, Dec. 1995.

[21] Object Management Group (OMG), *The Common Object Request Broker: Architecture and Specification.* Revision 1.2, Dec. 1993.

[22] H. Fujiwara, ''DAVIC Activities,'' *Standards and Common Interfaces for Video Information Systems (Critical Review), SPIE Photonics East '95 Symposium*, Philadelphia, Oct. 1995.

[23] Bell, G., Parisi, A., and Pesce, M., ''The virtual reality modeling language,'' Version 1.0 Specification.

[24] Mark Pesce, *VRML: Browsing and Building Cyberspace*, New York, Macmillan Publishing, Aug. 1995.

[25] Andrea L. Ames, David R. Nadeau, and John L. Moreland, *The VRML Sourcebook*, New York: Wiley Computer Publishing.

[26] http://java.sun.com/progGuide/noMoreC/index.html

[27] B. Markey, ''Emerging Hypermedia Standards,'' Multimedia for Now and the Future, Usenix Conference Proceedings, June 1991.

[28] F. Kretz and F. Colaitis, ''Standardizing Hypermedia Information Objects,'' *IEEE Communications Magazine*, p. 60, May 1992.

Chapter 2

MULTIMEDIA TECHNOLOGIES AND VLSI SYSTEMS

Horng-Dar Lin

Abstract

Multimedia technologies are exciting, dynamic, and far reaching. While the technologies are still growing and evolving, they have already changed how people work, learn, create, collaborate, communicate, and spend their leisure time. This phenomenon is attributed to technological advances in data processing, transport, and understanding of various human–media interactions. For example, digital video technology matured only after researchers understood how to discard visually insignificant components, how to compress the significant portion into data, how to transport the coded data safely and effectively, and how to regenerate video despite possible transport problems. It takes a long time to understand the science and principle behind these complex multimedia technologies. People enjoy multimedia products and services nonetheless because these complex processing, storage, and transport can be implemented at low cost. The main reason, of course, is the development of very large-scale integrated circuits (VLSIs).

This chapter deals with the technology components within the multimedia system and their implementations. Through the discussions, readers can find out what kind of roles VLSI plays within multimedia, what kind of design options are available, and what kind of design tradeoffs need to be considered. The discussion will include both the transport and the processing side. But first let's look at the big picture.

2.1 MULTIMEDIA SYSTEM AND TECHNOLOGY COMPONENTS

Multimedia systems and technologies have grown so fast that we see lots of variations in their complexity and diversity. For example, a simple case would be personal computer multimedia applications that rely mostly on playback of audio and visual information. The audio portion could be music or sound clips that are pre-stored or synthesized on the fly. The technology choices could be MPEG or wave-table, for example. Similarly, the visual information could be text, picture, video, or graphics. Again they can be stored or synthesized based on various technology choices or standards. Such types of multimedia systems can be modeled as shown in Fig. 2.1. Note that the visual block may contain multiple types of source materials such as text, images, video, and graphics. Each type of source material could be retrieved, reconstructed, and displayed in full parallel and only needs to be coordinated properly by the control block. Such a control block responds to users' requests and accommodates source programming and system variations. Other media materials perceivable to human sensory systems follow the same controlled playback structure as the audio and visual media.

The multimedia playback system usually follows predefined scripts in playing back the audiovisual information created by original authors. In such a case, the retrieval and

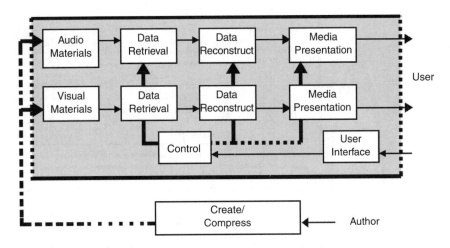

Figure 2.1   Example of a multimedia playback system.

playback of the audiovisual material is well defined. Once the user picks the playback script and parameters, the control block adapts to the performance of the hardware platform and exercises well-controlled media storage retrieval and playback. Because most of the interactions are within a well-controlled local system, such multimedia playback systems usually are not as complicated as general multimedia communication systems.

In general, a multimedia system not only retrieves information but also delivers information. This is no different from how humans communicate by carrying on two-way conversations. The interesting part is that in multimedia communication systems people do not have to be in the same room to communicate through different media. Voice, gestures, body language, documents, slide shows, pictures, movies, and many other forms of communications can be transported through multimedia communication networks, just like two persons can speak on the phone. Figure 2.2 shows a complete multimedia communications system that contains bidirectional links and likely also involves multiple parties. Note that the purpose of multimedia terminals in shaded boxes is just like today's phones. And, yes, the multimedia terminals could be very different, just as the phones can be different and people can still talk. A multimedia terminal includes bidirectional links to send and receive information through the communication network. Because general communications networks are more complex and more dynamic than a storage readback system, a communication network interface is required at both the source end and the destination end to coordinate the generation, transport, and consumption of multimedia information through the link. The control blocks at both ends need to consider the overall communications, which include the compression, transport, and reconstruction of the multimedia materials.

General multimedia communications systems match the models described in Figs. 2.1 and 2.2. For example, multimedia learning on the PC platform matches the model in Fig. 2.1, while virtual classroom learning matches the model in Fig. 2.2. That is, in virtual classroom learning, the instructor could deliver the course through the multimedia network, while the

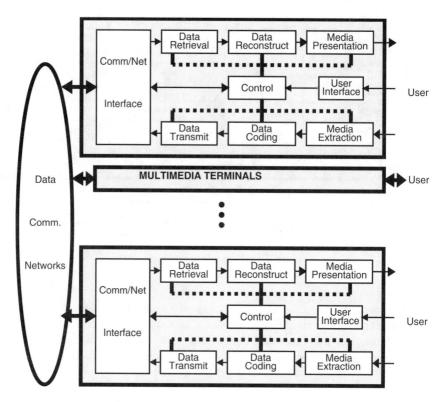

Figure 2.2   Example of a multimedia communications system.

students could ask questions and talk to other students in group assignments through the network as well. As another example, digital video discs follow the first model, while digital cable systems follow the second model. The source end of the digital cable system could be a server that stores and reprograms multimedia materials received from other source ends. It could also respond to user requests to deliver information dynamically. In addition, users could use the more advanced cable network to transport data or to communicate with other users or servers.

Although complex, the multimedia playback and communications systems share common technology-building blocks. Obviously, both systems consist of coordinated unidirectional links of a single medium. The basic model of the unidirectional single-medium link is shown in Fig. 2.3. Information flows through the extraction, representation, exchange, reconstruction, and presentation phase. The technological elements within the flow include two main categories as identified in different shaded regions in Fig. 2.3. One category is technological elements involving processing of information. This processing could include formatting, enhancement, compression, decompression, analysis, and synthesis. The other category is technological elements involving transport of information. This includes not just the information exchange itself, but also proper ways of representing, reconstructing,

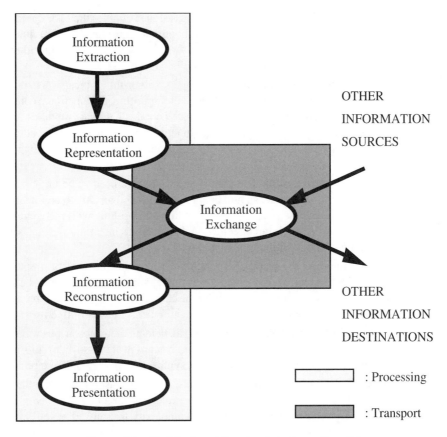

Figure 2.3 Model of a unidirectional single-medium link.

sequencing, storing, retrieving, protecting, sharing, and signaling information. These two categories of technological elements serve different objectives. The technology for media processing concentrates on physiological effectiveness and processing effectiveness. The technology for media transport focuses on bandwidth effectiveness and robustness of infrastructure. The media processing and transport technologies, however, rely on a third technology, VLSI technology, to achieve performance and cost-effectiveness.

The VLSI technology not only implements but also creates a bridge between what is theoretically optimal and what is economically feasible. It is much more than just the IC process technology. It includes technologies in the area of algorithm, architecture, VLSI design, circuits design, IC process, and manufacturing. For readers interested in implementation of multimedia systems, the main focal area includes the following:

- **Application algorithm design.** Although most systems and standards have functionally equivalent algorithms to perform specific functions, the implementation can vary significantly. The algorithm targeted for a specific application can be modified for performance and cost-effectiveness. For example, the task could be choosing finite bit precision or developing suboptimal algorithms that are much more cost-effective but still deliver high quality. Or in some cases the algorithm is modified from a sequential algorithm to a parallel algorithm.

- **Algorithm to architecture mapping.** An algorithm typically consists of different functional components. To implement the algorithm, the functional components need to be mapped to the architecture, which contains hardware modules for performing the processing. In many cases, the functional components can be computed in parallel. This requires structuring and sequencing the interactions among the hardware modules as well.

- **Architecture design.** The architectural modules need to be organized physically. The design, of course, should be integrated with algorithm to architecture mapping. In addition, quite often there are multiple algorithms with different requirements mapped to a single architecture. A balanced architectural design is important in such multi-algorithm implementation.

- **Architecture to circuits on silicon.** The architecture can be implemented with different circuit components. For example, storage elements may be implemented as registers or memories of different characteristics. The mapping again requires joint consideration of architectural requirements and cost-effectiveness of circuits.

- **Circuits techniques.** For a given circuit element there are various ways of designing the actual circuits. In semicustom and custom designs, such circuits achieve much higher density or speed than circuits synthesized from standard circuit libraries.

- **VLSI design methodology and tools.** A major reason for the continuing progress of VLSI technology is the ability to explore different designs and manage the design complexity. The VLSI design complexity has moved beyond the millions of transistors mark and soon will be in the tens of millions or even higher complexity. These complex VLSI chips often implement a complete system on silicon. Like any complex system, VLSI systems require a rigorous design methodology and tools to automate and maintain design quality.

Implementing multimedia systems in VLSI requires multidiscipline expertise. Often the best results are based on a full understanding of application algorithms, architectural tradeoffs, available circuit techniques, and design methodologies. The following sections discuss various VLSI applications in multimedia systems and architectural examples in media transport and media processing.

2.2 MULTIMEDIA TRANSPORT AND VLSI

VLSI applications for transporting multimedia information depend on the nature of the information exchange itself. The information exchange may happen at three levels of granularity: micro, local, or remote as shown in Fig. 2.4. The micro transport refers to the information exchange within the multimedia terminals. Specifically, the transport includes exchanges of various compressed, decompressed, and control data among the communi-

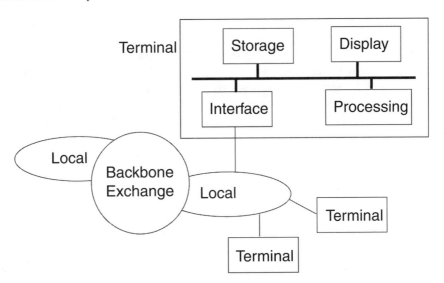

Figure 2.4   Media transport levels.

cations interface, storage subsystem, display subsystem, and processing subsystem. Note
that the micro transport may include several levels of communications hierarchy. For example, a processor in the processing subsystem may need to retrieve information through
a local bus within the processing subsystem, through a PCI bus to the storage subsystem, and then finally through a SCSI interface to a specific storage element. The local
transport involves data communications through the terminal interface with other multimedia terminals in a local area network. In this case, the multimedia terminals are more
tightly coupled and the delay is not excessive. In contrast, the remote transport requires
communications through multiple networks of unpredictable nature. The delay could be
significant as well.

Regardless of whether the communications are micro, local, or remote, VLSI systems
are common in the following three main application areas:

- **Physical level.** This area includes data signaling, coding, and modulation. Their
  function is to map logical symbols into physical signals so that digital symbols can
  be communicated through physical communication media. VLSI examples include
  modems, codecs, and transceivers for wired and wireless communications as well as
  various mixed-mode ICs for storage systems. These VLSI systems contain modules
  like filters, equalizers, amplifiers, modulators, demodulators, echo cancelers, spread
  spectrum communicators, scramblers, encoders, decoders, phase lock loops, and
  other timing recovery mechanisms. For example, an encoder that codes data into
  digital symbols (or codewords) can protect the data against noise, signal distortion,
  or interception during the transport.

- **Link level.** This area includes formatting, segmenting, packing, switching, routing, and sequencing of data. The function is to provide a connection for an information stream based on digital symbols. For example, the VLSI system could perform the data formatting function, which provides the conversion between raw data and structured data packets or between differently structured data packets. VLSI could also be designed for the segmentation and reassembly function, which provides the conversion between messages and a sequence of data packets. Switching and routing are common in systems that provide connections dynamically for the duration of the message. In this application, the VLSI often follows the control of a higher-level VLSI system for establishing connections and monitoring data packets.

- **Protocol and application.** This area includes network access control, handshake, error recovery, bandwidth control, encryption/decryption method control, and data network management. VLSI examples include traffic shapers, protocol engines, traffic policing chips, and communications/network controllers.

Each application area presents a multitude of choices. For example, just the transceiver alone leads to dozens of wired and wireless modulation and coding techniques. Common error control codes range from parity bits, cyclic redundant codes, convolutional codes, trellis codes, and Reed-Solomon codes. At higher levels, the choices narrow down to a few mainstream network standards. Among these network standards the ATM (asynchronous transfer mode) standard is the most natural choice for transporting multimedia materials. Unfortunately, the pace of multimedia network evolution is much slower than media processing. The existing network infrastructure places burdens on network evolution since maintaining cross-network compatibility through translations is hard and expensive. As a result, the media transport network today still lacks sufficient bandwidth and quality-of-service support. Ethernet is still the predominant choice today, with fast Ethernet and FDDI (Fiber Distributed Data Interface) gaining progress in the local transport. Since the ATM receives strong support from wide area communications providers, the remote transport usually involves heterogeneous networks with different protocols.

In real VLSI systems, a single IC may contain functions that span across the physical, link, and protocol levels. Some ICs may implement multiple standards at the same level. A typical network IC may include the following functions:

- Data and packet synchronization.
- Data formatting.
- Buffering.
- Header lookup and identification.
- Routing and switching.
- Packet filtering and policing.
- Format translation and header translation.
- Error detection and correction.
- Other packet processing such as segmentation and assembly control.

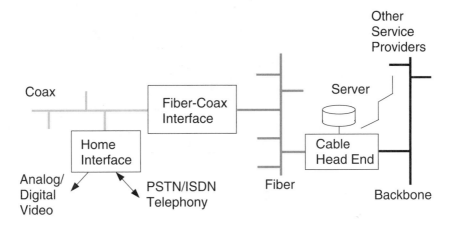

Figure 2.5   The fiber-coax digital cable system with multiple services.

The design of network ICs is, of course, highly application dependent. We will use examples to illustrate various architectures in different applications.

Let's consider the digital cable system that promises carrying multiple services and providing multimedia information access. Figure 2.5 shows the fiber-coax proposal. Here the assumption is that the information flow is highly asymmetric. Most users receive high-bandwidth broadcast video from the head end, while each user still has a low-bandwidth analog or digital telephony for information access. The digital telephone may carry voice, data, or compressed video over a common communication interface. The backbone and the fiber connections provide cost-effective mechanisms to transport volume broadcast media information and user traffic. The fiber-coax interface converts high-speed fiber connections to local cable connections and aggregates local user traffic. The home interface handles bidirectional information flow. An example architecture is shown in Fig. 2.6. The hybrid separates bidirectional signals with downstream signals feeding the audio/video tuner and the telephony demodulator. The audio/video stream can be decoded for various broadcast, education, and entertainment applications. The telephony channel may contain traditional telephone connections and data connections of different data formats. However, they can share the same downstream channel, and they only need to be decoded and formatted differently. The upstream channel contains similar mixed traffic as well.

Although bidirectional, the digital cable system is still a broadcast-type network. General multimedia communications are more symmetric because the information does not necessarily come from just a few fixed-source locations. In addition, a general network supports numerous parallel sessions, which naturally balance out the traffic flow. A network such as that shown in Fig. 2.5 cannot support symmetric multimedia communications effectively. The network architecture shown in Fig. 2.7 is more suitable for these types of applications. Conceptually, three types of network elements are involved in the transport. The access point provides network connectivity for terminals. Traffic from individual terminals are combined at the concentrator. The local traffic is switched directly among local

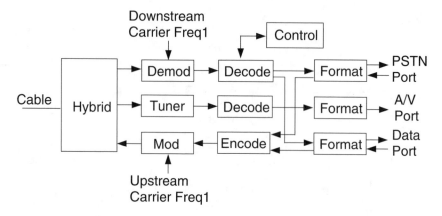

Figure 2.6   An example architecture of the home interface.

terminals and servers. Other types of traffic destined for remote terminals and servers are concentrated into high-speed channels and are fed to the switching network. The switching network contains switches and concentrators capable of routing data packets to their destinations. Note that the access point, the concentrator, and the switch all carry bidirectional traffics.

An example architecture of the access point is shown in Fig. 2.8. The purpose of the access point is to extract traffic from the network and to inject traffic to the network according to the protocols. The incoming packet from the network is buffered in the input queue while the header of the packet is examined. After the header lookup, the access point VLSI can determine whether the packet is destined for the local node or for other network nodes. The packet may go directly to the local I/O queue for the local node, to the output queue to the network, or into a packet buffer temporarily. Similarly, incoming

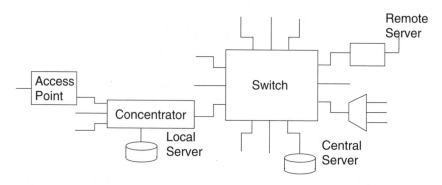

Figure 2.7   Multimedia network architecture.

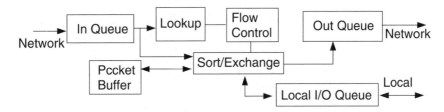

Figure 2.8   An example architecture for access point VLSI.

local packets are buffered in the local I/O queue and then may go to the output queue or the packet buffer. The decision depends on the types of packets, the current queue status, and the flow control.

The concentrator in principle is a switch with asymmetric link speeds and typically connects many low-speed links with a few high-speed links. The concentrator can be thought of as a low-speed switch with a multiplexer/demultiplexer for combining nonlocal traffic. Nonswitching concentrators are no more than just dumb multiplexers/demultiplexers. In this case, the dumb concentrator usually directs traffic to a local switch for local traffic handling.

The switch is one of the most critical components in network performance. For this reason, many different switch designs have been proposed over the years. The switch architecture depends on two major design choices: the switching fabric and the buffering. The switching fabric is the mechanism through which data are exchanged. The data exchange mechanism can be time, space, memory, or hybrid. Time-based switching uses a shared medium on a time-division multiplexing basis; different data exchanges and transfers occur at different time slots. Space-based switching accommodates data exchanges and transfers with separate connections. This is common in most multistage switches wherein multiple paths are provided for a given input-output pair to avoid collisions. Memory-based switching uses a common memory to accommodate data exchanges. Memory accesses, which constitute the data exchange mechanism, can be time-multiplexed into the same memory port or provided in parallel through separate ports. In the hybrid-switching scheme, various time-based, space-based, and memory-based switching can be combined.

Another main design consideration in the switch design is the buffering scheme. Buffers are used in the switch to smooth out traffic variations and to alleviate potential collisions in transferring data from input ports to output ports. The buffering scheme dictates the size and utilization of the buffer within the switch. The switch may buffer data at the input, at the output, at the cross-point, with a shared buffer, or with a hybrid scheme. Depending on the buffering scheme and the architecture, the switch requires buffers of different throughput rates. For example, consider the switch architectures in Fig. 2.9. In Fig. 2.9*a*, data are buffered at the input and output. The output buffers may use higher-throughput buffers to reduce collisions, but in general the buffer throughput need not scale with the number of input ports. Figure 2.9*b* shows a cross-point buffering scheme. In this case, a dedicated buffer is used for each input-output pair. Obviously, the buffer throughput need only match the input throughput rate, but the buffer size must accommodate peak traffic variations at

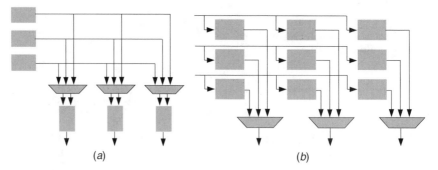

Figure 2.9   Example low-throughput-buffer architecture.

the input port and the target output port. Because the variation could be significant, the buffer utilization is quite low in normal cases.

Some other switch architectures use high-throughput shared buffers for different cost-performance tradeoffs. For example, the switch in Fig. 2.10a uses only output buffering. To accommodate simultaneous input port accesses, the buffer throughput must scale with the number of input ports. Obviously, the architecture is effective for low-speed or small switches but is expensive for other applications. The shared-buffer switch in Fig. 2.10b has even higher buffer throughput requirements. In principle, the switch is equivalent to an output-buffer switch with all the output-buffers merged together. The buffer utilization is better because of the buffer sharing. However, the buffer throughput needs to scale with both the number of input ports and the number of output ports. To build a more scalable switch, one may use a switch architecture that looks like Fig. 2.10c. The architecture uses buffers that need not scale with the number of input or output ports. It combines a block of cross-point buffers in Fig. 2.10b into a high-throughput shared buffer. In effect, it improves the buffer utilization of the cross-point block through buffer sharing [10].

We have reviewed various VLSI applications in asymmetric and symmetric multimedia transports. VLSI designs for multimedia transports depend on the protocols, standards, and performance requirements involved. In the past, the design focus has been on optimizing the

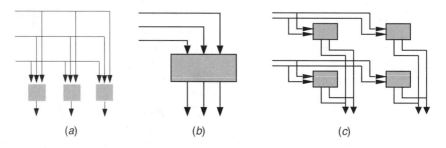

Figure 2.10   Example high-throughput-buffer architecture.

network ICs for specific standards and protocols. However, in reality most multimedia transports involve a heterogeneous network environment. The transport could be through dial-up connections or leased line connections. It could involve local area networks or wide area networks. Driven by the continuous effort toward providing uniform, transparent connectivity for global users, the network itself must accommodate various standards and operates across different types of networks seamlessly. VLSI has again come to the rescue. Recently, more VLSI systems have been designed to support multiple standards and heterogeneous networks. Unless all the network nodes are capable of handling multiple standards, transporting information across different types of networks always requires a gateway to assist the cross-handling of packet formats and protocols. In the local area network environment, a gateway or any point where traffic is concentrated could pose as a network performance bottleneck. In contrast, local area network switches capable of handling multiple standards are one of the more likely candidates for addressing both the performance bottleneck and the heterogeneous network transport problem.

2.3 MULTIMEDIA PROCESSING AND VLSI

VLSI systems for processing multimedia information include the extraction, presentation, reconstruction, and presentation of information as previously discussed in Fig. 2.3. More specific examples include the following types of processing:

- Sampling: This relates to converting analog signals to digital raw data according to the nature of the media information.
- Regeneration: This relates to recovering signals from sometimes corrupted or insufficient digital sampled data.
- Filtering: This relates to removing unwanted signal components from media data. For example, filtering often helps remove noise or shapes signals for better regeneration.
- Signal Enhancement: Some signal processing is done to enhance audiovisual features or effectiveness of presentation. Examples include synthesized acoustics, surround sounds, or image contrast enhancements.
- Format Conversion: Media can be represented in different formats, resolutions, sampling rates, and precisions. Signal processing is often necessary because of the heterogeneity of source and destination terminals.
- Data Compression: This signal processing is to reduce the amount of data needed for transmitting and storing media information. Various algorithms and standards provide different tradeoffs between the compression ratio and the quality.
- Data Decompression: This is the reverse procedure for data compression. In addition, often there are other algorithms for correcting errors or hiding other transport anomalies in retrieved compressed data.
- Composition: Sometimes media information are rendered directly from synthesis models. Another type of composition is to derive a composite media presentation from multiple media sources.

Actual media processing varies significantly from media type to media type. The three areas that receive most attention are audio, video, and graphics. In audio processing the compression, decompression, and synthesis are relatively simple. Because of its low sampling rate requirements, most audio processing can be implemented with general microprocessors or digital signal processors (DSPs). In contrast, video processing is much more complex. The complexity depends on processing algorithms, image resolutions, and frame rates. Many VLSI systems have been developed to provide higher processing power at lower cost. Video processing does not necessarily involve compression and decompression of video images. For example, video processing can be applied to track objects and positions, to interpret gestures, or to detect scene changes. Graphics, especially 3-D graphics, also require complex processing. However, unlike video processing where there are real-time requirements, graphics processing often has its visual quality set according to the processing power available at acceptable presentation rates. The processing consists of geometry transformation, rendering, anti-alias filtering, and generation of other visual effects. Some VLSI systems have been developed for high-end graphics, but most systems still use general microprocessors because there is no hard real-time performance constraint.

Many media processing standards have been developed for multimedia communications. While the graphics standards are still evolving, the H.26X standards are clearly the mainstream audiovisual compression standards. The H.261 and H.263 standards are the video conference standards for ISDN and low bit rates. The H.262 standard encompasses the MPEG family of video standards which have been applied to multimedia PC, VCR, digital TV, and even high-definition TV. The earlier MPEG-1 standard has been developed primarily for digital storage media such as CD-ROM. The standard is optimized for SIF noninterlaced video at 1.5 Mbit/s with features for random access and fast forward/reverse trick mode play. The MPEG-2 standard extends the MPEG-1 standard to support interlaced video, higher resolutions, higher coded bit rates, and various scalability. Both MPEG standards and the H.261/H.263 standards have many common processing requirements.

H.26X video processing requires a significant amount of processing power. Depending on the profile and level selected, the range of processing power also varies a lot. For example, the performance requirement for MPEG main-profile, low-level decoding applications is relatively low and can be implemented in software on general microprocessors. To encode main-profile, main-level video in real time, however, requires performance well into 10,000 million operations per second. Such high performance is often delivered through special video processing hardware.

Like many systems, an H.26X processing system typically uses a combination of software and hardware modules to implement various processing tasks. The main tasks include:

- Video preprocessing such as filtering and format conversions.
- Motion estimation.
- Motion compensation.
- DCT and IDCT (Inverse DCT).
- Quantization and inverse quantization.
- Bit-stream encoding and decoding.

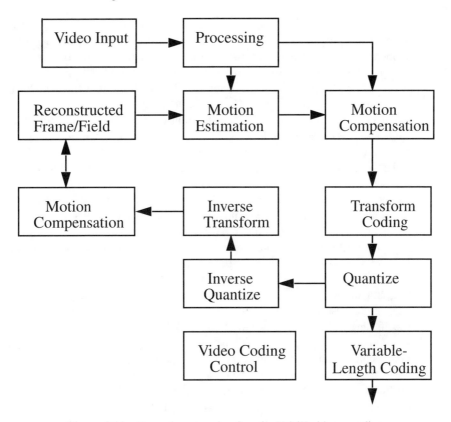

Figure 2.11   Example processing flow for H.26X video encoding.

- Coding control.
- Video postprocessing.

For a given application, a flow of tasks can be constructed. Figure 2.11 illustrates the H.26X video encoding flow. Note that the tasks involve processing of different data types. At the video input, data are typically a stream of pixels or scanlines. Filtering and preprocessing operates on pixels directly. Motion estimation, motion compensation, transform coding, and quantization are all block-based processing. Variable-length coding takes a block of quantized data and generates a bit stream. In designing the overall system, functionality as well as manipulation of data types must be carefully considered. The H.26X encoding itself includes a decoding loop and therefore shares common modules with the decoder. However, the nature of some modules could be quite different. For example, in the encoder design, the input is usually a constant-rate video input with a constant or variable rate bit-stream output. In the decoder design, the time it takes to process a single frame or field of image could vary significantly. Choice of processing algorithms for implementing a given task also sets different architectural requirements.

After the flow of tasks for the target application is established, the tasks can be mapped to three basic types of architectures: generic processor, custom data path engine, and application-specific processing engine. A generic processor could be a processor based on Complex Instruction Set Computing (CISC), Reduced Instruction Set Computing (RISC), or any other "all-purpose" architecture. In this style, the implementation often involves software compiled from high-level codes or programmed in the assembly language. A custom data path engine is one with its instruction set specially designed for certain classes of applications. Typical examples of such custom data path engines are today's audio digital signal processors (DSPs). The instruction sets and architectures of these DSPs are tuned to make them extremely efficient in filtering and similar applications. However, these instruction sets also make DSPs harder to program and less suitable for generic data processing. Application-specific processing engines are special-purpose hardware dedicated to specific functions. For example, these could be transform engines for DCT and IDCT or motion estimator engines for performing motion vector search.

Obviously, the three choices represent different tradeoffs of flexibility and efficiency. For example, application-specific processing engines are not as flexible as generic processors, but they are much more efficient. For a complex system, mix and match is often the name of the game. For example, coding control maps naturally to a generic processor, while motion estimation for high-resolution video is often implemented with an application-specific engine for performance reasons.

Other media processing ICs have similar architectural options in implementing their processing tasks. In fact, so do network ICs in general. That is, generic media processing or media transport tasks can be mapped to a general processor, a custom data path engine, or an application-specific processing engine. However, the emphasis may be slightly different. For example, in media transport the focus is usually more on movements of data, buffering, and memory-related aspects. Since the architectural options are the same as media processing and media communications ICs, the following discussion will use video media processing to illustrate the architectural options and design tradeoffs in detail.

2.4 ARCHITECTURAL OPTIONS

2.4.1 Generic Processor

The simplest form of implementation is based on compiled software codes. This approach is suitable for applications that do not demand high processing power or for those that have no real-time constraints. As opposed to implementing hardware modules, the focus is on building software modules.

Many traditional generic processors have started to incorporate new instructions to assist multimedia processing. For example, in the UltraSparc design [15], the instruction set has been extended to include many video processing functions. A single pixel distance instruction compares two 64-bit registers, each holding eight 8-bit components, calculates eight absolute differences between the corresponding components in parallel, and accumulates the absolute differences. Note that commands like these are more for application-specific computing than for generic computing. However, the same pixel distance calculation done in generic form takes more than 20 subtract, absolute, and add operations to complete.

This is a good indication that generic computing is not as effective as custom commands. Some ICs resort to high clock rates to compensate for the performance as an alternative [16].

2.4.2 Custom Data Path Engine

Custom data path engines are special-purpose processors that are based on application-specific commands. These application-specific commands deliver higher performance for certain types of calculations. However, these commands are less convenient to learn and use effectively for general computing tasks. Most generic processors have standard compilers that apply advanced compiler technologies to optimize code performance. This is possible because the instruction set is simple and generic. Custom data path engines such as DSPs have complicated commands and are difficult to optimize automatically.

The design of such custom data path engines is largely dependent on the target applications. The reason is obvious. The instruction set is limited. Within the limited set of commands there must be a careful balance between generic-type commands and special commands. The architecture must also be carefully tuned in order to achieve maximum performance.

Media processing operations usually involve lots of parallelism. There are two ways to leverage this parallelism for high-performance computing engines: through parallel execution and through pipeline execution. In parallel execution, independent tasks are assigned to separate processing units that operate in parallel. In pipeline execution, the independent tasks are subdivided and then are processed as in an assembly line in an industrial plant. Several tasks are processed simultaneously but all at different stages. In reality, the implementation could be combinations of parallel and pipeline executions on a single high-performance engine or on multiple computing engines. For example, one way to get high performance on a single computing engine is through the very-long-instruction-word (VLIW) architecture. In VLIW architecture, the highly pipelined computing engine can execute complicated commands that yield to high parallelism. For implementations with multiple computing engines, the single-instruction multiple data (SIMD) architecture and the multiple-instruction multiple data (MIMD) architecture are two popular choices. In the SIMD architecture, the computing engines perform the same instruction on their local data synchronously. Such synchronous execution provides opportunities for hardware sharing and thus saves implementation costs. However, the form of parallelism is quite rigid. In contrast, the MIMD architecture allows different computing engines to execute independently. This provides more flexibility at the expense of additional overhead for controlling these independent engines.

To date, many special-purpose engines are SIMD and VLIW based. The parallelism within these engines is at instruction or subinstruction level. The MIMD architecture is more popular with coarse-grain parallelism, although there are certain fine-grain implementations as well. For example, consider Texas Instruments' MVP processor [17] as illustrated in Fig. 2.12. It contains multiple special-purpose DSP cores and memory banks connected through a crossbar switch. It also contains a master processor and other supporting units like video and transfer control. The MIMD architecture is suitable for executing different coarse-grain tasks on different DSPs. For example, one DSP engine could be computing motion estimation, while another is computing the DCT routine. Or all the en-

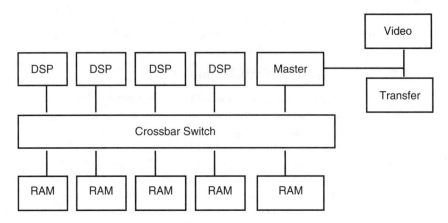

Figure 2.12   Coarse-grain MIMD architecture example.

gines could be computing DCT routines for different blocks independently. In contrast, a video signal processor by Philips employs a MIMD architecture with a finer grain of parallelism [18]. As illustrated in Fig. 2.13, the processor consists of arithmetic units, memory units, branch units, and output units interconnected with a crossbar switch. These units are fully independent, but they need to be carefully synchronized for performance reasons. From the programmer's view, the MIMD parallelism at this level corresponds to a resource scheduling problem. Good software programming tools are quite useful in improving code efficiency.

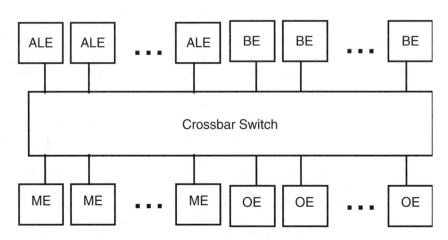

Figure 2.13   Fine-grain MIMD architecture example.

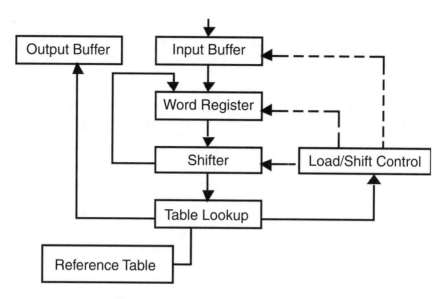

Figure 2.14   Example application specific engine: variable-length decoder.

2.4.3   Application-Specific Processing Engines

Application-specific processing engines are data processing units optimized for specific functions. For example, such engines could be a DCT engine for efficient DCT and IDCT processing, a quantization processor for quantization and inverse quantization, a variable-length encoder for encoding Huffman codes, a variable-length decoder for decoding Huffman codes, and so on. Because these engines are specifically tuned for a given function or functions, they are much more efficient in implementing the desired processing.

These application-specific processing engines differ significantly from generic microprocessors and DSPs. There are no instruction cache, instruction decode, or data paths that execute decoded instructions. Instead, the processing itself is captured directly in hardware. For example, consider building a variable-length decoder. The functionality of the decoder is to recognize codewords embedded in a stream of bits and to convert these codewords into proper data. Because the codeword boundaries are not aligned to fixed positions, the decoder needs to decide how many bits to discard for each decoded codeword. Figure 2.14 illustrates a conventional design. Conceptually, the input bit stream is stored in an input buffer with bits aligned at fixed wordlength boundaries. The initialization process includes loading data into the word register so that the word register contains at least the first codeword plus some trailing bits. The content of the word register is then compared against a lookup table without any bit shifting to determine the codeword size and the corresponding output value. The size of the codeword is fed back to the shift/load control, which keeps a running count of the next leading bit position within the word register. The shifter relies on this running count to discard the decoded bits and to align the new leading bits for looking up the next codeword. If the number of valid bits within the word register drops below a certain threshold, the valid bits are shifted up and loaded in the word register together with new data bits from the input buffer. The running count is adjusted accordingly to reflect the new leading bit position.

An application-specific processing engine like the variable-length decoder described above obviously lacks flexibility; it is quite difficult to compute DCT on a variable-length decoder and vice versa. The architecture style is also quite different; signal and data flow in prescribed directions and functional blocks work synchronously. The result is a highly efficient implementation that cannot be reused for other purposes.

The properties of these processing engines clearly display a range of tradeoffs between efficiency and flexibility. Generic processors are the most flexible; they are designed for general tasks. Custom data path engines are more specialized; they are like generic processors modified for certain sets of tasks. These engines achieve high performance for the tasks they are designed for at the expense of programming. The programmers need to understand the data path engines in order to write efficient programs. Application-specific processing engines have computing structures matched to the tasks they are designed for. These application-specific engines are compact and highly efficient. There is practically no need for software development since most of these engines have hardwired controllers and sequencers.

2.5 MORE VLSI EXAMPLES

In deciding the architecture for the overall VLSI system, there is no reason to be purist. Mix-and-match often works best in most situations, especially when the application is well defined. For example, many video processing ICs include all three types of engines: generic processors, custom data path engines, and application-specific processing engines. Consider AT&T's AVP-III video codec chip [22] illustrated in Fig. 2.15. The architecture contains multiple hardware modules connected with multiple buses. The main computing engines

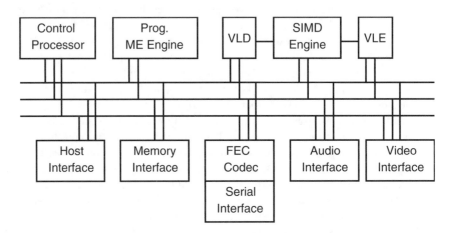

Figure 2.15   Example mix architecture.

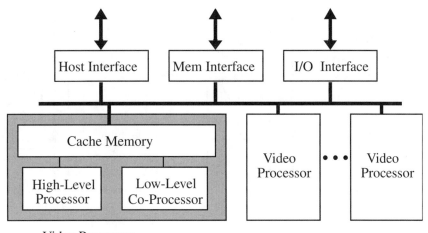

Figure 2.16   High-level/low-level multiprocessor architecture.

are on the top part of this figure. The control processor is a generic processor that not only controls the chip but also performs generic processing. The SIMD signal processor is a custom data path engine that can be programmed to perform DCT, IDCT, filtering, interpolation, and other tasks that have high processing regularity. The motion estimator engine, the variable-length decoder, and the variable-length encoder are application-specific processing engines. These application-specific engines are made relatively programmable so as to accommodate different video standards and processing requirements.

There are other ways of combining programmable engines. For example, consider the architecture shown in Fig. 2.16. Here the processing is divided into high-level general tasks and low-level tasks, with a high-level/low-level processor pair implementation [19]. The low-level processor implements computationally intensive but structured processing. The low-level processor runs relatively independently but is still under the control of a high-level processor. The high-level processor implements general tasks that have little structure or tasks that require lower processing performance. The processor pair forms an independent video processor, and the overall VLSI system is still an MIMD architecture consisting of multiple video processors. Compare this to the MVP MIMD architecture in Fig. 2.12. The low-level processor plays a similar role as the DSP in the MVP architecture. However, these low-level processors do not run under the control of a centralized master processor but rather work with a local high-level processor.

2.6   DESIGN ISSUES

Given the basic architecture choices, there are many ways to build a media transport or media processing IC for specific applications. The first step is to look at the requirements for these applications and then characterize processing tasks. Next, media processing al-

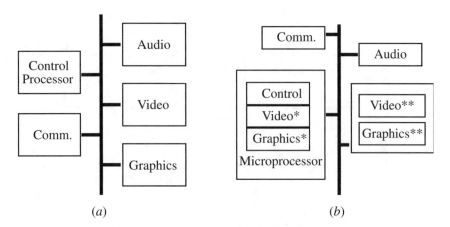

(a)   (b)

Figure 2.17   Architectural choice examples.

gorithms need to be developed in order to define each task completely. The designer then decides what kind of architecture makes sense. Various architectural options can be explored. The evaluation process consists of mapping processing tasks to different hardware architectural options. Obviously, application-specific engines address processing needs for the tasks completely. For tasks mapped to generic processors or custom data path engines, some software considerations need to be included as well. For example, audio processing tasks could be handled by the control processor or the SIMD signal processor in Fig. 2.15, but the cycle counts and software development difficulties are quite different. After deciding the architecture and mapping between the tasks and hardware modules, the designer could go ahead with software and hardware implementations. The rest of the design is nothing but a structured exercise for an experienced software/hardware design team.

Multimedia systems use VLSI to address different facets of multimedia communications. All these VLSIs have different performance and architectural requirements as is further illustrated in the references and examples in [7,9,14,23,28]. But the basic principle of VLSI architecture design remains the same: partition, map, and optimize. A hierarchical design flow from the top algorithmic level down to the final IC implementation often improves the quality of the design. As VLSI systems grow more complex, the design flow itself becomes even more critical.

In putting together a VLSI system, other architectural tradeoffs can be made. For example, consider the media processing systems in Fig. 2.17. Here the two architectures illustrate a choice between single-function and multiple-function partition. They also illustrate a choice in the high-level versus low-level partition. In Fig. 2.17a the architecture contains single-function modules in which each module performs all tasks for the given function, whether it's video, audio, or graphic processing. The architecture in Fig. 2.17b divides audio, video, and graphics processing function into various submodules. Some of

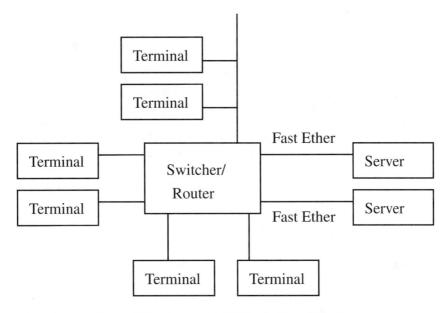

Figure 2.18   An example LAN switching application.

the submodules are combined and implemented in a multifunction chip. Other submodules of lower processing requirements are mapped to a high-level processor.

Media transport VLSI systems face similar design choices and architectural trade-offs, but most implementations to date focus on generic processors and application-specific engines only. Implementing with generic processor addresses an area in which flexibility is important, while implementing with application-specific engine addresses an area in which performance is important. However, the VLSI design considerations do differ somewhat from the media processing VLSI, even though the architectural choices are similar. The design depends on the required communications quality as well as on the network choices. Some examples and discussions can be found in [28], with more emphasis on ATM networks. There are also extensive VLSI efforts toward switched Ethernet and fast Ethernet as alternative solutions to revamping the local area network infrastructure. An example application is illustrated in Fig. 2.18. The server in general can be a file server or a communication server that links to other high-speed remote servers. The network standards involved could be Ethernet, Token Ring, FDDI, fast Ethernet, or ATM. A heterogeneous switcher/router VLSI system like this implements the switching concentrator function discussed earlier in Section 2.2. High-level architectural choices for media transport VLSIs parallel but sometimes differ from the example depicted for media processing in Fig. 2.17. For example, some may involve a high-level protocol versus a low-level media access partition. Others may involve buffering and throughput tradeoffs.

2.7 CONCLUSIONS

Different types of multimedia systems have been identified based on the multimedia playback model and the multimedia communication model. Regardless of the differences, these multimedia systems consist of common technological components that are realized by low-cost high-performance VLSI systems. The VLSI technology itself includes algorithm design, architecture design, circuits design, algorithm-to-architecture mapping, design methodology, and tools. This chapter presents key application areas of VLSI multimedia systems in two categories: media transport and media processing. In media transport, various VLSI systems have been applied to micro, local, and remote transports at the physical, link, and protocol levels. Various network structure and VLSI architecture examples have been discussed. In multimedia processing, VLSI audiovisual applications have been examined. VLSI architectural options were discussed to provide a complete picture of design possibilities. We have also examined various design issues such as the design steps and other high-level architectural tradeoffs.

Looking ahead, the trend of multimedia VLSI systems will continue to improve its integration level, its flexibility, and its performance. Integration is essential in reducing the overall cost and the form factor. Cost reduction brings the technology to the mass market. Smaller form factor makes it even more convenient to use and personalize the multimedia technology. Diverse applications and standards will continuously drive the VLSI systems to deliver higher flexibility to satisfy different needs. Multimedia systems depend on their overall system performance to achieve effective, quality communications. This includes both transport and processing performance for high audiovisual realism. Such high-quality communications are needed in entertainment, learning, consumer communications, collaborations, and presentations. The challenges ahead definitely require significant efforts devoted to improving the network performance for media transport and achieving higher-quality, yet affordable, media processing. VLSI will continue to be the catalyst in the success of multimedia communications.

References

[1] CCITT Study Group XV, Recommendations H.261, Video Codec for Audiovisual Services at px64 Kbits/s, Report R37, July 1990.
[2] ISO/IEC JTC1/SC29/WG11, Recommendation H.262, Generic Coding of Moving Pictures and Associated Audio, ISO/IEC 13818-2, Mar. 25, 1994.
[3] W. B. Pennebaker and J. L Mitchell, *JPEG: Still Image Data Compression Standard*, New York: Van Nostrand Reinhold, 1993.
[4] J. D. Foley et al., *Computer Graphics: Principle and Practice*, 2nd ed., Reading, MA: Addison-Wesley, 1992.
[5] P. Newman, ''ATM Technology for Corporate networks,'' *IEEE Communications Magazine*, pp. 90–101, Vol. 30, No. 4, Apr. 1992.
[6] K. Asantani, ''Standardization of Network Technologies and Services,'' *IEEE Communications Magazine*, pp. 86–91, Vol. 32, No. 7, July 1994.
[7] L. Goldberg, ''ATM Switching: A Brief Introduction,'' *Electronic Design*, pp. 87–103, Dec. 16, 1994.

[8] R. Rooholamini et al., "Finding the Right ATM Switch for the Market," *IEEE Computer Magazine*, pp. 16–28, Vol. 27, No. 4, Apr. 1994.

[9] E. W. Zegura, "Architectures for ATM Switching Systems," *IEEE Communications Magazine*, pp. 28–37, Vol. 31, No. 2, Feb. 1993.

[10] M. Katevenis, P. Vatsolaki, and A. Efthymiou, "Pipelined Memory Shared Buffer for VLSI Switches," *SIGCOMM'95*, Cambridge, MA.

[11] P. Oechslin et al., "ALI: A Versatile Interface Chip for ATM Systems," *Proc. Globcom'92*, Orlando, FLA., Dec. 6–9, 1992.

[12] J. M. Smith et al., ed., special issue on High Speed Computer/Network Interfaces, *IEEE Journal on Selected Areas in Communications*, Vol. 11, No. 2, Feb. 1993.

[13] S. K. Rao et al., "A Real-Time p*64/MPEG Video Encoder Chip," *ISSCC Digest of Technical Papers*, pp. 32–33, San Francisco, Feb. 24–26, 1993.

[14] B. Ackland, "The Role of VLSI in Multimedia," *IEEE Journal of Solid-State Circuits*, Vol. 29, No. 4, Apr., 1994.

[15] A. Chamas et al., "A 64b Microprocessor with Multimedia Support," *ISSCC Digest of Technical Papers*, pp. 178–179, San Francisco, Feb. 15–17, 1995.

[16] T. Inoue et al., "A 300MHz 16b BiCMOS Video Signal Processor," *ISSCC Digest of Technical Papers*, pp. 36–37, San Francisco, Feb. 24–26, 1993.

[17] K. Balmer et al., "A Single Chip Multimedia Video Processor," *Proceedings of the CICC*, San Diego, pp. 91–94, May 1–4, 1994.

[18] H. Veendrick et al., "A 1.5 GIPS Video Signal Processor (VSP)," *Proceedings of the CICC*, San Diego, pp. 95–98, May 1–4, 1994.

[19] K. Herrmann et al., "Architecture and VLSI Implementation of a RISC Core for a Monolithic Video Signal Processor," in *VLSI Signal Processing*, VII, pp. 368–377, New York: IEEE, 1994.

[20] S. C. Purcell and D. Galbi, "C-Cube MPEG Video Processor," *SPIE, Image Processing and Interchange*, Vol. 1659, 1992.

[21] Integrated Information Technology, Video Communications Processor VCP, Preliminary Information, 1995.

[22] D. Brinthaupt et al., "A Programmable Audio/Video Processor for H.320, H.324, and MPEG," *ISSCC Digest of Technical Papers*, pp. 244–245, San Francisco, Feb. 8–10, 1996.

[23] P. Pirsch, N. Demassieux, and W. Gehrke, "VLSI Architectures for Video Compression—A Survey," *Proc. IEEE*, pp. 220–245, Feb. 1995.

[24] I. Tamitani et al., "LSI for Audio and Video MPEG Standards," *NEC Research and Development*, Vol. 35, No. 4, Oct. 1994.

[25] T. Mastsumura et al., "A Chip Set Architecture for Programmable Real-Time MPEG2 Video Encoder," *Proc. CICC*, Santa Clara, pp. 393–396, May 1–4, 1995.

[26] J. Armer et al., "A Chip Set for MPEG-2 Video Encoding," *Proc. CICC*, pp. 401–404, Santa Clara, Calif., May 1–4, 1995.

[27] C-Cube Microsystems, VideoRISC Processor product information, 1995.

[28] H.-D. Lin, "Multimedia Processing and Transmission in VLSI," in *Microsystems Technology for Multimedia Applications: An Introduction*, eds. B. Sheu et al., p. 313, New York: IEEE Press, 1995.

<table>
<tr><td>Chapter
3</td><td># INTRODUCTION TO RESEARCH ON MULTIMEDIA TECHNIQUES IN TELECOMMUNICATION LABORATORIES</td></tr>
</table>

INTRODUCTION TO RESEARCH ON MULTIMEDIA TECHNIQUES IN TELECOMMUNICATION LABORATORIES

I-Chang Jou

Abstract

With the maturity of multimedia techniques and the rapid development of telecommunication networks and services, the combination of multimedia and communications will become the key technology of future information and telecommunications. Telecommunication Laboratories (TL) keeps track of research directions in Europe, the United States, and Japan, and positions itself in promoting new techniques of combining multimedia and communications. In this situation, the goal is to develop new telecommunication services for multimedia, promote telecommunication networks and services, and help advance multimedia communication techniques for the domestic information and communication sectors. Given this research pursuit, this chapter focuses on the following items: the development of multimedia telecommunication services, ATM (asynchronous transfer mode) broadband experimental networks and their applications, intelligent input/output techniques and their associated multimedia applications, and the development of multimedia customer premises equipment.

3.1 DEVELOPMENT OF MULTIMEDIA TELECOMMUNICATION SERVICES

Telecommunication Laboratories' mission with regard to multimedia is to cater to the construction of the new telecommunication networks and to provide new multimedia telecommunication services.

3.1.1 ISDN Distance Learning System

In order to promote the commercialization of the Integrated Services Digital Network (ISDN) [1–6], Telecommunications Laboratories (TL) focuses on the research and development of the distance learning system. A pilot PC-based system has been established, and its architecture is shown in Fig. 3.1.

This PC-based system uses the ISDN network to provide bidirectional multimedia distance learning services, which contain the functions of teaching material editing, on-line supplementary teaching material inputting, synchronous teaching flow control [7], full-color lecture transmission and display, pen-talking lecturing, and video communication. The techniques used in this system include H.261 videophones, image capturing/compression

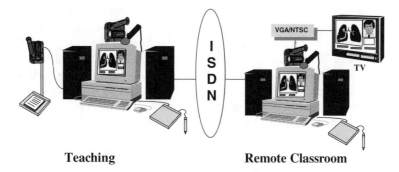

Teaching   **Remote Classroom**

Figure 3.1 System architecture of ISDN distance learning.

functions, ISDN communication techniques, a PC-based presentation development system, and complicated development and integration of software and hardware.

Instructors can use the system to edit teaching materials and transmit them to the remote student terminals. The teaching host controls the display and sequence of the lecture in the student terminals, and takes advantage of audio, pointer, and pen to illustrate and explain the teaching content. Instructors can also use the video overhead and scanner to input teaching materials in real time. Students cannot only passively learn by watching the television set but also actively talk to the lecturers through the videophone.

In addition to the above 128 Kbps version of the distance learning system, TL is also developing another higher level system (Fig. 3.2), which uses five ISDN BRI (Basic Rate Interface) lines: one BRI for lectures, one for voice, and three for video. The system can operate with full-color lecture, 384 Kbps video, and CD-quality audio. It supports high-quality distance learning application at reasonable cost.

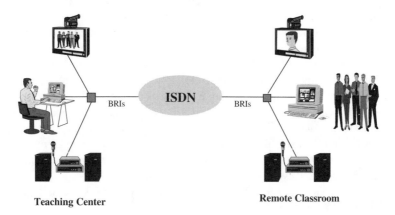

Teaching Center   **Remote Classroom**

Figure 3.2 Architecture of the higher level distance learning system.

The video part of this system (which we ourselves developed) uses three ISDN BRI connections and can support 384 Kbps bandwidth videoconferencing. The terminal part of the videoconference system follows the standards of the ITU-T H.320 series and ISDN. With regard to hardware, it uses two add-on cards on the personal computer. The bandwidth of the communication can be adjusted from one to three BRIs to support different videoconferencing qualities under the user's requirements. This system has been jointly developed by several companies, and we hope that the techniques can be transferred to more telecommunication and computer companies.

The system supports full-color lectures, electronic share whiteboard, and CD-quality music. Thus, the teacher can teach and play music as the background at the same time. In addition, with a 384 Kbps bandwidth high-quality video signal, the system can support professional distance learning, conference, training, and education. We demonstrated the system at the 1995 Information Show in Taiwan and connected the show booths in Taipei, Taichung, and Kaoshiung with the office of Telecommunication Laboratories located in Chungli. The system uses the economic ISDN to create an environment of the distance learning multimedia classroom, which will be an applicable system on the National Information Infrastructure (NII) in the near future.

TL has been cooperating with National Taiwan University, Taipei, in a research project entitled "Intelligent Computer Aided Education," which is sponsored by the National Science Council (NSC) of Taiwan. The system is undergoing a field trial connecting Taiwan University Hospital and Chin-Shan Community Medicine Training Center. We will assess the practical usage of the system during the period September 1995–June 1996. In addition, we will promote the system gradually and extend the system architecture and its functions to match different user requirements. We believe that the system will provide general users a high-quality, affordable, and easy promotional teaching services. Therefore, the system will further enhance our intensive promotion of NII.

3.1.2 Multimedia ISDN Teleshopping System

In May 1995, the Directorate General of Telecommunications (DGT) of Taiwan started the commercial ISDN services, which include multimedia communication services that integrate audio, data, image, and video. Because of its diversified characteristics, the promotion of ISDN is more complicated than the traditional audio services. In order to successfully promote ISDN services, the DGT intends to use the ISDN teleshopping system as an introductory multimedia service to potential customers.

The ISDN teleshopping system combines the software and hardware techniques of PC Windows, ISDN services, and Internet browsing, and sells goods directly on-line. It provides both sellers and buyers an electronic communication channel for transaction. Sellers can build a database for their products, which are presented in multimedia forms. With a user-friendly interface, customers can easily browse the products, quickly obtain item descriptions, and even order the products on-line.

Shown in Fig. 3.3 is the system configuration of this system. It consists of three parts: client, public network, and server.

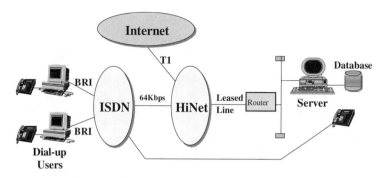

Figure 3.3   System configuration of the ISDN teleshopping system.

3.1.2.1   Client

An ISDN accessible PCIT (PC based ISDN Terminal) (see Section 3.4 for more details) with Internet software on a PC Window is introduced. This system hooks up with a server by accessing HiNet via ISDN and then through the Netscape Navigator software. Equipped with wider bandwidth offered by ISDN, the user is better off in accessing multimedia information over the Internet, and at the same time talking to the merchandise suppliers on the same pair of ISDN wires to find out more about the product and service.

A Packet driver was developed for PCIT to access HiNet over ISDN. This driver contains a PPP (Point-to-Point Protocol) implementation and is able to obtain necessary routing information from an ISDN router (e.g., an Ascend product on MAX) on HiNet with PPP, ensuring higher data correctness. Other software was also developed to facilitate the dial-up procedure, which includes calling up the HiNet representative address, supplying the user name and password for connection establishment, and so on. Figure 3.4 shows a software module diagram on the client side. It is deployed on a Windows environment.

3.1.2.2   Public Networks

The public networks include ISDN, HiNet, and leased lines. The ISDN routers need to be installed on HiNet for clients to access HiNet via the ISDN BRI communication port and to set up connections. On the server side, a leased line of 128 Kbps is deployed, and a class-C network user is assigned to the server through the router.

3.1.2.3   Server

Pentium PC is adopted for the server. With the help of software on Windows, the Web server is set up. Well-designed multimedia documents are prepared by authoring tools in HTML and are ready for the client's access. The teleshopping database is set up on MS Access, a very easy-to-learn and easy-to-use software that can be retrieved through

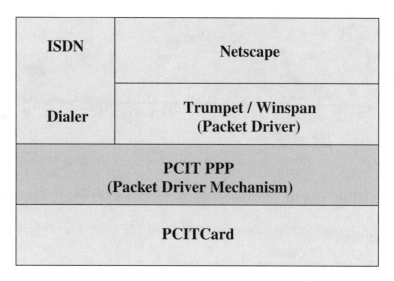

Figure 3.4   The software module diagram on the client side.

a program in Visual Basic over the standard Web server called interface CGI (Common Gateway Interface) for the multimedia information offered.

This system is adequate for the sale of all kinds of commodities, such as food, clothes, houses, transportation, and entertainment. A lot of other derived applications can also be created on top of this system—for instance, personal ads concerning friendship and love, political propaganda, and commercial information. We continue working with Pacific Rehouse Corporation on the project that is building up a real estate database for client access.

3.2 ATM BROADBAND EXPERIMENTAL NETWORK AND APPLICATIONS

To satisfy users' increasing demands for network bandwidth and to provide the appropriate broadband applications, TL has devoted considerable effort to developing ATM-based broadband equipment, such as ATM Virtual Path (VP) switches, ATM multiplexers, ATM LAN (local area network) switches, and ATM hubs. The Hsin-Chu Experimental Network of NII, deployed by using ATM equipment, was ready when the Prime Minister of Executive Yuan officiated over the opening ceremony on July 14, 1995. The construction of an islandwide ATM network covering 10 different locations was completed in June 1996.

3.2.1 Network Topology

The ATM Broadband Experimental Network in Taiwan was introduced in two phases. The first phase was based on VP switches, and the second on virtual circuit (VC) switches.

In the first phase, development of the ATM VP switch system was completed, and deployment of the broadband service trial based on this VP switching system has now been undertaken. The ATM VP switch system includes two major parts—an ATM VP switch node and an ATM multiplexer node [8,9,10]. The ATM switch has a five-Gbps system capacity and a 32 × 32 switching fabric based on the shared memory principle, and each inlet/outlet operates at 155/45 Mbps separately. It also uses permanent virtual connection (PVC) to provide cell relay service using SDH (Synchronous Digital Hierarchy) OC-3c and DS3/PLCP UNI/NNI interfaces. The ATM multiplexer is connected to an ATM switch by means of UNI interface and provides multiplexing functionality with DS1, DS3, Ethernet, and Frame Relay access interfaces. The ATM multiplexer provides electronic-optical and SDH/ATM signal conversion.

The islandwide broadband service trial is underway [10]. Installation of a total of 10 VP systems, as shown in Fig. 3.5, will be completed in three phases by June 1996. The ATM VP systems in Nan-er (Taipei), Chungli, and Kuan-Tung (Hsin-chu) were deployed in June 1995; the VP switch systems in Taichung, Tainan, Kaoshiung, and Tung-ssu (Taipei) were installed at the end of 1995; and finally the deployment in Ai-Kuo (Taipei), Hwa-Lien, and Nan-Kang (Taipei) will be worked out by June 1996. After the first service trial, an ATM VC-based field trial will be initiated in July 1997. This field trial will be built on the ATM VP-based backbone established in the first stage with additional equipment, for example, ATM VC switches, ATM multiplexers, and the interworking unit (IWU). The Science Based Industrial Park (SBIP) ATM LAN switch-based, high-speed data service provides services for organizations and companies in the SBIP area. The network is connected to the Internet through HiNet.

3.2.2　Services and Applications

Two kinds of services, DS1 and DS3 circuit emulations, are provided during the first field trial. To support the services on circuit emulations, the OC-3 and DS-3 multiplexers are usually installed at the user site and connected to a VP switch by either OC-3c UNI or DS-3 UNI. The related applications promoted in this trial are as follows.

1. Videoconference
   By using the point-to-point and multipoint videoconference, users in different locations can hold a meeting that is much like a face-to-face conference. Users' equipment, for example, video codec, connects to the ATM network using DS1 or DS3 transmission rates.

2. Distance Learning
   A distance learning application trial will interconnect seven universities in Taiwan by using the DS3 transmission rate. Three universities—National Taiwan University, National Tsing-Hua University, and National Chiao-Tung University—have already been connected to the trial network. Through this application, the goal of educational resources sharing can be reached.

3. LAN Interconnection
   In order to attain the benefits of resource sharing, users can use the high-speed transmission capability of the ATM network to connect local computers to remote computers

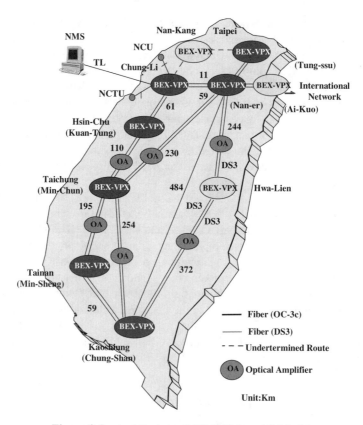

Figure 3.5   Architecture of ATM VP-based field trial.

and servers. In this trial, users connect their equipment, for example, a router, to an ATM network through DS1 and Ethernet interfaces.

4. Video-on-Demand (VOD)
   Using advanced video compression technology, video data are compressed and stored on video servers. Users can retrieve the video information from a remote video server and display VHS-quality programs on local TV. This application uses the DS1 transmission rate.

5. Multimedia Applications
   Through the DS1 transmission capability offered by the trial network, users can produce their own multimedia applications, such as Karaoke and desktop videoconferencing.

6. Image Transfer and Retrieval
   This application can be used in various fields, such as teleshopping, medical image archiving, and retrieval.

3.3 INTELLIGENT TECHNOLOGY AND MULTIMEDIA APPLICATIONS

As the combination of computer and communication (C&C) steadily gains popular consensus, new technologies are eagerly anticipated to satisfy people's needs and to help create the brand-new information world. At TL, the DSP (digital signal processing) group has been combining C&C to develop intelligent technology and help provide better, more advanced telecommunication services and multimedia applications. With these applications, we realize the advantages of applying DSP technologies to telecommunication services, which include (1) greater correctness and reliability of signal transmission; (2) more efficient networking by compression of voices, images, and video signals; and (3) new provision of practical and convenient services offered by our multimedia applications. Accordingly, we are convinced that research and development of intelligent digital signal processing technologies have been and will continue to play a vital role, either in the digitization process of telecommunication techniques, or in reaching the lower fee and highly proficient telecommunication services.

Aiming at these two goals, the DSP project has planned to meet the needs of future telecommunication digital services and the requirements of the national information infrastructure (NII). Specifically, the focus has been on the development of intelligent I/O capability and related core technologies, while the applications emphasize the R&D of communication and information processing systems, which are settled to satisfy user expectations in real time with multimedia power.

To demonstrate the success of applying core technologies developed by the DSP project to practical services, the Intelligent Wide-area Document Process System (IWDPS) is designed to open up a new and evolutionary field of telecommunication services. This system integrates existing DSP core technologies in TL, and, by networking the digital information on the telecommunication, it provides an outstanding multimedia facility that is fully integrated to meet users' needs. The IWDPS will be in Section 3.3.9.

In the remainder of this chapter, we will present the core technologies developed by the DSP group, together with their features and applications. These include (1) the intelligent pen-based input technique; (2) the Gin-Ih Chinese character (from Taipei and Mainland China) recognition system; (3) the intelligent and automatic official document processing system; (4) the intelligent computer speech synthesis; (5) the intelligent Chinese speech recognition system; (6) the trademark and commercial logo information processing system; (7) the interactive telecommunication training system; and (8) video-on-demand services. Finally, we summarize these technologies of the IWDPS system and the DSP group's future plans.

3.3.1 Intelligent Pen-Based Input Technique

For years, the most challenging task of introducing Chinese to computer processing has been the input methodologies of Chinese characters, which commonly suffer from (1) complicated rules to specify a character, (2) requirement for professional training, (3) long-term practicing, and (4) difficulty of writing documents on the fly. The pen-based method relieves most of these difficulties. In addition, a pen-based system has the following features [14]:

- It is independent of the order of strokes.
- Connected (Chinese) characters are allowed.
- Up to 7000 Chinese characters are recognized.
- There is a correct rate of over 95.2
- Recognition speed reaches 50 CPS (characters per second) on Intel 486-66.

Figure 3.6 illustrates the application of pen-based technology to telecommunication services. On-line users can write down their scripts in either Chinese or English, and can send them across the PSTN or ISDN to the Message Controller linked to the pen-based kernel at the other end of the network. At this end, services are provided to recognize the scripts and respond to users' requests. This technique has also been applied to commercial products with good outcomes. More specifically,

- Since July 1993, the technique has been transferred to over 11 companies.
- A successful commercial product was co-developed with COMJET Information Systems Corporation: Chinese On-line Hand-writing Recognition on Demand (Jan. 1994).
- An integrated Chinese/English pen-based system was designed for the Data Communication Institute (DCI) (Feb. 1994).
- The technique is embedded in the telecommunication services of the Central Taiwan Telecommunications Administration (CTTA), DGT, Corporate Planning Department, DGT, and the Long Distance Telecommunications Administration (LDTA) DGT.

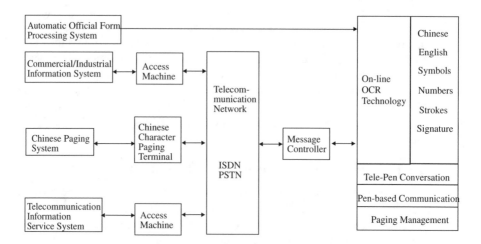

Figure 3.6 Overview of the Intelligent Pen-Based Input.

3.3.2 Gin-Ih Chinese Character Recognition System

Recognition for Chinese characters is the most complex task among optical character recognition (OCR) techniques. The OCR technique developed by the DSP group not only gracefully tackles this problem, but also aims at recognizing different fonts and styles of both English and Chinese characters simultaneously. More impressively, it can at the same time handle Chinese characters from Taipei and those from Mainland China. The automatic input of Chinese characters into their electrical forms has been the most successful achievement in the AI field. The architecture of the Gin-Ih system is shown in Fig. 3.7, where the system is divided into three parts: document analysis, OCR, and language model. In the first part, heterogeneous documents are first segmented with their tables, graphs, and text components. In the second part, the Gin-Ih system is equipped with the most sophisticated OCR engine developed by the DSP group. The Gin-Ih system also accommodates a language model processor and a postprocessing module to help improve the accuracy of recognition. In brief, the Gin-Ih system has the following features [15]:

- Ability to recognize different fonts.
- Automatic document layout analysis.
- Recognition of up to 13,053 Chinese characters.
- Correct rate of segmentation exceeding 98%.
- Correct rate of recognition of over 94%.
- Recognition reject rate of about 6%.
- Processing speed of over 16 CPS on Intel 486–66.
- Automatic candidate vocabulary analysis and correction.
- Language model covering 27,000 words.

The Gin-Ih Chinese OCR system has been actively used by several official government bureaus and effectively helps officers to handle a vast amount of printed Chinese documents. These applications include:

- A utility that translates scientific documents and official papers between Taipei and Mainland China for the Mainland China Affairs Association (June 1994).
- A core technology transfer to the industry of interests (Oct. 1994).
- A provision to the Planning Department of TL to save numerous typing efforts.

3.3.3 Intelligent and Automatic Official Document Processing System

In this system, we combined a newly developed technique of document analysis for official documents based on the core OCR technology [16]. Its development is justified by the need to translate enormous official documents in their paper forms into their electrical forms. Users of the system simply scanned the paper, and this system automatically takes

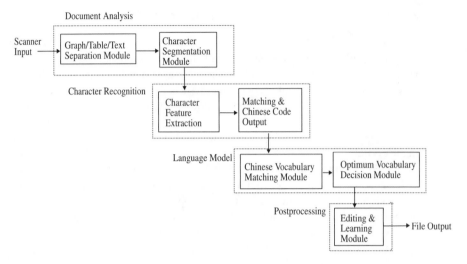

Figure 3.7   An overview of the Gin-Ih Chinese Character Recognition system.

over the frame extraction and the character recognition jobs. Furthermore, a database is maintained to solve the registration processing problem of these paper documents, and thus saves much of the human's load. As depicted in Fig. 3.8, this system consists of two parts: the Official Document Analysis and the OCR (described in the previous subsection). In the first part, tables are obtained through the "line and the field extraction process," while the data are from the "character segmentation process," and then organized into records by calling the OCR modules (the second part). The features are:

- Capability of processing general official documents.
- Recognition rate of over 93% and rejection rate of about 7%.
- Recognition speed of over 10 CPS on Intel 486-66.
- Capability of recognizing multiple Chinese fonts.
- Capability of on-line learning.
- Recognition of 13,053 Chinese characters, and 182 English letters and symbols.
- Minimum character size of 2.2 mm × 2.2 mm under a resolution of 400 dpi.
- Advanced recognition technique, including confirmation and classification, feature extraction and matching, and English/Physics features.
- User-friendly interface.
- Capability of processing skewed (under 3 degrees) documents.
- Embedded editor allowed (e.g., PE II).

The primary application of this system is for relieving human intervention in converting printed Chinese archives into computer files. Current applications include:

- Announcement and contract-seeking with the industry (Oct. 1994).
- Integration with DGT's "Chinese Electrical Official Document System version 1.6" (Apr. 1995).

3.3.4 Intelligent Computer Speech Synthesis System

In this system, users are required to listen to computer-synthesized Chinese sentences directly from the printed text without listeners reading the text [16]. Another goal of this technique is to help the blind access the colorful world. In Fig. 3.9, the input text, usually a sentence in Chinese, will be first analyzed by the Sentence Processing module, where the special symbols and vocabularies will be properly handled. The sentences obtained are then passed to the kernel module, in which databases of both the language and the speech will be referenced to generate the speech file output. The features of this system include:

- Clear and natural voices in Chinese.
- Tunable speech speed and volume.
- Purely software; no DSP chips needed.
- Supporting D/A functions of the Sound Blaster cards.

The application has been widely accepted in the community, for example:

- Cooperation with the Switching Technology Lab, TL, to support the automatic measuring process of Northern Taiwan Telecommunications Administration (NTTA).
- 50 packs provided to the Chi-Ming School for the Blind, helping blind students listen to articles on papers and access computers (June 1995).

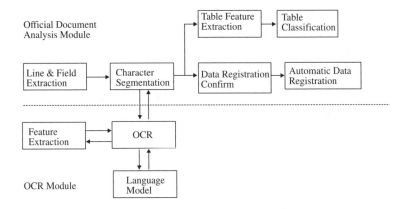

Figure 3.8   System overview of the Intelligent and Automatic Official Form.

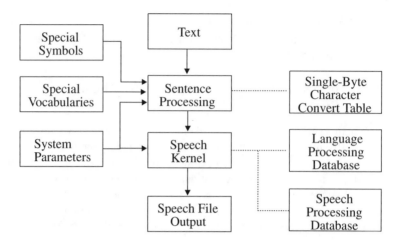

Figure 3.9   Overall architecture of the Intelligent Computer Speech Synthesis System.

- Part of the integrated Vocal Indexing System for Adult Education project, held by the Taipei City Library (June 1994).
- Embedded in the automatic climate telephone reporting service of the Central Weather Bureau (1994).
- Joint development of communication and information processing products, and technique transfers to interested industrial companies.

3.3.5   Intelligent Chinese Speech Recognition System

As a front-end interface for human access to computerized services, Chinese speech recognition could be the most convenient and friendly utility among others. Consequently, it has the greatest potential to increase add-on values to the telecommunication services. Our DSP group has developed a robust Chinese speech recognition system that effectively supports many useful applications. As Fig. 3.10 shows, the system can work under either normal or adverse environments. Acquired voice will be analyzed first in the small word size mode, then the large word size mode, and finally the speech understanding mode to extract the information carried by the speech. In all three modes, a mechanism that improves recognition under adverse environments accompanies the recognition process. This system:

- Is not specific to certain speakers.
- Recognizes a word instead of characters.
- Continuously inputs acceptable syllables.
- Has 1500 default vocabularies.
- Has a correct rate of over 98% (in five candidates).

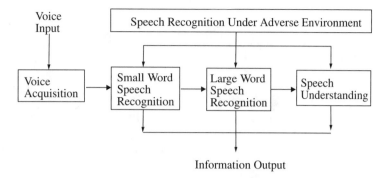

Figure 3.10 Overview of the Intelligent Chinese Speech Recognition System.

- Has a recognition speed of less than 0.7 second for its hardware version and less than 1.5 second for its software version.

The developed speech recognition technique has also achieved many spectacular honors, including [16]:

- A speech library of 100 persons, intended for research use by TL and affordable to other academic studies.
- An authorized license of the "Balanced-Sentence" technique.
- A 10-year patent of the "Fast search-and-recognition algorithm."
- 1000-person vocal services of telephone transfer and query system (a trial version in TL).
- Plans to support local/long-distance telephone services.
- Plans to present a 1000-name vocal telephone transfer and query the trial version with keyword spotting support.

3.3.6 Trademark and Commercial Logo Information Processing System

Basically, this system lessens the heavy load of human management for trademark and commercial logo registration. It seeks to utilize computer powers to perform analysis and search, while promptly and accurately finding or helping to determine whether a trademark or logo was registered in the library. As seen in Fig. 3.11, this approach provides remote access so that both the companies and the trademark reviewers can easily examine registered logos over either the PSTN or ISDN network. The approach has the following additional features:

- Automatic backup capability.
- Service provided on LAN, PSTN, and ISDN.

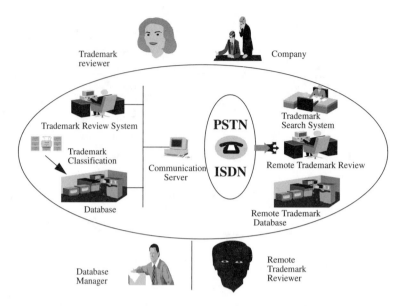

Figure 3.11   Overview of the Trademark and Commercial Logo Information
                  Processing System.

Applications and achievements include the following.

- It is cooperating with the Central Standard Bureau on the draft version of the Chinese Commercial Patterns Classification Standard.
- It provides the Commercial Pattern Classification/Indexing Aid System, Class 40 to the Central Standard Bureau (Sept. 1994).
- It will soon be an ATM service.
- The ISDN Trade Mark and Commercial Logo Information System will be a demo system.

3.3.7   Interactive Telecommunication Training System (ITTS)

Based on the use of personal computers and access to PSTN or ISDN, the ITTS tries to provide an improved facility for traditional telephone and tele-facsimile services. Both the caller and callee connected to each other via the ITTS can exchange text, pictures, charts, and tables interactively in real time, along with their voices. In Fig. 3.12, we show a typical application of ITTS: one central classroom is away from remote classrooms, which share the same courses at the same time. From the central classroom, signals are transmitted via a multiport bridge and modems to the local classrooms via the PSTN network. Its features include:

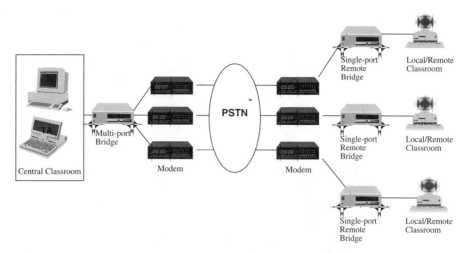

Figure 3.12   Overview of the ITTS System.

- File handling.
- Simultaneous editing on the spot.
- Interactive two-way drawing.
- On-line communication settings.
- On-line OCR.
- On-line signal CODEC.

For its applications, the ITTS serves as a powerful tool for real-time effective training courses:

- It supports the Telecommunication Training Institute (TTI) with simultaneous remote training courses in Pan-Chiao, King-Man, and Pen-Hu (Sept. 1994).
- TTI has adopted it as a standard remote training course system (Feb. 1995).

3.3.8   Video-on-Demand (VOD) Services

In an effort to provide an interactive video service, the VOD technique developed by the DSP group uses the asymmetric digital subscriber lines (ADSL) to transmit MPEG videos at VHS qualities [17]. Shown in Fig. 3.13, the existing telephone circuitry suffices to carry up to 1.544 Mbps compressed videos and other information using ADSL. On the video-sending end, Video servers provide their video programs via FDDI and bridge those signals to ADSL, on their way to the user end. Its features are:

- Video MPEG compressed to 1.5 Mbps.
- Video server on FDDI networks, able to serve 450 persons with 32 programs.

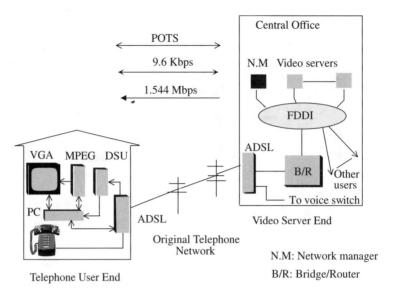

Figure 3.13   Overview of the VOD System.

- All VCR functions supported: play, fast forward, fast rewind, still, slow play, and even zoom-in and zoom-out operations.

The VOD application developed by the DSP group also provides the HIFAX tele-facsimile service to DCI, with A4 to B4 and B4 to A4 resolution conversion.

3.3.9   IWDPS and Future Works

The DSP group has been researching and developing practical and useful core technologies. With these technologies, we have successfully constructed systems that are tightly coupled to the telecommunication services and have also demonstrated the effectiveness of the technologies. In addition to providing human interface to telecommunication, the developed techniques also demonstrate the ability to handle multimedia in their applications.

Among these applications, we have constructed the Intelligent Wide-area Document Processing System, or IWDPS, to provide a brand-new integrated telecommunication service. The overview of IWDPS is depicted in Fig. 3.14, where we observe that intelligent I/O capabilities have been integrated into the front and back end of the system. To help secure data communication and provide multiple access in fast search, IWDPS adds security control, browsing control, and fuzzy search in this service. To sum up, the IWDPS successfully integrates:

- Chinese/English OCR, printed and/or handwritten.
- Intelligent speech synthesis that converts messages received via networking into speeches in real time.

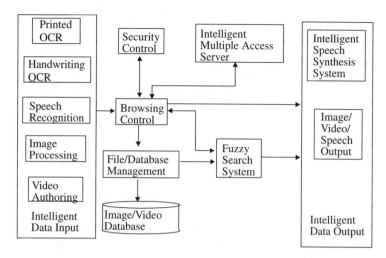

Figure 3.14   Overview of the IWDPS System.

- Multimedia interface.
- Security subsystem.
- Intelligent fuzzy-search subsystem.

In the future, we believe that only by a tighter combination of computers and communications can we develop more useful and powerful add-on values to the telecommunication services. The intelligent I/O capability, together with the multimedia processing capability, will be two very important factors that achieve highly user-friendly goals. Finally, we are pleased to cite some potential applications undertaken by the DSP group:

- **Express News Browsing System**: By integrating the OCR, the handwritten OCR, and the Intelligent Computer Speech Synthesis technologies, this system will demonstrate the ability to promptly input the headlines of the news (and some immediate messages for commercial use) into computer files on the users' fingertips via ISDN networks. When necessary, users of this system are allowed to access the up-to-date information and enjoy them with multimedia facilities such as computer-synthesized speeches.

- **Intelligent Virtual Library**: This library provides ITTS functions as well as electronic library functions. With the low cost of PSTN, users of the library enjoy lifetime learning.

- **Networking Information Service for the Disabled**: Serving as a social welfare utility, this system offers easy access to the Intelligent Virtual Library for the blind and those unable to hear or see clearly. The service can be constructed by using our core technologies together with the dot-readers for the blind developed by Dam-Kang University, Taiwan.

3.4 DEVELOPMENT OF MULTIMEDIA CUSTOMER SYSTEMS

The purpose of developing multimedia customer premises equipment is to catch up with the construction of high-speed networks and to promote networking services. The techniques being used can be transferred and shared by domestic industry to promote Taiwan's global competitiveness economically.

3.4.1 PC-Based ISDN Terminal

With the use of self-developing ISDN add-on cards, PC can connect to ISDN BRI and provide 2B+D multimedia communication functions. The ISDN protocols used by PCIT-1 include ITU-T Q.921, Q.931, V.110, and V.120 [18,19], which not only meet the DGT specifications but also provide the interface of MS-Windows application programs. PCIT-1 has passed the conformance test of DGT and been transferred to many domestic companies. On the other hand, PCIT-1 is also the key basis for the development of other multimedia terminal systems and multimedia telecommunication services.

In order to let users access multimedia information quickly from the Internet through ISDN, we also developed a Point-to-Point (PPP) driver program for PCIT-1. Thus, PC can connect to the Internet by ISDN at the rate of 144 Kbps. Since the interface of PCITPPP is based on the Packet Driver, PCIT-1 can emulate a general network card and use the available network softwares.

3.4.2 PC-Based ISDN Videophone System

Given the R&D experience with regard to ISDN and multimedia communication, we initiated a series of projects named ISDN Video-PC, aiming at development of PC-based ISDN videophone and videoconferencing.

The PC-based ISDN videophone was the product of a joint project in which six local entrepreneurs participated, and it was completed and transferred in December 1994. The software implementation conforms to ITU-T visual communication protocols H.320 series recommendation (H.320, H.261, H.242, H230, H.221 [20]) and ISDN communication protocols Q.921 and Q.931 on Microsoft Windows environment. It provides TAPI [21] and MCI high-level API [22].

To improve the system's speed, different media—video, audio, data, and signaling—are transferred on different buses. Compressed video stream is carried over a proprietary parallel bus V-bus, while compressed audio stream, as well as signaling, is by way of a serial bus instead of system bus. As for data stream, its amount is much less than those of audio and video data, and their content consists of the PC file or message on a PC environment. It is natural to convey data stream over the system bus. The data flow and the relative location of each bus of the system at runtime are shown in Fig. 3.15.

3.4.3 384K Videoconference System

With experience in the PC-based ISDN videophone and the requirements from private sectors, we launched research of the higher communication bandwidth videoconference

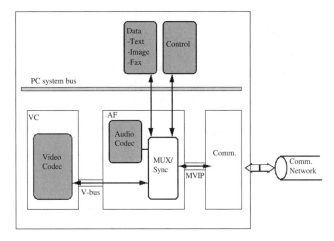

Figure 3.15   Data flowing view of ISDN Video-PC.

system. The system supports not only the videophone function but also multipoint video-conferences. The communication bandwidth of the system can be as high as three ISDN BRI; that is, six B channels with 384 Kbps bandwidth are available for higher quality video signals (CIF, 30 frames/sec). In addition, the size and cost of the hardware are also reduced. The system architecture is shown in Fig. 3.16. It consists of two add-on cards—one for ISDN BRI access and the other for audio/video compression. It supports not only one individual but also a group of people to do a rollabout videoconference. We joined forces with several companies to develop the system.

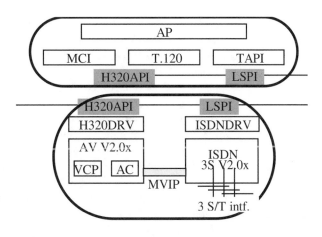

Figure 3.16   System   architecture   of 384K videoconference system.

3.4.4 Single-Board PC-Based ISDN Videophone System

To sharpen its competitive edge, a single-board PC-based ISDN videophone was developed. It combines video, audio compression module, H-Protocol module, and communication module into one, taking up only one PC slot, and the PCI bus was adopted. However, the videophone system is equipped with only one ISDN interface, offering 128 Kbps bandwidth. System designers are allowed to choose different system configurations, depending on requirements to meet demands in price and speed and the need for a flexible structure.

3.5 CONCLUSION

At the time when NII is being promoted and the DGT is in charge of constructing telecommunication networks, TL with its experience in multimedia communication will continue to develop more multimedia telecommunication services and techniques and support the construction of NII.

References

[1] S. L. Hsian et al., "A Workbench System for Multimedia Service on ISDN," *Proceeding of 8th International Joint Workshop on Computer Communication*, pp. D2.3.1–D2.3.7, Dec. 1993.

[2] M. K. Chang et al., "The Design of ISDN Video-PC," *Proceeding of 1994 Pacific Workshop on Distributed Multimedia Systems*, pp. 177–185, Feb. 1994.

[3] P. Y. Chang et al., "IAP: An ISDN Application Platform for Multimedia Communication," *Proceeding of 14th Int. Telecommunications Symposium*, pp. 115–123, 1994.

[4] L. Ludwing, "Multimedia in ISDN and BISDN: A Paradigm Shift Driver by User Technology and Applications," *Bellcore Digest*, 1989.

[5] C. Nicolaou, "An Architecture for Real-time Multimedia Communication Systems," *IEEE Journal on Selected Areas in Communications*, Vol. 8, No. 3, pp. 391–400, Apr. 1990.

[6] C. S. Thachenkarye, "Integrated Services Digital Networks (ISDN): Six Case Study Assessments of a Commercial Implementation," *Computer Networks and ISDN Systems*, Vol. 31, pp. 921–932 , 1993.

[7] P. Hoepner, "Synchronizing the Presentation of Multimedia Objects," *Computer Communications*, Vol. 15, No. 9, pp. 557–563, Nov. 1992.

[8] Lung-Sing Liang et al., "The Broadband Service Trial with Related Technologies Development in Taiwan," *Proceeding of International Telecommunication Symposium*, Vol. 3, pp. 115–121, Taiwan, Sept. 1994.

[9] Lung-Sing Liang et al., "Hardware Reliability and Availability Prediction of a Broadband Switching System," *Proceeding of 1st IEEE International Workshop on Broadband Switching System*, pp. 296–305, Poland, Apr. 1995.

[10] Heng-Yuan Hsu et al., "Performance Analysis and Buffer Dimensioning of an ATM Multiplexer," *Proceeding of International Symposium on Intelligent Networks and Broadband ISDN*, pp. 128–135, Beijing, China, Apr. 1994.

[11] "The Proposal of Video-On-Demand (VOD) Trial," Proposed by DGT, Taiwan.

[12] Herry Y. H. Lin, "Planning and Design of the Interactive Video System (IVS)," Technical Report of TL, Dec. 1993.

[13] Herry Y. H. Lin, "Implementation and Testing for the Interactive Video System (IVS)," Technical Report of TL, June 1994.

[14] K. S. Chou et al., "Knowledge Model Based Approach in Recognition of On-line Chinese Characters," *IEEE Journal on Selected Area in Communication*, Vol. 12, No. 9, pp. 1566–1575, Dec. 1994.

[15] C. S. Miou et al., "An Optical Chinese Character Recognition System Using a New Pipelined Matching and Sorting VLSI," *Optical Engineering*, Vol. 32, No. 7, pp. 1623–1632, July 1993.

[16] B. S. Jeng et al., "The Study on Speech Processing and Character Recognition at Telecommunication Laboratories," *Proceeding of IEEE ISSIPNN'94*, pp. 137–141, Hong Kong, Apr. 1994.

[17] I. C. Jou et al., "The Applications of a Video Cream on Demand System in Digital Subscriber Loop," *Proceeding of Telecommunication Symposium*, pp. 82–102, 1994.

[18] ITU-T Recommendation Q Series.

[19] ITU-T Recommendation V Series.

[20] ITU-T Recommendations H.320, H.261, H.242, H.230, H.221.

[21] Microsoft Telephony Application Program Interface (TAPI).

[22] Microsoft Media Control Interface (MCI).

PART

II

SUBMICRON ELECTRONIC TECHNOLOGIES

MEMORY ARCHITECTURES TECHNOLOGY FOR MULTIMEDIA SYSTEMS

Yoichi Oshima, Bing J. Sheu, and Steve H. Jen

Abstract

In the era of multimedia, highly integrated semiconductor memory systems will play a crucial role in facilitating information flow, storage, and transmission. A variety of multimedia applications require advanced storage methods that enable storage of a huge quantity of data, a high processing throughput rate, and operability with long-lasting battery power. In order to meet these strict requirements for multimedia applications, three major trends in memory technologies have emerged. First, increasingly higher density memories are required. This is an essential issue for semiconductor memory technology. With higher density memory, advanced multimedia application can be created. Second, development of low-power design-oriented memory is very beneficial. Since low-power consumption is a fundamental demand for a variety of portable equipment such as notebook PCs, wireless communication equipment expands the flexibility of multimedia systems. Third, high data throughput is an indispensable performance item for multimedia applications that need to deal with motion picture data. For the purpose of satisfying the demand by advanced high-speed clocked CPU which can handle motion picture data, memory technologies have to develop high throughput data memory chips that outperform conventional memory. Because of the close relationship between memory technologies and multimedia system applications, system design engineers should understand what memory technologies are. It is also important for memory engineers to understand how memory is used in multimedia applications. For that purpose, this chapter describes recent developments and trends in memory technology as well as key concepts of memory technology for multimedia applications.

4.1 OVERVIEW OF THE SEMICONDUCTOR MEMORY INDUSTRY

An overview of the semiconductor memory industry can provide a useful opportunity to understand both the present and historical background of this exciting and attractive industry. Based on this analysis, it may be possible to predict future trends. Three essential factors needed to analyze the situation are technology, market, and cost.

4.1.1 Technology Trend

From the technological viewpoint, a critical ultimate goal is to provide higher density memory. Figure 4.1 shows the capacity trend for each type of semiconductor memory [1]. Advances have been maintained at their astonishing pace since 1970. This is one evidence that memory technology is always fiercely pushed to produce the densest versions. In order

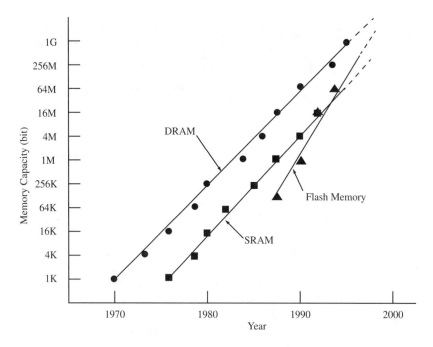

Figure 4.1   Semiconductor memory capacity trend.

to support this rapid growth, advanced process technologies have contributed to the whole period. However, the current situation reveals some changes. Figure 4.2 depicts the trend of DRAM (Dynamic Random Access Memory) design rules [2]. Although future process technologies will still play an important role, it will be recognized as almost reaching the leading edge, in terms of reducing the device feature size. In fact, the process technology gap between the laboratory and mass production level differs from what it was at the beginning of the1990s. The super performance chips made by advanced process technology have to wait a long time to be in real products. In other words, achievement of advanced process technology is not the only factor that influences the decision to move the next-generation devices. Thus, the semiconductor memory industry has to consider other aspects as well during the development of technology.

4.1.2 Market Forecast

From the birth of the semiconductor memory, the computer industry has been its largest customer. The more computers needed memory, the higher density semiconductor memories were provided. The capacity of memory was the first-priority requirement. However, recent computers, which play a major role in multimedia systems, require high-performance memory as well as high-density memory in order to realize satisfactory performance. Figure 4.3 shows the block diagram of components in a multimedia system [3]. Because computers in multimedia system have to manage a huge amount of data at high speed in a variety of situations, memory, which is the essential element of the computer, is required, both in terms

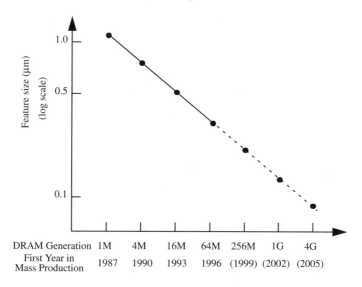

Figure 4.2   DRAM design rule trend.

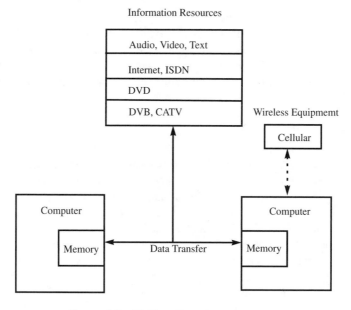

Figure 4.3   Multimedia system components.

of large capacity and high performance in a variety of multimedia equipment. A high data transfer rate for the management of moving picture data and low-voltage power operability for wireless/portable equipment are high-priority requirements for semiconductor memory.

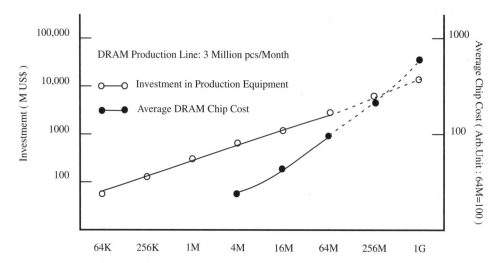

Figure 4.4   Prospect for investment in production equipment and average DRAM chip cost.

Fortunately, the future semiconductor memory market is still very optimistic. One research analysis has predicted that the market size in the year 2000 would be 2.3 times as large as the present market [2]. In order to realize this number, creation of the new market will be the highest priority challenge for the semiconductor memory industry. Whether or not this industry will enjoy this bright future really depends on the creation of new profitable markets, such as multimedia applications.

4.1.3   Cost Analysis

Cost is another crucial issue for the semiconductor memory industry. If cost is not carefully considered, both memory suppliers and users have to face serious problems. Research and development (R&D) investment, production equipment investment, and manufacturing expenses are three major elements of total cost. First, R&D investment, which is very important for the advanced technology industrial field, is becoming a heavy financial burden even for international-scale large companies. One analysis estimated that the R&D investment for 1G DRAMs would be 10 to 15 times as large as that of 1M DRAMs [2]. It is very important for management decision makers to know how to overcome this problem.

Second, the production equipment investment influences the product price itself. Figure 4.4 shows the investment trend in production equipment [2]. The increase in production equipment investment is expected to continue at least for the next few generations.

Third, design cost will increase as well as other factors. For example, CAD tools have to handle a huge amount of data and complicated logic. Workstations and microchip testers will also require a much more powerful computing performance. These requirements will certainly result in higher cost. In order to provide reasonably priced memories, the semiconductor industry needs careful assessment of each portion.

For R&D investments, the introduction of cooperation and joint ventures among the leading technology companies could be one good solution to the problem of how to best use their resources and share the financial burden. Some companies have already adopted this mutual partnership system. In addition, focusing on the development of cost-reduction technology is beneficial. For example, the SOI structure and high dielectric insulator will have a good chance to reduce production costs remarkably, because of the simplification in the fabrication process.

For the production equipment investment, the most important factor is investment timing. Without a proper match between demand for the products and supply ability, the result will be an unstable market, which is very inconvenient for both memory suppliers and users. Since memory is not a one-generation product, but is for successive generations, a smooth transition between the current and the next generation is beneficial for memory suppliers and users. Indeed, there is no absolute answer for this problem. However, careful planning and a variety of products will help reduce the risk. In addition, improvements of production yield, chip count per wafer, and wafer size can substantially reduce the investment cost.

In order to reduce design cost, adoption of a core cell built up systematically for each application field will be possible. Development of reliable device modeling can also contribute to the optimization process.

In summary, to realize a profitable future, development of advanced technology, creation of a market in the multimedia industry, and careful consideration of cost are required. Satisfaction of these three key requirements will benefit not only the semiconductor memory industry but also the multimedia industry.

4.2 KEY ELEMENTS FOR MEMORY

Most semiconductor memories for implementing multimedia applications can be categorized as DRAM, SRAM, and nonvolatile memories. With regard to market volume, DRAM is the most widely used memory because of the cost per bit performance. Let's take DRAM as an example to understand the internal structure of the memory system.

Figure 4.5 shows the block diagram of a DRAM system. In principle, function for all types of memory is very simple. It requires only writing the data in a certain address, preserving it for a certain period of time, and reading the data. Let's follow this simple scheme in Fig. 4.5. In the read operation, the memory chip needs to set up the address data. In DRAM, compared to other memory technologies, it adopts a unique address input scheme. It is called the address multiplex scheme. In this scheme, the address data are divided into two portions, defined as row address and column address, respectively. According to the enable address signals, each address is stored in an address input buffer by individual timing. Therefore, the number of address pins needs one-half of the whole address digits. On the other hand, two sequential address inputs are necessary. After obtaining the address information, the stored data that are selected by the row address are read by sense amplifiers to amplify the signals. Then, the column address is used to transmit the amplified signals to the output buffers. In the write operation, the input data are stored in a certain address. Although the advanced memory chips (which we will discuss later) have more complicated

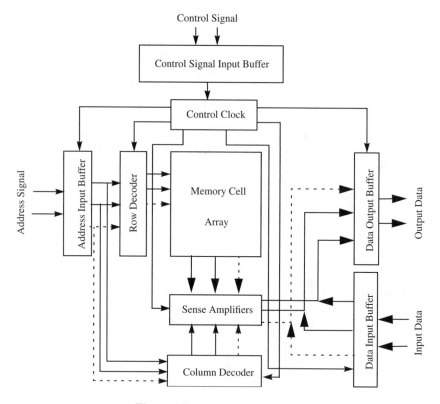

Figure 4.5   DRAM system block.

operations, the basic scheme still remains the same. Therefore, it is very important that we understand this simple operation before considering any advanced operation mode for applications.

4.2.1 Memory Cell

Indeed, the memory cell is the most important element in semiconductor memory design, and many device engineers and process engineers focus on this field. For application

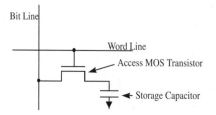

Figure 4.6   DRAM memory cell.

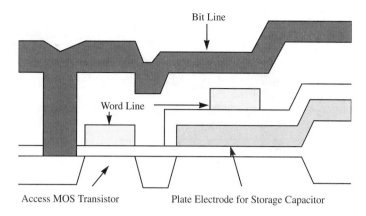

Figure 4.7   DRAM memory cell (cross-sectional view).

engineers, it is not necessary to understand this technology in detail. However, it is still beneficial to have basic knowledge of memory cells. Accordingly, we would like to provide a brief overview of each type of memory cell. Figure 4.6 shows the schematic diagram of the basic memory cell for DRAM, and Fig. 4.7 shows the cross section of a conventional planar DRAM cell.

Since minimum area consumption is allowed to achieve the high-density DRAM, the structure of the cell capacitor is modified into a vertical dimension for the advanced memory cell instead of the conventional plane capacitor. Figures 4.8 and 4.9 show two present well-known, fundamental three-dimensional capacitor cells. To achieve the required minimum value of capacitance, both approaches have been successful in minimizing the area consumption and fabrication process complexity. Furthermore, a variety of shapes of capacitor electrodes have been investigated in order to obtain larger capacitance in a small area for higher density DRAM [4–7]. Figure 4.10 shows the advanced three-

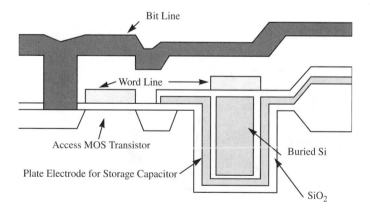

Figure 4.8   Trench capacitor cell (cross-sectional view).

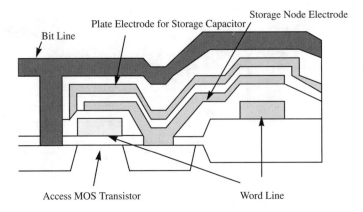

Figure 4.9 Stacked capacitor cell (cross-sectional view).

dimensional capacitor cell. This type of capacitor will play a main role for 64M DRAM and the higher density version. In addition to the above-mentioned approaches, thinner capacitance with high dielectric insulator [8,9] and enlarged surface area by micro villus patterning of electrodes technology [10] have been investigated for the next-generation memory cells.

Figure 4.11 shows the schematic diagram of a conventional SRAM (Static Random Access Memory) memory cell. Compared to DRAM, SRAM has superior speed performance. Therefore, it is preferred that SRAM be located near the CPU, which demands

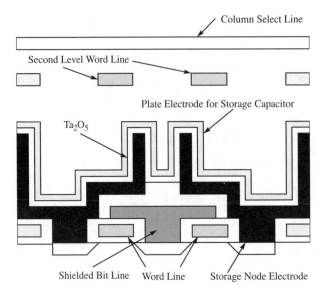

Figure 4.10 Advanced three-dimensional capacitor cell (cross-sectional view).

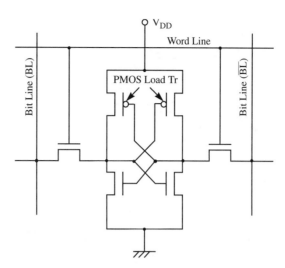

Figure 4.11   CMOS load SRAM cell.

quick response to its access request. However, SRAM needs more elements to store the data. It obviously has a disadvantage in terms of area efficiency. A pMOS load transistor is the pull-up device needed to supply leakage current. It is required to provide considerably high resistance in order to minimize power dissipation. Not only bulk CMOS load but also thin-film transistor (TFT) CMOS load [11] has been investigated to achieve reliable high resistance.

Figure 4.12 shows a cross section of three different types of nonvolatile memory cell. One of them, EPROM, played a major role during the early history of nonvolatile memory . Since this device requires ultraviolet light to erase the data, it has become an almost historical device. The second device is EEPROM. Instead of optoelectronic energy, this device can be controlled by only an electric signal. It was developed as the successor to EPROM. However, EEPROM has the inherent disadvantage that two transistors are required for each memory cell to avoid overerasing case. In this case, the threshold voltage of memory cell is too low to cut off by the voltage of control gate. Therefore, it causes normally-on cell. A recent remarkable innovation in the nonvolatile memory field was the Flash EEPROM. In the early days, EEPROM's main target was to replace the magnetic hard and floppy disks. These markets are attractive enough to accelerate its research for the semiconductor memory industry. Conventional EEPROM faces two tough obstacles. Cost is one important reason why EEPROM did not replace magnet hard disks as memory devices. For this aspect, Flash EEPROM could become competitive, because Flash EEPROM uses a single transistor per bit. With the simplified configuration, the Flash EEPROM has made a great contribution to solving the cost problem for EEPROM. In addition, Flash EEPROM provides a function to perform block erase and rewrite, which is a primary operation for disks. The second obstacle is reliability. At present, this is the most focused issue for Flash EEPROM. Since Flash EEPROM uses a high electric field to inject electrons into a floating gate, the reliability of thin oxide is one of the crucial issues for memory cell improvement. In order to solve this problem, active research has been pursued.

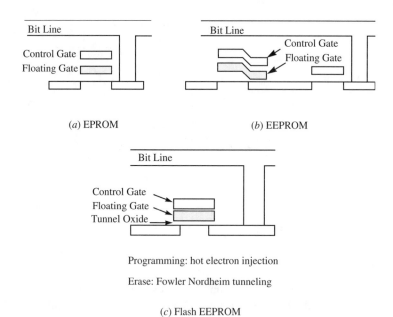

(*a*) EPROM   (*b*) EEPROM

Programming: hot electron injection

Erase: Fowler Nordheim tunneling

(*c*) Flash EEPROM

Figure 4.12   Nonvolatile memory cell (cross-sectional view).

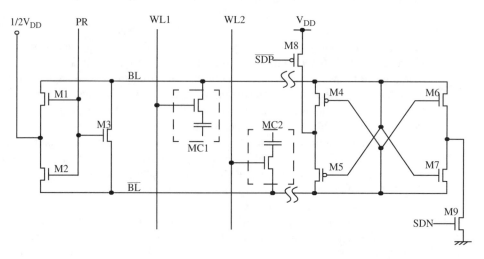

Figure 4.13   Conventional sense amplifier block.

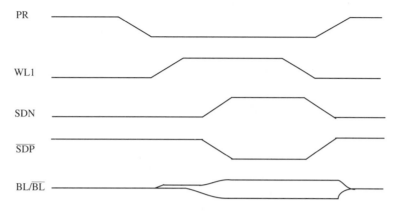

Figure 4.14   Sensing scheme timing chart.

4.2.2 Sense Amplifier

A sense amplifier is as important as the memory cell because its performance affects the whole chip performance considerably. The sense amplifier reads data from the storage cell and magnifies the signal level up to the appropriate logic level to be treated by a conventional logic block. Let's take the DRAM sense amplifier as an example. Figure 4.13 shows the schematic diagram of a conventional sense amplifier for DRAM.

This circuit block operates as follows. At the initial condition, assume that the "H" level is stored in MC1. A bit-line pair is precharged and equalized by M1, M2, and M3, and other MOS transistors are turned off. First, M1, M2, and M3 turn off to set up the preparation stage for sensing. Then, selected word line (WL1) by row address rises up. As a result, one MOS access transistor and one storage capacitor are connected to the bit line. This action causes the imbalance of the bit-line pair. The voltage of the bit line changes slightly because of storage charge in the MC1 capacitor, whereas the other bit line remains at the same level. This difference can transmit to the sense node. Sense amplifier driver transistors M8 and M9 turn on in order to activate the amplification function. Then, a small signal between the bit-line pair becomes a large signal level by the cross-coupled MOS transistors. The basic function is simple; however, optimizing the size and timing for each clock is an essential issue for the DRAM system designer. Figure 4.14 shows the timing diagram for the sensing operation.

4.3 LOW-POWER DESIGN TECHNOLOGY

Low-power memory technology is increasingly important not only for the new multimedia applications but also for general memory use [12]. Since the current trend for the memory market is to explore outdoor usage, the battery-operable feature is a crucial requirement for memories. In general, total power consumption of the DRAM chip (P), which is operated at V_{DD} and cycle time t_{RC}, can be expressed as follows.

$$P \cong \sum C_j \cdot (\frac{\Delta V_j}{\Delta t}) \cdot V_{DD} + I_{DC} \cdot V_{DD} \tag{1}$$

$$\cong \Delta Q_T \cdot \frac{V_{DD}}{t_{RC}} + I_{DC} \cdot V_{DD} \tag{2}$$

$$\cong \frac{(C_{BT} \cdot \Delta V_D + C_{PT} \cdot \Delta V_P) \cdot V_{DD}}{t_{RC}} + I_{DC} \cdot V_{DD} \tag{3}$$

$$\cong (\Delta Q_{BT} + \Delta Q_{PT}) \cdot \frac{V_{DD}}{t_{RC}} + I_{DC} \cdot V_{DD} \tag{4}$$

where C_j = Capacitance of node j
$\quad \Delta V_j$ = Voltage variation at node j
$\quad \Delta Q_T$ = Total charge of the chip during one cycle
$\quad \Delta Q_{BT}$ = Total charge of bit lines during one cycle
$\quad \Delta Q_{PT}$ = Total charge of peripheral blocks during one cycle
$\quad I_{DC}$ = DC current component
$\quad C_{BT}$ = Total capacitance for bit lines
$\quad \Delta V_D$ = Bit-line charged level
$\quad C_{PT}$ = Total capacitance for peripheral blocks
$\quad \Delta V_P$ = Voltage variation for peripheral blocks

As these equations show, there are several effective methods to reduce power consumption. Special care with supply voltage V_{DD}, bit-line capacitance charge Q_{BT}, and DC current component I_{DC} could minimize the power consumption significantly.

4.3.1 Lowering Operating Voltage

Supply voltage is one of the common issues in the memory development trend. Therefore, semiconductor engineers have to keep an eye on which external power supply value will be adopted as the standard. Figure 4.15 shows the conventional internal and external power supply values for several generations of DRAM. Use of lower operation voltage is a simple and effective approach to reducing power consumption. In fact, for 64K DRAM, the supply voltage changed from 12V to 5V. The 3.3V will be used starting from 64M DRAM. Although the most suitable external power supply values should be chosen, compatibility with existing chips is always a big obstacle. One solution to this problem is to adopt separate external and internal power supply values. For example, use of 4V for internal power supply and 5V for external power supply was adopted in 16M DRAM. A further advanced solution to obtain wide operation, functionality, and performance of DRAM from the battery-power supply level (1.8V) to high end of LVTTL level (3.6V) was proposed by using the advanced V_{DD} detection technique to compensate the back-gate bias generator (V_{bb}) and word-line voltage level generator (V_{pp}) [13].

Figure 4.16 shows the diagram of V_{DD} detection using the V_{ref} generator. Figures 4.17 and 4.18 show the compensation schemes for frequency and capacitance, respectively. Depending on the external voltage, the output logic was set to either "H" or "L." The combination of these three output signals determines the external voltage level. The signals

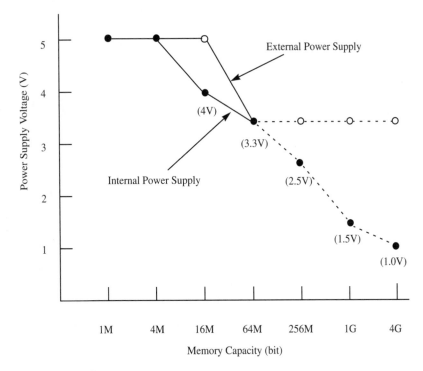

Figure 4.15   Internal and external power supply trend for DRAM.

are also used to decide the suitable frequency and capacitance for V_{bb} and V_{pp} circuits. In order to operate memory in a wide range of external voltage supply, these approaches are very useful.

4.3.2 Charging Capacitance Reduction

Partial activation is the key concept for reducing charging capacitance [12]. Figure 4.19 shows the block diagram of partial activation of a multidivided array. The more memory cell array is divided, the more reduction of power is achieved. However, the number of partitions is limited because of the refresh cycle. The refresh cycle is defined as the refresh operation times and the interval period. For example, 4096 (4K) or 8192 (8K) refresh cycles are required in 64 ms for 64-M bit DRAM. Therefore, one partition should be 64M/4096 or 8192 = 16K or 8K memory array. The other limitation is increasing the number of decoder blocks. In order to solve this problem, the sharing-decoder approach is quite successful. New advanced interconnection techniques can realize the sharing-decoder method. In addition, this scheme was introduced to peripheral circuits. The Address Transition Detector (ATD) is the common technology used to prevent unnecessary activation. Only during the period when an address transition occurs do appropriate peripheral circuits blocks become activated. This technology has been adopted in peripheral circuits since 64K SRAM and remarkably has contributed to minimizing the power consumption for many types memories.

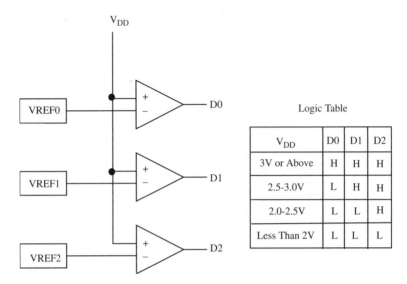

Figure 4.16 V_{DD} detection using the V_{REF} generator.

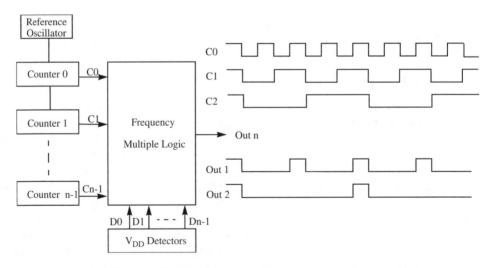

Figure 4.17   Block diagram of frequency compensation.

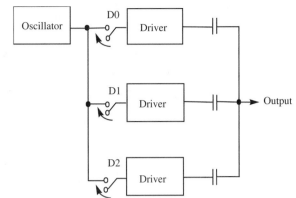

Figure 4.18 Block diagram of capacitance compensation.

Another practical approach is to limit the bit line and internal I/O swing while minimizing the effect on speed performance [14]. This approach can be valuable, especially for high-speed memory.

4.3.3 DC Leakage Current Reduction

Recent low-voltage operability trends have required advanced technology to minimize DC current. Since the threshold voltage of transistors will be forced to lower value in low-voltage operations, it is easy to cause substantial subthreshold current as the DC leakage current problem. Figure 4.20 shows the cross-sectional plot of a CMOS inverter for low voltage, and Fig. 4.21 shows the $I_{ds} - V_{gs}$ characteristics for low-voltage operation. Assume that the input of the CMOS inverter is connected to the ground potential. In this case, pMOS

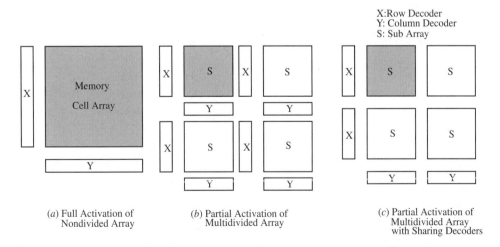

X:Row Decoder
Y: Column Decoder
S: Sub Array

(*a*) Full Activation of
Nondivided Array

(*b*) Partial Activation of
Multidivided Array

(*c*) Partial Activation of
Multidivided Array
with Sharing Decoders

Figure 4.19   Block diagram of partial activation.

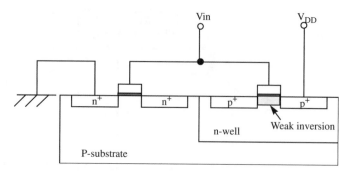

Figure 4.20   Cross section of a CMOS inverter for low-voltage operation.

is ON, and nMOS is OFF condition. Note that the nMOS transistor is operated in the weak inversion region. Under the low-power operation condition, the value of subthreshold current I_s cannot be neglected. Figure 4.21 shows that the leakage current increases from I_s to I_s^*. Therefore, if the subthreshold current is not carefully considered, it can cause a serious problem as the DC power consumption.

In order to avoid this problem, control of the gate voltage was proposed [15]. In fact, shifting V_{gs} from 0 to V_{gs}^* reduces the subthreshold current significantly.

The switched-source-impedance scheme, instead of direct control of the gate voltage, was proposed for subthreshold current reduction for scaled threshold voltage [16]. Figure 4.22 shows the switched-source-impedance scheme. The impedance is located at the source of the transistor involving subthreshold current. The switch turns on during active

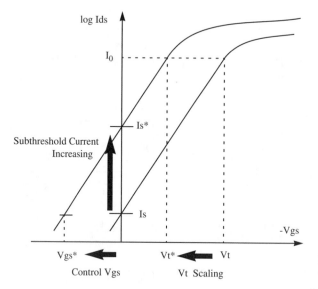

Figure 4.21   Subthreshold current characteristics for V_t scaling.

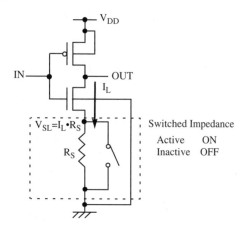

Figure 4.22 Switched-source-impedance scheme.

periods to maintain conventional CMOS circuits function, and it turns off during the inactive
period. The nMOS subthreshold leakage current in the active period is approximately

$$I_{L0} = \frac{I_0}{W_0} \cdot W \cdot 10^{\frac{-V_{T0}}{S}} \tag{5}$$

where V_{T0} is the V_T of nMOS without body effect, I_0/W_0 is the current density at V_T, W
is the channel width of nMOS, and S is the subthreshold swing and is expressed as

$$S = \frac{kT \cdot \ln 10}{q} \left(1 + \frac{C_D}{C_{OX}}\right) \tag{6}$$

where k is the Boltzmann constant, T is absolute temperature, q is the electronic charge,
C_D is the capacitance of the depletion layer, and C_{OX} is the capacitance of the gate oxide.
On the other hand, in the standby period, two mechanisms reduce the subthreshold
current. First, the back-gate bias of $-V_{SL}$ enhances V_T by ΔV_T, and current is reduced
from I_{L0} to I_{L1}:

$$I_{L1} = \frac{I_0}{W_0} \cdot W \cdot 10^{-\frac{(V_{T0}+\Delta V_T)}{S}} \tag{7}$$

$$= \frac{I_0}{W_0} \cdot W \cdot 10^{\frac{-\{V_{T0}+K(\sqrt{V_{SL}+2\phi}-\sqrt{2\phi})\}}{S}} \tag{8}$$

where K is the body-effect parameter and ϕ is the surface inversion potential. Second, the
gate-source voltage of nMOS becomes negative, $-V_{SL}$, and the current is further reduced
from I_{L1} to I_{L2}:

$$I_{L2} = \frac{I_0}{W_0} \cdot W \cdot 10^{\frac{-\{V_{SL}+V_{T0}+K(\sqrt{V_{SL}+2\phi}-\sqrt{2\phi})\}}{S}} \tag{9}$$

Therefore, the reduction ratio I_{L2}/I_{L0} is calculated by

$$\frac{I_{L2}}{I_{L0}} = 10^{\frac{-(V_{SL}+\Delta V_T)}{S}} \tag{10}$$

$$= 10^{\frac{-\{V_{SL}+K(\sqrt{V_{SL}+2\phi}-\sqrt{2\phi})\}}{S}} \tag{11}$$

Figure 4.23 illustrates the subthreshold current reduction mechanism.

With optimized selection of the source resistance, this scheme works very efficiently. In addition, the dependence of the current on temperature could be improved, because this circuit has immunity against the V_T fluctuation, which becomes very large with device scaling.

Decoded drivers, which were adopted from the above concept, were reported in [17]. Figure 4.24 shows the schematic diagram of DC current reduction for the decoded driver, and Fig. 4.25 shows the timing chart of DC current reduction for the decoded-driver scheme. Instead of locating at the nMOS source side, the impedance is located at the pMOS side to control the pMOS subthreshold current. Because the total gates of the decoded drivers occupy more than half of the whole chip, this approach revealed significantly improved result in terms of DC leakage current reduction.

Considering low-power operation, minimization of the subthreshold current is becoming extremely important because improvement in this performance can achieve long and stable data storage, which is an essential requirement of DRAM. For the purpose of realizing future high-density memory, DC leakage current reduction undoubtedly becomes crucial.

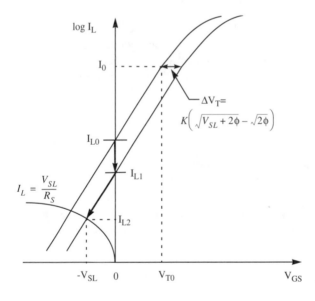

Figure 4.23 Mechanism of subthreshold current reduction.

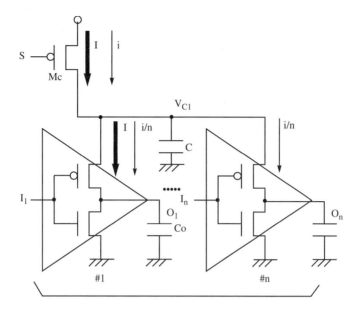

Figure 4.24   Schematic diagram of DC current reduction for decoded driver.

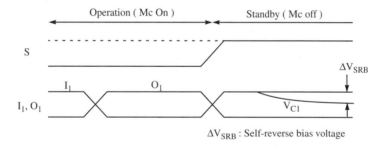

ΔV_{SRB} : Self-reverse bias voltage

Figure 4.25   DC current reduction for the decoded driver scheme.

4.4   HIGH-THROUGHPUT TECHNOLOGY

Since the CPU's speed performance has been dramatically increased, DRAM is under pressure to achieve fast response. A variety of useful approaches can be categorized in three ways: multibit data output, high-frequency control clock, and advanced interface technology. These approaches are selected with careful consideration for cost per bit performance, which is the most important factor for any type of memory chip. Figure 4.26 shows the recent prospect market map for memory, according to speed performance and capacity. Instead of common memory devices, several advanced approaches, such as Extended Data Out (EDO) DRAM, synchronous DRAM (SDRAM), and Rambus DRAM (RDRAM) will

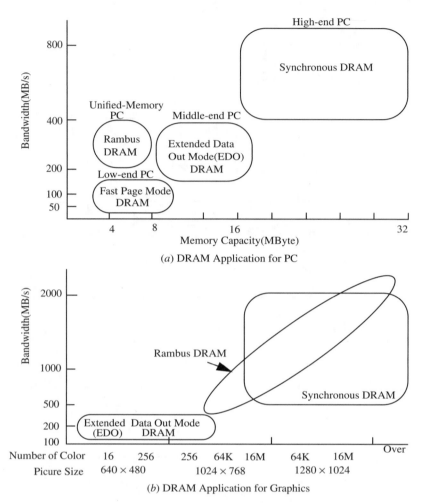

Figure 4.26 DRAM application for PC and graphics.

play the main role in the future memory market. Although the purpose of new approaches is to achieve high data throughput, each approach has unique features.

4.4.1 MultiBit DRAM

Increasing the number of data output structures is a simple and straightforward approach to achieving a high data throughput performance. This approach has already been adopted and has been successful for a variety of memories. In fact, $\times 4$, $\times 8$, $\times 16$ bit DRAMs are very popular products in the commercial market. Recently, achievement of $\times 32$ bit 16M DRAM for mass production was reported [18]. In order to realize the large number of multibit structures, development of an advanced data output buffer has become an indispensable

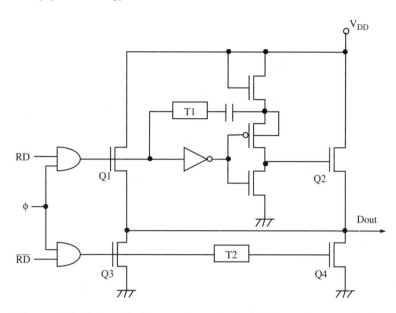

Figure 4.27   Schematic diagram of capacitor-boosted-type data output buffer.

issue. Basically, three inherent problems are associated with multibit memory: increase of switching noise, increase of power consumption, and increase of chip area. Therefore, the data out buffer is designed to minimize these effects. Switching noise is caused by the parasitic inductance, which is the wire line between the external pin and internal pad on the chip. The more the data output buffer is activated, the more output signal is distorted by the noise. Power consumption is proportional to the number of activated data output buffers. In order to solve the problem, some useful approaches can be used. Adoption of multiple power supply lines and ground lines can prevent noise interference. Minimization of the physical wire length can reduce the parasitic inductance. Lowering the power supply voltage can help reduce power consumption. In practice, a combination of these approaches will produce stable performance memories. Figure 4.27 shows the schematic diagram of a capacitor-boosted-type data output buffer [19]. At the initial stage, $Q1$ and $Q3$, which are small drive-ability transistors, turn on to avoid abrupt voltage transition that causes considerably large noise. After reaching a certain output level, $Q2$ and $Q4$, which have relatively large drive ability, turn on to speed up. $T1$ and $T2$ are used to set the certain delay time. Since the gate voltage of $Q2$ is boosted by capacitor coupling, a full V_{DD} level output signal can be achieved.

4.4.2 Fast Page Mode DRAM

In order to understand the high-frequency control clock approach. let's review the conventional DRAM. The current majority of DRAM is Fast Page mode DRAM. Although there are similar performance modes, such as Static Column mode and Nibble mode, the Fast Page mode dominates the market. There are three fundamental operation modes: read,

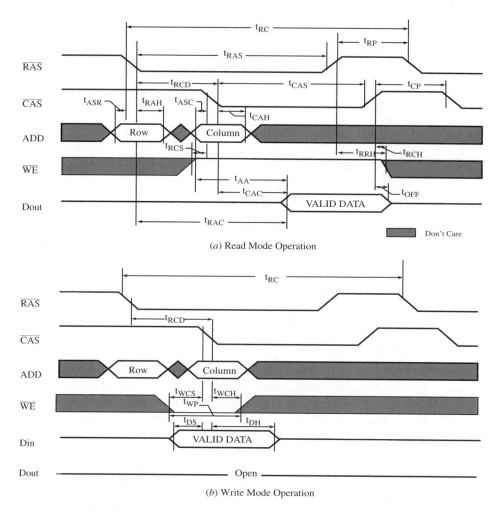

Figure 4.28   Fundamental DRAM operation scheme.

write, and refresh. The user needs to set up control signals such as $\overline{RAS}$, $\overline{CAS}$, $\overline{WE}$, $\overline{OE}$, and address signals in order to activate the proper mode. $\overline{RAS}$ is the signal to strobe the row address data, whereas $\overline{CAS}$ is the signal to strobe the column address data. Since DRAM adopted multiplex addressing, the user sets both data on the same address pins at different points in time. $\overline{WE}$ is defined as the Write Enable signal. Thus, $\overline{WE}$ is inactive in the read mode and active in the write mode. $\overline{OE}$ is defined as the Output Enable signal. This signal is used for ×4, ×8, and ×16 bit operation chips. Figure 4.28 shows the timing diagram of standard read and write operations, and Table 4.1 lists several main specifications for conventional 16M DRAM (t_{RAC} = 60 ns version, 5V, ×1)[20].

Access time is the most important specification item for DRAM. There are four kinds of access time: t_{RAC}, t_{CAC}, t_{AA}, and t_{OEA}. Thus, users must know which access time they

Table 4.1 Selected Specifications for 16M DRAM

	Parameter	min (ns)	max (ns)
t_{RC}	Random Read–Write Access Time	110	—
t_{RP}	Pulse Duration, $\overline{RAS}$ high (precharge)	40	—
t_{RAS}	Pulse Duration, $\overline{RAS}$ low	60	10,000
t_{CP}	Pulse Duration, $\overline{CAS}$ high	10	—
t_{CAS}	Pulse Duration, $\overline{CAS}$ low	15	10,000
t_{RCD}	$\overline{RAS}$–$\overline{CAS}$ Delay Time	20	45
t_{ASR}	Row Address Setup Time	0	—
t_{RAH}	Row Address Hold Time	10	—
t_{ASC}	Column Address Setup Time	0	—
t_{CAH}	Column Address Hold Time	10	—
t_{RAC}	$\overline{RAS}$ Access Time	—	60
t_{CAC}	$\overline{CAS}$ Access Time	—	15
t_{AA}	Column Address Access Time	—	30
t_{RCS}	Read Command Setup Time ($\overline{CAS}$ ref)	0	—
t_{RRH}	Read Command Hold Time ($\overline{RAS}$ ref)	0	—
t_{OFF}	Output Buffer Turn-off Delay Time	0	15
t_{WCS}	Write Command Setup Time (Early Write)	0	—
t_{WCH}	Write Command Hold Time	10	—
t_{WP}	Write Pulse Duration	10	—
t_{DS}	Data Setup Time	0	—
t_{DH}	Data Hold Time	10	—

are concerned with. First, t_{RAC} is defined as the time from $\overline{RAS}$ low to the valid data output. This is the longest access time among them. This access time is generally used to classify the version. Second, t_{CAC} is defined as the time from $\overline{CAS}$ being low to the valid data output. With the condition that data is accessed at the same row address, DRAM can offer the minimum access time, t_{CAC}. Third, t_{AA} is defined as the time from the column address setup to the valid data output. The t_{AA} is a useful specification for the Static Column mode, which can produce data by column address transition. Fourth, t_{OEA} is defined as the time from $\overline{OE}$ being low to the valid data output. Note that t_{OEA} is usually equal to t_{CAC}. The t_{OEA} is a valuable specification for $\times 4$, $\times 8$, and $\times 16$ bit DRAM.

The refresh operation is a unique feature of DRAM. This unavoidable operation adds to the complexity of DRAM. The refresh operation is equivalent to row address block activation. In other words, data are read out on the bit line and stored back to the same memory cell. For this operation, the column address block is not activated. If the user sends the specific row address, the chip can be refreshed by the $\overline{RAS}$-only refresh mode. If the user sets up $\overline{CAS}$ low before $\overline{RAS}$ low (CBR), the internal counter provides the specific row address instead of the external row address and starts the refresh operation. Figure 4.29 shows the refresh operation timing diagram, while Table 4.2 lists the refresh cycle specifications for the 16M DRAM (t_{RAC} = 60 ns version, 5V, $\times 1$)[20]. In addition

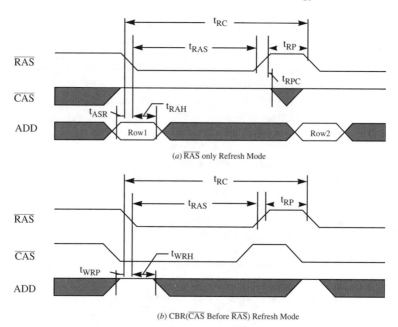

Figure 4.29   Refresh mode timing diagram.

to the above-mentioned operation modes, there are operation modes such as read-modify-write mode, hidden-refresh mode, and so on. Data-books provide detailed information on various operation modes.

In order to achieve a high throughput rate, the Fast Page mode is useful. In this mode, access time is just the $\overline{CAS}$ access time (t_{CAC}), although random access is limited to the selected row address. This is based on the characteristics of parallel structure of DRAM memory cell array. In this mode, every data cell that is connected to the selected word line is amplified and sent to the bit line. The external column address data is used to select the data on the bit line. Theoretically, it is possible to fetch the whole data which is connected to the selected word line successively. This operation does not require the user to repeat the word line boosted operation and sensing operation. This access time is the same as $\overline{CAS}$ access time (t_{CAC}), which is defined as the column address access time. Figure 4.30 shows the Fast Page read cycle mode, and Table 4.3 lists the typical 16M DRAM Fast Page mode specifications ($t_{RAC} = 60$ ns version, 5V, ×1)[20].

4.4.3 Extended Data Out Mode (EDO)

With recent progress the throughput rate has been improved efficiently. The technique involved is called Extended Data Out (EDO) mode, or Hyper Page mode. With simple modification on data output buffers, data throughput performance can be increased. Figure 4.31 shows the read cycle timing chart in the EDO mode, and Table 4.4 lists the related specifications ($t_{RAC} = 60$ ns version, 5V, ×4)[20]. The difference between the conventional Fast

Table 4.2 Selected Specifications for 16M DRAM Refresh Mode

	Parameter	min (ns)	max (ns)
t_{RC}	Random Read–Write Access Time	110	—
t_{RP}	Pulse Duration, $\overline{RAS}$ high (precharge)	40	—
t_{RAS}	Pulse Duration, $\overline{RAS}$ low	60	10,000
t_{CRP}	$\overline{CAS}$–$\overline{RAS}$ Precharge Time	5	—
r_{RPC}	$\overline{RAS}$ Precharge $\overline{CAS}$ Active Time	0	—
t_{ASR}	Row Address Setup Time	0	—
t_{RAH}	Row Address Hold Time	10	—
t_{REF}	Refresh Time	—	64/128 ms
t_{CSR}	$\overline{CAS}$ Setup Time ($\overline{CAS}$ Before $\overline{RAS}$)	5	—
t_{CHR}	$\overline{CAS}$ Hold Time ($\overline{CAS}$ Before $\overline{RAS}$)	10	—
t_{CP}	Pulse Duration, $\overline{CAS}$ high	10	—
t_{WRP}	$\overline{WE}$–$\overline{RAS}$ Precharge Time ($\overline{CAS}$ Before $\overline{RAS}$)	10	—
t_{WRH}	$\overline{WE}$–$\overline{RAS}$ Hold Time ($\overline{CAS}$ Before $\overline{RAS}$)	10	—

Page mode and the EDO mode is the data output control. In the Fast Page mode, output data is reset by rising $\overline{CAS}$; however, output data can be maintained until next $\overline{CAS}$ falling edge in EDO mode. This unique feature enables DRAM to be used efficiently in terms of data throughput. Figure 4.32 (page 146) shows the comparison of conventional Fast Page Mode DRAM with the word interleave technique and the EDO mode. In the Fast Page mode, the minimum value of pulse duration of $\overline{CAS}$ high cannot be used because some period of time is needed to reset the data after the $\overline{CAS}$ rising edge. Although the word interleave technique is used, it cannot achieve the same performance as the EDO mode. This modification considerably improves the DRAM speed performance in terms of the data throughput rate. Since the technology trend of the control DRAM is toward the synchronous operation, this

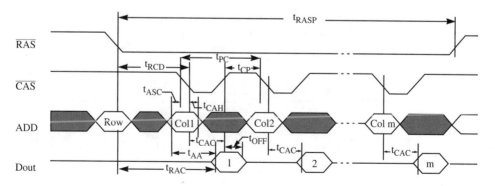

Figure 4.30 Fast Page read cycle mode.

Table 4.3 Selected Specifications for 16M DRAM Fast Page Mode

	Parameter	min (ns)	max (ns)
t_{RP}	Pulse Duration, $\overline{RAS}$ high (precharge)	40	—
t_{RASP}	Page-mode Pulse Duration, $\overline{RAS}$ low	60	400,000
t_{RCD}	$\overline{RAS}$–$\overline{CAS}$ Delay Time	20	45
t_{PC}	Page-mode Read Cycle Time	40	—
t_{CP}	Pulse Duration, $\overline{CAS}$ high	10	—
t_{ASC}	Column Address Setup Time	0	—
t_{CAH}	Column Address Hold Time	10	—
t_{RAC}	$\overline{RAS}$ Access Time	—	60
t_{OFF}	Output Buffer Turn-off Delay Time	0	15

synchronization capability is a great advantage for EDO. In production, EDO also has an advantage because it can be manufactured based on the current Fast Page mode DRAM, with small modification rather than making another chip design. In addition, full compatibility with the conventional Fast Page mode makes EDO an acceptable product in the commercial market. Therefore, in practice the EDO scheme could be recognized as a suitable bridge between the Fast Page mode and Synchronous DRAM.

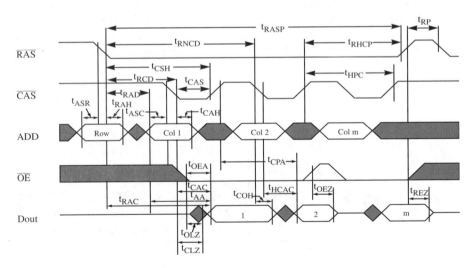

Figure 4.31 16M DRAM Extended Data Out mode read cycle.

Table 4.4 16M DRAM Extended Data Out Mode Specifications

	Parameter	min (ns)	max (ns)
t_{RNCD}	Hyper Page-mode $\overline{RAS}$-Next $\overline{CAS}$ Delay Time	60	—
t_{RASP}	Hyper Page-mode Pulse Duration, $\overline{RAS}$ low	60	200,000
t_{RHCP}	Hold Time, $\overline{RAS}$ High to $\overline{CAS}$ Precharge	35	—
t_{CSH}	Delay Time, $\overline{RAS}$ Low to $\overline{CAS}$ High	40	—
t_{HPC}	Hyper Page-mode Cycle Time	25	—
t_{CPA}	Column Precharge Access Time	—	35
t_{OEA}	$\overline{OE}$ Access Time	—	15
t_{HCAC}	Hyper Page-mode $\overline{CAS}$ Access Time	20	—
t_{COH}	Output Data Hold Time	5	—
t_{OLZ}	Delay Time, $\overline{OE}$ Low to Output in Low-Imp.	0	—
t_{RAC}	$\overline{RAS}$ Access Time	—	60
t_{CAC}	$\overline{CAS}$ Access Time	—	15
t_{AA}	Column Address Access Time	—	30
t_{CLZ}	Delay Time, $\overline{CAS}$ Low to Output in Low-Imp.	0	—
t_{OEZ}	Output Disable Time after $\overline{OE}$ High	0	15
t_{REZ}	Output Disable Time after $\overline{RAS}$ High	0	15

4.4.4 Synchronous DRAM

Although the EDO mode approach has improved speed performance, it cannot reach the level expected by memory application designers. As one of the future memory technologies, Synchronous DRAM (SDRAM) has been proposed to improve throughput performance by introducing synchronous operation to DRAM [21]. Figure 4.33 presents comparative data for throughput performance between SDRAM and EDO DRAM.

In the SDRAM operation, the read or write operation is set by command, which is a combination of levels of input pins at the rising edge of the clock. The command is decoded by the command decoder and starts to operate according to the decoded signal. Figure 4.34 shows how to set up commands, such as active, read/write, and precharge, by the input pin level. By adopting the command input scheme, the designer only has to pay attention to the setup time and hold time of each input signal related to the clock rising edge. It significantly contributes to high-performance system design. SDRAM requires initial conditions to set several important characteristics of the chip, such as CAS latency, length of burst data, and address generation type. The CAS latency is the number of required clocks after receiving the read command to produce the first data. The length of burst data is defined as the consecutive number of data. Address generation can be classified into two types: sequential and interleave.

Because of the synchronous operation, SDRAM has several crucial advantages that enhance its performance. First, all input signals are latched by the clock. System designers

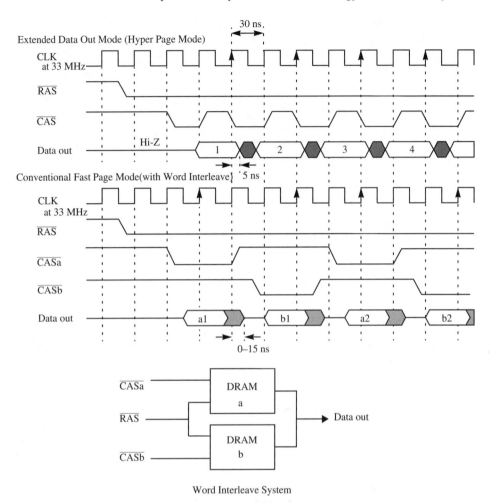

Figure 4.32 Comparison of EDO and Fast Page mode by word interleave operation.

do not have to worry about complicated timing problems, such as signal skew. In addition, pipeline operation, which is defined as the parallel operation for sequentially separated blocks, can be more efficient than asynchronous operation. Figure 4.35 shows the timing chart of pipeline operations, and Fig. 4.36 (page 149) shows the diagram for the internal circuit structure of pipeline operations. According to the control clock, each segment of column block is operated in parallel. Although access time for the first data remains the same, this approach can improve access time from the second piece of data to the last one. Furthermore, the synchronous operation allows the implementation of multibank configurations on the chip, instead of using several discrete chips. In fact, the multibank structure

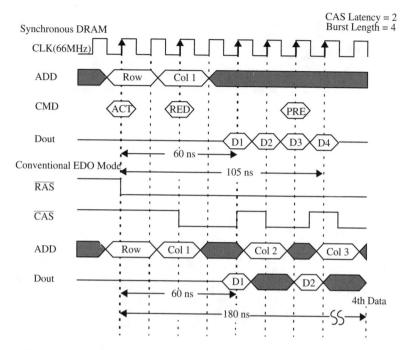

Figure 4.33 Comparison of operation methods of SDRAM and EDO mode
DRAM.

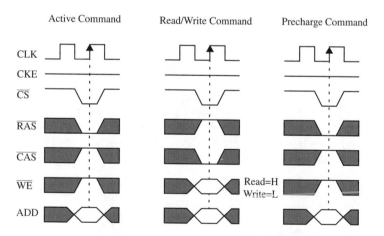

Figure 4.34 Command input SDRAM.

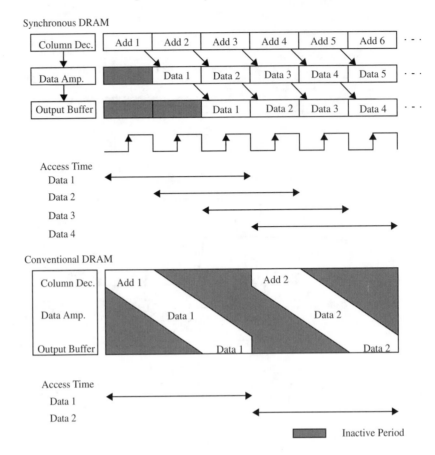

Figure 4.35 Comparison of pipeline process of SDRAM and DRAM internal process.

can provide a non-precharged period for users, because some banks can be accessed while others are in the precharged period. Figure 4.37 (page 149) shows the block diagram of a two-bank scheme. If Bank B is active, data are produced from only the Bank B memory cell array. During this period, Bank A is prepared for the next active period through precharging. This hidden multibank technique helps the designer to use memory in a very convenient manner.

Without doubt, SDRAM could play a major role in high performance, and it will be useful in high-speed multimedia applications.

4.4.5 Rambus DRAM

Besides the improvement of the DRAM chip performance itself, development of a high-performance interface is the future alternative approach. Rambus DRAM (RDRAM)

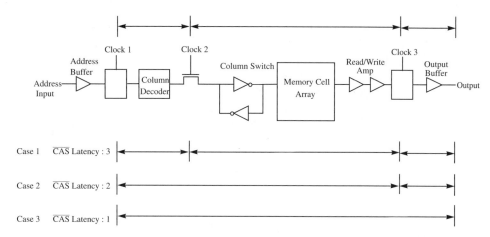

Figure 4.36   Internal pipeline structure of SDRAM.

was proposed to provide the optimized interface solution for data transfer between the CPU and memory [22]. In order to achieve this goal, RDRAM has adopted a new scheme for memory architecture. Figure 4.38 shows a comparison between a conventional memory hierarchy and the Rambus system. The system-on-a-chip approach is the target goal for RDRAM. RDRAM adopts a 9-bit data bus. Since there is no specified address bus, a request packet that includes the command to set the bus for address bus should be sent to the chip first through the control bus when a chip is accessed. After the request packet come the acknowledge and data packets. Because the initial condition has to be set, it will be late for the first data access. However, once the transfer condition is set, data access is achieved at considerably high speed, such as at 500 MB. For the purpose of stable data input and output, the phase-locked loop (PLL) circuit is located on the chip to synchronize operations between the chip and the external clock. Sense amplifiers in the memory array are used for cache memory to realize fast response. Figure 4.39 shows the block diagram of the read cycle operation for RDRAM. Since Rambus is not yet widespread, its high performance could be suitable for multimedia applications that require high-

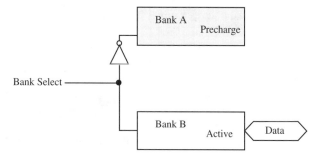

Figure 4.37   Multibank   structure   of SDRAM.

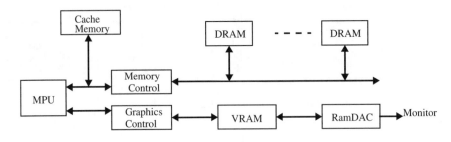

(*a*) Conventional Memory System

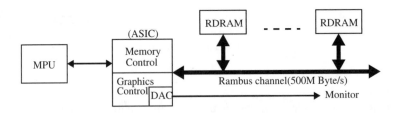

(*b*) Rambus Memory System

Figure 4.38 Comparison of conventional memory system and RDRAM system.

end memory. In the future, an increase in demand might make it available for low-end applications too.

4.4.6 Ramlink and Synclink

Ramlink was proposed as the input/output interface for the Scalable Coherent Interface (SCI), which was originally designated as the interface technology for the multiprocessor system [23]. IEEE adopted this interface technology as the standard bus interface

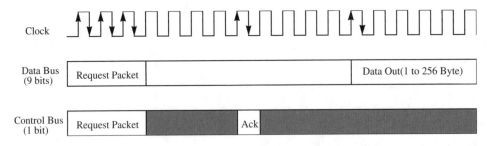

Figure 4.39 RDRAM operation scheme.

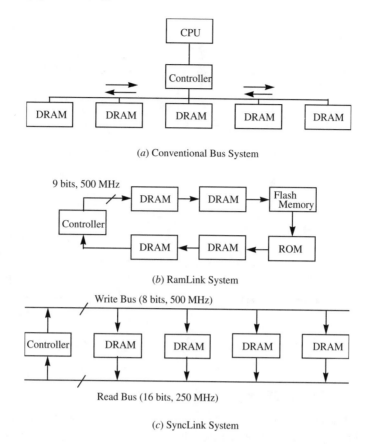

(a) Conventional Bus System

(b) RamLink System

(c) SyncLink System

Figure 4.40   Comparison of conventional bus, Ramlink, and Synclink system.

in March 1992. Signal amplitude is limited from 0.25V to 0.4V or 0.2V to 0.5V. The data are transmitted by synchronous operation at both the rising and falling edges of the control clock. Figure 4.40 shows the comparison of the conventional bus system and the new interface technology: Ramlink and Synclink. In Ramlink, data can be transmitted between the memory array by protocol control. It uses a ring topology, rather than a bus, to reduce round-trip travel time and loading problems. Instead of adopting the large number of bit-width approach, Ramlink adopted the 9-bit width to prevent signal skew problems. Synclink adopted two separate bus systems, one for the read bus, and the other for the write bus. Owing to independent controllability, each reading and writing operation can be controlled simultaneously. In addition, because the valid data is output from DRAM, PLL can be removed from the memory chip, although PLL is located in the chip for RDRAM. Compared with Rambus, Ramlink and Synclink have the advantage of flexibility. Beyond the gigabyte data transfer rate, this system solution-oriented approach will help realize the system's high-speed performance.

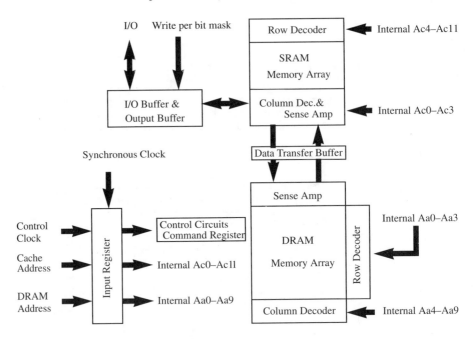

Figure 4.41   Block diagram of CDRAM.

4.4.7 Cache DRAM

Cache DRAM (CDRAM) is memory that has both DRAM array and SRAM array on a chip. Since sense amplifiers, which are flip-flop circuits to amplify and latch the signal, in DRAM are recognized as cache memory if the selected address hits the column address, a small modification enables CDRAM to be realized. Besides the above simple method, there are some alternative approaches, including the adoption of additional SRAM cell to connect the bit line. Figure 4.41 shows this type of approach, in which the small capacity of independent SRAM is integrated into the DRAM array and the transfer buffer is located between the cache and main memory [24]. The speed performance of CDRAM ensures good access speed for random access (about 100 MHz) until hitting the cache. If data are not stored in the cache, which is called miss-hit, then a copy-back operation is required. Thus, block data in cache (SRAM) are written into the main memory (DRAM). In order to speed up the copy-back operation, a data transfer buffer plays an important role. This data transfer buffer can send expected data from DRAM to SRAM and to copy-back simultaneously. It can reduce the required time for copy-back by about one-third, compared with the conventional copy-back operation time.

4.4.8 Video RAM

One well-known application-specific memory is Video RAM (VRAM). Because of the requirement for high-quality display, VRAM has been adopted as an important element in multimedia systems.

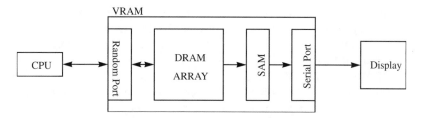

Figure 4.42 Block diagram of VRAM.

Figure 4.42 shows a diagram of the VRAM whose most distinctive characteristic is the dual-port scheme. Each port is designed to have a specific function. One port is the Serial Access Memory (SAM) block, which manages the serial data from VRAM to the display. The other port is the random access port to communicate with the CPU. These two ports are operated asynchronously and independently. Therefore, VRAM achieves efficient

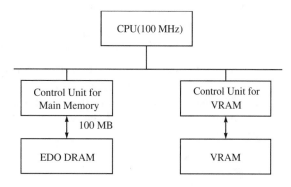

(*a*) Conventional Memory System (with VRAM)

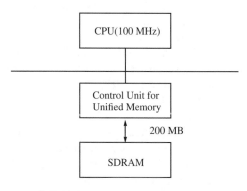

Figure 4.43 Comparison of the conventional memory system and the unified memory system.

(*b*) Unified Memory System (with SDRAM)

data transfer between the CPU and VRAM without interrupting the data transfer operation from VRAM to the display. "Line memory," "field memory," and "frame memory" are based on the same concepts but classified by the amount of storage capacity. Although current VRAM is attractive in terms of speed performance, cost per bit is very high. Since SDRAM has achieved a competitive speed performance, future conventional VRAM could be replaced by SDRAM if SDRAM were to become popular in the market. Figure 4.43 shows the system improvement that accompanies adoption of SDRAM. Providing the same speed performance is maintained, the unified memory system including SDRAM can reduce memory costs considerably. On the other hand, VRAM will be developed in specific applications, such as 3-D graphics accelerators.

4.5 SUMMARY

The future relationship between memory technology and multimedia applications is expected to be closer than what it is today. Therefore, memory system engineers should consider the application field as well as the enabling technology, and multimedia application engineers should explore the dependence of multimedia systems on memory advances. This mutual influence between two key technologies promises a bright future not only for the two technology fields but also for users.

Acknowledgments

Yoichi Oshima wishes to acknowledge Hiroyuki Taguchi of Sanyo Electric Co. Ltd., and Akira Kobayashi, Mitsuo Kawamoto, Takeo Takiuchi, Takuya Imai, and Akira Syoyama of the Japanese Patent Office for their helpful support. The warm encouragement offered by Yoshitaka Hirabayashi and Haruyoshi Uchino of the Japanese Patent Office is greatly appreciated.

References

[1] T. Masuhara et al., "VLSI Memories: Present Status and Future Prospect," *The Journal of the Institute of Electronics, Information and Communication Engineers*, Vol. E74, No.1, pp. 130–141, 1991.

[2] H. Komiya, "Future Technological and Economical Prospects for VLSI," *IEEE International Solid-State Circuits Conference*, pp. 16–19, San Francisco, Feb. 1993.

[3] H. Sasaki, "Multimedia Complex on a Chip," *IEEE International Solid-State Circuits Conference*, pp. 16–19, San Francisco, Feb. 1996.

[4] T. V. Rajeevakumar and G. B. Bronner, "A Novel Trench Capacitor Structure for ULSI DRAMs," *IEEE Symp. on VLSI Tech. Dig.*, pp. 7–8, Oiso, Kanagawa, Japan, May 1991.

[5] D. Kenney et al., "A Buried-Plate Trench Cell for 64-Mb DRAM," *IEEE Symp. on VLSI Tech. Dig.*, pp. 14–15, Oiso, Kanagawa, Japan, May 1991.

[6] T. Kaga et al., "Crown-shaped Stacked-Capacitor Cell for 1.5-V Operation 64-Mb DRAM's," *IEEE Trans. on Electron Devices*, Vol. 38, pp. 255–261, Feb. 1991.

[7] H. Watanabe et al., "A Novel Stacked Capacitor with Porous-Si Electrodes for High Density DRAMs," *IEEE Symp. on VLSI Tech. Dig.*, pp. 19–20, Honolulu, June 1994.

[8] K. Kashihara, T. Okudaira, and H. Itoh, ''A Novel Metal-Ferroelectric Insulator-Semiconductor (MFS) Capacitor Using PZT/$SrTiO_3$ Layered Insulator,'' *IEEE Symp. on VLSI Tech. Dig.*, pp. 49–50, Kyoto, Japan, May 1993.

[9] K. W. Kwon et al., ''Ta_2O_5/TiO_2 Composite Films for High Density DRAM Capacitors,'' *IEEE Symp. on VLSI Tech. Dig.*, pp. 45–46, Kyoto, Japan, May 1993.

[10] J. H. Ahn et al., ''Micro Villus Patterning Technology for 256Mb DRAM Stack Cell,'' *IEEE Symp. on VLSI Tech. Dig.*, pp. 12–13, Seattle, WA, May 1992.

[11] K. Ishibashi et al., ''A 6-ns 4-Mb CMOS SRAM with Offset-Voltage Insensitive Current Sense Amplifiers,'' *IEEE Journal of Solid-State Circuits*, Vol. 30, No. 4, pp. 480–485, April 1995.

[12] K. Itoh et al., ''Trends in Low-Power RAM Circuit Technologies,'' *IEEE Symp. on Low Power Electronics*, pp. 84–87, San Diego, CA, Oct. 1994.

[13] S.-M. Yoo et al., ''Variable Vcc Design Techniques for Battery-Operated DRAM's,'' *IEEE Journal of Solid-State Circuits*, Vol. 28, No. 4, pp. 499–503, Apr. 1992.

[14] B. S. Amrutur and M. Horowitz, ''Techniques to Reduce Power in Fast Wide Memories,'' *IEEE Symp. on Low Power Electronics*, pp. 92–93, San Diego, CA, Oct. 1994.

[15] T. Sakata et al., ''Subthreshold-Current Reduction for Multi-gigabit DRAM's,'' *IEEE Journal of Solid-State Circuits*, Vol. 29, No. 7, pp. 1136–1144, July 1994.

[16] M. Horiguchi et al., ''Switched-Source-Impedance CMOS Circuits for Low Standby Subthreshold Current Giga-scale LSI's,'' *IEEE Journal of Solid-State Circuits*, Vol. 28, No. 11, pp. 1131–1135, Nov. 1993.

[17] T. Kawahara et al., ''Subthreshold Current Reduction for Decoded-Driver by Self-Reverse Biasing,'' *IEEE Journal of Solid-State Circuits*, Vol. 28, No. 11, pp. 1136–1144, Nov. 1993.

[18] H. Koinumai and T. Kimura, ''×32 Bit 16M DRAM Structure,'' *Nikkei Microdevices*, pp. 84–85, June 1995.

[19] M. Aoki et al., ''New DRAM Noise Generation under Half-Vcc Precharge and Its Reduction Using a Transposed Amplifier,'' *IEEE Journal of Solid-State Circuits*, Vol. 24, No. 4, pp. 889–894, Aug. 1989.

[20] Texas Instruments MOS Memory Data Book, June 1995

[21] Y. Takai et al., ''250 M Byte/s Synchronous DRAM Using a 3-Stage-Pipelined Architecture,'' *IEEE Journal of Solid-State Circuits*, Vol. 29, No. 4, pp. 426–431, Apr. 1994.

[22] N. Kushiyama et al., ''500 M Byte/sec Data-Rate 512 K Bits ×9 DRAM Using a Novel I/O Interface,'' *Symp. on VLSI Circuits Dig.*, pp. 66–67, Seattle, WA, May 1992.

[23] S. Gjessing et al., ''A RAM link for High Speed,'' *IEEE Spectrum*, Vol. 29, No. 10, pp. 52–53, Oct. 1992.

[24] K. Dosaka et al., ''A 100MHz 4Mb Cache DRAM with Fast Copy-back Scheme,'' *IEEE Journal of Solid-State Circuits*, Vol. 27, No. 11, pp. 1534–1539, Nov. 1992.

Chapter

5

ADVANCED CMOS IMAGING

Bryan Ackland and Alex Dickinson

5.1 PART I: SINGLE-CHIP MULTIMEDIA CAMERA

Abstract

Multimedia applications based on video and still images will create a huge demand for compact, low-cost, low-power cameras. Recently developed image sensors based on standard CMOS meet these requirements by enabling the construction of integrated camera subsystems in which sensor array, A/D, timing, control, video signal processing, and even lenses are integrated on a single die. This chapter examines the requirements of a low-cost multimedia camera, reviews the architecture and operation of silicon image sensors, proposes an architecture for a single-chip camera, and discusses applications of this CMOS camera technology.

5.1.1 Introduction

The development of low-cost video camera technology has, for many years, been driven almost exclusively by the camcorder (3 million units per year in the United States) and security (1 million units per year) markets. The typical product is a multichip camera subsystem consisting of a Charge-Coupled Device (CCD) sensor, clock drivers, and analog signal processing devices to provide color balance and exposure control. Output is analog National Television System Committee (NTSC) or Phase-Alternative Line System (PAL). This picture is changing rapidly.

Recent advances in video compression and digital networking technology, combined with the ever-increasing power of PCs and workstations, are creating enormous opportunities to develop new multimedia products and services built on sophisticated voice, data, image, and video processing. This will create a significant demand for compact, low-cost, low-power electronic cameras for video and still image capture. These cameras will be a standard peripheral on all PCs bundled for multimedia applications. Given that more than 60 million PCs will be sold in 1996, a sizable new market for electronic cameras is being created.

Existing NTSC cameras are not well suited to digital multimedia applications:

- They are too expensive, with Original-Equipment Manufacturer (OEM) costs typically being greater than $100. Experience with the development of CD-ROM players suggests that as the OEM cost of a peripheral falls below $50, the vast majority of PCs will ship bundled with the peripheral.
- They are too large to be mounted inconspicuously on (or in) a PC monitor.

156

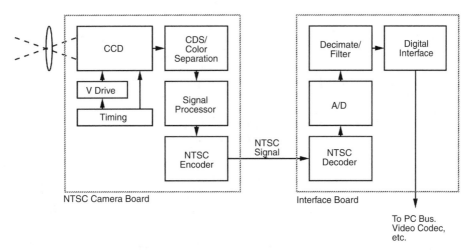

Figure 5.1 Conventional multimedia camera.

■ They consume too much power for portable applications. CCD sensors require high-voltage, high-current clocks; a CCD-based camera subsystem will typically consume 1 to 2 watts.

■ Video data are output in encoded analog raster scan format. This limits both the flexibility of the camera and the cost of the overall system. In multimedia systems based on camcorder-type cameras, additional circuitry must be included to convert from the NTSC-style output of the camera to the digital format required by the application, as shown in Fig. 5.1. This circuitry will frequently cost more than the camera itself.

What is needed is a camera technology that can be customized to particular applications such as desktop video, still scene, and document imaging. Cost, size, and power constraints require integrating the image sensor along with analog and digital signal processing and interfacing elements onto the same physical die, as shown in Fig. 5.2. Input to the chip is an image focused onto a sensor array. Output is a (possibly compressed) digital stream that connects seamlessly to the specified multimedia platform.

5.1.2 CCD Sensors

Any solid-state imaging device consists of an array of sensing elements combined with some form of transport mechanism to deliver these sensor outputs to the periphery of the die. Sensors used in commercial devices include photodiodes, MOS capacitors, charge injection devices, and bipolar phototransistors. All of these devices use essentially the same light-sensing mechanism. Photons penetrating a depletion region generate electron-hole pairs. These are swept away by the electric field across the depletion region and generate a small photocurrent.

Except under very bright light conditions, it is not possible to use this photocurrent directly. Even at 100% conversion efficiency, a 10 μm sensor illuminated at 1 lux will

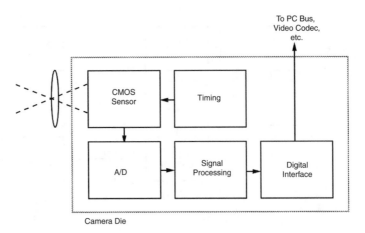

Figure 5.2   Multimedia camera on a chip.

generate a photocurrent of only 70 fA. In order to achieve a reasonable signal-to-noise ratio, these currents are usually integrated over a period of time (typically 15 ms) to produce an accumulated charge output. For the above example, a charge of 10^{-15} coulombs (60,000 electrons) would be accumulated in this time.

The CCD provides a simple mechanism for transporting these small charge packets out of the array. A CCD is a linear array of MOS capacitors that function as a charge domain shift register when driven by a set of multiphase clocks. In low-cost cameras, interline transfer, as shown in Fig. 5.3, is the most commonly used architecture. Adjacent to each column of sensors is a vertical CCD. Accumulated charge is transferred from the sensor to the corresponding CCD bucket. These charges are then shifted vertically, one line at a time, into a horizontal shift register. A single line is scanned out from the horizontal shift register onto a capacitor that converts each charge packet to a voltage for subsequent amplification and buffering.

CCD sensors have improved dramatically since their introduction in the 1970s. Scientific arrays of 4096 x 4096 resolution with dynamic noise levels of 3 to 5 electrons and a dynamic range of over 80 dB have been demonstrated. Low-cost commercial devices typically provide 640 x 480 pixel resolution, with a signal-to-noise ratio of 45 dB. One advantage of CCD sensors is the high fill factor (ratio of light sensitive area to total pixel area) that can be obtained, even for small pixels. This is because the only extra area required is that of the CCD register. State-of-the-art sensors use pixel sizes of 5 μm x 5 μm, which approaches the optical diffraction limit. A second advantage of these systems is their lack of pattern noise. This is caused by variations in offset and gain from one pixel to another. In a CCD, all image information travels through closely matched paths in the charge domain and then shares the same charge-to-voltage output stage.

CCDs, however, have a number of disadvantages in multimedia applications. Most of these disadvantages stem from the need to maintain a very high charge transfer efficiency (CTE) within the CCD shift register. CTE is a measure of the percentage of electrons that are successfully transferred from one bucket to another in one CCD shift cycle. In a 640 x

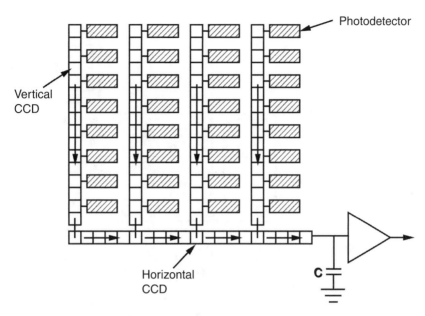

Figure 5.3   Interline transfer CCD.

480 sensor, a single charge packet may be shifted 1100 times. Even with a CTE of 0.9995, this will result in a 40% loss of charge by the time the packet reaches the output stage. Commercial devices typically require a CTE of 0.99995 or greater.

One way of increasing CTE is to use large voltages (12–15V) on the CCD clock lines. This, in turn, leads to high-power dissipation. Much work has been done recently on developing low-voltage CCD processes that will be better suited to multimedia applications. Both SONY [1] and Philips [2] have reported low-power consumer grade sensors in which most of the high-speed clock circuitry is driven at 3.3V.

Another approach is to carefully tune doping profiles so as to maximize charge-carrying capacity and minimize charge loss during transfer. This has led to processes that provide excellent CCD performance but are not at all suitable for producing standard digital VLSI circuits. Digital camera proposals based on CCDs [3] typically require at least three separate die: one for the sensor, a second for analog clock drivers and A/D, and a third for the digital signal processing components. Kodak [4], however, has recently reported a 2 μm process that supports high-quality CCDs, along with NPN bipolar and conventional CMOS devices. Such a process allows for the possibility of integrating all camera functions onto a single chip at a cost of four extra mask layers and three extra implants.

5.1.3 CMOS Sensors

An alternative approach is to design the sensor as a two-dimensional addressable array of sensors [5–8]. The architecture is very similar to that used in conventional random access memories. A bit line is associated with each column of sensors as shown in Fig. 5.4. A row-

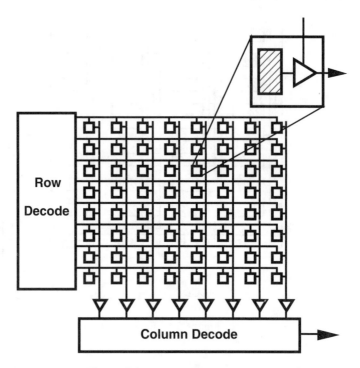

Figure 5.4   Active pixel sensor array.

enable line allows each sensor in a selected row to place its output onto its bit line. A multiplexer at the end of the bit lines allows for individual column addressing. This is an old idea dating back to the early 1970s, but one that, until recently, has not found commercial application. The difficulty arises from the very small charge generated at each pixel. From our previous example, a charge of 10^{-15} coulombs placed on a 2 pF bit line generates a voltage change of only 500 μV. Such a small signal is very susceptible to noise. What is needed is a simple amplifier at each pixel to provide buffering, as shown in Fig. 5.4; this is commonly referred to as an active pixel sensor (APS) array.

In the early 1970s, with sensor sizes of 25 μm and design rules of 5 μm, it was clearly not possible to include an amplifier at each pixel. Today, with sensor sizes of 10 μm and process design rules at 0.5 μm, we can build a three-transistor precharge/amplify/select circuit, as shown in Fig. 5.5, and still achieve a fill factor of over 25%. One advantage of APS sensors is that they can be powered from a single 3.3 V (or lower) supply and do not require external multiphase clock generators. This leads to reduced system costs and significantly reduced power dissipation. Integrated CMOS cameras with a total power dissipation under 10 mW have been reported. Silicon processing costs are also reduced because of the huge volumes associated with generic digital CMOS production. Another advantage is the flexibility that is provided by a random access sensor addressing scheme. No longer is one constrained to access pixels in a serial order

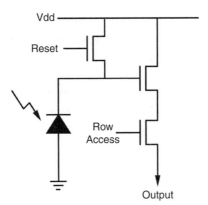

Figure 5.5 Active pixel circuit.

determined by the architecture of the CCD pipeline. This makes it much simpler to introduce alternative forms of pixel access, such as that required to support electronic pan and zoom.

Arguably the most important advantage of the CMOS APS approach, however, is the ability to integrate much of the camera timing, control, and signal processing circuitry onto the same silicon die. A CIF (352x288) sensor array can be built in 0.5 μm CMOS in less than 11 mm^2 of active area. Even assuming a modest die size of 30 mm^2, this leaves significant area for these system functions, plus the ability to add extra circuitry which will customize the camera for a particular application.

One particular problem associated with APS arrays is the existence of significant levels of fixed-pattern noise. Unlike CCDs, in which all charge packets travel essentially the same signal path and use the same output amplifier, each pixel in an APS array has its own amplifier. Gain and offset variations between these amplifiers lead to a static pattern noise that appears as a background texture on the image. The eye is very sensitive to small amounts of pattern noise (1–2% is clearly visible), particularly if it is aligned along vertical or horizontal lines, as is the case with noise contributed by column output stages.

Fortunately, the ability to integrate signal processing electronics onto the same die provides a number of solutions to this problem. Fixed-pattern noise can be significantly reduced by the use of a simple correlated double sampling (CDS) technique as shown in Fig. 5.6. Each column output stage contains two sample-and-hold capacitors. One is used to sample the pixel reset level, and the other is used to sample the signal level (after integration). By subtracting the reset level from the signal level, much of the pixel amplifier offset is removed. A second level of CDS can be applied to eliminate offset in the column amplifier. A combination of these two techniques can reduce fixed-pattern noise from 5% to 0.1%. Alternatively, digital techniques can be employed to reduce the level of pattern noise. The offset level for each column, for example, could be stored in a RAM and digitally subtracted from the output signal on a column-by-column basis. These techniques can reduce the pattern noise to a level where it is imperceptible under the room-light (or brighter) levels of illumination found in most multimedia applications.

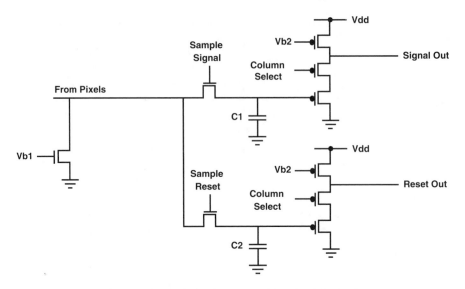

Figure 5.6   CDS fixed-pattern noise reduction circuit.

5.1.4   Single-Chip Camera

The basic architecture of a "camera on a chip" for multimedia applications is shown in Fig. 5.7. The detailed functionality of each module will depend on the nature of the application. Of particular significance is the degree of autonomy required of the camera. At one extreme—that represented by a conventional video camera—the camera operates in a stand-alone mode, calculating exposure times and color balance and producing a stream of video information at a predetermined frame rate. A more flexible model, however, is one in which camera functionality is partitioned between the camera hardware (simple, per-pixel operations) and software (complex, per-frame operations) in an intelligent host (e.g., PC), thereby reducing the cost of the camera hardware and increasing the functionality of the overall system.

The camera is no longer autonomous, instead having a symbiotic relationship with the host and the host application, as shown in Fig. 5.7. Exposure control, for example, may be partitioned between the camera, which maintains summary statistics on intensity derived from examining each pixel, and the host, which makes use of the summary statistics to calculate a suitable exposure time, which is then passed back to the camera. In the remainder of this subsection, we briefly examine the implementation of each of the modules shown in Fig. 5.7.

5.1.4.1   Sensor Array

The sensor array is comprised of a two-dimensional array of pixels that can be randomly addressed through adjacent row and column decoders. An emerging standard for

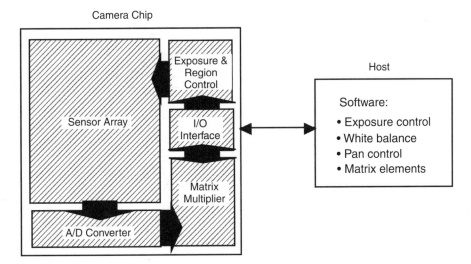

Figure 5.7   Camera hardware/software partitioning.

video telephony is Common Intermediate Format (CIF) at 288 by 352 pixels, somewhat less than NTSC resolution but sufficient for many compressed video and snapshot applications.

5.1.4.2 Exposure Control

The standard video frame rate is 30 frames per second. Multimedia applications, however, typically operate at 10 to 15 frames per second. These numbers suggest per frame exposure times of approximately 60 to 100 milliseconds. These, however, are maximum exposure times that are only used in moderate- to low-light conditions. As lighting conditions intensify, it is necessary to reduce the effective exposure time to ensure that the sensors do not saturate (exceed their maximum charge capacity). Long exposure times may also lead to high levels of dark current pattern noise. The exposure control block generates timing signals to set the interval between resetting a row of pixels and reading the accumulated charge. This correct exposure time is calculated to maintain a specified distribution of pixel brightness levels. This calculation can be performed either by on-board circuitry or by software running on the host.

5.1.4.3 Region Control

A specific region of the sensor may be read simply by presetting the counters that drive the row and column decoders to values that represent the origin of the region of interest at the start of every new frame. Electronic panning may then be implemented by altering the preset values to the new window origin under user (or application) control.

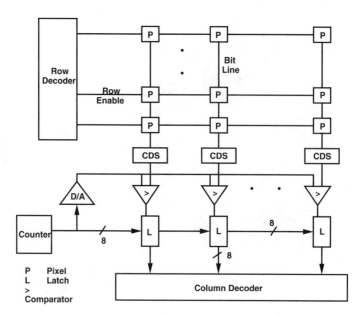

Figure 5.8 Per-column, single-slope A/D converter.

5.1.4.4 A/D Conversion

Traditionally, digital cameras have used a single A/D converter that operates at the pixel rate (3 M pixels/sec for CIF, 30 frames/sec). Eight-bit resolution is sufficient provided that Automatic Gain Control (AGC) and gamma correction have already been performed in the analog domain. Having the converter on the same die as the sensor, however, allows for alternative A/D solutions. Researchers at Stanford [9] have described a CMOS camera in which a sigma-delta A/D converter is effectively integrated into each pixel, allowing for digital readout at the cell level. The sensor capacitance conveniently performs the summing and integrating function. This considerably simplifies signal readout but leads to larger pixel sizes and reduced sensitivity since the raw sensor current is now the input to the A/D.

Alternatively, a simple low-speed single-slope converter may be placed at the output of every column, as shown in Fig. 5.8. A comparator compares the column output against a reference. The reference voltage is a ramp derived from a counter feeding a D/A converter. When the column comparator senses equality between the column signal and the reference, the counter output is recorded in a register associated with each column. At the end of a single conversion cycle (one row of video), the registers contain digital values representing the analog output of each column, and may be sequentially (or randomly) addressed to generate a digital output signal from the chip. Note that additional signal processing (AGC, gamma correction) may be performed by modifying the slope and shape of the reference ramp.

5.1.4.5 Video Signal Processing

Additional signal processing is usually required to compensate for variations in processing and operating conditions. These may be performed in either the analog or digital domain. Automatic Gain Control (AGC) is required in moderate- to low-light conditions where the camera is running at its maximum exposure time. Gain may be added into the signal path to increase the apparent brightness of the scene. This has the effect, however, of also amplifying noise, so the total gain will be limited by the signal-to-noise ratio of the array. Gamma correction is required to compensate for display nonlinear response. One implementation simply uses the digital value of the video signal to address a lookup table containing the corrected signal values.

Finally, it is usually necessary to perform color correction (white balance) to compensate for nonideal response in the sensors and color filters. This may take the form of a simple gain control on each component channel. Digital processing, however, provides a more flexible solution in the form of a color transformation matrix:

$$
\begin{bmatrix} R' \\ G' \\ B' \end{bmatrix} = \begin{bmatrix} X_{1,1} & X_{1,2} & X_{1,3} \\ X_{2,1} & X_{2,2} & X_{2,3} \\ X_{3,1} & X_{3,2} & X_{3,3} \end{bmatrix} \begin{bmatrix} R \\ G \\ B \end{bmatrix} \tag{1}
$$

This transformation is applied to each R/G/B sample to allow for crosstalk and response variation between the three color channels. It can be used to correct significant errors in sensor spectral response and color filter response, and therefore it simplifies the task of color filter array specification. In addition, such a matrix can be used to generate alternative color space formats (e.g., YCrCb, YUV).

5.1.4.6 Bus Interface

To maximize the value of integration, it is necessary to select an appropriate digital interface and implement that interface on-chip. Clearly, the interface is highly application dependent, with choices from a simple proprietary unidirectional data stream for connection directly to a video codec to more complex bidirectional standards such as IEEE 1394 (Firewire) for connection to a PC.

5.1.5 Back-End Manufacturing Steps

Although the concept of a single-chip camera is based on fabricating the entire device on a single die in a standard CMOS process, a number of additional or "back-end" steps must be included to complete the overall manufacturing process, as follows.

5.1.5.1 Packaging

Chip packaging costs are a significant portion of the complete costs of a sensor. A sensor package must

- Have a transparent, hermetically sealed lid.
- Be able to adequately dissipate sensor power.
- Be manufactured (including chip placement) to tolerances sufficient for inclusion in an optical system.

The relatively high power dissipated by CCD sensors and their sensitivity to thermal stress have often required the use of costly ceramic or precision plastic packages. The much lower power requirements of CMOS arrays permits the use of conventional plastic packages, considerably lowering the cost of the completed part.

5.1.5.2 Testing

Testing optical devices requires more complex facilities than those used for standard digital parts. Additional test issues include:

- Providing a controlled optical source for photodetector stimulation.
- Digital tester inputs capable of verifying that a good output lies in a range of values rather than a single value.

5.1.5.3 Color Filter Arrays

In order to construct a single-sensor color camera, it is necessary to pattern the sensor surface with a suitable mosaic of color filters. Two color systems are available: additive (red, green, blue) and subtractive (magenta, cyan, yellow). Subtractive filters have the advantage that they let more light onto the sensor and provide greater sensitivity. Additive filters lead to simpler color processing. Filters are typically made from dyed polyamide, each color being lithographically defined and etched in turn to create an individual filter square over each pixel. Various patterns, such as the one shown in Fig. 5.9, have been proposed. Typically, patterns are chosen to emphasize the luminance (or green) resolution, while chrominance (or red/blue) resolution is sampled at lower resolution. Depending on the pattern chosen, various amounts of buffering (typically, one to two lines) and processing (addition/subtraction) may be needed to derive the required per-pixel output data from the raw array data.

5.1.5.4 Microlenses

Because the fill factor of a pixel is typically around 30%, considerable gains in sensitivity can be achieved by constructing a lens over the entire pixel to focus light onto the active area. These microlenses may be fabricated by patterning and etching polyamide to form a cylinder over each pixel, then heating the material until it flows to form a spherical lens over the pixel.

5.1.5.5 Housing and Optics

In addition to the single silicon die, a complete camera will require a simple PC board (perhaps including a voltage regulator), a plastic housing, lens, cabling, and connector.

R	G	R	G	R	G
G	B	G	B	G	B
R	G	R	G	R	G
G	B	G	B	G	B
R	G	R	G	R	G
G	B	G	B	G	B

Figure 5.9   Color mosaic pattern.

Recent developments in the production of precision injection-molded plastic asphere lenses suggest that a high-quality multi-element lens can be produced at a fraction of the cost of glass spherical lenses. For simple fixed-focus applications, these may be attached directly to the camera chip package.

5.1.6   Evolution of Single-Chip Cameras

Work on single-chip cameras is presently concentrating on the production of low-cost color video cameras for multimedia applications. As the CMOS sensor array technology evolves and process line widths continue to decrease, we expect to see the following developments.

- CMOS image sensor arrays will become ''standard cells'' much like any other chip layout component. For example, an image sensor and a video encoder may be combined, together with some ASIC ''glue'' to create an application-specific product.
- More sophisticated use will be made of application/camera interaction, resulting in increased image quality and new features (e.g., automatic head tracking supported by electronic pan and zoom).
- Higher resolution sensors for document image capture applications such as fax will become available.
- Very high-resolution sensors for all-electronic consumer still camera applications will be developed.
- Very low-cost, low-resolution sensors will allow ''intelligent'' machine vision functions to be added to consumer items such as automobiles and home appliances.

We believe that the product life cycle of the digital clock may provide some indication of the future of cameras. Initially a relatively costly stand-alone device, digital clocks became cheap enough to be combined with radios, and then eventually became standard features of a wide range of products from microwave ovens to VCRs. Similarly, the high levels of integration enabled by the development of CMOS image sensor technology will drive consumer electronic cameras from their present stand-alone (camcorder) form to being a ubiquitous feature of everyday life.

References

[1] F. Fujikawa et al., "A 1/3-inch 630k-pixel IT-CCD Image Sensor with Multi-Function Capability," *Proc. IEEE Intl. Solid State Circuits Conf.*, pp. 218–221, Feb. 1995.

[2] J. Bosiers et al., "Design Options for 1/4''-FT-CCD Pixels," *Proc. IEEE Workshop on Charge-Coupled Devices and Advanced Image Sensors*, Apr. 1995.

[3] S. Wang et al. "A Real-Time Signal Processor for Use with the Interline Transfer Color CCD Imager," *Proc. IEEE Workshop on Charge-Coupled Devices and Advanced Image Sensors*, Apr. 1995.

[4] R. Guidash et al., "A Modular, High Performance, 2 5m CCD-BiCMOS Process Technology for Application Specific Image Sensors and Image Sensor Systems on a Chip," *Proc. IEEE Intl. ASIC Conf. & Exhibit*, pp. 352–355, Apr. 1994.

[5] D. Renshaw et al., "ASIC Vision," *Proc. IEEE Custom Integrated Circuits Conf.*, 1990, pp. 7.3.1–7.3.4.

[6] E. Fossum, "Active Pixel Image Sensors—Are CCD's Dinosaurs?", *Proc. SPIE*, Vol. 1900, pp. 2–14, 1993.

[7] C. Jansson et al., "An Addressable 256x256 Photodiode Image Sensor Array with an 8-bit Digital Output," *Analog Integrated Circuits and Signal Processing*, Vol. 4, pp. 37–49, 1993.

[8] A. Dickinson et al., "Standard CMOS Active Pixel Image Sensors for Multimedia Applications," *Proc. Conf. on Advanced Research in VLSI*, pp. 214–224, Mar. 1995.

[9] B. Fowler et al., "A CMOS Image Sensor with Pixel Level A/D Conversion," *Proc. IEEE Solid State Circuits Conf.*, pp. 216–218, Feb. 1994.

5.2 PART II: CMOS IMAGE SENSOR TECHNOLOGY

Eric R. Fossum

Abstract

CMOS active pixel sensors (APS) have performance competitive with CCD technology, and offer advantages in on-chip functionality, system power reduction, cost, and miniaturization. This section discusses the requirements for CMOS image sensors and their historical development. CMOS devices and circuits for pixels, analog signal chain, and on-chip analog-to-digital conversion are reviewed and discussed.[1]

[1]Earlier versions appeared in the 1995 International Electron Devices Meeting Digest of Technical Papers and the Proc. 1997 International Symposium on VLSI Technology, Systems and Applications, Taipei, Taiwan.

5.2.1 Introduction

Today there are many kinds of electronic cameras with very different characteristics. Camcorders are the most well-known electronic camera and capture images with television resolution at 30 frames per second. Digital "still" CCD cameras capture higher resolution images (e.g., 1280 x 1024 pixels) at slower frame rates. These cameras, while presently expensive for consumer applications, are expected to rapidly drop in price. Monochrome low-resolution (e.g., 300,000 pixels) CCD cameras are very inexpensive. Spaceborne, high-resolution scientific CCD cameras occupy the opposite end of the spectrum.

New markets are emerging for digital electronic cameras, especially in computer peripherals for document capture and visual communications. If the cost of the camera can be made sufficiently low (e.g., $100 or less per camera), it is expected that most personal computers will have at least one camera peripheral. Even less expensive cameras will find automotive and entertainment applications. Wireless applications of cameras will require ultra low-power operation. Very small cameras (e.g., less than 10 cm^3) will also permit new markets.

Despite the wide variety of applications, all digital electronic cameras have the same basic functions. These are (1) optical collection of photons, that is, a lens, (2) wavelength discrimination of photons, that is, filters, (3) detector for conversion of photons to electrons, for example, a photodiode, (4) a method to read out the detectors, for example, a CCD, (5) timing, control, and drive electronics for the sensor, (6) signal processing electronics for correlated double sampling, color processing, and so on, (7) analog-to-digital conversion and (8) interface electronics. In a CCD-based system, these functions often consume several watts of power (e.g., 1–5 W) and, for example, are a major drain on a camcorder battery. The volume and mass of the electronics and power supply constrains the level of miniaturization achievable with the system.

Over the past five years, there has been a growing interest in CMOS image sensors. The major reason for this interest is customer demand for miniaturized, low-power, and cost-effective imaging systems. CMOS-based image sensors offer the potential opportunity to integrate a significant amount of VLSI electronics on-chip and reduce component and packaging costs. It is now straightforward to envision a single-chip camera that has integrated timing and control electronics, sensor array, signal processing electronics, analog-to-digital converter, and full digital interface. Such a camera-on-a-chip will operate with standard logic supply voltages and consume power measured in the tens of milliwatts [1,2]. This section reviews CMOS image sensor technology and the roadmap to achieve a camera-on-a-chip imaging system.

5.2.2 Historical Background

Before CMOS APS and before CCDs, there were MOS image sensors. In the 1960s numerous groups were working on solid-state image sensors, with varying degrees of success, using NMOS, PMOS, and bipolar processes. For example, in 1963, Morrison reported a structure (now referred to as a computational sensor) that allowed determination of a light spot's position using the photoconductivity effect [3]. The *scanistor*, reported in 1964 by IBM [4], used an array of n-p-n junctions addressed through a resistive network to produce an output pulse proportional to the local incident light intensity. In 1966, Westinghouse reported a 50 x 50 element monolithic array of phototransistors [5]. All of these sensors had an output signal proportional to the instantaneous local incident light intensity and did not perform any intentional integration of the optical signal. As a consequence, the sensitivity of these devices was low, and they required gain within the pixel to enhance their performance.

In 1967, Weckler at Fairchild suggested operating p-n junctions in a photon flux integrating mode [6]. The photocurrent from the junction is integrated on a reverse-biased p-n junction capacitance. Readout of the integrated charge using a PMOS switch was suggested. The signal charge, appearing as a current pulse, could be converted to a voltage pulse using a series resistor. A 100 x 100 element array of photodiodes was reported in 1968 [7]. Weckler later called the device a *reticon* and formed Reticon to commercialize the sensor.

Also in 1967, RCA reported a thin-film transistor (TFT) solid-state image sensor using CdS/CdSe TFTs and photoconductors [8]. The 180 x 180 element array included self-scanning complementary logic circuitry for sequentially addressing pixels. A battery-operated wireless camera was also reported to have been constructed to demonstrate the array.

Also active at that time was Plessey in the UK. In a 1968 seminal paper, Noble described several configurations of self-scanned silicon image detector arrays [9]. Both surface photodiodes and buried photodiodes (to reduce dark current) were described. Noble also discussed a charge integration amplifier for readout, similar to that used later by others. In addition, the first use of a MOS source-follower transistor in the pixel for readout buffering was reported. An improved model and description of the operation of the sensor was reported by Chamberlain in 1969 [10]. The issue of fixed-pattern noise (FPN) was explored in a 1970 paper by Fry, Noble, and Rycroft [11].

Until recently, FPN was considered the primary problem associated with MOS and CMOS image sensors. In 1970, when the CCD was first reported [12], its relative freedom from FPN was one of the major reasons why it was adopted over the many other forms of solid-state image sensors. The smaller pixel size afforded by the simplicity of the CCD pixel also explains its embrace by industry.

Since the CCD's inception, the main focus of research and development has been on CCD sensor performance. The camcorder market has driven impressive improvements in charge-coupled device (CCD) technology. Criteria include quantum efficiency, optical fill factor (fraction of pixel used for detection), dark current, charge transfer efficiency, smear, readout rate, lag, readout noise and full well, that is, dynamic range. A desire to reduce cost and optics mass has driven a steady reduction in pixel size. HDTV and scientific applications have driven an increase in array size. Recently, emphasis has been placed on improved CCD functionality, such as electronic shutter, low-power, and simplified supply voltages. There have been several reports of integrating CMOS with CCDs to increase CCD functionality [13,14,15], but with the exception of some line arrays, the effort has not been fruitful because of both cost and the difficulty of driving the large capacitive loads of the CCD.

While a large effort was applied to the development of the CCD in the 1970s and 1980s, MOS image sensors were only sporadically investigated and were compared unfavorably to CCDs with respect to the above performance criteria [16]. In the late 1970s and early 1980s, Hitachi and Matsushita continued the development of MOS image sensors [17,18] for camcorder-type applications, including single-chip color imagers [19]. Temporal noise in MOS sensors started to lag behind the noise achieved in CCDs, and by 1985, Hitachi combined the MOS sensor with a CCD horizontal shift register [20]. In 1987, Hitachi introduced a simple on-chip technique to achieve variable exposure times and flicker suppression from indoor lighting [21]. However, perhaps because of residual temporal noise, which is especially important in low-light conditions, Hitachi abandoned its MOS approach to sensors.

In the later 1980s, while CCDs predominated in visible imaging, two related fields started to turn away from the use of CCDs. The first was hybrid infrared focal-plane arrays that initially used CCDs as a readout multiplexer. Due to limitations of CCDs, particularly in low-temperature operation and charge handling, CMOS readout multiplexers were developed that allowed both increased functionality and performance compared to CCD multiplexers [22]. A second field was high-energy physics particle/photon vertex detectors. Many workers in this area also initially used CCDs for detection and readout of charge generated by particles and photons. However, the radiation sensitivity of CCDs and the increased functionality offered by CMOS [e.g., 23] have led to subsequent abandonment of CCD technology for this application.

In the early 1990s, however, two independently motivated efforts have led to a resurgence in CMOS image sensor development. The first effort was to create highly functional single-chip imaging systems where low cost, not performance, was the driving factor. This effort was spearheaded by separate researchers at the University of Edinburgh in Scotland (later becoming VVL) and Linkoping University in Sweden (later becoming IVP). The second independent effort grew from NASA's need for highly miniaturized, low-power, instrument imaging systems for next-generation deep space exploration spacecraft. Such imaging systems are driven by performance, not cost. This latter effort was led by the U.S. Jet Propulsion Laboratory, with subsequent transfer of the technology to AT&T Bell Labs, Kodak, National Semiconductor, and several other major U.S. companies, and the startup of Photobit. The convergence of the efforts has led to significant advances in CMOS image sensors and the development of the CMOS active pixel sensor (APS). It has performance competitive with CCDs with respect to read noise, dynamic range, and responsivity but with vastly increased functionality, substantially lower system power (10–50 mW), and the potential for lower system cost.

Contributing to the recent activity in CMOS image sensors is the steady, exponential improvement in CMOS technology. The rate of minimum feature size decrease has outpaced similar improvements in CCD technology (see Fig. 5.10). Furthermore, sensor pixel size is limited by both optical physics and optics cost, making moot the CCD's inherent pixel-size advantage for most applications. Recent progress in on-chip signal processing (and off-chip DSP) has also reduced CMOS image sensor FPN to acceptable levels. In addition, the transition from analog imaging and display systems to digital cameras tethered to PCs permits digital FPN correction, with negligible system impact.

There are three predominant approaches to pixel implementation in CMOS: passive pixel, photodiode-type active pixel, and photogate-type active pixel. These are described below. There are also several ways to make p-n junction photodiodes in CMOS [24], but generally n+ diodes on a p/p+ epi substrate in an n-well process give the most satisfactory results.

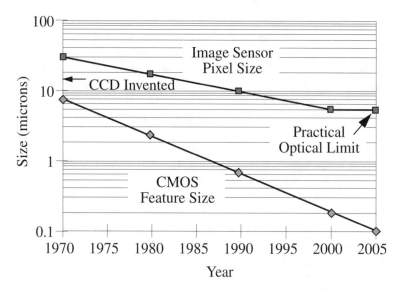

Figure 5.10   The steadily increasing ratio between pixel size and minimum feature size permits the use of CMOS circuitry within each pixel.

5.2.3   Overall Architecture

The overall architecture of a CMOS image sensor is shown in Fig. 5.11. The image sensor consists of an array of pixels that are typically selected a row at a time by row select logic. This can be either a shift register or a decoder. The pixels are read out to vertical column busses that connect the selected row of pixels to a bank of analog signal processors (ASPs). These ASPs perform functions such as charge integration, gain, sample-and-hold, correlated double sampling, and FPN suppression.

More advanced CMOS image sensors contain on-chip analog-to-digital converters (ADC). In Fig. 5.11, the ADCs are shown as column-parallel ADCs; that is, each column of pixels has its own ADC. The digital output of the ADCs (or analog output of the ASPs) is selected for readout by column select logic that can be either a shift register or a decoder. A timing and control logic block is also integrated on-chip. This digital block is readily defined at a high level using tools such as VHDL and implemented on-chip using automated synthesis and place-and-route tools.

The CMOS image sensor architecture of Fig. 5.11 permits several modes of image read-out. Progressive-scan readout of the entire array is the common readout mode. A *window* readout mode is readily implemented where only a smaller region of pixels is selected for readout. This increases access rates to windows of interest. A *skip* readout mode is also possible where every second (or third, etc.) pixel is read out. This mode allows for subsampling of the image to increase readout speed at the cost of resolution. Combination of skip and window modes allows electronic pan, tilt, and zoom to be implemented.

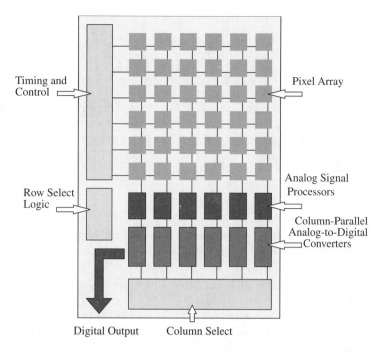

Figure 5.11   CMOS APS integrates timing and control, ADC, and other circuitry on the same chip.

5.2.4 Pixel Circuits

Pixel circuits can be divided into *passive* pixels and *active* pixels. The active pixel sensor (APS) contains an active amplifier. There are three predominant approaches to pixel implementation in CMOS: photodiode-type passive pixel, photodiode-type active pixel, and photogate-type active pixel.

5.2.4.1 Passive Pixel Approach

The photodiode-type passive pixel approach remains virtually unchanged since first suggested by Weckler in 1967 [6,7]. The passive pixel concept is shown in Fig. 5.12. It consists of a photodiode and a pass (access) transistor. When the access transistor is activated, the photodiode is connected to a vertical column bus. A charge integrating amplifier (CIA) readout circuit at the bottom of the column bus keeps the voltage on the column bus constant and reduces kTC noise [9]. When the photodiode is accessed, the voltage on the photodiode is reset to the column bus voltage, and the charge, proportional to the photosignal, is converted to a voltage by the CIA. The single-transistor photodiode passive pixel allows the highest design fill factor for a given pixel size or the smallest pixel size for a given design fill factor for a particular CMOS process. A second selection transistor has sometimes been added to permit true X-Y addressing. The quantum efficiency of the passive pixel (ratio of

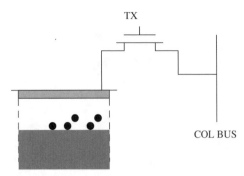

Figure 5.12 Passive pixel schematic and potential well. When the transfer gate TX is pulsed, photogenerated charge integrated on the photodiode is shared on the bus capacitance.

collected electrons to incident photons) can be quite high due to the large fill factor and absence of an overlying layer of polysilicon such as that found in many CCDs. This passive pixel is the basis for arrays produced by EG&G Reticon, Hitachi [17], Matsushita [18], and more recently, by Edinburgh University and VLSI Vision in Scotland [25,26], Linkoping University and IVP in Sweden [27,28,29], and Toyohashi University [30].

Much larger pixels have been used for document imaging [31]. Page-sized image sensors ($7.7''$ x $9.6''$) using amorphous silicon and constructed with a passive pixel architecture have been demonstrated with a dynamic range of $10^4 - 10^5$.

The major problems with the passive pixel are its readout noise level and scalability. Readout noise with a passive pixel is typically of the order of 250 electrons r.m.s., compared to commercial CCDs that achieve less than 20 electrons r.m.s. of read noise. The passive pixel also does not scale well to larger array sizes or faster pixel readout rates. This is because both increased bus capacitance and faster readout speed result in higher readout noise.

5.2.4.2 *Active Pixel Approach*

It was quickly recognized, almost as soon as the passive pixel was invented, that the insertion of a buffer/amplifier into the pixel could potentially improve the performance of the pixel. A sensor with an active amplifier within each pixel is referred to as an active pixel sensor or APS. Since each amplifier is only activated during readout, power dissipation is minimal and is generally less than a CCD. Non-CMOS APS devices have been developed that have excellent performance, such as the charge-modulation device (CMD) [32], but these devices [33,34,35] require a specialized fabrication process. In general, APS technology has many potential advantages over CCDs [36] but is susceptible to residual FPN and has less maturity than CCDs.

The CMOS APS trades pixel fill factor for improved performance compared to passive pixels using the in-pixel amplifier. Pixels are typically designed for a fill factor of 20 to 30%, similar to interline-transfer (ILT) CCDs. Loss in optical signal is more than compensated by reduction in read noise for a net increase in signal-to-noise ratio and dynamic range. Microlenses are commonly employed with low fill factor ILT CCDs [37,38] and can recover some of the lost optical signal. The simple, polyimide microlens refracts incident radiation

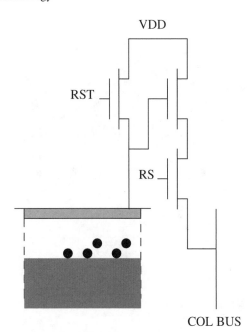

VDD

RST

RS

COL BUS

Figure 5.13 A photodiode-type active pixel sensor (APS). The voltage on the photodiode is buffered by a source-follower to the column bus, selected by RS-row select. The photodiode is reset by transistor RST.

from the circuitry region of the pixel to the detector region, but with the loss in the microlens material and the inherent sensitivity of the CMOS APS to lateral carrier collection, the effective improvement in sensitivity with a microlens may be twofold.

5.2.4.3 *Photodiode-type APS*

The photodiode-type (PD) APS was described by Noble in 1968 [9] and has been under investigation by Andoh at NHK in Japan since the late 1980s [39,40,41] in collaboration with Olympus and, later, Mitsubishi Electric. A similar device with an a-Si:H overlayer to improve effective fill factor was described by Huang and Ando in 1990 [42]. A diagram of the PD-APS is shown in Fig. 5.13.

The first high-performance PD-APS was demonstrated by JPL in 1995 in a 128 x 128 element array that had on-chip timing, control, correlated double sampling, and fixed-pattern noise suppression circuitry [43]. The chip achieved 72 dB dynamic range with FPN less than 0.15% saturation. A 640 x 480 PD-APS with 5.6 μm x 5.6 μm pixels and on-chip color filter arrays and microlenses was described by Toshiba in 1997 [44], and a 800 x 1000 element PD-APS was reported by VLSI Vision, also in 1997 [45].

More complicated pixels can be constructed to improve functionality and, to a lesser extent, performance. Hamamatsu reported on an improved sensor that used a transfer gate between the photodiode and the source follower gate [46]. The transfer gate keeps the photodiode at constant potential and increases output conversion gain by reducing capacitance but introduces lag. The Hamamatsu sensor also improved fixed-pattern noise using a feedback technique. More complication was added by the Technion to permit random access

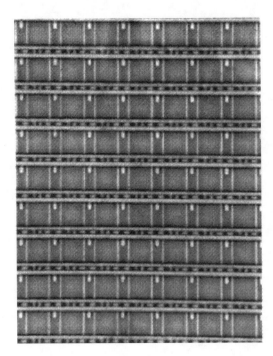

Figure 5.14 Closeup of 11.9 μm pixel photodiode-type active pixels used in the 1024 x 1024 array shown in Fig. 5.20.

and electronic shuttering with a significant increase in pixel size [47]. Similar work was reported recently by Stanford University [48]. A method for individual pixel reset for regional electronic shutter was presented by JPL [49]. Current-mode readout of CMOS APS has been investigated [50] and reported by Polaroid [51]. Gain and offset FPN remain a challenge in current mode.

Photodiode-type APS pixels have high quantum efficiency, for there is no overlying polysilicon. The read noise is limited by the reset noise on the photodiode since correlated double sampling is not easily implementable without frame memory and is thus typically 75 to 100 electrons r.m.s. The photodiode-type APS uses three transistors per pixel and has a typical pixel pitch of 15x the minimum feature size (see Fig. 5.14). The photodiode APS is suitable for most mid- to low-performance applications. The output signal remains constant for the same optical flux, to first order, since a decrease in detector area is compensated by an increase in conversion gain. Its S/N performance decreases for smaller pixel sizes since the reset voltage noise scales as $1/C^{1/2}$, where C is the photodiode capacitance. A tradeoff can be made in designed pixel fill-factor (photodiode area), dynamic range (full well), and conversion gain (μV/e^-). Lateral carrier collection permits high responsivity even for small fill-factor [52] at the possible expense of pixel-to-pixel crosstalk.

5.2.4.4 Photogate-type APS

The photogate APS was introduced by JPL in 1993 [53,54,55] for high-performance scientific imaging and low-light applications. The photogate APS combines CCD benefits

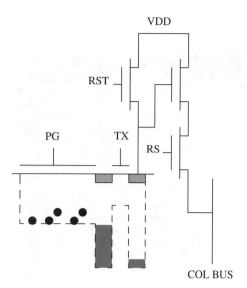

VDD

RST

PG   TX

RS

COL BUS

Figure 5.15 Photogate-type APS pixel schematic and potential wells. Transfer of charge and correlated double sampling permits low-noise operation.

and X-Y readout, and is shown schematically in Fig. 5.15. Signal charge is integrated under a photogate. For readout, an output floating diffusion is reset, and its resultant voltage is measured by the source-follower. The charge is then transferred to the output diffusion by pulsing the photogate. The new voltage is then sensed. The difference between the reset level and the signal level is the output of the sensor. This correlated double sampling suppresses reset noise, 1/f noise, and fixed-pattern noise due to threshold voltage variations.

The photogate and transfer gate ideally overlap using a double poly process. However, the insertion of a bridging diffusion between PG and TX has minimal effect on circuit performance and permits the use of single poly processes [56]. (Approximately $100\ e^-$ of lag has been attributed to the bridging diffusion [57]). A 256 x 256 element CMOS APS with 20.4 μm pixels implemented using a 1.2 μm n-well process with on-chip timing and control logic with 13 e^- r.m.s. read noise was reported by JPL [58]. This sensor required only 5V and clock to produce analog video output (see Fig. 5.16). Variable integration time and window of interest readout are commanded asynchronously. Arrays as large as 1024 x 1024 with 10 μm pixel pitch in a 0.5 μm process have been developed by a JPL/AT&T collaboration [59] (Fig. 5.17).

The photogate-type APS uses five transistors per pixel and has a pitch typically equal to 20x the minimum feature size. Thus, to achieve a 10 μm pixel pitch, a 0.5 μm process must be employed. A 0.25 μm process would permit a 5 μm pixel pitch. The floating diffusion capacitance is typically of the order of 10 fF, yielding a conversion gain of 10–20 μV/e^-. Subsequent circuit noise is of the order of 150–250 μV r.m.s., resulting in a readout noise of 10–20 electrons r.m.s., with the lowest noise reported to date of 5 electrons r.m.s. [52]. The advantage in read noise for the photogate pixel is offset by a reduction in quantum efficiency, particularly in the blue, due to overlying polysilicon.

PIXEL ARRAY

Figure 5.16   A JPL 256 x 256 element PG-APS with on-chip timing and control circuits (left side) and analog signal chain including fixed-pattern noise suppression (bottom).

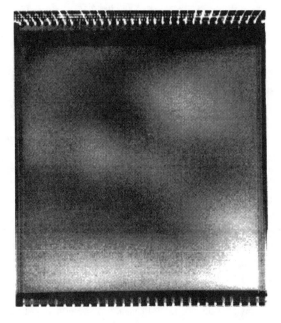

Figure 5.17   1024 x 1024 element photogate CMOS APS with 10 μm pixel pitch fabricated using 0.5 μm design rules by AT&T/JPL.

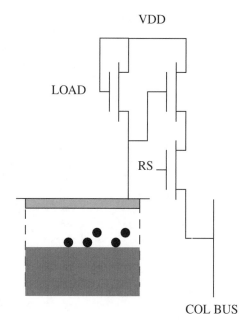

Figure 5.18 Logarithmic pixel schematic circuit.

5.2.4.5 *Logarithmic Pixels*

In some cases, nonlinear output of the sensor is desirable. Nonlinear output permits an increase in intrascene dynamic range as the photosignal is companded. Gamma-correction (basically a square-root transform) is one example of companding. A second example is logarithmic transformation, where the output signal from the pixel is proportional to the logarithm of the photosignal [60,61,62]. An example of this type of pixel circuit [63] is shown in Fig. 5.18.

The photodiode voltage self-adjusts to a level such that the load transistor current is equal to the photocurrent collected by the photodiode. This results in a logarithmic transformation of the photosignal for typical light levels and wide intrascene dynamic range. The logarithmic pixel permits true random access in both space and time since it is a nonintegrating pixel. Drawbacks to this nonintegrating approach include slow response time for low-light levels and large fixed-pattern noise (e.g., 60 mV). Although able to cover over six orders of magnitude in incident light level, the sensor has a small signal-to-noise ratio (45 dB) due to temporal noise and small voltage swings.

A nonintegrating 512 x 512 element photodiode-type APS was reported by IMEC with a 6.6 μm pixel pitch [64]. This sensor operates in a nonintegrating current mode with logarithmic response. FPN was corrected by means of a hot-carrier-induced threshold voltage shift. A 2048 x 2048 element logarithmic pixel sensor with 7.5 μm pixel pitch has also been reported [65].

5.2.4.6   Other Pixels

The pinned photodiode, developed for interline transfer CCDs, features high-quantum efficiency (especially in the blue), low dark current, and low-noise readout. The pinned photodiode has been combined with CMOS APS readout by JPL/Kodak to achieve high-performance pixel response [66].

A photogate CMOS APS with a floating-gate sense amplifier that allows multiple nondestructive, doubly sampled reads of the same signal was developed by JPL for use with oversampled column-parallel ADCs [67].

A floating-gate sensor with a simple structure was reported by JPL/Olympus [68]. This sensor used a floating gate to collect and sense the photosignal and features a compact pixel layout with complete reset.

Significant work has been done on retina-like CMOS sensors with nonlinear, adaptive response. While their utility for electronic image capture has not yet been demonstrated, their very large dynamic range and similarity to the response of the human eye offer intriguing possibilities for on-chip intelligent imaging [69,70].

5.2.5   Analog Signal Processing

On-chip analog signal processing can be used to improve the performance and functionality of the CMOS image sensor. A charge integration amplifier is used for passive pixel sensors and sample-and-hold circuits typically employed for active pixel sensors. JPL has developed a delta-difference sampling (DDS) approach to suppress FPN peak-to-peak to 0.15% of saturation level [43]. Other examples of signal processing demonstrated in CMOS image sensors include smoothing, using neuron MOSFETs [71], motion detection [72,73], programmable amplification [74], multiresolution imaging [75], video compression [76], dynamic range enhancement [77], discrete cosine transform (DCT) [30], and intensity sorting [78]. Continued improvement in analog signal processing performance and functionality is expected. Other computational-type optical sensors have been demonstrated that use CMOS analog signal processing [79,80].

5.2.6   On-chip Analog-to-Digital Converter (ADC)

To implement a camera on-a-chip with a full digital interface requires an on-chip analog-to-digital converter (ADC). There are many considerations for on-chip ADC. The ADC must support video rate data that range from 0.92 Msamples/s for a 320 x 288 format sensor operating at 10 frames per second for videoconferencing to 55.3 Msamples/s for a 1280 x 720 format sensor operating at 60 frames per second. The ADC must have at least 8b resolution with low integral nonlinearity (INL) and differential nonlinearity (DNL) so as not to introduce distortion or artifacts into the image (see Fig. 5.19). The ADC can dissipate only minimal power, typically under 100 mW, to avoid introduction of hot spots with excess dark current generation. The ADC cannot consume too much chip area or it will void the economic advantage of on-chip integration. The ADC cannot introduce noise into the analog imaging portion of the sensor through substrate coupling or other crosstalk mechanisms that would deteriorate image quality.

CMOS image sensors with on-chip single-slope ADC have been reported [29,81], as has related work in on-chip ADCs for infrared focal-plane array readout [82,83,84]. There

Figure 5.19 Unprocessed image taken from a Photobit 256 x 256 element sensor with on-chip ADC operating at 30 fps. Note no blooming from light and lack of other artifacts.

are many considerations for implementation of on-chip ADC [85,86]. The ADC can be implemented as a single serial ADC (or several ADCs, e.g., one per color) that operate at near video rates [10 Msamples/s]. The ADC can also be implemented in-pixel [87,88,89] and operate at frame rates [e.g., 30 samples/s]. We have been pursuing column-parallel ADCs where each (or almost each) column in the pixel array has its own ADC (see Fig. 5.11) so that each ADC operates at the row rate [e.g., 15 Ksamples/s]. In this architecture, single-slope ADCs work well for slow-scan applications (Fig. 5.20) but dissipate too much power for video rates. Oversampled ADCs require significant chip area when implemented in column-parallel formats [67]. A successive approximation ADC has a good compromise of power, bit resolution, and chip area. On-chip ADC enables on-chip DSP for sensor control and compression preprocessing.

5.2.7 Impact of CMOS Scaling Trends

The future prospects for CMOS image sensors are bright. Rapid progress has been made in realizing cost-effective pixel sizes (see Fig. 5.21). The effect of predictable trends in CMOS technology, based on the industry standard technology roadmap, were examined by Fossum and Wong of JPL/IBM [90,91]. To at least 0.25 μm minimum feature sizes, it appears that the standard CMOS process will permit the fabrication of high-performance CMOS image sensors.

The most obvious problem, but the easiest to correct, is the trend toward the use of silicides. Silicides are optically opaque and detrimental to image sensing. A silicide-blocking mask is already available in some processes. The switchover to silicon-on-insulator (SOI) technology will be problematic for the sensors due to the minimal absorption of photons in thin silicon films, but such a switchover is not expected to generally occur until beyond 0.25 μm minimum feature sizes. Active pixel sizes at the "practical lens limit"

Figure 5.20 A JPL 1024 x 1024 photodiode-type CMOS APS with 1024 column-parallel single-slope ADCs for slow-scan scientific applications.

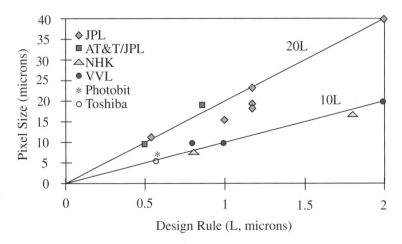

Figure 5.21 Scaling trend in pixel size versus design rule. It is expected that pixel pitch must be between 5 μm and 10 μm to be competitive.

(e.g., 5 μm) will be readily achievable in 0.25 μm CMOS. Passive pixel sizes well below that size will also be achievable.

Below 0.25 μm, "off" transistor currents may be of concern. Dark current is expected to minimally increase from 0.5 μm processes to 0.25 μm processes. This will likely be compensated by a steady improvement in wafer and process quality control. Intrinsic fixed-pattern noise may increase due to threshold voltage mismatch, but FPN suppression circuitry will likely become more sophisticated as well. A switch from LOCOS to shallow trench isolation would likely improve sensor performance. Deep trench isolation would be useful to reduce crosstalk. Reduced power supply voltages will reduce analog circuitry "headroom," but is partially offset by concomitant reduction in threshold voltages. Increases in DRAM chip size will drive improvements in process control as well as stepper field size—useful for larger format image sensors.

It is inevitable that when CMOS image sensors capture a significant share of the electronic imaging market, process deviations from standard CMOS will be made to permit product differentiation and improved performance. This is already the case with analog CMOS for capacitors and isolation. Use of the pinned photodiode [66] will improve quantum efficiency and decrease dark current. Double poly will permit efficient implementation of capacitors.

5.2.8   Roadmap for Camera-on-a-Chip

All the component technologies needed to realize a CMOS electronic camera-on-a-chip have been developed. Single-chip cameras based on the lower performance passive pixel are already available. Higher performance single-chip cameras based on the CMOS APS technology are expected to emerge shortly. Improvement in on-chip ADC technology to take advantage of the high dynamic range is needed. Back-end processes for color filter arrays and microlenses are nearly as complicated as the standard CMOS process and add significantly to cost. A single-chip color camera can be expected in the next year or two. Standards for digital cameras need to be developed to enable the wider development of the technology.

It can be anticipated that both CCD and CMOS-based imaging systems will converge to two-chip solutions. The CMOS imaging system is probably best partitioned into an image acquisition and compression preprocessing sensor, and a separate compression and color interpolation/filter DSP and frame buffer chip. CCD imaging systems will likely evolve to a CCD with a separate single CMOS IC for timing, control, drivers, signal processing, ADC, and compression DSP. However, the low-power and functionality advantages of the CMOS image sensor will permit continued market insertion of CMOS-based imaging technology.

5.3   CONCLUSIONS

Highly miniaturized imaging systems based on CMOS image sensor technology are emerging as a competitor to CCDs for low-cost visual communications and multimedia applications. CMOS active pixel sensor (APS) technology has demonstrated noise, quantum efficiency, and dynamic range performance comparable to CCDs with greatly increased functionality and much lower system power. CMOS image sensors with on-chip timing and control, and analog-to-digital conversion are enabling one-chip imaging systems with a full digital interface. Such a "camera-on-a-chip" may make image capture devices as ubiquitous in our daily lives as the microprocessor.

Acknowledgments

The author gratefully acknowledges the assistance of colleagues in North America, Asia, and Europe too numerous to name individually in the preparation of this manuscript. The assistance of J. Nakamura and J. Li in tracking down papers is greatly appreciated. The stories told to me of the early days of MOS imaging devices by G. Weckler, R. Dyck, and S. Chamberlain were interesting and are also appreciated. The author appreciates the support of his former group at JPL, the present group at Photobit, and especially S. Kemeny in the preparation of this updated manuscript.

References

[1] E. R. Fossum, "CMOS Image Sensors: Electronic Camera on a Chip," *1995 IEEE International Electron Devices Meeting Tech. Dig.,* pp. 17–25, 1995.

[2] B. Ackland and A. Dickinson, "Camera on a Chip," *1996 International Solid State Circuits Conference Dig. of Tech. Papers,* pp. 22–25, 1996.

[3] S. Morrison, "A New Type of Photosensitive Junction Device," *Solid-State Electronics,* Vol. 5, pp. 485–494, 1963.

[4] J. Horton, R. Mazza, and H. Dym, "The Scanistor—A Solid State Image Scanner," *Proc. IEEE,* Vol. 52, pp. 1513–1528, 1964.

[5] M. A. Schuster and G. Strull, "A Monolithic Mosaic of Photon Sensors for Solid State Imaging Applications," *IEEE Trans. Electron Devices,* Vol. ED–13, pp. 907–912, 1966.

[6] G. P. Weckler, "Operation of p-n Junction Photodetectors in a Photon Flux Integration Mode," *IEEE J. Solid-State Circuits,* Vol. SC–2, pp. 65–73, 1967.

[7] R. Dyck and G. Weckler, "Integrated Arrays of Silicon Photodetectors for Image Sensing," *IEEE Trans. Electron Devices,* Vol. ED–15(4), pp. 196–201, 1968.

[8] P. K. Weimer, G. Sadasiv, J. Meyer, L. Meray-Horvath, and W. Pike, "A Self-Scanned Solid-State Image Sensor," *Proc. IEEE,* Vol. 55, pp. 1591–1602, 1967.

[9] P. Noble, "Self-Scanned Silicon Image Detector Arrays," *IEEE Trans. Electron Devices,* Vol. ED–15(4), pp. 202–209, 1968.

[10] S. G. Chamberlain, "Photosensitivity and Scanning of Silicon Image Detector Arrays," *IEEE J. Solid-State Circuits,* Vol. SC–4(6) pp. 333–342, 1969.

[11] P. Fry, P. Noble, and R. Rycroft, "Fixed Pattern Noise in Photomatrices," *IEEE J. Solid-State Circuits,* Vol. SC–5(5), pp. 250–254, 1970.

[12] W. S. Boyle and G. E. Smith, "Charge Coupled Semiconductor Devices," *Bell Syst. Tech. J.,* Vol. 49, pp. 587–593, 1970.

[13] R. Dawson, J. Preisig, J. Carnes, and J. Pridgen, "A CMOS/Buried-n-Channel CCD Compatible Process for Analog Signal Processing Applications," *RCA—Review,* vol. 38, No. 3, pp. 406–435, 1977.

[14] D. Ong, "An All-Implanted CCD/CMOS Process," *IEEE Trans. Electron Devices,* Vol. ED–28(1), pp. 6–12, 1981.

[15] C. Anagnostopoulos, C. Ludden, G. Brown, and K. Wong, "An Integrated CMOS/CCD Sensor for Camera Autofocus," *Electronic Imaging '88: International Electronic Imaging Exposition and Conference. Advance Printing of Paper Summaries. Inst. Graphic Commun,* Waltham, MA, 2 vols. xxxviii+1272, pp. 159–163 Vol. 1, 1988.

[16] R. Melen, "The Tradeoff in Monolithic Image Sensors: MOS vs. CCD," *Electronics,* Vol. 46, pp. 106–111, May 1973.

[17] S. Ohba et al., "MOS Area Sensor: Part II—Low Noise MOS Area Sensor with Anti-Blooming Photodiodes," *IEEE Trans. Electron Devices,* Vol. ED–27(8), pp. 1682–1687, 1980.

[18] K. Senda, S. Terakawa, Y. Hiroshima, and T. Kunii, "Analysis of Charge-Priming Transfer Efficiency in CPD Image Sensors," *IEEE Trans. Electron Devices,* Vol. ED–31(9), pp. 1324–1328, 1984.

[19] M. Aoki et al., "A 2/3-inch Format MOS Single-Chip Color Imager," *IEEE Trans. Electron Devices,* Vol. ED–29(4), pp. 745–750, 1982.

[20] H. Ando et al., "Design Consideration and Performance of a New MOS Imaging Device," *IEEE Trans. Electron Devices,* Vol. ED–32(5), pp. 1484–1489, 1985.

[21] T. Kinugasa et al., "An Electronic Variable Shutter System in Video Camera Use," *IEEE Trans. Consumer Electronics,* Vol. CE–33 pp. 249–255, 1987.

[22] For example, see *Infrared Readout Electronics, Proc. SPIE,* Vol. 1684, 1992.

[23] B. Dierckx, "XYW Detector: A Smart 2-Dimensional Particle Sensor," *Nuclear Instruments and Methods in Physics Research,* Vol. A275, p. 527, 1989.

[24] P. Aubert, H. Oguey, and R. Vuillemier, "Monolithic Optical Position Encoder with On-chip Photodiodes," *IEEE J. Solid-State Circuits,* Vol. SC–23, pp. 465–472, 1988.

[25] D. Renshaw, P. Denyer, G. Wang, and M. Lu, "ASIC Image Sensors," *IEEE Intl. Symposium on Circuits and Systems,* pp. 3038–3041, 1990.

[26] P. Denyer, D. Renshaw, G. Wang, and M. Lu, "CMOS Image Sensors for Multimedia Applications," *IEEE Proc. Custom Int. Circuits. Conf.,* pp. 11.5.1–11.5.4, 1993.

[27] K. Chen, M. Afghahi, P. Danielsson, and C. Svensson, "PASIC—A Processor-A/D Converter Sensor Integrated Circuit," *IEEE Intl. Symposium on Circuits and Systems,* pp. 1705–1708, 1990.

[28] R. Forchheimer, P. Ingelhag, and C. Jansson, "MAPP2200: A Second Generation Smart Optical Sensor," in *Image Processing and Interchange, Proc. SPIE,* Vol. 1659, pp. 2–11, 1992.

[29] C. Jansson, O. Ingelhag, C. Svensson, and R. Forchheimer, "An Addressable 256 x 256 Photodiode Image Sensor Array with an 8-bit Digital Output," *Analog Integrated Circuits and Signal Processing,* Vol. 4, pp. 37–49, 1993.

[30] S. Kawahito, M. Yoshida, M. Sasaki, K. Umehara, Y. Tadokara, K. Murata, S. Doushou, and A. Matsuzawa, "A Compressed Digital Output CMOS Image Sensor with Analog 2-D DCT Processors and ADC Quantizer," *1997 International Solid State Circuits Conference Dig. of Tech. Papers,* pp. 184–185, 1997.

[31] X. Wu, R. Street, R. Weisfield, D. Begelson, W. Jackson, D. Jared, S. Ready, and R. Apte, "Large Format a-Si:H 2-Dimensional Array as Imaging Devices," *1995 IEEE Workshop on CCDs and Advanced Image Sensors,* Dana Point, CA, Apr. 20–22, 1995.

[32] K. Matsumoto et al., "A New MOS Phototransistor Operating in a Non-destructive Readout Mode," *Jpn J. Appl. Phys.,* Vol. 24, No. 5, pp. L323–L325, 1985.

[33] A. Yusa et al., "SIT Image Sensor: Design Considerations and Characteristics," *IEEE Trans. Electron Devices,* Vol. ED–33(6), pp. 735–742, 1986.

[34] N. Tanaka et al., "A 310 Pixel Bipolar Imager (BASIS)," *IEEE Trans. Electron Devices,* Vol. ED–37(4), pp. 964–971, 1990.

[35] J. Hynecek, "A New Device Architecture Suitable for High Resolution and High Performance Image Sensors," *IEEE Trans. Electron Devices,* Vol. ED–35(3), pp. 646–652, 1988.

[36] E. R. Fossum, "Active Pixel Sensors—Are CCDs Dinosaurs?," in Charge-Coupled Devices and Optical Sensors III, *Proc. SPIE,* Vol. 1900, pp. 2–14, 1993.

[37] Y. Ishihara and K. Tanigaki, "A High Sensitivity IL-CCD Image Sensor with Monolithic Resin Lens Array," *1983 IEEE International Electron Devices Meeting Tech. Dig.,* pp. 497–500, 1983.

[38] Y. Sano, T. Nomura, H. Aoki, S. Terakawa, H. Kodama, T. Aoki, and Y. Hiroshima, "Submicron Spaced Lens Array Process Technology for a High Photosensitivity CCD Image Sensor," *1990 IEEE International Electron Devices Meeting Tech. Dig.,* pp. 283–286, 1990.

[39] F. Andoh, K. Taketoshi, J. Yamazaki, M. Sugawara, Y. Fujita, K. Mitani, Y. Matuzawa, K. Miyata, and S. Araki, "A 250,000 Pixel Image Sensor with FET Amplification at Each Pixel for High Speed Television Cameras," *1990 International Solid State Circuits Conference Dig. of Tech. Papers,* pp. 212–213, 1990.

[40] H. Kawashima, F. Andoh, N. Murata, K. Tanaka, M. Yamawaki, and K. Taketoshi, "A 1/4 Inch Format 250,000 Pixel Amplifier MOS Image Sensor Using CMOS Process," *1993 IEEE International Electron Devices Meeting Tech. Dig.,* pp. 575–578, 1993.

[41] M. Sugawara, H. Kawashima, F. Andoh, N. Murata, Y. Fujita, and M. Yamawaki, "An Amplified MOS Imager Suited for Image Processing," *1994 International Solid State Circuits Conference Dig. of Tech. Papers,* pp. 228–229, 1994.

[42] Z-S. Huang and T. Ando, "A Novel Amplified Image Sensor with a-Si:H Photoconductor and MOS Transistors," *IEEE Trans. Electron Devices,* Vol. ED–37(6), pp. 1432–1438, 1990.

[43] R. H. Nixon, S. E. Kemeny, C. O. Staller, and E. R. Fossum, "128 x 128 CMOS Photodiode-Type Active Pixel Sensor with On-chip Timing, Control and Signal Chain Electronics," in Charge-Coupled Devices and Solid-State Optical Sensors V, *Proc. SPIE,* Vol. 2415, pp. 117–123, 1995.

[44] E. Oba, K. Mabuchi, Y. Iida, N. Nakamura, and H. Miura, "A $\frac{1}{4}$-inch 330k Square Pixel Progressive Scan CMOS Active Pixel Image Sensor," *1997 International Solid State Circuits Conference Dig. of Tech. Papers,* pp. 180–181, San Francisco, Feb. 1997.

[45] P. Denyer, J. E. Hurwitz, D. J. Baxter, and G. Townsend, "800k-Pixel CMOS Sensor for Consumer Still Cameras," in Solid-State Sensor Arrays: Development and Applications, *Proc. SPIE,* Vol. 3019, pp. 115–124, 1997.

[46] M. Kyomasu, "New MOS Imager Using Photodiode as Current Source," *IEEE J. Solid-State Circuits,* Vol. 26(8), pp. 1116–1122, 1991.

[47] O. Yadid-Pecht, R. Ginosar, and Y. Diamand, "A Random Access Photodiode Array for Intelligent Image Capture," *IEEE. Trans. Electron Devices,* Vol. 38, No. 8, pp. 1772–1780, 1991.

[48] C. Aw and B. Wooley, "A 128 x 128 Pixel Standard CMOS Image Sensor with Electronic Shutter," *IEEE J. Solid-State Circuits,* Vol. SC–31(12), pp. 1922–1930, 1996.

[49] O. Yadid-Pecht, B. Pain, C. Staller, C. Clark, and E. R. Fossum, "CMOS Active Pixel Sensor Star Tracker with Regional Electronic Shutter," *IEEE J. Solid-State Circuits,* Vol. 32, No. 2, pp. 285–288, 1997.

[50] B. Pain and E. R. Fossum, unpublished.

[51] R. D. McGrath, V. Clark, P. Duane, L. McIlrath, and W. Washkurak, "Current-Mediated, Current-Reset 768 x 512 Active Pixel Sensor Array," *1997 International Solid State Circuits Conference Dig. of Tech. Papers,* pp. 182–183, 1997.

[52] O. Yadid-Pecht, B. Pain, B. Mansoorian, and E. R. Fossum, "Optimization of Active Pixel Sensor Noise and Responsivity for Scientific Applications," Solid-State Sensor Arrays: Development and Applications, *Proc. SPIE,* Vol. 3019, pp. 125–136, 1997.

[53] S. Mendis, S. Kemeny and E. R. Fossum, "A 128 x 128 CMOS Active Pixel Image Sensor for Highly Integrated Imaging Systems," *1993 IEEE International Electron Devices Meeting Tech. Dig.,* pp. 583–586, 1993.

[54] S. Mendis, S. E. Kemeny, and E. R. Fossum, "CMOS Active Pixel Image Sensor," *IEEE Trans. Electron Devices,* Vol. 41, No. 3, pp. 452–453, 1994.

[55] S. K. Mendis, S. E. Kemeny, R. C. Gee, B. Pain, Q. Kim, and E. R. Fossum, "CMOS Active Pixel Image Sensors for Highly Integrated Imaging Systems," *IEEE J. Solid-State Circuits,* Vol. 32, No. 2, pp. 187–197, 1997.

[56] S. Mendis, S. E. Kemeny, R. Gee, B. Pain, and E. R. Fossum, "Progress in CMOS Active Pixel Image Sensors," in Charge-Coupled Devices and Solid State Optical Sensors IV, *Proc. SPIE,* Vol. 2172, pp. 19–29, 1994.

[57] E. R. Fossum, unpublished, 1996.

[58] R. H. Nixon, S. E. Kemeny, B. Pain, C. O. Staller, and E. R. Fossum, "256 x 256 CMOS Active Pixel Sensor Camera-on-a-Chip," *IEEE J. Solid-State Circuits,* Vol. 31, No. 12, pp. 2046–2050, 1996.

[59] A. Dickinson, S. Mendis, B. Ackland, D. Inglis, K. Azadet, P. Jones, and E. R. Fossum, unpublished, 1995.

[60] S. G. Chamberlain and J. Lee, "A Novel Wide Dynamic Range Silicon Photodetector and Linear Imaging Array," *Proc. IEEE Custom Integrated Circuits Conf.,* pp. 441–445, 1983.

[61] C. Mead, "A Sensitive Electronic Photoreceptor," *1985 Chapel Hill Conference on VLSI,* pp. 463–471, 1985.

[62] J. Mann, "Implementing Early Visual Processing in Analog VLSI: Light Adaptation," in Visual Information Processing: From Neurons to Chips, *Proc. SPIE,* Vol. 1473, pp. 128–132, 1991.

[63] N. Ricquier and B. Dierickx, "Pixel Structure with Logarithmic Response for Intelligent and Flexible Imager Architectures," *Microelectronic Engineering,* Vol. 19, pp. 631–634, 1992.

[64] N. Ricquier and B. Dierickx, "Active Pixel CMOS Image Sensor with On-chip Non-uniformity Correction," *1995 IEEE Workshop on CCDs and Advanced Image Sensors,* Dana Point, CA, Apr. 20–22, 1995.

[65] B. Dierickx, D. Scheffer, G. Meynants, W. Ogiers, and J. Vlummens, "Random Addressable Active Pixel Image Sensors," AFPAEC Europto, *Proc. SPIE,* Vol. 2950, p. 1, 1996.

[66] P. Lee, R. Gee, M. Guidash, T. Lee, and E. R. Fossum, "An Active Pixel Sensor Fabricated Using CMOS/CCD Process Technology," *1995 IEEE Workshop on CCDs and Advanced Image Sensors,* Dana Point, CA, Apr. 20–22, 1995.

[67] S. Mendis, B. Pain, R. Nixon, and E. R. Fossum, "Design of a Low-Light-Level Image Sensor with an On-chip Sigma-delta Analog-to-Digital Conversion," in Charge-Coupled Devices and Optical Sensors III, *Proc. SPIE,* Vol. 1900, pp. 31–39, 1993.

[68] J. Nakamura, S. E. Kemeny and E. R. Fossum, "A CMOS Active Pixel Image Sensor with Simple Floating Gate Pixels," *IEEE Trans. Electron Devices,* Vol. ED–42(9), pp. 1693–1694, 1995.

[69] Visual Information Processing: From Neurons to Chips, *Proc. SPIE,* vol. 1473, 1991.

[70] C. H. Koch and H. Li (eds.), *Vision Chips: Implementing Vision Algorithms with Analog VLSI Circuits,* IEEE Computer Press, 1995.

[71] J. Nakamura and E. R. Fossum, "Design of an Image Sensor Using a Neuron MOSFET with Image Smoothing Capability," in Charge-Coupled Devices and Solid State Optical Sensors IV, *Proc. SPIE,* vol. 2172, pp. 30–37, 1994.

[72] A. Dickinson, B. Ackland, E-S. Eid, D. Inglis, and E. R. Fossum, "A 256 x 256 CMOS Active Pixel Image Sensor with Motion Detection," *1995 International Solid State Circuits Conference Dig. of Tech. Papers,* pp. 226–227, 1995.

[73] A. Simoni, G. Torelli, F. Maloberti, A. Sartori, S. Plevridis, and A. Birbas, "A Single-Chip Optical Sensor with Analog Memory for Motion Detection," *IEEE J. Solid-State Circuits,* vol. 30(7), pp. 800–805, 1995.

[74] Z. Zhou, S. E. Kemeny, B. Pain, R. C. Gee, and E. R. Fossum, "A CMOS Active Pixel Sensor with Amplification and Reduced Fixed Pattern Noise," *1995 IEEE Workshop on CCDs and Advanced Image Sensors,* Dana Point, CA, Apr. 20–22, 1995.

[75] S. E. Kemeny, B. Pain, R. Panicacci, L. Matthies, and E. R. Fossum, "CMOS Active Pixel Sensor Array with Programmable Multiresolution Readout," *1995 IEEE Workshop on CCDs and Advanced Image Sensors,* Dana Point, CA, Apr. 20–22, 1995.

[76] K. Aizawa, H. Ohno, Y. Egi, T. Hamamoto, M. Hatori, and J. Yamazaki, "On Sensor Video Compression," *1995 IEEE Workshop on CCDs and Advanced Image Sensors,* Dana Point, CA, Apr. 20–22, 1995.

[77] O. Yadid-Pecht and E. R. Fossum, "Readout Schemes to Increase Dynamic Range of Image Sensors," *NASA Tech. Briefs,* Vol. 21, No. 1, pp. 32–33, Jan. 1997.

[78] V. Brajovic and T. Kanade, "New massively Parallel Technique for Global Operations in Embedded Imagers," *1995 IEEE Workshop on CCDs and Advanced Image Sensors,* Dana Point, CA, Apr. 20–22, 1995.

[79] J. Kramer, P. Sietz, and H. Baltes, "Industrial CMOS Technology for the Integration of Optical Metrology Systems (Photo-ASICs)," *Sensors and Actuators,* Vol. A34, pp. 21–30, 1992.

[80] R. Miyagawa and T. Kanade, "Integration-time Based Computational Sensors," *1995 IEEE Workshop on CCDs and Advanced Image Sensors,* Dana Point, CA, Apr. 20–22, 1995.

[81] A. Dickinson, S. Mendis, D. Inglis, K. Azadet, and E. R. Fossum, "CMOS Digital Camera with Parallel Analog-to-Digital Conversion Architecture," *1995 IEEE Workshop on CCDs and Advanced Image Sensors,* Dana Point, CA, Apr. 20–22, 1995.

[82] U. Ringh, C. Jansson, and K. Liddiard, "Readout Concept Employing Novel On-chip 16 Bit ADC for Smart IR Focal Plane Arrays," *Infrared Readout Electronics III, Proc. SPIE,* Vol. 2745, pp. 99–109, 1996.

[83] M. Dahlin et al., "Development of High Speed IR Sensor Chip Technologies," in *Infrared Readout Electronics III, Proc. SPIE,* Vol. 2745, pp. 22–39, 1996.

[84] Z. Zhou, B. Pain, R. Panicacci, B. Mansoorian, J. Nakamura, and E. R. Fossum, "On-Focal-Plane ADC: Recent Progress at JPL," *Infrared Readout Electronics III, Proc. SPIE,* Vol. 2745, pp. 111–122, 1996.

[85] B. Pain and E. R. Fossum, "Approaches and Analysis for On-Focal-Plane Analog-to-Digital Conversion," *Infrared Readout Electronics II, Proc. of SPIE,* Vol. 2226, pp. 208–218, 1994.

[86] G. Torelli, L. Gonzo, M. Gottardi, F. Maloberti, A. Sartori, and A. Simoni, "Analog to Digital Conversion Architectures for Intelligent Optical Sensor Arrays," *Advanced Focal Plane Arrays and Electronic Cameras, Proc. SPIE,* Vol. 2950, pp. 254–264, 1996.

[87] W. Mandl, J. Kennedy, and M. Chu, "MOSAD IR Focal Plane per Pixel A/D Development," *Infrared Readout Electronics III, Proc. SPIE,* vol. 2745, pp. 90–98, 1996.

[88] B. Fowler, A. Gamal, and D. Yang, "A CMOS Area Image Sensor with Pixel-level A/D Conversion," *1994 International Solid State Circuits Conference Dig. of Tech. Papers,* pp. 226–227, 1994.

[89] B. Pain and E. R. Fossum, "Design and Operation of Self-biased High-Gain Amplifier Arrays for Photon-Counting Sensors," in *Infrared Readout Electronics III, Proc. SPIE,* Vol. 2745, pp. 69–77, 1996.

[90] E. R. Fossum and P. Wong, "Future Prospects for CMOS Active Pixel Sensors," *1995 IEEE Workshop on CCDs and Advanced Image Sensors,* Dana Point, CA, Apr. 20–22, 1995.

[91] P. Wong, "Technology and Scaling Considerations for CMOS Imagers," *IEEE Trans. Electron Devices,* Vol. 43, No. 12, pp. 2131–2142, 1996.

Chapter
6

CAD OF MULTIMEDIA SYSTEMS

Abeer Alwan, Charles Chien, Etan Cohen, Leader Ho,
Rajeev Jain, Greg Pottie, and John Villasenor

Abstract

This chapter describes CAD tools for multimedia system design. The tools allow for rapid algorithm simulations using a functional model library and scripting procedures that automate iterative optimization of algorithm parameters. Implementation tools are linked into the algorithm design environment to allow efficiency in generating hardware designs from algorithm descriptions. Examples from image, speech, and channel coding, and from modem design illustrate how the data flow simulation in the CAD environment can be exploited for simulating and designing each of these components in a wireless system.

6.1 INTRODUCTION

Multimedia communication systems involve signal processing systems, such as those needed to compress speech and video signals, and communication systems to transmit the signals over wireline or wireless channels. Given the application requirements in terms of (a) available transmission bandwidth (or storage capacity) and (b) desired quality—usually measured in PSNR (Peak Signal-to-Noise Ratio) or MOS (Mean Opinion Score), choices have to be made about appropriate signal processing and communication algorithms as well as their parameters. These choices are not always obvious and require extensive simulations, with actual data samples and models of the transmission channels. Whether we design a system with known algorithms or develop new algorithms that offer better quality versus bandwidth tradeoffs, the iterative simulation procedure can be very time consuming.

This chapter describes the application of CAD tools to the design and optimization of a set of algorithms for a wireless multimedia communication device. The tools have been developed to increase productivity in multimedia system design by allowing rapid simulations of algorithms using a functional model library and scripting procedures to automate iterative optimization of algorithm parameters. Implementation tools are also linked into the algorithm design environment to allow efficiency in generation of hardware designs from the algorithm description. Whereas hardware synthesis for digital logic designs from boolean description is very common with current CAD tools, the synthesis of signal processing and communication hardware systems from algorithm description is still a challenging and unsolved problem. The CAD environment presented here provides back-end tools that can link the algorithm simulation environment to hardware design tools.

Section 6.2 gives a brief overview of the CAD tools for algorithm simulation and optimization. Section 6.3 describes the application of the tools to algorithm design for four subsystems in a wireless communication device: video compression, speech compression, channel coding, and spread-spectrum modem. Section 6.4 shows an example of the implementation tools for a Reed-Solomon channel codec.

6.2 THE CAD ENVIRONMENT: DSP CANVAS

The overall design goal in a wireless multimedia communication system is to achieve an acceptable quality for speech and video transmission while satisfying a maximum bit-error-rate constraint (BER) for data transmission. For an end-user device, it is additionally important to minimize the implementation complexity and power consumption. For each subsystem there are several tradeoffs in the algorithm design that allow optimization of the implementation. For example, the video compression simulations (Section 6.3.1) are combined with channel coding to minimize the error protection complexity while achieving acceptable PSNR over a range of BER values; the speech simulations (Section 6.3.2) are used to minimize filter complexity in a subband codec while achieving acceptable perceptual quality; the channel coding simulations (Section 6.3.3) are used to minimize the precision required in the metric calculations for Viterbi decoding while keeping the error probability within a desired constraint; and the digital modem simulations (Section 6.3.4) are used to minimize the wordlengths of costly elements such as multipliers and Direct Digital Frequency Synthesizer (DDFS) while satisfying output SNR constraints.

These design tradeoffs require a large number of iterative simulations in floating-point as well as fixed-point descriptions of the algorithms. To allow designers to effectively explore these tradeoffs and optimize the overall system, two design tools are being applied: the JetStream data flow simulator and the SystemSolve tools.

6.2.1 The JetStream Data Flow Simulator

The most basic of simulation paradigms is the programming language. Many designers write C language programs to simulate the signal processing or communication algorithms. There are various ways to make this process more efficient (reusable code, subroutine libraries), but it is inherently inefficient in that it requires the designer to translate a data flow (inherent in a multimedia system) to program flow. DSP Canvas provides a data flow simulator (JetStream) that exploits object-oriented techniques to provide two important features for multimedia system simulation.

MultiDomain Data Flow Scheduling. While data flow scheduling allows the designer to rapidly specify the signal processing algorithm, the simulation speed can degrade due to the overhead of scheduling all the blocks during simulation runtime. In multimedia systems, it is usually possible to schedule the execution of some blocks a priori when the simulation code is compiled because their schedule does not depend on runtime conditions. This is called static scheduling. For example, in a subband speech or video coder, the filterbanks can be scheduled statically since their functionality does not depend on the actual inputs. On the other hand, the execution of a run-length coder must be dynamically scheduled since the functionality is data-dependent and cannot be determined until runtime. The distinction between static and dynamic data flow scheduling has been recognized before, but other simulators require the designer to manually partition the design into static and dynamic portions to reduce simulation time. In the JetStream simulator, an algorithm has been developed that automatically partitions the system and generates the simulation code with appropriate use of static scheduling wherever possible.

Finite-Wordlength Analysis and Signal Representation. In multimedia systems, different types of signals must be handled—speech, video, and modulated bit streams. Furthermore, for implementation in digital circuits, signals must be represented by a fixed-point notation. Several fixed-point types exist, including those defined by the user. The particular type chosen has an impact on the system performance as well as the implementation complexity. Thus, the simulator must allow the designer to experiment with different signal types and different fixed-point representations. Traditionally, it has been necessary to write different models for the same function to handle the different signal types. Furthermore, when simulating with fixed-point representations, it is important to be able to assign different wordlengths (accuracy) to different signals or functions. For example, the accuracy required in a scalar quantizer algorithm may be higher than in a discrete cosine transform function. In JetStream, the model for each function does not have to assume a priori the nature of the signals. These can be determined at runtime by the designer without requiring any change in the model itself. This use of object-oriented data typing reduces the need for multiple model libraries or multiple descriptions of the system for simulation purposes, thereby reducing the design time.

6.2.2 SystemSolve: Iterative Simulation and Optimization Tool

To explore the various tradeoffs in multimedia systems requires the execution of a very large number of simulations, the collation of results from these simulations, and their analysis by the user in a coherent manner. These simulations have to be duplicated every time the top-level specifications are modified, increasing the total number of simulations even further. Extracting the system performance and optimizing various algorithm parameters can be very time consuming.

The SystemSolve tool in DSP Canvas provides a graphical scripting language that allows a designer to specify a sequence of simulation commands to execute while varying parameters of the design, for example, compile and run a simulation and postprocess its results while varying the input SNR of a system. Furthermore, the designer can specify an objective function of the parameters that needs to be optimized subject to specified

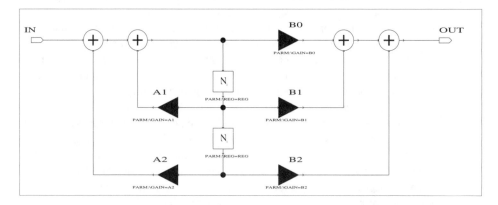

Figure 6.1   DSP Canvas schematic for a second-order biquad filter.

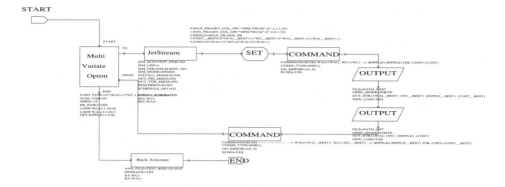

Figure 6.2   DSP Canvas flowchart for the optimization of the biquad filter
coefficient wordlength.

constraints. SystemSolve can invoke optimization tools to guide the iterative search. A
simple example that demonstrates the time savings provided by SystemSolve is discussed
next.

   Example. The simple biquad filter example in Fig. 6.1 illustrates the use of scripting
for automatic optimization. Figure 6.2 shows a flowchart for the simulation script that is
created by the user with the DSP Canvas user interface. The ''multivariate optimization''
box is used to specify: (a) the parameters to be varied in the optimization: the filter coefficient

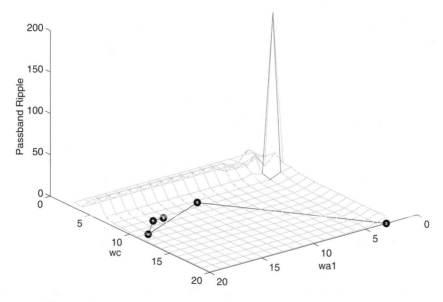

Figure 6.3   IIR biquad optimization-bandpass ripple versus quantization.

precision (wc) and the multiplier accuracy (wai); (b) the design constraint: the passband ripple; and (c) the cost function indicating the relative cost of the operators as a function of the parameters.

When DSP Canvas executes this optimization script, in each iteration of the simulator the parameters are varied and the filter frequency response is analyzed (using JetStream). The "SET" function extracts the passband ripple value and feeds it back to the multivariate optimization function, which decides the next set of values for the parameters to be simulated. In each iteration, DSP Canvas attempts to minimize the cost function. At the end of the iterations, DSP Canvas generates a plot of the minimum of the cost function and the path (Fig. 6.3). The constraint function (passband ripple) versus the hardware parameters is also plotted in Fig. 6.3 to illustrate that DSP Canvas successfully traverses the surface of the constraint function as it approaches the minimum. The plot also shows how DSP Canvas avoids an exhaustive search of the surface and gets to the minimum in a few moves. The scripting allows any number of parameters to be varied in sequence or in parallel. In a complex design such as a modem, video, or speech codec, scripting can save substantial time.

6.3 USING DSP CANVAS TO DESIGN AND EMULATE A MULTIMEDIA, WIRELESS COMMUNICATION SYSTEM

The combination of fast simulation using static-cum-dynamic scheduling and automated iterations with built-in optimization substantially reduces the algorithm development time for the various signal processing and communication functions in a multimedia system. The sections below describe the complexity of the algorithm development for each function and illustrate the application of the system simulation in analyzing and developing the algorithm.

The four basic components of a multimedia communication system are video codec, speech codec, channel codec, and modem. Each of these has many design alternatives which need to be analyzed for a given system specification. In this section we show how the data flow simulation in DSP Canvas is exploited for simulating and designing each of these components in a wireless system.

6.3.1 Video Coding Algorithm Design

6.3.1.1 Design Considerations

Wireless communication systems involve constraints that differ substantially from those found in wireline systems. For example, in order to reduce complexity and increase robustness, algorithms for wireless video will place less emphasis on motion compensation and more on intraframe coding. These algorithms will also have to employ low-complexity transforms and quantization schemes, and to utilize coding and synchronization techniques allowing not only protection from random or bursty bit errors, but also recovery from deep fades in which the signal is lost for several seconds or more. The algorithms should be adaptive to allow adjustment to changing bandwidth allocations from the network and to changing error characteristics of the channel. Finally, error protection, packetization, and other transfer protocol aspects affect both the video coding and the network, and should be designed to enable optimal performance in both.

Under the general umbrella of wireless video systems there is a range of distinct applications that place different requirements on the video coding algorithms and hardware. One possible application consists of remote monitoring in which the wireless unit transmits but does not receive video. By contrast, in a portable transceiver to be used for transmitting and receiving video, it is necessary to use a higher frame rate and to design an algorithm in which both the encoding and decoding can be performed with low complexity [8]. Another application consists of a wireless terminal that is optimized for receiving video (as opposed to supporting fully symmetric two-way video) [2].

No single coding algorithm is likely to be optimal across all wireless video applications. Each application reflects a different set of requirements on bandwidth, complexity, robustness, and functionality. For the design example described here, we consider interactive multimedia applications and are therefore concerned with algorithms that enable both high functionality and low complexity in a network of wireless transceivers. The complexity constraint is dominant in this design, and two-way, rate-adaptive coding is performed at low bit rates ranging from 60 to 600 Kbps.

6.3.1.2 Design Environment

To facilitate rapid exploration of design options, a model library was constructed in DSP Canvas containing a large set of image coding modules. Modules in this library are grouped by class; for example, the transform class includes wavelet, Fourier, and discrete cosine transforms, and the entropy coding class includes Run-Length, Huffman, and Arithmetic coders. There is also a set of channel models to allow simulation of random and bursty transmission environments. To construct an image coding system, a schematic containing the appropriate models is drawn. Figure 6.4 shows an example of a schematic and displays a number of algorithmic features that are included to respond to the cost/power/complexity of a wireless system. One of the most basic design decisions in a wireless image transmission system concerns the use of motion compensation. From an image quality standpoint, the advantages of motion compensation are large. While the precise coding gain due to motion compensation depends on the video content and the frame rate, one can expect between a factor of three and ten improvement in compression efficiency when the redundancy between successive frames in a video sequence is utilized. Unfortunately, this image quality gain comes at the price of a large increase in complexity. Because of this complexity penalty, the system in Fig. 6.4 is a pure intraframe system in which each frame is coded independently. This eliminates the need for frame memory in the encoder and for the costly computations associated with block matching and other motion compensation algorithms. Intraframe coding also eliminates the risk of transmission errors that propagate across multiple frames.

The transform constitutes one of the most important elements of a compression algorithm. While transforms themselves do not perform any compression, they furnish an alternative representation of image data that can be efficiently compressed in the subsequent quantization step. The block Discrete Cosine Transform (DCT) is the transform employed in the JPEG [17] and MPEG [7] compression standards, as well as in video conferencing standards such as H.261. The DCT performs well when low-compression ratios are used, but at high-compression ratios only the lowest frequency DCT coefficients from each 8-pel by 8-pel block are retained, resulting in severe blocking artifacts in the reconstructed im-

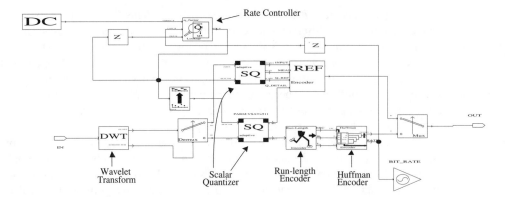

Figure 6.4   Schematic description of a low-complexity wavelet based encoder
in DSP Canvas.

age. Wavelet transforms offer an alternative to the DCT and can lead to efficient still-image
compression if the appropriate filters are used.

The intraframe coding scheme illustrated in Fig. 6.4 is based on a six-level Discrete
Wavelet Transform (DWT), followed by scalar quantization, Run-Length coding (RLC),
and Huffman coding. Each of these steps has been modified in the DSP Canvas coding
models to increase its functionality in a wireless system. Since the DWT represents the
most computationally intensive step in an intraframe subband coder, the length and nature
(floating point versus integer) of the filter coefficients will have a significant effect on
the overall power requirements. We performed a study of filterbanks and identified short
(a total of eight low-pass and high-pass taps) integer-coefficients filters [15] that require
approximately two-thirds less chip area than the more commonly used 16-tap 9/7 wavelet
filter. Measured in terms of PSNR, we observe that the compression performance of the
filter we are using is within 0.5 dB of that of the 16-tap filter at the data rates of interest.

6.3.1.3 Exploring Tradeoffs: An Example
Using Error Protection

One of the most powerful attributes of the design environment is the ability to rapidly
explore design tradeoffs and establish optimal operating parameters. Figures 6.5 and 6.6
provide an illustration of this capability. The issue being addressed in this example is error
protection; for example, as a function of the channel error characteristics, what is the best
way to perform channel coding? The figures illustrate results for three approaches to achieve
robustness: (1) no error protection at all, which is the most bandwidth efficient but also the
most vulnerable to errors, (2) equal error protection, in which all parts of the encoded video
bit stream are protected equally, and (3) unequal error protection, in which the depth of
error protection varies with the visual importance of the data. It is, of course, expected that
unequal error protection will give the best quality in poor transmission environments. The
simulation environment allows calculation of the marginal improvement enabled by a more

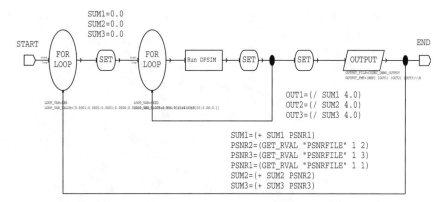

Figure 6.5   DSP Canvas script used to explore various error protection
schemes over different channel error rates.

sophisticated error protection approach, which then can be weighed against the increases
in implementation complexity.

Figure 6.5 shows the scripting entry that is used to perform this exploration. Two loops
are indicated in the figure: the outer loop increments the bit-error rate (BER), and the inner
loop is used to run the simulation (labeled DFSIM) many times so that the results of many

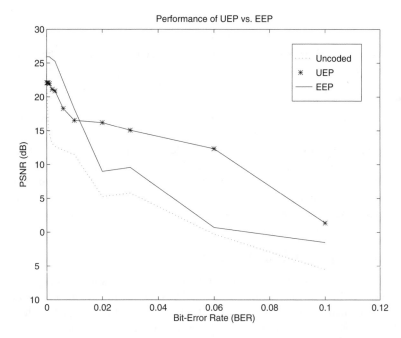

Figure 6.6   Results obtained from the script in Fig. 6.5. UEP: unequal error
protection; EEP: equal error protection.

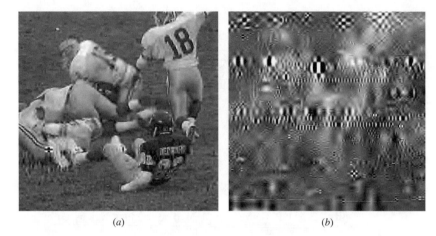

              (*a*)   (*b*)

Figure 6.7   Illustration of the importance of error protection in wireless multimedia communications. These images were compressed to 0.46
bits/pixel, using the wavelet scheme described earlier. This corresponds to a frame rate of 15 frames/sec. if the video bandwidth
is 450 Kbps. The channel BER in this example is 0.003. In the
image on the left, some of the bandwidth was allocated to error
protection using punctured convolutional codes that exploit the
hierarchical nature of the wavelet decomposition. The image on
the right is unprotected.

trials can be averaged. At each iteration, an image is input into the encoder in Fig. 6.4 to
generate a compressed bit stream. Appropriate error protection is added, and the bit stream
is then corrupted according to the channel model. Image decoding is performed, and the
PSNR of the decoded image is calculated.

    Figure 6.6 plots the results of using this scripted parameter exploration for the three
error-handling approaches identified earlier. As expected, the image quality (indicated by
PSNR) degrades as the channel error rate increases. In particular, the plot indicates that
in the critically important BER range from 0.01 to 0.1, the advantage of unequal error
protection over equal error protection is several dBs. The conclusion is that the relatively
modest complexity increase associated with unequal error protection is justified from an
image quality standpoint. Figure 6.7 illustrates the importance of using error protection in
wireless transmission.

6.3.2   Speech Codec Design

    Design of high-quality speech coders for wireless networks is just as challenging a
task as wireless video coding, since good quality should be maintained with low-power consumption under time-varying channel conditions and limited bandwidth. The design should
account for a number of parameters such as bit rate, delay, power consumption, complexity,
quality of coded speech, and channel characteristics. Available bandwidth will depend on

network protocols. Depending on the application, a set of parameters are optimized. For example, in certain applications delay in the range of 40 ms can be tolerated, whereas the bit rate should be kept low. In other applications, the design should yield minimum power consumption and the bit rates can be as high as 64 Kbps. Simulation tools that allow the user to analyze the quality/complexity/delay tradeoff of different codecs in a wireless, and possibly dynamically reconfigurable, network are essential but, currently, nonexistent. In our work, a set of simulation tools that allow for such a design has been implemented within the DSP Canvas.

In the past, speech codec design has been driven mostly by bandwidth-efficiency considerations, the target application being telephonic where the channel does not vary considerably with time and the signal-to-noise (SNR) is relatively high. For example, coders based on Code Excited Linear Prediction (CELP) are popular because of their low bit rates. The performance of these coders, however, deteriorates significantly in the presence of background noise, and the coders' complexity is high. Because of significant and time-varying degradations in wireless channels, adaptivity and noise robustness are highly desirable features in a wireless speech compression algorithm.

6.3.2.1 Design Modules

The design modules that have been developed range in complexity from basic units such as first-order filters to complicated blocks such as tree-structured filterbanks. The modules constitute a library that can be used to build speech processing systems, such as pitch detectors, analysis and synthesis systems, or coders. Examples of modeled functions include preemphasis (used to boost the high-frequency content of the signal analyzed), LPC (linear predictive coding), cepstrum (both real and complex), zero-crossing rate, adaptive bit allocation, and adaptive quantization.

A schematic of a simple subband speech coder is shown in Fig. 6.8*a*, and a block diagram of the coder as viewed in DSP Canvas is shown in Fig. 6.8*c*. Figure 6.8*b* shows two speech waveforms of the same sentence, uncompressed and compressed versions, that were generated with the simulation environment. The parameters that can be manipulated by the user include (1) analysis and synthesis filterbanks, including the filter order and choice of IIR or FIR filters, (2) number of bits assigned to each band, and hence, a choice of overall bit rates, and (3) type of quantizer. For example, the user can be prompted for the desired bit rate and the minimum number of bits per band. With appropriate channel models, one can also evaluate the performance of the coder under different channel conditions.

6.3.2.2 Perceptually Based Speech and Audio Coder

With the assistance of the integrated CAD environment, we developed a speech and audio compression scheme suitable for wireless communications which has the following characteristics: (1) low delay, (2) adaptive bit allocation and quantization, and (3) noise robustness.

The coder is a perceptually based and scalable subband coder. It consists of four components: analysis/synthesis filterbanks, a perceptual model, a bit allocation block, and a

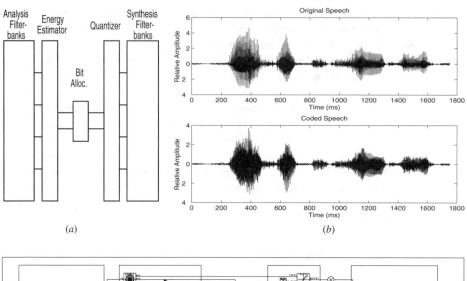

(a)   (b)

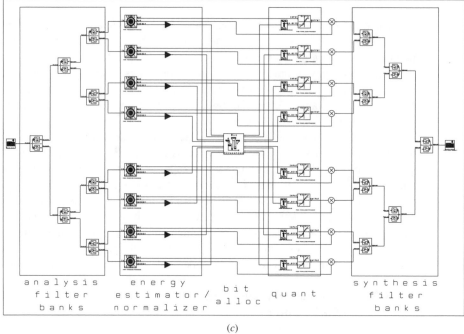

(c)

Figure 6.8   (a) Simplified representation of a speech subband coder. (b) Time
waveforms of a speech sentence as viewed in DSP Canvas. (c)
Schematic of speech coder in DSP Canvas.

quantization block. Low delay is achieved by using an eight-channel IIR, instead of the commonly used FIR, filterbank. The perceptual model ensures that encoding is optimized to the human listener and is based on calculating the signal-to-mask ratio in short time-frames of the input signal. The model adaptively estimates the audibility of quantization noise. More resources can then be allocated to the frequency bands where a greater SNR is needed to mask quantization noise. The bit allocation scheme translates the SNR prescribed by the model into a bit assignment used for quantizing the subband samples. Finally, the subband energies are quantized using a Max-Lloyd quantizer. Subjective listening tests, using quiet and noisy input signals, indicate that in error-free conditions, the coder at 12 Kbps has comparable performance to that of QualComm Code Excited Linear Prediction (QCELP) (the speech service option for wideband spread spectrum digital cellular system [EIA/TIA/IS-95]) at 8 Kbps and a Global Systems for Mobile (GSM) 6.10 coder (a standardized lossy speech compression algorithm employed by most European wireless telephones [14]) at 13 Kbps. For speech in background noise, however, the coder, at 12 Kbps, outperforms QCELP significantly, and for music, it outperforms both QCELP and GSM.

A detailed description of the coder can be found in [11]. The coder has been implemented in software. In addition, a simplified, energy-based version of the coder has been implemented on a TMS320C50 DSP board, controlled by a PC, that allows for real-time processing. Protocol routines have been developed on both the DSP and the PC for speech coding and decoding.

6.3.3 Channel Coding

Channel codes are used in many digital communications systems to ensure reliable transmission of information. With properly designed channel codes, less power is required to transmit the same information over a noisy channel for a specified error probability than in uncoded transmission. Power savings can be especially dramatic for wireless multi-access systems, resulting in large gains in system capacity. Due to the interactions with other systems components, it is essential in any CAD system for the design of high-performance communications to include channel codes. In the following section, we briefly describe the Forward Error Correcting (FEC) coding components included in DSP Canvas.

Error control codes may be based either on block codes such as cyclic codes, or trellis codes, which are generated using a finite state machine. The choice of which code to use depends on such factors as the decoding complexity, end-to-end delay, storage requirements, and redundancy versus coding gain. Reed-Solomon (RS) codes are a type of cyclic code operating over finite fields $GF(q)$, where q is usually chosen to be a power of 2. These codes are specified in a variety of standards from CD players to deep space applications. They are popular because of their efficient error correction capability and the existence of well-structured decoding algorithms suitable for VLSI implementation. All of the popular trellis codes make use of convolutional codes, and most such decoders use the Viterbi algorithm (VA). Convolutional codes and their derivatives are especially useful when a moderate error probability (10^3 to 10^6) is desired, and the decoder has access to the actual received channel symbols rather than a sequence of bits. These codes are used in voice-band modems and are proposed for a variety of video standards in conjunction with RS codes. In the following, we give more detail on RS and trellis decoders, and discuss how they may be combined together with interleaving to achieve highly effective error suppression.

6.3.3.1 Reed-Solomon Codes

The block length of an RS code over GF(q) is fixed at $q - 1$ symbols. For example, if $q = 256$, each symbol is a byte, and the block length is 255 bytes. RS codes can be constructed with different levels of error protection.

With r redundant symbols per block, the code can correct $r/2$ random symbol errors. It is possible to reduce the rate of an RS code by limiting the number of information bits per block and putting in a prefix of zeros (deleted at the encoder output). The decoder may then operate as normal. This enables the creation of RS codes of arbitrary block length, which can be useful in combination with variable-rate source coding schemes.

A variety of decoding techniques may be used for RS codes, all yielding the same error correction performance [1]. We have implemented the Berlekamp-Massey algorithm, including the possibility of correcting erasures, for RS codes over GF(2^m), $m = 4$ to 8, for arbitrary redundancies and rate reduction through information symbol deletion. The user may also specify a particular primitive polynomial to use to construct the finite field. The decoding procedure amounts to solving a set of nonlinear equations. This is transformed into two sets of linear operations, where first the locations of the errors are determined using the Berlekamp-Massey algorithm, and then the error magnitudes using the Forney algorithm. Both of these algorithms avoid a costly matrix inversion using the special algebraic properties of the code. The Berlekamp-Massey algorithm requires recursive construction of a shift register circuit which generates the observed set of syndromes. The coefficients for the multipliers in this circuit may be viewed as the coefficients of a polynomial; the roots of this polynomial in GF(q) are the inverses of the locations of the errors. The factorization of this so-called error locator polynomial is accomplished through an exhaustive search of all $q - 1$ possible solutions (the Chien search). The Forney algorithm requires further operations involving the creation and evaluation of polynomials at the error locations.

Our software implementation provides user access to intermediate stages in the decoder to facilitate testing alternative hardware implementations. For example, the Euclidean algorithm turned out to be more convenient in hardware than the Berlekamp-Massey algorithm for an application involving variable speed transmission (as detailed later), and it was helpful to be able to verify that the correct error locator polynomial was being produced.

6.3.3.2 Trellis Codes

Trellis codes are generated by a finite state shift register circuit. For each set of input bits, there is a corresponding output set or transition that depends on both the current inputs and contents of the shift register memories. The shift register contents define the state, while the output bits label a channel symbol or sequence of channel symbols. Thus, the code can be thought of as a series of transitions between different states, the set of transitions determined by the inputs given an initial state. This is drawn as a code trellis, a graph with one node for each state at each encoder interval, and the set of transitions between states drawn as edges. A sequence of connected edges is called a path, and only the channel symbols corresponding to such paths can actually be transmitted. The code is designed so that the distance between paths in the trellis is made as large as possible, minimizing the error probability. The maximum likelihood decoding procedure is to find the path through the trellis that is at minimum distance from the actual received sequence of channel symbols. This is accomplished using the Viterbi algorithm (VA) [1].

In a variation known as trellis-coded modulation, the labels attached to the transitions in the trellis diagram denote a collection of signal points known as cosets [6]. A large constellation of signal points is divided into sets of cosets such that the distance between members of any given coset is much larger than the smallest distance between points in the original constellation. Then the purpose of the convolutional code is to protect the sequence of cosets from error. The actual signal point in a coset does not need any coding, if in decoding we first determine the coset sequence using the Viterbi algorithm. This technique is used in the V.32 and V.34 voice-band modems because one low-rate convolutional code may be specified to work with a variety of signal constellations in the same family. In addition, the redundancy inherent in the code may be accommodated by expanding the signal constellation rather than by sending more symbols; thus, the bandwidth requirements remain the same as uncoded transmission. The only modification to the Viterbi decoder in this case is that the branch metrics must be computed based on the closest member of each coset to the received symbol.

We have implemented encoders and decoders for rate-1/2, rate-2/3, and rate-3/4 convolutional codes. Trellis-coded modulation based on these codes is supported for QAM and PAM constellations to enable experimentation in a variety of wireless system designs.

6.3.3.3 Concatenated Code Example

The broadcast HDTV standard for the United States [HDTV Standards, 1995] specifies the use of a concatenated code, with an inner trellis code, an outer RS code, and convolutional interleaving in between to break up long error bursts, as shown in Fig. 6.9. Concatenation is an approach that results in very high coding gain at low-error probabilities with fairly simple component codes, at the price of latency. The interleaving is done on a symbol (byte) basis rather than bit by bit, since the RS code corrects symbol errors. In addition, the inner

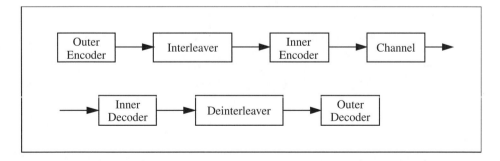

Figure 6.9   Concatenated coding system.

code may operate in one of two different modes, based on whether there is interference from NTSC television stations. With interference present, a comb filter is placed in the receive path, nulling out the luminance and chrominance carriers but effectively creating a partial response characteristic. The variation on the Viterbi algorithm used in such situations is known as Reduced State Sequence Estimation (RSSE) [5]. The comb filter is regarded as creating an intersymbol interference trellis, which is concatenated with that of the trellis code. In decoding, an eight-state RSSE approach that also takes into account the noise correlation can lead to significant performance improvement over other techniques. All of these components have been implemented in DSP Canvas.

One important issue that is conveniently addressed in DSP Canvas is the number of bits of precision required in the various metric calculations in the Viterbi decoder. Clearly, any VLSI implementation can be simplified by reducing the number of bits, but reduced precision and dynamic range for the path distances can cause an elevated error probability. We were able to easily determine values that yielded very small performance degradations, for both modes of the Viterbi decoder in HDTV.

6.3.4 A Direct-Sequence Spread-Spectrum Modem Design

This section describes the simulation of a direct-sequence spread spectrum modem to illustrate the essential design steps needed to achieve an optimized fixed-point digital implementation of the modem functions.

6.3.4.1 Modem Components

The spread-spectrum modem example consists of a modulator/demodulator, and a PN (Pseudo Noise)-code synchronizer. In the transmitter, the baseband modulator spreads the data with a Gold sequence and modulates the spread signal onto a RF carrier. The modulation employs Binary Phase Shift Keying (BPSK). In the receiver, the received signal is filtered and downconverted to an Intermediate Frequency (IF), amplitude adjusted by an automatic gain control, filtered, and then converted to a digital IF signal for processing in the digital receiver, which includes a Costas-loop coherent demodulator and a PN synchronizer (Fig. 6.10).

6.3.4.2 Coherent Demodulator

With coherent BPSK demodulation, the required SNR is 9.6 dB to achieve a BER better than 0.001% for a reliable data link. For the Costas-loop demodulator, the SNR is a function of the loop resonant frequency (ω_n) and the damping factor (λ), which are related to the loop filter coefficients, C_1 and C_2 (Fig. 6.11):

$$\frac{C_1}{C_2} = \frac{2\lambda}{\omega_n T_s} \tag{1}$$

The design goal is to determine the values for C_1 and C_2 which best meet the 9.6 dB SNR requirement. These coefficient values can be represented by powers of two

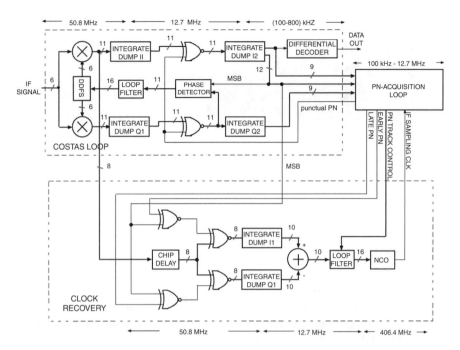

Figure 6.10 A direct-sequence spread-spectrum digital receiver.

($C_1 = 2^{-m}$ and $C_2 = 2^{-n}$), where m and n directly impact the bit precision required in the implementation of the loop filter. Therefore, m and n need to be minimized. Although using linear approximation, a closed-form expression can be found that relates m and n to the SNR; optimized according to the cost function $min(max(m, n))$, the solution does not account for nonlinear large-signal behavior and finite wordlength effects. Therefore, simulation is needed to model these nonlinear effects.

Figure 6.12 illustrates the result of an exhaustive search that shows the SNR as a function of m and n. The values within the contour on the $m - n$ plane satisfy the desired SNR, and the optimum values are $m = 6$ and $n = 16$. With low-simulation overhead and optimized scheduling, the data flow simulation paradigm is particularly suitable for this

$$C_1 = 2^{-m}$$

$$C_2 = 2^{-n}$$

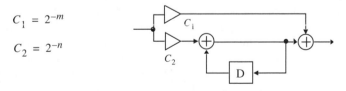

Figure 6.11 A second-order loop filter.

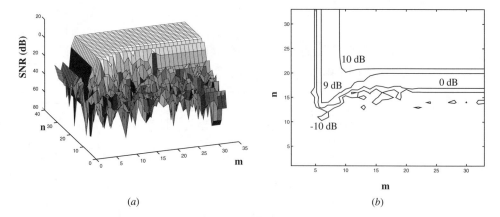

(a)   (b)

Figure 6.12   Simulated behavior of SNR versus m and n.

type of multiparameter search that requires a large number of simulation cycles. In this case, a total of 1000 simulations has been performed, each requiring 512,000 samples.

The loop filter optimization impacts the SNR performance and hardware complexity but has little influence on the speed performance of the receiver. For the receiver, the speed bottlenecks consist of two elements: the multiplier and the Direct Digital Frequency Synthesizer (DDFS) that operate at the IF sampling rate of 50.8 MHz. To meet this throughput requirement, the wordlength for each element has been minimized while minimizing the degradations due to quantization noise.

Figure 6.13 shows the simulation for the multiplier input wordlength versus output SNR for different input SNRs. The optimal precision is determined to be the point at which no further gain in SNR is obtained with increasing wordlength. In this case, the optimum is determined to be four bits for the IF input and six bits for the DDFS output. Figure 6.13 shows that deviation from the optimal wordlength results in a large penalty in both area and speed.

6.3.4.3 PN-Synchronization

PN-synchronization consists of an acquisition and a tracking block. The design of the PN-acquisition block highlights another key requirement in the simulation environment: namely, the ability to perform Monte Carlo analysis efficiently. The acquisition block helps to achieve the desired processing gain by locking onto the received PN sequence. In a code division multiple access application, as the number of users increases, the input SNR decreases, leading to a degraded user capacity. Not only does the BER degrade but also the amount of time required for the receiver to acquire the code lengthens, which has a negative impact on the network throughput. To evaluate the performance of the acquisition loop, the PN-acquisition probability is obtained using Monte Carlo analysis over 16 different multiple-access noise patterns. The results are shown in Fig. 6.14, where T_{acq} is the number of data bits allocated for acquisition. For the tracking block, the key design parameter is the

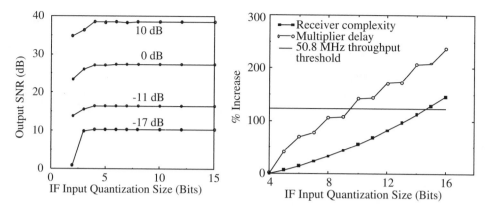

Figure 6.13 SNR and complexity as a function of IF wordlength.

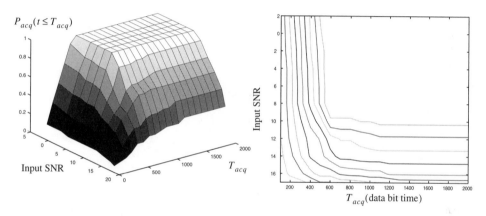

Figure 6.14 Monte Carlo analysis of probability of acquisition versus SNR and acquisition time.

oversampling ratio required for the desired SNR. The simulation sweep shows that a ratio of eight is sufficient in this case.

For further reading on the design and IC implementation of the transceiver, readers are referred to [3 and 4].

6.4 COMPUTER-AIDED IMPLEMENTATION OF MULTIMEDIA COMMUNICATIONS COMPONENTS

One of the challenges in multimedia communications system design is to seamlessly go from the system simulation of the algorithms for video, speech, channel coding, and modems to the actual implementation in integrated circuits. This involves the design of appropriate chip

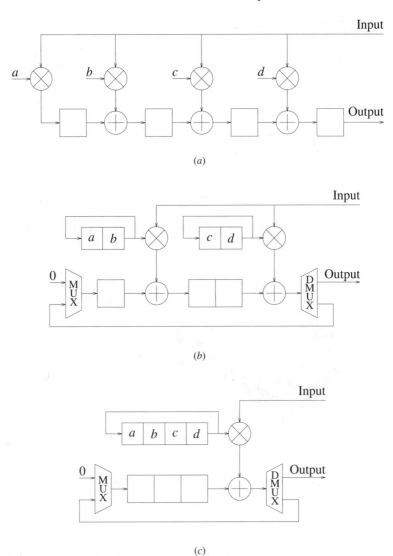

Figure 6.15 (*a*) Encoder, TF $=$ 1. (*b*) Encoder, TF $=$ 2. (*c*) Encoder, TF $=$ 4.

architectures for each algorithm and translation to a layout. Logic synthesis tools (such as Design Compiler from Synopsys) are available to generate layouts from a logic description. DSP Canvas system simulation, however, uses models at a much higher level than the logic level. While several attempts have been made at synthesizing DSP architectures from the system description of the algorithm, these techniques still need to mature further to produce useful designs. One of the CAD techniques developed in DSP Canvas for the specific

Table 6.1 Layout Dimensions for a 24Mb/s RS Codec

	Encoder	Syndrome	Euclidean	Chien	Forney
Height (λ)	4359	5115	8271	2697	2555
Width (λ)	2744	2688	4720	2064	1904
Area (mm^2)	4.306	4.950	14.054	1.991	1.751

multimedia and communication functions discussed in this chapter is to develop VHDL compilers targeted at specific parameterizable architectures. Such compilers have been developed for the two major communication functions within the DSP Canvas: modems and channel codecs.

In this section, we illustrate the implementation strategy with the example of a Reed-Solomon VHDL chip layout compiler. The inputs to the compiler include parameters of a Reed-Solomon codec as determined by the system simulation—the block length, symbol sizes, maximum correctable errors, primitive polynomial, and generator polynomial. It also

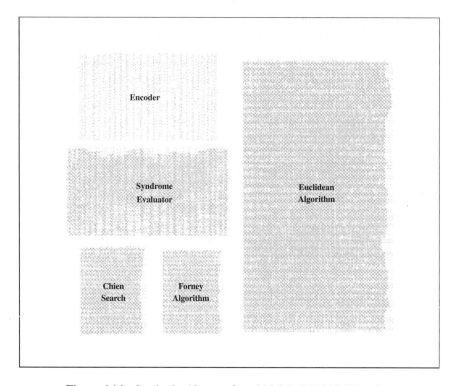

Figure 6.16 Synthesized layouts for a 24 Mb/s (255,235) RS codec.

Table 6.2 Layout Dimensions for a 12Mb/s RS Codec

	Encoder	Syndrome	Euclidean	Chien	Forney
Height (λ)	2027	2063	3939	1739	1411
Width (λ)	1448	1336	2176	1232	1160
Area (mm^2)	1.057	0.992	3.085	0.771	0.589

accepts many implementation-related parameters such as the desired sample rate; this is used to calculate the time-sharing factors for each individual operator (i.e., the finite field adders and multipliers) in the encoder and decoder. By varying the time-sharing factors, the correct point on the tradeoff curve of performance versus complexity is achieved for the architecture.

The compiler design cycle consists of two separate parts. The first involves the creation of a template file for a generic architecture that implements the functions in the codec for a known set of system parameter values. The second part mainly involves the writing of a program that transforms the architecture in the template files according to the desired parameter values to generate the appropriate VHDL outputs for each special case. The following figures illustrate all the possible transforms that can be performed to a generic two-error-correcting Reed-Solomon codec. For simplicity, only the encoder is shown, but the transforms apply to all decoder functions as well. The transforms correspond to different

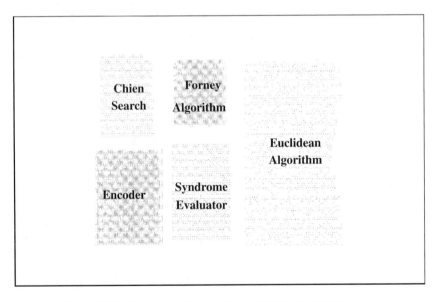

Figure 6.17   Synthesized layouts for a 12 Mb/s (31,23) RS codec.

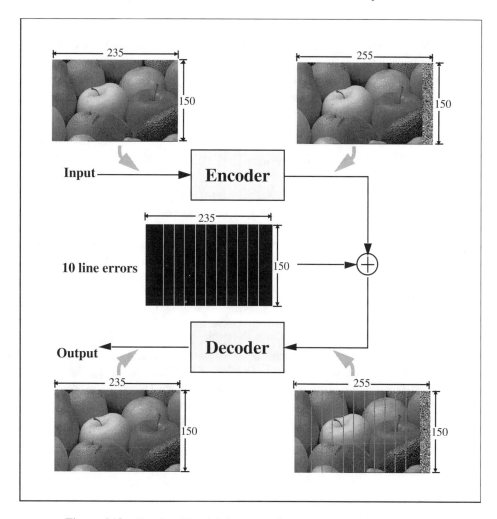

Figure 6.18   Simulated Reed-Solomon coding and decoding of images with
the chip design generated by the VHDL compiler.

symbol rate specifications, which result in different time-sharing factors (TF) as shown in
Fig. 6.15a–c.

Two layout examples are given next to illustrate the functionality of the Reed-Solomon
VHDL compiler. VHDL simulations (using Viewsim within the DSP Canvas-Viewlogic
environment) have been used to verify the VHDL designs. The complexity estimations are
based on the size of the layouts, synthesized using a 1.2 micron CMOS standard cell library.
The complexity comparisons are done on the five major components: encoder, syndrome
evaluator, Chien search, Forney algorithm, and Euclidean algorithms.

Design Example 1

Specifications: A (255,235) 10-error-correcting Reed-Solomon codec with a minimum throughput of 24 Mbits/s.

Design: The required symbol rate is 3 MHz for 8 bits/symbol. The symbol period is about 330 ns. The maximum value of time-share factors for all the components is 10. The layout dimensions are listed in Table 6.1, and the synthesized IC layout is shown in Fig. 6.16.

Design Example 2

Specifications: A (31,23) 4-error-correcting Reed-Solomon codec with a minimum throughput of 12 Mbits/s.

Design: The required symbol rate is 2.4 MHz for 5 bits/symbol. The symbol period is about 416 ns, and all five components can be interleaved. The Euclidean algorithm can be interleaved by a factor of 12. The maximal interleaving factor is 8 for the encoder, 8 for the syndrome evaluator, 4 for the Chien search unit, and 4 for the Forney algorithm unit. Note that this still assumes a conservative worst-case critical path of 30 ns for the Euclidean algorithm. This delay should be less for the (31,23) code due to the smaller symbol size. Therefore, the fully interleaved architecture should be capable of a throughput much higher than 12 Mb/s. The layout dimensions are listed in Table 6.2, and the synthesized IC layout is shown in Fig. 6.17.

Each VHDL design generated by the compiler can be simulated in DSP Canvas using Viewsim to verify the architecture design. The Reed-Solomon encoding and decoding of an image, for video transmission, is illustrated in Fig. 6.18 for the (255,235) 10-error-correcting VHDL design presented earlier. This simulation tests the maximum error correction capability of the (255,235) Reed-Solomon codec. By introducing 10 vertical lines of white pixels (greyscale = 255), each horizontal line of the image at the input of the decoder contains 10 corrupted pixels. The decoded image shown in Fig. 6.18 verifies that the VHDL architecture implementation of the (255,235) codec is capable of correcting a maximum of 10 symbol errors.

6.5 CONCLUSION

In this chapter, CAD tools that allow rapid algorithm simulations using a functional model library and scripting procedures were described. Implementation tools are linked into the algorithm design environment to allow efficiency in generating hardware designs from algorithm descriptions. Examples from image, speech, and channel coding, and from modem design illustrate how the data flow simulation in the CAD environment can be exploited for simulating and designing each of these components in a wireless system.

Future work will include parallelizing the simulation engine as well as the script and optimization engines to enhance simulation performance.

Acknowledgments

This work was supported in part by ARPA/CSTO Contract J-FBI-93-112, "Computer Aided Design of High Performance Wireless Networked Systems," by Sarnoff-TI MICRO project 93-075 and by NSF grant IRI93-09418. We thank Viktor Öwall, Philbert Bangayan, and Marcio Siqueira for their help with the figures.

References

[1] R. E. Blahut, *Theory and Practice of Error Control Codes*, Reading, MA: Addison-Wesley, 1984.

[2] A. Chandrakasan, A. Burstein, and R. Brodersen, "A Low Power Chipset for Portable Multimedia Applications," *Proceedings of the IEEE International Solid-State Circuits Conference, San Francisco*, pp. 82–83, Feb. 1994.

[3] C. Chien et al., "A 12.7 Mchips/sec All-Digital BPSK Direct-Sequence Spread Spectrum IF Transceiver," *IEEE Journal of Solid-State Circuits*, Vol. 29, No. 12, Dec. 1994.

[4] B.-Y. Chung, C. Chien, H. Samueli, and R. Jain, "Performance Analysis of an All-Digital BPSK Direct-Sequence Spread Spectrum IF Receiver Architecture," *IEEE Journal on Selected Areas in Communications*, Sept. 1993.

[5] M. V. Eyuboglu and S. U. H. Qureshi, "Reduced-state Sequence Estimation with Set Partitioning and Decision Feedback," *IEEE Trans. Comm.*, pp. 13–20, Jan. 1988.

[6] G. D. Forney Jr., "Coset codes—Part I: Introduction and Geometrical Classification," *IEEE Trans. Inform. Theory*, Sept. 1988, pp. 1123-1151.

[7] D. Le Gall, "MPEG: A Video Compression Standard for Multimedia Applications," *Comm. ACM*, Vol. 34, pp. 46–58, 1991.

[8] M. Khansari, A. Zakauddin, W. Y. Chan, E. Dubois, and P. Mermelstein, "Approaches to Layered Coding for Dual-rate Wireless Video Transmission," *Proceedings of the 1st Int. Conf. on Image Processing, Austin, TX, USA, 1994*, pp. 258–62, Vol. 1.

[9] David G. Messerschmitt, "A tool for structured functional simulation," *IEEE Journal on Selected Areas in Communications*, Vol. SAC-2, pp. 137–147, Jan. 1984.

[10] K. Shanmugan, "An Update on Software Packages for Simulation of Communication Systems (Links)," *IEEE Journal on Selected Areas in Communications*, Vol. 6, pp. 5–12, Jan. 1988.

[11] A. Shen, B. Tang, A. Alwan, and G. Pottie, "A Robust and Variable-Rate Speech Coder," *Proc. Int. Con. Acous. Speech Sig. Proc. (ICASSP) 1995*, Vol. I, pp. 249–252.

[12] M. K. Simon, J. K. Omura, R. A. Scholtz, and B. K. Levitt, *Spread Spectrum Communications*, 1st ed., Vol. 1, 1985.

[13] United States Advanced Television Systems Committee, *Digital Television Standard for HDTV Transmission*, Apr. 12, 1995.

[14] P. Vary et al., "Speech codec for the European Mobile System," *Proc. IEEE ICASSP*, p. 227, Apr. 1988.

[15] J. Villasenor, B. Belzer, and J. Liao, "Wavelet filter evaluation for image compression," *IEEE Trans. on Image Proc.*, Vol. 4, pp. 1063–1070, Aug. 1995.

[16] A. Vladimirescu, K. Zhang, A. R. Newton, D. O. Pederson, and A. Sangiovanni-Vicentelli, *SPICE User's Guide*, University of California at Berkeley, 1981.

[17] G. K. Wallace, "The JPEG Still Picture Compression Standard," *Comm. ACM*, Vol. 34, pp. 30–45, 1991.

DIGITAL LIBRARY
AND SERVERS

Chapter 7

THE TERADATA SQL3 MULTIMEDIA DATABASE SERVER

William O'Connell, David Schrader, and Homer Chen

Abstract

Multimedia applications—such as fingerprint matching, signature verification, face recognition, and speech recognition or translation—require complex abstract data-type support within database management systems. However, conventional databases are not designed to support multimedia. In this chapter, we describe several multimedia database challenges and explain how Teradata solves these problems with its SQL3 Multimedia Database system. A key component of this system is the Multimedia Object Manager, a general-purpose content-based multimedia server designed for the symmetric multiprocessor (SMP) and massively parallel processor (MPP) environments. The Teradata SQL3 Multimedia Database system allows users to define and manipulate user-defined functions (UDFs), which are invoked in parallel in the Multimedia Object Manager to analyze/manipulate the contents of multimedia objects. The two key characteristics of this subsystem are its support for content-based retrieval and multimodal integration. We provide an in-depth analysis of retrieval techniques using feature extraction and spatial indices. We also illustrate the power of multimodal integration by walking through the development of a complex application involving the generation of a "talking agent," which uses speech, image, and video data types within the database system.

7.1 THE STATE OF CLIENT/SERVER MULTIMEDIA APPLICATIONS

Advances in technology are allowing application developers to create interesting new applications using multimedia. Most of these applications exist today on client systems (PCs or workstations), which have increasing levels of hardware and software support for handling voice, image, and video data types. Server systems, by contrast, have only recently begun providing multimedia capabilities [1,2]. This chapter considers the problems of supporting multimedia applications in one of the most important software subsystems on a typical server, the database system.

An important driver for multimedia support in database systems will be the needs of future data warehouses and decision support systems. Such warehouses today contain traditional "coded" data: specifically, integers, character strings, real numbers, and boolean data that represent encoded information about customers and product sales. This limited set of native database data types necessarily imposes restrictions on what kinds of customer or sales information can be collected and encoded. As database customers gradually migrate their applications to contain more customer information (for example, pictures of frequent shoppers) and sales information (for example, product pictures and animation of sales activities across geographic areas), we expect data warehouses of the future to contain many multimedia objects. Builders of these data warehouses will have several new requirements:

217

- Ease of use. This requirement will threaten SQL unless the language can be gracefully extended to support multimedia objects.
- Integrated languages. These must express queries on both coded data and multimedia data. Computing on voice, pictures, and videos will become common.
- Scalability of both coded and multimedia data (for example, much coded data and less multimedia, or vice versa).
- Good optimization options for storage costs.
- Better communication channels among clients and servers. These are needed to support fast transfer of multimedia objects.
- Extending the Call Level Interface (CLI) for large multimedia objects.
- Enhanced security definitions for abstract data types, large multimedia objects, and feature extracts.

A heated debate is underway in the database industry about which of the following approaches best satisfies customer needs:

- Use object-oriented database management systems (OODBMSs).
- Extend the relational model.

OODBMSs have some of the basic functionalities needed to support multimedia database requirements. However, there are two large obstacles for OODB vendors: backward compatibility with large amounts of legacy information (much of it in relational tables), and performance and scale-up concerns. Although OODBMSs have modeling capability superior to relational systems, this modeling generality becomes a performance disadvantage, since comparable algebraic optimization techniques for performance acceleration are not yet well understood.

The extended relational approach, referred to as *object-relational* [3], augments the traditional relational model with object-oriented extensions (for example, abstract data types and methods). The object-relational approach combines the benefits of relational algebra with functionality for multimedia objects. To satisfy object-oriented requirements on the query language, database vendors are moving toward the SQL3[1] standard [4]. Each vendor implements its own subset of SQL3. We refer to the Teradata dialect as multimedia SQL, or MM-SQL.

Where today's relational database management systems provide extensions for richer types, the facilities are typically primitive. In most cases, the database is little more than a file system that simply stores and retrieves large objects, called binary large objects (BLOBs). As a result, the client's application usually manipulates multimedia data with little or no help from the database server. The client interprets the semantic content and manipulates the BLOB.

With either approach, OODBMSs or the extended relational model, there is a large class of applications requiring content-based database queries on large numbers of multimedia objects. Fraud-prevention applications, for example, include best-case matching

[1] SQL3 is still in draft format.

of fingerprints or faces, in which a sample object is supplied to the database system, and the closest N matches to that target are returned from the database server to the user. The database server may run a query on multiple nodes, scanning millions of objects to compute the best N matches. Other applications of content-based analysis include:

- Tumor recognition in a set of magnetic resonant images (MRIs)
- Speech recognition on a stored audio clip
- Keyword searching in a document

The client-server approach to multimedia has several advantages. Not only can large amounts of multimedia data be shared, but content-based processing is often computationally intensive and therefore amenable to the scale-up and speed-up advantages that SMP and MPP hardware systems offer. Moving the computation from the client to the server significantly reduces network traffic. Finally, a database approach to multimedia objects, as opposed to a file approach, yields the advantages of transaction consistency, data integrity, and data modeling.

7.2 DATABASE SUPPORT FOR MULTIMEDIA APPLICATIONS

The support that database management systems provide multimedia applications can be broadly classified into two categories:

- Support for storage/retrieval of multimedia objects (query by reference)
- Support for content-based querying (query by content)

Database management systems that provide storage/retrieval of multimedia objects face a variety of technical issues:

- **New capacity requirements.** Multimedia objects are orders of magnitude larger than coded data items.
- **New user interfaces with delivery attributes.** Some multimedia objects, like audio and video, have special requirements for guaranteed real-time capture and playback. Many systems skirt this issue by treating the real-time object as a file and requiring that the client copy the file completely into the client filespace before playback. Some systems provide the ability to stream or buffer multimedia objects through various communication network channels, some of which offer real-time delivery guarantees.
- **New processing requirements.** While simple store and retrieve operations on a multimedia object are not particularly difficult, augmenting the standard relational operators to cover large multimedia objects presents some new design options. For example, a ''SELECT *'' operator that returns four rows, each containing a video, will not delight the user if all videos are played back simultaneously!

- **New data placement requirements.** Multimedia objects may impose new requirements for relation partitioning and storage hierarchy placement (for example, optical disk).

- **New database administrator options.** Multimedia introduces new compression and decompression options, as well as the occasional need to ignore read-only multimedia objects during archives and back-ups.

Database management systems that provide content-based querying face all of these issues, as well as new challenges:

- **Support for user-defined types and functions.** Since the database vendor cannot anticipate all the algorithms that might be used to compute on multimedia objects, the vendor must provide techniques for database users to define new data types and identify them to the database query optimizer and plan generator.

- **Support for defining and precomputing multimedia feature extracts and indices.**

- **Support for controlling and scheduling the invocation of user-defined types and functions.** User-defined functions may require special security handling, and running them in a parallel environment introduces new scheduling problems.

- **Support for multimodal queries.** When a sequence of operations on multimedia objects occurs, pipelining these multimedia operations can provide quantum speedups in processing.

7.3   PROGRAMMING A MULTIMEDIA DATABASE SYSTEM

The developer of a multimedia database system application faces four challenges:

- Defining new multimedia data types to the system
- Using these data types to create multimedia tables
- Loading multimedia objects and computing feature extracts
- Writing SQL queries, which include multimedia terms as predicates in the WHERE clause, and as projections (result materialization)

7.3.1   Defining New Multimedia Data Types

Each multimedia object is an instance of an application-defined abstract data type (ADT). Each ADT has one or more functions defined in it, which we called multimedia functions, abbreviated MMF. Suppose a programmer wants to define a new data type which is a face. The MM-SQL for this type specification is shown in Fig. 7.1.

```
CREATE VALUE TYPE FACE_IMAGE
(
    PUBLIC faceAttributes  FACE_EXTRACT  VIRTUAL SET WITH
                    createFaceExtract( face FACE_IMAGE )
                    <code invoking createFaceExtract()>,


    PUBLIC FUNCTION compareFace( this_image FACE_EXTRACT,
                    reference  FACE_EXTRACT ) RETURNS Real
                    <code invoking compareFaceExtract()>,
    PUBLIC FUNCTION convertGrayScale( face FACE_IMAGE )
                    RETURNS FACE_IMAGE
                    <code converting to gray scale>
);
```

Figure 7.1   Face data type definition.

Each method, or MMF, in the FACE_IMAGE ADT operates on one or more attributes of the ADT. One such method, **compareFace**(), is used to compute a distance metric between two faces.[2] This function accepts two parameters:

1. The image in the database that is to be evaluated.
2. A sample, or reference, image used to compare against other images in the database.

For many multimedia data types, computation does not occur on the base object but rather on information extracted from the raw object. This information is called a feature extract. A base object may have multiple feature extracts. For example, a picture can have color feature extracts, texture extracts, or objects-in-picture extracts. Note that feature extracts can be either at a low semantic level (like color extracts, which are based on easily computed representational attributes of the picture) or at a high semantic level (like determining what people are in a picture).

Each derived feature extract is represented as an attribute, such as the *faceAttributes* attribute shown in the FACE_IMAGE data type. In this case, the attribute is defined as a FACE_EXTRACT data type with two available functions: **createFaceExtract**() and **compareFaceExtract**(). The MM-SQL for this type specification is shown in Fig. 7.2. These are the functions that understand the semantics of the feature extracts. Since the *faceAttributes* attribute is a derived attribute in the FACE_IMAGE ADT definition, the deriving function must also be indicated. By using the VIRTUAL declaration in Fig. 7.1, the deriving function is specified using the SET WITH definition.[3] In this example, the derived attribute

---

[2]The Face data type definition has place holders for the functions' code. In the case of C/C++ code, the object code is loaded through an *install* data definition language construct. SQL3 does not define this interface.

[3]The SQL3 standard may abandon the "VIRTUAL SET WITH" syntax for declaring a virtual attribute. In such the case, the attribute is set using normal function invocation syntax.

```
CREATE VALUE TYPE FACE_EXTRACT
(
  PUBLIC extract   Real(1600),


  PUBLIC FUNCTION createFaceExtract( face FACE_IMAGE )
                  RETURNS  FACE_EXTRACT
                  <code to do feature extraction>,
  PUBLIC FUNCTION compareFaceExtract( this_image FACE_EXTRACT,
                  reference  FACE_EXTRACT ) RETURNS Real
                  <code to compare feature extracts>
);
```

Figure 7.2   Face data type definition.

faceAttributes is set (populated) with the function **createFaceExtract**(). This function takes the current ADT object as a parameter and sets the ADT's *faceAttributes* attribute with face characteristics of the object. The feature extract definition allows storage space for 1600 "Real" data types to represent the feature extract.

7.3.2   Using These Data Types to Create Multimedia Tables

Once the appropriate definitions for ADTs are in place, the application author can then use these types as columns in a relational table. For example, the FACE_IMAGE data type can be used to construct a relation of information about known or suspected terrorists, as is shown in Fig. 7.3.

7.3.3   Loading Multimedia Objects and Computing Feature Extracts

Once the type definitions are in place, the next step in the process of creating a multimedia database is to populate it by loading the multimedia objects. During this step, physical design decisions (e.g., object placement) and performance decisions (e.g., index selection) become important.

In addition, the load process is an appropriate time for computing feature extracts on multimedia objects. The feature extracts themselves must be stored, and decisions must be made about feature extract indices.

```
CREATE TABLE terrorists( name char(40), face FACE_IMAGE, ...)
...
```

Figure 7.3   Relational table with multimedia datatype as column.

```
SET ANSWER_SET MAX_RETURN=5


SELECT name, face, compareFace(face..faceAttributes,
                              targetFace..faceAttributes)
FROM    terrorists
WHERE   compareFace(face..faceAttributes,
                    targetFace..faceAttributes) < 0.05
ORDER BY 3 ASC
```

Figure 7.4   MM-SQL fragment—Predicate use of MMF.

7.3.4 Writing SQL Queries That Include Multimedia Terms

With all table definitions and objects in place, the application author can next use MM-SQL to write queries. Multimedia functions can be used in two places in SQL3 queries. One use is within a SELECT statement as a predicate in the WHERE clause. The other is as part of result materialization (e.g., projection).

For example, an application might be written to compare the faces of people passing through security systems at an international airport to a database of known or suspected terrorists. In this face recognition system, a database query is generated when each person steps onto a metal detector floorboard where the camera angle and duration of face exposure are known and can be controlled. Such things as hats and sunglasses can be removed by the security personnel to ensure adequate face exposure. For each person passing through the metal detector, the system returns the top N matches in the terrorist database. For each record returned, the system also computes a distance measure. If the distance measure is sufficiently small (the person walking through the metal detector seems to match the image of a known terrorist), then the application can notify appropriate security personnel.

A MM-SQL query that returns at most the top five matches to a target face is shown in Fig. 7.4. This example illustrates an optimizer *pragma*,[4] which is an indication to the *answer set* manager that at most five answers should be returned. If there are more than five matches in the answer set, then the first five in the set are returned. Since the set is in ascending order, the top five matches are returned. The "ORDER BY 3 ASC" says to order the returned tuples in ascending order based on the third column in the projection list. The function **compareFace**() returns the difference between a current face and the target face. In this case, all faces within a distance of 0.05 of the target face meet the predicate MMF's condition.

In addition, since the function signature of **compareFace**() expects two FACE_EXTRACT parameters to be passed to the function, the query passes the references of the

---

[4]Pragmas are optimizer directives explicitly specified by the application/user. In this case, the "answer set" pragma is not defined in the SQL3 draft. It limits the returned answers to a subset of the answer set.

```
SELECT name, convertGrayScale(face)
FROM   terrorists
WHERE  compareFace(face..faceAttributes,
       targetFace..faceAttributes) < 0.05
```

Figure 7.5   MM-SQL fragment—Projection use of MMF.

FACE_IMAGE ADT attribute names. Accessing ADT attributes is accomplished by using the two-dot notation, *face..faceAttributes*.[5] In this case, *face* is the ADT, and *faceAttributes* is an attribute of that ADT. This technique distinguishes ADT attribute references from normal relational tuple variables.

An example of the use of an MMF as a projection qualifier on multimedia objects is shown in Fig. 7.5, in which qualifying tuples return the black and white version of color images in the terrorist database. Since the optimizer pragma has been removed from this same example, all matches within a 0.05 distance of the target face will be returned.

7.4 TERADATA ARCHITECTURE FOR MULTIMEDIA APPLICATIONS

To support content-based analysis, we have extended the Teradata relational database engine with multimedia capabilities. This new database is called the Teradata Multimedia DBMS. A two-tier server architecture shown in Fig. 7.6 provides the missing functionality needed to support multimedia applications. The four components of the Teradata Multimedia DBMS architecture are

1. A Federated Coordinator
2. A Relational Database Manager
3. A Multimedia Object Manager
4. A Real-Time Object Manager

7.4.1 Federated Coordinator

The first architectural component, the Federated Coordinator, is an MM-SQL processor. MM-SQL is a Teradata dialect of the SQL3 query language standard that supports user-defined functions (UDFs) and a subset of abstract data type (ADT) capabilities [4]. MM-SQL allows a user to specify and invoke user-defined functions in both the predicate and projection parts of an SQL statement. The Federated Coordinator also coordinates three types of underlying resource managers, as shown in Fig. 7.6 [5].

---

[5]The SQL3 draft is not clear on what type of dot notation will be used for ADT attributes.

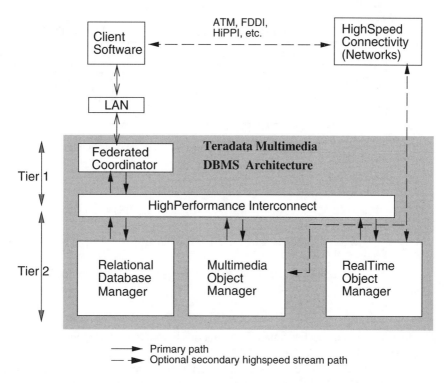

Figure 7.6   Teradata multimedia database architecture.

The Federated Coordinator, which is the entry point into the Teradata Multimedia Database system, has four functions:

1. Query decomposition: splitting an MM-SQL query into queries for each of the underlying resource servers
2. Query planning: optimizing the planned order of invocations and materializations of results
3. Query execution control and transaction management
4. Selection of appropriate communication pathways

The Federated Coordinator parses and splits a MM-SQL3 query into the appropriate relational and multimedia query parts. Before generating an execution plan, the query parts are optimized based on such factors as object-relational joins, network costs, data location, query caches, MMFs in the predicate, and pragmas. Once optimized, an execution plan is generated, referred to as *execution-steps*, and dispatched. To control the parallel execution of resource managers, the Federated Coordinator manages the query execution using the *X/Open distributed transaction processing* application programming interface (API) [6].

Alphanumeric Attributes				Multimedia Attributes	
patient_id	patient_name	age	scan_date	mri_scan	audio_notes
4078	McDonald	59	061596	<MRIIcon>	<Audio_icon>
⋮		⋮		⋮	

Figure 7.7   Multimedia patient relational table.

```
SELECT patient_name, age, rotateMRI(mri_scan, 0.45)
FROM   patients
WHERE  age > 45 AND FindTumor(mri_scan) > 0.13
```

Figure 7.8   SQL query containing predicate and projection MMFs.

In many ways, the Federated Coordinator is similar to numerous heterogeneous object managers [5].

The Federated Coordinator runs queries in two passes. The first pass evaluates predicates in the WHERE clause. These may include predicates on both alphanumeric data and multimedia objects. At the end of the first pass, the system returns a results table in which icons are displayed in the multimedia columns. (The icons either are defined by the user when creating the ADT or are defaults displayed by the system.)

In the second pass, the system retrieves the value of a selected object when its associated icon is selected (e.g., by point-and-click). The system may also evaluate any projection MMFs at this point. The object is then presented to the user/application via the appropriate displayer on the client.

Suppose that a database has been created which contains patient records, as illustrated in Fig. 7.7. Each record in this table represents one patient.

Next, suppose that the MM-SQL statement in Fig. 7.8 is executed. This example requests the patient's name, age, and rotated MRI scan for each patient who is over 45 and has a tumor size greater than 0.13 cm.

In this example, the Federated Coordinator begins by retrieving all tuples from the table *patients*, where the *age* is greater than 45. Because a MMF appears in the SQL predicate (**FindTumor**()), this MMF is invoked during the first pass to further qualify the results set. The Federated Coordinator does this by forwarding all the resulting *mri_scan* attribute OIDs[6] from the qualifying relational tuples to the Multimedia Object Manager, which runs the MMF to further qualify each tuple by determining if the MRI scan contains

[6]Even though multimedia objects are stored in the object manager, their OIDs are stored in the relational table attribute column representing the object.

patient_name	age	mri_scan
McDonald	59	\<MRIIcon\>
Peterson	62	\<MRIIcon\>
Johnson	55	\<MRIIcon\>

Figure 7.9 Results of the QUERY.

tumors that are larger than 0.13 cm. Ordinarily, predicates on traditional coded data are evaluated first. Next, the predicates on multimedia data are evaluated, since these can be computationally much more complex.

At the end of the first pass, the system returns the results table shown in Fig. 7.9.

An end user may inspect this table and wish to see the full representation (as opposed to the icon) for a particular patient. Clicking on the icon causes the Federated Coordinator to issue a request to materialize the multimedia object. In cases where one or more MMFs are in the SQL projection list, they are invoked on the object during this second pass. In the example in Fig. 7.8, the projection UDF **rotateMRI**() is performed on the *mri_scan* attribute object when it is retrieved for viewing in the second pass.

7.4.2 Relational Database Manager

The second architectural component of the system is a relational database system. Any SQL2 entry-level database server can be used for this component [7,8]. This server accepts SQL commands and generates data streams of tuples in response. Multimedia objects are treated as references in the relational table. These references, called ObjectIDs or OIDs, point to multimedia objects stored in one of the two multimedia resource managers.

The Federated Coordinator was designed to be nonintrusive to the database system. By this, we mean that there are no ''back doors'' between the Federated Coordinator and the relational database. For the rest of this chapter, we assume that an MPP-based Teradata DBMS is used as the relational database component.

7.4.3 Multimedia Object Manager

The third architectural component of the Teradata Multimedia DBMS, and the main focus of the rest of this chapter, is a Multimedia Object Manager. This resource manager stores, retrieves, and manipulates non-real-time multimedia objects [9]. Some multimedia functions (MMFs) are part of the base multimedia object system; these are called system-defined functions (SDFs). The Multimedia Object Manager is also ''programmable.'' Users can develop their own user-defined functions (UDFs) on multimedia objects and add those to the Multimedia Object Manager's Multimedia Function Library. When the Federated Coordinator processes an MM-SQL query, it creates a plan that requests the storage, retrieval, or manipulation of multimedia objects in the Multimedia Object Manager. The Federated Coordinator can cause the Multimedia Object Manager to run a program that invokes SDFs or UDFs.

7.4.4 Real-Time Object Manager

The fourth architectural component of the Teradata Multimedia DBMS is a real-time object manager. Objects that have real-time delivery constraints, like video and audio, can be placed in third-party video or audio servers controlled by the Federated Coordinator. In this case, a query to the Federated Coordinator produces a results table containing columns referencing objects in a video or audio server. A request to play back each object results in a request to the video or audio server, using Federated Coordinator playback options.

If a system designer wants to compute on audio or video objects stored in a Real-Time Object Manager, the object must first be copied into the Multimedia Object Manager. Indexing of audio or video can be done ''off-line,'' and the results used later as part of a query to ''find all videos containing the following keyword.'' The Multimedia Object Manager stores and computes on keywords during the first pass of the Federated Coordinator. Playback in real time is part of the second pass and may stream objects directly from the Real-Time Object Manager to the Client.

7.4.5 System Configuration Options

The Teradata Multimedia DBMS provides several options for system configuration. Figure 7.10 shows the mapping of the components of the Teradata Multimedia DBMS onto a sample NCR MPP hardware server platform. The Federated Coordinator and some parts of the Teradata DBMS, such as the Interface Processors (IFPs), run on the nodes at the top of the picture; these components are needed for query compilation. Query processing, done by the Teradata runtime engine as well as the Multimedia Object Manager, appears on the nodes in the lower part of the figure.

The most interesting system configuration options are available when the Teradata DBMS is chosen as the relational database component, since the Teradata DBMS and the Multimedia Object Manager share several characteristics:

- Both run on virtual processors (vprocs). Each vproc has its own CPU, memory, and disk space. The number of vprocs is configurable and not necessarily equal to the number of physical CPUs. Each vproc operates independently and in parallel with other vprocs.

- Both run on symmetric multiprocessing (SMP) or massively parallel processing (MPP) hardware architectures.

- Both are shared-nothing architectures [10] that maximize parallel computation through logical vertical partitioning of resources [9].

As shown in Fig. 7.10, the number of nodes used by the Teradata database engine and the Multimedia Object Manager are independently configurable and based on expected relation or set cardinalities and object sizes. Each resource manager may be scaled *independently* of the other by adding more processing nodes.

In addition, because individual hardware faults have a higher probability of occurrence on high-end systems, these systems have stringent data availability requirements. To improve availability, each resource manager has multiple hardware data paths to each physical storage device, shown for simplicity as a single dashed line in the figure. This technique

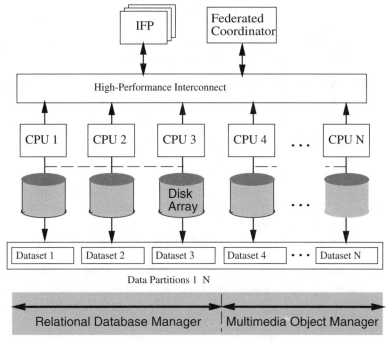

Number of nodes are configurable and scalable per manager type.

Figure 7.10   Shared-nothing database architecture.

was initially introduced in the Teradata database to increase data availability in case of path failures (e.g., a lost physical node) [7]. Each physical node can access all disk arrays within its clique, where the total number of nodes is typically divided into cliques of three to four SMP nodes.

Using vprocs as addressable logical processors improves data availability by making the system more manageable in system reconfiguration and more fault-resistant. This flexibility allows addressable vprocs to be moved between physical nodes within the same clique during hardware faults and between cliques when the machine scales [9]. Cliques of size C are configured with $C * (C - 1)$ vprocs, where each node contains $\frac{C*(C-1)}{C}$, or M vprocs. Cliques of multiple processing nodes with failover capabilities can be defined to handle individual processor failures. To handle cases of storage device failures (e.g., a failed disk), data redundancy may be specified. Fast failover techniques to reestablish data addressability are used to mitigate failures.

7.5   MULTIMEDIA OBJECT MANAGER OVERVIEW

The Multimedia Object Manager stores, retrieves, and analyzes the content of multimedia data on SMP or MPP platforms. The goal of the Multimedia Object Manager development team was to build a highly reusable key technology platform that leverages expertise in both the Teradata parallel database system and core AT&T Bell Labs competencies in multimedia.

In this section, we cover the Multimedia Object Manager design principles and describe this component of the Teradata Multimedia DBMS in more detail.

7.5.1 Multimedia Object Manager Design Principles

NCR's experience with the massively parallel Teradata database has proven useful in designing the Multimedia Object Manager. The Teradata database is the world's largest commercial decision support system (DSS), consisting of more than 4 terabytes of on-line user data at our largest customer site. Experience with this database shows that careful attention to scale-up and speed-up during design is important, since users inevitably capture more data than initially expected and the applications written against these data grow increasingly complex over time.

Accordingly, the design goals for the Multimedia Object Manager were:

- To create a flexible software platform that is application-independent and extensible.
- To use programmable agents to provide flexible approaches to computation.
- To provide content-based object analysis through system-defined multimedia functions.
- To provide extensibility through support for user-defined multimedia functions.
- To support an easy-to-use file-system-like API for access to very large objects.
- To give administrators extensive support for large object data placement.

7.5.2 Multimedia Object Manager Architecture

Figure 7.11 shows a high-level picture of the Multimedia Object Manager architecture. The three main components of the Multimedia Object Manager are the following:

- The Computation Engine, which launches agents and controls their computation
- The Multimedia Object Storage Engine, which stores and retrieves multimedia objects under the direction of agents
- The Multimedia Function (MMF) Library, which contains all user-defined and system-defined multimedia function definitions

These components run on top of a special-purpose operating system layer, which runs on top of Unix in both the SMP and MMP configurations.

7.5.3 Computation Engine

The computation engine uses programmable agents as its primary approach to controlling computation [11,12,13]. Each program submitted by a Multimedia Object Manager driver (e.g., by the Federated Coordinator) is interpreted within the Computation Engine and can cause one or more threads of computing activity in the system. Program execu-

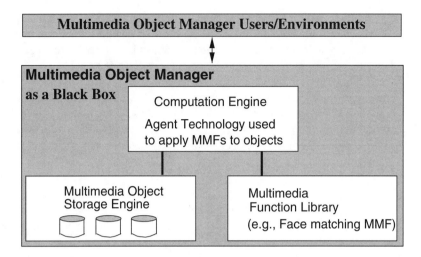

Figure 7.11 Architecture—Multimedia Object Manager as a black box.

tion is accomplished through the use of agents. Before being dispatched, the agents are programmed with the sequence of objects to visit and what operations to perform on each object. Each agent attempts to invoke the UDFs as close to the physical location of multimedia objects as possible to prevent large object movement on the interconnect. The idea is to move computation instead of data.

Each agent runs in one or more vprocs. A vproc is a virtual processor. Each node in the system may have one or more vprocs. For a sequential program, the agent starts at one vproc and sequentially processes objects at that location. When an operation on a nonlocal object is discovered, the interpreter at that vproc packages up the program context and *migrates* the agent to another vproc at a remote site, where computation on that vproc's interpreter continues. In a program that includes set operators on multimedia objects, the agent *clones* itself (copies itself onto one or more remote vprocs). The operators are then invoked in parallel on all relevant vprocs.

The migration and cloning of agents provide a powerful model of computation for a parallel environment. Agent cloning is a form of a scatter operation. The results of all the cloned agents are returned to the cloning agent; this is a form of a gather operation. These scatter/gather operations can be done recursively by one or more cloned agents, forming a computational tree structure. As in the case of a tree structure, results propagate back to the root agent. The completion of the gathering operation returns the results to the Federated Coordinator initiating the request, where the results are merged with relational database query results.

This computation model offers several opportunities for computation placement optimization. Agent migration is used when an agent operation requires one or more objects not residing on the same vproc and the operands are all located at a remote location. In this case, the agent is moved along with its current state information; this is less costly than moving large multimedia objects over the interconnect. The migrating agent's context is piggybacked along with the event that is sent to its new location (vproc).

If an agent operation requires one local object and one or more objects that are remote, then either agent migration or remote object access (ROA) can be used. In the former case, agent migration occurs and the local object is attached so that computation may proceed at the remote vproc that contains the other operands. Alternatively, the optimizer may elect to keep the agent at the current vproc and issue a ROA for the remote object(s). In both cases, objects are moved over the interconnect. The decision of where to execute an agent is based on the cost of transmitting objects and agent context over the interconnect.

7.5.4 Multimedia Object Storage Engine

Objects in the system are maintained in a parallel persistent storage system. Object location is hidden from the external user. Furthermore, as the system is reconfigured, objects may move from one vproc to another transparently. To enhance performance and reliability, the storage system exploits parallelism, data availability, and partitioning strategies. Application data stay available despite hardware component failures by allowing objects to be accessed through adjacent physical nodes during node faults [9]. Also, to improve performance on various types of access patterns and to increase total storage capacity, several partitioning strategies can be used to distribute objects across the shared-nothing vprocs on the MPP [14].

The Multimedia Object Storage Engine is based on the Bell Labs Storage System (BeSS). BeSS provides persistent storage/allocation, concurrency control, and recovery [15,16,18]. The system's memory mapping techniques provide near-memory-speed pointer dereferences (for memory-resident objects). BeSS also offers extensive support for large objects, including capabilities for striping across disk volumes and efficient logging of byte ranges of large multimedia objects [9,17]. In addition, the server maintains a distributed cache on each physical node. The system manages both the cache coherency and the shared virtual memory addresses for the cache frames so that processes can map cache frames directly into their address space to eliminate unnecessary data copying. Security measures ensure that only appropriate data in the cache are accessed. This provides performance enhancements that not only eliminate data copying but also allow processes to access data cached on memory shared by other processes [15].

Objects in the Multimedia Object Storage Engine are grouped into directories. Each directory also specifies a physical set of vprocs to contain the objects in that directory. Objects in a directory share a Placement Policy, which specifies a function to map any object onto one vproc. In particular, each object is mapped first into an Object Key, then the Object Key is used to calculate a Placement Key, and finally a Placement Key is used to identify a vproc.

Users may specify their own functions for computing Object Keys. The type of Placement Policy used for a set of objects in a directory is specified by the creator of the table that uses those objects.

Several Placement Policies are supported:

- **Random.** An object is placed on a randomly selected vproc within the directory. No ObjectKey is required.

- **Hashing.** An ObjectKey is computed for the object. The ObjectKey is hashed using a system or user-defined hashing function to calculate a vproc.

- **Value Partitioning.** An ObjectKey is computed for the object. The space of Object-Keys is partitioned into disjoint subsets. All ObjectKeys in a partition map to the same PlacementKey, which may be further mapped to one or a set of vprocs.

Not all requests are best served by the same placement strategy. Both Random and Hashing Placement Policies result in roughly uniform distributions of objects across vprocs. Both are advantageous for queries that access sets of objects. For example, a UDF to compare a target fingerprint against a set of fingerprints might benefit from random placement of the fingerprint set across all vprocs, to maximize parallelism.

Value Partitioning is useful for UDFs with nonuniform object accesses, that is, UDFs that exhibit small working sets. In this case, remote object references can be avoided by ensuring that subsets of objects used together are colocated in the same vproc. Value Partitioning is well suited for range queries, where many parallel subqueries operate on subsets of the directory over different subranges. These subranges span a portion of the directory and can contain similar (or dissimilar) objects grouped near each other. Value Partitioning is also good for multidimensional spatial objects (also referred to as Spatial Partitioning), in which feature extracts are used as ObjectKeys. Similar objects, that is, those that are "close" to one another in 1-D, 2-D, or in general N-dimensional space, can be physically placed in storage according to their physical spatial representations.

Both the directory identifier and the object's Placement Key are part of the logical OID. The directory number and the Placement Key are logical, not physical. The system computes vprocs from Placement Keys dynamically, which handles the case of reconfiguration of vprocs. The remainder of the logical OID is used by the node's object storage manager to locate the object within the vproc. This scheme allows objects to be relocated. When a system scales, the system migrates objects physically to keep the load balanced without affecting existing OIDs.

7.5.5 Multimedia Function (MMF) Library

The Multimedia Library consists of system-defined functions (SDFs) and user-defined functions (UDFs).

SDFs are UDFs that have been system-certified, that is, guaranteed to conform to system rules about invocation, exception handling, and resource utilization. The database administrator may limit applications' access to SDFs (e.g., royalties may be charged or special permissions may be needed to use certain classes of SDFs). The system provides a library of SDF building blocks reusable as predicates or projections in SQL queries.

UDFs are not system-certified. Application developers typically write UDF algorithms on client systems in stand-alone test mode. When satisfied with their correctness, these developers use utilities to load UDF code into the system. Since UDFs represent untrusted code, security information is associated with these functions, indicating that they require special system handling at invocation.

Initially, the Multimedia Function Library contains SDFs that have low semantic power. Examples include compression and decompression algorithms for video and image objects, simple keyword searching for text objects, and color or texture matching for images. The Multimedia Function Library also contains full facilities for writing and installing higher-powered UDFs. As multimedia technology matures and higher-level semantic algorithms become widespread, semantically rich algorithms will be added to the multimedia library as SDFs. These may include algorithms to index a video for instances of a certain person, to search text using semantic nets for associations, and to match on image shape or content.

An application developer loads and executes UDFs in the multimedia database to achieve good performance, as opposed to defining, linking, and invoking them in the application. By executing the UDFs in the server, the application benefits from set-based parallel function invocations over all appropriate objects on all relevant vprocs on range queries. Executing UDFs in the server also minimizes the need to send large amounts of multimedia data over a local or wide area network to be analyzed by the application.

7.6 CONTENT-BASED RETRIEVAL

Since multimedia objects may be "uninteresting" without the extraction of semantic content, object attributes (features) are used to represent important characteristics of an object. Some features, such as an image's width and intensity or the title of a video, are easily encoded and stored in traditional relational databases. Other features are more complex and cannot be represented easily within a single relational table entry. Examples of such complex features include facial characteristics, voice patterns in an audio file, pressure characteristics of a handwritten signature, fingerprint characteristics, and time-series information. From a database perspective, these features are derived objects, and their primary value is that it is easier to compute on these features than on the base objects directly.

Suppose a user of a system is looking for image objects in a database that contains sunsets. One method for solving this query is to have a human annotate each image with text describing its content. Another approach is to specify an ADT of type *image* which may include computationally derived features such as color histograms, color means, texture maps, and shapes. A query *find an image* that *"contains a sunset like this one"* could use one, all, or some combination of these features to compute pairwise distances between the target object and each object of type image in the relation. Suppose a programmer decides to use color means. Using the RGB spectrum, one can compute a 3-D feature extract from each 2-D image, $f_i = \{r_i, g_i, b_i\}$, where r_i is the red mean intensity of the image, g_i is the green, and b_i is the blue, respectively. When comparing two images, the system calculates the "distance" between them using their feature extracts. If the distance is small, then the pictures are a potential "match." If the distance is larger than some threshold, then the pictures are not. Using color means, a query can find all images that *potentially* have sunsets in them, represented by a high concentration of red, with low levels for blue and green, as specified by a sample picture. If a picture in the database has too much blue or green in it, then the feature distance between it and the sample image will be high, and it will not be included in the response set.

Although this example is oversimplified, it illustrates the use of feature extracts to reformulate a query on base objects. Image recognition is a very active research area in its infancy, but early products are appearing that have this kind of generalized rudimentary searching capability [22,23,32], or specific capabilities for geographic information systems [1,24]. As research improves, new algorithms providing deeper semantic content extraction and computation will make advanced queries feasible.

The rest of this section provides an overview of content-based retrieval. Topics include feature extraction, querying on features, acceleration of queries via indices, and architecture to support content-based queries. For a more comprehensive treatment of this information, see [29].

7.6.1 Feature Extraction

The essence of feature extraction is to map a multimedia object to a point in some N-dimensional space [33]. The dimensionality depends on the type of feature extraction. For example, using the color mean image extraction mentioned earlier, we find three features in the extract: the levels of red, green, and blue means, respectively. The point can be expressed as a vector (20,80,80), a point in 3-D space. A fingerprint, for example, can be encoded as a 50 integer vector, representing a point in 50-D space.

An object may have one or more feature extracts. For example, an image may have feature extracts representing brightness and color, shape measures describing an object's shape characteristics, and texture measures used to discriminate between the surface finish of a smooth or coarsely textured object/image. In general, a domain-specific *feature extraction algorithm* extracts an N-dimensional feature extract from the object, where there is one dimension per feature. Each feature extract represents an attribute of the object in some N-dimensional space.

The user must specify a feature extraction algorithm to compute each feature extract. Feature extraction is usually done off-line, since it may be computationally intense and would have a dramatic impact on query response times. Feature extraction during object insertion into the database, or in background mode after insertion, is preferred.

If an object is updated, its feature extracts may need to be regenerated since the key features of the object may have changed.

7.6.2 Querying on Features

Users can make various queries on feature extracts. These depend on the dimensionality of the feature extract. In the 1-D case, one can ask if a given point is in an existing set, whether a given point is in a given range of values, what points lie in a given range, what the distance is between two points, and how many points lie within a certain distance of a given point. In the 2-D case, one can ask if a given point is in an existing set, whether a point is in a rectangle specified by two other points, or in a circle defined by a target point and a radius, whether two regions intersect, and so on. In 3-D, the analogous queries deal with boxes and spheres. In general, there are both point and spatial queries.

Multidimensional querying is an active research field; additional information about point, range, all-pair, and nearest neighbor queries may be found in [25,26,29].

An important characteristic of these queries, unlike traditional database queries, is that they are necessarily ''fuzzy.'' For example, consider two fingerprints from the same finger of the same person, taken at different points in time. The raw images of these fingerprints are likely to be quite similar, but they will not match, pixel for pixel. That means that there will be some small difference between the feature extracts that are computed from these

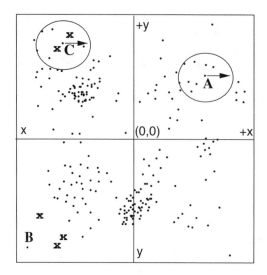

Figure 7.12   Range and nearest-neighbor queries in two-dimensional space.

images. The consequence is that exact match queries must be treated as range queries, with some small distance threshold specified for "exact" matching.

There are many ways of computing distance functions. A typical choice for determining the distance between two such feature points A and B is the Euclidean distance:

$$\text{Distance}(A, B) = \sqrt{(a_1 - b_1)^2 + \cdots + (a_n - b_n)^2}$$

In some cases, the feature extract cannot be treated as a logical vector of feature measurements where the Euclidean distance provides the relative closeness in promixity of the two points. A feature extract f_i may often be logically viewed as a vector of vectors. In such case, there is no direct mapping to a point in N-dimensional space. A typical choice for determining the difference between two feature extracts in this case is the Cartesian product (cross product), $f_x \times f_y$, where the vector of vectors is viewed as a set of vectors. The Euclidean distance is taken on all ordered pairs whose first component comes from f_x and whose second comes from f_y.

Figure 7.12 illustrates sample feature points in a 2-D feature space. Such a picture might represent the state of a database of multimedia objects whose 2-D feature extracts have been plotted. Note that some of the feature extract points are near each other, forming clusters of points. Other parts of the space may be sparse.

Given a way of computing distances between feature extracts in some N-dimensional space, we can now create queries on features. There are two techniques, which we call

- *Range* (R) queries
- *Nearest-neighbor* (NN) queries

In a range query, the R determines the circumference around a reference point. For example, a query may ask to see all fingerprints within a certain proximity of a reference fingerprint. The number of matches returned is determined by the number of points falling in the circumference dictated by R.

In a nearest-neighbor query, the parameter specifies the NN points closest to the reference point. For example, a query may be ask to see the top 10 fingerprint matches to a reference fingerprint; NN will limit the answer set to 10 points, independently of how close they may be to the reference point.

Figure 7.12 illustrates three queries. First, a range query is shown for point A to illustrate a result that returns all points within a given distance R from A. The nearest-neighbor query on point B returns the $NN = 3$ nearest-neighbors of point B. A combination range— nearest-neighbor query using reference point C and $NN = 2$—returns only the nearest two points to point C, provided they are within the specified R distance.

Hence, R is used to bound the degree of distance between the returned points and a reference point, and NN is used to control the number of matches. A combination of the two can be used to give the best precision and recall [29]. R and NN can be used to tune queries to achieve appropriate measures of recall and precision, two important concepts in pattern matching. These have been defined [29] as

$$\text{Recall} = \frac{\text{Retrieved\_and\_Relevant}}{\text{Total\_Relevant\_in\_Collection}} \tag{1}$$

$$\text{Precision} = \frac{\text{Retrieved\_and\_Relevant}}{\text{Total\_Retrieved}} \tag{2}$$

Equation (1) defines the percentage of relevant features returned from the database, whereas Eq. (2) defines the percentage of relevant features from the retrieved set.

Optimal algorithms will yield 1.0 (100%) on both recall and precision. Algorithms that yield 100% on recall but poorly on precision will produce many false positives, although no relevant points will be ignored. Algorithms that do poorly on recall will ignore many relevant features. As recall increases, precision tends to decrease. A good algorithm will maintain 100% recall, while minimizing false positives, which indicates that precision should also be close to 100%.

Figure 7.13 illustrates this concept using sets, where A is all features in the collection; set B is all relevant features in the collection; set C is the set of features retrieved by the

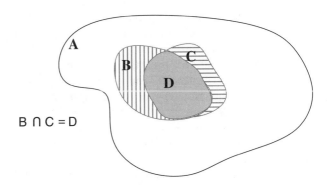

$B \cap C = D$

Figure 7.13 Recall and precision sets.

query; and set D is the set of relevant (''correct'') features retrieved. The best algorithms will result in $C \supseteq B$, such that $D \equiv B$ and the difference between B and C is minimized.

For example, suppose we are interested in *all books on database hashing*. Suppose the query returned 20 books on hashing, but only 16 were on *database hashing*. In addition, suppose this query missed seven books that were on *scatter distribution*, which is an old name for *database hashing*. The query's precision is:

$$\text{Precision} = \frac{16}{20} = 80\%$$

The query's recall is:

$$\text{Recall} = \frac{16}{16 + 7} = 69\%$$

Note that 20% of the books returned were false positives. However, the query's recall was only 69%; it did not retrieve 31% of the books that were of interest. In this case, a precision of 80% is offset by the low recall of the matching algorithm, which indicates that we will miss many features that we are interested in.

A query's recall and precision is determined by both the effectiveness of the feature extraction algorithm itself, along with the R and NN used to control the number of points matching the reference point when running the query.

7.6.3 Acceleration of Queries Via Indices

Since feature extracts are data, they can be indexed much like database keys so that computations on feature extracts run quickly. In most cases, feature extracts map directly to a point in space. However, feature extracts may be more complex than described earlier, and in many cases are logically represented as a vector of vectors, sometimes called a codebook.

Indexing high-dimension feature extracts requires spatial partitioning and indexing strategies. Various forms of spatial access methods (SAMs) exist, such as the following:

- Space-filling curves [29]
- R-trees (and their variants) [28]

Two-dimensional methods like z-ordering, linear quadtrees, and Hilbert curve techniques are used in the first approach and work well in two-dimensional space, but fail to scale well to higher dimensions. R-trees seem more promising and are more robust in higher-dimensional space.[7] An R-tree is an extension of the B-tree for multidimensional objects, where objects are represented by their minimum bounding rectangle (MBR). The number of points required to represent the MBR is its dimensionality. For example, in two-dimensional space the MBR is represented by two points, (x_{lower}, y_{lower}) and (x_{upper}, y_{upper}), for the opposite upper and lower corners of the rectangle.

R-tree nonleaf nodes contain (*ptr, MBR*) pairs, where *ptr* is a pointer to the child node and *MBR* is the rectangle that covers all objects in its subtree. Leaf nodes contain (*obj_id, MBR*) pairs, where *obj_id* is a pointer to the object and *MBR* represents the object in some dimensional space, which we later refer to as a point in N-dimensional space.

---

[7]Spatial dimensions above 20 are still a research area.

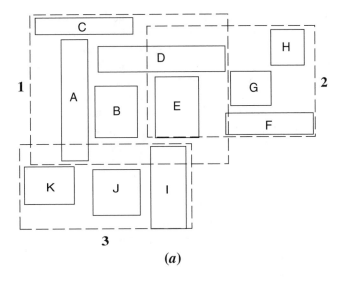

(a)

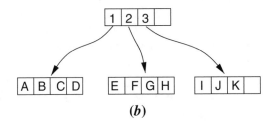

(b)

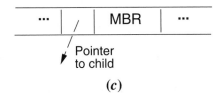

(c)

Figure 7.14   R-tree spatial access method.

Figure 7.14 illustrates two levels of MBRs for nonleaf R-tree nodes: (*a*) shows the logical MBRs in 2-D space, (*b*) shows the associated physical structure of the R-tree where nodes are disk pages, and (*c*) shows the key/value pair of each nonleaf node. The primary innovation of R-trees over B-trees is that nonleaf nodes may overlap, which guarantees good space utilization and tree balance.

The downside to using R-trees is that the feature extract must be mapped to an N-dimensional point, which is represented as an MBR. In N-dimensional space, the feature extract can represent a collection of spatial data types {*Point, Line, Region,...*}. Not all extracts map directly. This requires a feature space reduction algorithm, which is lossy and may lead to false positives. However, feature space reduction will not reduce the query recall but may affect precision, since false positives may be returned from the index access. To overcome this downside, an additional mapping can be kept by the object manager, which maps the reduced feature extract back to its original form.

One recently suggested approach to feature space reduction is the *FastMap* algorithm, used to map a high-dimension feature extract to a lower N-dimensional point [27]. This approach defines minimum bounding rectangles (MBRs) in a lower dimension space so that they can now be indexed. This FastMap technique loses some information with respect to distance maintenance (some false positives will be searched), but, overall, this is an improvement since high-dimension feature extracts cannot be indexed efficiently. In this case, large dataset search spaces are drastically reduced over straight sequential scans. The key to the FastMap technique is to produce a mapping giving the best distance-maintaining function between the original feature extracts and their corresponding points in some N-dimensional space. The FastMap technique can be applied to the extract to reduce its dimensionality for indexing. However, since this technique is lossy, the original extract can be kept for actual comparisons. In this case, a secondary mapping would be required to map the returned points from the index to the original feature extract. This technique would allow indexing to drastically reduce a large search space but allow the system to adequately throw out false positives returned from the spatial index.

7.6.4 Teradata Architecture to Support Content Queries

We conclude this section with a description of how the Teradata Multimedia DBMS has been extended to support content queries. Figure 7.15 illustrates the connection between ADT object definitions and the corresponding objects, both base objects (in this case, images) as well as the feature extract objects, and their indices.

Each ADT declaration defines attributes for each feature extract that can be used as a term in a query. Figure 7.15 shows a user-specified table attribute labeled *Image* as well an *Image Type* specification, which contains several UDFs. In this example, UDF_2 computes on two feature extracts, so these two feature extracts must be defined as types also, including UDF definitions on them to do feature extraction as well as comparison for the feature extract definitions f_1 and f_2.

When a row is inserted into the table, the image attribute value in the row is assigned an object id, OID, and is loaded into the Multimedia Object Manager. Since an index is kept on OIDs, it is also updated. Feature extraction UDFs UDF_{f11} and UDF_{f21} are run on the image to compute feature extract values, labeled O-f_1 and O-$f2$ in this figure. If indices have been specified on the feature extracts, these are updated as part of the load step. When UDF_2 is invoked in a predicate query, it will invoke UDFs UDF_{f12} and UDF_{f22} to do the actual feature extract comparisons.

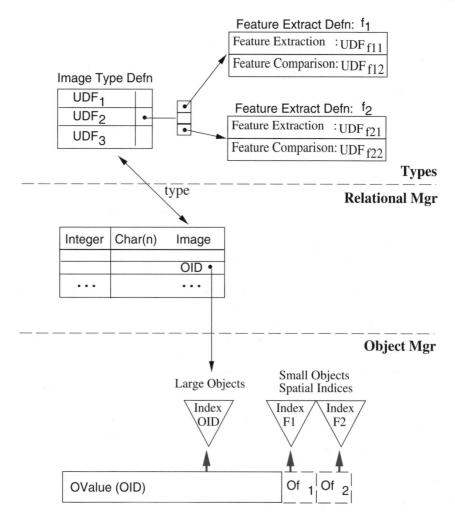

Figure 7.15   Object linkage to feature extracts.

The user must also specify, during setup, indexing and placement options for all objects. Earlier we discussed Placement Policies for base objects. These can also be used for feature extracts. The feature extracts and their indices are not necessarily placed on the same vproc as the corresponding ADT object "O-Value (OID)," since they may be partitioned spatially if they are indexed.

When a query references an object attribute in a SQL predicate, perhaps as part of a range or nearest-neighbor query fragment, the system maps the UDF invocation onto the corresponding feature extracts and distance UDFs, using feature extract indices if available and feature extract values to compute answer sets.

```
SET ANSWER_SET MAX_RETURN=5


SELECT name, face, compareFace(face..faceAttributes,
                               targetFace..faceAttributes)
FROM   terrorists
ORDER BY 3 ASC
```

Figure 7.16   MM-SQL fragment.

Figure 7.1 showed the attribute *faceAttributes* derived by calling the function **create-FaceExtract**(). This SQL also shows that this attribute has a function **compareFaceExtract**() used to compare feature extracts between two facial images. The query shown here in Fig. 7.16 uses a nearest-neighbor of 5, while range defaulted to the whole search space. Earlier SQL fragments showed different combinations of nearest-neighbor and range. Figure 7.5 illustrates a query using a range of 0.05, and nearest-neighbor defaulted to the whole search space. Figure 7.4 showed a SQL fragment combining both a nearest-neighbor and range values.

Using Fig. 7.4 as an example, if we know that any distance greater than 0.05 between two faces is not a good match, then we can eliminate those matches without even looking at them. However, if we don't want to see any more than the best five matches, we can limit the answer space to within zero to five of the best potential matches. If no matches are returned, then there are no potential matches.

Finally, a query may update an ADT object with derived feature extracts. If this is done, a ripple effect occurs and all derived metadata (like feature extracts and their indices) must be recomputed or updated. The same holds true for new bulk-loaded ADT objects.

7.7 MULTIMODAL QUERIES

In addition to content-based retrieval of object attributes, the Teradata Multimedia DBMS supports multimodal transformations and computations on multimedia objects. ''Multimodal'' means that a query or update may require sequences of operations on more than one data type.

7.7.1 Multimodal Examples

A typical simple multimodal transformation is text to speech. Stored text can be synthesized as an audio file through the use of text-to-speech algorithms in the database. This example is accomplished through the use of a *text* MMF, which produces an instance of a new object of type *audio*, subtype *speech*.

A more complex multimodal example, which we will come back to later in this chapter, is the generation of ''talking heads'' by the database system. In this case, a text object is converted into synthesized speech and a face is ''morphed'' to create a video in which the

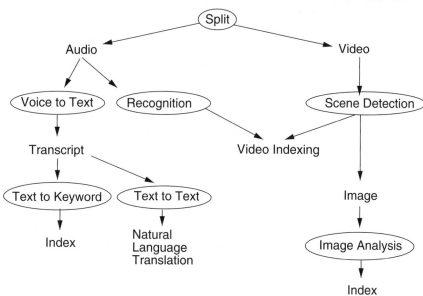

Figure 7.17 Data-type transformations on a videoconference.

lips match the speech. This multimodal example uses four data types: text, speech, image, and video.

A third example is shown in Fig. 7.17. In this case, the database system contains one or more videoconferences, which have been digitized and inserted in the database. Each videoconference has some number of coded attributes: for example, the TIME and DATE of the conference, perhaps also the LOCATION, the PARTICIPANTS, LANGUAGE, and TOPIC AREA.

In preprocessing the videoconference, the Multimedia Object Manager can create feature extracts and indices to accelerate later queries. For example, the audio portion of a video might be run through a speech recognizer, which might annotate the video with text. This text can be keyword-indexed. The audio portion might also be run through a voice recognizer that annotates the audio with the name of each person who spoke. Furthermore, the text might be run through a natural language translator that converts text from English to Chinese. This, too, might be indexed. The video channel can be preprocessed to do major scene detection, effectively dividing the video stream into a set of video snippets, each of which can be video-indexed. Each snippet might be run through a face recognizer that indexes the frames in which particular individuals are speaking. Using the video object's feature extracts, we can generate and accelerate the following types of queries:

- Retrieve a video starting at the location where "Alan Chow" first started talking.

- Retrieve all meetings that "Wayne Boyle" attended and the subject "Multimedia Object Manager" was discussed.

- Retrieve transcripts in Chinese for all videoconferences where "DEFECT 2789" was discussed by anyone.

If enough of these transformations can be done in real time, then applications like real-time teleconferencing between speakers of foreign languages with system-supplied language translation might become reality.

7.7.2 Multimodal Technical Challenges

From a database designer perspective, the following new requirements on the server are necessary to support multimodal queries:

- Transformational functions to convert objects of one data type into another
- Connection functions to "pipe" the output of one function to another
- Optimizing functions for multimodal graph execution
- Graphical or standard query creation facilities

7.7.2.1 Transformational Functions

To use the Teradata Multimedia DBMS to build multimodal applications, the Multimedia Function Library must be populated with some transformational functions. This set of functions can be used by application developers to bridge between data types and build sequences of operations. Sample transformational multimedia functions include

- Video to audio
- Audio to speech (screening out background noise)
- Speech to text
- Text to text (for example, natural language translation)
- Text to speech
- Speech to audio
- Audio and image sequence to video

Note that while each transformation is useful in its own right, the sequence of transformations provides many options for unique applications.

7.7.2.2 Connection Functions to Pipe Results

To build complex graphical representations of multimedia computation, the Multimedia Object Manager supports the ability to connect the inputs and outputs of different multimedia functions (MMFs) through Unix-like pipes. Data flows through the graph based on the concept of data-driven computation, which means computation is driven by the availability of data. Users can create graph structures of computation in which each vertex represents a MMF invocation and edges represent paths of data flow.

To support parallelism, the Multimedia Object Manager provides three new constructs:

- A broadcasting operator (scatter operation)
- A merge operator (gather operation)
- Pipes

The broadcast operator makes a copy of the data on its input edge to all instances of its output edge. The merge operator copies data on any input edge to the single output edge. Using these constructs, the user or system can dynamically alter multimodal graphs to provide parallel instances of agents running MMFs, thereby using the parallel compute and storage available in an SMP or MMP.

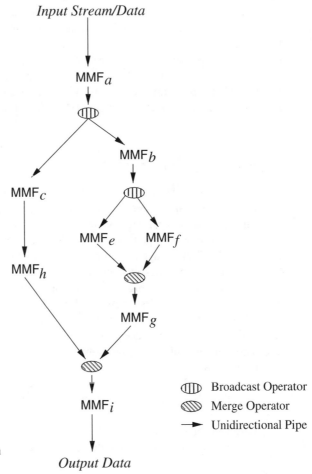

Figure 7.18   Multimodal connection graph.

Figure 7.18 shows an 8-vertex MMF graph that has been augmented with two broadcast and two merge vertices. The connectivity of each graph vertex is limited only by system resources. The Multimedia Object Manager does not limit the number of unidirectional edges on a vertex or the size of the graph.

A pipe supports one-way data flow with built-in flow control so that readers block if the pipe is empty and writers block if the pipe is full. A broadcasting operator sends identical copies of an incoming data stream to N outgoing one-way pipes; this assists in parallelizing computation. The merging operator collects N input data streams and demultiplexes the incoming data stream into an output stream.

7.7.2.3 *Optimization of Multimodal Graph Execution*

Multimodal graphs can be created either by the MM-SQL plan generator or by explicit, perhaps iconic, scripting languages. In either case, the system can optimize graphs by rewriting queries using a rule base of allowable optimizations. Both static analysis and dynamic, runtime-dependent optimizations are possible. For example, if a data type already has some feature extracts defined, these might be used to accelerate a query by rewriting the graph to use feature indices. Another static example is rewriting a query to reduce intermediate results. In the dynamic optimization case, the query might be mapped to lightly loaded vprocs, and prefixes or suffixes of the query graph can run on the client if the server is heavily loaded and the client can run the same MMFs.

7.8 TALKING AGENTS EXAMPLE

This chapter concludes with an example of how to use the Teradata SQL3 Multimedia DBMS to create ''talking agents,'' which illustrates the power of a multimodal system.

Studies on user experiences show that a ''talking head'' with an intelligible voice and lifelike video is more compelling and effective as a human–computer interface than a talking computer [30]. Talking agents can be used in kiosks, automatic teller machines, distance learning, training environments, and system management applications.

The creation of a talking agent multimodal application involves two processes, four data types, and eight UDFs (shown in Table 1.1). The two processes are Agent Creation and Talking Agent Generation, and the four data types are image, text, speech, and video.

The Agent Creation process involves creating a database of selectable human agents. Each agent that will ultimately be shown to an end user requires 17 images in this database, which forms the base image set from which mouth morphing is done. Each agent in the database is given an agentID, which is used in the second process.

The Talking Agent Generation process involves six steps, A through F, shown in Fig. 7.19.

Given a user-selectable agentID and some text, Talking Agent Generation involves a sequence of multimodal transformations resulting in a ''talking agent'' that can be played

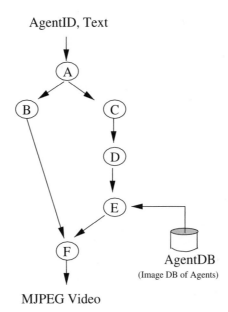

AgentID, Text

MJPEG Video

AgentDB
(Image DB of Agents)

Figure 7.19 *CreateTalkingAgent()* defined graph.

on a client platform. The process of creating a talking agent consists of transforming the existing agentID's images, along with the input text data, into a new data type called video. The UDFs on the four data types are shown in Table 7.1.

The Talking Agent Generation process is initiated by an application invoking the **CreateTalkingAgent**() function, as in Fig. 7.20.

The next sections describe the processes in more detail.

Table 7.1 Talking Agent User Defined Functions

Step	UDF	Input	Output	Type
1	CreateNewAgent	AgentDB, 17 Images	AgentID	Image
2	CreateTalkingAgent	AgentID, Text	M-JPEG Video	System
2A	TextToPhoneme	Text	PhonemeSeq	Text
2B	PhonemeToSpeech	PhonemeSeq	Audio	Speech
2C	PhonemeToViseme	PhonemeSeq	VisemeSeq	Speech
2D	StructDeformation	VisemeSeq, AgentID	WireFrameSeq	Image
2E	ImageSynthesis	AgentDB, WireFrameSeq	Video	Image
2F	AudioVideoSplice	Audio, Video	M-JPEG Video	Video

```
CREATE TABLE agent( name char(40), talkingAgent VIDEO, ...)
...


UPDATE agent
SET talkingAgent = CreateTalkingAgent(agentID, textFile);
...
```

Figure 7.20   Creating a Talking Agent.

7.8.1 Agent Creation

To generate lifelike talking heads, images of real people are used. (Studies are also underway within AT&T Bell Labs to determine the most effective uses of synthetic heads.)

The first step is to create a database of images of the actors with various mouth positions. Human speech is produced as a sequence of sounds by the vibration of vocal cords. Every speech sound belongs to one of the two main classes known as vowels and consonants. The basic linguistic units of speech sounds are called phonemes. A typical classification of the basic sounds of American English, together with their phonetic symbols, is shown in Table 7.2.

Similarly, the basic units of mouth shapes for classifying the speech in the visual domain are called visemes (visual phonemes). Each phoneme is associated with one viseme, which represents a sequence of one or two distinct, visible mouth shapes, such as the position of lips, tongue, teeth, jaw, and cheek in uttering the speech sound. In this work, we classify

Table 7.2   Phone to Viseme Mapping

Phone	Visemes	Phone	Visemes	Phone	Visemes
h#	(8, 0)	ey	(1, 13)	p	(9, 0)
aa	(1, 0)	f	(17, 0)	r	(12, 0)
ae	(2, 0)	g	(13, 0)	s	(11, 0)
ah	(3, 0)	hh	(15, 0)	sh	(11, 0)
ao	(4, 0)	ih	(13, 0)	t	(13, 0)
aw	(1, 12)	iy	(6, 0)	th	(10, 0)
ax	(5, 0)	jh	(11, 0)	uh	(12, 0)
ay	(2, 6)	k	(13, 0)	uw	(12, 0)
b	(9, 0)	l	(14, 0)	v	(17, 0)
ch	(11, 0)	m	(9, 0)	w	(12, 0)
d	(13, 0)	n	(13, 0)	y	(13, 0)
dh	(10, 0)	ng	(16, 0)	z	(11, 0)
eh	(2, 0)	ow	(7, 0)	zh	(11, 0)
er	(5, 0)	oy	(7, 13)		

the mouth shapes into 17 groups; see Table 7.2. For example, the mouth shapes of /m/, /b/, and /p/ are similar and, hence, are classified into one group.

To create these images, an actor is asked to utter different sounds of a spoken language while a digital image of each mouth position is captured. The head-and-shoulder images of this person speaking words that contain each of these phonemes are captured and processed to locate features such as lip contours and jaw position. From this, a set of 17 base images, or visemes, is generated. The baseImage, visemeNumber pairs are then inserted into the Agent database.

7.8.2 Talking Agent Generation

The second and more complicated process is to create a talking agent video from input text. A block diagram representing the logical runtime sequence is illustrated in Fig. 7.21. Each stage in the figure represents a logical processing step that occurs during the creation of the talking head. The runtime UDFs from Table 7.1 are shown mapped to the logical sequence in the figure from where they are invoked. The (slightly simplified) logical sequence consists of four parts:

- A text converter that transforms the input text into voice and also generates a phoneme sequence associated with the synthesized voice
- A posture generator that uses the phoneme sequence to drive the facial expressions.
- A structure deformation that uses the facial expressions to drive a wireframe facial model

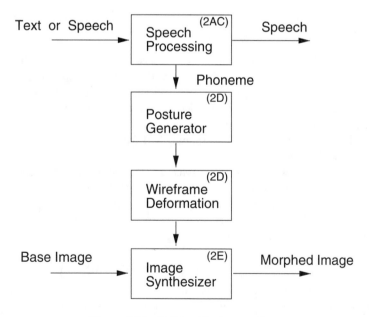

Figure 7.21 Talking Head generation.

- An image synthesizer that maps a person's face onto the deformed wireframe model to produce the desired facial movements conforming to the speech sound.

The text is first converted into a sequence of phonemes, and this sequence is then converted into a sequence of posture specifications. The system uses the table entries—together with knowledge about the intonation, rhythm, and emphasis—to render the table values into a continuous viseme sequence with transitional frames between different posture specifications suitably interpolated [31]. The extent to which interpolation should be performed from posture to posture is sound-dependent. For example, quick mouth closure between vowel sounds is perceptually important and hence is retained without alteration.

The talking-head image sequence is generated using a polygonal wireframe model, which is adapted to the shape of the face. In our current implementation, we use the facial model developed by the University of Tokyo. This wireframe model comprises a lattice of approximately 500 polygonal elements, of which approximately 80 are used to represent the lips and the inner mouth area. The lip contour is represented by six control points: two at the corners and one at the middle of the top and bottom edge of each lip. The head-and-shoulder image is texture-mapped onto the wireframe model. By rotating and translating the wireframe model, a realistic impression of a moving talking head is produced. In addition, vertices of the model in the cheek area are moved accordingly with the lip movement.

A demo of this work was shown in October 1995 at Partners, the Teradata Database User's Group meeting, held in Anaheim, California. More complicated UDFs could be added to this demo to include facial expressions, eye movements, and other more life-like characteristics.

7.9 SUMMARY

Multimedia applications will require increasing levels of support from database systems as computing on multimedia objects becomes possible. In this chapter, we described some of the problems that database system and application developers face in developing and running complex multimedia-enabled applications. Examples of the SQL3 language with user-defined type specifications highlighted some of the problems and language issues. Additional problems arise when running SQL3 in a parallel environment, such as Teradata. We described the architecture and implementation of a new system that provides solutions to these problems and allows multimedia objects to be treated much like traditional coded data. Some interesting problems regarding feature extracts and multidimensional indexing were described, and the approaches Teradata is taking to solve these were sketched. Finally, we illustrated the power of this system by explaining the steps required to create a complex application like a talking agent.

Acknowledgments

The authors gratefully recognize the assistance of many people in the preparation of this chapter: Catherine Anderson, Grace Au, Felipe Cariño, Glenn Linderman, Pekka Kostamaa, Jane Minogue, Eric Petajan, Gary Roberts, Cam Watson, and Darrell Woodcock.

References

[1] M. Bell, "The Montage Extensible Datablade Architecture," *Proc. of ACM-SIGMOD*, Vol. 23, No. 2, p. 482, June 1994.

[2] J. Wu, A. Narasimhalu, B. Mehtre, C. Lam, and Y. Gao, "CORE: Content-based Object Retrieval Engine for Multimedia Systems," *Multimedia Systems Journal*, Vol. 3, pp. 25–41, 1995.

[3] M. Loomis, "Moving Objects into Relational Systems," *Proc. of the Database World & Client/Server World*, Vol. 1, June 14, 1993.

[4] J. Melton et al., "Database Language SQL (SQL3)," ISO/ANSI Working Draft, ANSI X3H2-92-93-091 and ISO/IEC JTC1/ SC21/WG3/DBL YOK-003, Feb. 1993.

[5] F. Carino, W. Sterling, and I. T. Ieong, "Moonbase—A Complete Multimedia Database Solution," *Proc. of the ACM Multimedia Conference Workshop on Multimedia Database Management Systems*, San Francisco, Oct. 1994.

[6] F. Carino, W. Sterling, and I. T. Ieong, "Distributed Transaction Processing: The TxRPC Specification," *X/Open Snapshot*, X/Open Company Ltd., XoSpecs@xopen. co.uk, Draft 1.3, Dec. 1992.

[7] F. Carino, W. Sterling, and P. Kostamaa, "*Industrial Database Supercomputer Exegesis—DBC/1012, The NCR 3700, The Ynet and the BYNET,*" Emerging Trends in Knowledge and Database Systems, IEEE Adv. Computer Science Book, Chapter 8, 1994.

[8] W. Sterling, F. Carino, and C. Boss, "Multimedia Databases and Servers," *AT&T Technical Journal*, pp. 54–67, Sept./Oct. 1995.

[9] W. O'Connell, I. T. Ieong, D. Schrader, et al., "Teradata Content-Based Multimedia Object Server for Massively Parallel Architectures," *Proc. of ACM-SIGMOD*, Montreal, Canada, June 1996.

[10] M. Stonebraker, "The Case for Shared Nothing," *IEEE Data Engineering Bulletin*, Vol. 9, No. 1, pp. 4–9, Mar. 1986.

[11] M. Geneserethm and S. Ketchpel, "Software Agents," *Comm. of ACM*, Special Issue on Intelligent Agents, Vol. 37, No. 7, pp. 48–53, July 1994.

[12] G. Agha, *Actors: A Model of Concurrent Computing in Distributed Systems*, Cambridge, MA: MIT Press, 1986.

[13] G. Thiruvathukal, W. O'Connell, and T. Christopher, "Towards Scalable Parallel Software: Interfacing to Non-von Neumann Programming Environments," *Proc. of the SIAM'95*, San Francisco, Feb. 1995.

[14] S. Ghandehardizadeh and D. DeWitt, "Hybrid-Range Partitioning Strategy: A New Declustering Strategy for Multiprocessor Database Machines," *Proc. of the 16th VLDB*, Brisbane, Australia, pp. 481–492, 1990.

[15] A. Biliris and E. Panagos, "A High Performance Configurable Storage Manager," *Proc. of the IEEE 9th Int'l Conference on Data Engineering*, Taipei, Taiwan, pp. 35–43, Mar. 1995.

[16] A. Biliris, W. O'Connell, and E. Panagos, "*BeSS Reference Guide,*" Release 0.9, Technical Report, AT&T Bell Laboratories, Dec. 1995.

[17] A. Biliris, "An Efficient Database Storage Structure for Large Dynamic Objects," *Proc. of the IEEE 8th Int'l. Conference on Data Engineering*, Phoenix, pp. 301–308, Feb. 1992.

[18] A. Biliris, T. Funkhouser, W. O'Connell, and T. Panagos, "BeSS: Persistent Objects for Virtual Environments," *Proc. of ACM-SIGMOD*, Montreal, June 1996.

[19] C. Faloutsos, N. Koudas, and I. Kamel, "Declustering Spatial Databases on a Multi-Computer Architecture," Technical Report TM 950720-07, AT&T Bell Laboratories, Sept. 1995; *Proc. Extending Database Tech.*, France, Mar. 1996.

[20] M. Olson, "Cover Your Assets," Illustra Information Technologies, Inc., *Proc. of ACM-SIGMOD*, Vol. 24, No. 2, San Jose, CA, p. 453, 1995 .

[21] J. Gray and A. Reuter, *Transaction Processing: Concepts and Techniques*, Morgan Kaufmann Publishers, 1993.

[22] M. Flickner, H. Sawhney, W. Niblack, et al., "Query by Image and Video Content: The QBIC System," *IEEE Computer*, Vol. 28, No. 9, pp. 23–32, Sept. 1995.

[23] V. Ogle and M. Stonebraker, "Chabot: Retrieval from Relational Database of Images," *IEEE Computer*, Vol. 28, No. 9, pp. 40–48, Sept. 1995.

[24] D. DeWitt, N. Kabra, J. Luo, J. Patel, and J. Yu, "Client-Server Paradise," *Proc. of the 20th VLDB*, Santiago, Chile, 1994.

[25] T. Brinkhoff, H. Kriegel, and B. Seeger, "Efficient Processing of Spatial Joins Using R-trees," *Proc. of ACM SIGMOD*, Washington, DC, pp. 237–246, May 1993.

[26] N. Roussopoulos, S. Kelley, and F. Vincent, "Nearest Neighbor Queries," *Proc. of ACM-SIGMOD*, San Jose, CA, pp. 71–79, May 1995.

[27] C. Faloutsos and K. Lin, "FastMap: A Fast Algorithm for Indexing, Data-Mining and Visualization of Traditional and Multimedia Datasets," *Proc. of ACM-SIGMOD*, San Jose, CA, pp. 163–174, May 1995.

[28] I. Kamel and C. Faloutsos, "Parallel R-trees," *Proc. of ACM-SIGMOD*, May 1992.

[29] C. Faloutsos, "*Searching Multimedia Databases by Content*," Boston/London/Dordrecht: Kluwer Academic Publishers, Sept. 1996.

[30] S. Morishima and H. Harashima, "A Media Conversion from Speech to Facial Image for Intelligent Man-Machine Interface," *IEEE Journal of Selected Areas in Communications*, Vol. 9, No. 4, pp. 594–600, May 1991.

[31] D. Hill, A. Pearce, and B. Wyvill, "Animated Speech: An Automated Approach Using Speech Synthesized by Rules," *The Visual Compute*, Vol. 3, pp. 277–289, 1988.

[32] C. Faloutsos, R. Barber, M. Flickner, J. Hafner, W. Niblack, D. Petkovic, and W. Equitz, "Efficient and Effective Querying by Image Content," *Journal of Intelligent Information Systems*, Vol. 3, No. 3/4, pp. 231–262, 1994.

[33] H. V. Jagadish, "A Retrieval Technique for Similar Shapes," *Proc. of ACM-SIGMOD*, pp. 208–217, 1991.

Chapter
8

VIDEO INDEXING AND RETRIEVAL

Yin Chan, Shang-Hung Lin, and S.-Y. Kung

Abstract

Thanks to technological advancements in image/video capturing, data storage, compression, personal computing, and networking, an ever-growing amount of digital images and videos are becoming accessible to the general user. To take advantage of the rich information content of these media, data management systems that allow efficient and effective storage, indexing, and retrieval of these data are essential. Conventional data management systems, which excel in dealing with alphanumeric data, do not handle image/video data well. To accommodate these multimedia data, researchers have suggested the content-based indexing and retrieval paradigm. In this chapter, we describe the computation of different image and video features that researchers proposed to characterize the contents of images/videos and to allow efficient indexing and retrieval. In particular, we describe the computation and use of low-level features such as color, texture, shape, and motion, as well as high-level features such as human faces. Empirical results and prototypes are illustrated to show the effectiveness of these features. Limitations and tradeoffs of different features are discussed.

8.1 INTRODUCTION

The advent of various affordable technologies for image/video capturing, data storage, high bandwidth/speed transmission, together with the introduction of image/video compression standards such as JPEG[1], H.261[2], and MPEG[3], have greatly increased the availability of digital images and videos to the general user. Compared with text data, image and video data are much richer in information content. The old saying "A picture is worth a thousand words" is an understatement for images, let alone videos.

State-of-the-art text processing technology makes authoring, searching, and the like with text so easy that we tend to take it for granted. In order to take advantage of the abundance of information in video data, we would like to see similar techniques for video at our disposal. As in text processing, a first requirement is that video data be retrieved reasonably fast from archives before manipulating, viewing, and so on, can be applied. Hence, efficient video data management to enable rapid indexing and retrieval is very important.

In contrast to text data, video data occupy much more storage space. A one-minute color video clip with a frame rate of 30 frames per second and resolution of 352×240 pixels, for example, takes up 435 megabytes of storage in an uncompressed form. Assuming an aggressive compression ratio of 100:1, which is achievable but gives rise to noticeable picture quality degradation, a 100-minute movie eats up the same amount of space in a compressed format. The huge appetite for storage space of video data poses a challenge to current database management technology.

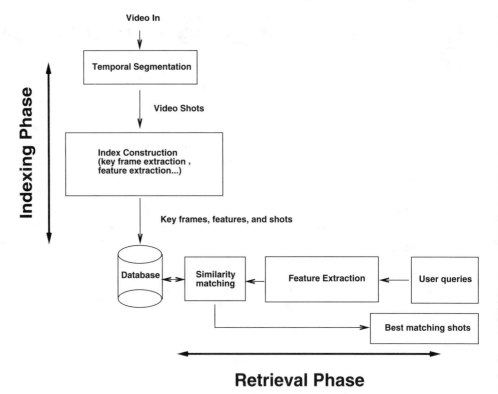

Figure 8.1   Block diagram of a video database management system for content-based video indexing and retrieval.

Traditionally, the database research community has concentrated on the development of management systems for alphanumeric data. In these systems, data are arranged into *fields*. Some *key fields* are used as indices for fast retrieval. The associated techniques work well with numeric data and short alphanumeric data. Current commercial database systems support image/video data indexing and retrieval by using keywords and text associated with images/videos. This approach is suitable only with images/videos that have already been annotated. There are a few problems with this approach. On the one hand, the unconstrained problem of automatically annotating images and videos is beyond the reach of current image/video understanding technology. On the other hand, manual annotation is very time consuming, if not impossible, when the data set is large, which is almost the rule in realistic image/video databases. Therefore, it is not generally affordable except possibly in restricted domains. Another problem with manual annotation is that there is no agreed-upon vocabulary for annotating these data and the interpretation of graphical data is very subjective. Hence, the nonalphanumeric nature of video data calls for new techniques for indexing and retrieval.

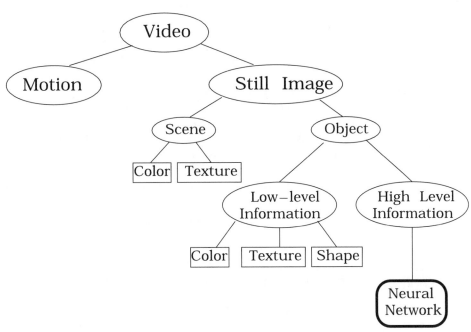

Figure 8.2   A hierarchy of features characterizing video content for content-based video indexing and retrieval.

There are a number of major issues here. The first one is how we select features used as indices into image/video databases so that those indices enable fast insertion and search. The second concern is how well these features characterize the content of videos and images so that they can be used to describe what we want to retrieve in query time. Another issue is how easy these features can be computed from images and videos. To answer these questions, researchers have suggested using image features such as colors, textures, and shapes and temporal features such as motion trajectories, which are computable using current technologies, to "describe" the content of image and video data and to be used as indices into image/video databases to enable content-based retrieval of visual data.

Figure 8.1 shows a system diagram that most current research prototypes such as the QBIC (Query By Image Content) [22] and SWIM (Show me What I Mean) [14] use. Video streams are first processed by a temporal segmentation method (sometimes referred to as *scene change detection* in the literature). In Section 8.2, we introduce some prominent methods to divide video data into chunks called "shots," which are the basic video units for further processing. The goal of this step is to address the issue of video data as being extremely voluminous. *Shots* provide a compact representation of video data. And the reduction in size from videos to shots makes efficient video processing realizable.

Index construction is the next step following temporal segmentation. In this phase, features are extracted from video shots as indices into video databases. Figure 8.2 depicts a hierarchy of methods to extract features that are commonly used to characterize video data content for content-based indexing and retrieval. Due to the abundant temporal redundancy within a "shot," usually a few key frames and motion information are extracted from a shot to represent the content of the shot. In Section 8.3, we will introduce some of the motion features that can be used to characterize temporal contents of shots. In Section 8.4.1, we will describe how still image features such as colors and textures are computed from key frames and used to index videos. For better content understanding, object detection/recognition is deemed very critical. In Section 8.4.2, still image features that can be used to characterize objects are described. These range from low-level features such as shapes, colors, and textures to more complex features such as facial patterns for human detection/recognition.

Subsequent to index construction, original video data, together with features extracted, are saved in some video database systems. At time of query, the feature extraction procedure is performed on the query video datum presented by the user. Then a search engine will compare these features with those stored in the database. Best matches are retrieved and displayed to the user.

8.2 TEMPORAL SEGMENTATION OF VIDEO SEQUENCES

There exists much temporal redundancy in videos, and indeed, if video data were processed as if they were unrelated sequences of images, much computing power and time would be wasted. Specifically, video frames within the same "shot," which is a sequence of images showing one event, exhibit much temporal redundancy. Precisely this redundancy makes the compression ratio of videos much higher than that of images. Commonly, video data are segmented into "shots," which are then treated as basic video units for further processing such as feature extraction and key frame extraction for indexing and retrieval purposes.

The simplest video shot boundaries to detect are those at abrupt scene changes. In contrast, special effects such as fade-in, fade-out, and dissolve [6] are more difficult to detect. Figure 8.3 shows an abrupt scene change and Fig. 8.4 depicts a dissolve. The basic idea to detect an abrupt scene change is to use some kind of difference metric to test the dissimilarity of adjacent frames. If the dissimilarity is above some threshold, a scene change is declared.

Otsuji et al. [4] use brightness data to detect scene change. Two metrics are attempted, that is, frame-based histogram difference and pixel-based interframe difference histogram. The first metric is used to detect change in brightness distribution. Here a 16-level brightness histogram is generated for each frame. Then differences between histograms of two consecutive frames are summed to form *FHDsum*. These sums are compared against a threshold to detect scene change [5]. The second metric is to measure change in motion. For each pair of adjacent frames $(N - 1)$ and N, an interframe difference image is formed. Afterward, a

Figure 8.3   An abrupt scene change.

Figure 8.4   A special effect *dissolve*.

16-level histogram, *IDH(N)*, for this difference image is generated. For each *IDH(N)*, they set a counter *IDHa(N)*, which tells how many pixels undergo changes larger than a certain threshold. Using a preset threshold $\delta IDHa_{\text{cut}}$, we can declare a scene cut at frame N if the following two predicates are both true:

$$\delta IDHa_{\text{cut}} < IDHa(N) \; - \; IDHa(N-1)$$

$$\delta IDHa_{\text{cut}} < IDHa(N) \; - \; IDHa(N+1)$$

Special effects are not considered in this experiment. To tackle them, Zhang et al. [7] propose a *twin-comparison* method. While abrupt scene changes are easy to detect due to the distinctively high dissimilarity between two consecutive frames, frame differences during the course of a special effect are only slightly higher than differences within a shot. Lowering the detection threshold will not work because large object or camera motion also entails higher interframe differences triggering "false-positive" detection. To illustrate the twin-comparison method, let's consider a special effect called *dissolve* in which one scene X is gradually changed into scene Y (cf. Fig. 8.4). This method makes use of two thresholds, T_b and T_s. Any frame exhibiting a frame difference with the previous frame higher than T_b is declared a scene change. If the difference is lower than T_b but higher than T_s, then this frame is registered as the potential start frame F_s of a gradual transition, which is a dissolve in this example. This frame is then compared to subsequent frames. It was observed that the difference between the first frame of a gradual transition and subsequent frames during the transition generally increases. The potential end frame F_e of a gradual transition is detected when the interframe difference between two consecutive frames drops below T_s. If the difference between F_s and F_e is higher than T_b, a gradual transition (scene change) is declared. Let $D_{i,j}$ denote the frame difference between frames F_i and F_j. The twin-comparison method can be illustrated as

```
if D_{i,i+1} > T_b
    declare scene change between F_i and F_{i+1}
else if D_{i,i+1} > T_s {
    s = i
    e = i
    while (D_{e,e+1} > T_s) {
        e = e + 1
    }
    if D_{s,e} > T_b
        declare scene change between F_s and F_e
}
```

The introduction of JPEG and MPEG standards leads to the existence of compressed video data. The ability to process video data without decompressing them first is very important to reducing computation time. To this end, a number of techniques have been proposed. Arman et al. [8] use DCT (Discrete Cosine Transform) coefficients of Motion JPEG compressed data for scene change detection. Given a series of 8×8 DCT coefficient blocks B_i, where $1 \leq i \leq n$, in a single JPEG compressed frame F, a subset of blocks β_j, $1 \leq j \leq \rho$ where $\rho \ll n$, are chosen a priori. This subset of blocks is chosen so that they correspond to k connected regions in each frame. The distribution of these blocks is fixed for all frames, sequences, and experiments. Furthermore, for each block, a subset $C_j = \{c_1, c_2, \ldots, c_\alpha\}$ of the 63 AC coefficients are selected so that they are randomly distributed among the 63 AC coefficients. Subsequently, a vector is formed for each frame using C_j's of all the blocks β_j, that is, $\vec{V}_F = \{c_1, c_2, \ldots, c_l\}$ where $l = \alpha \times \rho$. A similarity metric between two frames ψ apart is defined as the inner product of the corresponding vectors:

$$\Psi = \frac{\vec{V}_F \bullet \vec{V}_{F+\psi}}{\left|\vec{V}_F\right| \left|\vec{V}_{F+\psi}\right|}$$

A scene change is declared from frame F to frame $F + \psi$ if $1 - |\Psi| > t$, where t is a threshold and $0 \ll t < 1$. The accuracy and speed of this method are affected by a number of parameters. For example, ρ determines the number of blocks involved in the calculation. On the other hand, k determines how the ρ blocks are distributed in a frame. Other parameters include the number of AC coefficients used and their distributions. For more discussions on the effects of these parameters on performance, please refer to [8].

Yeo and Liu [9] developed a scene change detection method applied to *DC sequences*. For Motion JPEG and MPEG coded sequences, DC sequences are formed by sequences of spatially reduced images constructed using the DC coefficients of each frame. Effectively, images are reduced by a factor of $N \times N$, where N is the block size used in the compression step, N is typically 8 or 16. The construction of DC sequences requires little computation when compared with full decompression. In addition, Yeo reported, spatially reduced DC images capture enough information content for scene change detection purposes, while facilitating much faster detection than if the original sequences were used. One drawback of using a global threshold to detect scene changes is that in the case of a large object or camera motion, false alarms can be triggered. Yeo and Liu argue that a local view should be more realistic. They suggest the *sliding window* concept in which *2m* frames are spanned and *2m* - 1 interframe differences are examined at the same time. Let $f_i(j, k)$ denote the luminance value of the pixel located at coordinate (j, k) of frame F_i, and let $M \times N$ be the frame size. The dissimilarity metric that they used is the sum of absolute luminance difference between two consecutive frames:[1]

$$D_i = \sum_{j=0}^{M-1} \sum_{k=0}^{N-1} |f_i(j, k) - f_{i+1}(j, k)| \tag{1}$$

[1] It was reported that using the sum of squares of differences yielded similar results and absolute differences were used for the sake of fast computation

A scene change is declared from frame F_i to frame F_{i+1} when both of the following conditions are satisfied:

- D_i is maximum within a window of size $2m - 1$ centering at D_i.
- D_j is the second largest difference, and $D_i \geq n D_j$.

For $3 \leq m \leq 20$ and $1.5 \leq n \leq 3.5$, the reported results are satisfactory. To handle gradual transitions, Yeo and Liu parameterize them as linear transitions from scenes s_1 to s_2 from time t_1 to t_2 as

$$
s_t = \begin{cases} s_1 & t < t_1 \\ \frac{(s_2 - s_1)(t - t_1)}{t_2 - t_1} + s_1 & t_1 \leq t < t_2 \\ s_2 & t \geq t_2 \end{cases}
$$

Defining a new interframe difference sequence that compares frames k time units apart and selecting k so that $k > t_2 - t_1$, they show that gradual transitions of the above-mentioned form show up as "plateaus" of height $|s_2 - s_1|$, which enable effective detection of gradual transitions such as dissolve, face-in, and face-out.

Instead of working on spatially subsampled videos, Ahn and Oh [10] proposed to perform detection on temporally subsampled videos. The key observation is that scene change intervals are usually in the order of a few to tens of seconds. Assuming a frame rate of 30 frames per second, very often there are 100+ frames between consecutive scene changes. They suggest a binary search strategy to search for scene change. Given a skip factor S, a video sequence is broken down into chunks of $S + 2$ frames. The dissimilarity between frame F_i and F_{i+S+1} is compared against a preset threshold t. If the dissimilarity is smaller than t, one can declare that there is no scene change within these $S + 2$ frames and move on to the next chunk. Otherwise, the $S + 2$ frames are separated into two subsequences, and scene change search is performed for each subsequence consisting of ($\lfloor S/2 \rfloor + 1$) frames. The dissimilarity metric used is the *histogram comparison method* [7]:

$$
HD_{\text{sum}}(i) = \sum_{j=0}^{n-1} |H_i(j) - H_{i+S+1}(j)|
$$

where n is the number of intensity levels and H_i denotes the intensity histogram of frame F_i. An adaptive scheme whereby S is adaptive is also experimented with. If $HD_{\text{sum}}(i) < t$, then the next skip factor S_{next} is increased to

$$
\frac{S_{\text{current}} \times t}{HD_{\text{sum}}(i)}
$$

Special effects are not treated in Ahn's experiments.

8.3   MOTION-BASED INDEXING AND RETRIEVAL METHODS

After temporal segmentation, we have video shots. Because of the temporal redundancy within a shot, one or a few key frames, together with some motion features such as motion vectors, are enough to capture most of the information content of a shot.

Lee and Kao [11] proposed using moving objects and tracks as indices into videos. They define a video record as a subsequence of video sequence that starts at the frame where some object appears and ends at the frame where the object disappears. *Interactive annotation* is employed to identify objects of interest in their system. After the manual annotation step, object tracking is carried out. *Optical flow* computation is used to calculate one of the four classes of motion types:

1. **Translation at constant depth**
    North, Northeast, East, Southeast, South, Southwest, West, Northwest

2. **Translation in depth**
    Zoom-in, Zoom-out

3. **Rotation at constant depth**
    Clockwise, Anticlockwise

4. **Rotation in depth**
    Rotation-to-left, Rotation-to-right, Rotation-upward, Rotation-downward

Defining any two motion types that come from the same class as *conflicting*, Lee and Kao represent object motion tracks as ordered (using time of occurrence) subsets of motion types that don't contain conflicting elements within the same subset. In this representation, each subset of motion types denotes the motion of an object during one time unit, for example, the duration of a frame. {North, South} is a conflicting subset, for instance, because an object cannot both move along these two directions simultaneously while {North, Zoom-in} is not. {{North, Clockwise}, {Northwest, Zoom-in}} represents one valid motion track while {{Northwest, Zoom-in}, {North, Clockwise}} gives another valid track.

Ioka and Kurokawa [12] adopted a block-based motion tracking approach for indexing videos using motion information. First, the motion of different blocks is tracked for a certain period of time. This step takes into account the traceability of each block and the reliability of its calculated motion. The standard deviation of the intensity values of a block is used as a measure of the traceability. The reliability of calculated motion is computed using the history of the displaced frame difference, and the vector smoothness is compared with corresponding former motion vectors of the block. Blocks passing the traceability test are tracked using a block matching algorithm similar to those employed in MPEG encoding. The tracking is terminated when either a block moves out of the frame or its reliability is lower than a certain threshold. Subsequent to obtaining the motion vectors of individual blocks, trajectories of these blocks are represented using the following formulas:

$$T_s < t < T_s + T_l$$
$$\begin{cases} x_t = S_x + \sum_{i=0}^{t-T_s-1} V_{xi} \\ y_t = S_x + \sum_{i=0}^{t-T_s-1} V_{yi} \end{cases}$$

where T_s and T_l represent the starting time and duration of the trajectory of a block, (x_t, y_t) are the coordinates of the block at time t, (S_x, S_y) are the coordinates of the block at the starting time, and (V_{xi}, V_{yi}) are the motion vector between times $(T_s + i)$ and $(T_s + i + 1)$. Object trajectories are calculated based on the assumption that trajectories of blocks belonging to the same object are similar. The similarity measure between the trajectories of two blocks α and β is the mean Euclidean distance between their coordinates in every frame when their lifetimes overlap [12]:

$$d = \frac{1}{t_{ovl}} \sum_{i=0}^{t_{ovl}} \sqrt{ \begin{aligned} &((S_x^\alpha + \textstyle\sum_{k=0}^i V_x^\alpha) - (S_x^\beta + \textstyle\sum_{k=0}^i V_x^\beta))^2 + \\ &((S_y^\alpha + \textstyle\sum_{k=0}^i V_y^\alpha) - (S_y^\beta + \textstyle\sum_{k=0}^i V_y^\beta))^2 \end{aligned} } \tag{2}$$

A clustering algorithm is used to group similar trajectories. Trajectories closest to the means of the clusters are taken to represent moving objects in a scene. At time of query, Eq. (2) is also used to match user-presented trajectories and those found in video sequences.

For object-based motion tracking, only a small number of features are needed. And it is a common desire to have true motion vectors. Based on these two requirements, Chen et al. [38] noticed that the minimum residue criterion adopted by block-matching algorithms (BMA), which are widely used in motion- compensated video coding, often misses the true motion vectors, due to many practical factors (e.g., affine warping, image noises, object occlusion, lighting variation, and existence of multiple minimal residues). Hence, they proposed a new tracking method:

First, they disqualify some of the reference blocks that might be too unreliable to track by taking into account the variance of the blocks.

Second, they adopt a multi-candidate prescreening to provide some robustness in selecting motion candidates.

Third, assuming the true motion field is piecewise continuous,[2] they determine the motion of a feature block by moving all its neighboring blocks with it in the similar direction. This enhances the chance that some minority incorrect motion vectors can be corrected by the majority motion vectors. Besides, their method in principle can track more flexible affine-type motions, such as rotating, zooming, and sheering.

8.4 IMAGE-BASED INDEXING AND RETRIEVAL METHODS

Besides temporal information, *key frames* is another important part of video shot content. Two classes of methods that compute still image features as indices are described in this section:

- Global-scene-based methods (cf. Section 8.4.1)
- Object-based methods (cf. Section 8.4.2)

---

[2]There should be a good degree of motion similarities between the neighboring blocks. Therefore, the motion vector can be more robustly estimated if the global motion trend of an entire neighborhood is considered, as opposed to that of one feature block itself.

Furthermore, in Sections 8.5 and 8.6, we will highlight two object-based methods using a neural network approach to extract human objects (faces) for browsing and indexing purposes.

8.4.1 Global-scene-based Methods

By far the two most popular global-scene-based classes of features for image content characterization are colors and textures.

8.4.1.1 Color Histograms

Color histograms are invariant to rotation about the viewing axis, translation. They change only slightly with scaling, viewing angle, and occlusion [13]. Color spaces that have been experimented with by various researchers include *RGB* space, *YIQ* space, *opponent color* space, and *MTM* (Mathematical Transform to Munsell) space. It has been reported that the *opponent color* and *MTM* spaces work well for this purpose [13,14] when evaluated by subjective viewing.

After selecting an appropriate color space, another issue is color quantization. Assuming that a color is coded in a three-component vector, with each component represented in 8 bits, there are $2^{8 \times 3} = 16M$ possible colors. To shrink the number of colors to a reasonable size so that histogram generation and manipulation can be performed with fair complexity, a usual practice is to quantize each color axis to the range of a few tens. Further reduction can be achieved by some vector quantization method [13,15]. After color quantization, a color histogram can be generated by counting, for each color bin, the number of pixels that belong to that color.

To measure the similarity of two color histograms, a few metrics have been proposed. One is the *histogram intersection* method [13]:

$$H(I, M) = \sum_{j=1}^{n} \min(I_j, M_j)$$

where n is the number of color bins and I and M are the two color histograms. Results reported in [13] show that the *histogram intersection* method is very insensitive to the number of bins. Specifically, the effectiveness of the histogram intersection method changes little over the range of 64 to 8125 bins. Therefore, aggressive color quantization, for example, from $2^{8 \times 3}$ to 64, still allows good retrieval quality. An interesting property of the *histogram intersection* metric is that it is equivalent to the *city block* metric when the corresponding images of the two histograms under consideration are of the same size [13]:

$$\sum_{i=1}^{n} M_i = \sum_{i=1}^{n} I_i \;\Rightarrow\; 1 - H(I, M) = \frac{1}{2 \sum_{i=1}^{n} M_i} \sum_{i=1}^{n} |I_i - M_i|$$

A drawback of the *histogram intersection* metric is that the similarity between the colors represented by two bins is not accounted for. Obviously, *red* and *purple* are more alike than *red* and *green*. To remedy this, a weighted form of distance between two histograms I and

$M, D(I, M) = (I - M)^T A (I - M)$, can be used [15] with $A(i, j) = 1 - d(c_i, c_j)/d_{\max}$, where c_k denotes the kth color(bin) in the histogram, $d(c_i, c_j)$ is the Euclidean distance between the two colors in an appropriate color space, and $d_{\max}$ is the maximum distance among all the possible color pairs.

It has been observed that after color quantization, a small number of bins usually account for a majority of pixels of an image. Therefore, color histograms can be approximated by selecting a small but fixed number of bins containing the most pixels. Experiments show that this approximation gives comparable retrieval quality [13,16].

8.4.1.2 Texture Classification

One of the most popular models for measuring texture is the one proposed by Tamura et al. [25]. It is used in projects such as QBIC [22] and SWIM [14]. Computational measures for *coarseness*, *contrast*, *directionality*, and the like, which approximate human perceptions of textural patterns, are used as similarity metrics. Coarseness is a measure of the granularity of a pattern. It is computed using a moving window of varying sizes. Contrast is a measure of the vividness of a pattern, and it is calculated using distribution of intensity values of the pattern such as the dynamic range, standard deviation σ, and kurtosis α_4 defined as

$$\alpha_4 = \frac{\mu_4}{\sigma_4}$$

where μ_4 is the fourth central moment. Directionality, on the other hand, tells if a pattern has a dominant direction. It can be computed by using a histogram of local edge probabilities against their direction angles, that is, counting the number of edge points at each quantized angle. Similarity between two textural patterns can be defined as some weighted Euclidean distance in the three-dimensional texture space formed by the three quantities, namely, coarseness, contrast, and directionality.

8.4.2 Object-based Methods

Despite encouraging empirical results showing the effectiveness of global features, it has been recognized that for better content understanding, which is the key to content-based indexing and retrieval, object detection/recognition is critical. A drawback of global image features is that even though they are easier to compute, they do not carry enough content information to facilitate effective content-based retrieval. A color histogram, for example, can only tell us about the color distribution of an image. It can't tell, for instance, an image dominated by a large blue car from one showing a blue sky. This is not to say that global image features are not useful. In fact, they can be used as some kind of information filters that help to retrieve potential candidate images/videos quickly. More sophisticated algorithms or human operators can then work on the smaller set of retrieved images/videos. Consider the example where we want to search for a video clip showing President Clinton jogging on a beach on a sunny day. An examination of color histograms would give us those clips (using key frames) dominated by blue (sea and sky) and white (sand and cloud). This much smaller set of videos retrieved can then be examined by the user or an advanced algorithm to decide which one satisfies the query.

To make our presentation clearer, some terminologies need to be defined. By *object detection*, we refer to the identification of a general class of objects, such as cars, human beings, and computers. On the other hand, we use *object recognition* to refer to the process of distinguishing one individual from another *within* the same general class, such as telling one person from another. We contend that the object detection/recognition technique is a very useful next step toward better content understanding. Knowing that there is a person or a dog, and so on, tells us more about an image than knowing that an image is dominated by red and green. These techniques make object-related queries such as ''find me a video clip having a red car speeding across the screen'' possible when combined with global and motion features. Moreover, spatial and temporal relationships among objects detected can provide us with even more complicated queries, as one can imagine.

Unlike global-feature-based methods, which do indexing based on the features extracted from the whole image, object-based indexing methods characterize videos and images according to the presence of objects. In what follows, we will first describe several methods used to extract objects from images. These methods are designed to help identify objects of interest and don't provide object detection/recognition abilities. Afterward, computation of *features* to characterize the shapes, colors, and textures of objects will be discussed.

Compared with other objects, human objects in general attract more attention. In Section 8.5, we will introduce the topic of how facial features can be computed to characterize people. A system that utilizes a neural network face recognition technique to aid browsing of videos will be described. Finally, we will introduce a video shot classification scheme that makes use of face detection techniques for indexing and browsing purposes in Section 8.6.

8.4.2.1 Shape Analysis

Automatic object detection and recognition in general are difficult problems. In the content-based video/image indexing and retrieval domain, a number of methods along that direction have been proposed. In the QBIC project [22], unsupervised background/foreground segmentation methods were successfully applied to restricted classes of images such as those appearing in retail catalogs and museum art collections where backgrounds are not very complex. An interactive tool based on some *flood-fill* algorithm (sometimes referred to as *seed-fill* or *region growing* in the literature since the filling of a region starts at a *seed* pixel in the interior of that region) was constructed to help identify objects. The user just needs to use a pointing device to select an exterior point and an interior one with respect to an object. The tool will then grow a region by gathering connected pixels whose color values are within a certain threshold of the interior pixel. The region so obtained is taken as *the object* the user wants to identify. The threshold is dynamically calculated. It was reported that for objects with reasonably uniform surface in distinctive background, the results are satisfactory. In addition, an interactive object outlining tool that allows the user to draw a curve close to the boundary of an object was implemented. Using the *snake* model [29], which is an energy-minimizing spline guided by internal energy and external energy influenced by nearby image gradients, the tool pushes the user-drawn curve toward the boundary of the intended object. The above tools help to identify objects of interest *without* providing knowledge as to what the objects are.

After extracting objects from the background, we need to compute features to describe them. It has long been recognized that various *moments* can be an effective means to describe shapes. For an image $I(x, y)$, moment of order $(i + j)$ is defined as

$$m_{ij} = \sum_x \sum_y x^i y^j I(x, y)$$

And the *central moments* are

$$\mu_{ij} = \sum_x \sum_y (x - \overline{x})^i (y - \overline{y})^j I(x, y)$$

where

$$\overline{x} = \frac{m_{10}}{m_{00}} \quad \text{and} \quad \overline{y} = \frac{m_{01}}{m_{00}}$$

Defining the *normalized central moments* as

$$\gamma_{ij} = \frac{\mu_{ij}}{\mu_{00}^{\rho_{ij}}}$$

where

$$\rho_{ij} = \frac{i + j}{2} + 1 \quad \text{where } i + j \geq 2$$

a set of *invariant moments* that are invariant to translation, rotation, and scaling can be derived [18]:

$$\Phi_1 = \gamma_{20} + \gamma_{02}$$
$$\Phi_2 = (\gamma_{20} - \gamma_{02})^2 + 4\gamma_{11}^2$$
$$\Phi_3 = (\gamma_{30} - 3\gamma_{12})^2 + (3\gamma_{21} - \gamma_{03})^2$$
$$\Phi_4 = (\gamma_{30} + \gamma_{12})^2 + (\gamma_{21} + \gamma_{03})^2$$
$$\vdots$$

Moment-based methods are used in a number of research projects [15,19,20,17].

Zhang [14] uses summation of turning angles to characterize shapes. A set of tangent angles around the perimeter of an object is used to match it against other objects in the QBIC project [22]. One advantage of these *turning angle methods* is that they are invariant to translation, rotation, and scaling.

Jain and Vailaya [21] employ *edge-direction histograms* as a measure of shape attributes. The histogram intersection method is used to determine the similarity of images. This metric is invariant to translation only. Normalizing the histograms with respect to the total number of edge points makes it invariant to scaling. On the other hand, rotation of object shifts the bins of the histograms. Performing histogram intersection over all possible shifts, though being computation-intensive, solves the rotation invariance problem.

Sclaroff and Pentland [23] argue that shape similarity should be better modeled using the deformation between two objects. Hence, they choose the Finite Element Method to model the energy needed to change (bend, squeeze, etc.) one shape to another and use the energy amount as a dissimilarity measure. This approach has the merit that it is invariant to translation, rotation, and scaling.

Other metrics for characterizing shapes include **circularity** computed as ($perimeters^2/area$), **area** represented by the number of pixels in the binary image, **major axis of orientation** represented by the *principal vector* calculated using boundary pixels of an object, and **eccentricity** computed as the ratio between the smallest and largest eigenvalues of the covariance matrix of the boundary pixels.

8.4.2.2   Color-based Methods

After objects are extracted from the background, we can also characterize them by their color features similar to those described in Section 8.4.1.

Another approach appears in [16] where Gong et al. chose to use a small set of pre-defined object colors that appear frequently in color imagery such as those of human faces, sunny sky, or forest. It was observed that the *hue* components of these colors in the MTM(HVC) color space [24] fall into narrow ranges despite different illuminations. Hence, the *hue* values are used to detect these predefined objects in color images and videos. Since objects outside the predefined set may show colors similar to those in the set, a limitation of this approach is that the objects detected aren't necessarily what the user intends to get. In addition, we can only hope to retrieve images that have objects of these predefined colors.

8.4.2.3   Texture Classification

Similarly, objects can also be characterized by the textural features described in Section 8.4.1 once they are extracted from the background.

8.4.2.4   Neural-Network Methods

Compared with other objects, human objects in general receive more attention. In the following two sections, we will show how features can be computed to characterize human objects. Specifically, two systems will be used to illustrate how these features can be computed and used for browsing and indexing purposes:

- Video browsing system using human faces (cf. Section 8.5)
- Video shot classification using human faces (cf. Section 8.6)

8.5   VIDEO BROWSING SYSTEM USING HUMAN FACES

People are the center of attention in a lot of video. Political scientists want to study video capturing various activities of politicians; film study students wish to analyze the presentation styles of actors/actresses; movie-goers want to browse through parts of movies and know what parts/roles are played by whom before deciding a purchase in a movie-on-demand scenario. People make up a great deal of information content in most video, and the ability to extract it is crucial to applications such as video indexing and browsing.

In the *PICTION* project [30], captions associated with newspaper photos were used to help detect the existence of particular individuals. The limitations of this approach are that captions are not always available and people whose existence can be detected are restricted to those mentioned in the captions.

To address these limitations, we propose to use object recognition techniques to recognize people of interest. In particular, a video browsing scheme using human faces was proposed [35]. This scheme organizes the video data based on the presence of human faces and allows users to retrieve all the video clips that contain the persons whom the user requests to see. Figure 8.5 shows the system diagram of this video browsing scheme. There are three steps in this system:

- Scene change detection (cf. Section 8.2)
- Face detection and annotation (cf. Section 8.5.1)
- Face recognition and browsing using faces (cf. Section 8.5.1)

The first step of this face-based video browser is to segment the video sequence by applying some temporal segmentation algorithm. Afterward, a face detector implemented by a special type of neural network, called PDBNN (Probabilistic Decision-Based Neural Network), is invoked to find the segments (shots) that most possibly contain human faces. From every video shot, a representative frame (Rframe) is chosen and is fed into the face detector. Those representative frames from which the detector gives high face detection confidence scores are annotated and serve as the indices for browsing. In the browsing step, a face recognizer (also implemented by PDBNN) is built to find all the shots that contain persons of interest based on the user's request. Since temporal segmentation has been described in Section 8.2, we will omit this step from the discussion. In Section 8.5.1, we will describe the PDBNN neural network approach for face detection and recognition that is used in this system. In Section 8.5.2, experimental results will be used to illustrate how we apply this face recognition technique for the browsing of people of interest.

8.5.1 Face Detection and Recognition

Over the past 20 years, researchers have worked on the problem of human recognition by machines. Applications of this technology range from surveillance systems to static matching of photos such as those in passports and driver's license. A general assumption is that the environment in which the photos are taken are controlled (lighting, uniformed background). An excellent survey paper in this area is Chellappa et al., 1995 [26]. For applications such as image/video indexing and browsing, a mechanism for detecting human faces in cluttered scenes is also very important. In recent years, several research groups have put their efforts into this topic [27,28]. In this browsing scheme, we adopt a unified method to tackle both face detection and face recognition problems. A *probabilistic* variant of the Decision Based Neural Network [32], or PDBNN, is used to implement both the face detector and face recognizer in this scheme.

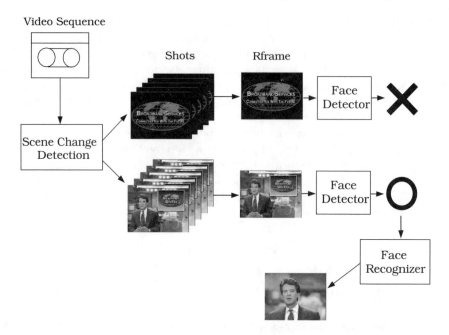

Figure 8.5 PDBNN face-based video browsing system. Scene change algorithm divides the video sequences into several shots. The face detector examines all the representative frames to see whether or not they contain human faces. If they do, the face detector passes the frame to the face recognizer to find out whose face it is.

8.5.1.1 Probabilistic Decision-based Neural Networks

The probabilistic DBNN (PDBNN) is a modular neural network with probabilistic discriminant functions. It has been used to implement the pattern detector and recognizer for many applications. The subnets of the probabilistic DBNN are designed to model the log-likelihood functions of object classes (i.e., $p(\mathbf{x}|\omega_i)$). For a K-class recognition problem, a PDBNN recognizer contains K class subnets. Several clusters (or neurons) are in one subnet. If the neuron transfer function is Gaussian, then the class likelihood function $p(\mathbf{x}|\omega_i)$ is modeled as a mixture of Gaussian distributions ($p(\mathbf{x}|\omega_i) = \sum_{r=1}^{R} P(\Theta_r|\omega_i)p(\mathbf{x}|\omega_i, \Theta_r)$), where $\Theta_r = \{\mu_r, \Sigma_r\}$ denotes the parameter set for the cluster r, $P(\Theta_r|\omega_i)$ denotes the prior probability of cluster r when input patterns are from class ω_i, and $p(\mathbf{x}|\omega_i, \Theta_r)$, for simplicity sake, is assumed as a D-dimensional Gaussian distribution with uncorrelated features, that is,

$$p(\mathbf{x}|\omega_i, \Theta_r) = \frac{1}{(2\pi)^{D/2} \prod_d^D \sigma_{rd}} \exp\left(-\frac{1}{2} \sum_{d=1}^{D} \frac{(x_d - w_{rd})^2}{\sigma_{rd}^2}\right)$$
$$\sim N(\mu_r, \Sigma_r)$$

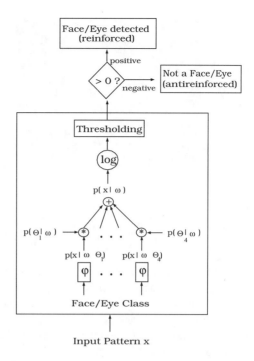

Figure 8.6 Schematic diagram of probabilistic DBNN for deformable object detection.

where $\mu_r = [w_{r1}, w_{r2}, \cdots, w_{rD}]^T$ is the mean vector and diagonal matrix $\Sigma_r = diag$ $[\sigma_{r1}^2, \sigma_{r2}^2, \cdots, \sigma_{rD}^2]$ is the covariance matrix.

The training scheme for PDBNN follows the LUGS principle. The Locally Unsupervised (LU) phase for the probabilistic DBNN can adopt several unsupervised learning schemes (e.g., VQ, k-mean, EM...). As for the Globally Supervised (GS) learning, the reinforced/antireinforced learning is applied to **all** the clusters of the global winner and the supposed (i.e., the correct) winner, with a weighting distribution proportional to the degree of possible involvement (measured by the likelihood) by each cluster.

PDBNN can also be used for pattern detection. For a PDBNN pattern detector, only one subnet is required in the network. (Take face detection, for example; the subnet represents the face class; cf. Fig. 8.6.) If, for an input pattern **x**, the discriminant function value of the subnet is larger than the threshold, then **x** is recognized as a face. Otherwise, it is considered a nonface.

In our experiment, we first use PDBNN to detect a face in an image. The approximate location of the face is shown inside the thin white box in Fig. 8.7. Search windows for both eyes, depicted by the thick white boxes, are subsequently estimated, inside which the eye detector is applied. The localization of eyes is crucial because it allows us to more accurately normalize the face size and reorient the face image. The normalization and reorientation are critical in the recognition step.

After a face is detected, properly located, and normalized, a subimage corresponding to the face region will then be cropped and downsampled to a 14×10 pixelmap. Edge-filtering and histogram modification techniques are then used to extract two types of features from

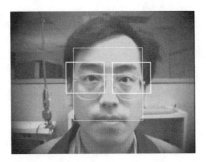

Figure 8.7   The thin white box represents the rough location found by the face detector. Based on the location of the face, the searching windows for locating eyes are assigned, as illustrated by the two thick white boxes.

the pixelmap: the "edge" feature and "intensity" feature. Finally, this feature vector is fed into a PDBNN face recognizer for pattern recognition.

The PDBNN face recognizer is usually trained in batch mode, but it is also capable of doing on-line training. As we mentioned in previous paragraphs, the PDBNN recognizer has K different subnets if there are K persons to be recognized, as shown in Fig. 8.8. Usually, the network is trained to recognize a particular group of persons (e.g., "all the 1996 Oscar nominees" or "all the congressmen in the United States") in the preparation stage. However, due to its modularity property, the PDBNN recognizer allows the system users to add new subnets to the original PDBNN, so that the new subnets can be trained to recognize the persons who are not in the original group.

8.5.2   Experimental Results

A preliminary experiment is conducted by using a four-minute News Report sequence. This sequence is sampled at 15 frames/sec and has spatial resolution of 320×240. Three persons appear in this sequence: an anchorman, a male interviewee, and a female interviewee. Our goal is to find out all the frames that contain the anchorman. The sequence is divided into 32 segments. Their representative frames are illustrated in Fig. 8.9a. The anchorman's face appears in seven of them (four in the frontal view and three in the side view). The PDBNN face detector and eye localizer mentioned in the previous section are again applied here to locate the face location on each Rframe. It takes about 10 seconds to process one frame. We have also built a PDBNN recognizer to recognize the anchorman. About 2 seconds' length of frames (32 frames) are used as training examples. It takes about one minute for the network to learn all the training examples and only seconds to process all the index frames. The experimental result shows that the four segments that contain the anchorman's frontal view images are successfully recognized with very high confidence scores (Fig. 8.10), and no other video segments are misrecognized as the anchorman's clips.

Notice that since our approach requires the appearance of both eyes, the three side-view segments of the anchorman cannot be recognized. The task of overcoming this limitation is considered as our future work. As to processing speed, we observe that the face detection step needs much more time than the face recognition step. For this News Report sequence, the system takes about 5 minutes (32 Rframes x 10 seconds/frame) in the detection step.

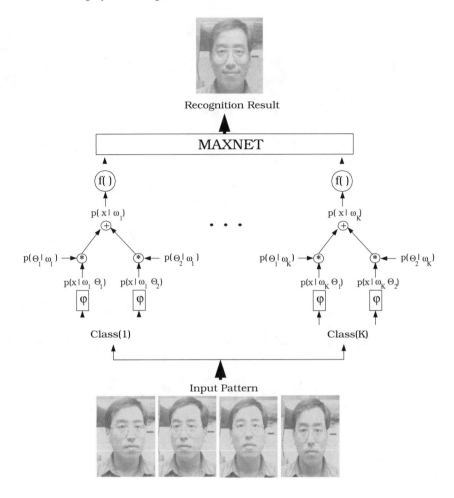

Recognition Result

$f()$: posterior type—normalization operator
likelihood type—log operator

Figure 8.8   Structure of a PDBNN face recognizer.

The reason for this long processing time is that in the face detection step, a multiresolution search is used so that the detector is capable of locating faces with different sizes. Several methods can be applied to reduce the total processing time. For example, we can reduce the number of Rframes by roughly merging similar Rframes based on their color histogram or shape similarity. Nevertheless, since the task of face detection is to locate and annotate faces in the sequence, it needs to be run only once. Therefore, this face detection time does not affect the system's on-line performance where only the annotated frames are processed by the face recognizer.

(a)

(b)

Figure 8.9   (a) Representative frames of the shots of the news sequence. (b) Shots containing frontal faces.

Figure 8.10   Representative frames of anchorman found by PDBNN face recognizer.

8.6 VIDEO SHOT CLASSIFICATION USING HUMAN FACES

Assuming that faces are already located, machine recognition can be done very quickly and accurately, as we showed in the previous section. But we cannot expect a recognizer to work for too many people. One problem is that training time will be too long. A second problem is that the performance of a recognizer will degrade as the collection of people whom it needs to categorize grows too large. Therefore, we could only afford using a recognizer for small sets of people of great interest such as famous politicians, actors/actresses, and infamous terrorists.

Nevertheless, it is reasonable to expect that a face detector is readily available. And we can still make good use of a face detector for people-related indexing and browsing purposes. As we discussed earlier, videos contain much redundancy within shots. When individual objects are concerned, redundancy may even spread across shots; that is, the same object may appear at different shots within the same video sequence. This is even more likely for human objects, especially main characters. We reason that if shots where the same person appears could be grouped together, it would be very beneficial to human-related browsing and queries. Here we illustrate a scheme [37] to use frontal facial images of people as their identities to classify video shots; that is, shots containing similar identities are put into the same group. The choice of frontal facial images as identities is for practical reasons. And we believe that the techniques developed for clustering video shots using frontal facial images could be generalized if other forms of human identities were reliably available.

Potential applications of this scheme include video indexing and browsing. Given a video sequence, for example, we can create an index structure for each face cluster. This structure contains the center and radius (e.g., Euclidean or Mahalanobis distance) of the cluster as well as indices into the shots that contain a facial image belonging to this cluster. The radius here is used as a similarity metric measuring the likeliness between an unknown face (in a membership sense) and the ''representative'' of the group of faces in a particular cluster. And the center of a cluster is chosen as the ''representative'' in our scheme. Any search for a certain face could then be sped up by checking its distance to the center of the cluster in the face space, instead of searching every single frame or key frame of the shots in the sequence. Thus, a successful grouping of video shots provides tremendous search speed-up considering the abundant temporal redundancy in videos. The importance of the speed-up is even more critical in a browsing environment where a user wants to navigate a video database in search for interesting people.

This scheme can also be very helpful in algorithms for constructing hierarchies of video shots for video browsing purpose. One such algorithm [34], for example, proposes using global color and luminance information as similarity measures to cluster video shots in an attempt to build video shot hierarchies. Their similarity metrics enable very fast processing of videos. However, in their demonstration, some shots featuring the same anchorman fail to be grouped together due to insufficient understanding of image content. For this type of application, we believe that the existence of similar objects, and human objects in particular, should provide a good similarity measure. As will be reported later, in contrast, our scheme successfully classifies these shots to the same group.

8.6.1 System Configuration of Video Classification

Figure 8.11 shows the block diagram of this scheme. A video stream is first processed by a temporal segmentation algorithm into shots. Then a face detector and an eye locator are applied to every shot to locate faces and corresponding eyes. The facial images extracted

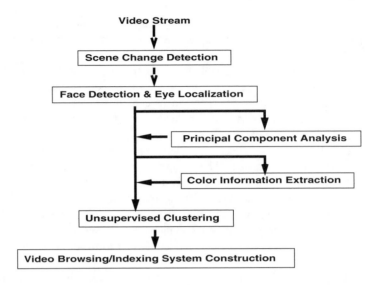

Figure 8.11   Video shot classification scheme using faces.

can then go through one of several routes to be clustered. One route is that facial images are directly processed by an unsupervised clustering algorithm. Alternatively, they can be operated on by principal component analysis (PCA) to extract the most important features, and then the clustering algorithm can be applied in a reduced feature space formed by a few principal components. A third choice is for the images to pass a color information extraction step before being clustered. Clothes and hair color statistics could be helpful when facial images don't provide enough information for clustering. In other words, color statistics can form an additional feature space where auxiliary clustering is performed. After the clustering phase, images belonging to the same group are assumed to belong to the same person and this information can then be used in further video processing such as indexing and browsing. Since the first two steps of this scheme are the same as those in the browsing system described in Section 8.5, we will only elaborate on the clustering phase in the following section.

8.6.2 Clustering of Facial Images

To effectively distinguish one face from another, the part of the face that contains the eyes and nose, as shown in Fig. 8.12, is selected as a facial pattern that is to be input to the clustering algorithm. It has been shown that this part of the face is least deformable and provides enough information to distinguish faces [35].

To cluster facial images, each face pattern is first reoriented and normalized to a fixed size using the locations of both eyes. Afterward, it is concatenated row-by-row into a d-by-1 (d is the number of pixels in the face pattern) pattern vector $\mathbf{x}_i$ (for $i = 1$ to N, where N is the total number of the selected facial patterns). An unsupervised clustering algorithm can then be applied to these vectors.

Figure 8.12 Least deformable part of face used in clustering face images.

8.6.2.1 Principal Component Analysis

Alternatively, similar to the eigenface idea [36], PCA can be used to reduce the dimensions of the original face pattern vector space and retain most of the significant features. From the covariance matrix R of the face pattern vectors, we can define a projection matrix $P_s = [\mathbf{v}_1 \ \mathbf{v}_2 \ \ldots \ \mathbf{v}_s]$ to project the original (high) d-dimensional face patterns into (low) s-dimensional subspace through equation $\mathbf{w}_i = P_s^T (\mathbf{x}_i - \mathbf{m})$, where the column vectors of P_s are the principal components of R and $\mathbf{m}$ is the mean value of all the face pattern vectors. For face patterns belonging to different people, their projected subspace patterns should differ by a certain amount. A clustering algorithm can then be used to cluster these subspace patterns into different groups. One advantage of using PCA is that the reduction in dimensionality of face pattern space speeds up clustering computations.

8.6.2.2 Color Information Extraction

Clothes and hair colors can often be very strong cues distinguishing one person from another. Similar to the floodfill algorithm employed by the QBIC project, here we use a region-growing algorithm to gather statistics on clothes and hair color. A unique feature of our method is that given the location of both eyes from the eye detector, the location of *seed pixels* can be automatically calculated instead of being selected manually. Let us use Fig. 8.13 to illustrate how we calculate the seed points, given the location of both eyes, that is, e_l and e_r. The seed points that we are seeking are h intended for getting hair color (forehead skin color in case the person is bald), and s_l and s_r intended for fetching left and right shoulder clothes color(s). Assign m_e to be the midpoint between the two eyes and m_s to be the midpoint between the two shoulder seed points, that is,

$$m_e = \frac{e_l + e_r}{2}$$

$$m_s = \frac{s_l + s_r}{2}$$

It has been observed that a person's head usually tilts one way or another while the body chunk remains relatively straight. To obtain more reliable positions of the shoulder seed points, we model the face and the shoulders by two triangles, that is, $\triangle e_l e_r p$ and $\triangle s_l e_r p$, joined by a pivot point p. We further assume that the shoulder triangle's bottom always remains horizontal, while the face triangle can rotate about p. We also define the three

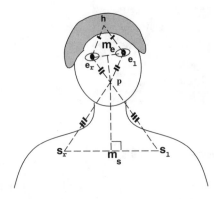

Figure 8.13 Given the location of both eyes, seed pixels are computed for region-growing algorithms to collect clothes and hair color statistics.

triangles $\triangle e_l e_r h$, $\triangle e_l e_r p$, and $\triangle s_l e_r p$ to be isosceles. Let $d(x, y)$ be the Euclidean distance between two points on the plane. Using the following assignments:

$$d(m_e, h) = \alpha d(e_l, e_r)$$

$$d(m_e, p) = \beta d(e_l, e_r)$$

$$d(m_s, p) = \gamma d(e_l, e_r)$$

$$d(s_l, s_r) = \delta d(e_l, e_r)$$

where α, β, γ, and δ are constants that could be experimentally predetermined, we can see that the locations of points h, p, s_l, and s_r can be uniquely calculated.

Subsequent to calculating the seed points, a region-growing algorithm is applied. Region color statistics are then used to form color vectors. Auxiliary clustering can subsequently be performed on these vectors.

8.6.2.3 Clustering Implementation Issues

When performing data clustering, three issues are of particular concern:

- Distance measure
- Number of clusters
- Cluster radius length(s)

For sake of simplicity, our current implementation uses Euclidean distance. Mahalanobis distance could also be used. If a K-mean type clustering algorithm is used, then the number of clusters needs to be provided. For some type of video sequences, such as movies and TV series, because we have knowledge of the cast, and thus the number of people involved, K can be assumed known. However, this assumption is invalid for general videos. In this case, the following heuristic could be used. We start with a small K and iteratively apply the

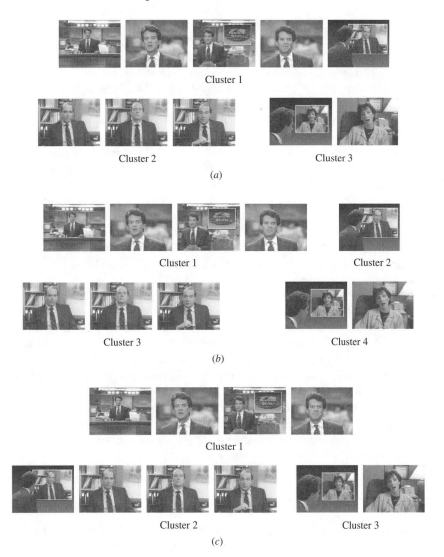

Figure 8.14   (*a*) Video shot classification result using $K = 3$. (*b*) Using $K = 4$. (*c*) Using clothes and hair colors.

K-mean clustering algorithm. A ''sudden'' decrease in magnitude of the cluster radii would indicate a suitable K. If a vector quantization type clustering algorithm is used, one needs to supply the cluster radius. Here one could make use of the variances of facial images from the same shots. The idea is that faces which are very spatially and temporally close can be assumed to belong to the same person. In other words, we can say with high confidence that faces detected from consecutive frames with close face sizes and locations belong to the same person. For empirical performance of these heuristics, please refer to [37].

8.6.2.4 Preliminary Experimental Results

In the four-minute news video sequence that we experimented with, there are three people, that is, anchorman, male and female interviewees. Since the face detector at hand detects only frontal faces, images containing frontal faces were used in our experiment. There are 32 shots whose representative frames are shown in Fig. 8.8a. Ten of these shots, depicted in Fig. 8.8b, contain frontal faces. We used the K-mean clustering algorithm to group 40 images from these 10 shots. Because of changing lighting conditions and varying angle of faces, we expect that images from one person may form more than one cluster.

In our experiments, same clustering results were obtained regardless of whether PCA was used. Figure 8.14a shows the result of $K = 3$. One shot containing the male interviewee was misclassified as one containing the anchorman. Other shots were correctly classified. Figure 8.14b depicts the outcome of $K = 4$. Here the shot that was misclassified when $K = 3$ was separated from the anchorman shots and formed a new cluster. The anchorman and female interviewee shots were accurately clustered. By using color statistics alone, all 10 shots were accurately classified as illustrated in Fig. 8.14c.

8.6.2.5 Remarks

When the number of people involved in the clustering scheme is small, we expect that facial images form simple clusters, each of which corresponds to one person. But when the number gets larger, it is less likely that this will happen. Facial patterns from different people will tend to overlap. Hence, we don't expect an unsupervised clustering algorithm such as K-mean and VQ (Vector Quantization) to work well. Actually, this is precisely the challenging problem being attacked by recognition systems based on sophisticated supervised learning algorithms such as PDBNN. However, since our goal is to classify shots belonging to *one single video sequence*, the number of people should not be too large in general. Therefore, the method proposed should work well.

8.7 PROTOTYPE EXEMPLARS

Recent years have seen a growing interest in content-based image and video indexing and retrieval. Promising research results have been put together to form prototypes. We are going to highlight two of the large research prototypes here. It is worth mentioning that some techniques of the first prototype have already been transferred to IBM's Ultimedia Manager product.

The QBIC project[3] [22] is a content-based image and video data retrieval system developed at the IBM Almaden Research Center. It facilitates user queries based on a number of features

- Example images
- User-drawn sketches and drawings

---

[3]Readers can try out their demo at the WWW site: *wwwqbic.almaden.ibm.com*

- Color histograms
- Textural patterns
- Camera and object motion

For video data, scene change detection is first performed. Then key frames and motion objects are extracted and camera motion is analyzed. Afterward, key frames are treated as regular images. Computable features such as colors, shapes, and textures are then extracted from images. These image features, together with motion attributes, are then saved in the database. This is the population phase. In the query phase, appropriate features are first computed from the user-presented image/video (e.g., selected color composition, a sketch, a previously retrieved image). Subsequently, a match engine searches the database and retrieves the best matches ordered in terms of some distance in some appropriate feature space. Besides completely specified queries like ''Give me video clips of 40% blue and 60% white,'' or ''Find me images whose shape look like this one,'' partial queries such as ''Show me images containing 20% of red and 40% of green; I don't care about the rest of the color composition'' are also supported. Furthermore, queries based on a weighted combination of multiple features such as ''Give me video clips containing a round object moving from left to right, having 50% purple, and with a background textured like this'' are allowed too.

The SWIM project [14], developed at the ISS of the National University of Singapore, is another prototype with a similar mission. Low-level image features such as colors, textures, and shapes, as well as motion attributes, are used as indices. Moreover, SWIM also provides a video browsing environment that allows the user both *sequential* and *random* access to video streams. A hierarchical structure of video shots can be formed where shots similar in visual content are grouped into clusters on each level. This browser is valuable to a user who wants to navigate the video database.

Acknowledgments

The authors would like to thank Y. K. Chen, Yun-Ting Lin, and Heather Yu for valuable comments on the drafts of the chapter. Some results presented here are from the authors' research work supported in part by an NSF Graduate Research Fellowship.

References

[1] G. K. Wallace, ''The JPEG Still Picture Compression Standard,'' *Communication of ACM*, Vol. 34, No. 4, pp. 30–44, 1991.

[2] M. Liou, ''Overview of the pX64 Kbits/s Video Coding Standard,'' *Communication of ACM*, Vol. 34, No. 4, pp. 59–63, 1991.

[3] D. L. Gall, ''MPEG: A Video Compression Standard for Multimedia Applications,'' *Communication of ACM*, Vol. 34, No. 4, pp. 46–58, 1991.

[4] K. Otsuji, Y. Tonomura, and Y. Ohba, ''Video Browsing Using Brightness Data,'' *Visual Communications and Image Processing*, SPIE, Vol. 1606, pp. 980–989, 1991.

[5] Y. Tonomura, ''Video Handling Based on Structured Information for Hypermedia Systems,'' *ACM, Proc. International Conference on Multimedia Information Systems '91*, pp. 333–344, 1991.

[6] D. Bordwell and K. Thompson, *Film Art: An Introduction*, New York: McGraw-Hill, 1993.

[7] H. J. Zhang, A. Kankanhalli, and S. W. Smoliar, "Automatic Partitioning of Full-motion Video," *Multimedia Systems*, Vol. 1, pp. 10–28, July 1993.

[8] F. Arman, A. Hsu, and M. Y. Chiu, "Feature Management for Large Video Databases," *Storage and Retrieval for Image and Video Databases*, SPIE, Vol. 1908, pp. 2–12, 1993.

[9] B. L. Yeo and B. Liu, "A Unified Approach to Temporal Segmentation of Motion JPEG and MPEG Compressed Video," *Proc. Second International Conference on Multimedia Computing and Systems*, May 1995.

[10] H. S. Ahn and I. S. Oh, "Fast Shot Detection from Video Images using Large and Adaptable Skip Factors," *Proc. Second Asian Conference on Computer Vision*, Vol. 2, pp. 489–493, 1995.

[11] S. Y. Lee and H. M. Kao, "Video Indexing—An Approach Based on Moving Object and Track," *Storage and Retrieval for Image and Video Databases*, SPIE, Vol. 1908, pp. 25–36, 1993.

[12] M. Ioka and M. Kurokawa, "A Method for Retrieving Sequences of Images on the Basis of Motion Analysis," *Image Storage and Retrieval Systems*, SPIE, Vol. 1662, pp. 35–46, 1992.

[13] M. J. Swain and D. H. Ballard, "Color Indexing," *International Journal of Computer Vision*, Vol. 7, No. 1, pp. 11–32, 1991.

[14] H. J. Zhang, "SWIM: A Prototype Environment for Image/Video Retrieval," *Proc. Second Asian Conference on Computer Vision*, Vol. 2, pp. 519–523, 1995.

[15] W. Niblack, R. Barber, W. Equitz, M. Flickner, E. Glasman, D. Petkovic, P. Yanker, C. Faloutsos, and G. Taubin, "The QBIC Project: Querying Images by Content Using Color, Texture, and Shape," *Storage and Retrieval for Image and Video Databases*, SPIE, Vol. 1908, pp. 173–187, 1993.

[16] Y. H. Gong, H. J. Zhang, H. C. Chuan, and M. Sakauchi, "An Image Database System with Content Capturing and Fast Image Indexing Abilities," *Proc. International Conference on Multimedia Computing and Systems*, Boston, pp. 121–130, 1994.

[17] M. K. Hu, "Visual Pattern Recognition by Moment Invariants," *IRE Transactions on Information Theory*, pp. 179–187, Feb. 1962.

[18] R. C. Gonzalez and R. E. Woods, *Digital Image Processing*, Reading, MA: Addison-Wesley, 1992.

[19] T. Y. Hou, A. Hsu, P. Liu, and M. Y. Chiu, "A Content-based Indexing Technique Using Relative Geometry Features," *Image Storage and Retrieval Systems*, SPIE, Vol. 1662, pp. 59–68, 1992

[20] G. Taubin and D. B. Cooper, "Recognition and Positioning of Rigid Objects Using Algebraic Moment Invariants," *Geometric Methods in Computer Vision*, SPIE, Vol. 1570, pp. 175–186, 1991.

[21] A. K. Jain and A. Vailaya, "Image Retrieval Using Color and Shape," *Proc. Second Asian Conference on Computer Vision*, Vol. 2, pp. 529–533, 1995.

[22] M. Flickner, H. Sawhney, W. Niblack, J. Ashley, Q. Huang, B. Dom, M. Gorkani, J. Hafner, D. Lee, D. Petkovic, D. Steele, and P. Yanker, "Query by Image and Video Content: The QBIC System," in *Computer*, pp. 23–32, Sept. 1995.

[23] S. Sclaroff and A. Pentland, "A Finite-element Framework for Correspondence and Matching," in *Proc. 4th International Conference on Computer Vision*, pp. 308–313, 1993.

[24] M. Miyahara and Y. Yoshida, "Mathematical Transform of (R,G,B) Color Data to Munsell (H,V,C) Color Data," *Proc. of SPIE Visual Communication and Image Processing*, 1001, pp. 650–657, 1988.

[25] H. Tamura, S. Mori, and T. Yamawaki, "Textural Features Corresponding to Visual Perception," *IEEE Transactions on Systems, Man, and Cybernetics*, Vol. SMC–8, No. 6, pp. 460–473, 1978.

[26] R. Chellappa, C. L. Wilson, and S. Sirohey, "Human and Machine Recognition of Faces: A Survey," *Proceedings of the IEEE*, Vol. 83, No. 5, May 1995.

[27] H. A. Rowley, S. Baluja, and T. Kanade, "Human Face Detection in Visual Scenes," *Technical Report CMU-CS-95-158*, School of Computer Science, Carnegie Mellon University, 1995.

[28] T. Poggio and K. K. Sung, "Finding Human Faces with a Gaussian Mixture Distribution-based Face Model," *Proc. Second Asian Conference on Computer Vision*, Vol. 2, pp. 435–440, 1995.

[29] M. Kass, A. Witkin, and D. Terzopoulos, "Snakes: Active Contour Models," *International Journal of Computer Vision*, pp. 321–331, 1988.

[30] R. K. Srihari, "Combining Text and Image Information in Content-based Retrieval," *Proc. IEEE International Conference on Image Processing*, pp. 326–329, Washington, DC, 1995.

[31] Mourad Cherfaoui and Christian Bertin, "Two-stage Strategy for Indexing and Presenting Video," *Proc. SPIE, Storage and Retrieval Image and Video Databases II*, Vol. 2185, pp. 174–184.

[32] S. H. Lin, S. Y. Kung, and L. J. Lin, "A Probabilistic DBNN with Applications to Sensor Fusion and Object Recognition," *IEEE Neural Networks for Signal Processing V*, Boston, Aug. 1995.

[33] S. W. Smoliar and H. J. Zhang, "Content-based Video Indexing and Retrieval," *IEEE Multimedia*, pp. 62–72, 1994.

[34] M. M. Yeung, B. L. Yeo, W. Wolf, and B. Liu, "Video Browsing Using Clustering and Scene Transitions on Compressed Sequences," *Proc. SPIE, Multimedia Computing and Networking, 1995*.

[35] S. H. Lin, Y. Chan, and S. Y. Kung, "A Probabilistic Decision-based Neural Network for Locating Deformable Objects and Its Applications to Surveillance System and Video Browsing," *Proc. of ICASSP, 1996*.

[36] M. Turk and A. Pentland, "Eigenfaces for Recognition," *Journal of Cognitive Neuroscience*, Vol. 3, No. 1, 1991.

[37] Y. Chan, S. H. Hung, Y. P. Tan, and S. Y. Kung, "Video Shot Classification Using Human Faces," *IEEE International Conference on Image Processing*, Lausanne, Switzerland, 1996.

[38] Y. K. Chen, Y. T. Lin, and S. Y. Kung, "A Feature Tracking Algorithm Using Neighborhood Relaxation with Multi-Candidate Pre-Screening," *IEEE International Conference on Image Processing*, Lausanne, Switzerland, Sept. 1996.

Chapter 9

CONTENT-BASED IMAGE RETRIEVAL—RESEARCH ISSUES[†]

Harold S. Stone

Abstract

This chapter surveys the research problems and directions in the field of image retrieval by content-based query. The central problem is to find high-speed methods for finding which images within a large collection best match a given image template. To be of practical use, a solution should be able to do detailed analyses at a rate of about 1000 images per second, which, when coupled with descriptor-based search techniques to select candidates for analysis, will enable effective search of libraries containing millions of images.

An attractive approach is to perform the search on compressed versions of the images. Reduction in data volume reduces I/O time, and should reduce processing time as well. Fourier-domain compression and wavelet compression are the major directions for this research.

The advantage of Fourier-domain compression is that it provides an efficient computational means to determine which position within an image best matches a specified pattern. However, the cost of performing Fourier transforms is a computational bottleneck, forcing researchers to consider other alternatives that may yield faster searches.

Wavelet compression has the advantage that correlation peaks can be detected in the wavelet domain, thus eliminating the need to invert the wavelet transform. But searching within a wavelet transform is more costly than in a Fourier domain. One might obtain the best of both transforms by combining Fourier transforms with wavelet functions.

For both wavelet and Fourier-domain computations, architectural support can reduce access-time delays to near zero on critical paths within the memory hierarchy because all of the accesses are known in advance. Memory-access time is the main source of performance degradation in the memory hierarchy. It may be possible to use the knowledge of future reference patterns to schedule data movement at various levels of the memory hierarchy in order to reduce the access time delay to zero for the critical accesses. Ideally, image streams will arrive at an arithmetic unit just in time to be processed, and the results will be returned to an external disk (or other form of memory) just as the write head reaches the region where the data are to be written.

The gains from both architectural support and processing of compressed images may yield the performance improvement required to meet our goal.

9.1 EXECUTIVE SUMMARY

The evolution of digital technology has created vast libraries of machine-processable information. Today these libraries are being tapped on a global scale, enabled by advances in data compression, text searching algorithms, communications, and networking. Text retrieval has reached a high level of sophistication, but image retrieval has lagged far behind. Most image retrieval is descriptor-based, and only recently have researchers investigated content-based queries [4,7,8,9,10,11,15,16].

Image-query systems that are based on image content typically preprocess images to obtain a set of descriptors and use these descriptors to search an image database. This avoids the cost of doing content analysis while performing a query, but it limits content searches to searches for which descriptors exist. Consequently, this approach is not useful for libraries in which images are rich in interesting details that are too numerous to summarize compactly by descriptors. Examples of such images are satellite and medical images. It is not apparent what descriptors capture all of the useful information necessary to respond to any reasonable query of the image data. For these images, the image data themselves may have to be analyzed in order to respond to a query. Descriptors can be used effectively to help limit the search, so it is generally a good idea to attach descriptors to each image to the extent possible. Content analysis can be performed on the collection of images whose descriptors satisfy a query.

Image retrieval as described here is a daunting problem. Consider, for example, earth satellite images. NASA Goddard Space Flight Center currently has more than 30 terabytes of data on-line and another 30 terabytes "near" on-line (on mountable tape cartridges). This is the equivalent of 60 million images, spanning about 20 years. When the Earth Orbiting Satellite (EOS) is launched later in this decade, it will produce image data at a rate of 1 petabyte per year, which is roughly 1 billion images per year. As technology advances, the rate of acquisition will increase. By 2010, the image repository may hold 25 billion images covering 35 years of historical data. In addition to the absolute number of images increasing, we expect the resolution of the images to increase in time as well. This could increase the number of pixels in the library by a factor of 4 to 16 over our estimates if linear resolution doubles or quadruples by 2010.

Clearly, content-based search on the full repository is overkill. A content-based query should use descriptors to focus a search on a geographical region, on a set of dates and times, and on other factors that may be relevant. With descriptors, a researcher should be able to produce a much smaller candidate set of images to view, but the size of that set depends on the query, the image library, and the descriptors available. If there are only a few responses, there is no need to do further content analysis, and the user can view all responses very quickly. This may be true as well if the number of responses is 100, although the viewing may be more tedious. With 1000 to 10,000 responses, the query almost certainly requires automatic content analysis to select the most relevant images. With more than 10,000 responses, the user may supply additional descriptors to focus the search on a smaller set. A reasonable goal, therefore, is to be able to analyze sets of 1000 to 10,000 images automatically, for which a processing rate of 1000 images per second provides a very good response time for human interaction.

If we use algorithms that take 10,000 operations per pixel to extract information, and images contain 1 million pixels, the processing load for the query is 10 teraoperations per second! This is unattainable today and may be difficult to attain at low cost even in the longer term, say, even by the year 2010. To achieve our goal, we need to perform automatic content analysis at a cost of no more than 100 operations per pixel. This reduces the processor requirement to 100 gigaoperations per second, which should be achievable by 2010 within server machines, and possibly within low-cost desktop machines. As a base point, we assume that in 1996 a low-cost Pentium-class computer runs at a rate equivalent to 250 to 500 megaoperations. If computer throughput doubles every two years, in 14 years comparable machines will run about 128 times faster. This produces a throughput of roughly 32 to 64 gigaops in the low-cost range. One level up are servers, which should be two to four times faster, at least, than low-cost commodity machines.

We believe that content-based query of images can open archives for queries that are otherwise impossible to perform. For example, a person should be able to gain insight quickly into the earth's environment, weather and climate, oceans, and resources. Historical data allow the researcher to examine specific regions over time periods that span from the mid-1970s to the present. Content-based query is useful because it can allow the user to ask for cloud-free days for searches that involve land use so that the items of interest are known to be visible. For rainfall measures and other information regarding precipitation and cloudy days, the user should ask for pictures with at least a certain fraction of cloud cover.

Medical imaging applications also produce large volumes of data, although the volume is small when compared to that of satellite images of the earth. Content-based search of X rays, CAT scans, MRI scans, and other image data can be used to find images that show similar pathologies. When a physician sees something unusual, he or she should be able to query the database for examples that have the same visual appearance. The physician can then examine the patient histories for diagnosis and treatment information.

In this chapter, we consider a number of approaches to content-based image querying. Specifically, we explore techniques that combine image search and image compression. Our objective is to accelerate search by operating in a compressed domain to the extent that this is possible. We also speculate on the characteristics of the problem that can lead to architectural support for image query.

We explore compression schemes in the spatial-frequency domain where the idea is to replace small Fourier coefficients by 0s to create sparse data structures. Processing sparse data in the frequency domain is computationally efficient, not only because the data volume is small, but also because it is often less costly to perform convolutions and correlations in the frequency domain than in the pixel domain. We show that a number of image-matching criteria that depend on correlations can be calculated quickly in the frequency domain. These criteria include the use of Euclidean distance [17], differences in average intensity [17], the correlation coefficient of a pattern with an image [21], and edge-detection criteria [2]. Stone and Shamoon [18] showed how to reduce the effects of occlusion in calculating the first two criteria, and the techniques they describe carry through to the others mentioned here.

These criteria indicate not only the presence of a match, but also the location of the best match within an image. If the query takes the form ''Find the images for which the pattern match may be at any location of the image,'' the correlation is essential, and Fourier-domain processing is an efficient way to perform the correlation, provided that the number of pixels in the pattern is at least $O(\log N)$ for images of size $N \times N$ pixels. If the query takes the form ''Find the images for which the pattern match is at location (i, j) in the image,'' then the transforms between pixel domain and Fourier domain are unnecessary and costly.

To foster the use of Fourier-domain techniques, we show how to modify a sequence of operations so that the nonlinear operations come after all linear operations are completed. The effect of this change in sequencing is to permit the linear operations to be done first in the Fourier domain and then followed by the nonlinear operations in the pixel domain, with a Fourier transform performed only at the point in the sequence where the operations change from linear to nonlinear. If the operations were to alternate between linear and nonlinear, it would be necessary to perform transforms at each point where the operations change between linear to nonlinear, provided that this is faster than pixel-domain operations.

The modifications we suggest do not preserve the matching criteria because the non-linear operations do not, in general, commute with the linear operations. Nevertheless, the modifications produce new criteria that appear to be as useful for image search as the original criteria.

This chapter explores some of the problems in searching JPEG-encoded data in the compressed domain. The fact that JPEG encoding partitions an image into 8×8 subimages greatly complicates matters. JPEG stores the transforms of the subimages, but we need the transform of the full image to do correlation. We show how to go directly from a JPEG encoding to a Fourier transform, without first reproducing a pixel representation of an image. The objective in performing this operation is to start with sparse data and end with sparse data, without decompressing data at any intermediate step. The scheme described here remains to be tested on JPEG-encoded images to determine if it retains enough sparsity to maintain a speed advantage. Also, we have not evaluated how well search criteria perform when used on images that have been compressed with lossy compression techniques as compared to searches on uncompressed images.

For the class of queries that ask whether a certain feature is present at a specific location, the use of Fourier-domain processing is not warranted. The matching can be done more efficiently by looking only at the given specific location in each image. For example, the query "Find the set of images containing clouds that obscure the subimage in position x of an image" does not require correlation over other areas of the image to establish the presence of clouds in position x. Wavelet decompositions are potentially useful for this type of query. They lend themselves to multispectral analysis, which has the potential for permitting matching to be done by looking at a few subbands of a wavelet representation instead of looking at all subbands. The results of wavelet-domain matches directly correlate with coordinates of the original image, so that it is not necessary to leave the wavelet domain to interpret a matching function.

We show that for image searches, the compression of wavelet representations through sequence subsampling can distribute key features to different subbands depending on the phase of the subsampling. This greatly complicates the search because the query algorithm cannot readily determine in advance how to limit the search to specific subbands. To avoid the subsampling problem, we may have to compress subband data by schemes other than subsampling. The idea is to be able to focus a query on particular subbands because the information, if present in the image data, will lie in a particular subband representation with certainty.

In considering the various approaches, we speculate on what architectural support will be useful for fast image queries and how this might be similar to, or different from, the current trends in computer architecture. Our findings are that image-query support should take advantage of the fixed pattern of data access to eliminate access delays throughout the memory system. That is, the computer system should be able to schedule data movement from archival storage to high-speed disk storage, to main-memory, cache-memory, or other high-speed buffer memory, and then to the processor registers. The goal is to schedule data transfers so that data will arrive where they are to be processed just in time to be processed.

To meet this goal, at each level in the memory hierarchy the data must be requested in advance of their actual need. In fact, if the access time at a particular device is T, the request for the data must reach the device at least T seconds before they are required so that the data can be accessed and delivered in time. The supporting hardware and software have to identify future accesses and issue requests for those accesses well in advance. If this can be done successfully, the access time will drop dramatically because requests for data will reach their target memories well after the access for the data has been triggered.

In an ideal situation, data movement might be done with an effective access time near zero throughout the memory hierarchy, although it is more likely that only the bottleneck level of memory will have an effective access time of zero. This requires a combination of prefetching and pipelining, and is unusual today in the extensive use of prefetching. Image accesses are totally predictable over long periods of time, whereas accesses produced by typical programs today are not nearly as predictable. The trends today are to find techniques that reduce access latency by using multiple threads of execution and large caches. While we expect to see today's trends to continue for general workloads, as image processing becomes an important application, we expect to see access scheduling and prefetching to be incorporated into machine architecture as well. Eventually, image processing support may dominate the system design.

The remainder of this chapter discusses the application area, Fourier methods, wavelet methods, and hardware assists.

9.2   IMAGE QUERY BY CONTENT—THE CHALLENGE

The opening section gave some examples and speculated that image-understanding methods may require processor throughput of as much as 10 teraoperations per second. This section looks more deeply into the nature of image queries and image retrieval to consider how we might reach our goal of analyzing 1000 images per second.

Descriptor-based search of images is extremely efficient. The examination of 100 bytes of descriptors may be sufficient to determine whether or not an image of 1 million bytes matches a query. The volume of information in the descriptor is four orders of magnitude less than the data in the full image. Consequently, descriptor-based search is the preferred method of query when descriptors are available.

There are two problems with descriptors, however. One problem is to determine which descriptors to use, and the second is to create the descriptors for an existing database. We are not sure how to solve the first problem, but even if we could, the second problem is a major challenge and may be insurmountable. Let's focus attention on the effort required to add descriptors to an existing data set, and then return to the question of what descriptors should be added.

The feasibility of adding descriptors to existing image libraries depends on the size of the library and on the cost per image to create the descriptors. If the library holds a few thousand images, it may be quite reasonable to make the investment to add descriptors to all the images. On the other hand, if the library holds millions of images, the cost of adding the descriptors is nontrivial. A 10-million image library holds 10 terapixels (at 1 megapixel per image). If the cost of adding descriptors is 10,000 operations per pixel, the cost of retrofitting new descriptors to the full library is about 100 petaoperations. At 1 gigaoperation per second, this is 1157 days, or a little over three years. A 1000-processor complex of gigahertz processors could complete this task in less than two days, but this is excessively costly by today's measures and will continue to be so for the next several years.

Our assumptions are based on the cost of a library with 10 million images. But image libraries are growing by orders of magnitude as well. If the growth rate of the data exceeds the growth rate of processing power, it may never be economical to retrofit a growing library for descriptor queries. For sufficiently rapid growth rates, we cannot ignore the cost of adding descriptors to newly acquired images, even if we abandon the idea of adding descriptors to images already acquired. It may be prohibitively expensive to create full-content image descriptors, and we may therefore have no choice but to do image analysis in real time while responding to an image query.

At this point we explore the question of what descriptors to use. We expect to maintain some descriptors for every image library because we have to exploit the power of descriptors to limit search when this is possible and practical. For satellite images, there are obvious descriptors that should be attached, including date, time, geographic location, satellite, and instrument. These do not require content analysis. Similarly, for medical images, the descriptors should include patient information, diagnosis, medical history, treatment, attending physician information, and so on. What additional information describes the content of the image?

Consider Fig. 9.1, an image of the Black Hills located in the northwestern United States. What aspects of the image merit recording? This is very much dependent on what queries will be made. Figure 9.2 shows some descriptive information about Fig. 9.1. This figure characterizes Fig. 9.1 by land use, with each distinct shade of gray representing a different type of use. Although this information came from other sources than the image itself, it is quite reasonable to add such information to every image entered in the database if it were available and inexpensive to compute.

Figure 9.3 shows the result of a content query for which a descriptor would not be known in advance. Figure 9.3*a* shows the query in the form of a rectangular pattern drawn in the forest area of Fig. 9.1. Figure 9.3*b* shows the regions of Fig. 9.1 that match the pattern to within a given threshold in each of two ways—intensity and texture. The thresholds were set to give a reasonably good visual characterization of the forested areas of Fig. 9.1 that are similar to the forested area in the rectangular pattern. The area picked up by the query depends very much on the initial pattern as well as on the thresholds. Although this search was very successful, its success was mostly due to the fact that a small visual pattern captured the idea of forest used to create ground truth. Note that some regions of Fig. 9.1 that are categorized as forest by ground truth in Fig. 9.2 are visually quite different from other forest regions, and they are not identified as forest regions by the

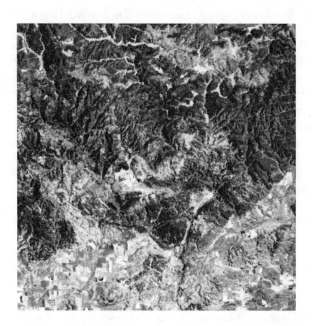

Figure 9.1   Black Hills image.

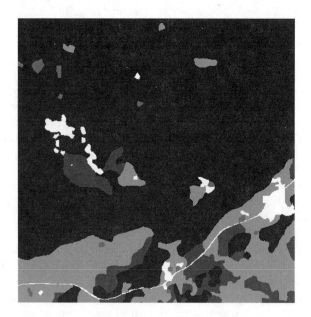

Figure 9.2   Ground truth for the image in Fig. 9.1.

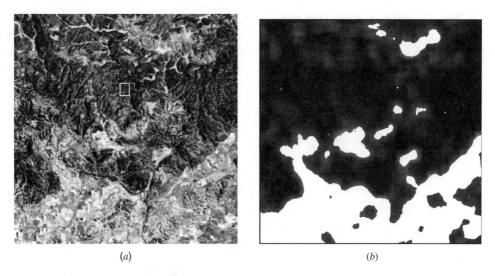

$$(a) \qquad\qquad\qquad\qquad\qquad\qquad\qquad (b)$$

Figure 9.3   (a) The "forest" pattern. (b) Search with $T_{\text{texture}} = 0.230$, $T_{\text{intensity}} = 0.108$.

search in Fig. 9.3b. We doubt that any single visual pattern can be used to match ground truth for the forest region of Fig. 9.1.

Here is a situation in which a query can be phrased in an enormous number of possible forms. In this case, the user found some interesting detail and asked "What looks like this?" But a user might select the pattern from any image in the library, and the pattern could be of any size. Is it possible for some small set of descriptors to capture the majority of the interesting queries that could be asked of this image? For Fig. 9.1, probably not.

Figure 9.3 demonstrates that the ability to form such content queries may have great value. If the characterization of forest area in this image were robust enough to serve as an area measure, we could query images taken on the same date for the last 20 years, find the cloud-free subset, and then find the regions in those images that match the pattern. By counting the dark pixels in the match data, we could obtain a general idea of the trend in forest cover in the region over the last 20 years, and this could be done, in principle, as part of the query mechanism without human intervention. Our goal is to be able to do this type of query on a compressed form of the image without relying on content descriptors assigned to the image by a preprocessor. Of course, if ground-truth information such as the data in Fig. 9.2 were available, the query engine should use it.

Our goal is to perform this sort of content analysis on 1000 images per second at reasonable cost. This is unachievable today, but we might achieve it through research innovations and faster hardware that will be available in the future. The effect of research will be to hasten the point at which the goal is attained or to make the goal attainable if it presently is not. The constraints force the query system to limit the type of processing that can be done in the image analysis in order to meet the performance requirement.

The requirement for high performance almost certainly precludes a query engine that attempts to understand the image. We focus on template matching techniques in the hope that they will prove to be powerful enough to extract useful images from large libraries. But we cannot expect to recognize structures, roads, towns, and rivers from underlying cognitive models of what these look like. Hence, we do not expect the query engine to be able to process the query:

Find images in which there is a road that runs along a river and stops at a town on the river.

The notions of "road," "river," and "town" are abstract notions satisfied by many different visual images. We can give individual examples of a road, a river, and a town, or a few different examples, but our approach is unable to create a query that recognizes these features by understanding images. We give up cognition of abstract forms in return for fast processing speed.

QBIC [15] uses template matching techniques based on color, texture, and shape. These criteria provide a good basis for content queries, but there is much room for new research. A query system should be able to mimic retrieval by the semantics of the query to the extent that this is possible. A user may well wish to recover images in which roads are parallel to rivers, and may find it frustrating and difficult to express this notion in terms of color, texture, and shape of sample images. What criteria and what compositions of those criteria are needed to give the user the power needed to construct the queries that the user actually needs?

If the user would benefit from the use of image understanding, why not use image understanding as a basis of the image analysis? This is a perfectly acceptable approach in the right timeframe, but its acceptability depends on overall cost and performance of the query system. Our goal is to analyze images at the rate of 10^9 pixels per second. The image analysis algorithm determines the number of operations per pixel, and this in turn determines the performance required and overall cost of the system to meet our goal. If image understanding can be done for a cost of 100 operations per pixel, that may be sufficiently low to attain our goal, and we need not look elsewhere for a solution. On the other hand, if image understanding requires 10,000 operations per pixel, we are in a totally different regime. In this case, we must seek other ways to solve the problem at reasonable cost within the next 10 to 15 years.

Although we have focused on particular types of image libraries, the utility of content-based image search extends well beyond those. The use of digital video is beginning to grow. It can create enormous libraries, far greater than the satellite image and medical libraries that we have mentioned in this section. In fact, the data rate from the EOS satellite is roughly equivalent to uncompressed video from a single digital video feed. If digital video cameras are as prevalent in the future as analog cameras are today, it is easily conceivable that video image libraries will reach 10^{18} pixels by the year 2000. Almost surely, the images will be stored in compressed format, and retrieval by image content will be a major means of library access if it meets cost and performance goals.

9.3 FOURIER-TRANSFORM TECHNIQUES

In this section, we examine techniques for image matching that are based on operations performed in the frequency domain. There are two reasons for taking this approach:

1. Images can be stored in compressed form by using Fourier transforms with small coefficients replaced by 0s. Compression reduces the cost of storage, I/O, and may reduce computation requirements as well.

2. Convolution and correlation operations can be done faster in many cases if the data are first transformed into the frequency domain and the corresponding operations are performed in that domain.

In the discussion that follows, all formulas are given for one-dimensional variables. They extend in obvious ways to two dimensions.

Consider a query of the form:

Find if pattern $\mathbf{p}$ is present in image $\mathbf{x}$ for each $\mathbf{x}$ in the candidate set $\mathbf{C}$, and if the pattern is present, indicate where in each image it occurs.

This type of query involves a pattern matching operation in all possible pattern positions within an image. When the location of the pattern is unknown, Fourier techniques offer processing efficiencies, because the cost per pixel to examine an entire $N \times N$ image is only $O(\log N)$ times more costly than to examine a single location for a match. But if the query is a simpler query of the form:

Find if pattern $\mathbf{p}$ is present at position $(i_0, \ j_0)$ in image $\mathbf{x}$ for each $\mathbf{x}$ in the candidate set $\mathbf{C}$,

it is more efficient to restrict the image analysis to the neighborhood of coordinate (i_0, j_0). The Fourier transform should not be used in this case because of the overhead of $O(\log N)$ times as many operations per pixel. In the discussion that follows, we focus on the first type of query, namely, those that ask where a pattern occurs in an image.

9.3.1 Convolution and Correlation Operations

In matching images, we need to have various measures of the quality of a match between an image and a pattern. The pattern serves as the key to a search, and the result of the search is a collection of images that match the pattern best. Convolution plays a significant role in determining the quality of a match, and the well-known convolution theorem [cf. Lim, 1990, pp. 142–145] allows us to do the convolution operations in the Fourier domain. Let us review convolution and the convolution theorem briefly, and show how to exploit the convolution theorem to compute a number of matching criteria that are useful in image search.

The circular convolution of two N-vectors $\mathbf{x} = (x_0, x_1, \ldots, x_{N-1})$ and $\mathbf{y} = (y_0, y_1, \ldots, y_{N-1})$, written $\mathbf{x} \circ \mathbf{y}$, is defined by the equation:

$$(\mathbf{x} \circ \mathbf{y})_j = \sum_{i \in N} x_{(j-i) \bmod N} \, y_i \tag{1}$$

where $\sum_{i \in N}$ denotes $\sum_{i=0}^{N-1}$.

The convolution theorem shows that this is equivalent to point-by-point multiplication in the Fourier domain. Specifically, we let $\mathbf{X}$ and $\mathbf{Y}$ be the Fourier transforms of $\mathbf{x}$ and $\mathbf{y}$, respectively. The convolution theorem is:

$$\mathbf{F}(\mathbf{x} \circ \mathbf{y})_j = (\mathbf{X})_j (\mathbf{Y})_j, \tag{2}$$

where $\mathbf{F}$ denotes the discrete Fourier transform. The Fourier-domain computation in one dimension requires only N multiplications, whereas the convolution requires N^2 multiplications, so that there is a net improvement in processing performance by calculating the convolution in the Fourier domain, provided that the cost of transforms back and forth between the domains is small. Since the transforms require only $O(N \log N)$ operations, for all but small values of N it is faster to compute convolutions in the Fourier domain. For two-dimensional images, the number of operations required to perform the convolution of two $K \times K$ images is $O(K^4)$ in the pixel domain and reduces to $O(K^2 \log K)$ when Fourier transforms are used. If we let $N = K^2$ denote the number of pixels in an image, the complexity of convolution grows as N^2 and $N \log N$, respectively, in the pixel and frequency domains for both one-dimensional and two-dimensional formulations.

In image-query applications, most measures of interest use correlations rather than convolutions, where the correlation of $\mathbf{x}$ and $\mathbf{y}$, denoted as $\mathbf{x} \star \mathbf{y}$, is defined as

$$(\mathbf{x} \star \mathbf{y})_j = \sum_{i \in N} x_{(j+i) \bmod N} \, y_i \tag{3}$$

The convolution theorem for the correlations is:

$$\mathbf{F}(\mathbf{x} \star \mathbf{y})_j = (\mathbf{X})_j (\mathbf{Y}^*)_j \tag{4}$$

where $\mathbf{Y}^*$ is the complex conjugate of $\mathbf{Y}$.

Query operations often require matching a small pattern $\mathbf{p}$ with a large image $\mathbf{x}$. We assume that $\mathbf{p}$ is an M-vector, the image is an N-vector, and $M < N$. In this case, convolution and correlation require $O(MN)$ operations. To do these operations in the Fourier domain, we extend $\mathbf{p}$ to length N by appending $(N - M)$ 0s, before taking transforms. The cost remains $O(N \log N)$ in the Fourier domain, and the cost of taking the transforms and inverse transform dominates the cost of the computation. For values of M on the order of $\log N$ or smaller, the convolution and correlation might be done faster in the pixel domain, depending on actual values of constant coefficients hidden by the "big-Oh" notation.

9.3.2 Frequency-domain Computation of Discrimination Functions

In this section, we consider typical matching criteria. We show how to modify widely used matching criteria to exploit Fourier-domain processing as much as possible.

Correlation is most often associated with matched filters [20], where it is the basis of a detector that maximizes the signal-to-noise ratio when extracting a known signal from a received signal contaminated by noise in highly constrained contexts. For image matching, correlation is useful but not optimal because areas of an image that do not match the pattern do not have the statistics of additive white Gaussian noise. Moreover, at places where a pattern appears in an image, most likely in a distorted form, the distortions are not adequately captured by the assumptions of the model for which the matched filter is optimum. Even though the use of correlation is not provably optimum in our context, it is a powerful way to compare images, and it is a component of all the comparison criteria described in this section.

Among the criteria that are commonly used in image matching is the Euclidean distance between an image and a pattern. Stone and Li [17] call this the *texture criterion* because it tends to represent the texture of a pattern. It is the sum of the squares of differences of pixel values. In the jth position of an M-vector pattern $\mathbf{p}$ relative to an N-vector pattern $\mathbf{x}$, the texture criterion is defined by the following formula:

$$S(j) = \frac{1}{M} \sum_{i \in M} (p_i - x_{i+j})^2, \qquad 0 \leq j \leq N - M - 1 \tag{5}$$

$$= \frac{1}{M} \sum_{i \in M} p_i^2 - 2 \sum_{i \in M} p_i x_{i+j} + \sum_{i \in M} x_{i+j}^2, \qquad 0 \leq j \leq N - M - 1 \tag{6}$$

The expanded form of the texture discriminant has three summations. The first term is independent of j and need not be computed separately for each value of j. The second term is a correlation, as is the third term. In fact, the third term can be written

$$\sum_{i \in M} x_{i+j}^2 h_i = \mathbf{x}^2 \star \mathbf{h} \tag{7}$$

where $\mathbf{h}$ is an N-vector ''window,'' whose first M coordinates are 1s and whose remaining $(N - M)$ coordinates are 0s.

Note that last two terms in Eq. (6) can be computed in the Fourier domain and added together there before transforming them back to the pixel domain. Because the point-by-point multiplications in the Fourier domain are much less costly than inverse transforms, especially if both $\mathbf{x}$ and $\mathbf{x}^2$ are stored in compressed form in the Fourier domain, then the major contributor to the cost of evaluating this discriminant is the cost of the transform back to the pixel domain. The inverse transform is used to find peaks of the discriminant in the pixel domain. For uncompressed images of size 256×256 to size 1024×1024, the cost of an inverse transform is somewhere in the range of 50 to 100 operations per pixel. The point-by-point multiplications in the frequency domain and nonlinear thresholding in the pixel domain add a few more operations per pixel, but are typically less costly than a Fourier transform. There is a small reduction in computation of the inverse-transform computation due to compression in the frequency domain, but the reduction depends strongly on the amount of compression and the extent to which the nonzeros cluster in the frequency domain.

Stone and Shamoon [18] showed that the texture discriminant in Eq. (6) can be modified to reduce the effects of occlusions in images. An occlusion is a visual artifact that obscures an underlying pixel. In satellite images, an occlusion is usually the result of a cloud, shadow, or data dropout. Because occluded pixels are dramatically different from the value that would be observed in the absence of an occlusion, occlusions tend to severely distort the discriminant calculation. Encoding occluded pixels as 0s effectively removes them from the middle term in Eq. (6). Similarly, by replacing the window mask $\mathbf{h}$ with a mask of the window whose 1s correspond to valid pixels in the pattern and whose 0s correspond to invalid pixels, the effects of occluded pixels in the pattern can be removed from the third term of Eq. (6). The first term of Eq. (6) also needs to be modified to remove the effects of occluded pixels in the image, and this is done by correlating $\mathbf{p}^2$ with an occlusion mask for the image just as the third term correlates $\mathbf{x}^2$ with an occlusion mask of the pattern. The first term becomes

$$\sum_{i \in M} m_{i+j} p_i^2 = \mathbf{m} \star \mathbf{p}^2 \qquad (8)$$

where $\mathbf{m}$ is a binary N-vector mask whose 1s indicate valid pixels in the image and whose 0s indicate occluded pixels.

In attempting to do as much as possible in the frequency domain, the calculation of the first term requires an occlusion mask for the image and an additional point-by-point multiplication in the frequency domain. The transform of the occlusion mask for the image can be precomputed and saved in compressed form so that this does not have to be computed as part of the query. The cost of the query is dominated by the cost of the inverse transform. Note that the normalization constant M in Eq. (6) is not independent of j in the presence of occluded pixels. At position j, the normalization factor is equal to the number of valid terms in the summations for the jth pixel. This can be computed by correlation operations on the occlusion masks. Therefore, the normalization factors can be computed in the frequency domain and transformed back to the pixel domain where the pixel-by-pixel normalizations are done. The impact on processing cost is that two inverse Fourier transforms are required— one for the normalizing factor and one for the three-term sum—instead of just one inverse transform when there are no occlusions.

We can gain about a factor of 2 by taking advantage of the fact that the images and patterns contain real numbers rather than complex numbers. It is well known that two real matrices can be combined into a single complex matrix and then transformed into the frequency domain with a single Fourier transform. Once in the frequency domain, the individual transforms can be extracted from the composite transform. Conversely, two Fourier transforms of real data can be joined in the frequency domain and separated into their individual images in the pixel domain [cf. Blahut, 1985, pp. 66–69]. Consequently, by batching the inverse transforms into pairs of inverse transforms, we can reduce the number of operations per pixel by nearly a factor of 2.

Another discriminant function that is used frequently in image processing applications is the correlation coefficient from statistics and probability. The correlation coefficient $\rho(j)$ of an M vector pattern $\mathbf{p}$ and an N-vector image $\mathbf{x}$ at position j is given by the formula:

$$\rho(j) = \frac{M \sum_i p_i x_{i+j} - (\sum_i p_i)(\sum_i x_{i+j})}{\{M \sum_i p_i^2 - (\sum_i p_i)^2\}\{M \sum_i x_{i+j}^2 - (\sum_i x_{i+j})^2\}^{1/2}}, \tag{9}$$

$$0 \leq j \leq N - M - 1$$

The numerator consists of one correlation of $\mathbf{p}$ with $\mathbf{x}$, and the computations of $\sum p_i$ and $\sum x_{i+j}$. In the absence of occlusions, the sum of p_i is independent of j and can be computed once for a pattern and used repeatedly in all image searches for all values of j. The sum of x_{i+j} must be recomputed for each j and can be computed efficiently by incremental updating. To compute $\sum_{i \in M} x_{i+j}$ for $j + 1$ given the value of the sum for j, to the latter sum add $-x_j + x_{j+M}$. (The formula is a little more complex in two dimensions but still requires fewer operations to evaluate than is required by an inverse transform from the frequency domain to the pixel domain.)

To evaluate the denominator, note that the sums $\sum p_i$ and $\sum x_{i+j}$ appear in both the numerator and denominator so that they can be computed just once for both purposes. The other two sums are $\sum p_i^2$ and $\sum x_{i+j}^2$. In the absence of occlusions, the first sum is independent of j, and the second can be computed incrementally as indicated above. Consequently, in the absence of occlusions, Eq. (9) requires only one inverse transform, plus a few operations per pixel in both the Fourier and pixel domains. The various nontransform operations are negligible relative to the cost of the inverse transform.

If there are occlusions, the summations of the first and second powers of p_i are not independent of j, and the summations of the first and second powers of x_{i+j} do not lend themselves to incremental evaluations. In this case, we can compute the four sums by correlations with occlusion masks. This can be done in the Fourier domain, but all four sums need to be transformed back to the pixel domain in order to evaluate Eq. (9) because the terms combine nonlinearly. Hence, Eq. (9) has 2.5 times as many inverse transforms as Eq. (6)—five for Eq. (9) and two for Eq. (6). Since all of the discriminant components are real-valued, we can use the trick cited above to reduce the number of inverse transforms by a factor of 2 by combining pairs of Fourier representations before doing the inverse transforms.

The two criteria described above illustrate the power of performing processing in the compressed domain. For the texture coefficient, the terms can be combined in the frequency domain before transforming back. For the correlation coefficient, we do not have the luxury of combining data in the frequency domain, and the computation becomes much more costly when we have to compute several terms in the frequency domain and transform all of them back to the pixel domain for additional processing. In both cases, we hope to exploit the sparsity of compressed images in the frequency domain in order to accelerate processing.

In addition to the texture criterion, Stone and Li propose a second criterion that they call the *intensity discriminant*. It is a difference in average values of the image and pattern within a pattern-sized window, and it is defined mathematically to be:

$$I(j) = \left| \frac{1}{M} \sum_{i \in M} (p_i - x_{i+j}) \right|, \qquad 0 \le j \le N - M - 1 \tag{10}$$

This is somewhat different from the more usual L1 norm which has the form:

$$L_1(j) = \frac{1}{M} \sum_{i \in M} \left| (p_i - x_{i+j}) \right|, \qquad 0 \le j \le N - M - 1 \tag{11}$$

In Eq. (10) the differences are summed before taking the absolute value, whereas Eq. (11) sums differences after taking the absolute value. These discriminants are not mathematically identical, and it is not clear that one or the other is superior in discrimination power when used for image searching. In fact, both are sensitive to differences in average intensity and can be used about equally well to mask out regions of an image that differ from the intensity of a pattern. The advantage of Eq. (10) is that the computations can be done in the frequency domain and combined there. Stone and Li expand Eq. (10) to the form:

$$I(j) = \left| \frac{1}{M} \left(\sum_{i \in M} p_i - \sum_{i \in M} x_{i+j} \right) \right|, \qquad 0 \le j \le N - M - 1 \tag{12}$$

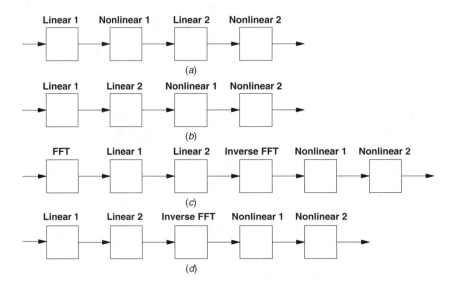

Figure 9.4 Reordering of linear and nonlinear operations. (*a*) Original order. (*b*) Reordered to place nonlinear operations after linear operations. (*c*) Fourier transform and inverse Fourier transform inserted around linear operations. (*d*) Operation sequence without the initial Fourier transform for data held in their Fourier-domain representations.

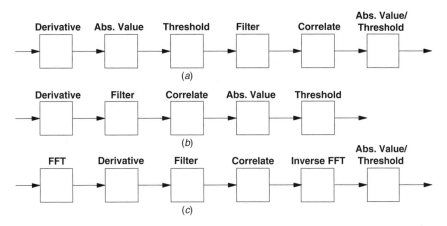

Figure 9.5   Example of reordering the operations of an edge-detection algorithm. (*a*) A prototypical edge-detection algorithm. (*b*) The edge-detection algorithm with the linear operations moved before the nonlinear operations. (*c*) The modified algorithm with transforms into and out of the frequency domain to speed up the linear operations.

As indicated earlier for Eq. (9), the first sum is independent of j in the absence of occlusions, and the second can be computed by correlating **x** with a window mask. In the presence of occlusions, both terms can be computed by correlations with occlusion masks. In either case, the operations can be done in the frequency domain and combined before performing the inverse transform. There is no apparent way to evaluate Eq. (11) in a similar way because the linear and nonlinear operations in the equation do not commute.

Figure 9.4 illustrates the ideas behind the differences in the two equations. Figure 9.4*a* shows a sequence of linear and nonlinear operations in a computation; this corresponds to the calculation of the L1 norm. Figure 9.4*b* shows a substitute computation in which the nonlinear operations are moved to the end of the computation. In general, the nonlinear and linear operations do not commute so that the computation of Fig. 9.4*b* is not identical or equivalent to the computation of Fig. 9.4*a*. Then the linear operations are performed in the frequency domain by inserting transforms into and out of the frequency domain as shown in Fig. 9.4*c*. Finally, Fig. 9.4*d* shows the computations starting in the frequency domain because the transforms are precomputed and the transform into the frequency domain is not required. Although the operations in Fig. 9.4*a* and 9.4*d* are not equivalent, the differences in practice may not be significant.

This general technique can also be applied to other image discriminants. Figure 9.5 illustrates classical ways to detect edges in images. In Fig. 9.5*a*, a typical set of operations is a derivative operation to highlight regions where intensity changes, followed by a nonlinear operation to take the absolute value of the derivatives and apply a threshold. After the nonlinear operations, the edges are broadened by a linear filtering operation. After the edges are filtered, the data may take part in other linear operations, such as correlations with the

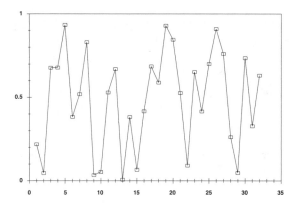

(*a*) Data input.

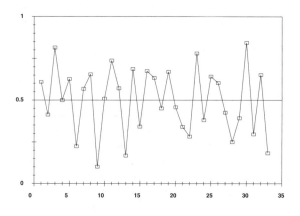

(*b*) Data after taking a derivative.

Figure 9.6   Prototypical edge-detector outputs.

edges of other images. Figure 9.5*b* shows the operations reordered so that the absolute value and thresholding operations are moved after the linear operations. (The nonlinear operations in Fig. 9.5*b* are not necessarily identical to those in Fig. 9.5*a*.) Figure 9.5*c* shows the same sequence of operations with transforms into and out of the frequency domain. If the data start in the frequency domain, the initial transform is not required.

Figure 9.6 shows a concrete example of this process. Figure 9.6*a* shows a function **x** whose edges are computed in Fig. 9.6*b* by means of the high-pass linear filter $y_i = x_i - x_{i-1}$. Figure 9.6*c* is the absolute value of **y** that is greater than a threshold value of 0.5 as described by the equation

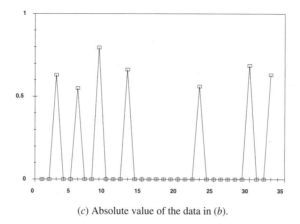

(*c*) Absolute value of the data in (*b*).

(*d*) Data after smoothing filter.

Figure 9.6   (*continued*)

$$z_i = \begin{cases} |y_i|, & \text{if } |y_i| > 0.5 \\ 0, & \text{otherwise} \end{cases} \tag{13}$$

Note that the peaks in Fig. 9.6*c* correspond to edges in Fig. 9.6*a*. Figure 9.6*d* shows Fig. 9.6*c* with its peaks broadened by filtering with the function $w_i = z_{i-1} + 2z_i + z_{i+1}$. Figure 9.6*e* shows Fig. 9.6*d* correlated with itself. Figure 9.6*f* is Fig. 9.6*e* with a threshold applied to zero out values less than 9. The major peak in Fig. 9.6*e* occurs at a point where the images are in registration. The thresholding operation in Fig. 9.6*f* makes the position of this peak apparent and also isolates two minor peaks. The filtering operation enables the

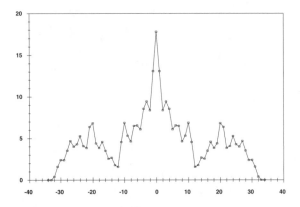

(*e*) Correlation of (*d*) with itself.

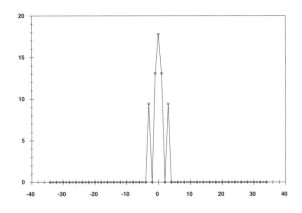

(*f*) Data from (*e*) after thresholding

Figure 9.6   (*continued*)

correlation to match edges in the image and pattern that are not in perfect registration. The filter broadens the edges to make overlaps occur where misregistration would otherwise produce no overlaps. The overlaps contribute to the correlation summation and are thereby factored into the matching computation.

Figure 9.7 illustrates how the operations of Fig. 9.6 can be reordered to do the linear ones before the nonlinear ones. Figure 9.7*a* and 9.7*b* repeat Fig. 9.6*a* and *b* to show the initial image and the image after high-pass filtering with the filter $y_i = x_i - x_{i-1}$. The nonlinear steps of taking the absolute value and thresholding the result that occurs next in Fig. 9.6 do not occur at this point in Fig. 9.7. Instead, Fig. 9.7*c* shows the broadening filter $z_i = y_{i-1} + 2y_i + y_{i+1}$, and Fig. 9.7*d* shows the correlation of Fig. 9.7*c* with itself. At this

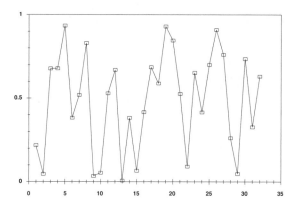

(*a*) Data input (same as Fig 9.6*a*).

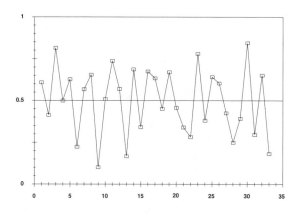

(*b*) Data after taking a derivative (same as Fig 9.6*b*).

Figure 9.7   Output from a prototypical edge-detector with linear operations performed before nonlinear operations.

point, the nonlinear operations occur. Figure 9.7*e* shows the result of the correlation, and Fig. 9.7*f* shows the correlation after applying a threshold of 5. Note that the major peak in Fig. 9.7*f* is identical in position to the major peak in Fig. 9.6*f*. The minor peaks are close in position but are shifted relative to each other. The fact that the correlations in Fig. 9.6*e* and Fig. 9.7*d* have different shapes is not important. What matters is the number of major peaks and their respective positions because these contain the information where the matches occur. Of less importance are their relative heights, because the height information is a

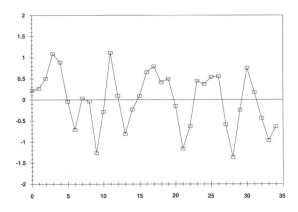

(*c*) Data in (*b*) after smoothing filter.

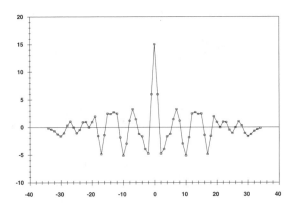

(*d*) Correlation of (*c*) with itself.

Figure 9.7   (*continued*)

measure of the relative quality of the match. Of no importance are the values of functions that lie well below the peaks because these values will be removed by a threshold operation.

The computations illustrated in Figs. 9.6 and 9.7 tend to produce the same major peaks and the same positions of those peaks for correlations when there is a match between an image and a pattern. They do not produce the same minor peaks, and they vary significantly in relative heights of peaks at off-registration points, but these differences are invisible if they fall below threshold. The quality of the discrimination depends on the signal-to-noise ratio of the discrimination functions prior to taking a threshold. This is a measure of the relative height of the peak where a match occurs as compared to the average energy in the

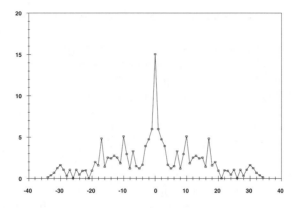

(*e*) Absolute value of the data in (*d*).

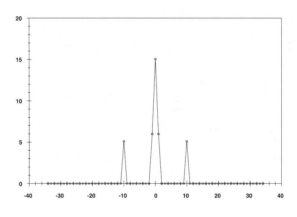

(*f*) Data from (*e*) after thresholding.

Figure 9.7   (*continued*)

clutter around the base line at positions where no match occurs. Figures 9.6*e* and 9.7*e* have roughly comparable signal-to-noise ratios for the running example, but this is not indicative of what might be the case in actual practice because the characteristics of images are quite different from the characteristics of the random numbers used in this example.

From a computational point of view, the computations in Fig. 9.7 can be done in the frequency domain, with only one inverse transform required if the image and pattern data are stored initially in their frequency domain representations. In the computations in Fig. 9.6 some nonlinear operations precede the correlation, with the result that the data should be in the pixel domain for the nonlinear operations, and then transformed into the frequency domain for the correlation and back to the pixel domain for the postcorrelation threshold operations.

The major contributor to the cost of computation in this example is the correlation operation. The other linear filter operations and nonlinear absolute value and thresholding operations require only a few operations per pixel (about 10 operations per pixel in this example). The correlation operation requires a number of operations per pixel equal to the size of the pattern. The Fourier transforms require between 50 and 100 operations per pixel for images in the range of interest. Hence, for patterns containing a few hundred pixels or more, the method depicted in Fig. 9.7 is very attractive when all of the linear operations are performed in the frequency domain. In fact, the linear operations take negligible time when compression creates sparse representations in the frequency domain. Moreover, the algorithm can apply a single linear filter operation to perform the two steps illustrated in Fig. 9.7b and c in one step. Consequently, the bulk of the work occurs in the inverse transform step.

As we pointed out earlier in this section, there is a significant gain in computation speed for large patterns, but not for patterns containing a number of pixels M of order log N or less. For small patterns, the correlation is computed more efficiently in the pixel domain than in the frequency domain, and there is little or no reason to operate in the frequency domain. Hence, in this case the two edge detectors have to be compared strictly on the quality of the results they produce because the difference in computation time is negligible.

The discussion above indicates that we can benefit significantly by doing computations in the frequency domain, but when we do, we have to pay the cost of transforming data back to the pixel domain. If we could stay in the frequency domain, we could avoid this cost, but unfortunately, we know of no other way to discover the peaks of a discriminant function and their positions in pixel space from a representation of the discriminant function in the Fourier domain. This problem remains an interesting challenge whose solution offers an opportunity to make significant reductions in processing time.

9.3.3   Searching JPEG- and MPEG-encoded Images

The last part of this section examines the possibility of searching JPEG- and MPEG-coded images in their compressed forms. Our results indicate that the compression does not lend itself well to search because of the images being partitioned into disjoint 8×8 subimages. However, it may be possible to do a fast conversion of a JPEG transform of an image into an FFT of the image without going back to pixels.

First, we review briefly JPEG coding techniques, and then we explore how to search JPEG-encoded images. JPEG encoding makes use of the assumption that in small regions of an image, color and intensity change rather slowly. Therefore, JPEG schemes partition images into disjoint regions of size 8×8, then transform these regions into the frequency domain and quantize the coefficients. The quantization tends to force small coefficients to 0 and reduce the number of bits required to represent the remaining coefficients. Run-length and Huffman coding techniques further reduce the bits required to represent the residual data. JPEG uses the discrete cosine transform instead of the discrete Fourier transform because the discrete cosine transform tends to produce greater compression.

MPEG is a compression scheme used for video and motion pictures that takes advantage of the frame-to-frame redundancy of image streams. MPEG uses JPEG to encode key frames, and encodes the frames between key frames by means of predictions and corrections.

The key element with respect to search is that both JPEG and MPEG reduce images first by partitioning images into disjoint regions and subsequently by transforming those regions independently. If a pattern appears in an image wholly within one 8×8 region, we could search the regions independently. This is rather unlikely and cannot be assured in advance of a search. Patterns are far more likely to extend across two or more 8×8 regions in some unpredictable way. Consequently, a search of a JPEG-encoded image must deal with pieces of keys contained within subimages. The complexity of dealing with the disjoint regions appears to be very high, and defeats our goal of fast search.

An alternative is to transform a JPEG-encoded image into a different representation that can be searched quickly. For example, we could transform the JPEG representation into a compressed Fourier representation and then use the techniques described above to perform the search. The following discussion shows how to perform such a transformation directly without going back to pixels. The reason for avoiding pixel representations is that the pixel representation is dense, and we would lose all advantages of starting with a compressed representation of the image if we had to go back to pixels in order to perform a search. The scheme we describe is only partially successful in reaching the goal, since we do not describe how to maintain sparsity in the intermediate representations. That is still an open problem.

To illustrate the difficulty, we describe a very simple version of the general problem. Take two column vectors, $\mathbf{x}^{(1)}$ and $\mathbf{x}^{(2)}$, both of length $N/2$, and transform them into a new domain by using the matrix $\mathbf{H}_{N/2}$ to produce two column vectors, $\mathbf{y}^{(1)}$ and $\mathbf{y}^{(2)}$, of length $N/2$, defined by

$$\mathbf{y}^{(i)} = \mathbf{H}_{N/2}\mathbf{x}^{(i)}, \qquad i = 1, 2 \tag{14}$$

The vectors $\mathbf{x}^{(1)}$ and $\mathbf{x}^{(2)}$ correspond to two subimages of an image, and the vectors $\mathbf{y}^{(1)}$ and $\mathbf{y}^{(2)}$ correspond to JPEG encodings of those subimages. For JPEG, the $\mathbf{y}$ vectors are actually two-dimensional of size 8×8, and the matrix $\mathbf{H}_N$ is the discrete cosine transform matrix for two-dimensional images of size 8×8.

We wish to build a new column vector $\mathbf{x}$ of length N that is the transform of the column vector formed by concatenating $\mathbf{x}^{(1)}$ and $\mathbf{x}^{(2)}$. Specifically, we want to compute

$$\mathbf{z} = \mathbf{F}_N \begin{bmatrix} \mathbf{x}^{(1)} \\ \mathbf{x}^{(2)} \end{bmatrix} = \mathbf{F}_N \begin{bmatrix} \mathbf{H}_{N/2}^{-1}\mathbf{y}^{(1)} \\ \mathbf{H}_{N/2}^{-1}\mathbf{y}^{(2)} \end{bmatrix} = \mathbf{F}_N \begin{bmatrix} \mathbf{H}_{N/2}^{-1} & 0 \\ 0 & \mathbf{H}_{N/2}^{-1} \end{bmatrix} \begin{bmatrix} \mathbf{y}^{(1)} \\ \mathbf{y}^{(2)} \end{bmatrix} \tag{15}$$

where $\mathbf{F}_N$ is the Fourier-transform matrix for vectors of length N.

This is equivalent to computing

$$\mathbf{z} = \mathbf{G}_N \begin{bmatrix} \mathbf{y}^{(1)} \\ \mathbf{y}^{(2)} \end{bmatrix} \tag{16}$$

where

$$\mathbf{G}_N = \mathbf{F}_N \begin{bmatrix} \mathbf{H}_{N/2}^{-1} & 0 \\ 0 & \mathbf{H}_{N/2}^{-1} \end{bmatrix} \tag{17}$$

The matrix $\mathbf{G}_N$ takes the data directly from the JPEG domain to the Fourier domain, without passing through the pixel domain as an intermediate step. The special form of the matrix $\mathbf{G}_N$ leads to computational efficiency if it is factored into a sequence of matrices. Both $\mathbf{F}_N$ and $\mathbf{H}_{N/2}$ factor into O(log N) sparse matrices, so that matrix multiplication by the factored form of $\mathbf{G}_N$ produces O(N log N) operations, whereas the general matrix multiple produces O(N^2) operations. If we use the fast algorithm factorization directly, then as an intermediate step, the algorithm produces a pixel representation, and we lose the benefit of image compression because the pixel representation is dense.

By taking advantage of commutativity, we can avoid creating a dense representation at an intermediate point in the computation. For example, if it were true that

$$
\mathbf{F}_N \begin{bmatrix} \mathbf{H}_{N/2}^{-1} & 0 \\ 0 & \mathbf{H}_{N/2}^{-1} \end{bmatrix} = \begin{bmatrix} \mathbf{H}_{N/2}^{-1} & 0 \\ 0 & \mathbf{H}_{N/2}^{-1} \end{bmatrix} \mathbf{F}_N \tag{18}
$$

then we could factor both $\mathbf{H}_{N/2}^{-1}$ and $\mathbf{F}_N$ into their fast decompositions, and perform the matrix-vector multiplication from right to left starting with the factors of $\mathbf{F}_N$ and completing with the factors of $\mathbf{H}_{N/2}^{-1}$. The total computation would take O(N log N) operations and at no point would there be an intermediate representation in pixels. Hence, there would be an opportunity to use the fast decompositions and retain sparsity. However, the matrices do not commute, and Eq. (18) is false. Nevertheless, a more limited form of commutativity holds. Some of the factors of $\mathbf{F}_N$ commute with the $\mathbf{H}$ matrix. So we can multiply by those factors, then by the $\mathbf{H}$ factors, and finally by the remaining $\mathbf{F}$ factors.

To show how the matrix factors commute, we first note that the matrix

$$
\mathbf{H}^{-1} = \begin{bmatrix} \mathbf{H}_{N/2}^{-1} & 0 \\ 0 & \mathbf{H}_{N/2}^{-1} \end{bmatrix} \tag{19}
$$

is block diagonal. For JPEG data, the blocks in the matrix $\mathbf{H}^{-1}$ have size 64×64, and they manipulate arrays of size 8×8 within a vector representation of a two-dimensional image. The entries of $\mathbf{H}^{-1}$ that lie outside the diagonal blocks are all 0s. The structure of the $\mathbf{H}^{-1}$ matrix in Eq. (19) has the form:

$$
\mathbf{H}^{-1} = \mathbf{I_2} \times \mathbf{H}_{N/2}^{-1} \tag{20}
$$

where $\mathbf{I}_k$ is a $k \times k$ identity matrix and the matrix operator $\times$ denotes the Kronecker (tensor) product. The Kronecker product of matrices $\mathbf{A}$ of size $k \times l$ and $\mathbf{B}$ of size $r \times s$ is given by

$$
\mathbf{A} \times \mathbf{B} = \begin{bmatrix} a_{11}\mathbf{B} & a_{12}\mathbf{B} & \dots & a_{1l}\mathbf{B} \\ a_{21}\mathbf{B} & a_{22}\mathbf{B} & \dots & a_{2l}\mathbf{B} \\ \dots & \dots & \dots & \dots \\ a_{k1}\mathbf{B} & a_{k2}\mathbf{B} & \dots & a_{kl}\mathbf{B} \end{bmatrix} \tag{21}
$$

The size of $\mathbf{A} \times \mathbf{B}$ is $klrs$. Later in this section, we make use of the following distributive property of tensor products:

$$(\mathbf{A} \times \mathbf{B})\,(\mathbf{C} \times \mathbf{D}) = \mathbf{AC} \times \mathbf{BD} \tag{22}$$

provided that the matrix products $\mathbf{AC}$ and $\mathbf{BD}$ exist; that is, the number of columns of $\mathbf{A}$ is equal to the number of rows of $\mathbf{C}$, and similarly for $\mathbf{B}$ and $\mathbf{D}$.

The fast factorization of the $\mathbf{F}_N$ breaks it up into a sequence of "butterfly" matrices, preceded by a "reverse binary" permutation matrix. Each butterfly matrix operates on vector elements that lie 2^i positions apart for various values of i. Using notation from Temperton [19], we give the factorization of a one-dimensional Fourier transform matrix $\mathbf{F}_N$ by

$$\mathbf{F}_N = \mathbf{PT}_k\mathbf{T}_{k-1}\ldots\mathbf{T}_1 \tag{23}$$

where $k = \log N$, the $\mathbf{P}$ matrix product is the reverse-binary permutation of N items, and the $\mathbf{T}$ matrices are butterfly matrices. In Temperton's factorization, $\mathbf{T}_i$ operates on pairs of indices that lie $N/2^i$ apart. The structure of each matrix $\mathbf{T}_i$ is

$$\mathbf{T}_i = \mathbf{I}_{2^{i-1}} \times \left[\mathbf{D}_{N/2^{i-1}}(\mathbf{W}_2 \times \mathbf{I}_{N/2^i})\right] \tag{24}$$

where $\mathbf{D}_{N/2^i}$ matrix is a diagonal matrix of size $N/2^i \times N/2^i$ and the matrix $\mathbf{W}_2$ is a 2×2 matrix.

To recast the problem at hand, we substitute Eq. (23) into Eq. (16) to obtain:

$$\mathbf{z} = \mathbf{G}_N \begin{bmatrix} \mathbf{y}^1 \\ \mathbf{y}^2 \end{bmatrix} = \mathbf{PT}_k\mathbf{T}_{k-1}\ldots\mathbf{T}_1 \begin{bmatrix} \mathbf{H}_{N/2}^{-1} & 0 \\ 0 & \mathbf{H}_{N/2}^{-1} \end{bmatrix} \begin{bmatrix} \mathbf{y}^{(1)} \\ \mathbf{y}^{(2)} \end{bmatrix} \tag{25}$$

We show below that the rightmost factor of $\mathbf{G}_N$ commutes with the $\mathbf{H}$ matrix, so that Eq. (25) can be rewritten as

$$\mathbf{z} = \mathbf{G}_N \begin{bmatrix} \mathbf{y}^1 \\ \mathbf{y}^2 \end{bmatrix} = \mathbf{PT}_k\mathbf{T}_{k-1}\ldots\mathbf{T}_2 \begin{bmatrix} \mathbf{H}_{N/2}^{-1} & 0 \\ 0 & \mathbf{H}_{N/2}^{-1} \end{bmatrix} \mathbf{T}_1 \begin{bmatrix} \mathbf{y}^{(1)} \\ \mathbf{y}^{(2)} \end{bmatrix} \tag{26}$$

The important point of Eq. (26) is that the $\mathbf{y}$ vector is moved one butterfly step into the frequency domain before the $\mathbf{H}^{-1}$ step is applied. We hope to retain sparsity in applying the butterfly because the resulting vector is in a frequency domain that is a composite of the Fourier frequency domain and of the $\mathbf{H}$ frequency domain (which is a discrete cosine domain in the case that $\mathbf{H}_N$ is a JPEG matrix). Therefore, there is a good chance that high-frequency coefficients will be small after a butterfly step and that many nonzeros introduced by the butterfly step will be small enough to be replaced by zeros.

To demonstrate that the matrix $\mathbf{T}_1$ commutes with the matrix $\mathbf{I}_2 \times \mathbf{H}_{N/2}^{-1}$ consider matrices $\mathbf{A}$ and $\mathbf{B}$ of sizes $s \times s$ and $r \times r$, respectively, and note that

$$
\begin{aligned}
(\mathbf{A} \times \mathbf{I}_r)\,(\mathbf{I}_s \times \mathbf{B}) &= \mathbf{AI}_s \times \mathbf{I}_r\mathbf{B} \\
&= \mathbf{I}_s\mathbf{A} \times \mathbf{BI}_r \\
&= (\mathbf{I}_s \times \mathbf{B})\,(\mathbf{A} \times \mathbf{I}_r)
\end{aligned}
\tag{27}
$$

The form of $\mathbf{T_1}$ according to Eq. (24) is $\mathbf{T_1} = \mathbf{D}_N \left(\mathbf{W}_2 \times \mathbf{I}_{N/2} \right)$, which commutes with $\mathbf{I}_2 \times \mathbf{H}_{N/2}^{-1}$.

To make use of this characteristic for JPEG images, we have to deal with two dimensions rather than one, and a typical image in the database is much larger than 8×8 pixels, not just twice as large in one or both dimensions. For this discussion, we assume that images have size $N \times N$, for $N \gg 8$, where N is a power of 2.

To consider the case for one dimension, note that it follows from Eq. (24) that all butterflies of points at least 8 pixels apart commute with the $\mathbf{H}^{-1}$ matrix. Specifically, for $k = \log N$ we have:

$$
\mathbf{z} = \mathbf{G}_N
\begin{bmatrix}
\mathbf{y}^1 \\
\mathbf{y}^2 \\
\vdots \\
\mathbf{y}^{N/8}
\end{bmatrix}
$$

$$
= \mathbf{P}\mathbf{T}_k \mathbf{T}_{k-1} \mathbf{T}_{k-2}
\begin{bmatrix}
\mathbf{H}_8^{-1} & 0 & \cdots & 0 \\
0 & \mathbf{H}_8^{-1} & \cdots & 0 \\
\vdots & \vdots & \vdots & \vdots \\
0 & 0 & \cdots & \mathbf{H}_8^{-1}
\end{bmatrix}
\tag{28}
$$

$$
\mathbf{T}_{k-3} \mathbf{T}_{k-4} \ldots \mathbf{T}_1
\begin{bmatrix}
\mathbf{y}^{(1)} \\
\mathbf{y}^{(2)} \\
\vdots \\
\mathbf{y}^{(N/8)}
\end{bmatrix}
$$

The three butterfly matrices that do not commute manipulate items 1-apart, 2-apart, and 4-apart, respectively. The ones that do commute manipulate items 8-apart or more.

The fact that permutation matrix $\mathbf{P}$ does not commute with $\mathbf{H}^{-1}$ is not a concern. The matrix $\mathbf{P}$ does not alter the number of nonzero entries and therefore has no effect on the sparsity of a sparse representation.

Moving all but three of the butterfly matrices to the right of $\mathbf{H}^{-1}$ keeps the intermediate vectors out of the pixel domain. There is an opportunity to maintain sparsity throughout the evaluation of Eq. (29) by checking the magnitude of each intermediate result as it is produced. A sparse-vector implementation should replace small coefficients by 0s, assuming that the loss of information does not measurably reduce the effectiveness of the search algorithm. In general, while performing a butterfly-matrix multiply, each nonzero in the input to the current iteration produces two nonzeros in the output for the next iteration. It is a matter of research interest to discover how to retain sparsity during each iteration and to determine if this can be done without impairing the effectiveness of the search on the resulting data.

In two dimensions, Eq. (29) takes the form:

$$\mathbf{z} = \mathbf{P}^{(r)}\mathbf{T}_k^{(r)}\mathbf{T}_{k-1}^{(r)}\cdots\mathbf{T}_1^{(r)}\mathbf{P}^{(c)}\mathbf{T}_k^{(c)}\mathbf{T}_{k-1}^{(c)}\cdots\mathbf{T}_1^{(c)}$$

$$\begin{bmatrix} \mathbf{H}_{8\times8}^{-1} & \cdots & & 0 \\ 0 & \mathbf{H}_{8\times8}^{-1} & \cdots & 0 \\ \vdots & \vdots & \vdots & \vdots \\ 0 & 0 & \cdots & \mathbf{H}_{8\times8}^{-1} \end{bmatrix} \begin{bmatrix} \mathbf{y}^{(1)} \\ \mathbf{y}^{(2)} \\ \vdots \\ \mathbf{y}^{(N^2/64)} \end{bmatrix}$$

$$= \mathbf{P}^{(r)}\mathbf{P}^{(c)}\mathbf{T}_k^{(r)}\mathbf{T}_{k-1}^{(r)}\mathbf{T}_{k-2}^{(r)}\mathbf{T}_k^{(c)}\mathbf{T}_{k-1}^{(c)}\mathbf{T}_{k-2}^{(c)}.$$

$$\begin{bmatrix} \mathbf{H}_{8\times8}^{-1} & \cdots & & 0 \\ 0 & \mathbf{H}_{8\times8}^{-1} & \cdots & 0 \\ \vdots & \vdots & \vdots & \vdots \\ 0 & 0 & \cdots & \mathbf{H}_{8\times8}^{-1} \end{bmatrix} \mathbf{T}_{k-3}^{(r)}\mathbf{T}_{k-4}^{(r)}\cdots\mathbf{T}_1^{(r)} \qquad (29)$$

$$\mathbf{T}_{k-3}^{(c)}\mathbf{T}_{k-4}^{(c)}\cdots\mathbf{T}_1^{(c)} \begin{bmatrix} \mathbf{y}^{(1)} \\ \mathbf{y}^{(2)} \\ \vdots \\ \mathbf{y}^{(N^2/64)} \end{bmatrix}$$

where the superscript (r) denotes a matrix that operates on rows, and the superscript (c) denotes one that operates on columns.

To see why this is true, using the results for commutation of Kronecker products, it is easy to show that the row butterfly matrices commute with all factors of the column matrices. Moreover, all but the first three row and column butterflies commute with $\mathbf{H}^{-1}$. So we can apply all but six of the butterfly operations in the $\mathbf{y}$ domain; then we apply the inverse $\mathbf{H}$ transform and follow with the remaining Fourier matrix factors. If we can maintain sparsity through the sequence of operations, we should be able to achieve a speed-up by operating on fewer nonzero data. As mentioned above, how to do this efficiently remains an open research question.

This brings us to the close of the discussion of JPEG transforms, which is the last subject for Fourier-based methods. The next section considers wavelet representations and how they might be exploited for image queries.

9.4 WAVELET TRANSFORM TECHNIQUES

In the prior section, we saw that Fourier methods offer a fast alternative to convolution and correlations in the pixel domain. In this section, we show that wavelet representations are especially attractive when correlation is not required because the location of a potential match within an image is known in advance. The main advantages of the wavelet representation are:

1. Peaks in discriminant functions are visible in wavelet domain representations of the same functions.
2. The location of peaks in the discriminant functions are very close to their locations in the wavelet representations of the discriminants.

These two characteristics indicate that we can obtain essential information from wavelet representations of discriminants without requiring inverse transforms back to the pixel domain. Recall that the major cost of Fourier processing is the cost of the inverse transform from frequency to pixel domain. The inverse transformation is required in the Fourier context because the Fourier representation does not directly display the peaks and positions of the pixel representation.

On the other hand, wavelet domain representations are not directly useful for queries that seek a match anywhere in an image. To search over all possible coordinate positions, one must search within a wavelet representation, which is equivalent to performing convolutions and correlations on wavelet representations. Consequently, the techniques for processing pixel representations in the Fourier domain carry over to the wavelet domain. If the wavelet representation is sparse or of reduced dimension, performing correlations and Fourier transforms on wavelet representations may be faster than corresponding operations performed in the pixel domain.

A typical wavelet decomposition process is shown in Fig. 9.8. Figure 9.8a shows a pixel representation of an image passed through two filters, $g(x)$ and $h(x)$, whose outputs are subsampled by a factor of 2. (This discussion assumes images are one dimensional to simplify notation. All results extend directly to two dimensions.) For wavelet decompositions, the filters obey certain mathematical properties that are described in detail in the literature [5,6]. For N pixels in the original image, each of two filters produces N transform points at its output. The composite opposite output doubles the number of points in the representation. The subsampling operations discard half the number of points from each filter, leaving N points in total in the representation. The filter functions can be chosen so that the remaining N points are sufficient to reconstruct the original N points faithfully to within roundoff error of the calculations. The benefit of the wavelet representation for compression is that $g(x)$ and $h(x)$ can often be selected in such a way as to create a representation in which most coefficients are small values [6]. When this occurs, the small values can be encoded as 0s or with relatively few bits. For our purposes, we are interested in creating as many 0s as possible to reduce the number of mathematical operations required.

Figure 9.8b shows the wavelet decomposition applied recursively for 2 stages to create four subbands, each with $N/4$ components. The outputs of the first stage contain high-resolution information, and the resolution diminishes by a factor of 2 at the output of the second stage. The decomposition can be continued for several more iterations, with each successive stage containing twice as many subbands, each with half as many points.

To achieve our objective of fast search, a general strategy would be to look for pattern matches by searching a few subbands rather than by looking at all data points. Because

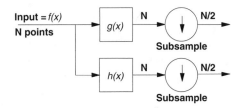

(*a*) A one-stage decomposition.

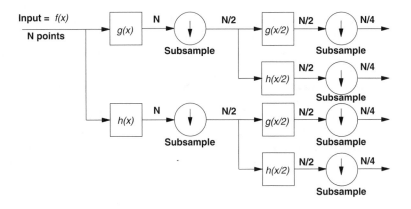

(*b*) A two-stage decomposition.

Figure 9.8   Wavelet decompositions.

the subbands examined may lie at different resolution levels of the decomposition tree, this type of image analysis is often called *multiresolution analysis.*

To improve the speed of searching, the decomposition is generally not carried out to uniform depth along each branch. Instead at each node in the decomposition tree, an algorithm chooses whether or not to decompose the subband, depending on the relative benefit of the additional work. For example, the tree can be very lopsided by decomposing only the $h(x)$ function at each stage, thereby creating a single path instead of a multiway branching path. Chang and Kuo [3] propose an adaptive decomposition technique that decomposes a subband based on the amount of energy within the subband. If the subband does not contain a minimum amount of energy, their scheme makes the subband a leaf node in the decomposition tree; otherwise they split it into two subbands by applying a wavelet decomposition at half the resolution of the present level.

Chang and Kuo indicate that their technique can be used for texture classification because the set of textures that they classify is well characterized by the decomposition tree produced by the texture. They select the subbands with the most energy and determine the position of these subbands in the decomposition tree. They classify sample patterns by the positions occupied by the five most dominant subbands, and report excellent success.

Although Chang and Kuo's results show that wavelet decomposition is useful for pattern classification, two major obstacles need to be addressed in order to apply their technique or something computationally similar to image query.

1. The class of images we wish to search has rich details that vary widely across the image. To find if a pattern matches an image in some particular position, it is necessary to isolate portions of the image in some way, and compare each of these portions individually with the pattern. In other words, we need to do the mathematical equivalent of the correlation of the pattern with regions of the image of similar size.

2. The energy contained within a subband and the structure of the information in that subband both depend on the phase of the subsampling. Hence, we cannot be certain that we can find a match with a specified pattern by examining only the subbands of an image that correspond to the dominant subbands of the pattern. The energy may be in a different subband of the image.

The first point is relevant because the application that we envision has characteristics that are quite different from the classification problem treated by Chang and Kuo. In their application, each texture sample contains only one texture, although they varied illumination and reduced detail in various samples to illustrate that the classification method can operate well in the presence of certain kinds of distortions. For satellite and medical images, the search problem is more like one of having images in which many different textures are present, with some found in relatively small regions. Our search problem is equivalent to one in which we ask a classifier to indicate the textures present in the image, and we expect a positive answer for each texture. We would like the individual textures within an image to reveal themselves in the subband data by showing up as unique characteristics within the subbands. Unfortunately, the subband data for a composite image may look dramatically different from the subband data for the individual textures that comprise the image. To discover locations where specific textures appear in small regions of an image requires high-resolution analysis within small windows of the image. This suggests that we need to work with compressed representations that retain high-resolution information, and that we need to perform correlations on those representations to locate where the best possible match lies within a representation.

In the best of circumstances, we could look in low-resolution subbands, say subbands with $N/64$ points. The subband may be sufficiently small that it is more efficient to correlate pattern information with the subband information directly rather than to pay the cost to transform into the frequency domain and back again to the wavelet domain. But since our images are highly cluttered and detailed, we are more likely to be forced to look at high-resolution subbands with $N/2$ or $N/4$ points to obtain the resolution we need. Within high-resolution subbands, the search for a match is relatively costly,

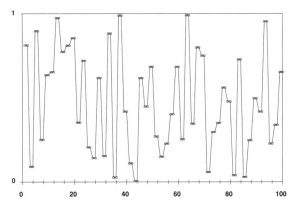

(*a*) Original image waveform.

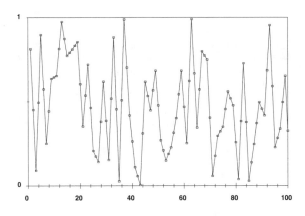

(*b*) Image waveform after low-pass filtering.

Figure 9.9   Waveforms produced by a wavelet decomposition.

and we may lose the benefit of a compact wavelet representation. Consequently, much depends on the ability to match detailed patterns in low-resolution representations of images.

We noted earlier that the distribution of feature information among subbands depends on the subsampling phase. Figure 9.9 illustrates this point. Figure 9.9*a* shows an image function, and Figs. 9.9*b* and 9.9*c* show filtered versions of the image. Figure 9.9*b* shows

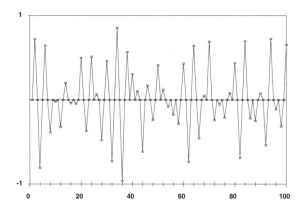

(*c*) Image waveform after high-pass filtering.

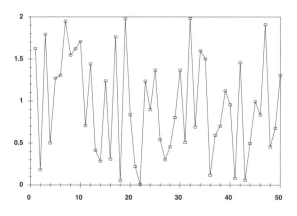

(*d*) Subsampled low-pass outout (even phase).

Figure 9.9   (*continued*)

the result of using the low-pass filter $h(i) = x_{i+1} + x_i$, and Fig. 9.9c shows the output of the high-pass filter $g(i) = x_{i+1} - x_i$. These two graphs depict the outputs before subsampling.

   To complete the decomposition, we subsample by a factor of 2. There are two possible phases for the subsamples. Figures 9.9c and *d* show subsampling for even values of *i*, and Figs. 9.9e and *f* show subsampling on odd values of *i*. In this case, the fea-

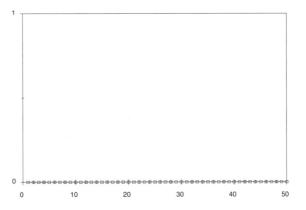

(*e*) Subsampled high-pass output (even phase).

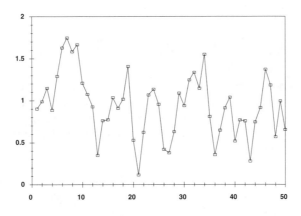

(*f*) Subsampled low-pass output (odd phase).

Figure 9.9   (*continued*)

tures of the signal are of the same period as the sampling rate. The information contained in the signal is distributed to particular subbands in a way that depends on the phase of the subsampling. Notice how different the distributions of energy are in the two sets of subsampled figures. Clearly, for this signal, we could not focus on one subband or the other in seeking a match, but would have to treat both subbands when seeking a match.

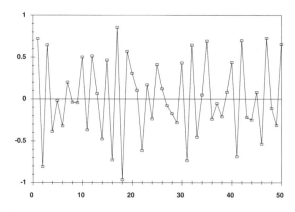

(*g*) Subsampled high-pass output (odd phase).

Figure 9.9   (*continued*)

This example illustrates the problem because the image function contains considerable energy in the frequency band of the subsampling rate. The phenomenon is not significant for data whose energy is widely distributed throughout the frequency domain. But image data may well contain local areas with significant energy at the subsampling rate.

The subsampling process presents a serious obstacle to pattern matching in the wavelet domain. Subsampling is a very powerful technique for compression but is disruptive for search. We seek other ways of compressing information in the wavelet domain that are compact and yet retain information about all data points in a subband. We need to avoid the loss of information associated with subsampling.

Mallat [13] and Mallat and Zhong [14] offer two alternatives to representing wavelet information. Mallat [13] introduces a representation based on zero-crossings of a wavelet transform that can be used to reconstruct the original image. The zero-crossing information, though sparse, contains enough information to yield reasonably good image reconstruction. Mallat suggests that the zero-crossing representation can be used directly in pattern-matching applications. This may be quite viable, especially for edge detection, which is readily available from the zero-crossing information retained by Mallat's approach.

Mallat and Zhong [14] propose to reconstruct signals from edge information embodied in wavelet decompositions that stem from smoothed first derivatives of a pixel representation of an image. The position of an edge in the image corresponds to the position of a peak in their particular wavelet decomposition. Their discussion describes wavelet decompositions that do not incorporate subsampling, so that they can avoid phase sensitivity problems. Their main concern is edge identification and image reconstruction rather than compression and pattern matching. At best, we can speculate that their techniques will be useful for image query, but this has yet to be established.

Kovesi [22] reports a slightly different wavelet-based strategy for image analysis. Kovesi produces both in-phase and quadrature components of a wavelet decomposition of an image, and from the two components computes the phase within each subband. Points where all subbands are phase coherent correspond to edges in the original image, and the location of phase coherence in the wavelet domain maps into a corresponding point in the pixel domain. Consequently, the phase information in the wavelet representation gives a direct pointer to the edges of the original image.

The trait common to the approaches used by Mallat [13], Mallat and Zhong [14], and Kovesi [22] is that the wavelet subbands retain all N points at every stage of the decomposition, rather than reduce the points through a subsampling process. Consequently, these methods ensure that feature information associated with a particular subband will be present in that subband in the representations. Mallat [13] compresses the subband information by recording zero-crossings and average values between zero-crossings, rather than by subsampling. This representation may prove to be more useful for image query. Neither Mallat and Zhang nor Kovesi address the use of their methods for image search, and this topic remains open for future study.

9.5 ARCHITECTURE SUPPORT FOR IMAGE QUERY

The ability to perform content search of 1000 images per second almost surely requires architecture support. This section looks at how this support might be provided and suggests that prefetching to reduce latency is a leading candidate.

There are several potential processing bottlenecks:

1. Raw CPU performance in operations per second
2. Memory latency
3. Memory bandwidth
4. I/O latency
5. I/O bandwidth

The *latency* of the memory system is a measure of the time delay between a request for data and the delivery time of the requested data. If the delivered data cannot be transferred in a single cycle, the latency measures the time between the request and the appearance of the first packet of the response. A similar definition holds for I/O latency. Bandwidth is a measure of the peak traffic that can be supported and is usually measured under zero-latency conditions.

Let us consider each of these factors in turn in order to determine where there are opportunities for architectural advances to support the image-query operations.

For raw CPU performance, we need 100 gigaoperations per second to perform 100 operations per pixel on 1000 images per second, where each image contains 1 million pixels. A high-performance computer today is likely to have a clock rate of 500 MHz and execute an average of three operations per clock cycle by using multiple arithmetic units and clever schemes to manage them. This achieves a performance of about 1.5 gigaoperations per second. We need another factor of 50 to 100 to meet our goal.

Where will this come from? From several sources. Clock speeds will continue to climb, albeit at a slower rate than historical rates. We should reach 2 GHz clock speeds by 2010, or about four times the clock speed of high-end machines today. The number of operations per cycle is not likely to increase beyond two or three for general workloads because of the significant amount of branching in such programs. But image processing has special characteristics. There is relatively little conditional branching other than at the ends of branches. Accesses tend to be made to local regions of a data structure. When the accesses are not local, as in some phases of the Fourier transform, the data can be gathered into a local structure for processing and restored to their original locations at the completion of processing. This enables the data to be held temporarily in a portion of the computer that is close to the arithmetic unit while the processor actively processes the data. Clearly, here is an opportunity to pick up a large gain in performance for image processing by exploiting the characteristics of image processing codes.

For linear arithmetic operations involving matrices and arrays, the processor needs to have several independent arithmetic units, so that it can perform many floating-point operations concurrently. For nonlinear operations, particularly thresholding, the processor needs high concurrency together with the ability to do a comparison and a selection operation based on the result of the comparison. The selection operation should be implemented without a conditional branch to avoid the delays of such branches.

If we could increase the number of operations per cycle from 3 to about 10, we would improve the processing rate by a factor of 3.3. This increase is far less than the factor of 12 to 25 that we need after taking into account the increases in clock speed that are likely to occur. We could still use additional speed-up, perhaps a factor of 10.

Parallelism is an obvious answer because the tasks are embarrassingly parallel. For individual images, each image requires an independent computation, so that each of N processors can be assigned $1/N$th of the images; thereafter, they can work independently without experiencing delays due to synchronization and contention. The discussion above indicates that five processors can achieve 100 gigaops if each processor completes 10 operations per cycle at a clock rate of 2 GHz. At present rates of improvement, this objective may be achievable by the year 2010 or sooner.

To achieve this type of throughput for image processing applications, it seems natural to organize the processors to operate on vectors of data. The instruction sequences executed within the processors may be identical in some cases, but, in general, it is probably a good idea to permit the instruction sequences to be nonidentical. Once we postulate that the instruction sequences can be different, there is only a marginal distinction in program models between building a single high-performance processor that supports multiple-independent instruction streams versus building a tightly integrated system consisting of individual processors. Both architectural models are reasonable to consider. Technology constraints will dictate which model to follow, or may make other alternatives not discussed here more attractive.

The memory system and external database storage system have a major impact on performance of the image-query system. The total bandwidth of the path from database storage through main memory to the processor must be sufficient to support access to 1000 images per second, which is approximately 1 gigapixel per second. Main-memory bandwidth for dynamic RAM has reached 1 byte every 2 nanoseconds for RAMbus, which is 500 megapixels per second at 1 byte per pixel of uncompressed image data. This assumes that successive accesses touch successive memory addresses, which is the normal case for accesses to images. We can expect the throughput of RAMbus to double in a few years, and we can gain additional bandwidth by using multiple independent RAMbuses. With high confidence, we believe that dynamic RAM will be able to support accesses to 3 bytes per pixel and concurrent two-way data traffic at a clock rate of 1 gigahertz.

Similarly, the database storage system has sufficient bandwidth if we have disk arrays with sufficient parallelism. The bandwidth of a system that uses a single head lags the bandwidth of dynamic RAM by about a factor of 10. Disk arrays make up for this discrepancy by putting together 8 to 10 drives and accessing them concurrently. Consequently, the throughput of disk arrays is close enough today to meet the goal to lead us to believe that disk arrays will be fully acceptable for an image-query system of the future. Of course, other, more attractive approaches may emerge. The point is that the throughput of the database storage system is unlikely to be a major problem.

For both the main-memory system and the database storage system, we need to deal with the delay in access to information. Latency is thus a critical element in limiting processor performance. The main advantage of cache memory, for example, is that it reduces average access time. An ideal cache memory permits a processor to obtain a new operand on every cycle with an access time to cache of one cycle. By comparison, today main-memory access times vary from 10 cycles to 50 cycles, and the trend is for the access-time delay to increase when measured in clock cycles.

Disk systems have made extensive use of cache memory to hide disk-access latency. When effective, it reduces disk-access latency measured in tens of thousands of machine cycles to a minimum latency on the order of tens or a few hundred cycles. Average latency is somewhat higher because of the high penalty for accesses to items not in cache.

Current trends are focusing on techniques for latency hiding. Cache techniques have been extremely effective in the past but may not work as well for general workloads in the future. One reason for this is that the working sets of general workloads are growing in time and may be growing faster than the growth of cache. Another reason is that some applications such as transaction systems have little reuse of data, so that caching is less effective. Consequently, techniques such as prefetching data and using multiple threads of execution per processor have been studied as possible mechanisms to reduce access time.

Image processing applications are ideally suited to latency hiding because the items accessed and the order of access are totally predictable in advance of the access. If a query is to examine 1000 images, then as each image file is opened and accessed, all future accesses on that file occur in a specific order, and the times of those accesses can be predicted fairly accurately. In principle, it should be possible to schedule accesses at every level of the memory and database hierarchy in a way that reduces access time to close to zero cycles.

In practice, only the bottlenecks in the memory system need to have zero-cycle access time. The processor can sustain small access-time delays at other levels of the hierarchy when the delays are completely overlapped by other processing. The scheduling algorithm needs to reduce average access time only to the point where it does not impair performance, because further reduction does not improve throughput.

We do not have a specific recommendation on how to schedule accesses to achieve zero latency. It is clear that software should be able to learn of the availability of various system resources such as buffers and controllers from the present time to some time in the future, and that the system should be able to modify the schedule for future operations based on current state information and new requests for service. The scheduler should be able to model and predict which events will be taking place throughout the system over long periods in the future, and should be able to schedule new events well in advance. If this is done well, data will be moved from secondary storage to main memory before a processor requests the data. At lower levels of the memory hierarchy, the data should be moved into the processor registers just in advance of when they are needed there for numerical operations. Because the data movement can be prescheduled, the computer system will work in a very different mode than do current systems, which tend to move after the processor issues requests for data. For example, image data may flow from main memory to the processor without being staged into a cache memory. Cached items such as instructions and search parameters may flow into cache before a processor requests them.

If the processing power of future processors increases rapidly because of the growth of applications involving images, multimedia, and similar kinds of data, we may discover that the conventional applications of today occupy a very small fraction of the system capacity. If this were to occur, evolving machine architecture would be skewed toward image applications, and design decisions would be biased to support such processing. For example, cache memory would become less important as a means of reducing latency in favor of prefetching data by using predictable access patterns.

This discussion suggests that a major change in the evolution of computer architecture might lie ahead of us. If present trends were to continue, the processor of 2010 would be strongly oriented to running multiple interacting threads of control with about equal balance between fixed-point and floating-point operations, and a high frequency of conditional branching. If image processing were to become the dominant application, the focus of system resources would be on independent streams of data, would involve heavy use of floating-point arithmetic, and would have relatively few conditional branches whose outcomes are difficult to anticipate. The differences in these two scenarios lead to rather different families of computer architectures. The future of computer architecture depends on how strongly image processing applications take root in everyday workloads.

9.6   SUMMARY AND CONCLUSIONS

The major finding of this chapter is that the processor demands for image-query applications of the future may be as high as 10 teraops with detailed content analysis. By using more efficient, but less powerful, means for analyzing images, the demand drops to 100 gigaops. This could be achievable at reasonable cost in 2010, particularly if the architecture supports image processing. To do so, we expect machines to exploit the characteristics of image processing, most notably the fact that access patterns are known well in advance of their occurrence.

The algorithmic improvements are likely to come from the ability to search images in their compressed form. Fourier-domain techniques are attractive to some extent. They can greatly reduce the total amount of computation required, but some of this benefit is offset by the cost of performing Fourier transforms. Wavelet representations support multiresolution analysis, which may prove to be very effective for quickly rejecting images that fail to match a query.

Important open questions are:

1. What criteria for matching should be used? We seek criteria that are meaningful to the user and compatible with the image representation.
2. What image representations are suitable for both compression and search?
3. What support from the underlying hardware would be useful in improving the performance of the query system?

Some progress toward solving each of these problems appears in the body of this chapter, but we are still quite far from solving the problems. This area of research presents significant challenges, and if they are successfully met, vast amounts of image information for daily use could open up.

Acknowledgments

The author is indebted to Drs. Talal Shamoon and David Waltz of NEC Research Institute for their helpful suggestions and critical review which aided in the preparation of this chapter.

References

[1] R. E. Blahut, *Fast Algorithms for Digital Signal Processing,* Reading, MA: Addison-Wesley, 1985.
[2] J. Canny, "A Computational Approach to Edge Detection," *IEEE Trans. on Pattern Analysis and Machine Intelligence,* Vol. 8, No. 6, pp. 679–698, Nov. 1986.
[3] T. Chang and C.-C. J. Kuo, "Texture Analysis and Classification with Tree-Structured Wavelet Transform," *IEEE Trans. on Image Processing,* Vol. 2, No. 4, pp. 429–441, Oct. 1993.
[4] I. J. Cox, S. Roy, and S. Hingorani, "Dynamic Histogram Warping of Images Pairs for Constant Image-Brightness," Research Report, NEC Research Institute, dated Feb. 1995.
[5] I. Daubechies, "The Wavelet Transform, Time-Frequency Localization and Signal Analysis," *IEEE Trans. on Information Theory,* Vol. 36, No. 5, pp. 961–1005, Sept. 1990.
[6] R. A. DeVore, B. Jawerth, and B. J. Lucier, "Image Compression Through Wavelet Transform Coding," *IEEE Trans. on Information Theory,* Vol. 38, No. 2, pp. 719–746, Mar. 1992.
[7] K. Hirata and F. Kato, "Query by Visual Example," *Advances in Database Tech. EDBT '92,* Vienna: Springer-Verlag, Mar. 1992.
[8] K. Hirata, Y. Hara, N. Shibata, and F. Hirabayashi, "Media-based Navigation for Hypermedia Systems," *Proc. ACM Hypertext '93,* pp. 159–173, 1993.
[9] B. Holt and L. Hartwick, "Visual-image Retrieval for Applications in Art and Art History," *Proc. SPIE, Storage and Retrieval for Image and Video Databases,* Vol. 2185, pp. 70–81, Feb. 1994.

[10] T. Y. Hou, A. Hsu, P. Liu, and M. Y. Chiu, "A Content-based Indexing Technique Using Relative Geometry Features," *Proc. SPIE, Image Storage and Retrieval Systems*, Vol. 1662, pp. 29–68, 1992.

[11] T. Y. Hou, P. Liu, A. Hsu, and M. Y. Chiu, "Medical-Image Retrieval by Spatial Feature," *Proc. IEEE International Conference on System, Man, and Cybernetics*, pp. 1364–1369, 1992.

[12] Jae S. Lim, *Two-Dimensional Signal and Image Processing*, Englewood Cliffs, NJ: Prentice-Hall, 1990.

[13] S. Mallat, "Zero-crossing of a Wavelet Transform," *IEEE Trans. on Information Theory*, Vol. 37, No. 4, pp. 1019–1033, July 1991.

[14] S. Mallat and S. Zhong, "Characterization of signals from multiscale edges," *IEEE Trans. on Pattern and Machine Analysis*, Vol. 14, No. 7, pp. 710–731, July 1992.

[15] W. Niblack, R. Barber, W. Equitz, et al., "The QBIC Project: Querying Images by Content Using Color, Texture, and Shape," *Proc. SPIE, Storage Retrieval for Image and Video Databases*, Vol. 1908, pp. 173–187, 1993.

[16] J. R. Smith and S.-F. Chang, "Automated Image-Retrieval Using Color and Texture," Research report, Center for Telecommunications Research, Columbia University, CU/CTR/TR 414-95-20, 1995.

[17] H. S. Stone and C.-S. Li, "Image Matching by Means of Intensity and Texture Matching in the Fourier Domain," *Proc. SPIE Conf. in Image and Video Databases*, San Jose, CA, Vol. 2670, pp. 337–344, Jan. 1996.

[18] H. S. Stone and T. Shamoon, "The Use of Image Content to Control Image Retrieval and Image Processing," Research report, NEC Research Institute, dated May 1995.

[19] C. Temperton, "Self-sorting in-place Fast Fourier Transforms," *SIAM J. Scientific and Statistical Computing*, Vol. 12, No. 4, pp. 808–823, July 1991.

[20] G. Turin, "An Introduction to Matched Filtering," *IEEE Trans. Information Theory*, Vol. IT–6, pp. 311–329, 1960.

[21] R. Y. Wong, E. L. Hall, and J. Rouge, "Hierarchical Search for Image Matching," *IEEE Conf. Decision Control*, Clearwater, FL, Dec. 1976.

[22] P. Kovesi, "Image Features from Phase Congruency," *Technical Report* 95/4. Computer Science Dept., Univ. of Western Australia, June, 1995.

Chapter 10

DATA STORAGE AND RETRIEVAL IN DISK-ARRAY-BASED VIDEO SERVERS

Ming-Syan Chen

Abstract

In response to the emergence of various multimedia applications, a significant amount of research effort has recently been expended on ways to deal with video data storage and retrieval in disk-array-based video servers. In this chapter, we examine various issues on video storage and retrieval in disk arrays. The issue of video replication in disk arrays is first discussed. Next we describe some prior studies on disk scheduling and examine methods to minimize the buffer requirement of the video server. The issue of storing scalable videos is then investigated. Finally, methods to support interactive viewing functions, such as pause/resume and fast browsing operations, for a disk-array-based video server are considered. An alternative model to support video viewing by video downloading is also discussed.

10.1 INTRODUCTION

Recent advances in technologies such as computing, storage, and communication have made possible the creation of several exciting multimedia applications [22,30]. Given the extremely large data size and high retrieval rates, the major challenges in handling multimedia data in a server are (1) to support very high-disk bandwidth for video retrieval, and (2) to provide very high-network bandwidth for data transmission [34]. ATM (asynchronous transfer mode) has been proposed as a solution to meet the demand for high-network bandwidth. On the other hand, disk arrays are employed to provide the disk bandwidth required for a video server [19,25,36]. For example, at HDTV resolution, the video data rate required is approximately 2 MB per second (even after compression). It is not desirable to store such a video in a single disk for two reasons. First, a 100-minute HDTV movie will require 12 GB of storage. Such a large disk is usually expensive. Second, playing a hot (i.e., frequently requested) movie from a single disk may cause a performance bottleneck. In fact, this problem also occurs when playing movies of normal VCR quality. Consequently, it is highly desirable to use data striping in a disk array to handle the storage and retrieval of video data [2,19]. In this chapter, we investigate various issues related to video data storage and retrieval in disk-array-based video servers.

Interactive TV and video-on-demand (VOD) have been identified as two important services made possible by advances in video compression and network transmission technologies [17]. In a VOD system, multimedia streams are stored on a storage server (the video server) and played out to the user station upon request. A significant amount of effort has been devoted to the design of a video server [10,24,27,28,32,36]. A video server for this purpose is expected not only to concurrently serve many clients (hundreds or more), but

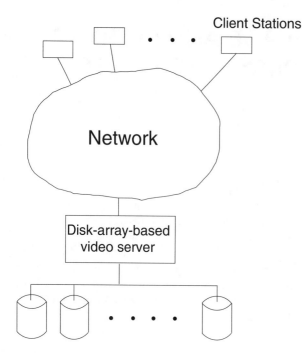

Figure 10.1 A disk-array-based video server.

also to provide many interactive features for video playout, such as pause/resume, backward play, and fast forward and fast backward play, which home viewers have been enjoying from the current VCR systems. Providing interactive features will unavoidably compromise the opportunity of batching requests and increase the system resource required. In addition, it is projected that similar to the current movie rental business, the movie request in a VOD environment will be highly skewed; that is, most of the requests are made for viewing a small number of hot movies. These factors, together with the importance of fault tolerance in real-time VOD applications, suggest that replicating certain frequently accessed movies in some disk arrays be a viable approach to providing the VOD service required [3,4,11]. It is worth mentioning that data replication in VOD system is employed primarily to support high I/O bandwidth required for multimedia data. This is in contrast to data replication in OLTP (On-Line Transaction Processing) systems, which are used mainly to provide fault-tolerance. The VOD system considered here is illustrated in Fig. 10.1, in which the disk-array-based video server is composed of many disk arrays. Each disk array is the unit to store a copy of a movie. If necessary, one movie may be replicated and stored in more than one disk array. In this chapter, we first examine the issue of video replication.

Next, the issue of disk scheduling is explored. It is noted that the number of video streams that can be supported by each disk or disk array for a given amount of buffer is an important parameter for system throughput. Conventional approaches to disk scheduling include round-robin (RR) scheduling [31] and SCAN scheduling [24] schemes. In [37], the grouped sweeping scheme (GSS) is proposed to deal with disk arm scheduling so as to minimize the buffer requirement. GSS can be viewed as a general scheme and covers SCAN-type elevator schemes and fixed-order round-robin schemes as its special cases.

The third issue we study is the storage of scalable video in a disk array. Layered video coding, referring to the encoding technique that accommodates at least two resolutions in a video stream, is capable of providing scalable video [12]. A scalable video stream permits the extraction of subsets of the full-resolution bit stream that may be decoded to create low-resolution videos [5,6,13]. In the broadcasting industry, it is desirable to support layered multiple resolutions from a video server since it allows a service provider (such as a video-on-demand company) to provide customers with different levels of service. Naturally, the resolution of a video ordered by a customer with an HDTV will be higher than that of a video ordered by a customer with a conventional TV. In addition, multiple-resolution encoding is useful for the computer industry for such applications as multiplatform decoding, which allows video to be decoded by platforms of different capabilities, and also multiwindow decoding where videos of different resolutions can be independently selected by decoders to produce videos for different window sizes. For this issue of scalable video storage, we will discuss methods that can reduce the buffer required and improve the system throughput.

Finally, the capability of fully interactive playout for a disk-array-based video server is studied. The interactive operations considered include pause/resume and fast forward/backward operations. For each VOD server, there is a maximum number of video disk streams that can be supported. This is referred to as the stream capacity of the server. Since the video requests are often skewed toward a small set of hot videos, enabling multiple viewing requests on the same video to share a common video stream can greatly increase the number of viewers supportable by the video server. This approach is referred to as batching of viewers. Through cleaver scheduling and buffering techniques, the concept of batching can be applied to support pause/resume VCR-like operations [39].

In addition to providing the basic pause/resume functions, it is highly desirable to provide the user with interactive functions such as fast forward (FF) and fast backward (FB). Two alternatives to support variable-rate video browsing in a disk-array-based video server, namely, a zig-zag sampling method and a staggered placement method, will be discussed [10].

As will be seen later, the interframe dependencies of MPEG make it prohibitively expensive to provide some interactive features over the network. Furthermore, such factors as skewed movie requests and peak-hour activities have made it very difficult, if not impossible, to have a cost-effective resource allocation (in terms of CPU, storage, and network bandwidth) in a VOD system. To date, the feasibility of providing interactive movie viewing over the network (including backbone and cable networks) is still unclear. Accordingly, in this chapter we discuss an alternative solution for the movie-on-demand service. This solution involves downloading of the video data into the storage of a player device located at the customer premise, so that the customer can view the video subsequently without further intervention from the network. Under the downloading model, a standard compressed stream can be transformed into the one optimized for efficient local playout. The growing market of multimedia applications and the fast advances of related technologies indicate that learning to handle video data in disk arrays in a cost-effective way is becoming an increasingly important problem.

The following sections discuss video replication in disk arrays; data retrieval in a disk; the issue of storing scalable video data; the approach of batching viewer requests to support pause/resume operations; methods to support fast forward and fast backward operations; and a downloading model to supply video to viewers.

10.2 VIDEO REPLICATION IN DISK ARRAYS

To employ the replication approach to VOD applications, the primary issue is to determine the placement of movie copies in disk arrays. Due to the nature of sequential access, it is desirable to decluster each movie copy into blocks and stripe them across a disk array. Basically, three replica declustering techniques have been proposed in the literature to improve fault tolerance, namely, *mirrored declustering*, *chained declustering*, and *interleaved declustering*. These declustering techniques are employed primarily to support random access applications, for example, database transaction processing [23]. In the VOD environment, the isochronous support for each continuous video stream imposes different requirements and hence calls for alternative replica declustering techniques. Although a movie placement method based on the bandwidth-to-space ratio was proposed in [15], the corresponding effect on fault tolerance was not explored.

10.2.1 Conventional Data Placement

As mentioned earlier, three basic replica declustering techniques have been proposed to improve fault tolerance. In the first of these techniques, mirrored declustering, the disks are organized into many identical disk arrays, and fault tolerance is then achieved by storing replicated data in these disk arrays. An example for storing two movie copies in two disk arrays under mirrored declustering is given in Table 10.1. While easy to implement and proper for random access applications, mirrored declustering is not suitable for sequential access applications, such as VOD, where losing a single disk in a disk array will render the whole striped array useless since the video delivery requires access to each disk in cyclical order repeatedly.

On the other hand, under the second technique, the chained declustering method, the primary data copy in disk i has a backup copy in disk $(i + 1)$ mod n, where n is the total number of disks employed. An example of chained declustering where the cluster size is

Table 10.1 A Double Redundant Data Placement with Mirrored Declustering

	Disk Array 1				Disk Array 2			
DISK	0	1	2	3	4	5	6	7
m0 - m3	m0	m1	m2	m3	m0	m1	m2	m3
m4 - m7	m4	m5	m6	m7	m4	m5	m6	m7

Table 10.2 Chained Declustering Disk Array with Double Redundancy

	Disk Array 1				Disk Array 2			
DISK	0	1	2	3	4	5	6	7
1st copy	m0	m1	m2	m3	m4	m5	m6	m7
2nd copy	m3	m0	m1	m2	m7	m4	m5	m6

shown in Table 10.2 where the cluster size is equal to the disk-array size, that is, 4. As shown in [21,23], for the random access pattern, the chained declustering method can achieve better fault tolerance and load balancing after failure than the mirrored declustering method. For example, when disk 1 fails under mirrored declustering (Table 10.1), access to m1 and m5 will need to be redirected to disk 5, resulting in a 100% workload increase at disk 5. With chained declustering (Table 10.2), when disk 1 fails, access to m0 and m1 can be evenly redistributed among all remaining disks in the same cluster [23]. Note, however, that using the chained declustering, it will be costly to dynamically change the number of replicas, since to do that, it would be necessary to change the number of disk arrays to stripe across for the existing copies.

In the third technique, interleaved declustering, the backup copy of the primary data in a disk is broken up into multiple subpartitions. Each subpartition is stored on a different disk within the same disk array—but not the disk containing the primary data [14]. It can be seen that for a similar reason as for chained declustering, adding/dropping movie copies dynamically is very costly under the interleaved declustering method. However, in real-time VOD applications, the number of copies stored for a video has to change as the demand for the video varies. With chained declustering and interleaved declustering, applications will need to be interrupted while adding/dropping data copies, thus making these two methods unfavorable for VOD applications.

10.2.2 Description of RMD Scheme

A replication method called *rotational mirrored declustering* (RMD) was proposed in [7] to support high data availability for disk arrays in VOD environments. In essence, RMD is similar to mirrored declustering in that multiple copies are stored in different disk arrays to increase the supportable throughput, however different they are from the mirrored declustering in that the data placements in different disk arrays under RMD are properly rotated. In this way, the capability of balancing workload upon disk failure is increased greatly, while maintaining the capability of dynamically adding/dropping data copies. The net effect of the rotation in replica placement is to achieve a different layout on striping for the replica from the original copy. Upon disk failure, the traffic to the failed disk can therefore be spread across all disks in the disk array containing the replica. This is in contrast to the conventional mirrored declustering, where the traffic to the failed disk can only be redirected to one of the disks in the array containing the replica. Combining the merits of

Table 10.3   A Double Redundant Data Placement Under RMD

	Disk Array 1				Disk Array 2			
DISK	0	1	2	3	4	5	6	7
m0 - m3	m0	m1	m2	m3	m0	m1	m2	m3
m4 - m7	m4	m5	m6	m7	m7	m4	m5	m6

both chained and mirrored declustering methods, RMD is particularly useful for storing multiple movie copies in a disk-array-based video server to support VOD applications. RMD was formulated as follows. Given a set of rn disks numbered $0, 1, 2, \ldots, rn - 1$, where n is the size (number of disks) of a disk array, the ith partition of the jth replica of a movie is placed on the disk numbered $d(i, j)$, where $d(i, j) = (i + \lfloor i/n \rfloor * (j - 1))$ mod $n + (j - 1) * n$.

A double redundant data placement based on RMD is shown in Table 10.3, where each disk array in the RMD declustering strategy contains a movie copy. Unlike the chained declustering method, RMD allows replica and disks to be added on-line while neither having to move data in the existing copy around nor affecting the disk arm movement on existing disks. For example, to add a new movie copy to the existing two copies shown in Table 10.3, a third data array will be allocated (either from an existing and available pool of disk arrays or adding a new disk array to the system) to the movie. The movie copy can then be loaded from tape to the newly allocated disk array without affecting the applications accessing the existing two movie copies. After the third movie copy has been loaded, the copy can then be made on-line for viewing. Table 10.4 illustrates the data placement with RMD after the third copy has been added. Consequently, users can incrementally add I/O capacity, I/O bandwidth, and the number of replicas without affecting existing services. This feature is particularly useful for VOD applications. Clearly, this feature is not available by the chained declustering method.

Table 10.4   A Triple Redundant Data Placement Under RMD

	Disk Array 1				Disk Array 2				Disk Array 3			
DISK	0	1	2	3	4	5	6	7	8	9	10	11
m0 - m3	m0	m1	m2	m3	m0	m1	m2	m3	m0	m1	m2	m3
m4 - m7	m4	m5	m6	m7	m7	m4	m5	m6	m6	m7	m4	m5

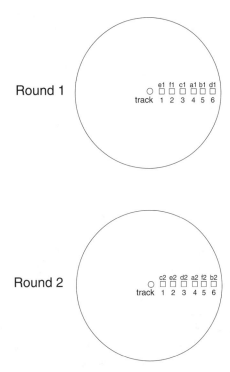

Round 1

Round 2

Figure 10.2 Illustrative scenarios for RR, SCAN, and GSS disk scheduling schemes.

10.3 DATA RETRIEVAL IN A DISK

The number of video streams that can be supported by each disk or disk array for a given amount of buffer is affected by the disk scheduling scheme employed. Here, we illustrate this concept by showing the operations under three disk scheduling schemes: fixed-order round-robin (RR) scheduling [31], elevator-type SCAN scheduling [24], and group sweeping scheduling (GSS).

In the RR approach, a request from each stream is served in a fixed order in each cycle of service. Since the blocks of different streams are scattered on a disk, the stream-based fixed-order servicing can incur a significant amount of seek (or disk arm movement) delay, resulting in performance degradation. For illustrative purposes, suppose six data streams are stored in the disk shown in Fig. 10.2. For stream a, a_1 is the first block and a_2 is the second block; $b_1, b_2, c_1, c_2, \ldots, f_2$ have similar meaning. The disk arm movement between two consecutive tracks is referred to as a *one-seek step*. Assume the disk arm is positioned in track 6 in the beginning. The effect of disk rotation is not considered here. Under RR, the block retrieval sequence and the number of corresponding seek steps required are shown in the first row of Table 10.5, where, for example, it took two seek steps to get a_1, and then, from the position of a_1, it took one step to get b_1, and so forth. The total number of seek steps incurred for these two rounds is 29.

Table 10.5   The Block Retrieving Scenarios Under
Three Disk Scheduling Schemes

	Round 1						Round 2					
RR	a_1	b_1	c_1	d_1	e_1	f_1	a_2	b_2	c_2	d_2	e_2	f_2
(block, step)	2	1	2	3	5	1	2	2	5	2	1	3
SCAN	d_1	b_1	a_1	c_1	f_1	e_1	c_2	e_2	d_2	a_2	f_2	e_2
(block, step)	0	1	1	1	1	1	0	1	1	1	1	1
GSS	b_1	a_1	c_1	d_1	f_1	e_1	a_2	b_2	d_2	c_2	e_2	f_2
(block, step)	1	1	1	3	4	1	3	2	3	2	1	3

In contrast, an elevator-type scheduling scheme can be used to reduce the number of seek steps required. This type of scheme, which is an adaptation of the classical SCAN algorithm [29], can effectively support a large number of simultaneous streams. In this approach, the ordering of retrievals is arranged according to their positions on the disk in such a way that the disk arm picks up the data as it scans from one end of the disk to the other end. As such, each service cycle requires only one maximum disk arm movement, which is independent of the number of retrieval streams. For the example placement in Fig. 10.2, the block retrieval sequence and the number of corresponding seek steps required under SCAN are shown in the second row of Table 10.5. Under SCAN, the number of seek steps incurred for these two rounds is 10.

Since under the SCAN algorithm, the ordering of service of a particular stream may be changed from the first to the last in two consecutive cycles, up to two cycles of retrieved data must be buffered. Playout of a stream can begin only at the end of the first service cycle. The round-robin scheme, on the other hand, requires the buffering of data from only one service cycle, and playout of a stream can begin at the end of its first retrieval. We note that the cycle time using the SCAN approach is typically smaller than that of the round-robin approach.

On the other hand, the group sweeping scheduling (GSS) provides a framework for minimizing the buffer requirement for VOD or multimedia storage management. It covers SCAN-type elevator schemes and fixed-order round-robin schemes as its special cases. GSS does not make any particular assumption on the layout of the data blocks for each stream on disk. Note that, on the one hand, we want to reduce the amount of seek delay, while on the other hand, we would like to minimize the worst-case bound on the times between two consecutive services to the same request stream. GSS tries to strike a balance between these two conflicting requirements. This concept is exploited in various VOD server designs and studies [20,35].

Essentially, GSS divides the number of media streams needed to be served, n, into g groups, and then performs (1) RR scheduling *between groups* and (2) SCAN scheduling *within each group*. In each cycle of service, GSS scans g times through the disk tracks from one end to the other, and serves the request streams in the ith group during the ith scan. Consider again the example placement in Fig. 10.2. Suppose $g = 3$, and group G_1 has streams a and b, group G_2 has streams c and d, and group G_3 has streams e and f. Under GSS, the block retrieval sequence and the number of corresponding seek steps required are shown in the third row of Table 10.5, and the number of seek steps incurred for these two rounds is 25.

Note that g is the tuning parameter whose value needs to be determined to optimize the buffer requirement. The optimal value of g can be derived for both the homogeneous case (i.e., all requests have the same playout rate) and the heterogeneous case [37]. The assignment of streams to groups is arbitrary in the homogeneous case, whereas the assignment needs to even out the buffer requirement among the groups in the heterogeneous case. The GSS approach provides a general formulation to cover a family of disk scheduling schemes. The traditional approach based on the fixed-order RR service scheme is a special case of GSS with $g = n$. Similarly, the SCAN scheduling scheme is a special case of GSS with $g = 1$.

10.4 STORING SCALABLE VIDEO DATA

Significant research effort has been focused on multiresolution coding, and this has led to the development of hierarchical coding techniques such as subband coding. The subband coding approach uses a bank of filters to decompose the original video into several frequency bands, resulting in a set of multiple-resolution videos [12]. For example, by dividing the frequency domain into four regions, the original video can be decomposed into four sets, say R1, R2, R3, and R4, where Ri is called rate i data. Here, R1 corresponds to the basic video (class 1), R1+R2 corresponds to class 2 video, R1+R2+R3 corresponds to class 3 video, and R1+R2+R3+R4 corresponds to the full-resolution video.

Video data of different rates can be stored separately to provide different resolutions of videos. An approach of staggering video blocks in the disk array based on data rates was proposed in [9] to deal with the storage of scalable video in a disk array. This approach, termed *rate staggering*, was devised to minimize the buffer space required at the server and improve the system throughput. The storage unit of video data is a block, which is composed of a sequence of frames.

An example of conventional scalable video placement, which employs disk striping (but not rate staggering), is shown in Table 10.6, where a disk array of eight disks is used and the ith block of the jth layer is denoted by $B_{i,j}$. An example for the scalable video placement with rate staggering is given in Table 10.7. As will be described later, the rate staggering approach has the following three advantages:

1. The intermediate buffer space required at the server is minimized.

2. Better load balancing is achieved due to finer scheduling granularity.

3. The disk bandwidth fragmentation is alleviated due to better bandwidth allocation.

Table 10.6 Scalable Video Placement with Disk
Striping, but without Rate Staggering

Disk No.	1	2	3	4	5	6	7	8
Rate 1	$B_{1,1}$	$B_{2,1}$	$B_{3,1}$	$B_{4,1}$	$B_{5,1}$	$B_{6,1}$	$B_{7,1}$	$B_{8,1}$
Rate 2	$B_{1,2}$	$B_{2,2}$	$B_{3,2}$	$B_{4,2}$	$B_{5,2}$	$B_{6,2}$	$B_{7,2}$	$B_{8,2}$
Rate 3	$B_{1,3}$	$B_{2,3}$	$B_{3,3}$	$B_{4,3}$	$B_{5,3}$	$B_{6,3}$	$B_{7,3}$	$B_{8,3}$
Rate 4	$B_{1,4}$	$B_{2,4}$	$B_{3,4}$	$B_{4,4}$	$B_{5,4}$	$B_{6,4}$	$B_{7,4}$	$B_{8,4}$

10.4.1 Rate Staggering for Scalable Video Data Storage

Let r be the number of different classes of video that the server can provide. When subband coding is used, the number r depends on the number of frequency bands and is usually flexible. The whole video data is divided into r partitions, called rate 1 data, rate 2 data, ..., and rate r data. The lowest quality video, referred to as class 1 video, requires only rate 1 data for playout. The second to the lowest quality video, referred to as class 2 video, requires both rate 1 and rate 2 data for playout. More generally, class i video requires all of rate j data, $1 \le j \le i$, for playout.

It is assumed that data retrieval proceeds in rounds. Let P (in byte/second) be the playout speed for the decoder to play out the full-resolution video, and let T be the one-round retrieval time by the disk array. Then, using the double buffering method (i.e., the buffer space is chosen to be twice that needed to accommodate the data retrieved in one round), the buffer space required by the server for a full-resolution stream is equal to $2TP$. As pointed out in [24], a larger block size will lead to a higher disk throughput, showing a tradeoff between the server buffer space required and the system throughput. Clearly, the choice of a larger storage unit can amortize the disk arm positioning overheads over a larger read time. Since such a choice of block size is system dependent, it is assumed that all blocks have the same block size, b (in bytes). The assumption for blocks containing

Table 10.7 Scalable Video Placement with Rate
Staggering

Disk No.	1	2	3	4	5	6	7	8
Rate 1	$B_{1,1}$	$B_{2,1}$	$B_{3,1}$	$B_{4,1}$	$B_{5,1}$	$B_{6,1}$	$B_{7,1}$	$B_{8,1}$
Rate 2	$B_{7,2}$	$B_{8,2}$	$B_{1,2}$	$B_{2,2}$	$B_{3,2}$	$B_{4,2}$	$B_{5,2}$	$B_{6,2}$
Rate 3	$B_{5,3}$	$B_{6,3}$	$B_{7,3}$	$B_{8,3}$	$B_{1,3}$	$B_{2,3}$	$B_{3,3}$	$B_{4,3}$
Rate 4	$B_{3,4}$	$B_{4,4}$	$B_{5,4}$	$B_{6,4}$	$B_{7,4}$	$B_{8,4}$	$B_{1,4}$	$B_{2,4}$

data of different rates to have the same size is deemed reasonable under subband encoding. However, more provision is needed to justify this assumption under MPEG encoding [12].

Let k be the displacement factor for staggering data blocks of different rates in the disk array. For example, the displacement factor in Table 10.7 is two. Clearly, $\lceil \frac{TP}{b} \rceil$ is the number of data blocks needed by a full-resolution video stream within the time duration T. Hence, in order to achieve load balancing among disks, the displacement factor k is designed to be $\lceil \frac{TP}{br} \rceil$. Such a placement by rate staggering can spread the workload of each stream evenly across disks.

Denote the buffer size of the end decoder as B_D. The maximal amount of data the end decoder can retrieve at a time is half its total buffer size (assuming that the other half is being used for playout). B_D thus has to be greater than or equal to $2\lceil \frac{TP}{b} \rceil b$. The data placement for scalable video in a disk array of n disks can be determined by a procedure in [9], where the displacement factor k is obtained as $\lceil \frac{TP}{br} \rceil$ first and block $B_{i,j}$ is placed in disk $d(i, j) = [(j-1)k + i]_n$. It can be verified from Table 10.7 that with $n = 8$ and $k = 2$, $B_{3,2}$ resides in disk $d(3, 2) = [2 + 3]_8 = 5$ and $B_{5,4}$ resides in disk $d(5, 4) = [6 + 5]_8 = 3$.

10.4.2 Advantages of Rate Staggering

In order to understand the advantages of rate staggering, let us first examine the video data placement given in Table 10.6. For ease of presentation, consider the scenario of serving one video stream and also assume the time required for each disk retrieval is proportional to the amount of data retrieved. Let the time required for one disk to retrieve one data block of size b be T_1. Suppose that the previously mentioned double buffering method is used and that the decoder of an end player, with a local buffer size $16b$, requires the playout speed $8b/T_1$ to play the full-resolution video. It can be seen that for the data placement in Table 10.6, all 32 blocks have to be retrieved in one round of retrieval (with the duration $4T_1$), which would require the available buffer size of $2 * 32b = 64b$ at the server.[1] Note that the server can only send $8b$ data to the end player at a time due to the limited buffer size of the decoder (i.e., $16b$). Given the placement in Table 10.6, the server has to retrieve all 32 blocks (4 blocks from each disk) in order to extract 8 blocks to send to the decoder for playout.

Table 10.8 Four Rounds of Full-Resolution Data Retrieval in a Disk Array with Rate Staggering

Disk No.	1	2	3	4	5	6	7	8
Round 1	$B_{1,1}$	$B_{2,1}$	$B_{1,2}$	$B_{2,2}$	$B_{1,3}$	$B_{2,3}$	$B_{1,4}$	$B_{2,4}$
Round 2	$B_{3,4}$	$B_{4,4}$	$B_{3,1}$	$B_{4,1}$	$B_{3,2}$	$B_{4,2}$	$B_{3,3}$	$B_{4,3}$
Round 3	$B_{5,3}$	$B_{6,3}$	$B_{5,4}$	$B_{6,4}$	$B_{5,1}$	$B_{6,1}$	$B_{5,2}$	$B_{6,2}$
Round 4	$B_{7,2}$	$B_{8,2}$	$B_{7,3}$	$B_{8,3}$	$B_{7,4}$	$B_{8,4}$	$B_{7,1}$	$B_{8,1}$

[1]With a technique of pipelining, the buffer space required may be reduced; however, it is still much larger than that needed by the case with rate staggering.

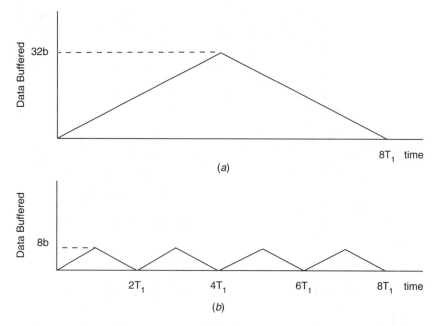

Figure 10.3   Illustration for the amount of data buffered in half of the buffer
space: (*a*) without rate staggering and (*b*) with rate staggering.

On the other hand, given the data placement in Table 10.7, one only has to retrieve
8 blocks in one round of retrieval (with the duration T_1), as shown in Table 10.8, which
requires the buffer size of $2 * 8b = 16b$ at the server, only a quarter of that required by the
case without rate staggering. Illustration for the amount of data buffered in half the buffer
space is shown in Figure 10.3. The above request from a decoder cannot be satisfied by a
server with an available buffer space within the range $[16b, 64b)$, unless the rate staggering
technique is employed. It can be seen that this advantage of using rate staggering still holds
when multiple streams are considered.

10.5 PROVIDING PAUSE/RESUME OPERATIONS WITH BATCHING AND BUFFERING

Recall that a maximum number of video disk streams can be supported in each VOD server.
This is referred to as the stream capacity of the server. Clearly, if we use one dedicated stream
to schedule each viewer, the number of viewers supportable at most equals to the stream
capacity of the server. Since the video requests are often quite skewed toward a small set of
hot videos, enabling multiple viewing requests on the same video to share a common video
stream can greatly increase the number of viewers supportable by the video server. This is
referred to as batching of viewers. Batching is most applicable when the VOD system does

not support any interactive functions; that is, each video is shown without interruption. The most straightforward method to explore the concept of batching is to delay the viewing and send the same stream to multiple clients. This is achieved by batching requests for the same movie which arrive within the same short time duration. Various policies for selecting the movie to be multicast were investigated in [16], and it was shown that the choice of a policy depends on the customer waiting time tolerance before reneging. In that study, it was found that one policy that schedules the movie with the longest outstanding request can outperform the other policy that chooses the movie with the maximal number of outstanding requests. In addition, the notion of batching can also be implemented by buffering [38]. Basically, the idea of buffering is to allow a video request to share the video stream of an earlier request, which has already started, by using buffering to bridge the time gap between their showing times. In contrast to the delayed scheduling approach, batching via buffering does not delay the earlier requests to form a batch. Instead, the later requests are made to catch up through buffering. This tends to provide better quality of service at the cost of an additional buffer requirement.

10.6 FAST FORWARD AND FAST BACKWARD FUNCTIONS

In addition to providing the basic "start/stop" functions, it is highly desirable to provide the user with VCR–like search or scan functions such as "fast forward" (FF) and "fast backward" (FB). There are several possible approaches to implementing these functions, some of which mimic the scan operation of an analog VCR or movie projector. However, as explained here, each of these approaches imposes additional resource requirements on the system. For example, consider the case that the video has to be scanned (forward) at three times the normal playout rate.

- The multimedia stream is retrieved and transmitted at three times the normal playout rate, and the end station filters and plays out the data. It is apparent that this solution requires additional resources (three times normal) at the storage system, the memory buffers, and the network. Moreover, it requires additional resources at the end station to process the incoming data.

- The storage system retrieves and transmits every third frame to the end station. This scheme also requires significant additional system resources since the multimedia file must now be indexed to retrieve individual frames and the amount of retrieved data is higher than normal due to the structure of the interframe coding (i.e., interframe dependencies in MPEG; see Section 10.6.1 for more details). In addition, the retrieval process for these frames may not be efficient since it is difficult to ensure individual frame alignment with track/block boundaries on the disk.

- The system switches over to a separately coded "scan forward" stream to provide the scan operation. This solution eliminates any additional read bandwidth or network bandwidth. However, it is extremely expensive in terms of storage space and inflexible in that it supports a fixed scan rate.

- A restricted form of FF can be provided for MPEG streams by playing out only those frames without interframe dependencies (**I** frames[2]). Since **I** frames are very large in size, the frame rate has to be reduced significantly in order to maintain a fixed network bandwidth. The end viewer will therefore have to ensure a slower frame playout rate during FF and also the inflexibility of FF speed.

As a result, after requesting the browsing function, the viewer may have to be put into a wait state, if the additional stream capacity required is not available. Such a problem exists even if a dedicated stream is allocated to each viewer during the normal playout.

Sampling is an approach designed to maintain the same playout rate during browsing as under normal showing. For the case of no interframe dependencies, if the video is placed on a single disk, to achieve an FF of m times the normal playout rate, one can simply sample every mth blocks. In a disk-array environment, we have an additional requirement to balance the load on the disks in the array. Specifically, we would like to retrieve one block from each disk during every round of retrieval. The traditional approach on video placement is to store the video blocks in a round-robin manner on the disk array. Uniform sampling generally will not be able to spread the load evenly. For example, suppose a disk array is composed of nine disks, numbered disks 0, . . . , 8. If we want to achieve FF with three times the normal rate, starting from disk 0 and sampling at every third block will put all the loads on disks 0, 3, and 6.

This load-balancing problem can be solved either by some nonuniform sampling technique or by a different placement method other than round-robin. In this section we describe two alternatives, namely, the zig-zag sampling method [10] and the staggered placement method [10]. Both approaches support variable-rate video browsing in a disk-array-based video server. To understand the reasons for the design of these two approaches, we will first review the data organization of MPEG.

10.6.1 MPEG Data Organization

The structure of the MPEG stream imposes several constraints on the video data storage and playout. An MPEG video stream consists of intraframes (I), predictive frames (P), and interpolated frames (B). In this stream, I frames are coded so that they are independent of any other frames in the sequence, and P frames are coded using motion estimation and have a dependency on the preceding I or P frame. On the other hand, B frames depend on two "anchor" frames: the preceding I/P frame and the following I/P frame. Since P and B frames use interframe compression, they are substantially smaller than I frames. Figure 10.4 shows the interframe dependencies in a sequence of MPEG frames, where the frames are numbered in temporal order. The arrows indicate the dependencies between frames. The interframe dependency implies that it is not possible to decode a P frame without the preceding I or P frame. Similarly, it is not possible to decode a B frame without the corresponding two-anchor frames (i.e., two P frames, or one I and one P frames). Figure 10.5 shows the differences between the order in which compressed frames are presented to the decoder (presentation order) and the order in which decompressed frames are presented to the viewer (temporal order). For normal forward playout, it is necessary to keep exactly

---

[2]Or **I** and **P** frames by using proper provision.

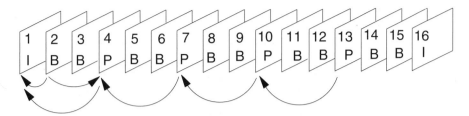

Figure 10.4   Interframe dependency in a sequence of MPEG frames.

two decompressed frames in the memory buffer for decoding a frame that references these two frames. For the example in Fig. 10.5, decompressed frames 1 (I frame) and 4 (P frame) are required to decode frame 2 (B frame). On the other hand, when decoding frame 5 (B frame), we need decompressed frames 4 and 7 (two P frames) and no longer need frame 1. Since decompressed frames are of the same size, we need buffer space for two decompressed frames to do the decoding for normal playout.

Video compression like MPEG imposes another problem on sampling. Since MPEG compression introduces interframe interdependency, uniform sampling at the frame level would make the decoding impossible. To remedy this problem, one approach is to sample only the independent frames. Since independent frames can be a lot larger in size than the dependent frames, this approach has a problem that to maintain the same data playout rate during the FF, more system resources will be required. Alternatively, one can sample at the segment level where a segment is a group of frames, starting from an independent frame and ending immediately before another independent frame [10]. Hence, the interframe dependency occurs mostly within the segment. To avoid additional load to the disk array and simplify the file system management, the striping unit over a disk array should be chosen similar to the sampling unit.

10.6.2   Segment Sampling Method

The zig-zag segment sampling method [10] assumes that media segments belonging to any multimedia stream are stored in a robin-robin manner on the disk array. It determines the retrieval order of segments for FF operations for any desired FF rate chosen by the viewer.

Temporal Order:	I	B	B	P	B	B	P	B	B	P	B	B	P	B	B	I	...
Frame Number:	1	2	3	4	5	6	7	8	9	10	11	12	13	14	15	16	

Presen./Storage Ord.:	I	P	B	B	P	B	B	P	B	B	P	B	B	I	B	B	...
Frame Number:	1	4	2	3	7	5	6	10	8	9	13	11	12	16	14	15	

Figure 10.5   Temporal order (to the viewer) and presentation order (to the decoder) of MPEG frames.

Table 10.9 A Fast Retrieval for a Disk Array of 9 Disks and FF Rate of 3

Disk No.	0	1	2	3	4	5	6	7	8
1st round	0*	1	2	3*	4	5	6*	7	8
	9	10*	11	12	13*	14	15	16*	17
	18	19	20*	21	22	23*	24	25	26*
2nd round	27	28	29*	30	31	32*	33	34	35*
	36	37*	38	39	40*	41	42	43*	44
	45*	46	47	48*	49	50	51*	52	53
1st round segments	0	10	20	3	13	23	6	16	26
2nd round segments	45	37	29	48	40	32	51	43	35

The segments selected by this method are distributed uniformly across the disk array and can be shown to achieve a minimal variation on the number of segments skipped between every two consecutive retrieved segments. This holds for any disk-array size.

Table 10.9 shows the segment retrieval pattern under the zig-zag sampling method for the case of nine disks and a fast forward rate of 3. As the table shows, instead of retrieving segments whose numbers are multiples of three (which would make disks 1, 2, 4, 5, 7, and 8 idle), the zig-zag scheme properly shifts the data segments retrieved in some retrievals. For example, segment 10 is fetched instead of segment 9, and segment 20 is fetched instead of segment 19. Such shifting, though making the segments retrieved not perfectly uniformly distributed, ensures the maximal throughput is achieved. The group of segments retrieved in the first round of retrieval in Table 10.9 consists of segments 0, 10, 20, 3, 13, 23, 6, 16, and 26, which are then displayed in the order of 0, 3, 6, 10‡, 13, 16, 20‡, 23, 26, where ‡ indicates a shift for retrieved segment numbers.

10.6.3 Segment Placement Method

In contrast to the zig-zag segment sampling method that selectively retrieves segments from a disk array in which segments are stored in a round-robin manner, the staggered segment placement method [10] allocates segments to disks judiciously so that no special provision is needed for sampling and the segment can be completely uniformly sampled in an FF mode for some predetermined FF rates. The constraint is that the FF rate selected must be a submultiple of the disk-array size.

The segment placement function, $f(g, n)$, defines a mapping from media segment g to a disk, $k \in [0, n)$, in the disk array with n disks. Let $[x]_y$ denote x mod y for notational simplicity. Assuming that m is a submultiple of the number of disks n, that is, $[n]_m = 0$, the segment placement function is derived as follows: $f_2(g, n) = [g + \lfloor g/n \rfloor]_n$. The first term, that is, g within $[.]_n$, represents a regular scattering of the segments on the n disks and the second term, that is, $\lfloor g/n \rfloor$ within $[.]_n$, represents the staggered factor.

Table 10.10 Segment Layout on a Disk Array of Six Disks

Disk No.	0	1	2	3	4	5
1st round	0*	1	2*	3	4*	5
	11	6*	7	8*	9	10*
2nd round	16*	17	12*	13	14*	15
	21	22*	23	18*	19	20*

Table 10.10 shows the segment placement and retrieval pattern under the staggered placement method for the case of six disks and a fast forward rate of 2. The segment retrieved is indicated with an *.

This layout ensures that the media segments to be retrieved in a round all reside in different disks, so that the load imposed on the storage system by the retrieval process in FF mode is identical to the load under the normal operation.

Generally speaking, the zig-zag segment sampling method uses a simple round-robin placement policy and a sophisticated segment sampling strategy for retrieval. It can be used to provide FF retrieval at any desired rate with only a minimal deviation from the uniform sampling sequence. For certain FF rates m and the disk array size n where m and n are relatively prime, the sampling method produces a uniform sampling sequence. When the desired FF rates are known a priori, it is possible to simplify the segment retrieval process by using a more sophisticated segment placement method. The staggered placement method guarantees a uniform retrieval sequence that presents an evenly distributed load on the disk array. Although these methods have been described in the context of FF retrieval, they can also be applied to fast backward retrieval with some changes in the end station for playout. For example, in the first round of Table 10.9 the display order for fast backward will be 26, 23, 20, 16, 13, 10, 6, 3, and 0. Note that the VCR-like FF method considered here (i.e., a viewer locates the interested scene by scanning the video content) can in fact be used together with the time (or index)-based video browsing, which is expected to be widely available for digital video, to provide a most efficient video search.

To support browsing in a disk-array-based video server, [26] presented alternatives for providing FF in an optical storage system. This work does not consider the use of a disk array, and thus does not address the problem of balancing the load across the disks. As mentioned in [5], it is possible to support FF with data striping for certain specific stride rates. However, [5] deals with neither interframe dependencies in a compressed video nor disk load balancing for interactive browsing. With the purpose of providing FF/Reverse capabilities with a statistical quality-of-service guarantee, [18] proposed and analyzed by queue models two alternative schemes: one to delay the service and the other to immediately provide the service with a lower quality, in order to handle the situation of inefficient bandwidth. In addition, the MPEG-2 draft standard [1] proposes the creation of special **D** frames that do not have any interframe dependency to support video browsing. However, the **D** frames contain only the DC coefficients of the transform blocks and consequently have very poor resolution. In other related work, issues such as admission control and selection of service size to support multimedia applications are addressed in [31,36]. Disk scheduling schemes for optimizing the throughput of the DASD storage system are considered in [20,33,37].

10.7 DOWNLOADING: AN ALTERNATIVE TO REAL-TIME PLAYOUT

Finally, we discuss a model that involves downloading of the video data into the storage of a player device located at the customer premise, so that the customer can view the video subsequently without further intervention from the network. It can be shown that such a player device is economically feasible. Using the MPEG technique, a 100-minute MPEG-1 movie will occupy 1–1.5 GB of storage. Currently, the price of a 1.6-GB disk is slightly under $400, and it is expected that this cost will decrease rapidly in the years to come due to rapid increases in recording densities, thus falling into the price range of consumer products. With the current disk bandwidth (e.g., a SCSI disk), downloading a 100-minute MPEG-1 movie from the remote video server over the network to the disk of a client station will take only three to five minutes, close to the time for TV commercial breaks that is generally acceptable for end viewers. With video data stored in the player's storage, viewers can then enjoy all the interactive features for video viewing without incurring any server resources and network bandwidth. In addition, since downloading can be done prior to viewing, the effects of *skewed movie requests* and *peak-hour activities* can be minimized. In this model, video data are stored in the video server and transmitted to the player device upon request. The transmission may occur at high speed (either via ISDN or cable modem) so as to permit downloading of the entire movie within a few minutes of elapsed time. Under the downloading model, the VOD server is able to transmit videos out as fast as possible without explicit pacing. Also, since this is not real-time playout, the server has the flexibility of queuing up requests for downloading. Based on these trends, we believe that downloading digital movies into a player device at the customer premises for viewing is economical and desirable, and will be a competitive choice to real-time VOD.

This downloading model also allows us to perform stream conversion. As explained earlier, although the presentation sequence of MPEG obviates the need for storing compressed frames during forward playout, it does not address the problems of backward playout. For example, consider the case that a viewer decides to play backward when he is viewing frame 14 in Fig. 10.5. (At that moment we have decompressed frames 13 and 16 in the buffer.) He can then view frame 13. However, to decode frame 12, the decoder needs decompressed frames 10 and 13. To obtain decompressed frame 10, the decoder needs decompressed frame 7, which in turn requires decompressed frame 4 and frame 1. Thus, to decode a frame P during the backward playout, it is necessary to decode, in a reverse sequence, all the P frames until an I frame is reached. This reverse chained-decoding is required for backward playout, but not for forward playout, since a P frame is encoded based on the previous I/P frame. The buffer space required for backward playout thus increases significantly. (We need buffer space for five decompressed frames in this case.)

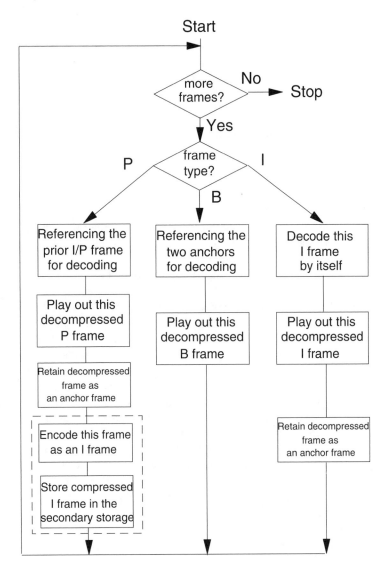

Figure 10.6 Execution flow for the decoder during the forward playout.

In order to facilitate backward playout, a transformation of the standard MPEG stream into a local compressed form was proposed in [8]. Specifically, after a P frame is retrieved, decompressed, and played out, we encode this frame as an I frame and store it back to the secondary storage. As mentioned before, since this P-I conversion is performed after a P frame is decompressed and played out, no extra cost is required for decoding. Also, since no motion estimation and compensation is required for compressing a single frame into

```
Orig. Frames Stored:     I  P  B  B  P  B  B  P  B  B  P  B  B  I  B  B  ...
Frame Number:            1  4  2  3  7  5  6  10 8  9  13 11 12 16 14 15


Frames Stored
After P/I Conv:          I  I  B  B  I  B  B  I  B  B  P  B  B  I  B  B  ...
Frame Number:            1  4  2  3  7  5  6  10 8  9  13 11 12 16 14 15
```

Figure 10.7   A snapshot for the result of P-I conversion.

an I frame, this I frame encoding can be done very efficiently. An execution flow for the decoder during the forward playout is shown in Fig. 10.6. Figure 10.7 shows a snapshot for the compressed frames stored in the secondary storage when the normal playout reaches frame 14 (when we keep decompressed frames 13 and 16 in the buffer and frame 13 is yet to be converted into an I frame).

Using the proposed P-I conversion, we see that the buffer space required for backward play will be the amount for storing two decompressed frames, that is, the same as required for forward play. For example, consider again the case where a viewer decides to play backward when he is viewing frame 14 (with decompressed frames 13 and 16 in the buffer). He next views frame 13 and is then able to view frame 12, which is decoded based on frames 10 and 13. With P-I conversion, frame 10 is now stored as an I frame in the secondary storage, and can be retrieved and decompressed by itself to be used for decoding frame 12. The reverse chained-decoding required for the backward playout in the original MPEG stream is thus avoided. After the P-I conversion, the temporal order (to the viewer) and presentation order (to the decoder) for backward playout are shown in Fig. 10.8.

The additional storage required due to this P-I conversion is small. Assuming that the ratio of frame sizes for I, P, and B frames is 5:3:2, Table 10.11 shows the additional secondary storage required for the P-I conversion and the MPEG-JPEG conversion (in terms of the percentage over the size of the original MPEG stream) for various MPEG streams. The frame ratio in Table 10.11 indicates the mix of I, P, and B frames in the MPEG stream. For instance, the MPEG stream in Fig. 10.4 has a frame ratio of 1:4:10. Consider this stream as an example. Since the ratio of frame sizes for I, P, and B frames is 5:3:2, the percentage of size increase by P-I conversion will be $\frac{5*5+2*10-(5*1+3*4+2*10)}{5*1+3*4+2*10} = 21.6\%$. On the other

```
Temporal Order:          I  B  B  I  B  B  I  B  B  I  B  B  I  B  B  I  ...
Frame Number:            16 15 14 13 12 11 10 9  8  7  6  5  4  3  2  1  ...

Presentation Order:      I  I  B  B  I  B  B  I  B  B  I  B  B  I  B  B  ...
Frame Number:            16 13 15 14 10 12 11 7  9  8  4  6  5  1  3  2
```

Figure 10.8   Temporal order (to the viewer) and presentation order (to the decoder) for backward playout.

Table 10.11 Additional Secondary Storage Required by P-I Conversion and MPEG-JPEG Conversion

Frame Ratio (I:P:B)	1:3:8	1:3:12	1:4:10	1:4:15
P-I conversion	20.0%	15.7%	21.6%	17.0%
MPEG-JPEG conv.	100.0%	110.5%	102.7%	112.7%

hand, the percentage of size increase by MPEG-JPEG conversion for this stream will be $\frac{5*15-(5*1+3*4+2*10)}{5*1+3*4+2*10} = 102.7\%$. Following the same procedure, we can obtain the numbers in other columns. While requiring the same amount of buffer for decoding, P-I conversion requires a significantly smaller amount of secondary storage than MPEG-JPEG conversion. From Table 10.11, we see that the additional secondary storage required by P-I conversion is small and fairly acceptable in view of the resulting benefits and the inexpensive nature of the secondary storage.

10.8 CONCLUSIONS

In this chapter, we examined various related issues and surveyed several recent studies. The issue of video replication in disk arrays was first discussed. Next we described some prior work on disk scheduling and examined methods to minimize the buffer requirement of the video server. The issue of storing scalable videos was investigated. Finally, methods to support interactive viewing functions, such as pause/resume and fast browsing operations, for a disk-array-based video server were considered. An alternative model to support video viewing by video downloading was also discussed. The issue of how to cost-effectively handle video data in a disk-array-based video server is expected to have growing importance.

Acknowledgment

Recent work done by Ming-Syan Chen is in part supported by National Science Council, Project No. NSC 87-2213-E-002-009 a nd Project No. NSC 87-2213-E-002-101, Taiwan, ROC.

References

[1] Generic Coding of Moving Pictures and Associated Audio. ISO/IEC Recommendation H.262, working draft, Mar. 1994.
[2] S. Berson, S. Ghandeharizadeh, R. Muntz, and X. Ju, "Staggered Striping in Multimedia Information Systems," *Proceedings of ACM SIGMOD,* Minneapolis, MN, pp. 79–90, May 1994.

[3] S. Berson, L. Golubchik, and R. R. Muntz, ''Fault Tolerant Design of Multimedia Servers,'' *Proceedings of ACM SIGMOD*, pp. 364–375, May 1995.

[4] W. A. Burkhard and J. Menon, ''Disk Array Storage System Reliability,'' *Proc. of Symposium of Fault-Tolerant Computing, FTCS-23*, pp. 432–441, June 1993.

[5] E. Chang and A. Zakhor, ''Scalable Video Data Placement on Parallel Disk Arrays,'' *IS&T/SPIE International Symp. on Electronic Imaging: Science and Technology,* Vol. 2185: Image and Video Database II, Feb. 1994.

[6] E. Chang and A. Zakhor, ''Variable Bit Rate MPEG Video Storage on Parallel Disk Arrays,'' *1st International Workshop on Community Networking Integrated Multimedia Services to the Home*, July 1994.

[7] M.-S. Chen, H. Hsiao, C.-S. Li, and P. S. Yu, ''Using Rotational Mirrored Declustering for Replica Placement in a Disk-Array-Based Video Server,'' *Proceedings of ACM Multimedia*, pp. 121–130, Nov. 1995.

[8] M.-S. Chen and D. D. Kandlur, ''Stream Conversion to Support Interactive Playout of Videos in a Client Station,'' *IEEE Multimedia*, Vol. 3, No. 2, Summer 1996.

[9] M.-S. Chen, D. D. Kandlur, and P. S. Yu, ''Using Rate Staggering to Store Scalable Video Data in a Disk-Array-Based Video Server,'' *Proc. IS&T/SPIE Symposium on Electronic Imaging—Conference on Multimedia Computing and Networking, SPIE*, Vol. 2417, pp. 338–345, Feb. 1995.

[10] M.-S. Chen, D. D. Kandlur, and P. S. Yu, ''Storage and Retrieval Methods to Support Fully Interactive Playout in a Disk-Array-Based Video Server,'' *Proceedings of ACM Multimedia*, Vol. 3, No. 3, pp. 126–135, July 1995.

[11] P. M. Chen, E. K. Lee, G. A. Gibson, R. H. Katz, and D. A. Patterson,'' RAID: High-Performance, Reliable Secondary Storage,'' *ACM Computing Surveys*, Vol. 26, No. 2, pp. 145–185, June 1994.

[12] T. Chiang and D. Anastassiou, ''Hierarchical Coding of Digital Television,'' *IEEE Communication*, Vol. 32, No. 5, pp. 38–45, May 1994.

[13] T.-C. Chiueh and R. H. Katz, ''Multi-Resolution Video Representation for Parallel Disk Arrays,'' *Proceedings of ACM Multimedia*, pp. 401–409, Aug. 1993.

[14] G. Copeland and T. Keller, ''A Comparison of High-Availability Media Recovery Techniques,'' *Proceedings of ACM SIGMOD, Portland, OR*, pp. 98–109, June 1989.

[15] A. Dan and D. Sitaram, ''An Online Video Placement Policy Based on Bandwidth to Space,'' *Proceedings of ACM SIGMOD*, pp. 376–385, May 1995.

[16] A. Dan, D. Sitaram, and P. Shahabuddin, ''Scheduling Policies for an On-Demand Video Server with Batching,'' *Proceedings of ACM Multimedia*, pp. 15–23, Oct. 1994.

[17] D. Deloddere, W. Verbiest, and H. Verhille, ''Interactive Video on Demand,'' *IEEE Communications Magazine*, Vol. 32, No. 5, pp. 82–88, May 1994.

[18] J. K. Dey, J. D. Salehi, J. F. Kurose, and D. Towsley. ''Providing VCR Capabilities in Large-Scale Video Servers,'' *Proceedings of ACM Multimedia'94*, pp. 25–32, Oct. 1994.

[19] G. R. Ganger, B. L. Worthington, R. Y. Hou, and Y. N. Patt, Disk Arrays: High-Performance, High-Reliability Storage Subsystems, *IEEE Computer*, pp. 30–37, Mar. 1994.

[20] D. J. Gemmell, ''Multimedia Network File Servers: Multi-Channel Delay Senstitive Data Retrieval,'' *Proceedings of ACM Multimedia*, pp. 243–250, Aug. 1993.

[21] L. Golubchik, J. C. S. Lui, and R. R. Muntz, "Chained Declustering: Load Balancing and Robustness to Skew and Failure," *Proceedings of the 2nd International Workshop on Research Issues in Data Engineering: Transaction and Query Processing, Tempe, AZ*, pp. 89–95, Feb. 1992.

[22] W. I. Grosky. "Multimedia Information Systems," *IEEE Multimedia*, pp. 12–24, Spring 1994.

[23] H.-I. Hsiao and D. J. DeWitt, "Chained Declustering: A New Availability Strategy for Multiprocessor Database Machines," *Proceedings of the 6th International Conference on Data Engineering*, pp. 456–465, 1990.

[24] D. D. Kandlur, M.-S. Chen, and Z.-Y. Shae, "Design of a Multimedia Storage Server," *Proc. IS&T/SPIE Symposium on Electronic Imaging—Conference on High Speed Networking and Multimedia Applications*. SPIE, Feb. 1994.

[25] R. Katz, G. Gibson, and D. Patterson, "Disk System Architectures for High Performance Computing," *Proceedings of the IEEE*, Vol. 77, No. 12, pp. 1842–1858, Dec. 1989.

[26] T. Mori, K. Nishimura, H. Nakano, and Y. Ishibashi, "Video-on-Demand System Using Optical Mass Storage System," *Japanese Journal of Applied Physics*, 1(11B):5433–5438, Nov. 1993.

[27] R. T. Ng and J. Yang, "Maximizing Buffer and Disk Utilizations for News on-Demand," *Proceedings of the 20th International Conference on Very Large Databases*, pp. 451–462, Sept. 1994.

[28] B. Ozden, A. Biliris, R. Rastogi, and A. Silberschatz, "A Low-Cost Storage Server for Movie on Demand Databases," *Proceedings of the 20th International Conference on Very Large Databases*, pp. 594–605, Sept. 1994.

[29] J. L. Peterson and A. Silberschatz, *"Operating System Concepts*, 2nd ed., Reading, MA: Addison-Wesley, 1985.

[30] S. Ramanathan and P. V. Rangan, "Architectures for Personalized Multimedia," *IEEE Multimedia*, Vol. 1, No. 1, pp. 37–46, Spring 1994.

[31] P. V. Rangan and H. M. Vin, "Designing File Systems for Digital Video and Audio," *Proceedings of the 12th ACM Symposium on Operating Systems*, pp. 81–94, Oct. 1991.

[32] P. V. Rangan, H. M. Vin, and S. Ramanathan, "Designing a Multi-User Multimedia On-Demand Service," *IEEE Communications Magazine*, Vol. 30, No. 7, pp. 56–65, July 1992.

[33] A.L.N. Reddy and J. Wyllie, "Disk Scheduling in a Multimedia I/O System," *Proceedings of ACM Multimedia*, pp. 225–233, Aug. 1993.

[34] A.L.N. Reddy and J. Wyllie, "I/O Issues in a Multimedia System," *IEEE Computer*, pp. 69–74, Mar. 1994.

[35] F. A. Tobagi, J. Pang, R. Baird, and M. Gang, "Streaming RAID—A Disk Array Management System for Video Files," *Proceedings of ACM Multimedia*, pp. 393–400, Aug. 1993.

[36] H. M. Vin and P. V. Rangan, "Designing a Multi-User HDTV Storage Server," *IEEE Journal on Selected Areas in Communication*, Vol. 11, No. 1, pp. 153–164, Jan. 1993.

[37] P. S. Yu, M.-S. Chen, and D. D. Kandlur, "Grouped Sweeping Scheduling for DASD-Based Multimedia Storage Management," *Multimedia Systems*, Berlin: Springer-Verlag, pp. 99–109, 1993.

[38] P. S. Yu and H. Shachnai, ''Return Based Viewer Scheduling to Support Video-on-Demand Applications,'' *IBM Research Report*, Yorktown Heights, NY, 1994.

[39] P. S. Yu, J. L. Wolf, and H. Shachnai, ''Look-Ahead Scheduling to Support Pause-Resume for Video-on-Demand Applications,'' *Proc. IS&T/SPIE Symposium on Electronic Imaging—Conference on Multimedia Computing and Networking, SPIE*, Vol. 2417, Feb. 1995.

PART

IV | **NETWORKING**

HIGH-SPEED LAN, MAN, AND ATM PROTOCOLS AS MULTIMEDIA CARRIERS

W. Melody Moh

Abstract

Multimedia applications integrate a variety of media, namely, audio, video, images, graphics, text, and data, each of which has different characteristics and quality-of-service (QoS) requirements. In this chapter, we study several existing (commercially available) and newly proposed LAN (local area networks), MAN (metropolitan area networks), and WAN (wide area networks), mainly ATM (asynchronous transfer mode) protocols, and evaluate their performance for multimedia communications. Specifically, for LAN protocols, we study 100Base-T Ethernets, Ethernet++ (the Priority Mode CSMA/CD Protocol), and 100VG-AnyLAN (the Demand Priority MAC Protocol), and compare their collision rates, delay, and throughput in supporting messages of different priorities. For MAN protocols, we first present the FDDI (Fiber Distributed Data Interface). Next, we study four reservation-based MAN protocols, including the IEEE 802.6 DQDB (Distributed Queue Dual Bus), the CRMA (Cyclic-Reservation Multiple-Access), the DQMA (Distributed-Queue Multiple-Access), and the FDQ (Fair Distributed Queue) protocols, and compare their performance under various delay and loss constraints.

For the ATM protocol, we first present several ABR (Available Bit-Rate) congestion control mechanisms and compare their performance in supporting messages of different burstiness. A new design, the MFRP (Modified Fast Resolution Protocol), is then proposed for ATM burst-level admission control. Its performance is evaluated against existing methods including the FRP (Fast Resolution Protocol), and the AFRP (Adaptive Fast Resolution Protocol). We believe that the simulation experiments and results presented in this chapter will provide important metrics of evaluating high-speed protocols for supporting multimedia traffic. They will also give insight for researchers to explore the essence of different high-speed protocols as multimedia carriers.

11.1 INTRODUCTION

''Multimedia'' is one of the buzzwords of the nineties and will continue to dominate into the next century. Multimedia systems integrate a variety of information sources, such as audio, voice, graphics, images, animation, and full-motion video, into a wide range of applications. They combine three major industries: computing, communication, and broadcasting.

Many applications, such as video mail, videoconferencing, interactive TV, and collaborative work systems, require networked multimedia. *Networked multimedia systems* can be viewed as a new generation of systems consisting of high-speed networks, including the Broadband Integrated Service Digital Networks (BISDN), conventional and high-performance networks, multimedia workstations, and personal computers [42]. They impose new requirements on network system components.

The complexity of multimedia applications stresses all the components of computer and communication systems. It requires great processing power to implement software codecs (coders-decoders) and multimedia file systems and databases. The computer architecture must provide high-bus bandwidth and efficient input/output processing. A multimedia operating system should support real-time scheduling and new data types. Storage and memory requirements include real-time access, very high capacity, and transfer rate. Finally, high-speed networks and protocols are necessary to provide fast data transfer guaranteed delivery and quality [42].

This chapter presents possible approaches and solutions for one of the requirements described earlier: high-speed networks as multimedia carriers. The following sections describe multimedia traffic characteristics and QoS (quality-of-service) requirements; conventional and new LAN technology, with a comparison of their performance for multimedia applications; MAN technology and their performance in supporting networked multimedia systems; and the new emerging technology specifically chosen for BISDN carrying multimedia: the ATM (asynchronous transfer mode) protocol.

11.2 MULTIMEDIA TRAFFIC CHARACTERISTICS, AND QUALITY-OF-SERVICE REQUIREMENTS

Traffic in a networked multimedia system can broadly be divided into two main categories: real-time and non-real-time. Real-time traffic, which includes voice and video, consists of continuous bit streams. It can be either constant bit rate (CBR) or variable bit-rate (VBR). It usually requires stringent time delay and delay jitter, but tolerates a small percentage of packet loss. Non-real-time traffic, which includes image, text, and computer data, is more "bursty." A bursty source can either be idle or active; when active, it generates variable-length messages at a very high rate. Non-real-time traffic can tolerate time delay but not packet loss [23]. To support multimedia applications, the underlying network must ensure that all (or at least most of) the messages meet their various QoS requirements.

Since different media and different applications have different requirements, multimedia services are usually parameterized. This allows for flexibility and customization of services, so that a new application could avoid implementing a whole new set of system services. The different requirements are termed quality of service (QoS) by the International Standards Organization (ISO) to specify how "good" networking services are—that is, to define parameterization.

11.2.1 QoS Specification

A networked multimedia system consists of three major abstraction layers: the application level (including all the application services), the system level (including the operating system and communication services), and the device level (including both network and multimedia devices) [42]. QoS specification should be considered in all three layers. Since this chapter focuses on networking support of multimedia systems, in the following we discuss only the QoS parameters most relevant to communication networks.

Table 11.1   Video QoS Parameter Examples

Medium	QoS Parameter	Range	Quality Characterization
Video		64 Kbps–2 Mbps	H.261 encoded videoconferencing
		1.2 Mbps	MPEG-1 VCR Quality
		2–4 Mbps	MPEG-2 broadcast quality TV
		3–6 Mbps	MPEG-2 compressed studio-quality TV
		140–166 Mbps	Uncompressed TV, PCM coding
		25–34 Mbps	HDTV lossy MPEG-2 compression
		around 500 Mbps	HDTV lossless compression
		≥ 1 Gbps	HDTV uncompressed quality
	Bit-error rate	$\leq 10^{-6}$	Long-term bit-error rate
	Packet loss rate	$\leq 10^{-2}$	Uncompressed video
		$\leq 10^{-11}$	Compressed video
	End-to-end delay	250 msec	Video telephony
		200 msec	JPEG video transmission
	Delay jitter	10 msec	Video telephony
		5 msec	JPEG video transmission
	Frame rate	30 frames/sec	NTSC format
	Frame width	≤ 720 pixels	Video signal MPEG coded
	Frame height	≤ 576 pixels	Vertical size
	Color resolution	8 bit/pixel	Grayscale resolution of 256 colors
	Compression ratio	2:1	Lossless compression of HDTV
		50:1	Lossy compression of HDTV
	Decoded buffer	$\leq 376, 832$ bits	MPEG related parameters

Tables 11.1–11.3 show some commonly used QoS parameters of video, audio, and data/image for different applications. They include some QoS parameters that are beyond the network level. For more detailed QoS specification, please refer to [18,19,42].

- *Delay*
  Delay (latency) includes the following terms: access delay, transit delay, transmission delay, propagation delay, latency, end-to-end delay, and round-trip delay. This network parameter is especially important for real-time synchronous applications. Round-trip delay is usually a metric of network latency especially for interactive applications. It is the time between the emission of the first bit of a data block until the block has been echoed by the destination and received by the original sender.

Table 11.2   Audio QoS Parameter Examples

Medium	QoS Parameter	Range	Quality Characterization
Audio	End-to-end delay	0–150 msec	Acceptable for most applications
		150–400 msec	May impact some applications
	Packet loss rate	$\leq 10^{-2}$	Telephone quality
	Bandwidth	16 Kbps	Telephone speech
		32 Kbps	Audio-conferencing speech
		64 Kbps	Near CD-quality audio
		128 Kbps	CD-quality audio
		192 Kbps	MPEG audio compressed
			Consumer CD audio
	Sample rate	8 kHz	Telephone voice quality
		44.1 kHz	CD audio
	Playback point	100–150 msec	
Audio/video	Sync skew	$+/-$ 80 msec	Lip synchronization
Audio/image	Sync skew	$+/-$ 5 msec	Music with notes

Table 11.3   Data and Image QoS Parameter Examples

Medium	QoS Parameter	Range	Quality Characterization
Data	Bandwidth	0.2 to 10 Mbps	File transfer
	End-to-end delay	1 sec	
	Packet loss	10^{-11}	
Image	File size	900 KB	Medium-size uncompressed
	Transmission time	9 sec	Over Ethernet
		2 min	Over ISDN
	File size	36 KB	Medium-size JPEG compressed
	Transmission time	0.3 sec	Over Ethernet
		5 sec	Over ISDN
	File size	4 MB	Large-size uncompressed
	Transmission time	40 sec	Over Ethernet
		10 min	Over ISDN
	File size	160 KB	Large-size JPEG compressed
	Transmission time	1.5 sec	Over Ethernet
		25 sec	Over ISDN

- *Delay jitter*

  Sometimes termed *delay variance*, delay jitter is the most critical characteristic of networks supporting time-dependent media streams. It is the variation (more specifically, the variance) of the end-to-end delay experienced in networks. It could be the difference between the actual delay and some target delay for the data flow, or the difference between the longest and the shortest delays observed over a period of time.

- *Loss/error rates*

  The error rates are measures of the network in terms of loss, alternation, duplications, and out-of-order delivery of data. It could be expressed as bit-error rate, packet-error rate (packet loss rate), or cell-error rate (cell loss rate). Text and compressed image and video usually require a more stringent error rate, whereas uncompressed image and video tolerate higher error rates.

- *Bandwidth*

  Sometimes also called *throughput, data rate*, or *transfer rate*, bandwidth is the bit rate at which two communicating end systems can exchange binary information, and which the network is capable of accepting and delivering. The units expressing bandwidth are bps (bits per second), Kbps, Mbps, and Gbps. Traffic could further be specified as *constant bit-rate* (CBR) or *variable bit-rate* (VBR) streams. (Please see Section 11.5 for more discussion on CBR and VBR traffic.)

- *Peak and average bit rates*

  The peak rate is the maximum number of bits contained in the stream over a short predefined period of time. The average bit rate is the number of bits contained in the stream averaged over a long period of time, generally the duration of a session. Other relevant parameters are the peak duration and the *burstiness ratio* (the ratio between the peak and average bit rates).

11.3 HIGH-SPEED LAN PROTOCOLS FOR MULTIMEDIA TRANSMISSION

A LAN (local area network) is characterized by (1) its span of at most a few kilometers and (2) a bandwidth of at least several Mbps [51]. The number of stations connected to a LAN is typically limited to 100. The basis of LAN communication is broadcasting using multi-access broadcast channels. Thus, the MAC (multiple-access control) sublayer is particularly important in these networks.

The two most popular conventional shared-medium MAC technologies are the Ethernet (IEEE 802.3) and the Token Ring (IEEE 802.5). Unfortunately, individual Ethernet segments or Token Rings connecting a hundred stations have insufficient bandwidth for real-time transmission of digital audio and video, except possibly the compressed telephony-quality sound. Thus, current low-speed shared-medium LANs, when used in their conventional mode, are not suitable for real-time multimedia applications, at least those applications involving audio and video [18,48].

11.3.1   Options to Improve LAN Performance

Many options have been considered to modify the current LAN technology so as to enhance its performance in order to better support multimedia applications. The following is a list of several major proposals.

1. Increase the bandwidth of Ethernet while keeping the same philosophy (100Base-T) [32].
2. Keep the frame format of Ethernet, increase the bandwidth, and change the multi-access protocol (100VG-AnyLAN) [1,43].
3. Keep the same MAC layer but add some extra feature to support high-priority real-time traffic (Ethernet ++) [15].
4. Connect Ethernet segments to a switch capable of switching Ethernet frames (100 Mbps Ethernet Switching).
5. Keep the Token Ring philosophy but introduce mechanisms that reserve some resources or better support isochronous traffic (Priority Token Ring) [10].
6. Replace Ethernet and Token Rings by FDDI, or further modify to support isochronism (FDDI-II) [2,39].
7. Use ATM technology for LANs (ATM LANs) [26,27].
8. Introduce ATM technology in parallel with the migration of existing LANs to a frame-switching structure (Hybrid LAN ATM cell switching and frame switching).

In the following subsections, we examine the first three options in greater detail and compare their performance in supporting heterogeneous multimedia traffic.

11.3.2   Enhanced Ethernet LAN Protocols

The idea of fast Ethernet is to make the most of the existing market of Ethernet (70% of LAN market throughout the world) and its simple principle, but to operate at a high data rate, that is, at 100 Mbps. In the following, we describe various competing technologies including the 100Base-T, the 100VG-AnyLAN, and the Ethernet++.

11.3.2.1   The 100Base-T Fast Ethernet

Fast Ethernet refers to a technology developed by a grouping of companies called the Fast Ethernet Alliance (which includes companies such as 3Com, Cabletron, David System, Digital Equipment Corporation, Grand Junction Networks, Intel, and SUN Microsystems Computer Corporation). Also known as 100Base-T, it offers throughput of up to 100 Mbps. It keeps the sharing mechanism used by the conventional Ethernet, the CSMA-CD (carrier-sensing multiple access with collision detection), but adapts the physical characteristics to operate 10 times faster [32]. Accepted by IEEE as a standard, it defines a media-independent interface (MII), which enables it to support various cabling types on the same Ethernet network.

Like the conventional 10 Mbps Ethernet, Fast Ethernet can be configured in switched or shared-media implementations. It requires new workstation adapter cards and new hubs or switches equipped with 100 Mbps transceivers. It can be used by existing Ethernet applications without requiring any change to the applications. Another major strength is that it can easily be added to shared-media and switched 10Base-T networks.

There are other variations of 10 Mbps or 100 Mbps Ethernets to improve their multimedia transmission capabilities: (1) Use of *hubs*: Connecting stations to hubs or intelligent hubs to form a star (as opposed to a bus) configuration. In this configuration each station has the full Ethernet bandwidth available. (2) *Dedicated Ethernet*: Dedicating a separate Ethernet LAN to transmit audio/video continuous data. Similar examples can be found in [8,16]. (3) *Switched Ethernet*: Connecting stations to switches that identify blocks of data and redirect them according to their destinations. This eliminates the collision problem in the original shared-medium algorithm.

11.3.2.2 100VG-AnyLAN: The Demand Priority MAC Protocol

The 100VG-AnyLAN technology has been proposed by another group of companies (including initially AT&T, Hewlett-Packard, Proteon, Kalpana, and Ungermann Bass). It has been standardized by IEEE and referenced as IEEE 802.12. Two main objectives have been established for this LAN technology. First, it should be able to use the unshielded twisted pair (UTP) wiring found in the popular 10Base-T and the shielded twisted pair (STP) used for Token Rings (IEEE 802.5). Second, the network should support new applications such as videoconferencing and remote training, while also providing backwards compatibility with the massive installed software base [53].

The 100VG-AnyLAN retains the frame format from the original Ethernet. Instead of CSMA/CD, it uses a deterministic protocol called *Demand Priority MAC* [1,53]. With the new protocol, each hub has a number of ports, and each port may be connected to a station; a station issues a request to its local hub when it has a frame to transmit. The hub checks for requests from its attached stations and indicates to one station that it may transmit a frame. Figure 11.1 shows the sequence of events that occur when a station sends a frame [53]:

1. Initially, the network is idle, so all stations send an IDLE signal to the hub, and the hub responds with IDLE.

2. When a station wishes to send some frame, it sends a REQUEST signal to the hub. The hub notes any requests and arbitrates between them on a round-robin basis. The hub then signals to the successful station that it may transmit. At this same time, the hub sends an INCOMING signal to all the other stations to notify them that there is an incoming frame.

3. The source station starts to transmit its frame to the hub. When the hub receives the destination address, it then forwards the frame only to the destination station and sends an IDLE signal to all the other stations. Note that the source station is still transmitting its frame.

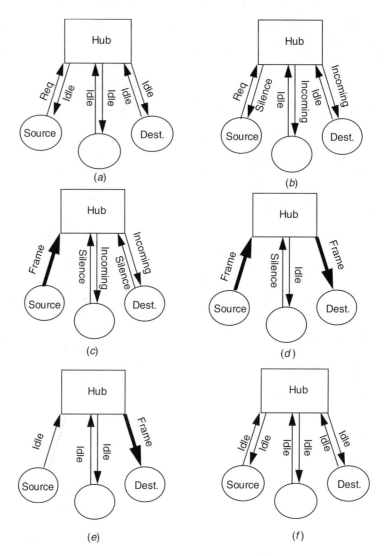

Figure 11.1   The demand priority MAC protocol.

4. When the source station finishes its transmission, it may send an IDLE signal or make another REQUEST if it has more frames to transmit.

5. When the hub finishes forwarding the frame to the destination, it can immediately select the next station.

The protocol is efficient as it avoids the collision problem in CSMA-CD, and yet there is no token propagation around the network as in Token Rings.

The demand priority protocol can be easily extended to support two priorities by providing two request signals: a normal-priority request (for conventional applications such as file transfers and remote print spooling) and a high-priority request (for delay-sensitive traffic such as voice and video). A hub will always serve a high-priority request before a normal-priority request. It serves each priority level in a round-robin order in which the available bandwidth will automatically be shared evenly among all stations currently active at the highest priority. A normal-priority request may be promoted to a high priority if it has waited longer than some fixed amount of time such as 250 msec. With two priority levels, the network can provide a service that guarantees bandwidth and bounds the access delay for high-priority real-time applications [20].

11.3.2.3 Ethernet++: the PM-CSMA/CD Protocol

An experimental priority MAC protocol for the support of real-time communications on Ethernet LANs has been specified, known as *Priority Mode CSMA/CD (PM-CSMA/CD)* [15]. The protocol employs a reserved cyclic access scheme with call admission control to provide a high-priority (HP) service class with real-time packet transport. The traditional CSMA/CD is used for standard-priority (SP) access, which supports non-real-time channel access. The dual protocol network has been named *Ethernet++*, referring to the addition of class-oriented media access mechanisms.

The PM-CSMA/CD protocol is based on Reservation CSMA/CD [13], with additional mechanisms for supporting a priority function. It is configured for HP interface access via N_{VC} virtual circuits; the admission is controlled via a virtual token on the basis of an assigned virtual circuit number. As a result, HP stations access the channel in a round-robin order. Since the protocol does not provide absolute preemptive channel access for HP stations, HP packet delay is dependent on SP traffic conditions. This nonpreemptive nature provides reasonable interpriority fairness and realizes zero protocol overhead for the priority function. In the next subsection, we study the performance (collision rate, delay, and link utilization) of HP and SP stations while supporting heterogeneous traffic.

11.3.3 Performance of Enhanced Ethernet Protocols

In this section, we present some simulation results comparing the performance (throughput, collision rate, and delay) of 100BaseT Ethernet, Ethernet++, and 100VG-AnyLAN while supporting both real-time and non-real-time traffic [35].

In the simulation, the traditional non-real-time (SP—standard-priority) traffic is represented by the Poisson process. The real-time (HP—high-priority) traffic is modeled close to a VBR (variable bit-rate) traffic, in which a VBR source is characterized by alternating idle and busy periods [43]. Busy periods are fixed-length (16 msec) intervals with isochronous arrivals of fixed-length packets: one packet after 31 slots on the bus. These busy periods are separated by idle periods, which are assumed to have exponentially distributed lengths, with a 16-msec average.

For each protocol studied, the high-priority load per station imposed on the MAC layer is 0 to 10 Mbps, with frame size (bytes) as indicated in Table 11.4.

Table 11.4   VBR Traffic Load per HP Station

Avg. VBR traffic load (Mbps)	0	2	4	6	8	10
Frame size (byte)	—	512	1024	1536	2048	2560

11.3.3.1 100 Mbps Ethernet versus Ethernet++

The simulation model is based on a 100 Mbps broadcast bus connecting 28 stations. The stations are subdivided into two priority groups: SP (standard-priority) and HP (high-priority) stations. The network and protocol parameters are listed in Table 11.5.

In the first set of simulations, the HP traffic load is kept at 48%, that is, 48 Mbps, while varying SP traffic load. Both SP and HP packet sizes are taken to be 2 KB. Figures 11.2 through 11.4 show the collision rate, SP mean delay, and HP mean delay, respectively, of Ethernet and Ethernet++. From Fig. 11.2, we can clearly see that Ethernet++ is able to reduce the collision rate since all the HP stations are scheduled to transmit using the virtual token. As a result, the HP stations experience near-constant delay despite the increasing SP load (Fig. 11.3). This is crucial since the most important objective of a multimedia network protocol is to ensure that real-time messages experience bounded delay. The cost is a slight increase in SP delay compared with that of the Ethernet (Fig. 11.4).

In the second set of simulations, the SP traffic load is kept constant at 52%, that is, 52 Mbps, while varying HP traffic load. Figures 11.5 through 11.7 show the collision rate, HP mean delay, and SP mean delay, respectively. Note that this set of results is similar to the previous set except that HP delay does increase slightly with increasing HP load; still the delay is bounded by 0.2 msec.

Table 11.5   Ethernet and Ethernet++ Simulation Parameters

Channel transmission rate	100 Mbps
Bus length	100 meters
Interstation spacing	Uniformly distributed
Frame payload	1500 bytes
Standard priority message size	2000 bytes
Minimum interpacket period	96 bits
Jam signal length	32 bits
Backoff slot length	512 bits
Reservation slot length	200 bits
Number of SP stations	22
Number of HP stations	6
SP traffic model	Poisson
HP traffic model	VBR

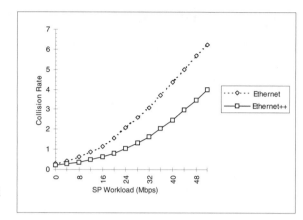

Figure 11.2   Collision rate (HP workload is 48 Mbps).

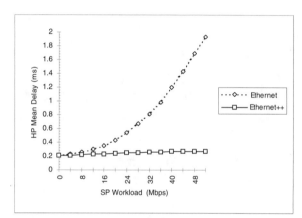

Figure 11.3   HP mean delay (HP workload is 48 Mbps).

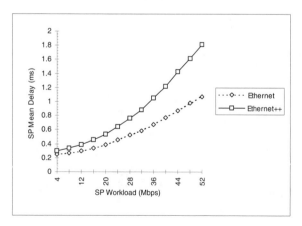

Figure 11.4   SP mean delay (HP workload is 48 Mbps).

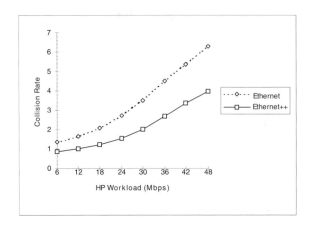

Figure 11.5   Collision rate (SP workload is 52 Mbps).

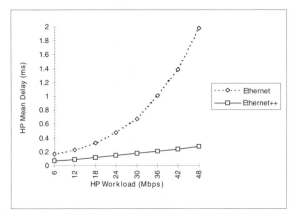

Figure 11.6   HP mean delay (SP workload is 52 Mbps).

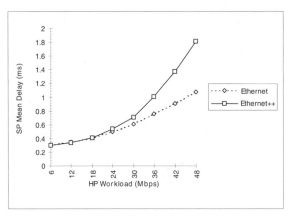

Figure 11.7   SP mean delay (SP workload is 52 Mbps).

Table 11.6   100VG-AnyLAN
Simulation Parameters

Channel transmission rate	100 Mbps
Hub-station distance	100 meters
Hub-hub distance	200 meters
Frame payload	1500 bytes
Standard priority message size	2000 bytes
Number of SP stations	22
Number of HP stations	6
Number of Hubs	3
SP traffic model	Poisson
HP traffic model	VBR
TTRT for HP stations	10 msec

11.3.3.2 100VG-AnyLAN

Two sets of experiments similar to those described above are carried out on 100VG-AnyLAN using demand priority MAC. Simulation parameters are listed in Table 11.6.

The mean delay of both SP and HP stations is measured while (1) HP traffic load remains the same (Fig. 11.8), and (2) SP traffic load remains the same (Fig. 11.9). We can see from Fig. 11.8 that HP delay does not increase with increasing SP load. On the other hand, SP delay sharply increases with increasing HP load (Fig. 11.9; note the logarithmic scale). Further simulation has indicated that HP mean delay does not experience such a

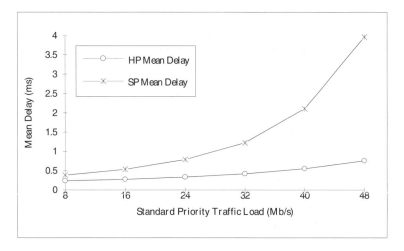

Figure 11.8   Mean delay versus standard-priority traffic load (high-priority traffic load = 48 Mb/s).

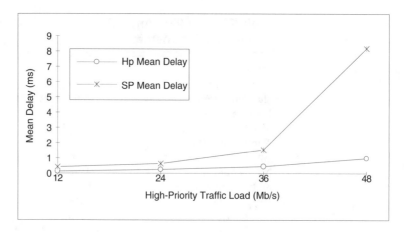

Figure 11.9   Mean delay versus high-priority traffic load (high-priority traffic load = 52 Mb/s).

sharp increase when SP traffic load is less than 50%. The long delay experienced by SP messages is due mainly to queueing delay [35]. This seems to be a major disadvantage of the demand priority MAC protocol, which implements absolute priority in which SP traffic might suffer very long delay. Note that the nonpreemptive nature of Ethernet++ provides a better interpriority fairness (Figs. 11.4 and 11.7).

11.4 HIGH-SPEED MAN PROTOCOLS FOR MULTIMEDIA TRANSMISSION

The current situation of the international communication environment is characterized by a diversity of technologically dissimilar and administratively autonomous subnetworks. On one hand, the Broadband Integrated Service Digital Networks (BISDN) are designated as a future communication network model to provide multimedia services. On the other hand, it is still realistic to expect that the heterogeneous network environment will persist because of diversity of needs and applications served, diversity of evolution in transmission technologies, multiplicity of administrative authorities, and various historical reasons [52].

A MAN (metropolitan area network) usually covers a range of 10–100 km. It uses a shared medium with distributed switching and Media Access Control (MAC). It has generally higher data rates than LAN (i.e., no less than 100 Mbps). The number of stations connected in a MAN is mostly in the thousands. The major services of a MAN include traditional functions such as interconnection of different LANs and host-to-host computer internetworking, and new services such as voice and video communication.

During the last decade, many high-speed MAN protocols have been proposed by IEEE, ANSI, and other research entities. These protocols include the Distributed Queue Dual Bus (DQDB) (IEEE802.6) standard proposed by IEEE [25] and its close relatives (to be discussed later), the Fiber Distributed Data Interface (FDDI) proposed by ANSI [3], and the Switched Multi-Megabit Data Service (SMDS) of Bellcore [21]. They are intended as backbone networks or metropolitan area networks (MANs) connecting diverse LANs to ATM WANs for BISDN.

In the following subsections, we first describe FDDI and FDDI-II, and then discuss DQDB and its three siblings, comparing their performance in supporting multimedia traffic.

11.4.1 Token-Based MAN Protocols: FDDI and FDDI-II

The FDDI (Fiber Distributed Data Interface) was originally proposed by ANSI (American Standard Institute) in 1982 as a high-speed LAN but achieved a span of up to 100 km. It is a high-performance fiber-optic network configured as a ring. It runs at 100 Mbps over distances up to 100 km and connects up to 500 stations.

FDDI supports different transmission modes that are important for communication of multimedia data. The *synchronous mode* allows a bandwidth reservation; the *asynchronous mode* behaves similar to the Token Ring protocol. It is further subdivided into *restricted mode* and *nonrestricted mode*, which includes Priority levels 0–7.

The FDDI-specific access protocol is the *Timed Token Rotation Protocol*, which supports two types of services: synchronous and asynchronous. Each station may be allocated a portion of the network bandwidth for its synchronous traffic. Upon receiving a token, a station can transmit messages in the synchronous mode for at least its preallocated time before releasing the token. Messages in the asynchronous mode are transmitted only if certain time constraints are met. This guarantees that the deadlines of all synchronous messages are met.

For audio and video transmission, the FDDI synchronous mode is quite adequate; yet the major critic is that the time spent on bandwidth reservation and token rotation is nonnegligible. As a result, its maximum channel utilization drops with increasing transmission speeds and network sizes [38]. This, along with other arguments, including the need for circuit-switching service, led to the introduction of an additional *isochronous mode* in *FDDI-II*.

FDDI-II integrates circuit-switched service (isochronous services) for delay-sensitive applications, such as voice and video, and packet services (synchronous and asynchronous services), as available in basic FDDI on the same physical medium. The resulting network is very good for the transmission of continuous data because of the isochronous service. The commercial relevance of FDDI-II as opposed to the original FDDI is still doubtful owing to the incompatibility of the two systems.

Much research has been done on the support of FDDI and FDDI-II for multimedia communication; for example, see [49]. Details of FDDI and FDDI-II are described in the standard document [3], as well as, for example, in [2,39].

11.4.2 Reservation-Based MAN Protocols: DQDB, CRMA, DQMA, and FDQ

Recently, high-speed protocols based on reservation schemes have attracted much attention, especially in Europe. Unlike FDDI, whose maximum utilization of the channel drops with increasing transmission speeds and network sizes, which makes it unsuitable

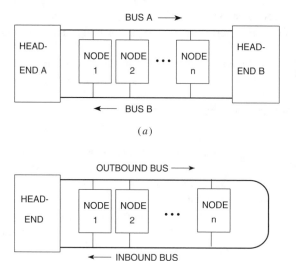

Figure 11.10 (*a*) Dual-bus configuration; (*b*) folded-bus configuration.

for very high-speed networks [38], reservation-based protocols do not waste capacity if there is a demand for it, and achieve high bandwidth efficiency independent of distance, transmission rate, and number of nodes. All of these protocols, taking advantage of advances in fiber-optic technology, can therefore operate at a transmission rate over 100 Mbps and may even go beyond 1 Gbps.

Figure 11.10 shows both the dual-bus and the folded-bus configurations used in the protocols. For simplicity, later in the performance study, we choose the folded-bus (single-bus) configuration for the simulation, since most of the protocols are described and evaluated in this configuration in their original proposals [29,38,41].

In the following, we describe four reservation-based MAN protocols: the DQDB (Distributed Queue Dual Bus) proposed by the group of IEEE 802.6 [25] and its three improved versions: the Cyclic-Reservation Multiple-Access (CRMA) and the Distributed-Queue Multiple-Access (DQMA) protocols proposed by IBM [38,41]; and the Fair Distributed Queue (FDQ) proposed by Kabatepe and Vastola [29].

Their access and request mechanisms are summarized in Table 11.7. The last row of the table indicates a few access refinement implemented in our simulation. For detailed descriptions of these four protocols, please refer to the original documents or proposals [25,29,38,41].

11.4.2.1 DQDB (Distributed Queue Dual Bus)

The DQDB medium-access protocol has been adopted as a MAN standard by the working group of IEEE 802.6 [25]. It is a high-speed integrated service protocol designed to accommodate traffic generated by a variety of information sources, as well as provided for the interconnection of LANs. An enormous amount of variations in design and performance

Table 11.7 Summary of Access/Request Mechanisms of All Four Protocols

Protocol	DQDB	CRMA	DQMA	FDQ
Transmission bus	Outbound	Outbound	Outbound	Outbound
Request bus	Inbound	Outbound	Inbound	Inbound
Transmission mechanism	Busy/free bit	Start (cycle-no.)	Busy/free bit	Busy/free bit
Request mechanism	R bit RC & CD counters	Reserve (cycle-no., cycle-length)	Request subfiled	A bit, I bit AD & CD counters
Request size	1 slot	Maximum of 255 slots per cycle	Maximum of 255 slots	1 slot
Request size used in this chapter	1 slot	Maximum of 150 slots per cycle	Maximum of 150 slots	1 slot
Slot size	53 bytes	71 bytes	71 bytes	unspecified
Slot size used in this chapter	53 bytes	53 bytes	53 bytes	53 bytes
Payload size per slot	44 bytes	44 bytes	44 bytes	44 bytes
Slot contiguity	No	Yes	Yes	No
Access refinement	No	Reservation-cancellation backpressure	Request-delay equalization	No

issues have been investigated [33,46]. In this subsection, we focus on the basic protocol proposed by IEEE [25].

The DQDB network consists of two high-speed unidirectional buses carrying information in opposite directions. Each network user is capable of transmitting and receiving information on both buses. Information segments (packets or cells) are transported in fixed-size slots that are continuously generated by the head of each bus. Since the media access protocol is identical for both network buses, only packet transmissions along bus A are described; access to bus B is identical.

DQDB uses two access control bits per slot, referred to as busy bit (B) and request bit (R). To request a free slot on bus A, the R bit of a slot on bus B is set from 0 to 1. Each station has two counters, which emulate a FIFO (First-In First-Out) request queue. Each time a node sees a passing R = 1 on bus B, it enqueues a request in its FIFO request queue. A node wishing to transmit will enqueue a *self-request* but only after the previously issued *self-request* has been serviced. The top entry of the request queue is removed each time a free slot passes that node on bus A. If the first entry is a *self-request*, the slot is set busy and the corresponding data segment is transmitted. Alternatively, if the top entry is a *request* (of other stations), the free slot is passed downstream for use by another node.

The enqueueing of a *self-request* is accompanied by a request submission on bus B, if the FIFO request queue is nonempty. This is accomplished by setting the R bit of a bus B slot from 0 to 1. Since a slot with R = 0 may not be available immediately, a counter is needed to keep track of outstanding request settings on bus B. Note also that each *self-request* is only for one slot, and a node may not enqueue a new *self-request* until the previous *self-request* is served. These limitations can result in severe throughput unfairness [54].

11.4.2.2 CRMA (Cyclic-Reservation Multiple-Access)

The most important mechanisms of CRMA are *cyclic reservation access* and *reservation-cancellation "backpressure"* which achieve high performance even at high speed and long distances. Design of the protocol is motivated by the throughput unfairness demonstrated in DQDB at high speeds or long distances and under the requirement of high-bandwidth utilization [38,41].

In CRMA, nodes access the bus according to cycles of slots. The nodes reserve slots at the beginning of each cycle, and the head-end station generates the cycle large enough to satisfy these reservations. The basic CRMA access mechanism, namely, the *cycle-reservation access* mechanism, is described as follows. Two access commands are used: *reserve (cycle number, cycle length)* and *start (cycle number)*. The head-end station periodically issues *reserve* commands, with the *cycle length* set to zero initially. As the *reserve* command passes a node on the outbound bus, the node can reserve slots in that cycle by augmenting *cycle length*. The node then stores this number as *reserve length*, associated with the *cycle number*, in a local reservation queue. When the *reserve* returns to the head end, a reservation containing the *cycle number* and *cycle length* is entered into a global reservation queue. This queue is served according to a FIFO discipline. The head-end station then issues *start (cycle number)*, followed by as many empty slots as requested in *reserve length*. When a station observes a *start* command on the outbound bus, it checks its local reservation queue. If there is an entry with a *cycle number* matching that of the *start* command, the node waits for the next empty slot. It then transmits segments in as many slots as its own *reserve length* associated with this *cycle number*.

The above *cycle-reservation access* mechanism is complemented by the *reservation-cancellation backpressure* mechanism to minimize the global reservation queue length in the head-end station and to achieve delay fairness. This mechanism monitors the total number of slots in the cycles queued at the head-end station, including the slots in the outgoing cycle which have not yet left the head end. The *reserve* command is inhibited when the return of this command increases this number beyond a certain threshold. In addition, all *reserve* commands that have been issued, but have not yet returned, are canceled. The generation of *reserve* commands is resumed when the number of reserved slots drops below the threshold.

11.4.2.3 DQMA (Distributed-Queue Multiple-Access)

DQMA [38] is an access protocol *generalizing* the DQDB distributed-queue approach to achieve throughput fairness. It is very similar to DQDB, with the major modification that each network node can reserve up to 255 *consecutive* slots for a single message. Each slot consists of a 2-byte access control field (ACF) which is formed by a *busy* bit, a 2-bit

Equalize, a 2-bit *Priority*, and an 8-bit *Request* subfield. Each node can thus request up to 255 empty slots in a single operation using the *Request* subfield. The *Equalize* subfield is used for the delay-equalization of the configuration, which will be described later.

The basic access mechanism is the *generalized-distributed-queue access*, described as follows. Each node contains a FIFO request queue. When a node has some message to transmit, it sets the *Request* subfield of an inbound bus slot from zero to the number of segments (slots) required to transmit the message. It also enqueues the number as a *local request* into its request queue. When a node observes a nonzero *request* on the inbound bus, it copies that into its request queue as an *external request*. When the head of its request queue is a *local request*, it transmits a segment in the next empty (nonbusy) slot on the outbound bus and decrements the *local-request* value. Once this value reaches zero, the *local request* is discarded. If, on the other hand, the head of queue is an *external request*, it decrements the value of *external request* for each empty slot on the outbound bus. The *external request* is discarded when the value reaches zero.

The above *generalized-distributed-queue access* mechanism does not guarantee that a node will transmit its packets in consecutive slots; an additional mechanism, called *request-delay equalization*, provides this slot contiguity. It is achieved by providing a delay element in front of each request queue. Both *external requests* and *local requests* pass through this delay element before they are inserted in the request queue. Generally, at each node, the delay is selected so that the propagation delay from the node's outbound bus access point to the entry point of its request queue is equal to b slot transmit time, where b is an integer selected, which is as small as possible, but no less than the round-trip bus latency normalized to the slot transmission time. In this implementation, the delay in the underlying bus structure is equalized so that the nodes attain a consistent view of the state of network.

11.4.2.4 FDQ (Fair Distributed Queue)

FDQ has been proposed by Kabatepe and Vastola [29]. It was motivated by two important results of DQDB: (1) The available capacity of a DQDB network under heavy load is *divided evenly among the active nodes* if and only if the steady-state average value loaded to the CD counter following each transmission is equal to the number of active downstream nodes and (2) the reservation mechanism in DQDB communicates to each station the number of active downstream nodes under the ideal conditions of zero propagation delay and an infinite bandwidth reservation channel [29]. The resulting protocol is extremely fair with respect to delay experienced by individual network nodes, even for networks of long-distance or high-transmission rate.

FDQ is a slotted system based on the unidirectional bus topology. A slot header contains a busy bit, an active (A) bit, and an inactive (I) bit, which are all initialized to zero. Nodes write into the slots in the outbound channel and may receive slots in both the inbound and outbound channels. When a node wants to transmit on a slot, it sets the busy bit to one. A and I bits can only be set in the inbound channel.

Each node has two counters, AD (Active Downstream nodes) and CD (Count Down). The AD counter, at any point in time, keeps a running count of the number of active downstream nodes. It is incremented by one for each A bit detected in the inbound channel, and decremented by one for each I bit observed by the node. When a node becomes active, it sets the first free A bit detected to one. It also loads the content of its AD counter to the CD counter. The CD counter is decremented by one for each free slot passing by the node in the outbound channel, and when it reaches zero, the node's segment is transmitted in the first free slot observed. As long as the node continues to have segments to transmit, it takes no action on the A and I bits of passing slots except reading them. When it finishes transmitting its segments and becomes idle, it sets the first free I bit observed in the inbound channel to one.

11.4.3 Throughput Performance

To study how well various network protocols support multimedia communication, it is important to integrate synchronous and asynchronous traffic into the same network, and measure the performance under various traffic settings, such as workload characteristics and traffic burstiness. In this subsection, we present some of our earlier study on the performance of the four reservation-based MAN protocols simultaneously supporting synchronous traffic (for various real-time multimedia applications) and asynchronous background traffic (for interactive terminal activities and computer data transfers) [36]. In particular, multimedia throughput is measured while changing the burstiness of asynchronous data traffic.

A single folded-bus network is assumed to be of (end-to-end) length 10 km with 20 network nodes evenly distributed. Slot size is chosen to be 53 bytes, compatible with the standard ATM cell size, which includes 9 bytes of header (for the ATM and the AAL layers) and 44 bytes of data. Since messages are generally much larger than a slot, they are divided into segments (each fits into a slot).

A constant bit rate (CBR) of 1.5 Mbps (similar bandwidth of an MPEG-1 video source) is used for synchronous (real-time multimedia) traffic. On the asynchronous traffic, we assume that data sources generate fixed-size messages following Poisson arrivals, and we consider three message sizes: 1, 10 and 100 KB.

11.4.3.1 Bursty Data Without Extended Delay

Figures 11.11 through 11.14 show S_{max}, the maximum number of streams (at 1.536 Mbps—workload for high-quality video conference) that can be supported when varying aperiodic data traffic with loads ranging from 10 Mbps to 50 Mbps, and data sizes of 1, 10, and 100 KB. Both DQDB and CRMA significantly reduce their throughput when more bursty data traffic (100 KB data size) is added. This effect is less significant in DQMA where adding 10 KB or 100 KB messages gives very similar results. FDQ here shows a performance superior to all the other protocols: burstiness of asynchronous traffic does not have any negative effect on its support of real-time traffic. As its name implies, the protocol is very fair: it gives equal bandwidth to each of the active heavily loaded nodes independent of traffic burstiness.

11.4.3.2 Bursty Data with Extended Delay

Figures 11.15 through 11.18 show the multimedia throughput (S_{max}) for various data sizes by changing delay constraint, D_{max} (deadline). All except the FDQ protocol (in which

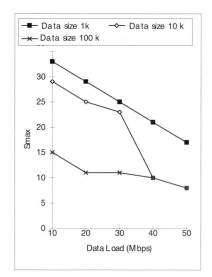

Figure 11.11 $S_{\max}$ versus data load, varying data size, for DQDB. Stream Rate $= 1.536$ Mbps, TxRate $= 100$ Mbps, $D_{\max} = 20$ms.

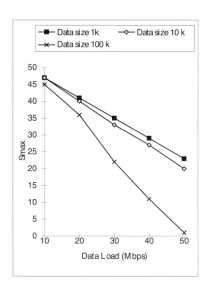

Figure 11.12 $S_{\max}$ versus data load, varying data size, for CRMA. Stream Rate $= 1.536$ Mbps, TxRate $= 100$ Mbps, $D_{\max} = 20$ms.

bursty data has almost zero effect on its synchronous traffic support) show some improvement in multimedia throughput when $D_{\max}$ is increased, from 25 msec to 250 msec.

Since interactive multimedia application (such as videoconferencing) can tolerate 100 to 200 msec or even longer delay owing to the ability of human eyes to tolerate some loss [14], our result here shows that all the reservation-based protocols, including DQDB (Fig. 11.15), are effective in integrating bursty data and multimedia streams, when delay constraint is properly relaxed.

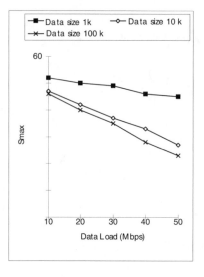

Figure 11.13 S_{max} versus data load, varying data size, for DQMA. Stream Rate = 1.536 Mbps, TxRate = 100 Mbps, D_{max} = 20ms.

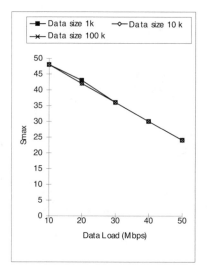

Figure 11.14 S_{max} versus data load, varying data size, for FDQ. Stream Rate = 1.536 Mbp s, TxRate = 100 Mbps, D_{max} = 20ms.

11.4.4 Delay Performance

To investigate the support of multimedia traffic on high-speed MAN protocols, in an earlier paper we examined two significant metrics: delay fairness and worst-case delay performance [34]. In this section, we present the results on delay fairness in supporting synchronous multimedia traffic—specifically, the access delay and message delay experienced by each network node when synchronous multimedia workload representing interactive education [17,49] (see Table 11.8) is offered to networks.

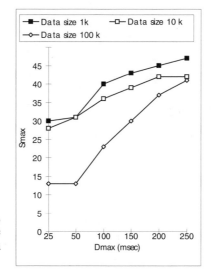

Figure 11.15 S_{max} versus data load, varying data size, for DQDB. Stream Rate = 1.536 Mbps, TxRate = 100 Mbps, Data Load = 16 Mbps.

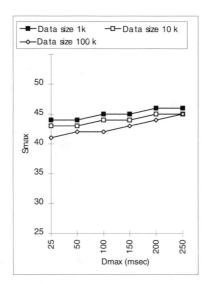

Figure 11.16 S_{max} versus Data Load, varying data size, for CRMA. Stream Rate = 1.536 Mbps, TxRate = 100 Mbps, Data Load = 16 Mbps.

Access delay is defined as the time between when a message arrives at the head of queue until its transmission begins. *Message delay* measures the time between the arrival of a message until its complete transmission. The results are shown in Figs. 11.19 and 11.20.

DQDB has performed much worse than all the other protocols. The upstream nodes experience significantly longer delay than downstream ones. This is the case since we are simulating a single-bus (folded-bus) configuration, and upstream nodes often yield to downstream ones. The CRMA protocol is shown to be a very fair protocol in dealing

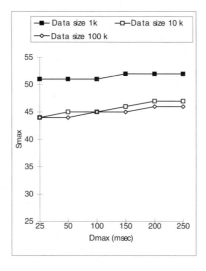

Figure 11.17 S_{max} versus Data Load, varying data size, for DQMA. Stream Rate = 1.536 Mbps, TxRate = 100 Mbps, Data Load = 16 Mbps.

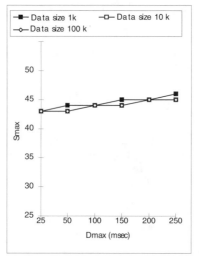

Figure 11.18 S_{max} versus Data Load, varying data size, for FDQ. Stream Rate = 1.536 Mbps, TxRate = 100 Mbps, Data Load = 16 Mbps.

Table 11.8 Workload Set for Interactive Education

Multimedia Application	Msg Length	Period	Deadline	Load
Workload	(bits)	(msec)	(msec)	(Mbps)
Audio (CD stereo)	47070	33.33	33.33	1.346
Graphics (512 × 512 × 4)	69905	33.33	33.33	2.000
Image (1024 × 1024 × 8)	69905	33.33	33.33	2.000
Text (80 × 25 × 8)	1067	33.33	33.33	0.031
Video (MPEG-like)	51200	33.33	33.33	1.500
Total				6.877

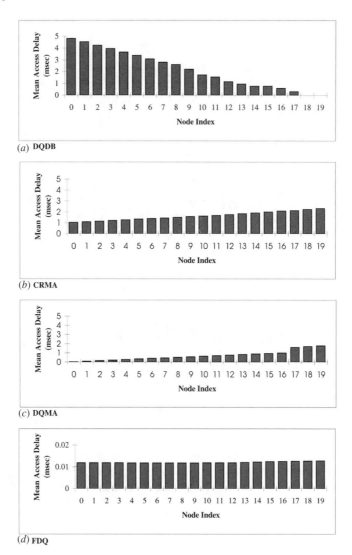

Figure 11.19　Mean access delay, multimedia traffic.

with uniform synchronous traffic, especially in terms of message delay. Because of its special request scheme, the DQMA protocol has shown very interesting results. Access delay in upstream nodes is less, due mainly to the fact that they can access free slots (generated by the head station) more quickly than downstream nodes, which have to wait for free slots to propagate from upstream. Message delay, on the other hand, is significantly larger when experienced by the upstream nodes since reservations are made in the inbound channel; downstream nodes thus have better chances of making a reservation (of up to 150

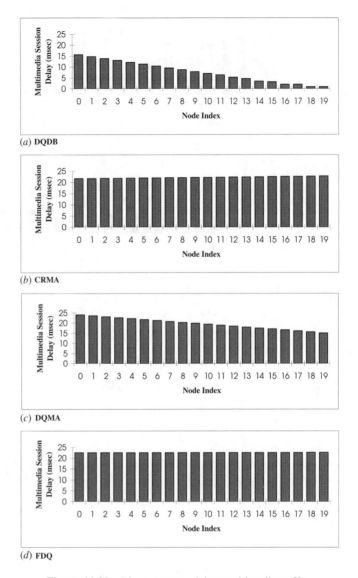

Figure 11.20   Mean message delay, multimedia traffic.

consecutive slots). FDQ proves itself to be an extremely fair protocol, in terms of both access and message delays.

   Comparing the result of throughput and delay fairness, one can clearly see a close connection between a protocol's fairness and its support of synchronous multimedia traffic among heterogeneous traffic. The ''fairer'' a protocol is under heavy bursty traffic, the better it is to support synchronous multimedia traffic in the midst of asynchronous bursty traffic.

11.5 THE ATM PROTOCOL

In the evolution from the current telecommunication networks toward the integrated broad-band communication network (also called the full-service network), some important directions and guidelines have recently been made. The new network is often referred to as the Broadband Integrated Service Digital Network (BISDN) since it is considered a logical extension of the ISDN. The most important factor for BISDN is the merging of a large number of teleservices with different (sometimes unknown) requirements. The most popular teleservices to appear in the future are video-on-demand, videoconferencing, high-speed data transfer, videophone, video library, home education/shopping/working, and HDTV (High-Definition TV).

The need for a flexible network and the progress in both technology and system concepts led to the definition of the ATM (asynchronous transfer mode) principle. It has been accepted as the ultimate solution for the BISDN by ITU-T (International Telecommunications and Telegraphy), formerly known as CCITT (International Consultative Committee for Telecommunications and Telegraphy). It has also been accepted as the technology to interconnect computers over LANs (ATM LANs) at the ATM Forum by the computer industry.

The ATM Forum was formed in October 1991 by a group of vendors, telecom operators, and users, with the goal of accelerating development and deployment of ATM products and services in the private environment. It concentrates on specifying customer premise equipment and private switching. Since then, the ATM Forum has continued to release ATM specifications [4,5,6]. There have also been numerous books and articles on ATM; examples include [40,45].

In this section, we first present ATM QoS and service classes for traffic management. Next, we describe several major ATM traffic control schemes, followed by a detailed description of control mechanisms and performance of several ABR (Available Bit-Rate) rate-based congestion controls. Finally, several burst-level admission controls schemes, including the FRP (Fast Reservation Protocol), the AFRP (Adaptive FRP), and our newly proposed MFRP (Modified FRP) and their relative performance, are presented.

11.5.1 ATM QoS and Service Classes

The ATM Forum has defined five numbered QoS classes and example applications, as summarized in Table 11.9 [4].

To relate traffic characteristics and QoS requirements to network behavior, the ATM Forum traffic management specification has further categorized and defined the following five traffic and service classes [6]:

1. *Constant Bit-Rate (CBR) Service*
   This class is used for emulating circuit switching. The cell rate is constant. It is for real-time applications with tightly constrained delay. Examples include video and voice applications.

2. *Real-Time Variable Bit-Rate (rt-VBR) Service*
   This class allows users to transmit at a variable rate. This includes real-time applications such as voice and video, with tight constraints on delay, but the transmis-

Table 11.9   ATM Forum QoS Classes

QoS Class	QoS Parameters	Application
0	Unspecified	"Best Effort," "At Risk"
1	Specified	Circuit Emulation, CBR
2	Specified	VBR Video/Audio
3	Specified	Connection-oriented data
4	Specified	Connectionless data

sions from sources are expected to be bursty. Examples include interactive compressed video.

3. *Non-Real-Time Variable Bit-Rate (nrt-VBR) Service*
   This class is for non-real-time applications that are also bursty but expect very low cell loss and a bound on cell transfer delay for all cells. Examples include multimedia e-mail.

4. *Available Bit-Rate (ABR) Service*
   This class is designed for normal data traffic such as file transfer and e-mail. Although the standard does not require the cell transfer delay and cell loss ratio to be guaranteed or minimized, it is still desirable for switches to minimize delay and loss. This is done by integrating several types of feedback from the network to control source transmission rate, in response to changes in the network traffic (see the next two subsections for details).

5. *Unspecified Bit-Rate (UBR) Service*
   These are non-real-time applications that do not require tight delay or loss constraints. These include file transfer, e-mail, and credit card verification. No traffic-related service guarantee is specified.

Only ABR traffic responds to congestion feedback from the network. The rest of this section is devoted to this class of traffic.

11.5.2   ATM Traffic Control

Traffic control and congestion control are two important functions of traffic management. Traffic control functions are carried out during normal network operations, that is, when there is no congestion. In an ATM network, traffic control includes connection admission control and usage parameter control (traffic policing). When congestion occurs, some congestion control function should be performed. In the following, we present a more detailed description of these controls.

11.5.2.1 Admission Control

This is the set of actions taken by the network in order to determine whether a connection can be granted or rejected. A connection request is granted only when sufficient resources are available to service the connection at each successive network element, based on its service category and QoS terms, while maintaining QoS demands of existing connections.

11.5.2.2 Usage Parameter Control

This is the set of actions that are performed by the network to monitor and control traffic. The UNI (User-Network Interface) detects violations of negotiated parameters and performs suitable actions to control them, whether or not these violations are intentional.

11.5.2.3 Congestion Control (Flow Control)

Flow control (also called Reactive Traffic Management) seeks to recognize congestion within the network as it develops, and attempts to limit the flow of new traffic into network accordingly.

Congestion occurs at a particular node of the network when too many cells are intended to pass through that node. Congestion in the network causes the quality of service to deteriorate from assured levels. The traffic condition at any ATM switch that is suffering congestion can be controlled by informing the sources (that are generating traffic intended to pass through that ATM switch) to reduce or stop generating cells until informed otherwise. In this way, flow control helps clear the congestion. The effectiveness of flow control depends on network bandwidth and the delay in informing the traffic sources.

In the following subsections, we describe (1) congestion controls for ABR traffic and (2) burst-level admission control for guaranteed-burst ABR traffic. The performance of several related control mechanisms is presented and compared.

11.5.3 Rate-Based ABR Congestion Control Schemes

The ATM Forum has adopted *rate-based control* for ABR traffic and defined referenced source and destination behaviors. ABR flow control occurs between two end-systems [6]. It involves a closed-loop control implemented by RM (Resource Management) cells which originate at the source end-system, reach the destination end-system, and are turned back to the source end-system. The RM cells are generated by the source either every N_{rm} (number of cells between two RM cells) cell or every T_{rm} (time between two RM cells) time unit. They carry information about network conditions to the source end-system after being turned around by the destination end-system.

The network feedback information is written into the RM cells by network elements. The network elements may do one of three things: (1) directly insert information into the RM cells when they pass, (2) indirectly indicate congestion conditions to the source end-system by setting EFCI (Explicit Forward Congestion Indication) bits in data cells, in which case the destination end-system inserts information into RM cells before turning them around, or (3) generate backward RM cells themselves.

The sources have to declare the maximum required bandwidth and the minimum bandwidth necessary for the connection at the time of connection establishment. These connection parameters are called the Peak Cell Rate (PCR) and the Minimum Cell Rate (MCR). The actual rate at which the source can generate traffic is the Allowed Cell Rate (ACR).

The ABR traffic control maintains an ACR for each source, which will be equal to the guaranteed MCR or higher, but never higher than PCR, throughout the lifetime of the connection. It provides rapid access to unused network bandwidth at up to PCR, whenever the network bandwidth is available [6]. Low cell loss is expected to result from ABR traffic control if the source and destination end-systems follow referenced behaviors.

The switch algorithm is not defined by the ATM Forum and hence many algorithms are possible. Using a standardized format for the RM cell and control algorithms, different switch architectures will be able to coexist. ATM switches can control the rate of the sources by one of several ways: relative rate marking, EFCI marking, or ER marking.

11.5.3.1 Relative Rate Marking

The source sends RM cells, with their CI bits reset, either a certain number of cells (N_{rm}) apart or a certain amount of time (T_{rm}) apart. The destination turns around the RM cells it receives from the source and sends them back to the source, using the same path. The switches on the path of the connection set the CI bit in these backward RM cells when there is congestion in the forward direction. When the source receives a backward RM cell with its CI bit set, it reduces its ACR by a factor of RDF (Rate Decrease Factor). The resulting ACR, if lower than the MCR, is replaced by MCR. If the source receives backward RM cells with reset CI bits, it increases its ACR by a factor of RIF (Rate Increase Factor) of its PCR [6].

11.5.3.2 Explicit Forward Congestion Indication (EFCI) Marking

The source sends its data cells with the EFCI bit reset at the rate of ACR. It also sends RM cells at some regular interval. When a switch in the path of the connection detects congestion, it sets the EFCI bit in the data cells. The destination, on receiving data cells with their EFCI bits set, will set the CI bit in the very next forward RM cell that it receives. It then turns the RM cell around. The source will react to RM cells with their CI bits set by reducing its ACR. The source will increase its ACR if it receives RM cells with their CI bits reset [6,24].

11.5.3.3 Explicit Rate (ER) Marking

The source writes the rate it desires in the RM cells it sends at regular intervals between data cells. The switch computes the fair share of bandwidth that should be allocated to each VC by monitoring the queue length. It updates the ER field of backward RM cells with the calculated fair share. The source will change its ACR to the value in the ER field of returning RM cells [6,7].

There are many variations of these schemes. A separate queue can be used at the switch for RM cells to speed up response. This queue can be given priority over the data queue to avoid RM cells being blocked due to congestion. Several *intelligent marking* schemes have been proposed so that different VCs can receive different feedback at the ER field according to their loading situation [50].

Active work has appeared in the literature on ABR congestion controls. Lee et al. [31] formally represent ABR source and destination behavior using an extended finite state machine model. Bonomi and Fendick [9] compare the EFCI with the ER scheme in terms of fairness. Ohsaki et al. [44] quantitatively evaluate the performance of all these three algorithms in terms of maximum queue length for persistent traffic. They vary propagation delay and the number of VCs to show the effectiveness of rate-based congestion control. Chang et al. [12] show that EFCI and ER switches can interoperate provided that the switch implementations conform to reference behavior in terms of congestion notification and usage of RM cells. Siu and Tzeng [50] describe an "intelligent marking" mechanism along with its analytical and simulation results. Jain [28] provides a survey on rate-based congestion control mechanisms and their recent advances.

11.5.4 Performance of ABR Congestion Control: The Effect of Bursty Source Traffic

In this subsection, we investigate both the effectiveness of rate-based ABR congestion control in the presence of bursty source traffic and the relationship between the burst time scale and the ABR control time scale. Two ABR congestion control schemes, the ABR Explicit Forward Congestion Indication (EFCI) and the ABR Congestion Indication (CI) schemes, are compared with Unspecified Bit-Rate (UBR) transport which makes no effort to control congestion. This is part of an earlier work in [22].

We consider two ATM switches, each connected to 50 end-systems. The simulation is repeated for two source traffic scenarios.

1. All sources with a short mean burst length (100 cells).
2. All sources with a long mean burst length (10,000 cells).

The burst length of the sources follows a geometric distribution around the mean value. The period between two bursts follows exponential distribution. The activity fraction was 1/16 for the bursty sources, resulting in a long-term traffic load of almost 85% (50 VCs × 96 cells/ms × (1/16)/353 cells/ms, since there are 50 VCs initiated by sources with PCR 96 cells/ms and the capacity of the backbone link is 353 cells/ms).

ABR Scheduler Parameters
PCR (Peak Cell Rate) is 96 cells/ms or 40 Mbps.
ICR (Initial Cell Rate) is taken to be the same as PCR.
MCR (Minimum Cell Rate) is 0.
N_{rm} (Number of data cells between two RM cells) is 32.
T_{rm} (Time between rate updates) is 20 ms.
RIF (Rate Increase Factor) is 1/256.
RDF (Rate Decrease Factor) is 1/16.

Table 11.10 ABR Congestion Controls (Mean burst length = 100 cells)

Congestion Control Scheme	Maximum Buffer Length (cells)	Mean Queueing Delay (msec)	No. of Cells Dropped	Link Utilization (%)
UBR	3600	1.1722	0	85.24
ABR EFCI	3600	2.7295	0	85.23
ABR CI	3700	1.8392	0	85.24

11.5.4.1 Short Bursty Traffic

Table 11.10 summarizes the results (maximum buffer length in terms of cells, mean queueing delay in msec, number of cells dropped, and link utilization percentage) of these simulations using a mean burst length of 100 cells. We can see that both ABR EFCI and ABR CI controls do not affect much of the maximum queue length compared with the UBR control.

11.5.4.2 Long Bursty Traffic

Table 11.11 summarizes the maximum buffer length, mean queueing delay, cell loss, and link utilization characteristics of the simulation with a mean burst length of 10,000 cells. As can be seen from the table, even a maximum buffer length of 50,000 (which is reasonable for OC3 links) is not adequate in this long-burst case for UBR control, which results in a significant loss of cells. On the other hand, ABR EFCI and ABR CI perform extremely well in inhibiting buffer occupancy and resulting in zero cell loss, the most important QoS criterion for ABR traffic.

The mean queueing delay values shown here resulting from ABR control are much higher than those from the UBR control. It has not, however, incorporated the delay caused by retransmission by the upper layers, which are needed for cell loss resulting from the

Table 11.11 ABR Congestion Controls (Mean burst length = 10,000 cells)

Congestion Control Scheme	Maximum buffer Length (cells)	Mean Queueing Delay (msec)	No. of Cells Dropped	Link Utilization (%)
UBR	50,000	49.6040	61694	85.49
ABR EFCI	6900	765.8332	0	70.14
ABR CI	1450	525.1764	0	75.46

UBR control. It also can be seen that ABR CI performs better than ABR EFCI in terms of delay and buffer occupancy.

From the results shown above, ABR control does not control high-frequency, short-length traffic bursts. It is, however, extremely effective in controlling low-frequency, long-length bursts. This is very desirable since it is the low-frequency behavior that results in extended periods of overload and corresponding queue loss. By controlling the low-frequency behavior, ABR control reduces queue lengths and minimizes cell loss due to buffer overflow.

ABR EFCI control is the simplest and most cost-effective ABR control to implement. Our results show that it is effective in minimizing buffer occupancy. ABR CI performs significantly better than ABR EFCI in terms of delay and maximum buffer length, since information about network conditions reaches the sources faster.

11.5.5 Burst-Level Admission Control Schemes

Iwata et al. [27] have described three ATM traffic classes and defined their respective control schemes. They are: the *best effort*, the *guaranteed burst*, and the *guaranteed stream* classes. In particular, the *guaranteed burst* class is for high-speed, long-burst file transfers. Since such transmission easily causes overload in the networks, this kind of traffic should be transferred with bandwidth reservation.

Burst-level admission control protocols allow sources to negotiate different peak rates for each burst on each link along the virtual circuit on a burst-by-burst basis. In the guaranteed burst class, the virtual circuit is initially established without bandwidth reservation. When a source has a burst to transmit with an established virtual circuit, the peak bandwidth required for each burst is declared to the network, in order to be reserved on a burst-by-burst basis with fast reservation protocols (FRPs) [11,47].

The FRP has been proposed for fast allocation of bandwidth or buffer resources for bursty traffic. There are many variations of burst-level control protocols. In the following, we describe three major variations of FRP: the original FRP, the AFRP (Adaptive FRP), and our new design, the MFRP (Modified FRP) [37].

11.5.5.1 FRP

A source using the FRP attempts to reserve bandwidth along its entire path using a request cell. It requests bandwidth at its peak rate of transmission. If the bandwidth requested by the source is available along the path, the source receives an acknowledgment (ACK) that the bandwidth has been reserved; the source then begins transmission of its burst. Once it has completed its transmission, the source sends a cell to release the reserved bandwidth. On the other hand, if the requested bandwidth is not available on one of the links along its path, the source receives a NAK (negative acknowledgment); it then backs off for a certain period and re-attempts after that.

11.5.5.2 AFRP

AFRP was first proposed by Ikeda and Suzuki [26]. A source using AFRP attempts to reserve bandwidth at its peak rate initially. If an ACK is received, it begins transmitting its burst and releases the reserved bandwidth once the transmission is completed. The source also increases its future request bit rate as follows:

$$NewRate = OldRate + (OldRate * IncrementFactor)$$
$$MeanRate \leq NewRate \leq PeakRate$$

On the other hand, if the requested bandwidth is not available, the source receives an NAK and backs off for some period of time. The source will then request again, after some random backoff, at the following reduced rate:

$$NewRate = OldRate * DecrementFactor$$
$$NewRate \geq MeanRate$$

11.5.5.3 MFRP

This scheme uses the idea of negotiated bandwidth allocation [37]. The bandwidth for transmitting a burst is first negotiated between source and network. Once a bandwidth is decided, it is maintained during the entire burst transmission. The high-level structure of MFRP is presented below, followed by a description of the algorithm.

MFRP
If (a burst is ready)
   SendRequest (ReqRate, MinRate)
Wait for Acknowledgment
If (*ACK (AllowedRate)* is received)
   Transmit at *AllowedRate*
Else if *NAK* is received
   Back off and later *SendRequest (ReqRate, MinRate)*

A source using the MFRP uses a request cell in the format of *SendRequest (ReqRate, MinRate)* to request bandwidth when a burst is ready. *ReqRate* indicates the requested rate. *MinRate* indicates the minimum bandwidth the source is willing to accept; it is usually equal to the mean rate of the burst. If a bandwidth greater than or equal to *MinRate* is available along the entire path, the request will be granted at *AllowedRate*, which is the maximum available bandwidth such that

$$MinRate \leq AllowedRate \leq ReqRate$$

Upon receiving the acknowlegment, the sender will start transmitting the burst at the granted rate, that is, *AllowedRate*. If, on the other hand, a NAK is received, it will back off for some period of time and re-send the same request, *SendRequest (ReqRate, MinRate)*.

Table 11.12 Summary of Three FRP Protocols

	FRP	AFRP	MFRP
Mechanism	Request peak rate	Back-and-forth rate negotiation	One-time rate negotiation
Blocking rate	High	Moderate	Low
Transmission time	Short	Moderate	Varies (depends on *AllowedRate*)
Extra overhead	None	Source keep track of current request rate and increase or decrease its next req. rate depends on ACK or NAK	One extra parameter at the request cell and the ACK

A summary of the newly proposed protocol and the two major existing protocols (FRP and AFRP), in terms of their major mechanism, protocol overhead, and various performance characteristics, is given in Table 11.12.

11.5.6 Performance of FRP, AFRP, and MFRP

In this section, the performance (blocking probability, average delay, and carried load) of FRP, AFRP, and MFRP is evaluated on a two-stage ATM network supporting *multirate* traffic. This is part of an earlier work in [37].

It is expected that in many applications of ATM networks, bursty traffic of different peak and mean rates will share the same network link. Table 11.13 shows three traffic types considered in this work. The peak rates of the traffic are taken similar to that in [30]. The mean rate was suggested as 0.125 of the peak rate in [26], but we take a more conservative approach to make it about 0.25 of the peak rate.

General network and protocol parameters are summarized in Table 11.14. Some specific parameters for AFRP and MFRP are as follows. We assume in AFRP that $Increment Factor = 0.125$ and $Decrement Factor = 0.5$ [26]. In MFRP, the $Min Rate$ is taken to be the mean rate of each traffic type. The $Req Rate$ is taken to be either the peak rate, or $1.25 \times Min Rate$. The two values result in similar performance except that the latter value gives slightly better blocking probability.

Figures 11.21 and 11.22 show the results of carried load and end-to-end delay, respectively. MFRP is expected to reduce the blocking probability since it is willing to accept any negotiated rate that lies between $Req Rate$ and $Min Rate$. As a result, MFRP also allows higher carried load (Fig. 11.21). What is more significant is that MFRP does not suffer from longer delay (Fig. 11.22). The major reason is that, by reducing blocking probability, backoff delay is largely avoided. (Note that the backoff delay is taken to be three times the

Table 11.13   Traffic Types

Traffic Type	Peak Rate (Mbps)	Mean Rate (Mbps)
Type 0	35	10
Type 1	55	15
Type 2	85	20

Table 11.14   Network and Protocol Simulation Parameters

Parameters	Values
Network	Two-stage
Traffic	Multirate
Source-switch distance	0.01 msec propagation time
Switch-switch distance (WAN)	5 msec propagation time
Arrival process	Random
Burst length	5 Mbits
Back-off period	$3 \times$ (mean burst transmission time)
ATM outlink capacity	155 Mbps
Traffic load	90–180 Mbps
Simulation time	10 sec

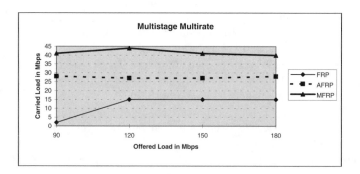

Figure 11.21   Carried Load of FRP, AFRP, and MFRP.

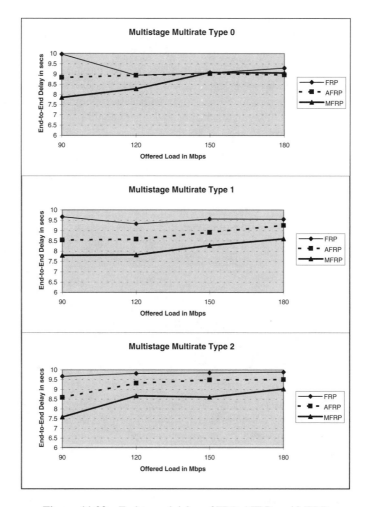

Figure 11.22   End-to-end delay of FRP, AFRP, and MFRP.

message transmission time using mean rate [30].) It can be concluded that the new protocol, MFRP, outperforms the existing protocols in all three performance criteria.

11.6 SUMMARY AND CONCLUSIONS

In this chapter, we have studied high-speed LAN, MAN, and ATM protocols for multimedia communications. We have first discussed multimedia traffic characteristics and QoS requirements. Traditional and more recent LAN protocols including the 100Base-T Fast Ethernet, 100VG-AnyLAN, and 100 Mbps Ethernet++ have been described. For MAN, we have described token-based protocols including FDDI and FDDI-II, plus four reservation-based protocols including DQDB, CRMA, DQMA, and FDQ. For ATM protocols, we have discussed QoS and traffic service classes proposed by the ATM Forum. Various ATM congestion control mechanisms for ABR traffic have been described. Existing and a new burst-level admission control mechanisms for the guaranteed-burst traffic have been presented. For each of the above network categories, we have studied and compared the performance of these protocols as multimedia carriers supporting heterogeneous traffic. We believe that the simulation results presented here could serve as significant indicators as to which network protocols would be more successful in carrying multimedia traffic. These simulation experiments would also provide valuable means to evaluate new protocols for multimedia communication.

Acknowlegments

Special thanks are due to the following former graduate students who are the co-authors of our earlier papers referred in the chapter and who have contributed significantly to the simulation study: Yu-Jen Eddy Chien, Yu-Feng Chung, Madhavi Hegde, Usha Rajgopal, Joanna Wang, Yi-Wen Wang, and Irene Zhang.

References

[1] A. Albrecht et al, "An Overview of IEEE 802.12 Demand Priority," *Proceedings of IEEE Globecom,* pp. 263–268, San Francisco, Nov. 1994.

[2] B. Albert and A. Jayasumana, *FDDI and FDDI-II Architecture, Protocols, and Performance,* Artech House, 1994.

[3] ANSI, "FDDI Token Ring Media Access Control (MAC)," ANSI draft proposal X3T9/84-100, Feb. 1986.

[4] ATM Forum, *ATM User-Network Interface Specification Version 3.0*, ATM Forum and Prentice-Hall, Sept. 1993.

[5] ATM Forum, *ATM User-Network Interface Specification Version 3.1*, ATM Forum, July 1994.

[6] ATM Forum, *ATM Traffic Management Specification Version 4.0*, ATM Forum, Oct. 1995.

[7] A. W. Barnhart, "Example Switch Algorithm for Section 5.4 of TM Specification," *ATM Forum Contribution 95-0195*, Feb. 1995.

[8] S. Bly, S. Bly, and S. Irwin, "Media Space: Bringing People Together in a Video, Audio, and Computing Environment," *Communications of the ACM,* Vol. 36, No. 1, pp. 28–45, Jan. 1993.

[9] F. Bonomi and K. W. Fendick, "The Rate-Based Flow Control Framework for the Available Bit Rate ATM Service," *IEEE Network Magazine*, Vol. 9, pp. 25–39, Mar./Apr. 1995.

[10] C. Bisdikian et al., "The Use of Priorities on Token-Ring Networks for Multimedia Traffic," *IEEE Network,* pp. 28–37, Nov./Dec. 1995.

[11] P. E. Boyer and D. P. Tranchier, "A Reservation Principle with Applications to the ATM Traffic Control," *Computer Networks and ISDN Systems,* Vol. 24, pp. 321–334, 1992.

[12] Y. Chang, N. Golmie, and D. Su, "Study of Interoperability Between EFCI and ER Switch Mechanisms for ABR Traffic in an ATM Network," *Proc. of the 4th Inter-*

national Conference on Computer Communications and Networks, pp. 310–315, Las Vegas, NV, Sept. 1995.

[13] J. Chen and V. Li, "Reservation CSMA/CD: A Multiple Access Protocol for LANs," *IEEE JSAC*, Vol. 7, pp. 202–210, 1989.

[14] I. Dalgic, W. Chien, and F. Tobagi, "Evaluation of 10Base-T and 100Base-T Ethernets Carrying Video, Audio and Data Traffic," *Proceedings of IEEE INFOCOM'94*, pp. 1094–1102, Toronto, June 1994.

[15] F. Edwards and M. Schulz, "A Priority Media Access Control Protocol for Video Communication Support on CSMA/CD LANs," *ACM Multimedia Systems,* pp. 243–255, Berlin: Springer-Verlag and ACM, 1995.

[16] F. Fish, R. Kraut, R. Root, and R. Rice, "Video as a Technology for Informal Communication," *Communications of the ACM,* Vol. 36, No. 1, pp. 48–61, Jan. 1993.

[17] E. Fox, "Advances in Interactive Digital Multimedia Systems," *IEEE Computer*, Vol. 24, No. 10, Oct. 1991.

[18] F. Fluckiger, *Understanding Networked Multimedia Applications and Technology*, Englewood Cliffs, NJ: Prentice-Hall, 1995.

[19] B. Furht, "Multimedia Systems: An Overview," *IEEE Multimedia,* pp. 47–59, Spring 1994.

[20] J. Grinham and M. Spratt, "IEEE 802.12 Demand Priority and Multimedia," *Proceedings of the 4th International Workshop on Network and Operating Systems Support for Digital Audio and Video,* pp. 75–86, Nov. 1993.

[21] C. Hernrick, R. Klessig, and J. McRoberts, "Switched Multi-megabit Data Service and Early Availability via MAN Technology," *IEEE Communications Magazine,* Vol. 26, No. 4, pp. 9–14, Apr. 1988.

[22] M. Hegde and W. M. Moh, "Effect of Burst Source Traffic on Rate-based ABR Congestion Control Schemes," *Proceedings of IFIP-IEEE International Conference on Broadband Communications*, pp. 135–146, Montreal, Quebec, Canada, Apr. 1996.

[23] I. Habib and T. Saadawi, "Multimedia Traffic Characteristics in Broadband Networks," *IEEE Communications Magazine*, pp. 48–54, July 1992.

[24] M. Hluchyj and N. Yin, "On Closed-loop Rate Control for ATM Networks," *Proceedings of IEEE INFOCOM '94*, pp. 99–108, Toronto, 1994.

[25] IEEE 802.6, *IEEE Standards for Local and Metropolitan Area Networks: Distributed Queue Dual Bus (DQDB) Subnetwork of a Metropolitan Area Networks (MAN),* Dec. 1990.

[26] C. Ikeda and H. Suzuki, "Adaptive Congestion Control Schemes for ATM LANs," *Proceedings of Infocom'94*, Toronto, pp. 820–838, June 1994.

[27] A. Iwata, N. Mori, C. Ikeda, H. Suzuki, and M. Ott, "ATM Connection and Traffic Management Schemes for Multimedia Internet-Working," *Communications of the ACM,* Vol. 38, No. 2, pp. 73–89, Feb. 1995.

[28] R. Jain, "Congestion Control and Traffic Management in ATM Networks: Recent Advances and a Survey," *Computer Networks and ISDN Systems*, Nov. 1996.

[29] M. Kabatepe and K. Vastola, "Exact and Approximate Analysis of DQDB under Heavy Load," *Proc. IEEE INFOCOM '92*, pp. 508–517, Florence, Italy, May 1992.

[30] B. G. Kim and P. Wang, "ATM Networks: Goals and Challenges," *Communications of the ACM,* Vol. 38, No. 2, pp. 39–44, Feb. 1995.

[31] D. Lee, K. K. Ramakrishnan, W. M. Moh, and A. U. Shankar, "Protocol Specification Using Parameterized Communicating Extended Finite State Machines—A Case Study of The ATM ABR Rate Control Scheme," *Proceedings of IEEE International Conference on Network Protocols* (ICNP'96), pp. 208–217, Columbus, OH, Oct. 1996. See also: D. Lee, K. K. Ramakrishnan, and W. M. Moh, "A Formal Specification of the ATM ABR Rate Control Scheme," to appear in *International Journal on Computer Networks and ISDN Systems.*

[32] L. Melatti, "Fast Ethernet: 100 Mbit/s Made Easy," *Data Communications,* pp. 111–113, Nov. 1994.

[33] B. Mukherjee and C. Bisdikian, "A Journal Through the DQDB Network Literature," *Performance Evaluation*, Vol. 16, pp. 129–158, Dec. 1992.

[34] W. M. Moh, Y.-J. Chien, I. Zhang, and T.-S. Moh, "Delay Performance Evaluation of High Speed Protocols for Multimedia Communications," *Proceedings of Fourth International Conference on Computer Communications and Networks (IC3N'95),* pp. 352–355, Las Vegas, NV, Sept. 1995.

[35] W. M. Moh, Y.-F. Chong, T.-S. Moh, and J. Wang, "Evaluation of High Speed LAN Protocols as Multimedia Carriers," *Proceedings of the IEEE International Conference on Computer Design,* Austin, Texas, October, 1996.

[36] W. M. Moh, T.-S. Moh, Y.-J. Chien, J. Wang, and Y.-W. Wang, "The Support of Optical Network Protocols for Multimedia ATM Traffic," *Proc. of the IEEE Singapore International Conference on Networks (SICON),* pp. 1–5, Singapore, July 1995.

[37] W. M. Moh, U. Rajgopal, and A. Dinesh, "Improved Burst-level Admission Control Schemes for ATM Networks," *Proceedings of the International Conference on Computer Communications and Networks (IC3N),* pp. 239–244, Washington, DC, Oct. 1996.

[38] H. Muller, M. Nassehi, J. Wong, E. Zurfluh, W. Bux, and P. Zafiropulo, "DQMA and CRMA: New Access Schemes for Gbits LANs and MANs," *IEEE INFOCOM,* pp. 185–191, San Francisco, June 1990.

[39] S. Mirchandi and R. Khana, *FDDI Technology and Applications,* New York: John Wiley & Sons, 1993.

[40] D. McDysan and D. Spohn, *ATM Theory and Application,* New York: McGraw-Hill, 1995.

[41] M. Nassehi, "CRMA: An Access Scheme for High-speed LANs and MANs," *IEEE SUPERCOMM/ICC '90,* pp. 1697–1702, Atlanta, GA, Apr. 1990.

[42] K. Nahrstedt and R. Steinmetz, "Resource Management in Networked Multimedia Systems," *IEEE Computer,* pp. 52–63, May 1995.

[43] J. Ottensmeyer and P. Martini, "Improving the Demand-Priority Protocol," *Proceedings of the Fourth International Conference on Computer Communications and Networks (IC3N'95),* pp. 369–376, Las Vegas, NV, Sept. 1995.

[44] H. Ohsaki, M. Murata, H. Suzuki, C. Ikeda, and H. Miyahara, "Rate-based Congestion Control for ATM Networks," *ACM SIGCOMM Computer Communication Review,* pp. 60–72, Apr. 1995.

[45] M. De Prycker, *Asynchronous Transfer Mode Solution for Broadband ISDN,* 3rd ed., Englewood Cliffs, NJ: Prentice Hall, 1995.

[46] M. Sadiku and A. Arvind, ''Annotated Bibliography on Distributed Queue Dual Bus (DQDB),'' *Computer Communication Review*, Vol. 24, No. 1, pp. 21–36, ACM Press, Jan. 1994.

[47] H. Suzuki and F. A. Tobagi, ''Fast Bandwidth Reservation Scheme with Multi-link and Multi-path Routing in ATM Networks,'' *Proceedings of Infocom '92*, Florence, Italy, pp. 2233–2240, May 1992.

[48] R. Steinmetz and K. Nahrstedt, *Multimedia: Computing, Communications and Applications,* Englewood Cliffs, NJ: Prentice Hall, 1995.

[49] A. Shah, D. Staddon, I. Rubin, and A. Ratkovic, ''Multimedia over FDDI,'' *Proceedings of 17th Conference on Local Computer Networks,* pp. 110–124, IEEE, Sept. 1992.

[50] K. Siu and H. Tzeng, ''Intelligent Congestion Control for ABR Service in ATM Networks,'' *ACM Computer Communication Review,* pp. 81–106, Oct. 1995.

[51] Tanenbaum, *Computer Networks,* 3rd ed., Englewood Cliffs, NJ: Prentice Hall, 1996.

[52] I. I. Venieris, J. D. Angelopoulos, and G. I. Stassinopoulos, ''ATM Traffic Transfer via Queue-Arbitrated DQDB,'' *Computer Communications*, Vol. 16, No. 12, pp. 746–758, Dec. 1993.

[53] G. Watson et al., ''The Demand Priority MAC Protocol,'' *IEEE Network Megazine,* pp. 28–34, Jan./Feb. 1995.

[54] J. Wong, ''Throughput of DQDB Networks under Heavy Load,'' Proc. EFOC/LAN '89, Amsterdam, The Netherlands, pp. 146–151, June 1989.

Chapter	# HIGH-SPEED OPTICAL
# 12	# INTERCONNECT FOR
	# MULTIMEDIA SYSTEMS

Chung-Sheng Li

Abstract

As the performance of multimedia systems continuously improves, it has become apparent that metal interconnects will be increasingly difficult to provide sufficient bandwidth at the board or backplane levels. Optical interconnect, with its almost unlimited bandwidth, has the potential to solve the I/O bottleneck problem currently faced by many multimedia systems. In this chapter, several promising optical interconnect architectures and technologies are discussed, and the potential advantages and challenges of using optical interconnects in a high-performance multimedia system are investigated.

12.1 INTRODUCTION

Multimedia has become omnipresent recently, owing to the rapid advances in VLSI, storage, and communication technologies. These technologies allow the delivery of high-definition video, images, and CD-quality audio to end users. As a result, multimedia applications such as World Wide Web, virtual reality, digital library, video on demand, and distance learning have become feasible. However, the unrelenting demand on the quality of these applications creates pressure for further performance improvement on the CPU and the communication bandwidth within the system. Thus far performance improvement has been realized by advances in (1) processor architectures such as the use of pipeline, superscalar, and parallel processing structures, and (2) VLSI technologies such as the feature-size reduction of CMOS. Yet the speed of devices is not the only criterion that determines the acceptance of a technology. When these devices are used in a multimedia system, problems of parasitics, circuit design, power consumption, and packaging often dominate over sheer speed. Therefore, it is insufficient to improve the performance of a system simply by choosing a faster device technology or a better system architecture. In particular, a number of factors such as the reflections due to electrical discontinuities of the transmission lines, crosstalk, skin effect, signal dispersion, and delta-I noise degrade the signal quality on metal interconnections [1,4] as clock speeds exceed 100 MHz. These factors lead to degradation that increases with the length and density of the interconnections as well as with the signaling rate on each conductor.

New technology is required to overcome these obstacles in order to create low-latency, high-bandwidth communication paths whose characteristics match the performance of multimedia systems. Different metal-based technology standards such as Rambus [2], Ramlink [3], and Scalable Coherent Interface (SCI) [5] have been proposed for parallel metal interconnects to meet the requirements of systems with clock speeds up to 500 MHz and are in the process of being implemented. Chip sets working up to 1.5 Gbps for bus-oriented serial metal interconnects have also been reported [6,7]. These systems show that with careful engineering such as the use of a controlled-impedance transmission line, fully differential signaling (SCI and Ramlink), and limiting the interconnection structure to point-to-point (SCI and Ramlink) can push the metal interconnection technology to higher bandwidths than could be supported with existing technology. Nevertheless, the cost of the new technology is initially high, and there is no guarantee that the solutions can be scaled to clock speeds higher than their present limits. If any of these interconnection technologies is going to succeed, it must be available at low cost in high volume, and it must be able to evolve to support future clock speeds of 1 GHz and beyond.

Optical interconnections provide an alternative technology to solve the interconnection problem. The multi-gigabit bandwidth allowed by this technology is more than sufficient for applications such as communications within a multimedia system for the foreseeable future. Furthermore, it is easier to control reflections in this technology for both point-to-point and multidrop structures than in metal links [1]. Optical links generally exhibit less ground-loop noise because fibers do not carry currents as do metal links. For these reasons, optical interconnections may be an attractive alternative technology for building high-speed board and backplane interconnections in future multimedia systems.

An optical link can be designed to be an almost one-to-one replacement for metal point-to-point or multidrop connections. The conventional line driver is replaced by a laser driver and an edge-emitting or surface-emitting laser diode/LED, or a laser diode and an external modulator such as a Mach-Zehnder interferometer, directional coupler, total internal reflection (TIR) modulator, spatial light modulator (SLM), self-electrooptic device (SEED), or vertical-to-surface transmission electrophotonic device (VSTEP) at the transmission end. The conventional line receiver is replaced by a light-sensitive device such as a PIN or metal-semiconductor-metal (MSM) photodetector and an amplifier at the receiving end. The light can be guided from the transmission end to the receiving end through single-mode or multimode fiber ribbon cable, polyimide, or silica-on-silicon channel waveguides, or free-space microlenses and/or holograms.

In this chapter, we survey a number of promising optical interconnect architectures and technologies. The goal is to investigate the potentials and limitations of optical interconnects. The rest of this chapter describes the existing metal interconnection hierarchy and potential impairments at high frequency; the advantages and drawbacks of optical interconnects; optical interconnect architectures and technologies; and recent research activities in this area.

12.2 EXISTING INTERCONNECTION HIERARCHY

Currently available packaging and interconnect technology at various packaging levels (as shown in Fig 12.1) are chips, single-chip modules (SCM), multichip modules (MCM), cards, boards, and backplanes [25]:

- *Chip-to-package interconnections*: These technologies include wire-bonding, tape automated bonding (TAB), and flip-chip bonding using solder ball.

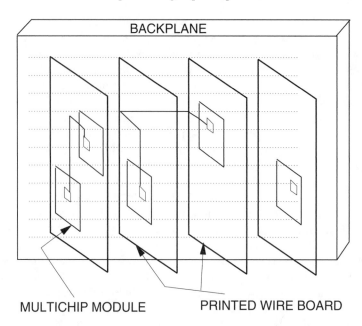

Figure 12.1   Packaging hierarchy. A typical packaging hierarchy, from bottom
                   to top, includes chips, multichip modules (MCM), cards, boards,
                   and backplanes.

- *Ceramic and plastic chip modules*: Each module made of ceramic or plastic en-
  capsulation contains a single chip (single-chip module or SCM) or multiple chips
  (multichip module or MCM). The interconnections on these modules can have multiple signal layers using thin-film or thick-film processing techniques.[1]

- *Package-to-board interconnections*: Existing technologies can be categorized as pin-
  through-hole (PTH), leadless chip carrier (LLCC), and surface mount technology
  (SMT). A through-hole on the printed-circuit board is provided for each pin of a
  chip package in PTH. Both mechanical joint and solder joint are feasible for this
  technology. On the other hand, both LLCC and SMT, which are more area efficient
  and provide better signal quality, require solder joint between each lead of a package
  and the pad on a circuit board.

- *Printed-circuit board*: This technology has been around since before 1960. The
  progress over the past 30 years includes the decrease in the through-hole diameter
  (from ~ 840 μm to ~ 350 μm), the increase in the through-hole density (from ~ 9

---

[1]Thin-film packaging refers to packages in which the conductor and insulators are fabricated
using deposition and patterning techniques similar to those used for fabricating integrated-circuit
chips.

to 64 cm^2), the increase in the number of signal planes (from $\sim$ 4 to 50), and the decrease of the interconnect width (from $\sim$ 250 μm to $\sim$ 50 μm).

As the speed of devices increases, existing metallic interconnect technology is no longer adequate because of its performance degradation at high frequency. Sources of performance degradation include

- Reflections
- Ground-loop noise
- Crosstalk among adjacent interconnects
- Frequency-dependent signal distortion

12.2.1 Reflections

A high-performance multimedia system requires more than one level of packaging and interconnects to accommodate complicated logic functions. A typical packaging hierarchy includes chips, single-chip modules (SCM), multichip modules (MCM), cards, boards, and backplanes. However, electrical discontinuities exist between any two packaging levels. Discontinuities may be primarily inductive (such as electrical connectors) or capacitive (such as stubs in a multidrop net and 90-degree bends in a microstrip line). Depending on the nature of the discontinuities and impedance changes, the resulting reflections may be either positive or negative.

Various methods exist to reduce the reflections resulting from impedance mismatch. For example, a termination resistor is usually placed at the receiving end of an interconnect in order to reduce the reflections. However, a perfect matching between the characteristic impedance of the interconnection and the impedance of the load is difficult to achieve because of the parasitic capacitance and inductance. If the round-trip propagation time between the source and the discontinuities is less than the rise time of the signal, these reflections can be absorbed by the interconnect driver with a net effect of an increased signal rise time. On the other hand, the waveform of the signal is severely degraded by the multiple reflections if the round-trip propagation time is longer than the rise time of the signal, resulting in a reduced noise margin or/and false switching.

12.2.2 Ground-loop Noise

The ground plane of a packaging system usually cannot achieve zero resistance and inductance. Any local injection of current from the devices changes the electrical potential at that point. For a single-ended interconnection, the receiving side has to rely on the potential of the local ground plane as a reference to determine the amplitude of the incoming signals. Any disturbance of the ground plane is therefore coupled into the received signal.

One way of alleviating this problem is to transmit differential signals so that the signal can be interpreted unambiguously at the receiving end of an interconnect. However, the required interconnect density has to be doubled, and thus more signal layers are necessary to accommodate the increased interconnect complexity. Some of the chips that are already pin-count-limited cannot afford this option either.

12.2.3   Crosstalk Among Adjacent Interconnects

For a given interconnect density, crosstalk between adjacent interconnects increases as the rise time of the signal decreases. Furthermore, crosstalk of the transmission lines with a TEM (Transverse Electromagnetic) or near-TEM structure,[2] such as slotted lines and microstrip lines, usually couple with switching noise and may consume the entire noise margin if they are not carefully controlled [8]. Therefore, either the interconnects have to be spaced farther apart or additional shielding lines have to be inserted between signal lines to reduce crosstalk to an acceptable level. In both cases, the effective interconnect density is reduced.

12.2.4   Frequency-dependent Signal Distortion

Packaging discontinuities introduce frequency-dependent signal distortion as a result of the inductive or capacitive nature of the discontinuities. Additional signal distortion is introduced by the dispersion and skin effect of metal interconnects.

The microstrip lines on a printed-circuit board are inherently dispersive, since they are incapable of supporting a pure TEM mode [9]. The mode's effective dielectric constant is a function of frequency, causing different frequency components of the signal to travel at a different speed. This effect becomes significant when the rise time of the waveform is smaller than 100 ps and the signal has to travel more than a few centimeters.

The skin effect also contributes to frequency-dependent signal distortion for metal interconnects when the thickness of the interconnects is large compared to the skin depth. Due to the skin effect, high-frequency components within the signal experience higher attenuation, yielding nonnegligible waveform distortion. In order to reduce the skin effect, the thickness of the metal has to be less than the skin depth of the metal.[3] A wider transmission line is thus required to accommodate signals with higher data rate while maintaining an acceptable DC and low-frequency loss, resulting in a net reduction of the interconnect density.

12.3   OPTICAL INTERCONNECTS

Because of the bandwidth bottleneck associated with the existing interconnect and packaging technology, optical interconnect using free-space, optical waveguides, or optical fiber thus becomes a viable and attractive alternative to increase the total system throughput. In this section, issues associated with using optical interconnect for high-speed digital systems are investigated. In particular, we will examine the potential problems and solutions of using dense optical interconnects for high-performance multimedia systems. In such systems, serialization of data cannot be employed to increase the channel density if the data rate of each channel is very high before serialization is introduced. Therefore, an interconnect technology with the capability of providing high density and high bandwidth is necessary for acceptance in digital systems.

---

[2]TEM mode is the fundamental mode supported by a transmission line such as a coaxial cable. The transmission line structures that can support TEM mode are said to have TEM structures.
[3]The skin depth of copper is 2 μm at 1 GHz and becomes 0.7 μm at 10 GHz.

12.3.1 Potential Advantages

Dense optical interconnects may offer the following advantages:

- *More sophisticated interconnection pattern*: Light beams from different sources do not interfere with each other upon crossing. Very sophisticated 2-D and 3-D interconnect patterns based on planar optical waveguide and free-space interconnect technologies, respectively, can thus be built from this principle, achieving a higher packaging density and shorter average signal propagation distance.

- *Electrical reflection reduction*: The reflections due to electrical discontinuities of a packaging system do not seriously affect the signal waveform as long as the round-trip propagation delay is less than the rise time of the signal waveform. Therefore, multiple reflections due to impedance mismatch between different levels of packaging can be reduced or eliminated by replacing metal interconnects on higher packaging levels (such as the boards and the backplanes) with optical interconnects so that the round-trip propagation delay of any metal interconnects is shorter than the signal rise time.

- *Higher bandwidth*: The bandwidth of the optical interconnects is mainly limited by the interface electronics and has the potential to achieve a multigigabit data rate with very little signal distortion.

- *Higher spatial density*: The potential spatial density of either optical-waveguide or free-space interconnect technology is an order of magnitude higher than what can be achieved by the current metal interconnect technology. (Line spacing between two thin-film metal interconnects is ≥ 25 μm with a propagation distance less than 7 cm and increases to ≥ 100 μm for longer distance in order to avoid large crosstalk between adjacent interconnects [25].)

- *Freedom from electromagnetic interference (EMI)*: The propagation of light does not generate EMI to interfere with the surrounding circuit, nor can it be affected by the EMI produced by the environment.

- *Breaking of groundloops*: By using optical interconnects, current is no longer transferred between the transmitters and receivers, and thus the disturbance on the ground plane is reduced. In addition, optical signals in an optical interconnect cannot be disturbed by the noise of the ground plane, and therefore the signal quality is improved.

12.3.2 Potential Problems

On the other hand, we also have to be aware of the potential problems if optical interconnects are used to replace metal interconnects:

- *Modal noise* [24]: When multimode waveguides or fibers are used in conjunction with highly coherent lasers, the coherent interference of different spatial waveguide or fiber modes gives rise to a speckle pattern. Fluctuations of the speckle pattern due, for example, to fluctuations in the spectrum of the optical source can lead to modal noise if a mode-selective loss (such as a bad connector) is present in the optical link.

Modal noise can cause a bit-error-rate (BER) floor which might not be tolerable in applications that require extremely low BER. Modal noise problems can be solved by either using a laser diode with large linewidth or premodulating the laser at a frequency comparable to the relaxation oscillation frequency of the laser diode [28].

- *Optical reflections* [27]: Index discontinuities are also unavoidable in waveguide or fiber interconnects. Reflections from the laser/waveguide interface might increase the linewidth as well as the relative intensity noise (RIN) of the laser. Other reflections due to the discontinuities along the optical path degrade the signals arriving at the receiver by reducing the eye opening and increasing the RIN.

- *Optical crosstalk*: Optical crosstalk can occur at the coupling between laser array and optical waveguide array, between adjacent waveguides, or between the waveguide array and the photodetector array as a result of the high packaging density required by the system.

- *Threshold uncertainty* [11]: The large number of interconnects within a digital system requires that all of the receivers be set at the same threshold. In practice, this threshold cannot be individually adjusted according to the characteristics of the source. This means there is no feedback between the driver and the receiver to adjust the laser output, which deteriorates with time. Local feedback might be able to correct for this problem, but the added logic circuitry would compete for chip area with other logic circuitry.

- *High density required for optoelectronic components*: Each typical single-chip module (SCM) may have over 100 signal-I/Os, while a multichip module (MCM) can have several hundreds to several thousand signal-I/Os. In order to provide optical interconnect in this environment, we have to be able to fabricate equally dense optoelectronic devices such as LD/LED, PIN/APD arrays, driver arrays, and receiver arrays.

- *Propagation delay* [11]: The propagation delay of light in waveguide is unlikely to go below the 5.0 ps/mm value currently available. This compares unfavorably with the 3.5–4.0 ps/mm for metal interconnects if suitable fabrication processes are developed to use expanded PTFE-type material as an insulator in multichip modules and boards. This seems to be a fundamental limitation for waveguide optical interconnects. However, metal interconnects suffer additional delay at each discontinuity as well as require longer settling time due to switching noise, crosstalk, and reflections. Therefore, propagation delay alone cannot be used to evaluate the performance of an interconnect technology.

- *Conversion delay*: Signals are useful only in their electrical forms. Therefore, electrical-to-optical (E/O) and optical-to-electrical (O/E) conversions are necessary for every interconnect, which always involve nonnegligible conversion delay.

- *Sensitivity to noise during E/O and O/E conversion*: Existing optical interconnect technology has more loss than metal interconnection for such distances, due to the insertion loss of the connector and scattering loss of the surface defects of a waveguide. Therefore, the receiver experiences more amplification and a higher

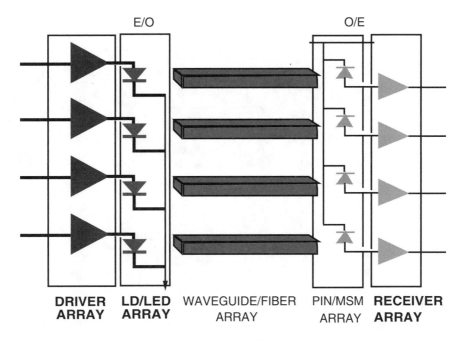

Figure 12.2   Structure of an optical interconnect system.

sensitivity to both power supply noise and electrical crosstalk. This problem is further aggravated by the high density required by a dense optical interconnect environment. In such an environment, there could be significant electrical interference either through the shared common power supply or through the parasitic inductance and capacitance.

■ *Thermal interactions*: Laser characteristics, such as the wavelength, threshold current, and differential quantum efficiency, are strongly affected by the operating temperature. Thermal interactions between adjacent lasers in a dense laser array could thus significantly degrade the system performance.

12.4 ARCHITECTURE OF OPTICAL INTERCONNECTS

Figure 12.2 shows the structure of a typical optical interconnect, which consists of a driver array, a laser diode or LED (LD/LED) array, a waveguide or fiber ribbon array, a photodetector array (p-i-n or MSM), and a receiver array. Using optical interconnects for high-bandwidth communication channels between boxes has been demonstrated, for example, in [83]. It is conceivable that optical interconnect can also be used within a box (at both the board and backplane levels), shown in Fig. 12.3.

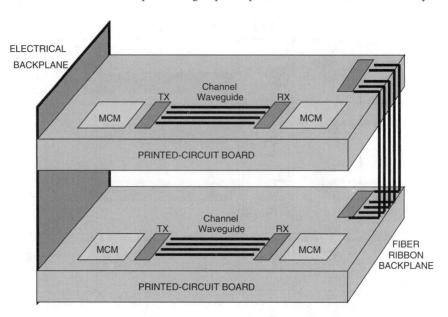

Figure 12.3 A packaging structure uses optical interconnect at board and backplane levels.

In this section, possible architectures for dense optical interconnects at the board and backplane levels are investigated. The constraints for designing the architecture of an optical interconnect system are:

- Compatibility with existing packaging technology
- Flexibility in fitting into the architectures of digital systems
- Fault tolerance
- Easy engineering change and fault diagnostics

In the following, we will first examine the available interconnect forms. Possible interconnect architectures at backplane, board, and multichip module level will then be investigated. Possible E/O and O/E conversion schemes will also be evaluated.

12.4.1 Interconnect Media

Media that can be used for optical interconnects include:

- *Free-space interconnect*: Light travels fastest in free space. In addition, free-space interconnects also offer the highest density and the most sophisticated interconnection patterns. Unfortunately, bulk optical elements such as lenses, holograms, and beam splitters, are usually unavoidable in free-space optical interconnects and thus make the alignment of optical beams very difficult and unstable with respect to environmental disturbances.

- *Optical fiber ribbon*: Optical fiber has the least loss compared with the other two media, and most of the technologies used in fabrication are already mature. Fiber ribbon cable also has the potential of providing reasonable interconnect density with regular interconnection patterns. However, fibers are incompatible with the existing packaging technology at the board or MCM level, and they are not suitable for interconnects with very short distance or complicated patterns due to the possibly excessive volume occupied by the fiber cable. A lot of research effort has thus been devoted to the development of compatible connector and packaging technologies to interconnect fiber ribbon and optical transceiver array.

- *Planar optic waveguide*: Passive planar optic waveguides are emerging as a viable alternative to optical fiber for very short-distance interconnects. It has a higher propagation loss than optical fiber ($0.01 \sim 0.5$ dB/cm as compared to 0.2 dB/km) but uses technologies that are compatible with existing PCB or MCM technology. Therefore, it is more suitable for short-distance dense interconnect applications. However, coupling of light into and from the waveguides is also difficult, and careful alignment cannot be avoided.

12.4.2 Backplane Optical Interconnects

The backplane provides a logical bus for all boards connected to it. Free space, fibers and planar waveguides are all suitable for backplane interconnects. An optical backplane can be achieved by using star couplers, as shown in Fig. 12.4. Each board in the architecture occupies one input port and one output port from each of the star couplers, so that signals input to any of the input port will be broadcast to all of the output ports. The total number of star couplers required can be greatly reduced by multiplexing several channels into a single waveguide with each channel using a different wavelength.

On the other hand, a topological bus can also be used to interconnect from one board to another, as shown in Fig. 12.5. The bus is either folded back at the end, or two independent buses are used because a unidirectional optical bus structure is usually easier to implement.

12.4.3 Board and Multichip-module Optical Interconnects

Board-level optical interconnects have to provide interconnects between different SCMs or MCMs, while MCM-level optical interconnects have to provide interconnects between unpackaged wire-bonded or solder-ball-bonded flipped chips. At the board level, the E/O and O/E conversion can be performed within an SCM/MCM, or through separate special-purpose E/O and O/E chips. Similarly, the E/O and O/E conversion at the MCM level can be performed within the chip where the logical signals are generated or via separate special-purpose E/O and O/E chips on an MCM.

If the E/O and O/E conversion is performed before the package is connected to the next higher level, as shown in Fig. 12.6, the electrical discontinuity can be minimized but the optical alignment is more difficult. On the other hand, more electrical discontinuity and thus more signal distortion are introduced if the E/O and O/E conversion is performed after

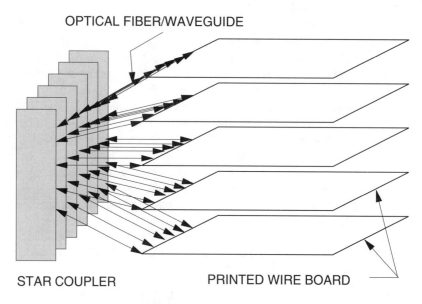

Figure 12.4   Optical backplane interconnects: Star couplers are used to combine and redistribute the data signals.

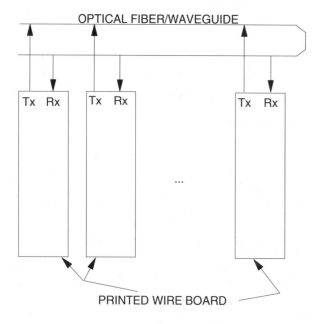

Figure 12.5   Optical backplane interconnects: A topological bus is used to provide a communication path between any two boards connected to the backplane.

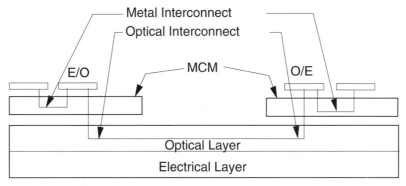

Figure 12.6   E/O and O/E conversion: Conversion is performed at the same packaging level as the electrical signal is generated.

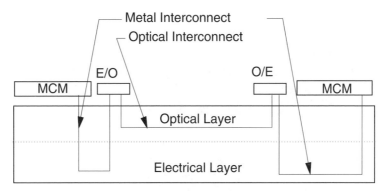

Figure 12.7   E/O and O/E conversion: Conversion is performed at the next higher packaging level.

the package is connected to the next level, as shown in Fig. 12.7. However, this is acceptable for applications that require only moderate data rates.

In both cases, there already exist multiple layers of metal interconnect that provide signal lines as well as power and ground plane. Optical interconnects can be developed on top of these metal interconnect layers in order to allow optical signals to propagate from one chip/module to another chip/module. In some cases, more than one optical layer may be necessary in order to provide sufficient interconnect density (such as at the MCM level) just similar to its electrical counterpart.

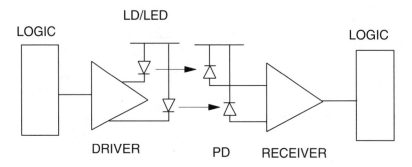

Figure 12.8   A fully differential optical interconnect architecture.

12.4.4 Fully Differential Optical Interconnect

As discussed earlier, optical interconnects for a digital system have the following potential problems:

- Threshold uncertainty
- Latency due to serialization/deserialization, encoding/decoding
- Sensitivity to the switching noise and power supply noise
- Sensitivity to the thermal interactions
- Sensitivity to the DC level of the data at the receiver

A fully differential optical interconnect architecture, as shown in Fig. 12.8, was proposed in [78,79,80] to minimize the detrimental effects arising from these potential problems. In this architecture, complementary optical signals are generated, transmitted, and received along two independent optical channels.

In a fully differential optical interconnect, the threshold voltage at the output of the receiver is always located at differential zero, which is halfway between two signal voltages of approximately equal amplitude but opposite sign, assuming two lasers at the differential transmitter have approximately the same average power and the attenuation along the differential path is similar. The threshold voltage is then independent of the actual power output of the lasers and the attenuation of the channel. Since both the laser drivers and receivers are fully balanced, the fluctuation of the current demands from the power supply is minimized, and thus the switching noise is reduced.[4] Furthermore, the differential structure for both drivers and receivers increases the common-mode rejection and thus reduces the sensitivity to the power supply noise. Therefore, differential optical interconnect is very attractive in a dense optical environment.

---

[4]An offset voltage is incurred when the laser output power or the attenuation is not balanced along the differential path.

12.5 TECHNOLOGIES FOR OPTICAL INTERCONNECT SYSTEMS

In a dense optical interconnect, electrical interactions among elements in a transmitter or receiver array due to high-density requirement might limit the system performance and will be the subject of this section.

12.5.1 Transmitter Array

A transmitter array usually consists of a driver array and a laser diode array (or LED array). These two components might be monolithically or hybrid integrated on the same substrate. Among possible interactions in a dense transmitter array are

- Electrical crosstalk between laser diodes due to the sharing of a common substrate
- Electrical crosstalk due to parasitic capacitance and mutual inductance between adjacent channels
- Switching noise due the sharing of a common power supply and ground

These interactions increase with the increase of channel density, modulation speed, and modulation current of the transmitter.

Crosstalk among laser array elements has been a subject of continuous interest. Fabrication and characterization of a one-dimensional, individually addressable laser or LED array has been reported in [29,30,31,33]. Recently, two-dimensional vertical cavity surface emitting laser (VCSEL) diode arrays or surface-emitting LED arrays have received a lot of attention and have emerged as a very promising light source for two-dimensional optical interconnects. The performance of these LEDs and laser diodes is reported in [32,38,39,40,41]. but the crosstalk data have yet to be established. Most of the laser or LED driver circuits were published in the late 1970s and early 1980s [42–48]. Recent laser driver circuit designs usually include monitoring circuits that calculate the peak and average of the laser output power in order to maintain a constant extinction ratio. Based on these designs, a driver array can be built by replicating the same design N times. Both monolithic integration [34] and hybrid integration [35,36] of the driver array with the laser array have been exploited. Crosstalk in these works is usually determined through experiments or simulations, but a systematic study of the crosstalk due to switching noise is yet to be addressed. However, this issue is important for choosing a suitable driver architecture to minimize overall interference.

12.5.2 Waveguide

It has been shown that passive waveguides based on silicon nitride [74] and polymers [75,76] are attractive for very short-distance interconnections, such as those between chips on a multichip module or on a printed-circuit board, or as backplane interconnections. Although suffering more loss than fiber, waveguides have the potential of providing much closer spacing and planar crossover geometries and can integrate modulators, optical amplifiers, and receivers on the same substrate as well [77]. The density of a waveguide array is limited mainly by the coupling-induced crosstalk between adjacent waveguides. In order to achieve the maximum density allowed by the required bit-error rate (BER), it

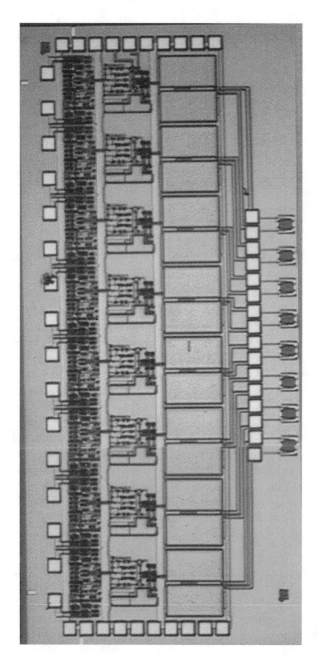

Figure 12.9   Photograph of an 8-channel receiver array with monolithically integrated MSM photodetectors.

is necessary to determine the power coupling among waveguides in an array structure and thus the incurred system penalty.

12.5.3 Receiver Array

Both hybrid integration and monolithic integration technology can be used to package a photodetector array with an amplifier array. Hybrid integration allows separate optimization of the processing technology for the photodetectors and amplifiers. This technology usually gives better device performance, at the expense of greater adjacent channel crosstalk and signal distortion introduced by the bonding wires. The photodetector array in a hybrid receiver array usually has a p-i-n structure and is made of Si, GaAs, or InGaAs/InP, depending on the wavelength of the light signals [36,54]. The amplifier array is made of Si bipolar [50] or GaAs MESFET. In a monolithic integration environment, both the photodetector array and the receiver array are integrated on the same semiconductor substrate. A planar process for the photodetectors is usually preferable for easier monolithic integration with other electronic circuits.[5] Metal-semiconductor-metal (MSM) with its planar structure has thus far emerged as the most popular structure for the photodetector array [56–71]. A fully monolithically integrated 8-channel 1.2 Gb/s array receiver is shown in Fig. 12.9. The pitch of MSM photodetector is 140 μm, and the pitch of the receiver array is 560 μm.

There have been a number of receiver array designs using either hybrid integration [36,37,50] or monolithic integration [35,51,52,53,55,73] technology. Up to 32 and 12 channels/chip have been achieved thus far with monolithic [81] and hybrid technology [82], respectively.

Electrical crosstalk between photodetectors in a p-i-n array has been previously examined in [26,54]. It was concluded in [26] that the common substrate of a p-i-n array introduces negligible DC crosstalk. A majority of the crosstalk came from the parasitic coupling between the bonding wires connecting between photodetectors and receivers.

12.6 RESEARCH ACTIVITIES ON OPTICAL INTERCONNECTS

Using optics for interconnections between VLSI systems was first suggested in [18,19]. Early systems are based mostly on free-space interconnects with the use of holographic optical elements (HOE) and spatial light modulators (SLM) to establish interconnect patterns. More recent systems have begun to use both optical fibers and planar waveguides [17]. An interprocessor optical link has been demonstrated between processor blocks in the Thinking Machines CM-2 at 400 Mbps [23]. The feasibility of board-level optical interconnect using polymer [13,14] and silica [22] has also been demonstrated recently. Both of these prototypes can demonstrate a bit rate higher than 300 Mbps. However, the problems associated with the high-density interconnect are yet to be addressed.

---

[5]A p-i-n structure usually has a vertical structure that requires the growing of a thick epitaxial layer in order to accommodate the intrinsic region of the p-i-n structure. The thickness of the intrinsic region is at least 2 μm in GaAs and 10 μm in silicon for efficient absorption of the light signals at $\lambda = 0.8$ μm. This process is usually incompatible with the processing steps used for electronic circuits that usually only require a thin epitaxial layer (≤ 2 μm).

A DC-coupled, fully differential optical interconnect system was proposed, analyzed, and simulated in [78,79] for connections within high-speed digital systems, specifically for board and backplane level interconnections. A chip set consisting of a 2.5-Gb/s bipolar differential laser driver, an 800-Mb/s GaAs MSM-preamp array, an 800-Mb/s GaAs MSM-preamp-postamp array, and a GaAs MSM-preamp array, with each preamp having a different bandwidth varying from 300 Mbps to 2 Gbps, has been designed, fabricated, and tested to serve as a vehicle for verifying the concept [80].

Between 1991 and 1994, ARPA supported the Optoelectronic Technology Consortium (OETC), which consists of Martin Marietta, AT&T, Honeywell, and IBM, to develop a 32-channel bus with a data transfer rate of 500 Mb/s [81]. This system uses 850 nm VSCEL for the transmitter array, MSM for the photodetector array, and GaAs E/D MESFET for the AC-coupled receiver and driver array. The data are Manchester coded due to the AC-coupled design at the receiver. A 32 × 1 multimode fiber ribbon cable with 62.5 μm core diameter, 125 μm cladding diameter, and 140 μm pitch is used between the transmitter and the receiver. A NIST-funded consortium consisting of IBM, 3M, and Lexmark is currently developing a 20-channel parallel optical interconnect, with a total throughput of 1 GB/s.

An ARPA-sponsored collaborative effort by the parallel optical link organization (POLO), consisting of HP, AMP, Du Pont, SDL, and the University of Southern California, will operate between 1994 and 1997. The objective of this program is to provide a 10–20 Gb/s parallel channel with a manufacturing cost of $10/channel [85]. A 10-channel DC-coupled parallel optical link, with each link operating at more than 500 MHz, using VCSEL polymer waveguide and bipolar receiver, has already been demonstrated [84].

In another ARPA-sponsored consortium consisting of GE and Honeywell, Allied Signals is currently working on the POINT project [86]. This project focuses on the batch processing and passive alignment between optical waveguides and traceivers for board and backplane applications.

In Europe, the European Strategic Programme for Information Technology (ESPRIT) sponsored OLIVES (Optical Interconnections for VLSI and Electronic Systems) between 1989 and 1992 and HOLICS (Hierarchical Optical Interconnects for Computer Systems) immediately after OLIVES. In HOLICS, 4-channel edge-emitting laser diode arrays, InGaAs/InP p-i-n photodetector array, and 8-channel and 12-channel 1 Gb/s receiver arrays have been developed for use in conjunction with 250 μm-pitch fiber ribbon cable [82].

12.7 SUMMARY

In this chapter, we have surveyed a number of promising optical interconnect architectures and technologies that can significantly improve the performance of high-throughput multimedia systems. These optical interconnect systems have already reached very high density (32 parallel channels), high data rate (1 Gb/s), low insertion loss, as well as low optical and electrical crosstalk. Some of these technologies have reached commercial maturity (such as fiber ribbon cable, MACII connectors, monolithically integrated photodetector, and receiver array). Other technologies, such as the packaging and transmitter array, still have a long way to go before they can reach the same level of reliability.

References

[1] H. S. Stone and J. Cocke, "Computer Architecture in the 1990s," *IEEE Computer Magazine*, Vol. 24, No. 9, pp. 30–38, Sept. 1991.

[2] M. P. Farmwald and D. Mooring, "A Fast Path to One Memory," *IEEE Spectrum*, pp. 50–51, Oct. 1992.

[3] S. Gjessing, D. B. Gustavson, D. V. James, G. Stone, and H. Wiggers, "A RAM Link for High Speed," *IEEE Spectrum*, pp. 52–53, Oct. 1992.

[4] E. E. Davidson and G. A. Katopis, "Chapter 3: Package Electrical Design," in *Microelectronics Packaging Handbook*, New York: Van Nostrand Reinhold, pp.111–165, 1989.

[5] IEEE P1594 Working Group, "Scalable Coherent Interface: Logical, Physical, and Cache Coherence Specifications," IEEE Standard Department, 1992.

[6] R. C. Walker, T. Hornak, C.-S. Yen, J. Doernberg, and K. H. Springer, "A 1.5 Gb/s Link Interface Chipset for Computer Data Transmission," *IEEE Journal of Selected Areas in Communications*, Vol. 9, No. 5, pp. 698–710, June 1991.

[7] R. Walker, J.-T. Wu, C. Stout, B. Lai, C.-S. Yen, T. Hornak, and P. Petruno, "A 2-Chip 1.5 Gb/s Bus-Oriented Serial Link Interface," *Proc. ISSCC*, pp. 226–227, 1992.

[8] G. A. Katopis, "Delta-I Noise Specification for a High-Performance Computing Machine," *Proceedings of the IEEE*, Vol. 73, No. 9, pp. 1405–1415, Sept. 1985.

[9] R. L. Veghte and C. A. Balanis, "Dispersion of Transient Signals in Microstrip Transmission Lines," *IEEE Transactions on Microwave Theory and Technique*, Vol. 34, No. 12, pp. 1427–1436, Dec. 1986.

[10] W. R. Blood, *MECL System Design Handbook*, Motorola, 1988.

[11] G. Arjavalingam and B. Rubin, "Electrical Considerations for Interconnections Inside a Computer," *Proc. SPIE*, Vol. 991, pp. 12–21, 1988.

[12] R. L. Khalil, L. R. McAdams, and J. W. Goodman, "Optical Clock Distribution for High Speed Computers," *Proc. SPIE*, Vol. 991, pp. 32–41, 1988.

[13] D. H. Hartman, G. R. Lalk, J. W. Howse, and R. R. Krchnavek, "Radiant Cured Polymer Optical Waveguides on Printed Circuit Boards for Photonic Interconnection Use," *Applied Optics*, Vol. 28, No. 1, pp. 40–47, Jan. 1989.

[14] D. H. Hartman, G. R. Lalk, and T. C. Banwell, "Board Level High Speed Photonic Interconnections: Recent Technology Developments," *Proc. SPIE*, Vol. 994, pp. 57–64, 1988.

[15] H. S. Stone, "Chapter 3: Pipeline Design Techniques," in *High-Performance Computer Architecture*, Reading, MA: Addison-Wesley, 1987.

[16] K. Hwang and F. A. Briggs, "Chapter 7: Multiprocessor Architecture and Programming," *Computer Architecture and Parallel Processing*, New York: McGraw-Hill, 1984.

[17] L. D. Hutcheson, P. Haugen, and A. Husain, "Optical Interconnects Replace Hardwire," *IEEE Spectrum*, pp. 30–35, Mar. 1987.

[18] J. W. Goodman, F. I. Leonberger, S.-Y. Kung, and R. A. Athale, "Optical Interconnections for VLSI Systems," *Proceedings of the IEEE*, Vol. 72, pp. 850–866, 1984.

[19] R. K. Kostuk, J. W. Goodman, and L. Hesselink, "Optical Imaging Applied to Microeletronic Chip-to-Chip Interconnections," *Applied Optics*, Vol. 24, pp. 2851–2858, 1985.

[20] J. Shamir, "Three-Dimensional Optical Interconnection Gate Array," *Applied Optics*, Vol. 26, pp. 3455–3457, 1987.

[21] A. W. Lohmann, "Optical Bus Network," *Optik (German)*, Vol. 74, pp. 30–35, 1986.

[22] Y. Yamada, T. Miya, M. Kobayashi, S. Sumida, and T. Miyashita, "Optical Interconnections Using Silica-Based Waveguide on Si Substrate," *Proc. SPIE*, Vol. 991, pp. 4–11, 1988.

[23] B. O. Kahle and E. C. Parish, "Optical Interconnects for Interprocessor Communications in the Connection Machine," *Proc. ICCD*, pp. 58–61, 1989.

[24] R. E. Epworth, "The Phenomenon of Modal Noise in Analog and Digital Optical Fiber Systems," *Proc. of 4th ECOC in Genova*, pp. 492–501, 1978.

[25] R. R. Tummala, R. W. Keyes, W. Grobman, and S. Kapur, "Thin Film Packaging," in *Microelectronics Packaging Handbook*, New York: Van Nostrand Reinhold, 1989.

[26] D. R. Kaplan and S. R. Forrest, "Electrical Crosstalk in p-i-n Arrays, Part I: Theory," *IEEE Journal of Lightwave Technology*, Vol. 4, No. 10, pp. 1460–1469, 1986.

[27] J. Gimlett and N. K. Cheung, "Effects of Phase-to-Intensity Noise Conversion by Multiple Reflections on Gigabit-per-Second DFB Laser Transmission Systems," *IEEE Journal of Lightwave Technology*, Vol. 7, No. 6, pp. 888–895, 1989.

[28] R. W. Huegli and C. M. Olsen, "Elimination of Modal Noise Bit-Error-Rate Floors by Strong Stimulation of the On-Level Relaxation Oscillations," IBM Research Report RC 16675, IBM, T. J. Watson Research Center, Mar. 1991.

[29] L. A. Koszi, B. P. Segner, H. Temkin, W. C. Dautremont-Smith, and D. T. C. Huo, "1.5 μm InP/GaInAsP Linear Laser Array with Twelve Individually Addressable Elements," *Electronic Letters*, Vol. 24, No. 4, pp. 217–219, 1988.

[30] J. P. Van Der Ziel, R. A. Logan, and R. M. Mikulyak, "A Closely Spaced (50 μm) Array of 16 Individually Addressable Buried Heterostructure GaAs Lasers," *Applied Physics Letters*, No. 41, p. 9, 1982.

[31] P. P. Deimel, J. Cheng, S. R. Forrest, S. J. Walker, P. H.-S. Hu, R. Huntington, R. C. Miller, J. R. Potopowicz, D. D. Roccassecca, and C. W. Seabury, "Electrical and Optical Integration of a Monolithic 1 x 12 array of InGaAsP/InP ($\lambda = 1.3\mu$m) Light Emitting Diodes," *Journal of Lightwave Technology*, Vol. 3, 1985.

[32] L. A. Koszi, H. Temkin, B. H. Chin, S. G. Napholtz, and B. P. Segner, "Fabrication and Performance of an InP/InGaAsP monolithic 12 x 12 element matrixed LED array," *Electronic Letters*, No. 23, pp. 284–286, 1987.

[33] D. Botez, J. C. Connolly, D. B. Gilbert, M. G. Harvey, and M. Ettenberg, "High-Power Individually Addressable Monolithic Array of Constricted Double Heterojunction Large-Optical-Cavity Lasers," *Applied Physics Letters*, No. 41, 1982.

[34] O. Wada, H. Nobuhara, T. Sanada, M. Kuno, M. Makiuchi, T. Fujii, and T. Sakurai, "Optoelectronic Integrated Four Channel Transmitter Array Incorporating AlGaAs/GaAs Quantum Well Lasers," *IEEE Journal of Lightwave Technology*, Vol. 7, No. 1, pp. 186–197, Jan. 1989.

[35] N. Yamanaka, M. Sasaki, S. Kikuchi, T. Takada, and M. Idda, "A Gigabit-Rate Five-Highway GaAs OE-LSI Chipset for High-Speed Optical Interconnections Between Modules or VLSI's," *IEEE Journal of Lightwave Technology*, Vol. 9, No. 5, June 1991.

[36] K. Kaede, T. Uji, T. Nagahori, T. Suzaki, T. Torikai, J. Hayashi, I. Watanabe, M. Itoh, H. Honmou, and M. Shikada, ''12-Channel Parallel Optical-Fiber Transmission Using a Low-Drive Current 1.3-μm LED Array and a p-i-n PD Array,'' *IEEE Journal of Lightwave Technology*, pp. 883–888, June 1990.

[37] Y. Ota, R. C. Miller, S. R. Forrest, D. R. Kaplan, C. W. Seabury, R. B. Huntington, J. G. Johnson, and J. R. Potopowicz, ''Twelve-Channel Individually Addressable INGaAs/InP p-i-n Photodiode and InGaAsP/InP LED Arrays in a Compact Package,'' *IEEE Journal of Lightwave Technology*, Vol. 5, No. 8, pp. 1118–1122, 1987.

[38] D. L. McDaniel, Jr., J. G. McInerney, M. Y. A. Raja, C. F. Schaus, and S. R. J. Brueck, ''Vertical Cavity Surface-Emitting Semiconductor Laser with CW Injection Laser Pumping,'' *IEEE Photonic Technology Letters*, Vol. 2, No. 3, Mar. 1990.

[39] R. S. Geels, S. W. Corzine, J. W. Scott, D. B. Young, and L. A. Coldren, ''Low Threshold Planarized Vertical-Cavity Surface Emitting Lasers,'' *IEEE Photonic Technology Letters*, Vol. 2, No. 4, Apr. 1990.

[40] Y. H. Lee, B. Tell, K. Brown-Goebeler, J. L. Jewell, C. A. Burrus, and J. M. V. Hove, ''Characteristics of Top-Surface-Emitting GaAs Quantum-Well Lasers,'' *IEEE Photonic Technology Letters*, Vol. 2, No. 9, Sept. 1990.

[41] J. L. Jewell, Y. H. Lee, A. Scherer, S. L. McCall, N. A. Olsson, J. P. Harbison, and L. T. Florez, ''Surface-Emitting Microlasers for Photonic Switching and Interchip Connections,'' *Optical Engineering*, Vol. 29, No. 3, Mar. 1990.

[42] M. Uhle, ''The Influence of Source Impedance on the Electrooptical Switching Behavior of LED's,'' *IEEE Transactions on Electron Devices*, Vol. 23, pp. 438–441, 1976.

[43] R. Olshansky and D. Fye, ''Reduction of Dynamic Linewidth in Single-Frequency Semiconductor Lasers,'' *Electronic Letters*, Vol. 20, pp. 928–929, 1984.

[44] L. Bickers and L. D. Westbrook, ''Reduction of Laser Chirp in 1.5 μm DFB Lasers by modulation pulse shaping,'' *Electronic Letters*, Vol. 21, pp. 103–104, 1985.

[45] M. A. Karr, F. S. Chen, and P. W. Shumate, ''Output Power Stability of GaAlAs Laser Transmitter Using an Optical Tap for Feedback Control,'' *Applied Optics* No. 18, pp. 1262–1265, 1979.

[46] P. W. Shumate, F. S. Chen, and P. W. Dorman, ''GaAlAs Laser Transmitter for Lightwave Transmission Systems,'' *Bell System Technical Journal*, Vol. 57, pp. 1823–1836, 1978.

[47] D. W. Smith and M. R. Matthews, ''Laser Transmitter Design for Optical Fiber Systems,'' *IEEE Journal of Selective Area Communications*, pp. 515–523, 1983.

[48] R. G. Schwatz and B. A. Wooley, ''Stabilized Biasing of Semiconductor Lasers,'' *Bell System Technical Journal*, Vol. 62, pp. 1923–1936, 1983.

[49] K. P. Jackson, C. Harder, P. Buchmann, and K. Datwyler, ''High-Speed Characterization of a Monolithically Integrated GaAs-AlGaAs Quantum-Well Laser-Detector,'' *IEEE Photonic Technology Letters*, Vol. 2, No. 11, Nov. 1990.

[50] Jorg Wieland and Hans Melchior, ''Optical Receivers in ECL for 1GHz Parallel Links,'' *SPIE Proceedings of International Symposium on Advances in Interconnection and Packaging*, Vol. 1389, pp. 659–664, 1990.

[51] M. Makiuchi, H. Hamaguchi, T. Kumai, M. Ito, O. Wada, and T. Sakurai, ''A Monolithic Four-Channel Photoreceiver Integrated on GaAs Substrate Using Metal-Semi-

conductor-Metal Photodiodes and FET's," *IEEE Electronic Device Letters*, Vol. 6, No. 12, pp. 634–635, 1985.

[52] J. D. Crow, "Optical Interconnects for High-Performance Data Processing Systems," *Proc. IOOC'89*, 1989.

[53] N. Yamanaka and T. Takada, "A 1.5 Gbit/s GaAs Four-Channel Selector LSI with Monolithically Integrated Newly Structured GaAs Ohmic Contact MSM Photodetector and Laser Driver," *IEEE Photonic Technology Letters*, Vol. 1, No. 10, pp. 310–312, 1989.

[54] M. G. Brown, P. H.-S. Hu, D. R. Kaplan, Y. Ota, C. W. Seabury, M. A. Washington, E. E. Becker, J. G. Johnson, M. Koza, and J. R. Potopowicz, "Monolithically Integrated 1 x 12 Array of Planar InGaAs/InP Photodiodes," *IEEE Journal of Lightwave Technology*, Vol. 4, No. 3, pp. 283–287, Mar. 1986.

[55] J. D. Crow, C. J. Anderson, S. Bermon, A. Callegari, J. F. Ewen, J. D. Feder, J. H. Greiner, E. P. Harris, P. D. Hoh, H. J. Hovel, J. H. Magerlein, T. E. Mckoy, A. T. S. Pomerence, D. L. Rogers, G. J. Scott, M. Thomas, G. W. Mulvey, B. K. Ko, T. Ohashi, M. Scontras, and D. Widiger, "A GaAs MESFET IC for Optical Multi-processor Network," *IEEE Transaction on Electron Devices*, Vol. 36, p. 263, 1989.

[56] L. Yang, A. S. Sudbo, R. A. Logan, T. Tanbun-Ek, and W. T. Tsang, "High Performance of Fe:InP/InGaAs Metal/Semiconductor/Metal Photodetectors Grown by Metalorganic Vapor Phase Epitaxy," *IEEE Photonics Technology Letters*, Vol. 2, No. 1, pp. 56–58, Jan. 1990.

[57] L. Yang, A. S. Sudbo, W. T. Tsang, P. A. Garbinski, and R. M. Camarda, "Monolithically Integrated InGaAs/InP MSM-FET Photoreceiver Prepared by Chemical Beam Epitaxy," *IEEE Photonic Technology Letters*, Vol. 2, No. 1, pp. 59–62, 1990.

[58] D. L. Rogers, J. M. Woodal, G. D. Pettit, and D. McInturff, "High-Speed 1.3 μm GaInAs Detectors Fabricated on GaAs," *IEEE Electronic Device Letters*, Vol. 9, No. 10, Oct. 1988, pp. 515–517.

[59] M. Ito and O. Wada, "Low Dark Current GaAs Metal-Semiconductor-Metal (MSM) Photodiodes Using WSIx Contacts," *IEEE Journal of Quantum Electronics*, Vol. 22, No. 7, pp. 1073–1077, July 1986.

[60] L. Figueroa and C. W. Slayman, "A Novel Heterostructure Interdigital Photodetector (HIP) with Picosecond Optical Response," *IEEE Electron Device Letters*, Vol. 2, No. 8, pp. 208–210, Aug. 1981.

[61] W. C. Koscielniak, R. M. Kolbas, and M. A. Littlejohn, "Performance of a Near-Infrared GaAs Metal-Semiconductor-Metal (MSM) Photodetector with Islands," *IEEE Electron Device Letters*, Vol. 9, No. 9, pp. 485–487, 1988.

[62] B. J. Van Zeghbroeck, W. Patrick, Jean-Marc Halbout, and P. Vettiger, "105 GHz Bandwidth Metal-Semiconductor-Metal Photodiodes," *IEEE Electron Device Letters*, Vol. 9, No. 10, pp. 527–529, Oct. 1988.

[63] H. Schumacher, H. P. Leblanc, J. Soole, and R. Bhat, "An Investigation of the Optoelectronic Response of GaAs/InGaAs MSM Photodetectors," *IEEE Electron Device Letters*, Vol. 9, No. 11, Nov. 1988, pp. 607–609.

[64] W.-P. Hong, G.-K. Chang, and R. Bhat, "High Performance :f.Al sub 0.15 Ga sub 0.85 As / In sub 0.53 Ga sub 0.47 As:ef. MSM Photodetectors Grown by OMCVD," *IEEE Transaction on Electron Device*, Vol. 36, No. 4, pp. 659–662, April 1989.

[65] W. Roth, H. Schumacher, J. Kluge, H. J. Geelen, and H. Beneking, "The DSI Diode— A Fast Large-Area Optoelectronic Detector," *IEEE Transactions on Electron Devices*, No. 6, pp. 1034–1036, June 1985.

[66] K. Nakajima, T. Iida, K.-I. Sugimoto, H. Kan, and Y. Mizushima, "Properties and Design Theory of Ultrafast GaAs Metal-Semiconductor-Metal Photodetector with Symmetrical Schottky Contacts," *IEEE Transactions on Electron Devices*, Vol. 37, No. 1, pp. 31–35, Jan. 1990.

[67] J. B. D. Soole and H. Schumacher, "Transit-Time Limited Frequency Response of InGaAs MSM Photodetectors," *IEEE Transactions on Electron Devices*, Vol. 37, No. 11, Nov. 1990, pp. 2285–2291.

[68] D. Kuhl, F. Hieronymi, E. H. Bottcher, and D. Bimberg, "High-Speed Metal-Semiconductor-Metal Photodetectors on InP/Fe," *IEEE Photonic Technology Letters*, Vol. 2, No. 8, pp. 574–576, Aug. 1990.

[69] O. Wada, H. Hamaguchi, L. Le Beller, and C. Y. Boisrobert, "Noise Characteristics of GaAs Metal-Semiconductor-Metal Photodiodes," *Electronic Letters*, Vol. 24, No. 25, pp. 1574–1575, Dec. 1988.

[70] T. Kikuchi, H. Ohno, and H. Hasegawa, "$Ga_{0.47}In_{0.53}As$ Metal-Semiconductor-Metal Photodiodes Using a Lattice Mismatched $Al_{0.4}Ga_{0.6}As$ Schottky Assist Layer," *Electronic Letters*, Vol. 24, No. 19, pp. 1208–1210, 1988.

[71] E. Sano, "A Device Model for Metal-Semiconductor-Metal Photodetectors and Its Applications to Optoelectronic Integrated Circuit Simulation," *IEEE Transactions on Electron Device*, Vol. 37, No. 9, pp. 1964–1968, Sept. 1990.

[72] W. C. Koscielniak, Jean-Luc Pelouard, and M. A. Littlejohn, "Intrinsic and Extrinsic Response of GaAs Metal-Semiconductor-Metal Photodetectors," *IEEE Photonic Technology Letters*, Vol. 2, No. 2, pp. 125–127, Feb. 1990.

[73] W.-P. Hong, G.-K. Chang, R. Bhat, H. Lee, C. Nguyen, and J. R. Hayes, "High-Functionality Waveguide/MSM/HEMT Integrated Receiver Prepared by One-Step OMCVD Grown on Patterned InP Substrates," *Proc. OFC'91*, p. 5, Feb. 1991.

[74] Stutius and W. Streifer "Silicon Nitride Films on Silicon for Optical Waveguides," *Applied Optics*, Vol. 6, No. 12, pp. 3218–3222, 1977.

[75] B. L. Booth "Low Loss Channel Waveguides in Polymers," *IEEE Journal of Lightwave Technology*, Vol. 7, No. 10, pp. 1445–1453, Oct. 1989.

[76] J. M. Trewhella "Polymeric Optical Waveguides," *Proc. SPIE*, Vol. 1177, pp. 379–386, 1989.

[77] M. Dagenais, R. Leheny, H. Temkin, and P. Bhattacharya, "Application and Challenges of OEIC Technology: A Report on the 1989 Hilton Head Workshop," *IEEE Journal of Lightwave Technology*, Vol. 8, No. 6, pp. 846–862, 1990.

[78] C.-S. Li and H. S. Stone, "Differential Board/Backplane Optical Interconnects for High-Speed Digital Systems Part I: Theory," *IEEE Journal of Lightwave Technologies*, Vol. 11, No. 7, July 1993, pp. 1234–1249.

[79] C. M. Olsen and C.-S. Li, "Differential Board/Backplane Optical Interconnects for High-Speed Digital Systems Part II: Simulation Results," *IEEE Journal of Lightwave Technologies*, Vol. 11, No. 7, July 1993, pp. 1250–1262.

[80] C.-S. Li, H. S. Stone, Y. Kwark, and C. M. Olsen, "Fully Differential Optical Interconnections for High-Speed Digital Systems," *IEEE Transactions on VLSI Systems*, Vol.1, No. 2, June 1993, pp. 151–163.

[81] Y.-M. Wong et al., "Technology Development of a High-Density 32-Channel 16 Gb/s Optical Data Link for Optical Interconnection Applications for the Optoelectronic Technology Consortium (OETC)," *Journal of Lightwave Technology*, Vol. 13, No. 6, pp. 995–1016, 1995.

[82] H. Karstensen, C. Hanke, M. Honsberg, J.-R. Kropp, J. Wieland, M. Blaser, P. Weger, and J. Popp, "Parallel Optical Interconnection for Uncoded Data Transmission with 1 Gb/s-per-Channel Capacity, High Dynamic Range, and Low Power Consumption," *Journal of Lightwave Technology*, Vol. 13, No. 6, pp. 1017–1030, 1995.

[83] J. W. Lockwood, H. Duan, J. J. Morikuni, S.-M. Kang, S. Akkineni, and R. H. Cambell, "Scalable Optoelectronic ATM Networks: The iPOINT Fully Functional Testbed," *Journal of Lightwave Technology*, Vol. 13, No. 6, pp. 1093–1103, 1995.

[84] K. H. Hahn and D. W. Dolfi, "POLO: A Gigabyte/s Parallel Optical Link," *SPIE Proc.*, Vol. CR62, Feb. 1996.

[85] W. S. Ishak, K. H. Hahn, B. L. Booth, C. Mueller, A. A. J. Levi, and R. Craig, "Optical Interconnects: The POLO Approach," *SPIE Proc.*, Vol. 2400, pp. 214–221, Feb. 1995.

[86] Y. S. Liu et al., "Polymer Optical Interconnect Technology (POINT): optoelectronic packaging and interconnect for board and backplane interconnects," *SPIE Proc.*, Vol. CR62, Feb. 1996.

Chapter 13

NETWORKS FOR THE PROFESSIONAL CAMPUS ENVIRONMENT

B. J. Sano and A. F. J. Levi

Abstract

This chapter describes the challenges of effectively utilizing distributed resources in a new Professional Campus Environment. In this environment, the synthesis and manipulation of multimedia data from physically distinct locations is a critical activity that requires development of advanced network technology. Such a network will make use of fiber-optic interconnects, high-throughput, low-latency data transfer protocols and visualization servers based on scalable clusters of high-performance workstations. Cost-effective delivery of high-resolution real-time image data is possible if the visualization clusters are interconnected via a very broadband backbone. We describe an approach that makes use of advanced networking technologies, including a multi-Gbps parallel fiber-optic link technology currently being developed as part of a Hewlett-Packard/USC program. The major challenge and goal of this campus-based network is to develop and demonstrate efficient Gbps data transfer within and between cluster servers. A long-term objective is to realize a practical networked interactive-visualization system capable of serving remote campus locations.

13.1 INTRODUCTION

In recent years, remarkable progress has been made in developing powerful, inexpensive desktop personal computers. The cost performance of these stand-alone units exceeds that of all other computer platforms due in part to economies of scale and intense competition between vendors. At the same time, advances have been made in long-distance communications. Telephone companies have slowly developed asynchronous transfer mode (ATM) [1] capability as the future solution to wide area networking (WAN). The Internet's World Wide Web, which makes use of telephone lines and Ethernet, has grown explosively. Web users are serviced by a plethora of products, all of which attempt to bypass conventional means of communication and distribution by delivering their services directly to the desktop personal computer. Examples include provision of long-distance telephone service, company advertising, and discount brokerage services. Because of the limited bandwidth of Ethernet and limitations to the underlying WAN communication infrastructure, much effort has been made to develop lossy compression techniques to meet the ever-increasing demands and expectations of Web users. True multimedia services to the desktop will require a cost-effective means of delivering video, audio, and data on-demand and in real time. However, services of this type will be developed and delivered to the user with as yet unknown levels of quality. Meanwhile, the need to provide product and content for this growing network will increase. In addition, new needs and expectations will be driven by the mere existence of even a low-quality communications infrastructure.

A new Professional Campus Environment will emerge from this situation to meet the multimedia needs of professional organizations. Campus entities such as hospitals, advertising agencies, video production houses, city government, museums, and technologically intensive manufacturing centers will require new networks capable of supporting the creation, distribution, storage, and retrieval of uncompressed, interactive, real-time multimedia services. These Professional Campus Environments are characterized by specialized groups of professionals who are interconnected and collaborate within a single network administration. Unlike traditional network environments, the quality of service within a Professional Campus Environment has direct impact on and is intimately coupled to product. Product is, of course, defined as output resulting from the professional activity. In a Professional Campus, large databases and computational resources are distributed within and between buildings and are required to communicate with Gbps rates and microsecond latencies. The minimum requirement for such networks is the ability to support digital video to the desktop. The common D1 (CCIR-601 [2]) digital video format used in production of NTSC programming requires sustained data transfer rates greater than 250 Mbps. At present, even high-performance workstations are unable to achieve and sustain such performance. Future users of the Professional Campus will require networks capable of supporting multiple desktop displays, each of which requires in excess of 1 Gbps sustained throughput. Such needs are far beyond anything available today or planned for the near future.

The term *campus* as used here loosely defines a broad class of professional settings in which specialized personnel are naturally partitioned into clusters or departments physically separated over a campus setting. A hospital is a good example of a Professional Campus. Within a hospital, medical specialists are partitioned into departments (e.g., administration, imaging, operating rooms, recovery, etc.). All of these specialized departments utilize computers for data storage, management, or processing. For example, CAT scan images are synthesized with the assistance of specialized computers. Computers are also used to store or transpose to film vast quantities of high-resolution images. Administration is another example of a specialized group of professionals. In this case, the staff is focused on processing numerous insurance and regulatory forms. They are also responsible for complex billing and accounting procedures. In a hospital environment, approximately 30% of the cost associated with delivering health care is directly attributable to the cost of processing information associated with a patient [3]. Such costs could be reduced considerably by providing a network that would enable a paperless information environment, including the delivery of multimedia data to specialists for diagnosis.

The challenge for networks in the future Professional Campus Environment is to develop a cost-effective and cost-scalable solution that delivers high quality of service to the application layer within the campus and yet effectively bridges to an ATM WAN environment. As will become clear in the following sections, while some individual components have the required bandwidth to communicate between entities of this network, there remain important bottlenecks in data flow due to system architecture, media access control, network flow control protocols, operating systems, and application software implementation which all conspire to severely limit perceived quality of service to the user. Starting from the lowest of the network layers, we describe the physical links, network interfaces, and network protocols for distributed visualization applications for the Professional Campus Environment.

13.2 ADVANCED FIBER-OPTIC PHYSICAL LAYER TECHNOLOGIES

Viewed as a system-level packaging problem, networking is merely a way to interconnect components of a distributed system. Because large systems are, by their very nature, constructed from a number of smaller components, cost-effective approaches to interconnection and packaging is a fundamental issue faced by any system designer. Often, the competitive advantage of a given system is determined by the system integration and interconnection strategy made by the system designer. Figure 13.1 illustrates, as a function of interconnection length scale, dominant interconnection technologies in high-performance systems [4].

Electrical interconnects are the solution of choice for intra- and interchip connections on length scales up to approximately 1 m. The reason for this is simply that no viable

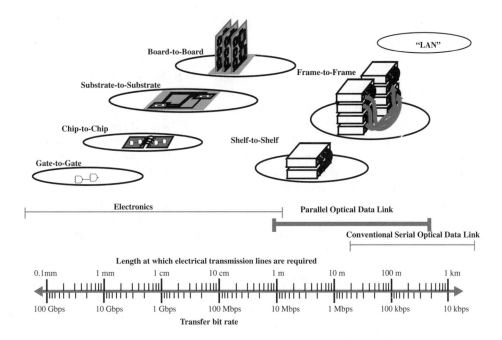

Figure 13.1 The insertion of parallel optical data links solves an I/O bottleneck for interconnects on length scales of 1 m to a few 100 m. Future applications for highly integrated parallel optic modules include insertion into systems with interconnect length scales of less than a meter.

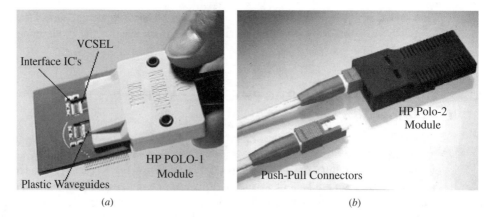

Figure 13.2   The left picture shows the HP POLO-1 Transceiver Module
which uses low-cost plastic components to deliver a very high-
performance physical layer for future fiber-optic networks. The
picture on the right is the more advanced HP POLO-2 Module
with a compact BGA package and push-pull fiber ribbon connectors.

cost-effective alternative has emerged. On length scales greater than several tens of meters,
conventional serial fiber-optic local area network (LAN) technologies such as Fiber Channel [5], ATM (OC12, OC48), and FDDI [6] have been successfully implemented in both
experimental and commercial campus environments.

As shown in Fig. 13.1, there exists an opportunity for advanced parallel fiber-optic
technologies to impact high-performance system design on length scales from 1 m to a
few 100 m. Parallel fiber-optic modules are a potentially low-cost solution to a specific
I/O bottleneck that has developed in large telecommunication and supercomputer systems
[7]. This bottleneck, which exists in electrical systems, arises because of the high density of relatively slow-speed electrical connections needed at the edge of cards, shelves
and between frames. Parallel optics with its high form-factor and high speed offers an excellent technical solution to this bottleneck. The cost of system implementation has been
driven down to an attractive level by advances in components such as Vertical Cavity Surface Emitting Lasers (VCSELs) [8] plastic waveguides, plastic array connectors [9], and
low-skew fiber-optic ribbons [10]. Figure 13.2 shows an example of just such a low-cost
transceiver developed by Hewlett-Packard called the Parallel Optical Link Organization
(POLO) Module.

It is possible to leverage this interconnection technology into other systems such as
workstation clusters needed for the Professional Campus Environment for length scales
that fit within and between buildings. New types of distributed computing resources with
new classes of service may naturally evolve as a consequence of integrating parallel optics
into otherwise electronic systems. Clearly, future systems will make use of fiber optics. The

exact form and extent of implementation will be determined by the cost and system benefit of available optical technologies. As illustrated in Fig. 13.1, in the future we anticipate that low-cost high-performance parallel optical interconnects will increasingly find use at shorted length scales and ultimately be inserted into the core of advanced computing and communications systems.

13.3 HIGH-PERFORMANCE NETWORK INTERFACES

The existence of low-cost fiber-optic solutions for system interconnects is only one aspect of the problem. Clearly, a fiber-optic physical layer has the ability to deliver high bandwidth to the desktop. However, high-performance network interfaces must also be available. Unfortunately, some implementations are intrinsically more expensive than others. A simple example involves solutions based on a central switch. Such approaches are not cost-scalable and are therefore not attractive to the user, because the user does not wish to pay for an expensive network switch that is never fully used. Rather, there must be either a modular switch design or a distributed switch that consists of identical elements and is scalable (at least to a reasonable degree). The concept of a cost-scalable system is important and must be addressed by the network system designer. The notion of a conventional centralized switched system does not survive in this scenario.

Shared-medium networks such as rings are a well-known solution to the domain of medium-scale cluster interconnects [11,12], and it is this approach that we have adopted in our experimental systems at USC. The ring is a undirectional slotted ring called the POLO Network [7]. Clusters within this network consist of machines distributed over part of the floor of a building. (If they sit on the same carpet, we might call them ''Carpet Clusters.'') The average length of the fiber-optic cable connecting adjacent nodes of the cluster might be 10 m, corresponding to a 50 ns signal delay. The performance of the POLO Module also permits even longer links up to several 100 m. However, balancing the node latency with an average fiber delay of 10 m requires developing network interfaces with individual ring node delays of less than 50 ns.

Figure 13.3 shows the data path for a single-chip Link Adapter (LA Chip) network interface developed at USC. The LA Chip is designed to provide all of the high-speed interface and media access control for the POLO Network. The chip contains the host interface and virtual channel identifiers (VCI) that assist in efficient (AAL-5) message demultiplexing at the device driver level. At the physical link level, the POLO Module provides a 10 Gbps signaling capability (i.e., 10 channels each signaling at 1 Gbps) for both the transmit and receive interfaces. At present, the unidirectional slotted ring has a bisection bandwidth in excess of 16 Gbps and is likely to be upgraded to 32 Gbps. To achieve this performance, separate clock and frame control channels have been allocated leaving an 8-wide data path for the POLO Network. Separating the clock channel simplifies clock extraction and distribution on-chip. The allocation of a separate frame control line simplifies detection on valid frames at the data link level and allows encoding of other control information (e.g., ring status) without interfering with the data path. This yields an 8 Gbps receive and transmit data rate per node for an aggregate 16 Gbps data bisection bandwidth per module.

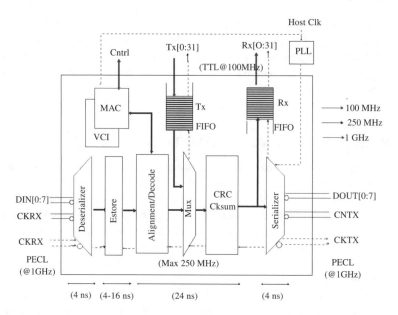

Figure 13.3   Block diagram of Link Adapter (LA) Chip which implements the Media Access Control (MAC) functions of the 10 Gbps POLO Network. High-speed bytewide PCEL interfaces directly attach to the POLO Module. The internal data path of the LA Chip contains all of the MAC functionality and network buffering.

Both the control and data channels are deserialized on-chip to a 250 MHz clock rate for further processing and buffering. Currently, a 0.8 micron CMOS version of the LA Chip has a minimum node latency of less than 50 ns. A future 0.5 micron CMOS design with modifications to the Media Access Control protocol will exhibit minimum node latencies of less than 15 ns, suitable for average interconnection lengths of less than 3 m.

Figure 13.4 illustrates a fabricated test die for the high-speed core of the physical link layer portion of the LA Chip. At this physical link level, an elastic store (estore) is used to compensate for clock variation between workstations and allow for large (e.g., 2 KB) packets to be sent over the links. No signal encoding of the data, control, or clock is used since the VCSELs are robust and d.c. coupled to the system. Once the complete header of a network packet is available to the media access controller, it processes the packet and consults a Virtual Channel Identifier (VCI) table for unicast and multicast mapping or uses a ring identifier to address the station.

The Media Access Control (MAC) design implements a slotted ring protocol for low-latency message transmission. Most of the cluster applications will have 16 to 32 nodes per ring. With a node latency and an average fiber delay of 50 ns each, this implies an average ring latency of 1.6 to 3.2 microseconds, and for random ring destination addressing with mean transmission length of half the ring circumference, the average packet latency is 0.8 to

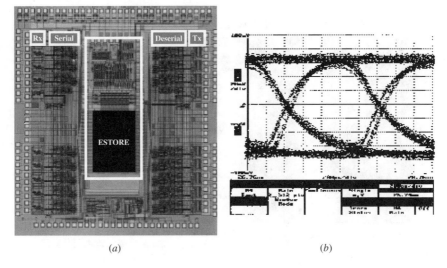

(a)   (b)

Figure 13.4   To the left is a photograph of a test die for the physical link
layer interface of the LA Chip. The die contains the PECL Rx,
deserializer, estore, serializer, and Tx circuitry. The die measures
4 mm x 4 mm in 0.8 micron CMOS. To the right is a measurement
eye diagram of error-free data passing through a PECL interface
as part of the physical layer.

1.6 microseconds. Application-to-application latency will depend on the number and size
of slots programmed and the nature of the messages along with the software overheads in
the operation system interface.

   The POLO Network has been optimized for applications that require the transmission
of large packets of information (e.g. high-resolution image data or pages of networked
memory), all within medium-scale clusters of high-performance workstation and personal
computers. Alternative cluster interconnects and experimental systems do exist (e.g., SCI
[11], Myrinet [13], or S-Connect [14]). However, these interconnects are optimized for low-
latency fine-grain message traffic and require costly interfaces or switches. In contrast, the
USC POLO Network is a very high-performance, cost-effective solution for interconnecting
a cluster. The network utilizes the broadband nature of the POLO Module to simplify the
organization and operations of the network interface.

   The first version of the USC POLO Network interface will replace link adapter functions such as the 1 Gbps experimental JetStream interface [15]. The new link adapter board
will contain the CMOS Link Adapter (LA Chip), which directly interfaces to the POLO
Module and to external synchronous FIFO buffers of the Afterburner host interface board
[16]. This design approach allows use of the LA Chip with generic bus architectures. For
example, Fig. 13.5 illustrates a future POLO Network card that will be able to interface
to the PCI standard bus or other "open" bus standards, thereby significantly increasing

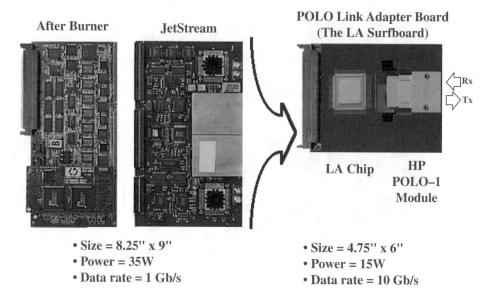

After Burner	JetStream	POLO Link Adapter Board (The LA Surfboard)

- Size = 8.25" x 9"
- Power = 35W
- Data rate = 1 Gb/s

- Size = 4.75" x 6"
- Power = 15W
- Data rate = 10 Gb/s

Figure 13.5   The POLO Network Interface replaces the function of JetStream and provides a 10-times increase in signaling rate. The POLO Interface fits on a single-sided board, which is smaller than the double-sided JetStream board.

the number of potential system platforms. The approach allows early demonstration of the POLO Network while leaving open other possible development paths.

13.4 NEW PROTOCOLS FOR LOW-LATENCY AND HIGH SUSTAINED THROUGHPUT

Even if the physical layer (fiber-optic components, lasers, network interface, etc.) has the required bandwidth, latency, and cost structure, the system designer may still reject the networked Carpet Cluster approach for other reasons. One important consideration is the ability of network protocols to provide the appropriate levels of service required by the user. Recall that our minimum requirement of interactive D1 digital video to any desktop requires sustained application-to-application one-way throughput of over 250 Mbps.

By reducing the number of physical memory data copies in Transmission Control Protocol (TCP), dramatically enhanced sustained application-to-application throughputs have been achieved in HP Series 700 workstations using the JetStream [15] experimental network. JetStream is a Gbps network developed by Hewlett-Packard Laboratories at Bristol, England, and is being used as an experimental network system at USC. As part of our system evaluation, we have performed a number of network tests and comparisons. The measured throughput as of function of message size for the JetStream network is illustrated in

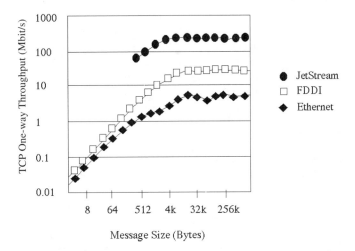

Figure 13.6   Measured sustained one-way TCP throughput on an HP 700 series workstation as a function of message size for the indicated
networks.

Fig. 13.6. A maximum sustained application-to-application throughput of 200 Mbps is measured for one-copy TCP. This is almost twice the throughput of a two-copy TCP but still
below the maximum theoretical throughput of the system bus (the Standard Graphics Connector bus) owing to limitations imposed by the memory and system bus controller within
the Series 700 workstations. Also shown in the figure are results of using conventional
Ethernet and FDDI networks.

The sustained throughput of all the networks saturates for message sizes of about
4 KB corresponding to main-memory page size. For applications that involve distributed
computing, retrieval of image-format data from multiple sources, and the like, it would
be beneficial if this saturation were to occur at much smaller message sizes since such
applications involve passing many small messages to establish and maintain data flow and
data process synchronization.

In addition to reducing the copying of data, an important technique that has been
shown to reduce message latency is the concept of active messages in which a process at the
receiving node can start before the complete message has arrived [17]. This is achieved by
including in the message the address of the function that is to be invoked upon arrival at the
destination. Another approach used by Hamlyn [18] creates a high-performance network
interface by implementing sender-based memory management. Ultimately, changes to the
operating system have to be made so that these methods of improving throughput and
reducing latency are both invisible to the user and safe to use in a multiprogramming
environment.

An interesting case in point is the concept of zero-copy protocol and the notion of
networked display (Fig. 13.7). Networked video will, under certain circumstances, only
require display and little if any destination processing. In this situation, it makes little sense

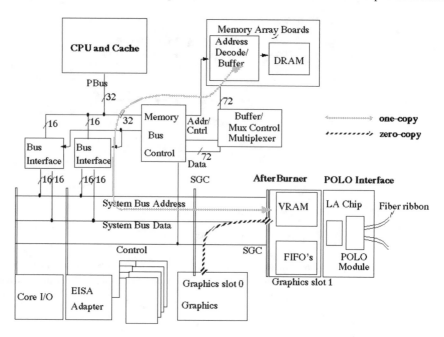

Figure 13.7   HP 755 with AfterBurner and JetStream Network Interface showing the concept of zero-copy to frame buffer of the graphics card
and the implementation of one-copy from the network to the
main memory.

to copy data first from the network to main memory and then to the display frame buffer.
Rather, a networked display should take data directly from the network. Overlay of a subset
of display can be provided by the host or the network. Unfortunately, simple display and
overlay do not allow rudimentary intelligent functions such as tracking of features or objects
in the video stream. This type of functionality requires computation by the processor and
hence, at least partial image-format data storage in main memory. At this point, it becomes
clear that a change in architecture could be of great potential benefit. In particular, it would be
helpful if the network, processor, frame buffer, main memory, and so on, were served more
democratically. By this we mean that the network, processor, display, and main memory
all have essentially equal access to what is traditionally the processor bus. In this situation,
processor performance might not be optimized, but the overall functionality and potential
utility of the networked system could be dramatically enhanced.

   Initial changes to system architecture which attempt to solve some of these difficulties
have already been implemented by a number of vendors. These new organizations are
designed to accommodate concurrent access or transfer at high-sustained data rates between
the processor, memory, and I/O. An example of this implementation is illustrated in Fig.
13.8. This architecture uses four data path switch chips, a control interface chip, and a PCI
controller chip to effectively form a switch-based architecture [19]. Ultimately, this six-

AlphaStation 600 Architecture

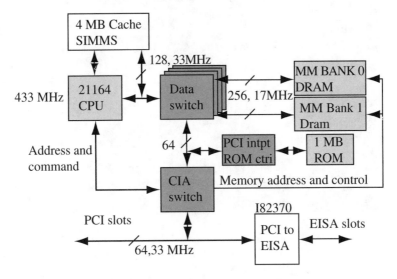

Figure 13.8   The Alpha 600 architecture uses a chip-set to implement a switching function within a workstation. The switch can be enhanced to a nonblocking switch with dedicated ports to processors, memory, I/O, and networks.

chip set will be replaced by a single nonblocking crossbar switch providing access between main memory, multiple processors, I/O, and high-bandwidth networks such as the POLO Network. The user-preceived improvement to quality of service in a Campus Network will manifest itself by the availability of new services, which are characterized by high-sustained data throughput between distributed system resources.

13.5 THE NEED FOR VERTICAL INTEGRATION FROM PHYSICAL LAYERS TO APPLICATION INTERFACES

Understanding and ultimately solving the quality of service issue for Carpet Clusters and the Professional Campus Environment require an unusual level of vertical integration. Target applications have to be developed, and these applications are used to drive the underlying operating system, network protocols, and physical layer. The central research issue is simultaneous optimization of hardware, protocols, parallel graphics, and computation architectures to meet the needs of future networked multimedia and visualization systems. Our approach has been to combine state-of-the-art hardware and software to demonstrate a specific distributed data-visualization application within a high-performance workstation-cluster environment. Figure 13.9 illustrates our specialized hospital visualization application

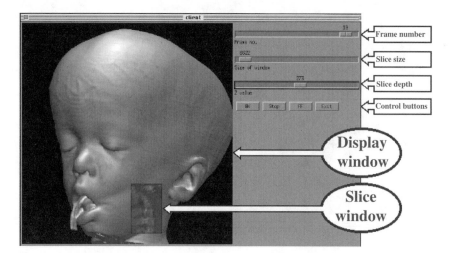

Figure 13.9   Illustration of a Graphical User Interface for a distributed medical
visualization application. Data flows over a high-performance
network from different locations on the Professional Campus.
The specialist accesses image data in real time and at interactive
rates.

implemented at USC with an experimental cluster of workstations, the JetStream interface,
and a POLO Module.

In this distributed medical application, a collection of CAT scan images of a child's
head have been volume rendered. The rendered images serve as orientation for slices of
the internal images. The doctor can rotate the head and then cut a slice window of the
volume image. This distributed visualization application uses three computers. One computer stores the raw CAT scan images and calculates the slice window requested by the
user. Another computer renders the volume image of the head and sends the images to a
third computer, which combines the volume rendered images along with the internal slice
images. This application illustrates many of the challenges associated with a Professional
Campus Environment. First, the computing, storage, and display platforms are physically
distributed among spatially separate departments. Second, the professionals demand large
high-resolution, lossless images because the quality of the images determines the quality
of diagnosis. Third, the timely delivery of these images and raw data is essential to the
efficiency of the professional (i.e., impacts time spent processing a patient). Combining all
three of these characteristics places considerable demand on any network for a Professional
Campus Environment.

Experimental results of this USC cluster (Fig. 13.10) indicate that a high-resolution
medical image of the volume and internal slices can be presented to the specialist at nearly
full frame rate (Fig. 13.11). However, as the slice window size increases to expose more of
the internal structure, the animation is slowed considerably. The slowdown occurs because
of the increased time required for calculating the slice image. Since in this three-machine

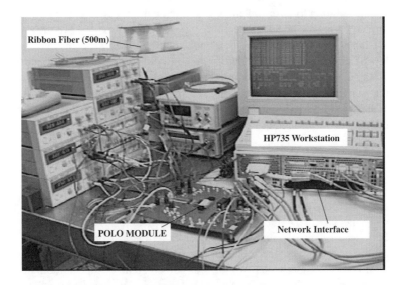

Figure 13.10   Photograph of the HP POLO-1 Module with two channels connected to the workstation interface. An HP 735 and 755 (not
shown) are used for the nodes in the network. The JetStream
board has SMA connectors for a 1 Gbps differential serial interface. These connectors are cabled to a prototype board containing the POLO Module.

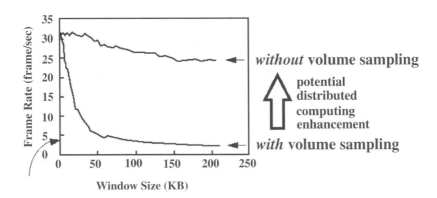

Figure 13.11   Experimental results of the frame rate versus slice window size
of the medical imaging application for a small cluster of workstations.

experiment only one computer is assigned this task, the overall display rate slows. The natural solution to this problem is to distribute the slice calculation task to other potentially unused computer nodes in the cluster. Unfortunately, in this experimental setting, none is available. But if there were such nodes, the 256 CAT scan images, each containing 128 KB of information (i.e., 32 MB/volume), could be distributed at startup in one second. Then slice calculation could proceed in parallel with small synchronization and command messages directing the computation. However, this procedure will saturate the experimental 1 Gbps network during startup for one-volume rendering and does not scale well with larger image sets or multiple users.

13.6 CONCLUSIONS

It is clear that even a 1 Gbps experimental network can barely handle a representative real-time, interactive Professional Campus application as demonstrated with the distributed CAT scan medical visualization server experiment. Although this is only one example, it illustrates many of the problems that Professional Campus Environments will pose for future advanced networks. We have described some of the technologies that will address these problems with a cost-effective slotted ring network called the POLO Network, which uses multi-Gbps parallel fiber-optic modules to interconnect computer clusters within and between buildings. Quality of service is achieved within our new workstation clusters by designing into the network interface hardware guaranteed bandwidth and latency at the Media Access Control level. In our specific, targeted medical visualization application, use of conventional high-performance graphics and computing is transformed into a new high-performance networked visualization system. In general, this type of medium-scale distributed computing will be of benefit to the broader scientific community and society by providing advanced cost-effective technologies well matched to important campus-based commercial activities such as CAD/CAM, multimedia creation, and other professional applications.

Acknowledgments

Part of this work is supported by DARPA under agreement MDA 972-94-0038. We also want to thank Professor Ulrich Neumann for help in developing the medical visualization code for the demonstration system.

References

[1] CCITT-I.361, ''B-ISDN ATM Layer Specification, Integrated Services Digital Network (ISDN), Overall Network,'' *International Telecommunications Union*, Geneva, 1993.
[2] CCIR Recommendation 601-2, ''Encoding Parameters of Digital Television for Studios,'' Vol. XI—Part 1, *International Telecommunications Union*, Geneva, 1990.
[3] B. Gilbert, Private Communications, *Mayo Foundation*.
[4] R. A. Nordin and A. F. J. Levi, ''A System Design Perspective on Optical Interconnection Technology,'' *AT&T Technical Journal*, Vol. 72, No. 5, pp. 37–49, 1993.

[5] ANSI X3.230:199x, "Fibre Channel—Physical and Signaling Interface (FC-PH)," *American National Standards Institute*, Aug. 1994.

[6] ANSI X3.148-1988, "Fiber Distributed Data Interface (FDDI)—Token Ring Physical Layer," *American Standards Institute*, Nov. 1988.

[7] K. H. Hahn, "POLO—Parallel Optical Links for Gbyte/s Data Communications," *45th Electronics Components and Technology Conference*, pp. 368–375, May 1995.

[8] K. H. Hahn et al., "Large Area Multi-Transverse Mode VCSELs for Modal Noise Reduction in Multimode Fibre Systems," *Electron Letters*, Vol. 29, pp. 1482–1483, 1993.

[9] T. Satke et al., "MT Multifiber Connectors and New Applications," *44th Electronics Components and Technology Conference*, pp. 994–999, May 1994.

[10] A. P. Kanjamala and A. F. J. Levi, "Sub-picosecond Skew in Multimode Fiber Ribbon for Synchronous Data Transmission," *Electron Letters*, Vol. 31, pp. 1376–1377, 1995.

[11] IEEE 1596-1992, "IEEE Standard for Scalable Coherent Interface (SCI)," *Institute of Electrical and Electronics Engineers*, 1993.

[12] I. Cidon and Y. Ofek, "MetaRing—A Full-Duplex Ring with Fairness and Spatial Reuse," em IEEE Trans. on Communications, Vol. 41, No. 1, pp. 110–120, 1993.

[13] N. Boden et al., "Myrinet—A Gigabit-per-second Local-Area Network," *IEEE Micro*, Vol. 15, No. 1, Feb. 1995,

[14] A. Nowatzyk et al., "S-Connect: From Networks of Workstations to Supercomputer Performance," *22nd Annual International Symposium on Computer Architecture*, pp. 71–82, June 1995.

[15] A. E. Edwards et al., "User-space Protocols Deliver High Performance to Applications on a Low-cost Gb/s LAN," *SIGCOMM94*, pp. 14–23, 1994.

[16] C. Dalton et al., "Afterburner," *IEEE Network*, Vol. 7, No. 4, pp. 36–43, 1993.

[17] T. von Eicken et al., "Active Messages: A Mechanism for Integrated Communication and Computation," *19th Annual International Symposium on Computer Architecture*, pp. 256–266, May 1992.

[18] G. Buzzard et al., "Hamlyn: A High-performance Network Interface with Sender-based Memory Management," *Hot Interconnects III*, Aug. 1995.

[19] Dileep Bhandarkar, "ALPHA Implementations and Architecture—A Complete Reference Guide," Digital Press, 1996.

MULTIMEDIA SIGNAL PROCESSING AND APPLICATIONS

Chapter 14

INTELLIGENT SPEECH/AUDIO PROCESSING FOR MULTIMEDIA APPLICATIONS

Oscal T.-C. Chen

Abstract

Intelligent speech and audio processing can provide efficient and smart interfaces for various multimedia applications. Generally, speech is the most natural form of human communication. Audio and music can enhance our emotional impacts and promote interest in multimedia applications. A successful interactive multimedia system must have the capabilities of speech and audio compression, text-to-speech conversion, speech understanding, and music synthesis. The main purpose of speech and audio compression is to provide cost-effective storage or to minimize transmission costs. Text-to-speech converts linguistic information stored as data or text into speech for the applications of talking terminals, alarm systems, and audiotext services. Speech understanding systems make it possible for people to interact with computers using human speech. Its success relies on the integration of a wide variety of speech technologies, including acoustic, lexical, syntactic, semantic, and pragmatic analyses. The applications of music processing for multimedia were mostly realized by means of the combination of music, graphics, video, and other media. Since musical sounds and compositions can be precisely specified and controlled by a computer, we can easily create artificial orchestras, performers, and composers. Nowadays, multimedia systems have become more sophisticated with the advances made in computer and microelectronic technologies. Many applications require efficient processing of speech and audio for interactive presentations and integration with other types of media. The application-specific hardwares are proposed to meet the high-speed, low-cost, lightweight, and low-power requirements. The design example of a speech recognition processor and system for voice-control applications is introduced. The industrial standards and commercial products of speech and audio processing are also summarized in this chapter.

14.1 INTRODUCTION

Multimedia is built on a group of infrastructure technologies that can coordinately manipulate and communicate the various media [1]. It integrates a variety of information sources, such as text, speech, graphics, music, image, audio, and video, into a wide range of applications, as shown in Fig. 14.1. This big picture shows multimedia as the merging technologies of computing, communication, and intelligent information processing for the applications of publishing, education, entertainment, industry, military, and medicine [2,3].

A computer platform with high-performance I/O devices, user-friendly software tools of information processing, and efficient communication networks is a fundamental multimedia system that can support the interactive use of speech, audio, still image, and motion video. Currently, speech and audio play important roles in multimedia applications, especially in point-of-sale or point-of-information systems [3]. A speech commentary can be

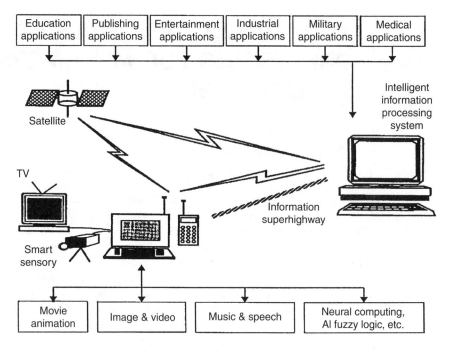

Figure 14.1 Multimedia systems.

used to narrate what is happening onscreen or to convey key concepts. Combined with pictures or animation, it can be used to explain an idea to the user in a more effective way than text or graphics alone. In addition, audio can be performed to attract customers' attention or to create a particular mood.

Traditionally, computers are used to process text and graphics with the help of keyboard and mouse. Today a multimedia system offers a rich range of interaction possibilities. The interaction devices give a user direct control over application behaviors. In order to achieve efficient communication between a person and a machine, an intelligent interface is required for a multimedia system. Speech processing is a core technology for realizing this service because speech is the most natural form of human communication. The development of an interactive multimedia system must have the capabilities of understanding fluently spoken speech, converting text to speech, and compressing speech data [4].

Multimedia combines speech, audio, and visual materials to enhance communication and enrich its presentation with creativity, conveying information and engaging the imagination [5]. It is not only adding intelligent interfaces, high-fidelity audio, and pretty pictures to the computers. Multimedia will eventually change the way we work and live. In the near future, we will have information sockets like power sockets in our homes where we can get audio, video, and plenty of information by just plugging in a terminal. Bell Atlantic, now merged with TCI, the largest cable-TV operator in the United States, together are bent on revolutionizing home entertainment and information services by turning Bell Atlantic's telephone network into an audio-video pipeline.

14.2 SPEECH/AUDIO COMPRESSION

In recent years, significant progress has been made in the digital processing of speech and audio information. Based on the interdisciplinary studies of signal processing, coding theories, and psychophysics, speech and audio signals can be encoded at various rates while maintaining high quality. Advances in these compression techniques have been accompanied by many industry standards for digital storage and communication in many diverse applications, such as consumer electronics, professional audio processing, telecommunications, broadcasting, and multimedia [6–9]. Although high bit-rate channels, networks, and devices become more easily accessible, low bit-rate coding is still very important. The main purpose of low bit-rate coding is to provide cost-effective storage or to minimize transmission costs, especially in the mobile radio channels and packet-oriented networks [10]. In addition, there is the critical need to share channel capacities between audio and video in audiovisual multimedia communications.

Speech compression can achieve a high compression rate because of the vocal tract production model and the advance in auditory perception [11]. Good to excellent results can be achieved with a bit rate as low as 0.5 bit per sample using the Code Excited Linear Prediction (CELP) model [12]. Interest in speech compression has been increasing owing to rapid depletion of available communication bandwidth in many applications. Uncompressed digitalized speech requires 64 Kbps at a sampling rate of 8 kHz and a resolution of 8 bits per sample, that is, 480 KB per minute of speech. Without compression, it is too expensive to store or transmit with today's technologies.

Audio signals have complex harmonic structures with sharp peaks in their spectra. They require relatively high-accuracy techniques to reproduce the original waveform as compared with the speech signals. Wideband audio compression is generally aimed at a quality that is nearly indistinguishable from consumer compact-disc audio. Subband and transform coding methods combined with sophisticated perceptual coding techniques dominate in this arena [8]. Nowadays, high-fidelity audio coding is required in the multimedia services and advanced digital TV [9,13,14].

14.2.1 Low Bit-Rate Speech Coding

Speech codec at a very low bit rate is becoming important in a wide range of applications, such as voice mail, mobile radio, cellular telephony, and secure voice systems [15]. The operation of the speech codec is basically to compress speech into highly compact information, capable of reproducing the original signal, for the purpose of transmission and storage. Important advances in speech compression algorithms have recently emerged and resulted in systems that provide high-quality digital speech at a bit rate as low as 2.4 Kbps [8]. Advances in microelectronic technologies and VLSI design have also kept pace with the increasing complexity of more recent algorithms [16,17,18]. The rapid technology transfer from research to product development continues to keep the pressure on researchers to find better and more efficient algorithms in order to meet the demanding objectives of users and industrial standard organizations.

Speech coding schemes can be broadly classified into three categories: waveform coders, vocoders, and hybrid coders [11]. Waveform coders are characterized by their attempt to preserve the general shape of signal waveform [19,20]. The success of waveform coding for speech has been limited to rates above 16 Kbps, but they are nevertheless very popular and will remain so because of their simplicity and ease of implementation. At the opposite extreme to waveform coders, vocoders are very speech specific in their principles, and no attempts are made to preserve the original speech waveform. A very popular vocoder standard is the U.S. government linear predictive coding algorithm (LPC-10) standard, which operates at 2.4 Kbps with poor speech quality [21]. This standard is targeted mainly at noncommercial applications, for example, secure military systems. To overcome the deficiencies of pure waveform and vocoding schemes, hybrid coding methods such as codebook excited linear prediction (CELP) and multiband excitation, have been developed. They incorporate the advantages offered by each of the pure schemes [22,23,24].

A speech codec can be characterized by three criteria: quality, data rate, and complexity. Speech quality is evaluated mostly by subjective measures, whereby listeners are asked to grade speech quality under different situations. Objective measures, such as signal-to-noise ratio, are not very useful for low bit-rate speech compression algorithms. From the implementation point of view, low-computation complexity is necessary to meet real-time and low-cost requirements [25]. Different speech compression models are studied in the research community to trade off quality, rate, and complexity. CELP is one of the popular models [7,8]. It offers a quality versus bit-rate tradeoff significantly better than most prior compression techniques for rates in the range of 4 to 16 Kbps. The U.S. Department of Defense has proposed a 4.8 Kbps coder based on the CELP model. It consists of three analysis steps: short-term prediction, long-term prediction, and codebook excitation [26]. Figure 14.2 shows the functional block diagram of the CELP coder.

In the CELP coder, the original speech signal is partitioned into analysis frames of around 20 to 30 ms. Short-term prediction (STP) analysis is performed on the speech frame to produce linear predictive coding (LPC) coefficients. It models the spectral envelope of the speech. This information is then removed from the speech for subsequent analysis. The long-term prediction (LTP) analysis is usually performed on subframes, around 5 ms to 7.5 ms to achieve higher resolution. The analysis can be performed by close loop or open loop [11]. The LTP extracts pitch periodicity from the speech. Once the parameters of the STP and LTP filters are found, a codebook vector is selected to model the speech residual. In the standard CELP, the excitation is selected from a codebook of random white Gaussian sequences. In the synthesizer, the scaled codebook vectors are fed into LTP and STP filters to produce the reconstructed speech.

In order to achieve lower bit rates, modified CELP methods have been proposed by many researchers [10,15,22]. These methods generally have more adaptive excitation structures and alternative approaches in the STP and LTP. In the STP, interframe delta coding can be explored to reduce the bit rate. Vector quantization can also be used to quantize the LSP (line spectrum pair) vectors. In the LTP, several approaches can be investigated to reduce bit rate and obtain reasonable speech quality. First, LTP analysis can be performed in a larger speech frame, around 10 ms to 15 ms. Speech frames can be classified into voiced, unvoiced, and transient. In some conditions, the LTP is not required for the unvoiced and transient frames because they have fewer periodic signals in the speech waveform. In the conventional methods, the LTP and codebook excitation were performed sequentially. The LTP can be performed with the codebook search simultaneously to achieve a better performance. When considering codebook excitation, the adaptive codebook scheme can be utilized to match the various characteristics of speech frames. On the other hand, the multiband excitation

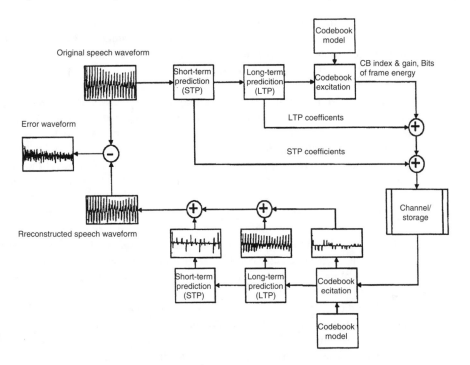

Figure 14.2 Functional block diagram of the CELP coder.

(MBE) coder [27] can yield a fair speech quality at bit rates of 2.4 Kbps and 1.2 Kbps. In this coder, the accurate and reliable pitch estimation and the unvoiced/voiced decision are very critical. The efficient quantization schemes of the spectral amplitude vector can be utilized to achieve a low bit rate. In order to improve speech quality, the speech formants need to be accurately modeled by the MBE coder.

Recently, the U.S. Department of Defense selected the mixed excitation LPC (MELP) vocoder [28] as a new federal 2.4 Kbps standard. This coder is based on the traditional LPC vocoder with either a periodic impulse train or white noise exciting an all-pole filter, but the coder contains four additional features [27]: (1) mixed pulse and noise excitation (2) periodic or aperiodic pulses (3) adaptive spectral enhancement and (4) pulse dispersion filter. These features allow the coder to mimic more of the characteristics of natural human speech. This MELP coder has been optimized for performance in acoustic background noise and in channel errors, as well as for efficient real-time implementation. Listening tests confirm that the enhanced 2.4 Kbps MELP coder performs as well as the higher bit-rate 4.8 Kbps FS1016 CELP standard [29].

14.2.2 High-Fidelity Audio Coding

Digital audio coding probably began in the early 1970s. Initial efforts simply used uniform or nonuniform quantization of audio signals. Today all the work in high-fidelity audio coding relies on either subband coding or transform coding [9]. In general, audio coding is a generic scheme. Unlike the vocal-tract model specially tuned for speech signals, the audio coding gets its compression without making assumptions about the nature of the audio source. Instead, the coder exploits the perceptual limitations of the human auditory system. Much of the compression results from the removal of perceptually irrelevant parts of audio signals.

In the transform coding, the overlapping block windows are utilized to cancel the time-domain alias. The scalar quantization and entropy coding are generally performed on the transformed signal components. Perceptual masking models determine adaptive bit allocations through the spectral components. Recently, a transform coding scheme called AC-3, developed by Todd et al. at Dolby Laboratories, was adopted for the multichannel audio portion of the forthcoming high-definition television terrestrial broadcasting standard of the U.S. Federal Communications Commission [14]. The algorithm operates at a range of bit rates as low as 32 Kbps per channel, with up to 5.1 channels where the 0.1 channel is a channel of low-frequency effects. The coder uses non-aliased filterbanks and perceptual masking. Other features include the transmission of a variable-frequency resolution spectral envelope and hybrid backward/forward adaptive bit allocation. The coder supports sampling rates of 32, 44.1, and 48 kHz and 19 monochannel bit rates from 32 to 640 Kbps.

Subband coding has also been the basis of effective audio coding methods. An early example of subband coding is the Telecommunication Standardization Sector of the International Telecommunication Union (ITU-T) G.722 standard that employs adaptive differential pulse code modulation (ADPCM) to code each of two subbands. For wideband audio compression, a coding scheme called masking pattern adapted subband coding and multiplexing was developed by Theile et al. [30]. Subsequently, a closely related algorithm called masking pattern adapted universal subband integrated coding, and multiplexing (MUSICAM) was adopted in Europe for use in digital audio broadcasting [31].

In the Motion Picture Experts Group (MPEG), the MPEG-1 coding standard supports bit rates of 250 Kbps for two-channel audio and 1.2 Mbps for video [13]. This standard can provide a three-layer audio coding algorithm for stereophonic audio. The layers I, II, and III define coding algorithms with increasing complexity and performance. The MPEG-2 audio coding standard is designed for multichannel high-fidelity audio [32]. In many features, it is compatible with the MPEG-1 audio coding. Recently, emerging activities of the International Organization for Standardization (ISO) have aimed at proposals for audio coding at low and very low bit rates. The basic audio quality will be more important than compatibility with existing or upcoming standards. Therefore, the MPEG-4 work addresses standardization of audiovisual coding at very low bit rates, allowing for a high degree of flexibility and extensibility.

Digital multichannel audio will improve stereophonic systems and will be of importance for both audio-only and multimedia applications. We can also expect further activities and developments in the field of digital surround systems. The enhanced multichannel representations can be implemented by making better use of interchannel correlations and interchannel masking effects to bring the bit rates further down. In order to achieve very low bit rates, the studies of enhanced perceptual models, an adaptive time/frequency resolution, scalar/vector quantizations, and analysis-by-synthesis coding strategies can be highly explored for the future audio coding.

14.2.3 Industrial Standards and Applications

The applications of speech and audio coding methods are used mostly in transmission and storage, such as wireless communication, videotelephony, computer archiving, solid-state storage, and interactive multimedia. For example, the AT&T VideoPhone 2500 operates over a single telephone line. It provides voice and color motion video by using a modem operating at 19.2 Kbps. A channel capacity of only 6.8 Kbps is used for coding voice. This example illustrates the importance of bit-rate reductions for the speech and audio components to provide acceptable overall bit rates. Table 14.1 lists various standards of speech/audio compression proposed by industry and government. Some of these speech/audio coders are briefly described as follows.

(1) 4.8 Kbps CELP coder (US Federal Standard FS 1016)

This coder is implemented by the linear-prediction-based analysis-by-synthesis method using the adaptive and stochastic codebooks. In the beginning, speech is sampled at 8 kHz and segmented in frames of 30 ms. Ten parameters of the short-term prediction are encoded as the values of line spectrum frequencies on a frame-by-frame basis. The LTP lag search is performed by an adaptive codebook search where the codebook is defined by previous excitation sequences and the lag determines the specific codevector. The stochastic codebook contains 512 sparse and overlapping codevectors. Each codevector consists of 60 samples, and each sample is ternary valued $(1, 0, -1)$ to allow for fast convolution. In the exhaustive two-stage search, the optimum excitation vector from the adaptive codebook is

Table 14.1 The Standards of Speech/Audio Compression

Standards	Bit rates (kbits/s)	MOS value	Coding techniques	Groups
LPC-10e	2.4	2.6	Vocoder	U.S. DoD's F.S. 1015
CELP	4.8	3.1	Analysis by synthesis (ABS)-CELP	U.S. DoD's F.S. 1016
CELP	8	3.9	ABS-CELP	
CELP	16	4.1	ABS-CELP	
IS54	8	3.5	ABS-VSELP	U.S. Telecom. Ind. Assoc.
GSM	13	3.5	ABS-RPE-LTP-LP	Europ. digital mobile group
G.711	64	4.3	PCM	ITU-T
G.721	32	4.1	ADPCM	ITU-T
G.722	48/56/64	3.7/4.0/4.1	ADPCM	ITU-T
G.723	24/32/40	—	DCME-ADPCM	ITU-T
G.727	16/24/32/40	—	Embeded-ADPCM	ITU-T
G.728	16	3.9	LD-CELP	ITU-T

selected; then a stochastic codebook is searched to match the remaining signal. The computational complexity of this 4.8 Kbps CELP coder was estimated at 16 million instructions
per second (MIPS). Its subjective quality can reach mean opinion score (MOS) 3.1 listed
in Table 14.1. The 4.8 Kbps CELP coder is robust to channel errors, and the background
noise is acceptably reproduced [26].

(2) 7.95 Kbps VSELP coder (IS54)

A vector-sum excited linear predictive (VSELP) coder has been chosen by the U.S.
Telecommunications Industry Association as one of the North American digital cellular
systems [33]. Speech sampled at 8 kHz is first preprocessed using a fourth-order high-pass
Chebyshev filter. The frame in the VSELP coder is 20 ms, and each frame is divided into
four 5-ms subframes. A tenth-order STP filter is applied, and then the LTP lag is searched
by using an adaptive codebook. The excitation is coded using gain-shape vector quantizers
where two stochastic codebooks are employed. This sum excitation approach makes the
codebook excitation more robust to channel errors. The net bit rate for source coding is 7.95
Kbps, and the total bit rate is 13 Kbps. The computational complexity of the VSELP coder
was reported to be more than 13.5 MIPS.

(3) 13 Kbps RPE-LTP-LP Coder (GSM)

The linear predictive coder of the regular-pulse excited long-term prediction, the so-
called GSM coder, is being used in the European cellular mobile radio system [34]. Speech is
sampled at 8 kHz and quantized at 13 bits/samples. The preprocessing involves preemphasis
and DC offset compensation. An eighth-order short-term prediction is performed at each
20 ms frame. The lag and gain parameters of the LTP are computed in every 5 ms subframe
and encoded at 7 and 2 bits, respectively. Since the excitation is modeled as a regular pulse
train, the optimum excitation signal is chosen in a simple search that avoids the complexity
of a full analysis-by-synthesis search. The net bit rate for source coding is 13.0 Kbps. The
data rate of signal is heavily protected against channel errors, which yield a total bit rate of
22.8 Kbps. The computational complexity of the GSM coder is around 5 MIPS.

(4) ITU-T G.722 standard

The ITU-T G.722 wideband speech coding algorithm supports a bandwidth of 7 kHz,
with a sampling rate of 16 kHz and bit rates of 48, 56 and 64 Kbps [35]. Based on a 24-
tap quadrature mirror filter, the 14-bit PCM representation of a wideband input signal is
split into two critically subsampled components called lower band and higher band. After
this decimation, each band is effectively sampled at 8 kHz, which allows for a combined
allocation of 8 bits per sample. For a higher band, the 2-bit backward adaptive Laplacian
quantizer is permanently employed. In a lower band, either a 4-, 5-, or 6-bit quantizer is used,
depending on the desired coding rates of 48, 56, and 64 Kbps. This coder has an overall delay
of around 3 ms, small enough to cause no echo problems in telecommunication networks.

(5) ISO/MPEG audio coding standard

Currently, international interests in audiovisual compression algorithms center on the
ISO/MPEG standardization [36]. The MPEG-1 audio coding standard supports sampling
rates of 32, 44.1, and 48 kHz and bit rates ranging from 32 to 448 Kbps per monophonic
or stereo channel. In the first stage, the audio signal is converted into spectral subband
components via an analysis filterbank. Each spectral component is quantized where the
number of quantizer levels for each component is obtained from a dynamic bit allocation
rule that is controlled by a psychoacoustic model [13]. The MPEG-1 audio standard consists

of three layers, I, II, and III, with increasing complexity, delay, and subjective performance. For example, a 48 kHz sampling rate is introduced as follows.

(a) Layer I contains the basic mapping of the digital audio signal into 32 subbands via polyphase quadrature mirror filters, an 8 ms frame length, very simple quantization, side information, and encoding. A simple form of stereo irrelevancy removal, called intensity stereo, is provided. Layer I shows an excellent performance at a bit rate of 192 Kbps.

(b) Layer II utilizes the same filterbanks but with a 24 ms frame length, constrained quantization values, and more sophisticated side information, for a higher coding efficiency. It is proposed to be suitable for the high-quality applications at 128 Kbps and with an intensity stereo at 96 Kbps.

(c) Layer III uses each of the 32 bands from the polyphase filters as an input of which frequency elements are determined by its perceptual content. In addition, entropy coding and more sophisticated quantizers are included. This layer is proposed to be used as a monophonic coder at 96 Kbps or as a stereo coder at 64 Kbps. An intensity stereo, and L-R, and L+R stereos are included in Layer III.

The MPEG-2 has two multichannel audio coding standards, one of which will be forward and backward compatible with the MPEG-1. Forward compatibility shows that the multichannel decoder can properly decode MPEG-1 mono or stereo signals. Backward compatibility shows that the MPEG-1 stereo decoder can deliver a correct stereo signal when decoding the MPEG-2 multichannel bit stream. Since the MPEG-1 has a bit-rate limitation, the MPEG-2 standard allows for a second bit stream to overcome this limitation and to provide compatible multichannel audio at higher rates. In the future MPEG-4 standard, low and very low bit rates are proposed for high-efficiency audiovisual transmission.

14.3   TEXT-TO-SPEECH CONVERSION

Text-to-speech (TTS) conversion transforms linguistic information stored as data or text into speech. The resulting speech must achieve a high degree of intelligibility and naturalness. The TTS is widely used in text-reading devices for blind people and digital voice storage for voice mail and voice response in the multimedia systems [37,38]. Any text-to-speech system consists of two major stages: text-to-parameters and parameters-to-sound. In the text-to-parameters stage, the linguistic information of the input text is interpreted as the parameters of sound production based on the words or subwords. The speech is produced by concatenating prerecorded words or subword segments such as syllables, morphemes, phonemes, diphones, or triphones with natural-sounding rhythm and intonation. Considering the parameters-to-sound, we need a type of sound-generating mechanism whose function is analogous to that of the human vocal tract. A mouth by itself cannot talk, so we require a module whose input is the text or other linguistic information and whose output drives the sound-generating mechanism.

A schematic of the human vocal tract is shown in Fig. 14.3. Air under pressure from the lungs flows through the trachea and the vocal cords in the larynx. This opening between the vocal cords is called the glottis, and the air flow as a function of time is called the glottal waveform. Vocal tract models based on the physical shape and the physiology of the sound production mechanism provide many scientific insights. The complex relationship

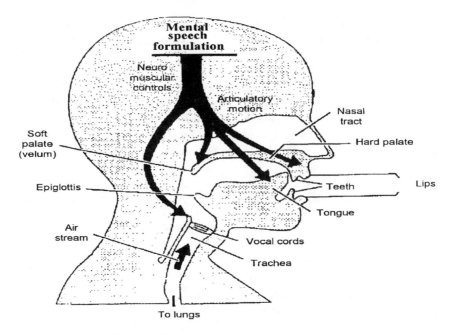

Figure 14.3   A schematic of human vocal tract.

between these physical parameters and the resulting speech waveform involves nonlinear equations. A small change in one of the model's parameters often makes a major change in the resulting sound. The most important acoustic parameters for speech synthesis are the fundamental frequency of the glottal waveform and the frequencies of the first three narrow bandwidth formants [39]. For a typical male voice, the fundamental frequency varies over about an octave centered around 120 Hz, while the first three formants vary around 500 Hz, 1500 Hz, and 2500 Hz, respectively. The fundamental frequency for a female voice typically falls closer to 200 Hz, while the formant frequencies are about 10% higher than those of a male voice. The source/filter model of speech production as shown in Fig. 14.4 is the most widely used model for acoustic phonetic research.

14.3.1   Text-to-Speech Synthesis

A thought can be written and verbalized so that text and speech are two distinct manifestations of the same idea. Text is a train of symbols that follow, more or less, the flow of corresponding speech sounds. The ability of machines to convert text strings to speech depends on these facts. When written language first came into being, it used a distinct symbol for each word as Chinese and other languages still do today. But word vocabularies commonly reach from several thousand to hundred thousand entries. If written symbols represent individual sounds rather than words, it is sufficient to realize the text-to-speech conversion using fewer sound parameters. This technique has been widely used in the TTS systems of different languages [40]. Generally, the process of converting text into speech

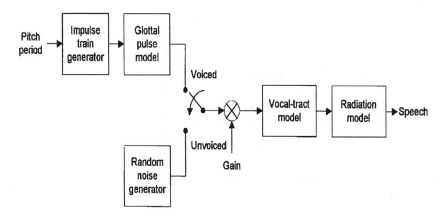

Figure 14.4   A source/filter model of speech production.

can break down into a number of stages. Figure 14.5 summarizes the English TTS processes discussed in the following six stages [38,41].

1. *Text normalization:* A text normalizer converts everything in the text stream to letters. It also spells out special symbols in full alphabetic form so that no ambiguity regarding pronunciation is passed on to succeeding stages. For example, "$900" becomes "nine hundred dollars" and "Dr." becomes either "doctor" or "drive," as appropriate.

2. *Identification of morphemes and exceptional cases:* This stage is to obtain a prescription for basic pronunciations of each word in the normalized text. Morphemes are the smallest syntactic units of a language. Pronunciation of a word is obtained by concatenating pronunciations for each of its morphemes. Some words in English are not pronounced in accordance with the basic rules. The word "of," for example, is the only case where a final "f" is pronounced "v," To say these words correctly, the system stores a phonemic transcription of their exact pronunciation in an exception dictionary.

3. *Letter-to-phoneme conversion:* A phoneme is the smallest distinguishable sound of a language. The letter-to-phoneme rules convert English spelling into phoneme transcriptions, which are a more exact representation of pronunciation. For example, the word "red" is represented as "r ε d".

4. *Prosody generation:* The prosody rules create the intonation or rhythm of sentences in the text. Most TTS systems attempt to synthesize a natural-sounding rhythm and an acceptable intonation, but they have somewhat robotic prosodies because the machine, unlike human speakers, follows rigid rules. However, end users can insert prosodic "diacritics" into a text to get special intonation patterns.

5. *Phonetic analysis:* A fine adjustment of phonemes must be accomplished to account for phenomena resulting from contextual influences at concatenated phoneme boundaries. The tuning of pronunciation takes place in the phonetic rules. For example, the phoneme "t" is pronounced differently in "tom," "atom," and "hat."

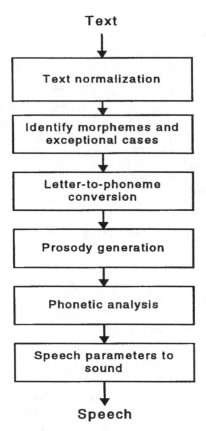

Figure 14.5 Text-to-speech synthesis.

6. *Speech parameters to sound:* From a phonetic transcription that includes embedded information to guide the conversion, parameters can be produced that drive a vocal tract model. A parametric speech representation is most convenient for speech synthesis because speech parameters can be controlled individually.

Although the TTS technology is quite mature and employed in many applications, the conversion system can be improved in the following [4,41]: (1) *Synthesis technology:* The commonly used LPC model is too simple to generate a high-quality speech. The acoustic waves of the air flow in the vocal tract are governed by a much more complicated nonlinear system than the LPC model. More advanced computational models need to be explored. (2) *Computational models of variability:* Explicit models of variability are needed to avoid speech monotony in synthesis of long monologues and long human–computer interactive sessions. (3) *Integration of synthesis and language understanding:* The synthesizer needs to understand what it is saying to achieve human-like impressions. Currently, our language models are not sophisticated enough to interpret the text completely as a human does. We need a more powerful representation of meanings to help the computational models.

14.3.2 Text-to-Speech Technology for Multimedia

The TTS is an important technology in multimedia systems for communicating from computers to humans through the natural human speech. Its applications consist of talking terminals, alarm systems, talking aids for the vocally handicapped, and reading aids for the blind. The TTS technology provides an effective speech interface to make users easily engage multimedia applications, especially listening electronic mails, story books, newspapers, commercial information, industrial activities, and so on. For example, audio-text services based on TTS technology allow users to retrieve information from public or private databases such as telephone directories, financial accounts, stock quotations, weather reports, reservations, sales orders, and inventory information [42]. While some of this information could be obtained by using recorded human speech, the TTS systems are appropriate when services access a large or regularly changing database. The TTS reduces storage requirement from 64 Kbps of a telephone-quality speech to a few hundred bits of an equivalent text sentence.

14.4 SPEECH UNDERSTANDING

Speech understanding systems make it possible for people to interact with computers using human natural speech. This interaction relies on speech techniques with acoustic, lexical, syntactic, semantic, and pragmatic analyses [43]. The simplicity and friendliness of the human speech interaction with a computer provide unskilled users easily engaging multimedia systems. Over the past decade, although progress in speech technologies has been impressive, significant obstacles remain [42]. Speech understanding systems must be robust in all environments, so that they can handle background or channel noise, unfamiliar words, new accents, new users, or unanticipated inputs. They also need to exhibit more intelligence of knowing when they do not understand or only partially understand something, and interacting with the user appropriately to provide conversational correction and prediction. They can integrate speech with other media, driving the user's intention by combining speech with gestures, eye movements, facial expressions, and other features [4].

The speech understanding process can be viewed as a mapping from a large amount of language pattern space to a condensed representation. The representation used in speech understanding is to provide useful knowledge for higher-level processing. When you are able to talk with your multimedia computer, it can reduce the amount of typing, leave your hand free, and allow you to move away from terminal or screen. It would also help in some applications if the multimedia computer could tell who was speaking. The approach for speaker recognition is similar to that of speech recognition. The speech recognition system tries to disregard who uttered a voice and to determine what was said. In contrast, the speaker recognition system tries to establish the identity of the talker or talker's group [44].

14.4.1 Automatic Speech Recognition

A speech recognition system performs by recognizing the phonemes or words, interpreting an individual word or sequence of words, and providing an appropriate response to

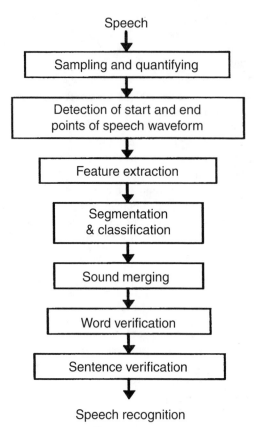

Figure 14.6 A speech recognition system.

the user [45]. In the past decade, the technologies of a speech recognition system have made rapid advances. A large number of significant methods and techniques have been developed and have been successfully employed in the system implementations [47,51,53]. However, the practical speech recognition systems needed to meet the quality requirements of humans are still challenges [4].

A speech recognition system is shown in Fig. 14.6. A recorded speech through a microphone is sampled and quantized as input data. The starting and endpoints of a digitized speech waveform are then determined. Feature extraction takes relevant information from the effective speech samples. It removes unwanted variations such as background noise and channel response. The dominant method of feature extraction in speech recognition systems is linear predictive coding [46]. It is based on the source/filter modeling of vocal tract for analyzing the resonant frequencies, formants. In English, the excitation information, pitch, is discarded. However, in a tonal language such as Chinese, a pitch is required in the recognition system to decide the tone as well as the vocal tract information. After the phonemes are recognized, the words are determined by the sound merging and verified by the neighboring words, such as the bi-gram and tri-gram grammars [47]. Finally, a correct sentence is verified by using a language model.

Template matching is a fundamental technique of pattern recognition and consists of three basic steps: (1) parameter generation, (2) pattern comparison, and (3) decision making. A sequence of feature vectors for each phoneme, word, or connected words in the speech database is generated as a template. An unknown speech pattern is compared with each template to find the closest match. In the speech recognition process, we require both a local-distance measure, which is defined as the spectral distance between two well-defined spectral vectors, and a global time alignment procedure, which compensates for different rates of speaking. The dynamic programming algorithm is an efficient way to accomplish time normalization and alignment. The template matching based on the dynamic programming algorithm is called the dynamic time warping (DTW) scheme. It is used to stretch or shrink the input pattern to minimize the distortion measure for each template according to the time-alignment path constraints [43].

Currently, the most popular statistical model used in speech recognition is the hidden Markov model (HMM) [48]. The underlying assumption of the HMM is that the speech signal can be well characterized as a parametric random process and that the parameters of the stochastic process can be determined in a precise, well-defined manner. For this procedure, training consists of estimating the parameters, means, and covariances of a probabilistic model for each word. To classify an unknown utterance, one computes the likelihood that was generated by each HMM model. The utterance is generally recognized as the word whose model gives the highest likelihood score. The principal advantage of the HMM over the template-based approach is that the HMM retains more statistical information of the speech patterns than templates. For continuous speech, a language grammar can be easily modeled by a state machine, which can be incorporated in the HMM framework. The HMM is being widely used in speech applications except that the applications are easily handled by the DTW based on considerations of computation cost.

In addition to the HMM and DTW, the neural network approaches for solving speech recognition problems are also very promising [49–53]. For example, the neural phonetic typewriter [49] provides a speech representation method to demonstrate the speech phonemes on the Kohonen feature map. The time-delayed neural networks [50] employ a multilayered neural architecture that is trained to solve the nonlinear time-warping problem in order to recognize consecutive spectral patterns of speech. Since temporal information processing is a major problem in the fixed network topologies, the many time-normalization preprocessing methods for the artificial neural networks have been studied in [51–53]. Generally, the neural network approaches can provide the speech recognition systems with capabilities of automatic knowledge learning and adaptation.

Another speech recognition approach is to model the human auditory system instead of the vocal tract. The motivation for investigating the physiological model is to gain an understanding of how the human auditory system processes speech, so as to be able to design and implement robust, efficient methods of analyzing and representing speech. This technique starts with a set of overlapping bandpass filters corresponding to the sensitivity of cochlear membrane, and then explores the modeling of nonlinear effects that occur in human auditory processing [43]. Beyond the auditory processing, it is important to understand how the brain processes the signals of neural activities along the auditory nerves in order to recognize speech. The auditory models of speech reception and the LPC models of speech production are quite successful in some applications of speech recognition. However, they are so primitive to represent the physiologies of speech production and hearing that many aspects remain to be solved in order to achieve a human-like speech recognition system [4,10].

Prosodic attributes such as pitch, stress, and duration provide valuable information that is usually discarded in most state-of-the-art speech recognition systems. Without prosody, we lose the clues to make speech fluent and well constructed. In order to understand the confused words, it is effective to incorporate prosodic parameters with spectrum features in the recognition process. In addition to identifying an individual word or sentence, the conversational context and grammatical constraints are also useful information to enhance speech recognition.

The occurrence of unknown or out-of-vocabulary words is one of the major problems frustrating the use of automatic speech recognition systems. It is very difficult to identify out-of-vocabulary words correctly and reject them because the conventional recognition methods only derive the most likely answer from the speech database. In real-world applications, a good rejection method needs to be developed for speech recognition systems, with capabilities of rejection and keyword spotting.

When communicating over a telephone channel, many ignored phenomena such as echoes, noise, and nonlinearities, arise and need to be addressed. It is very easy for humans to tell the difference between channel effects and original speech. In a speech recognition system, different channel conditions can often cause the system to break down. Most front-end processing employs simple spectrum estimations so that it cannot learn or adapt to channel variations. In order to make speech recognition deployable in real-world applications, channel robustness is the key issue to be figured out.

14.4.2 Speaker Recognition

In our daily life, we sometimes communicate with machines that always ask us to enter a personal password to confirm our identity. However, personal characteristics of an individual's voice can be used to help confirm an identity. Usually, speech waveforms convey various kinds of information, such as content meaning, voice characteristics, and speaker's emotional condition. Automatic speaker recognition is the process of automatically determining the speaker's identity based on the information conveyed by the speech waveform [44]. Speaker recognition technologies can be widely used in bank telephone services, credit card verification, and speech keys for control of access to a location or database. For these applications, speech is used as a signature or an identification card. Figure 14.7 shows a speaker recognition system. A speech utterance is processed by the acoustic analyzer to generate an input pattern. The similarity measure between an input pattern and each characteristic pattern in the database is performed for the decision process. When characteristic patterns need to be updated or modified, the feedback training process is utilized to adjust the speakers' identity database.

Speaker recognition can be classified by two disciplines of speaker verification and speaker identification [54,55]. Speaker verification is the process of accepting or rejecting a speaker's identity claim. The input utterance is accepted as the known voice by the registered speaker if its distortion of similarity measure is smaller than the threshold. Otherwise, an input utterance whose distortion is larger than the threshold is rejected. The threshold is usually set a posteriori for each individual speaker in the process of recognition training.

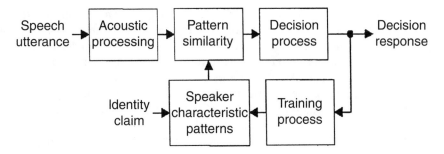

Figure 14.7   A speaker recognition system.

On the other hand, speaker identification is the process of determining whether an input utterance matches a speaker's voice whose identity is being claimed. Its accuracy depends on the number of registered speakers, whereas speaker verification accuracy does not.

The performance of the above two tasks is determined by the type of speech material used to claim an identity. The text-dependent systems require the recitation of a predetermined text, whereas the text-independent systems accept speech utterances of unrestricted text. In the text-dependent systems, one can make precise and reliable comparisons between two utterances of the same text by using adequate time alignment. This is not easily accomplished in the text-independent systems. Hence, the performance in the text-dependent system is far superior to that of the text-independent system. The text-dependent systems are used primarily in the applications of access control where the user is cooperative and consistent from session to session. The text-independent systems are needed in forensic and surveillance applications where the user is not cooperative and often not aware of the task [54].

The speech signal conveys information about the speaker in many ways. These include high-level features such as dialect, context, speaking style, and emotional state of the speaker, which are often used by human listeners to identify a person. In order to develop a high-performance speaker recognition system, the fundamental features in any specific application comprise (1) interspeaker or intergroup discrimination, (2) tolerance of intraspeaker variabilities, (3) characterizing from speech utterance, (4) stability over time, and (5) impostor and mimic resistance.

14.4.3 Applications of Speech Understanding for Multimedia

Speech understanding plays an important role in multimedia applications, especially in the human-to-machine interface. Current developments have created the opportunity to incorporate speech recognition into a computer interface in a way that allows for natural speech communication. To support the conversational way of speech interaction, multimedia systems must have adequate interaction protocols, fast response time, error correction, and user plasticity. In addition, the capabilities of word spotting, barge-in, robustness, and rapid deployment in speech recognition provide the basis for a range of successful applications [10]. *Word spotting* is to recognize command words within a fluent speech. *Barge-in* is the user's ability to speak over the voice prompts and be recognized correctly. *Robustness* is the ability to maintain a consistent level of performance for different users, backgrounds, handsets, and communications channels. Finally, the *rapid deployment* ability can create new services without the need for extensive vocabulary training. Some examples of commercial applications are introduced as follows.

To make a phone call, we always enter the telephone number or credit card number using keypads, but this method is not efficient for users. However, AT&T Bell Laboratories has developed a friendly interface for the telephone that lets users utilize both speech and keypad to communicate with a machine [56]. In addition to recognizing the numbers, the conversational content can be interpreted to the motion picture in a multimedia telephone [57]. This system lets a hearing-impaired person use a multimedia telephone that converts speech to lip movements like a normal person. In the application of voice banking service, the customer can communicate with the bank's multimedia computers by telephone based on speech input. This system can provide 24-hour service and reduce staff needed for answering questions. Recently, US ARPA's Air Travel Information System program has aimed at studying word-spotting applications. For instance, when a traveler says, ''Please show me all the flights from Los Angeles to New York,'' the speech recognition system only spots ''from Los Angeles'' and ''to New York'' to be understood; then the system queries the database and plays back the answer. In the other speech applications, a phonetic typewriter for Japanese words was developed for the speech-to-text conversion [58]. Another speech-to-text system based on the connected words for Chinese characters was also developed by Apple Computer. These systems can help users who are quickly typing documents where it is not efficient to generate a word using the current computer keyboard for nonalphabetical languages.

A multilingual speech recognition system for voice-control applications was proposed by Chen et al. [53]. In this approach, speech signals are sampled by using a 16-bit resolution at a rate of 20 kHz and then preemphasized by (1-0.98/z). The beginning and endpoints of each 3-second speech signal are determined based on the spectrum energy. The frame length is 25.6 ms, and the shift length is 12.8 ms where the 512-point Hamming window is used. The 16 cepstrum coefficients for each speech frame form a vector. The speech database is trained by using the learning vector quantization method. A user-friendly software system was developed with the capabilities of window management controlled by the keyboard, mouse, and speech commands. The tables for different functions of speech recognition are shown in Fig. 14.8. In the beginning of speech recognition, background noise is detected for compensation of speech input signals. The vector of a speech frame is generated from the processing of sampling, background noise deduction, preemphasizing, acoustic analysis, and cepstrum calculation. This system is used to recognize a short-period speech and not to understand the individual word or phoneme. Therefore, it is highly suitable for voice-control applications. The content of voice commands can be defined according to the practical applications. Since the language models are not implemented in this system, the different languages and dialects, such as English, Mandarin, Taiwanese, and Japanese, can be applied for voice-navigation applications such as remote controls, mobile telephones, and computer multimedia.

The major area of application for speaker recognition is in access control to information, credit, banking, machines, networks, cars, and building. Thus, the voice lock concept is

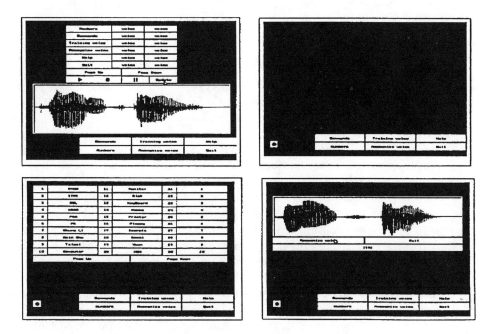

Figure 14.8   User-friendly window tables for speech recognition.

accomplished by speaker recognition technology that prevents access until the appropriate speech by authorized individuals is heard. With the advance of computers, networks, and other telecommunications systems, the need for security has grown to the point where speaker recognition is now an attractive alternative to electronic security in multimedia systems. The performance of a speaker recognition system is very sensitive to several factors, including microphones, transmission channels, background noises, and speaker conditions. Various technical solutions have been proposed for these factors [10,59]. However, currently there is no perfect solution that provides a robust system with high-performance recognition.

14.5   MUSIC PROCESSING

The applications of music processing for multimedia were realized primarily by means of the combination of music, graphics, video, and other media. With the advance of computer technologies, musical sounds and compositions can be precisely specified and controlled by a computer, so that we can easily create artificial orchestras, performers, and composers. Musical instrument digital interface (MIDI) is an industry-standard connection for computer and musical instruments [60]. It provides a way to record, play back, and synchronize the settings needed to control musical devices, such as expanders, synthesizers, keyboards, and MIDI instruments. The main purpose of music processing for multimedia applications is to enhance our emotional receptors and promote interest in learning or performing something. Today a variety of tools are available to support musicians who want to compose and edit music for the applications of music education, interactive fictions, user-engaging games, and virtual realities [61].

14.5.1 Representation of Music

During the past several years, one reason why music processing has advanced quickly is that music processing is computationally tractable. Music can be organized into rhythmic structures consisting of beats, measures, sections, and movements. Music pitch structure results in keys, scales, chords and progressions. At these high-level structures, music can be analyzed, manipulated, and synthesized by using a wide variety of techniques [62]. When employing some intelligent processes in computer music systems, we can artificially create professional music for responding in real time to human inputs. Recently, multimedia has provided the exciting integration of systems and media, which creates new opportunities for computer music in various applications.

MIDI is an international standard for musical data transfer between electrical instruments and computing devices. It is a protocol for music symbols that may represent note, velocity, channel specification, controllers, and messages to control a device. In order to make a sound, we have to put the MIDI message through a synthesizer. The major approaches to realize the synthesizer are frequency modulation (FM) and wavetable by pulse code modulation (PCM). In the FM synthesizer, one for making sound is named a carrier, and the other for changing the frequency of a sound is called a modulator. Attack, decay, sustain, and release are four primary elements required by the FM synthesizer to generate a music sound. In addition, we can achieve some music effects by changing sound volume, frequency, fading away, and vibrato. In the wavetable approach, the music is synthesized by concatenating the prestored sound units where these original sound units are modeled by the PCM scheme. A larger memory capacity in the wavetable synthesizer is required than those in the FM synthesizer when generating the same music. However, the music quality in the wavetable synthesizer is usually better than the other.

As the sound representation using the MIDI is compared with that using the audio coding schemes, musical representation is more abstract and compact than audio representation. Such musical representation reduces a lot of storage and transmission costs. It can also be easily synthesized with a fidelity and complexity suitable for the hardware realization. A further advantage is that musical representation is noise-free, whereas digital audio has inherent noise. In addition, the most significant advantage is that a musical representation makes possible many operations such as music synthesis, editing, and composition, which would be infeasible or require extensive processing for the audio data. However, it is not appropriate for a music representation to reproduce a specific performance like a concert. In other words, musical representations are the best for earlier stages of music production, while audio representations are preferred for the final music production [1].

14.5.2 Computer Music for Multimedia

Most applications of modern computer music are realized in the multimedia systems. The combination of music and other expressive media is an important factor in making products attractive and marketable. Figure 14.9 shows a music system for multimedia applications, which includes an electronic music keyboard, a synthesizer, a sequencer, and MIDI devices. The music is generated by keying notes on a keyboard of an electronic organ

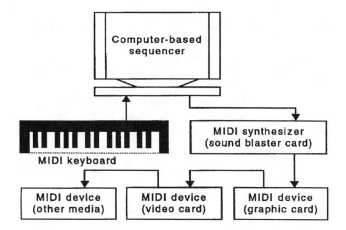

Figure 14.9 A music system for multimedia applications.

or a piano that is connected to a computer via the MIDI I/O ports. A sequencer in this computer is used to record the MIDI information rather than sound. This information can then be edited and sent to the MIDI synthesizer for playback. The computer outputs the music through a sound blaster card that is implemented by the FM synthesizer or wavetable. The other devices such as video, film, and graphic are synchronized with music using the MIDI information.

Computer music using the MIDI can be a good teaching tool. Music education based on the combination of music and the other media is an exciting application [63]. Interactive music education systems can provide an interesting model and testbed of new education techniques. Computer music also provides users with increasing interests in the multimedia applications of user-engaging games, interactive fictions, and virtual realities. The real-time performance is essential to computer music in these applications. Usually, music processing itself comes in different forms and places different kinds of demands on a system so that music output requires hard real-time scheduling to avoid glitches. Hence, new developments in scheduling, operating systems, and the MIDI protocol are useful to explore high-performance applications in music [64].

14.6 VLSI DESIGN FOR SPEECH/AUDIO PROCESSING

Multimedia systems have become more sophisticated with the advance of computer and microelectronic technologies. Many applications require efficient manipulation of speech and audio for interactive presentations and integration with other types of media [65]. Nowadays, speech and audio signals are easily incorporated into a multimedia computer with the introduction of sound boards for recording, processing, and playing. These add-in boards extend the computer's functions into telephony, facsimile, speech recognition, text-to-speech, music animation, and other speech and audio processing areas. Combinations of computers and sound boards become either general processing platforms or dedicated

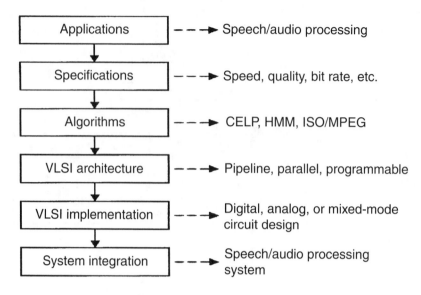

Figure 14.10   A top-down VLSI system design.

application systems, depending on what software is employed. In order to achieve real-time applications, the sound board usually has a specialized digital signal processor (DSP) or multiple DSPs for advanced speech and audio computing. The DSP is efficiently programmable when executing signal processing algorithms [65]. It is designed to have fast instruction cycle times, a high degree of parallelism, and sophisticated arithmetic units that execute in a single machine cycle. The DSP instructions are also utilized to optimize speech and audio processing operations. Currently, various commercial DSPs are available for advanced sound board designs.

In addition to the sound board, the application-specific hardware designs are preferred to realize the portable speech and audio products. The VLSI implementation undoubtedly plays a key role in developing the high-speed, low-cost, lightweight, and low-power applications [67]. Figure 14.10 shows a top-down VLSI system design. This design flow starts from the customer's needs in speech and audio applications. The system specifications, such as speed, quality, and data rate, are considered to develop the high-performance algorithm that is suitable for hardware implementation. Based on the pipeline, parallel, or programmable schemes, adequate VLSI architecture is explored to reach the high-throughput and cost-effective design. The best architecture is then implemented by using VLSI circuit design schemes. After the design is fabricated in a custom chip or masked on the field programmable gate array (FPGA) chip, the speech or audio system can be accomplished by integrating this chip with the other supporting components. The main challenge in the system design would be to optimize the architecture for the intended applications and implement only the necessary functions with a minimum number of chips at low cost.

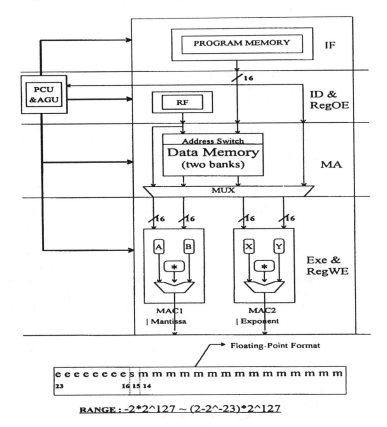

Figure 14.11   The functional blocks of the speech recognition processor.

14.6.1 VLSI Speech/Audio Processors

The VLSI technologies might be useful in developing new applications, improving reliability and safety, and systematizing various functional components. In the speech and audio hardware design, speed, cost, and power requirements are crucial. For instance, in the new personal multimedia communication systems where hand-held audio-video telephones are used, the battery consumption, cost, and size of the portable equipment have to be reasonable in order to make the product widely acceptable. Custom hardware implementations are often the solution whenever general-purpose systems cannot meet portability, compactness, cost, or performance requirements. In general, there are four different approaches in the custom VLSI design [68,69]: (1) application-specific integrated circuits (ASIC), (2) domain-specific programmable processors, (3) core-based ASIC, and (4) application-specific processors.

Real-time implementation of speech and audio processing is very important from a cost point of view. If the computation complexity of the speech or audio algorithm is fairly

Supported Addressing Mode :

Short immediate (0~256)

Direct.

Register direct.

Register indirect.

Index

Reverse index

Supplied Instruction Set :

Instr.	description	Instr.	description
LOAD	memory access	JME	jump if equal
STORE	memory access	JMG	jump if greater than
MOVE	register transfer	JML	jump if less than
SET	register initial	NOP	no operation
AND	logical op	ABS	absolute of ACC
OR	logical op	MAX	max of two Registers
NOT	logical op	MIN	min of two Registers
XOR	logical op	NORM	Fix.Pt. to F.Pt.
ADD	addition	SUBF	F.Pt. subtraction
SUB	subtraction	NORMF	F.Pt. normalization
MPY	multiplication	ADJF	F.Pt. adjustment
MAC	Mpy&Add	MPYF	F Pt. multiplication
MAS	Mpy&add	ADDF	F.Pt. addition
SHIFT	arithmetic shift	RPT	repeat block(loop)
JMP	jump	DMAMOV	DMA transfer

Figure 14.12   The instruction set and addressing mode of the speech recognition processor.

low, like the PCM or ADPCM, the ASIC approach can be used to design a single custom chip with a simple data path control. Otherwise, many chips or a very large-scale chip is required for the hardwired ASIC design but not encouraged. In the approach of domain-specific programmable processors such as commercial digital signal processing chips from Motorola DSP-5600/9600 and Texas Instruments TMS320C30/40, the computation is not efficiently performed as compared with the other three approaches. However, users can easily obtain these commercial DSPs and program them for any application. The core-based ASIC approach can improve some computation bottlenecks, but it will increase some communication costs between the CPU core and the ASIC part. The CPU core can be a general-purpose CPU or a DSP core that is not fully optimized for the speech and audio operations. Therefore, the performance of the whole core-based ASIC system cannot be highly improved. In the approach of application-specific processors, the instruction set will be optimized to match the algorithms and hardware environments so that the high-performance speech and audio systems when considering the integrated hardware-software constraints can be effectively realized.

Application-specific instruction-set processors [70] are programmable processors of which the architecture and instruction set are optimized to a specific application. Important

Table 14.2 The Comparison of the Commercial DSPs
and the Proposed Processor

Vendor	Model	Arithmetic			MAC speed
		Data (bits)	Acc. (bits)	Type	
Analog	ADSP-2100	16	40	fixed	60 ns
Devices	ADSP-21020	32/40	80	floating	40ns
AT&T	DSP16	16	36	fixed	25ns
	DSP32	32	40	floating	60ns
Motorola	DSP56000	24	56	fixed	50ns
	DSP56156	16	40	fixed	50ns
	DSP96002	32	96	floating	50ns
NEC	uPD77230	32	55	floating	150ns
	uPD77240	32	55	floating	90ns
Texas	TMS320C1x	16	32	fixed	100ns
Instruments	TMS320C2x	16	32	fixed	80ns
	TMS320C3x	32	40	floating	50ns
	TMS320C40	32	40	floating	40ns
	TMS320C5x	16	32	fixed	35ns
CCU Signal and Media Labs.	SAM-1	16 (24)	32	fixed & (floating)	25ns (50ns)

applications include multimedia, communications, and consumer products. These systems demand a more flexible design strategy in which hardware and software designs proceed in parallel, with feedback and interaction between the two. We are focusing on the design of hardware and software for speech and audio systems, in which the hardware typically comprises custom data paths, finite state machines, glue logic, and programmable signal processing units, and the software is the program running on the programmable components. The codesign task is to produce an optimal hardware-software design that meets the given specifications, within a set of design constraints such as real-time requirements, performance, speed, area, code size, memory requirements, power consumption, and programmability [71,72].

A design example of the speech recognition processor is described as follows [53]. The application-specific programmable processor is developed for low-cost, high-speed, and high-flexibility performances when considering the computational complexity of speech recognition and the cost of chip size. Figure 14.11 (page 453) shows the major functional blocks of the proposed speech recognition processor. A 24-bit floating-point operation or two 16-bit fixed-point operations can be performed in one clock cycle where the dual MAC units with 16-bit multipliers and 32-bit adders are implemented. This design provides users with more flexibility to handle floating-point or fixed-point operations in order to achieve

Table 14.3 The Commercial Products of Speech and Audio Coding

Product name	Audio decoder	Teleconference, audio coding	SCOP 4800	VM 1000	Low bit-rate synthesis IC
Related standard	MPEG-1 (layer I, II)	G.722	FED-STD 1016	GSM6.10	FED-STD 1016
Sampling frequency (Hz)	48k, 44.1k, 32k	16k	8k	8k	8k
Input resolution (bits)	16 (linear)	14 (linear)	8 (u-law)	8 (u-law)	8 (u-law)
Bit rate (bits/s)	96k, 128k, 160k, 192k per channel	64k, 56k, 48k	4.8k	10k	4.8k
Compression ratio	7.4:1, 5.5:1, 4.4:1, 3.7:1	3.5:1, 4:1, 4.7:1	13.3:1	6.4:1	13.3:1
Delay time	8.7 ms (layer I) 26.1 ms (layer II)	62.5 us	30 ms	20 ms	30 ms
Quality	Near CD	Audio	MOS 2.8-3	MOS 3-3.5	MOS 3
Algorithm	Subband coding	SB-ADPCM	Modified CELP	NREP-LTP	CELP decoder
Processor for real-time implementation	ADI ADSP2105 ADI ADSP2115	TI 320C30	TI 320C5X	ADI ADSP 2105	Full-custom design
Computational complexity	10 MIPS 16 MIPS	14.5 MIPS	18 MIPS	7 MIPS	N/A
Cost	U.S. $10 U.S. $15	U.S. $165	U.S. $50–60	U.S. $20–30	N/A
Applications	Digital audio broadcast	Teleconference, Multimedia	Security phone	Voice mail	Answer machine

maximum throughput. In the instruction set, there are 24 specific instructions and 6 parallel instructions that are optimized for the mathematical operations of the speech recognition method. The instruction set and addressing mode are shown in Fig. 14.12 (page 454). By using the TSMC 0.8 um CMOS technology, the critical delays of a 16-bit multiplier and a 32-bit adder can be smaller than 25 nsec [67]. The computation power can reach 40 MIPS at a system clock of 40 MHz. Table 14.2 illustrates the comparison of the commercial DSPs and the proposed processor. Our processor can perform the high-speed voice guidance, vocal feedback, and command verification in a superior way.

Table 14.4 The Commercial Products of Speech Recognition Processors

Product Name	D6106	HM2007	MSM6679	RSC-164	TC8860F	TC8864F & TC8861F	5A128 & 5S320
Company	DSP Comm.	HUALON Micro. Corp., Taiwan	OKI Semi. Group	Sensory Circuits Inc.	Toshiba Corp.	Toshiba Corp.	RICOH Corp.
Recognition method	Dynamic time warping (DTW)	N/A	DTW & hidden Markov model (HMM)	neural network (NN)	learning matching method	multiple similarity method	N/A
Price	U.S. $36.7	U.S. $25	U.S. $20	U.S. $3.75	U.S. $7.5	N/A	U.S. $10
No. of words	16–128 words	20 or 40 words	25 words	20–30 words	10 words	50 words	10 words
Characteristic	IW & SD	IW & SI	IW & SI / SD	IW & SI / SD	IW & SD	IW & SD	IW & SI / SD
Power Supply	5V	5V	5V	3–6V	4.5–5.5V	4.5–5.5V	5V ± 10%
Package	80-pin PQFP	48-pin plastic DIP	N/A	N/A	MFP44	FP100	80-pin plastic flat package
Spec.	ext. SRAM (1*32-2*128KB), ext. micro-controller	ext. 8KB SRAM, ext. micro-controller	no ext. CPU	ext. RAM, 4MIPS-8bit RISC processor	ext. 4K-bits RAM	N/A	N/A
Demo board	EVS6106	N/A	a serial port interface for PC	N/A	N/A	TBP88D64	N/A
Applications	handsfree voice dialer	toys	handicap aids, industrial controls	electronics learning aids, watches	toys	industrial controls, game	handsfree voice dialer, voice-control
Price of demo board	U.S. $500	U.S. $100	U.S. $876	N/A	N/A	N/A	U.S. $3000

(Note: isolated word: IW; speaker independent: SI; speaker dependent: SD)

14.6.2 Commercial Hardware Products

Various commercial hardware products of speech and audio processing have appeared in many multimedia applications. The manufacturers always try to find a high-performance and low-cost solution in order to make products marketable and profitable. Table 14.3 illustrates some commercial products of speech and audio coding based on industrial compression standards. These coding algorithms, including the subband coding, ADPCM, CELP, and GSM, are realized in the DSPs or full-custom processors. The delay time is estimated for the programmable processor to perform the corresponding codec algorithm. According to the values of delay time, these processors have enough computation powers to support their real-time applications. Table 14.4 summarizes the methods, capabilities, costs, manufactures, and applications of the speech recognition processors. The recognition schemes of the DTW, HMM, neural network, learning matching method, and multiple similarity method are implemented in their corresponding processors. The input words are pronounced discretely for these recognition engines. The features of vocabulary and speaker dependent or independent are crucial for users to choose the speech recognition processor. The hardware design schemes of these processors in Table 14.4

consist of the RISC-based CPU, DSP, and full-custom IC approaches. Some processors require external memories to store the speech patterns. Most of these processors with added speech I/O capabilities offer improved ease-of-use to customers for the voice-control applications.

14.7 CONCLUSIONS

In this chapter, intelligent speech and audio processing has been presented through the topics of compression, text-to-speech conversion, speech understanding, music processing, and VLSI design. These topics are introduced by the current technologies, technology bottlenecks, future directions, and their applications. The advances in algorithmic techniques for speech codec have resulted in a reasonable speech quality at a bit rate as low as 2.4 Kbps. The high-fidelity audio coding is achieved by using the multichannel approach based on transform or subband coding. The text-to-speech technology is quite mature and is employed in many applications such as talking terminals, alarm systems, and audiotext services. In speech recognition, the hidden Markov model is the most popular approach, with fairly good performance. The large-vocabulary, speaker-independent, and continuous speech recognition is still being explored by many researchers. The methods of speaker recognition are similar to those of speech recognition. However, there is no perfect solution which provides a robust system with high-performance speaker recognition. Different spoken languages have different vocal properties that need to be investigated individually, especially for the applications of text-to-speech conversion and speech understanding. By using the MIDI protocol, we can professionally create artificial music that can be synchronized and integrated with the other media. In order to achieve real-time operations of speech and audio processing, the VLSI design plays a key role in developing high-speed, low-cost, lightweight, and low-power applications. The application-specific instruction-set processor, of which the architecture and instruction set are optimized to a specific application, is proposed for high-performance computing. The design examples of the speech recognition processor and system for voice-control applications are presented in this chapter. The industrial standards and commercial products are also summarized. These speech and audio technologies provide efficient and smart interaction channels to make users easily engaging in the multimedia applications. In addition, a multimedia system that further incorporates auditory, visual, and gestural information to generate a rich texture of human-to-machine communication will facilitate the multimedia evolution.

Acknowledgments

The author would like to thank Dr. Yu-Hung Kao of Texas Instruments Corporation, in the United States, for the valuable discussion on speech processing; Hwai-Tsu Chang, Fang-Ru Hsu, Chia-Chang Hsu, and Yuh-Ren Yang of Computer Communication Research Laboratories, Industrial Technology Research Institute, Taiwan, for helping with the software and hardware designs of the speech recognition system; and Chih-Yung Chen and Kai-Ming Tsou of the Department of Electrical Engineering, National Chung-Cheng University, for help in preparing the materials.

References

[1] J. Jeffcoate, *Multimedia in Practice: Technology and Applications*, New York: Prentice Hall, 1995.

[2] S. Gibbs and D. Tsichritzis, *Multimedia Programming: Objects, Environments, and Frame Works*, Reading, MA: Addison-Wesley, 1995.

[3] B. Furht and M. Milenkovic, *A Guided Tour of Multimedia Systems and Applications*, IEEE Computer Society Press, Los Alamitos, California, 1995.

[4] R. Cole et al., "The Challenge of Spoken Language Systems: Research Directions for the Nineties," *IEEE Trans. on Speech and Audio Processing*, Vol. 3, No. 1, Jan. 1995.

[5] J. Koegel Buford, *Multimedia Systems*, Reading, MA: Addison-Wesley, 1994.

[6] R.-V. Cox, P. Kroon, J.-H. Chen, R. Thorkildsen, K. M. Odell, and D. S. Isenberg, "Speech Coders—From Idea to Product," *AT&T Technical Journal*, Vol. 74, No. 2, pp. 14–22, Mar. 1995.

[7] A. S. Spanias, "Speech Coding: A Tutorial Review," *Proceedings of the IEEE*, Vol. 82, No. 10, pp. 1541–1582, Oct. 1994.

[8] A. Gersho, "Advances in Speech and Audio Compression," *Proceedings of the IEEE*, Vol. 82, No. 6, pp. 900–918, June 1994.

[9] P. Noll, "Digital Audio Coding for Visual Communications," *Proceedings of the IEEE*, Vol. 83, No. 6, pp. 925–943, June 1995.

[10] L. R. Rabiner, "Applications of Voice Processing to Telecommunications," *Proceedings of the IEEE*, Vol. 82, No. 2, pp. 199–228, Feb. 1994.

[11] A. M. Kondoz, *Digital Speech Coding for Low Bit Rate Communications Systems*, New York: Wiley, 1994.

[12] R. Dettmer, "The Big Squeeze; A Celp Speech Codec," *IEE Review*, pp. 55–58, Feb. 1990.

[13] D. Pan, "A Tutorial on MPEG/Audio Compression," *IEEE Multimedia*, Vol. 2, pp. 60–74, Summer 1995.

[14] Advisory Comm. on Advanced Television Serv., "Grand Alliance HDTV System Specification," *Version 1.0*, 1994.

[15] B. S. Atal, V. Cuperman, and A. Gersho, *Speech and Audio Coding for Wireless and Network Applications*, Boston: Kluwer Academic Publishers, 1993.

[16] G. Nicollini et al., "A 5-V CMOS Programmable Acoustic Front-end for ISDN Terminals and Digital Telephone Sets," *IEEE Journal of Solid-State Circuits*, Vol. 29, No. 9, pp. 1035–1045, Sept. 1994.

[17] D. Haspeslagh, E. Moerman, Z. Chang, and J. Haspeslagh, "A 4/7 Khz Audio Bandwidth Selectable Digital Phone Interface (DPI) Chip with On-chip Analog Functions and Modem," *IEEE Journal of Solid-State Circuits*, Vol. 29, No. 8, pp. 914–920, Aug. 1994.

[18] N. Tsakalos and E. Zigouris, "Use of Single-Chip Fixed-point DSP for Multiple Speech Channel Vocoders," *Microprocessors and Microsystems*, Vol. 18, pp. 12–18, Jan. 1994.

[19] CCITT Red Book, *Recommendation G. 721*, Vol. 3.

[20] CCITT Yellow Book, Recommendation G. 711, Vol. 3.

[21] T. Tremain, "The Government Standard Linear Predictive Coding Algorithm: LPC-10," *Speech Technology*, pp. 40–49, Apr. 1982.

[22] Y. Shoham, "Constraint-stochastic Excitation Coding of Speech at 4.8 Kbps," *Proc. of Int'l Conf. on Spoken Language Processing*, pp. 645–648, Kobe, Japan, Nov. 1990.

[23] J. Chen, Y.C. Lin, and R. V. Cox, "A Fixed-point 16 kbps LD-CELP Algorithm," *Proc. of IEEE Int'l Conf. on Acoustics, Speech, and Signal Processing*, pp. 21–24, 1991.

[24] S. Yeldener, A. M. Kondoz, and B. G. Evans, "High Quality Multi-band LPC Coding of Speech at 2.4 Kbps," *IEE Electronics Letters*, pp. 1287–1289, July 1991.

[25] M. Ahmed and M. Al-Suwaiyel, "Fast Methods for Code Search in CELP," *IEEE Trans. on Speech and Audio Processing*, Vol. 1, No. 3, pp. 315–325, July 1993.

[26] J. Campbell Jr., T. Tremain, and V. Welch, "The Federal Standard 1016 4800 bps CELP Voice Coder," *Digital Signal Processing*, Vol. 1, pp. 145–155, 1991.

[27] T. Wang, K. Tang, and C. Feng, "A High Quality MBE-LPC-FE Speech Coder at 2.4 Kbps and 1.2 Kbps," *Proc. of IEEE Int'l Conf. on Acoustics, Speech, and Signal Processing*, Vol. 1, pp. 208–211, May 1996.

[28] A. V. McCree and T. P. Barnwell, "A Mixed Excitation LPC Vocoder Model for Low Bit Rate Speech Coding," *IEEE Transactions on Speech and Audio Processing*, Vol. 3, No. 4, pp. 242–250, July 1995.

[29] A. McCree, K. Truong, E. George, T. Barnwell, and V. Viswanathan, "A 2.4 Kbit/s MELP Coder Candidate for the New U.S. Federal Standard," *Proc. of IEEE Int'l Conf. on Acoustics, Speech, and Signal Processing*, Vol. 1, pp. 200–203, May 1996.

[30] G. Theile, G. Stoll, and M. Link, "Low Bit-Rate Coding of High-quality Audio Signals: An Instruction to the MASCAM System," *EBU Rev. Tech.*, No. 230, pp. 158–181, Aug. 1988.

[31] Y. Dehery, M. Lever, and P. Urcun, "A MUSICAM Source Codec for Digital Audio Broadcasting and Storage," *Proc. of IEEE Int'l Conf. on Acoustics, Speech, and Signal Processing*, Vol. 1, pp. 3605–3609, 1991.

[32] G. Robert, B. Karlheinz, and S. Gerhard, "Current and Future Standardization of High-quality Digital Audio Coding in MPEG," *Proc. of IEEE Workshop on Application of Signal Processing to Audio and Acoustics*, pp. 43–46, Oct. 1993.

[33] I. Gerson and M. Jasiuk, "Vector Sum Excited Linear Prediction (VSELP) Speech Coding at 8 Kbps," *Proc. of IEEE Int'l Conf. on Acoustics, Speech, and Signal Processing*, pp. 461–464, 1990.

[34] A. Potter, "Implementation of PCNs Using DCS 1800," *IEEE Communications Magazine*, Vol. 30, No. 12, pp. 32–37, Dec. 1992.

[35] P. Mermelstein, "G. 722, A New CCITT Coding Standard for Digital Transmission of Wideband Audio Signals," *IEEE Communications Magazine*, pp. 8–15, Jan. 1988.

[36] J. D. Johnston, "MPEG-audio Draft, Description as of Dec. 10, 1990 ISO/IEC JTC1/SC2/WG11," *MPEG COMPCON Spring 91*, pp. 336–337, Mar. 1991.

[37] S. Levinson, J. Olive, and J. Tschirgi, "Speech Synthesis in Telecommunications," *IEEE Communications Magazine*, pp. 46–53, Nov. 1993.

[38] M. O'Malley, "Text-to-speech Conversion Technology," *IEEE Computer*, Vol. 23, pp. 17–23, Aug. 1990.

[39] A. Breen, "Speech Synthesis Models: A Review," *Electronics & Communication Engineering Journal*, pp. 19–31, Feb. 1992.

[40] N. Sugamura, T. Hirokawa, S. Sagayama, and S. Furui, "Speech Processing Technologies and Telecommunications Applications at NTT," *Proc. of the 2nd IEEE Workshop on Interactive Voice Technology for Telecommunications Applications*, pp. 37–42, 1994.

[41] G. E. Pelton, *Voice Processing*, New York: McGraw-Hill, 1993.

[42] A. Syrdal, R. Bennett, and S. Greenspan, *Applied Speech Technology*, Boca Raton, FL: CRC Press, 1995.

[43] L. Rabiner and B.-H. Juang, *Fundamentals of Speech Recognition*, New York: Prentice Hall, 1993.

[44] R. Peacocke and D. Graf, "An Introduction to Speech and Speaker Recognition," *IEEE Computer*, pp. 26–33, 1990.

[45] J. Allen, "How Do Humans Process and Recognize Speech," *IEEE Transactions on Speech and Audio Processing*, Vol. 2, No. 4, Oct. 1994.

[46] J. R. Deller, J. G. Proakis, and J. H. Hansen, *Discrete-Time Processing of Speech Signals*, New York: Macmillan Publishing, 1993.

[47] K.-F. Lee, *Automatic Speech Recognition*, Boston: Kluwer Academic Publishers, 1989.

[48] L. Rabiner, "A Tutorial on Hidden Markov Models and Selected Applications in Speech Recognition," *Proceedings of the IEEE*, Vol. 77, No. 2, pp. 257–285, 1989.

[49] T. Kohonen, "The Neural Phonetic Typewriter," *IEEE Computer*, Vol. 21, pp. 11–24, 1988.

[50] A. Waibel, "Phoneme Recognition Using Time-delay Neural Networks," *IEEE Trans. on Acoustic, Speech, Signal Processing*, Vol. 37, pp. 1888–1898, 1989.

[51] N. Morgan and H. Bourlard, "Continuous Speech Recognition," *IEEE Signal Processing Magazine*, pp. 25–42, May 1995.

[52] S. Chen and W. Chen, "Generalized Minimal Distortion Segmentation for ANN-based Speech Recognition," *IEEE Trans. on Speech and Audio Processing*, Vol. 3, No. 2, pp. 141–145, Mar. 1995.

[53] O. T.-C. Chen, C.-Y. Chen, H.-T. Chang, F.-R. Hsu, H.-L. Yang, and Y.-G. Lee, "A Multi-lingual Speech Recognition System Using a Neural Network Approach," *Proc. of IEEE Int'l Conf. on Neural Networks*, June 1996.

[54] J. Naik, "Speaker Verification: A Tutorial," *IEEE Communications Magazine*, pp. 42–48, Jan. 1990.

[55] H. Gish and M. Schmidt, "Text-independent Speaker Identification," *IEEE Signal Processing Magazine*, pp. 18–32, Oct. 1994.

[56] D. Brens and B. Wattenbager, "Dialog Design for Automatic Speech Recognition of Telephone Number and Account Numbers," *Proc. of Second IEEE Workshop on Interactive Voice Technology for Telecommunications Applications*, pp. 117–120, Sept. 1994.

[57] F. Lavagetto, "Converting Speech into Lip Movements: A Multimedia Telephone for Hard of Hearing People," *IEEE Transactions on Rehabilitation Engineering*, Vol. 3, No. 1, pp. 90–102, Mar. 1995.

[58] T. Yamada, T. Hanazawa, T. Kawabata, S. Matsunaga, and K. Shikano, "Phonetic Typewriter Based on Phoneme Source Modeling," *Proc. of IEEE Int'l Conf. on Acoust. Speech and Signal Processing*, Vol. 1, pp. 109–172, May 1991.

[59] T. Matsui and S. Furui, "A Text-independent Speaker Recognition Method Robust Against Utterance Variation," *Proc. of IEEE Int'l Conf. on Acoustics, Speech and Signal Processing*, Vol. 1, pp. 377–380, May 1991.

[60] T. Dean, "Understanding MIDI," *IEEE Potentials*, pp. 10–11, 1994.

[61] A. Camurri and R. Dannenberg, "Computer-generated Music and Multimedia Computing," *Proc. of the Int'l Conf. on Multimedia Computing and System*, pp. 87–88, 1994.

[62] D. Baggi, "Computer-generated Music," *IEEE Computer*, pp. 6–9, July 1991.

[63] A. So, K. Tse, and W. Chan, "Musical Education in Hypermedia Environment," *Proc. of IEEE Int'l Conf. on Multimedia Engineering Education*, pp. 392–397, 1994.

[64] R. Dannenberg and D. Jameson, "Real-time Issues in Computer Music" *Proc. of Real-Time System Symposium*, pp. 258–260, 1993.

[65] W. Lee, Y. Kim, R. Gove, and C. Read, "MediaStation 5000: Integrating Video and Audio," *IEEE Multimedia*, pp. 50–61, Summer 1994.

[66] V. Madisetti, *VLSI Digital Signal Processors*, Boston: Butterworth Heinemann, 1995.

[67] N. Weste and K. Eshraghian, *Principles of CMOS VLSI Design: A Systems Perspective*, Reading, MA: Addison-Wesley, 1993.

[68] A. Kalavade and E. Lee, "A Hardware-Software Codesign Methodology for DSP Applications," *IEEE Design & Test of Computers*, pp. 16–28, Sept. 1993.

[69] D. Gajski, F. Vahid, S. Narayan, and J. Gong, *Specification and Design of Embedded Systems*, Englewood Cliffs, NJ: Prentice Hall, 1994.

[70] I.-J. Huang and A. Despain, "Synthesis of Application Specific Instruction Sets," *IEEE Transactions of Computer-Aided Design of Integrated Circuits and Systems*, Vol. 14, No. 6, pp. 663–675, June 1995.

[71] G. Micheli, "Computer-aided Hardware-Software Codesign," *IEEE Micro*, pp. 10–16, Aug. 1994

[72] P. Subrahmanyam, G. Micheli, and K. Buchenrieder, "Hardware-Software Codesign," *IEEE Computer*, pp. 84–87, Jan. 1993.

Chapter 15

SPEECH RECOGNITION IN MULTIMEDIA HUMAN–MACHINE INTERFACES USING NEURAL NETWORKS

Jhing-Fa Wang and Chung-Hsien Wu

Abstract

The past decade has been highlighted by the emerging technology of multimedia interface design. Intelligent multimedia interfaces can be developed that require very little computer sophistication on the part of the user. This chapter focuses on speech recognition systems applied to multimedia human–machine interfaces. There are a number of speech recognition systems on the market today, and some of them can be integrated into task-specific applications. However, speech recognition research still faces a few challenges in the area of multimedia human–machine interfaces. This chapter presents some approaches based on neural networks for Mandarin speech recognition. In practical applications, a robust Mandarin speech recognition system (VenusDictate) applied to multimedia interfaces is described.

15.1 INTRODUCTION

15.1.1 Motivation and Applications of Speech Recognition to Multimedia Systems

Speech is the most natural form of human communication. If computers could recognize and understand speech, automatic speech recognition would provide a comfortable and natural form of human–machine communication. Speech recognition has already proven useful for certain applications, and research has resulted in various achievements. Currently, speech recognition is often applied in voice entry of data or commands. Speech recognition over the telephone network has the greatest potential for growth. One ambitious goal is to implement automatic query systems that could be accessed through public telephone lines, because some telephone companies are concerned about the amount of time operators spend on the telephone. An even more ambitious plan is to recognize speech in one language and then to synthesize its content in another, on-line. Furthermore, speech recognition can help users control the personal workstation or interact with other applications remotely. Related applications occur in automatic transcription and intelligent human–machine interfaces.

Recently, multimedia has grown into a new technology combining computer, communication, and consumer electronics. The past decade has been highlighted by the emerging technology of multimedia interface design. Examples include speech recognition or understanding, vision, gesture recognition, intelligent graphics, speech synthesis, and information retrieval. Nevertheless, from a practical perspective, these systems operate in restricted environments. An effective and graceful interaction methodology has yet to be realized. Recent advances in speech recognition technology [1–8] have made it possible to build intelligent human–machine interfaces for multimedia systems. To support natural interaction, a speech recognition system needs to embody certain basic properties. This chapter addresses some key approaches in developing the Mandarin speech recognition system, VenusDictate, using neural networks.

15.1.2 Current State and Related Problems in Mandarin Speech Recognition

Mandarin speech is a syllabic language of which each syllable consists of an initial part and a final part. The initial part comprises an optional consonant. The final part comprises a vowel or diphthong nucleus before an optional medial and followed by an optional nasal. Although Mandarin speech recognition has been researched for only a few years, some encouraging results have been obtained. For the recognition of isolated syllables, research [1,5,9] has been made and extended to recognition for a large vocabulary size. For lexical tone and initial part recognition, Yang [9] and Liu [2] gave some answers based on the hidden Markov model (HMM) and the neural network (NN). For recognizing strings of connected words, more difficulties are involved, but a number of systems have been proposed [3,4,6,11, 12]. For the construction of a language model, Chien [10] and Wu [8] proposed language processing models, both integrating the unification grammar and Markov model. These systems can decode phonetic symbol sequences into the corresponding Chinese character sequences. In the wake of the above advances, recently a prototype Mandarin dictation system (Golden Mandarin III) was developed in the speech laboratory of National Taiwan University [11]. This system accepts utterances continuous within a prosodic segment which is composed of one or a few words. It also possesses various on-line learning capabilities for fast adaptation to a new user in acoustic, lexical, and linguistic levels. Several techniques, including PLU-based acoustic modeling, an N-best frame synchronous dynamic network searching algorithm, a three-stage hierarchical word classification algorithm, and a new word-class-based Chinese language model, are used. However, since the language model used in this system is not robust for all fields, errors will propagate if the prosodic segment contains word combinations that are not in the training corpus. In the meantime, a large-vocabulary Mandarin dictation system (Tangerine) has been developed at the Apple-ISS Research Center [12]. This system is a word-based Mandarin dictation system. The Mel-scale frequency cepstral analysis is adopted to describe the speech signal. A statistical language model is used to overcome the problem of homonyms in Chinese. For training this system, each speaker is asked to pronounce a training database that takes about three hours. Therefore, retraining the system to suit a new user is not a trivial task. In addition, a robust and practical Mandarin speech recognition system (VenusDictate) commercially available has been developed at National Cheng Kung University [13]. This system will be described in this chapter.

One of the most difficult aspects of speech recognition is its interdisciplinary nature. Consider some problems for Mandarin speech recognition in which fundamental research is needed:

1. For each Mandarin syllable, the initial part lasts for just a short duration compared to the final part, and the initial part is always affected by the final part. Low initial recognition rate is a severe problem for Mandarin speech recognition.

2. Since Mandarin speech is a monosyllabic and tonal language, increasing the vocabulary size introduces many acoustically similar words, thus increasing the error rate.

3. There exists a great deal of variability in speech: intraspeaker variability due to different speaking modes, interspeaker variability, and environment variability.

4. Coarticulation effects, high computational complexity, and high error rate undermine the performance for large-vocabulary continuous speech recognition.

5. There are no precise rules for finding the information at different levels of linguistic decoding (including syntax, semantics, and pragmatics).

15.1.3 The Potential of Neural Networks for Mandarin Speech Recognition

Neural networks have been studied for many years in the field of speech recognition. Current research is aimed at analyzing learning algorithms, building complete systems for speech recognition, and obtaining experience with these systems [14–20]. After many neural network classifiers have been applied to the problems of classifying static input patterns, excellent performance has been obtained using time-delay neural networks [21]. Performance for small vocabularies often slightly exceeds that yielded by high-performance experimental HMM recognizers. Neural networks with recurrent connections [22] have not been used as extensively for speech recognition problems as feed-forward networks because they are more difficult to train, analyze, and design. These nets typically yield good performance on small problems but require an extremely long training time. On the other hand, researchers are beginning to combine conventional HMM and Dynamic Time Warping (DTW) speech recognition algorithms with neural net classification algorithms [18]. This may lead to improved recognition accuracy as well as to new designs for compact real-time hardware. Linked predictive neural networks [23] can predict the next frame, and the predictive error is regarded as the matching distance. Kohonen compared a neural network classifier called learning vector quantization (LVQ) [24] to a Bayesian classifier and a K-Nearest Neighbor (KNN) classifier. Furthermore, Hamming nets [17] and Hopfield networks [25] were also adopted for speech recognition.

Although children learn to understand speech with little explicit supervision, it has proven to be a difficult task to duplicate with computers. Therefore, when highly parallel and adaptive methods such as neural networks are introduced, we assume their capabilities can best be utilized if the networks are made to adapt to the real data, finding relevant features in the signals. Thus, recently, researchers have placed great hopes on neural networks to perform speech recognition. Evidently, neural networks have the potential to provide massive parallelism, adaptation, and new algorithmic approaches to problems in speech recognition.

15.2 NEURAL NETWORKS FOR ISOLATED MANDARIN SPEECH RECOGNITION

A speech recognition system is a device that transcribes speech into text. The recognition system usually consists of two components: an acoustic component and a language processing component. For a Mandarin speech recognizer, the acoustic component matches the acoustic input to syllables in its vocabulary. The language processing component incorporates a language model that determines the most promising sentence hypotheses from a list of previously hypothesized words.

15.2.1 The Acoustic Signal Processor

For large-vocabulary speech recognition, as the number of recognition candidates becomes too large, a hierarchical recognition scheme is commonly chosen to overcome the problems of massive numbers of interconnection weights and long training time. Mandarin speech is a tonal and syllabic language. The basic units include 5 lexical tones, 21 initial parts, and 38 final parts for the constitution of 1300 Mandarin syllables. There are 408 phonologically allowed tone-independent syllables. Therefore, the lexical tone, initial part, and final part of each syllable can be separately adopted and recognized hierarchically. Accordingly, by using specific features in each decision level, a hierarchical approach for the 1300 Mandarin syllables is proposed, which adopts a pitch feature in the first level, a final part feature in the second level, and an initial part feature in the third level for lexical, final part and initial part recognition, respectively.

In order to deal with the initial part and hierarchical recognition problems described in the last section, an initial/final (I/F) segmentation algorithm is desirable to meet these purposes. Therefore, an efficient algorithm that simultaneously performs accurate I/F segmentation and pitch detection, driven by the special properties of Mandarin speech, is proposed. As an initial part is located, it will be enhanced by normalizing its duration and combined with the front end of the following final, alleviating the problems of short initial part duration and coarticulation. Consequently, this approach provides a better initial part recognition rate and thus makes possible the recognition of all Mandarin syllables hierarchically.

15.2.1.1 Pitch Detection and I/F Segmentation

For Mandarin speech, pitch detection and I/F segmentation are two important steps in the front end processing for hierarchical recognition. Although many pitch detection algorithms [26] have been proposed, most presently available pitch detection schemes cannot give perfectly satisfactory results across a wide range of speakers, applications, and operating environments. Besides, these algorithms cannot perform the I/F segmentation we need. Therefore, an algorithm that can simultaneously perform pitch detection and I/F segmentation is desirable. For Mandarin speech, the initial part lasts just a short while compared to the final part, and the peak amplitude of the initial part is much less than the peak amplitude of the final part. Moreover, it is well known that pitch periods change slowly with time.

Considering the above properties, a particular pitch detection and I/F segmentation scheme is proposed. This scheme is as follows:

1. Locate a 30 msec voiced interval from the middle of the syllable and calculate all the pitch periods within this interval.
2. Find all the peak positions backward and perform I/F segmentation.
3. Find all peak positions forward until the end of the speech signal.

One example of the pitch detection and I/F segmentation for the utterance /ma/ is shown in Fig. 15.1. This algorithm is based on purely time-domain processing, and some complicated and unnecessary computations used in the traditional approaches are omitted; most of the computations used in this algorithm are comparisons. Therefore, this algorithm can be implemented to operate very quickly on an ordinary IBM personal computer.

15.2.1.2 Feature Extraction

1. *Lexical tone:* For each syllable, the pitch period contour is normalized into eight pitch parameters. A pitch vector is formed by the concatenation of the offset and slope of the eight pitch parameters.
2. *Initial and final parts:* Speech data (sampled at a 10 kHz rate) are preemphasized and Hamming windowed. The linear predictive coding (LPC) derived cepstral vector is computed up to the twelfth component. Bandpass liftering [42] is then applied to the cepstral coefficients. A 20-dimensional feature vector, including 10 cepstral and 10 delta cepstral coefficients, is computed for each frame.

15.2.1.3 Recognition Using Neural Networks

Figure 15.2 gives the hierarchical taxonomy of Mandarin syllables and recognition phases. The well-known backpropagation (BP) neural network with two hidden layers is adopted for each recognition phase. One lexical tone network is used to decide the lexical tone of the input syllable. Five final networks, each corresponding to one lexical tone, are constructed to decide the most promising final part with respect to the input syllable. Finally, 5*38 initial part networks, each corresponding to one lexical tone and one final part, have to be trained for the initial part recognition. In the recognition process, one of 1300 syllables is fed into the lexical tone network first. The input syllable is classified into one of the five lexical tones and then fed to the corresponding final part network. The final part network is used to classify the input syllable into one of 38 final parts corresponding to the recognized lexical tone. The best two final parts are chosen as the final part candidates. Finally, the result of the recognition process is obtained by feeding the input syllable into the initial part network corresponding to the two recognized final parts to perform the initial part recognition. Therefore, the number of recognition candidates can be reduced from 1300 to 44, that is, 22 initial parts for each recognized final part (including one null initial part). The 10 most likely syllables, five containing the first most promising final part and five containing the second most promising final part, were chosen to minimize the problems

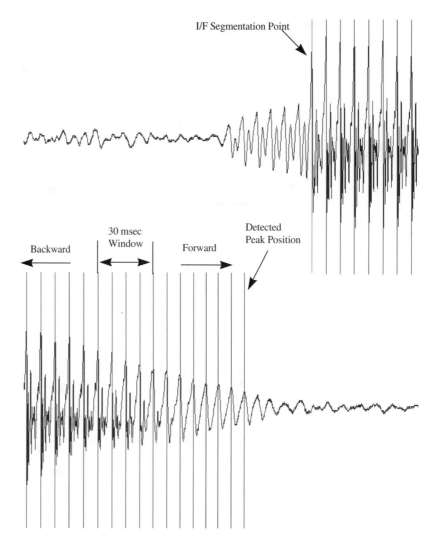

Figure 15.1 Pitch detection and I/F segmentation results for the utterance /ma/.

of recognition uncertainty and errors. The 10 recognized syllables are then passed to the language processing model in order to find the most promising sentence hypothesis.

15.2.2 The Language Processing Model

The language processing component incorporates a language model that determines the most promising sentence hypotheses from a list of previously hypothesized words. Conventionally, either grammatical or statistical approaches are used in language processing

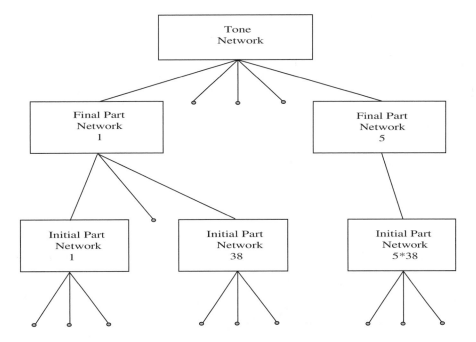

Figure 15.2   The hierarchical taxonomy of Mandarin syllables and the recognition phases.

models [10–13]. However, using either grammatical or statistical approaches alone results in a high degree of ambiguity and a large number of noisy word hypotheses in the word lattice, and subsequent incorrect identification and slow computation speed. Since the features of the grammatical and statistical approaches are basically complementary, several methods [9–11] have been proposed to combine these two approaches by combining the grammatical and statistical approaches sequentially. In this chapter, a language processing model using a hierarchical grammar-based Markov model is presented.

A block diagram of the language processing model is shown in Fig. 15.3. The model consists of three major units:

1. The word formation unit
2. The scoring unit
3. The hierarchical grammar-based Markov model

Due to the acoustic signal recognition uncertainty and errors, the language processing model accepts the 10 most promising syllables as the input. The word formation unit will look up the lexicon and find out all possible word hypotheses generating the corresponding word lattice. For each word hypothesis, the scoring unit then calculates a score using heuristic rules and a weighted unigram Markov model. The N most promising sentence hypotheses are chosen and fed to a hierarchical grammar-based Markov model. In the hi-

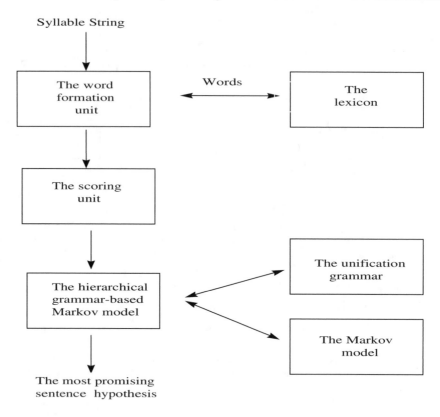

Figure 15.3 The block diagram of the language processing model.

erarchical grammar-based Markov model, a sentence hypothesis is valid only if it can be generated by the grammar rules. In addition, the hierarchical grammar-based Markov model will give each valid sentence hypothesis a score based on its likelihood. The final score is calculated as the weighted average of the output scores of the scoring unit and the output scores of the hierarchical grammar-based Markov model.

An experimental system for Chinese language recognition has been implemented and tested. In the training phase of the hierarchical grammar-based Markov model, primary school Chinese textbooks were used as the training database. In the testing phase, we randomly chose 812 test Chinese sentences from the primary school Chinese textbooks, newspapers, and children's books in Taiwan. All of these test sentences can be generated by the grammatical rules in our system. There are 5806 separate characters in the sentences, and the length ranges from 5 to 12 characters, with an average of 7.15 characters. System performance is evaluated using the following parameters:

1. The top 10-sentence correct rate is defined as the rate for which one of the top 10-sentence hypotheses is exactly the same as the expected correct sentence.

2. The top 1-character correct rate is defined as the correct comparison rate of the corresponding characters between the top 1-sentence hypothesis and the expected correct sentence.

For the 812 test sentences, a top 10-sentence correct rate of 94.2% and a top 1-character correct rate of 91.6% were obtained. Furthermore, an acceptable computation speed of about 0.38 second per character was achieved.

15.3 CONTINUOUS MANDARIN SPEECH RECOGNITION BASED ON NEURAL NETWORKS

Over the past years, although significant advances have been achieved in the field of isolated word recognition, the approaches used cannot be easily extended to continuous speech recognition. For recognizing strings of continuous words, there still remain a substantial number of unsolved problems, especially for large vocabulary. Approaches proposed in past years can be classified into two categories:

1. Segmentation prior to recognition—Segmenting recognizer
2. Joint segmentation and recognition—Nonsegmenting DTW recognizer

In the first category, several algorithms have been proposed for recognizing a string of connected words in order to alleviate both the computational complexity and massive storage problems. Zelinski and Class [27] proposed a segmentation algorithm based on a statistical estimation principle. Svendsen and Soong [28] proposed three different approaches that are based on template matching, spectral change detection, and constrained-vector quantization, respectively. Andre-Obrecht [29] proposed a statistical approach using an AR statistical model. However, as the speaking rate approaches that of continuous discourse (180–300 syllables/min), the performance of such a continuous speech recognizer falls dramatically. Coarticulation is the downfall of segmentation-based continuous speech recognition. In the second category, approaches to continuous speech recognition are all based on a recognition process where no segmentation is performed prior to recognition, and the basic strategy employed is the technique of dynamic time warping (DTW). Sakoe [30] proposed a two-level DP approach. Myers and Rabiner [31] proposed a level building approach. Ney [32] proposed a one-stage dynamic programming algorithm. Although each of these approaches differs greatly in implementation, all of them are similar in that the basic procedure for finding an optimal matching is to solve the time-alignment problem using the DTW method. These approaches can alleviate the effects of coarticulation, but computational complexity and misrecognition are still severe problems for long word string recognition. In this section, these two kinds of recognizers based on neural networks are explored separately.

15.3.1 Segmenting Recognizer for Continuous Speech

In the segmenting recognizer, a multilayer perceptron with a backpropagation learning algorithm is adopted. This section addresses the application of neural networks to a signal classification problem: the segmentation and recognition of continuous speech. Since multilayer perceptron can form any arbitrarily complex decision regions and can learn to discriminate continuous-valued signals, the segmentation problem can be formulated as a signal classification problem and can be solved by using the segmentation network to decide the boundaries between syllables. Similarly, speech recognition for segmented syllables can also be formulated as a classification problem and can be performed with a well-trained multilayer perceptron.

15.3.1.1 Feature Extraction for Segmentation

Of the various speech signal features, energy and spectral transitions have been shown to be successful for continuous speech segmentation [28]. Another speech feature, pitch period transition, has also been investigated. Pitch transition provides additional significant information for continuous speech segmentation. Therefore, in this approach, energy, spectral, and pitch-period transitions are adopted. In the feature extraction process, speech data are preemphasized by a +6 db/oct filter. The speech samples are then segmented into analysis frames by a Hamming window with a length of 128 samples and 64 samples of overlap to adjacent frames. The FFT algorighm is employed to compute the power spectrum. Melscale coefficients are computed from the power spectrum by computing log energies in each melscale energy band. The three feature transitions used in this approach are defined as follows.

1. Spectral Transition (ST): The time derivative of the log spectrum over the whole frequency range.
2. Energy Transition (ET): The time derivative of the instantaneous energy.
3. Pitch-Period Transition (PT): The pitch-period transition parameters expressed as the time derivative of pitch contour.

All the parameters for each contour derived above are normalized by subtracting the average parameters computed over each contour, respectively. Parameters are then normalized to lie between –1.0 and +1.0. The three parameters (i.e., ST, ET, PT) constitute one analysis frame for the following process.

For training the segmentation network, a data window is laid over some signal parameters and shifted along the time axis as shown in Fig. 15.4. The length of the data window has to be carefully chosen in order to achieve optimal performance of the segmentation procedure. If the window is too short, some word combinations that cannot be uniquely mapped into a window class will occur. The task of the segmentation network is formulated to solve the classification problem. There are three possible classes in each position of the data window.

1. Begin-transition (B) : A word boundary lies in the right of the data window.
2. End-transition (E): A word boundary lies in the left of the data window.
3. Nontransition (N): A word boundary or nonboundary lies in the data window.

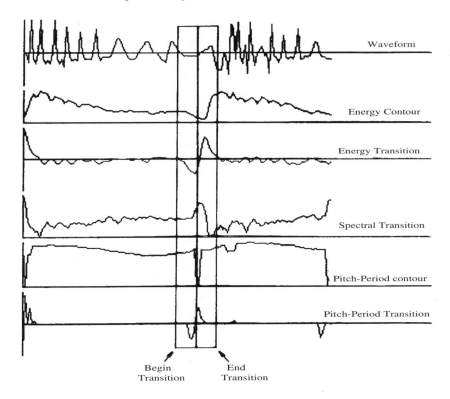

Figure 15.4 A sliding window in the training procedure of the segmentation network.

In the case of an increase in spectral transition and a decrease in energy and pitch-period transitions as shown in Fig. 15.4, the data window is regarded as a Begin-transition. Conversely, if the conditions are reversed, the data window is regarded as the End-transition class. The others are regarded as the nontransition class. In this approach, the training data must include words with the three possible transitions. The three training classes are manually determined according to the true word transitions. The speech data are taken from different speakers so that speaker-independent segmentation can be performed. In order to evaluate the performance of segmentation, a coincidence rate that denotes the percentage of automatically found boundaries coinciding with the manual segmentation results within a margin of 100 samples. The experimental results for continuous speech at different speaking rates are summarized in Table 15.1. From these results, the coincidence rate decreases as the speaking rate increases.

15.3.1.2 Recognition of Segmented Syllables

In the training process, the segmented syllables are used to train the isolated speech recognizer. In the recognition process, the segmented syllables are then fed to the isolated

Table 15.1 Segmentation Coincidence Rate for
Continuous Speech at Different Speaking Rates

| | Segmentation Coincidence Rate | | | |
| | SPEAKING RATE (SYLLABLES/MIN) | | | |
	120–140	140–160	160–180	180–200
Average coincidence rate	96.1%	94.8%	92.2%	89.3%

Mandarin speech recognizer described in the previous section to determine the recognition results. Experimental results are listed in Table 15.2. From these results, we find an interesting phenomenon, namely, that the recognition rate is higher than the coincidence rate. This reveals that some of the missegmented syllables are still correctly recognized. This result arises from the following two facts.

1. The unavoidable manual segmentation error in the training procedure lowers the coincidence rate.

2. The recognition network can cope with some uncoincident boundaries of the segmented syllables.

Compared with the statistical [29] and estimation principle approaches [27], this method involves fewer restrictions and greater reliability not only because of the selection of features but also the classification ability of neural networks. In addition, excellent regularity and massive parallelism for the architecture are extra bonuses.

15.3.2 Nonsegmenting DTW Recognizer Using Neural Networks

In the nonsegmenting recognizer, the backpropagation network and the Bayesian network are used separately to provide distance measure. For the backpropagation network, the main idea is to transform every vector in the feature space to a vector in some code space

Table 15.2 Recognition Accuracy for Continuous
Speech at Different Speaking Rates

| | Recognition Accuracy | | | |
| | SPEAKING RATE (SYLLABLES/MIN) | | | |
	120–140	140–160	160–180	180–200
Average recognition accuracy	84.6%	82.3%	79.1%	74.5%

in such a way that every template corresponds to a codeword in that code space. The code should preferably have the property that codes are uniformly distributed in the code space; that is, the distances between every pair of codewords are the same. With this transformation, the problem of classification is transformed into the coding problem of decoding a noisy codeword. For the Bayesian network, the main idea is to design a distance estimator based on the statistical Bayes theorem. After this, the one-stage dynamic programming algorithm is used to find the most promising syllable sequence.

Mandarin speech is a syllabic language in which there exist basic phonelike units (PLUs), including 21 initial parts and 38 final parts that constitute 1300 tone-dependent syllables. Considering the inter- and intrasyllable coarticulation, 99 initials and 38 finals are chosen as the context-dependent PLUs. For training data collection, in view of the special properties of Mandarin speech, the final parts of Mandarin syllables can be categorized into seven groups [33]. Besides this, the lexical tone also affects the properties of Mandarin syllables. Therefore, by suitably combining the initials, finals, and lexical tones, 176 syllables are obtained to comprise all the desired intrasyllable coarticulations with lexical tones instead of 1300 syllables. Meanwhile, a set of 483 balanced sentences are also designed to obtain the intersyllable coarticulations. Therefore, each PLU in the vocabulary appears in each possible phonetic context at least once in the training set. In this way, the acoustic variability at the beginning and at the end of each PLU can be modeled appropriately.

A block diagram of the continuous speech recognizer is shown in Fig. 15.5. In this recognizer, two distance estimation networks, backpropagation and Bayesian networks, are adopted separately to output the distances. These distances are then fed to the one-stage dynamic programming process. A short description of the modules involved in this system is given in the following section.

15.3.2.1 Presegmentation and Silence Deletion

In each utterance of syllable strings, there exist some silent intervals caused by the speaker pausing. A long silent interval (> 20 ms) is treated as a segmentation point and used to segment a long utterance into short speech intervals. Therefore, computation complexity of the one-stage dynamic programming is alleviated. Besides, a short silent interval (about 5 ms) is deleted to reduce the computation load and eliminate unreasonable matching.

15.3.2.2 Feature Extraction

Speech data (sampled at a 10 kHz rate) is preemphasized and Hamming windowed. The LPC-derived cepstral vector is computed up to the tenth component. Bandpass filtering is then applied to the cepstral coefficients. A 20-dimensional feature vector including 10 cepstral and 10 delta cepstral coefficients is computed for each frame.

15.3.2.3 Backpropagation Network

The backpropagation network is used to provide a distance measure of similarity. Each training pattern is normalized into M frames, and each frame is used to train its correspond-

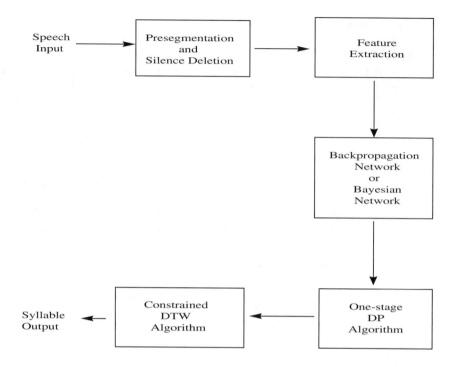

Figure 15.5　The block diagram of the nonsegmenting continuous speech recognizer.

ing backpropagation network. For each input vector, the responses of each backpropagation network are defined as the distances with respect to the input vector. The distances corresponding to all the networks are fed to the one-stage dynamic programming process to choose the most promising syllable sequences using the fast tree-trellis search algorithm [34,35].

15.3.2.4 Bayesian Network

The Bayesian network shown in Fig. 15.6 contains three layers [25]: the input, Gaussian, and mixture layers. An adaptive weight is associated with each input to the Gaussian layer. The Gaussian layer functions as a vector quantizer, and each Gaussian node is assigned to a particular codeword determined by the K-means algorithm [36]. Each mixture node represents one frame of the reference template; it accumulates the weighted outputs of the Gaussian nodes to respond to the similarity between the input vector and one frame of the reference template. For each input vector, the Gaussian node calculates the conditional probability represented by a Gaussian distribution with respect to one codeword. The output of the mixture node is the summation of the weighted outputs of the Gaussian

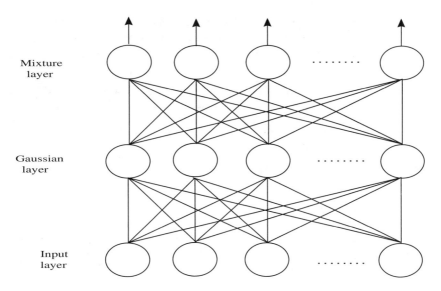

Figure 15.6   The architecture of the Bayesian network.

nodes. The mixture layer outputs are then transformed into distance measure and fed to the one-stage dynamic programming algorithm.

15.3.2.5 One-Stage Dynamic Programming

Since the one-stage approach requires much less warping memory and significantly less computation than the level building (LB) approach, the one-stage algorithm is generally employed to find the most promising syllable sequence. The one-stage dynamic programming approach carries out optimization using transition rules for the word interior and for the word boundaries to output a sequence of syllable candidates. Approaches to continuous speech recognition-based nonsegmenting algorithms (i.e., one-stage or LB) may insert short, spurious syllables into the output string, delete short syllables from the output string, or misinterpret two short syllables as a single erroneous syllable. These insertion, deletion, and misrecognition errors can be minimized by applying a constrained DTW algorithm to re-recognize syllable outputs with unreasonable length.

For speaker-dependent speech recognition, the training set consists of 483 balanced sentences. The segmental k-means algorithm is adopted for PLU modeling. The testing set consists of 500 sentences provided by the same speaker. Results for the systems using the backpropagation network and Bayesian network are listed in Table 15.3. From the experimental results, we find that systems using the Bayesian network outperform those using the backpropagation network. Besides this, most of the substitution errors result from those syllables that are different only in the initial part. The insertion errors occur in the sentences with a low speaking rate, and conversely, the deletion errors always occur in the sentences with a high speaking rate.

Table 15.3 Average Error Rates (%) for the Systems
Using Backpropagation Network and Bayesian Network

| | | Average Error Rate (%) | | | |
| | Type of Errors | SPEAKING RATE (SYLLABLES/MIN) | | | |
		120–140	140–160	160–180	180–200
Backpropagation	I	7.3	6.7	6.1	5.5
Network	D	3.6	4.5	5.8	7.2
	S	5.8	6.9	7.5	7.9
Bayesian	I	7.1	6.7	5.9	5.9
Network	D	3.6	4.3	5.6	7.0
	S	4.5	6.0	6.6	6.8

I : Insertion   D : Deletion   S : Substitution

15.3.3 Keyword Spotting Using Neural Networks

In the past decade, speech recognition technology has made rapid advances, supported by progress in speech technology as well as rapid gains in computing technology. However, most speech recognition systems that exist today are constrained in that the speech to be recognized must consist only of words from a predefined vocabulary. For telephony-based applications, it is naive to assume that users will adhere strictly to this protocol. Research has shown that it is extremely difficult to get users to speak only allowable words. With these constraints on the recognition systems, several methods for keyword spotting have been proposed for conversational speech monitoring over a long-distance telephone network [37–39]. In addition to telephone network-based services, recent investigation into the area of keyword spotting from continuous speech utterances has been driven by many diverse applications, for example, telemarketing and office automation [40,41].

While much research has been performed on the task of general keyword spotting, little of it has been published. Recently, research into algorithms that are able to spot keywords has been focused on constructing hidden Markov model (HMM)-based speaker-independent keyword spotting systems using either subword models or whole word models [38,39]. Typically, a keyword spotting system is trained using speech data that contain keyword and nonkeyword tokens from a training database. A limited-vocabulary recognition model consisting of keyword and nonkeyword garbage models is constructed. Recognition can be performed using the Viterbi algorithm [37]. Performance of these systems is dependent on the number of keyword models and the ability of the garbage models to absorb the extraneous nonkeyword speech utterances.

The block diagram of the keyword spotting system is shown in Fig. 15.7. In the cepstral analysis process, the input speech signal is sampled at 10 kHz with a preemphasis filter, $1-0.97\,z^{-1}$. A Hamming window with a width of 30 ms is applied to the speech signal every 10 ms. Fourteen LPC coefficients are computed for every 30 ms frame using the

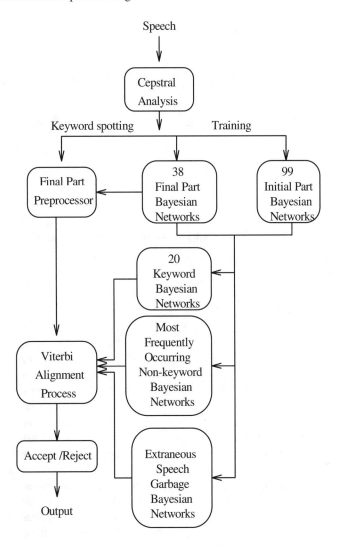

Figure 15.7 The block diagram of the keyword spotting system.

autocorrelation method. Finally, a set of 12 LPC-derived cepstral coefficients is computed from the LPC coefficients. Bandpass liftering is then applied to the cepstral coefficients. A 25-dimensional feature vector, including 12 cepstral and 12 delta cepstral coefficients and 1 delta energy, is computed for each frame. In the training process, each training Mandarin syllable is segmented into an initial part and a final part. The Bayesian network is used to model each PLU. For each keyword in the vocabulary, a whole word-based Bayesian network is constructed by concatenating the corresponding Bayesian networks of the PLUs of the keyword. The most frequently occurring nonkeywords are divided into pre-nonkeywords and post-nonkeywords. The pre-nonkeywords represent those nonkeywords generally spo-

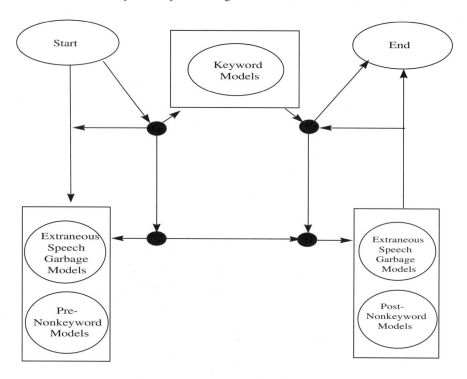

Figure 15.8   The grammar used in the keyword spotting system.

ken before the keyword. The post-nonkeywords represent those nonkeywords generally spoken after the keyword. Three kinds of garbage models including pre-nonkeyword, post-nonkeyword, and extraneous speech garbage models are constructed. The grammar used in the spotting process allows for any amount of extraneous speech followed by one of the vocabulary keywords and by more unconstrained extraneous speech. This is shown in Fig. 15.8. However, users sometimes provide responses consisting only of extraneous non-keywords or background noise. It is desirable to reject all the speech utterances with no keywords. This system is endowed with the ability to perform the task of rejection.

In order to assess the keyword spotting system performance, a query system to access directory information for a city name in the directory has been implemented. In our system, 20 cities in Taiwan are selected as the keywords and 27 most frequently occurring nonkey-words (13 pre-nonkeywords, 14 post-nonkeywords) are predefined. The training database was provided by 25 speakers (15 males, 10 females), each pronouncing 176 monosyllables and 483 balanced words or sentences once. We also recorded 750 utterances for testing spoken by the same speakers responding to requests for a city name in our vocabulary. All test utterances were assigned to one of the following categories. The percentage for each category in the testing database is also listed.

1. In-vocabulary city names, spoken in isolation (K): 38%
2. In-vocabulary city names, embedded before a phrase (K+N): 14%

Table 15.4 (a) Spotting Rates and (b) Rejection Rates
for Five Speech Utterance Categories

	Speech Utterance Category (percentage)			
	ISOLATED	EMBEDDED		
	K(38%)	K+N(14%)	N+K(18%)	N+K+N(18%)
Spotting rate(%)	97.2	92.3	94.1	90.3
Average(%)	97.2		92.2	

(*a*)

	Speech Utterance Category (percentage)				
	ISOLATED	EMBEDDED			NO KEYWORD
	K (38%)	K+N (14%)	N+K (18%)	N+K+N (18%)	N (12%)
Rejection rate(%)	3.2	8.6	5.9	11.1	95.6
Average(%)	3.2		8.5		95.6

(*b*)

3. In-vocabulary city names, embedded after a phrase (N+K):18%
4. In-vocabulary city names, embedded in a sentence (N+K+N):18%
5. Speech with no in-vocabulary city names (N): 12%

In this database, only 88% of the users provided an isolated city name or a city name embedded in a phrase or a sentence; 12% of user responses included no city names at all. All of these responses need to be rejected. In our experiments, the word spotting rate is defined as the ratio of the number of correctly accepted utterances to the total of both correctly plus incorrectly accepted utterances. The rejection rate is defined as the ratio of the number of utterances rejected to the total number of utterances.

The experimental results are listed in Table 15.4. The keyword spotting rate for the first category (K) was 97.2%, and the rejection rate was 3.2%. The spotting rate for the third category (N+K) was 94.1%, and the rejection rate was 5.9%. They were better than that of other categories. This is because the final part in these two categories can be easily detected. Consequently, we can obtain better performance in these two categories. It is reasonable that the first category (K) and the fourth category achieved the best and the worst spotting rates, respectively. The average spotting rates were 97.2% and 92.2% for isolated and embedded keywords, respectively. The average rejection rates were 3.2% and 8.5% for isolated and embedded keywords, respectively. For the fifth category (N), a rejection rate of 95.6% was obtained.

15.4 VENUSDICTATE: A ROBUST AND PRACTICAL MANDARIN SPEECH RECOGNITION SYSTEM FOR MULTIMEDIA APPLICATIONS

15.4.1 Introduction to VenusDictate System

In the Chinese language, there are at least 5000 daily used characters, each corresponding to a monosyllable, and at least 80,000 commonly used words [43]. Every word is composed of one or more characters. The total number of phonologically allowed syllables in Mandarin is only about 1300. Obviously, there is a one-to-many mapping from Mandarin syllables to Chinese characters. To correctly map syllables into texts, recognition with high accuracy for each syllable is required [44]. Unfortunately, this requirement is difficult to achieve, because there exist 38 easily confused sets. As described in the previous section, each Mandarin syllable can be decomposed into an initial part and a final part. In speech recognition, the final parts are stationary periodical signals with gradual change in pitch contours and can be correctly recognized within the top five candidates. However, the initial parts are frequently misrecognized for two reasons. First, the duration of the initial part is too short to be identified using a segmentation algorithm. Second, initial parts are pronounced slightly differently according to the individual's accent. Particularly for the retroflex sets in Mandarin syllables, even many native Chinese speakers cannot pronounce them precisely. Accordingly, the recognition rate of the initial parts is always much lower than that of the final parts. Generally speaking, it is enough to distinguish the Chinese words only by their final parts if their word lengths are longer than two characters.

It is also noticed that the total numbers of three-character and four-character words are 13,000 and 11,388, respectively, in our dictionary, which is composed of 80,000 frequently used words. The average numbers for three-character and four-character words with the same final parts are 0.23 (13000/38*38*38) and 0.005 (11388/38*38*38*38), respectively. This means that three- or four-character words with the same final parts are rare. Hence, words of length more than two characters can be determined using only the final parts. Conversely, for words of two characters or less, recognition for both the initial and final parts is needed. Therefore, a practical system called VenusDictate based on the above ideas has been constructed for Mandarin speech recognition. This system is commercially available on the market. Besides, it works well for most Chinese speakers even if they don't speak standard Mandarin.

15.4.2 System Description

15.4.2.1 I/F Segmentation and Syllable Recognition

The VenusDictate is a speaker-dependent Mandarin syllable recognition system. Users have to pronounce 408 syllables once for training. This takes about 10 to 15 minutes. The initial and final parts of each Mandarin syllable are extracted by using the I/F segmentation algorithm. The Bayesian networks are adopted to recognize each input syllable. The distances between input frames and reference frames are then computed using the DTW algorithm. Since the initial part is included for recognizing two-character words, a weighted

DTW algorithm is adopted to emphasize the importance of the initial part. The recognition process is speeded up by comparing only 38 final part networks instead of 408 initial part networks for those multicharacter words. However, for two-character words, all 408 initial part networks will be used to recognize the input syllable. In order to find the correct word hypothesis, the top five syllable candidates will be chosen for later processing.

15.4.2.2 Mapping Syllables to Texts

Since the words are recognized according to their length, the data structure for vocabulary searching is also designed based on the wordlength. The data structure is shown in Fig. 15.9. The starting index is the combination of the first two finals of a Chinese word. There is a total of 38*38 combination indices in the data structure. In order to speed up the vocabulary searching, a linked list data structure is adopted here. The nodes in each linked list are sorted by their corresponding attributes. For example, in the linked list for WORDNODEs, all nodes are sorted by the phonetic symbols of the final part. These arrangements can greatly increase the search speed in a dictionary. Owing to memory considerations, only the linked list is stored in memory. The texts of each word are stored on disk separately according to their lengths. Each word in the dictionary is represented by its BIG-5 code, phonetic symbols, and occurring frequency. The occurring frequency is used as an index to sort those word hypotheses with the same combination of finals. The occurring frequency is statistically obtained from a Chinese corpus with 100 million Chinese characters.

In order to evaluate the performance of VenusDictate, eight speakers including two children, five adults, and one female American who can speak a little Chinese were tested in three months. Each of them was asked to pronounce 408 syllables once for training and 200 computer-generated Chinese words of length two to five characters for testing. The experimental results are listed in Table 15.5. This table reveals that high recognition rates were obtained for long words. This is because few long words have the same combinations of final parts. In addition, a recognition rate of 91.0% for five-character words was achieved even for the female American.

15.4.2.3 Friendly Human–Machine Interface

For a practical application, we implemented this system on an IBM PC/AT. For ease of adaptation to other applications, the system was designed as a TSR (Terminate and Stay Resident) program. It takes only 48 KB of conventional PC memory. Hence, it can be applied to other application software. We have tested the program on various Chinese application software, such as PE II, HE II, and DBase III systems, and it works very well for each. The user-interface design is briefly described as follows. Once a Mandarin syllable has been pronounced and recognized, a red arrow will appear at the bottom of the screen and the user can continue to input the next syllable. If the user finds that the pronounced syllable is wrong, he can use the DEL key on the keyboard to delete the last pronounced syllable. After all syllables of a Chinese word have been pronounced, the system begins to match the possible word hypotheses. The 10 most promising word hypotheses will be shown at the top of the screen. The user can use the ''number'' key to choose the correct

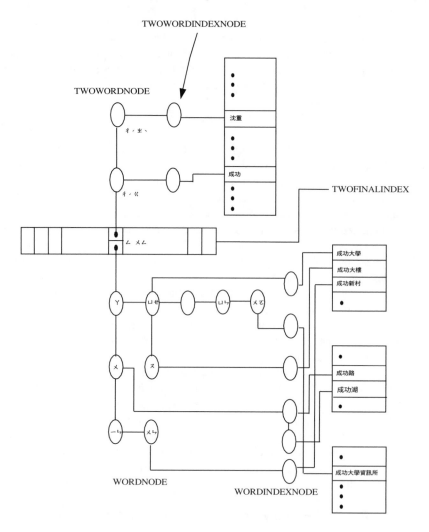

Figure 15.9   The linked list data structure in the dictionary.

Table 15.5   Top Five Recognition Rates for Words with Different Length

	Top Five Recognition Rates (%)			
	2-CHARACTER WORDS	3-CHARACTER WORDS	4-CHARACTER WORDS	5-CHARACTER WORDS
Children (2)	81.5	90.5	93.0	95.5
Adults (5)	84.0	95.0	98.5	100
American (1)	61.5	82.0	90.0	91.5

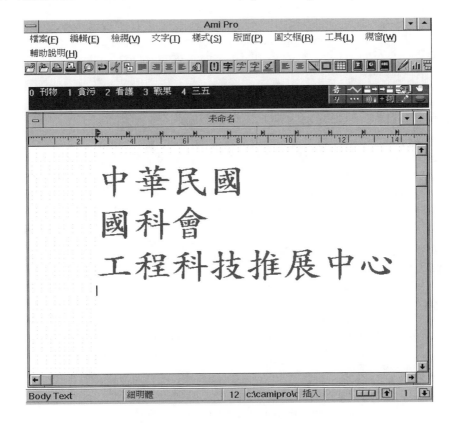

Figure 15.10   An example of the human–machine interface.

one. An example of the human–machine interface is shown in Fig. 15.10. If the correct one is not among the 10 word hypotheses, a menu for modifying the recognized syllables will appear on the screen and the user can easily modify the syllables to re-match the correct word. However, in some cases, the system will automatically match again by increasing the number of syllable candidates if the correct word is not found the first time. Besides this, an additional on-line vocabulary adding function is also designed to let users define their new words conveniently.

15.4.3 Applications to Multimedia Systems

Since VenusDictate has been implemented as a TSR program on an IBM personal computer, some Chinese text processing or data input-and-query application software such as PE II, HE II, and DBase III systems can be directly applied. Generally, this system can be easily applied to ''command-and-control'' multimedia applications. For example, a voice repertory dialer can allow a caller to place calls by speaking the name of someone in the repertory instead of dialing the digit codes. A directory listing retrieval system can provide access to directory information via spoken spelled items. A dictation machine that facilitates Chinese input has been much sought after. The VenusDictate system can perform just such a role. In addition, with a built-in syntax, an interesting application is to use a recognizer that can recognize the merchant identification number, credit card number, and address.

15.5 FUTURE TRENDS AND CONCLUSIONS

In this chapter, some neural network approaches for Mandarin speech recognition in multimedia human–machine interfaces have been presented. A number of speech recognition systems are on the market today, and capabilities range from recognition of isolated keywords to natural language. However, real-world multimedia human–machine interface systems require high accuracy and robustness. The high-level natural language systems are still impractical because they require perception of semantics and pragmatics. Robust methods, such as noise immunity learning, automatic training, and speaker adaptation, are necessary to eliminate ambiguities in acoustic processing. On the other hand, if the ambiguities cannot be eliminated at the acoustic level, high-level knowledge in fields such as semantics and pragmatics can be adopted to solve the problem of ambiguities.

Because it is not easy to overcome the ultimate challenge of speech recognition, our goal in this chapter is to present our research experience in Mandarin speech recognition. Having carried out this research in developing practical speech recognition systems for multimedia interfaces, the following issues present themselves as natural progressions for future study.

1. To develop better front-end acoustic-phonetic feature extraction
2. To improve acoustic/phonetic discrimination
3. To develop training algorithms to construct subword and word models automatically without excessive supervision
4. To develop networks that must include internal mechanisms to distinguish speech from background noise
5. To develop more rapid and incremental training techniques for large-vocabulary speech recognition
6. To develop algorithms and networks for the speaker-independent recognition of difficult sets or phonemes
7. To integrate the neural net approach with conventional approaches to training and classification
8. To develop high-level speech understanding systems that can learn and use syntactic, semantic, and pragmatic constraints

References

[1] J.-F. Wang, C.-H. Wu, S.-H. Chang, and J.-Y. Lee, "A Hierarchical Neural Network Model Based on a C/V Segmentation Algorithm for Isolated Mandarin Speech Recognition," *IEEE Trans. Signal Processing*, Vol. 39, No. 9, pp. 2141–2145, Sept. 1991.

[2] L. C. Liu, "A Study on the Recognition of Mandarin Consonants," Ph.D. Dissertation, Department of Electrical Engineering, National Tsing Hua University, 1990.

[3] D. B. Paul, "The Lincoln Robust Continuous Speech Recognizer," *Proc. IEEE ICASSP'89*, pp. 449–452, 1988.

[4] V. W. Zue et al., "The SUMMIT Speech Recognition System Phonological Modeling and Lexical Access," *Proc. IEEE ICASSP'90*, 1990.

[5] F. Liu, Y. Lee, and L. Lee, "A Direct-Concatenation Approach to Train Hidden Markov Models to Recognize the Highly Confusing Mandarin Syllables with Very Limited Training Data," *IEEE. Trans. Speech and Audio Processing*, Vol. 1, No. 1, pp. 113–119, Jan. 1993.

[6] X. Huang and K.-F. Lee, "On Speaker-Independent, Speaker-Dependent, and Speaker-Adaptive Speech Recognition," *IEEE. Trans. Speech and Audio Processing*, Vol. 1, No. 2, pp. 150–157, Apr. 1993

[7] K.-F. Liu and C.-H. Wu, "Phoneme-based Speaker-adaptive Mandarin Syllable Recognition Using Segmental Bayesian Networks," *Communications of COLIPS*, Vol. 4, No. 2, pp. 151–158, 1994.

[8] C.-H. Wu and J.-F. Wang, "A Language Processing Model for Mandarin Speech Recognition Using Scoring Unit and Grammar-based Markov Language Model," *Proceedings of 1994 International Conference on Computer Processing of Oriental Languages*, Taejeon, Korea, pp. 126–131, May 10–13, 1994.

[9] W. J. Yang, "A Study on the Implementation of Hidden Markov Model Based Speech Recognizer," Ph.D. Dissertation, Department of Electrical Engineering, National Tsing Hua University, 1988.

[10] L.-F. Chien, K.-J. Chen, and L.-S. Lee, "A Best-First Language Processing Model Integrating the Unification Grammar and Markov Language Model for Speech Recognition Applications," *IEEE. Trans. Speech and Audio Processing*, Vol. 1, No. 2, pp. 221–240, April 1993.

[11] R.-Y. Lyu et al., "Golden Mandarin (III)—A User-adaptive Prosodic-segment-based Mandarin Dictation Machine for Chinese Language with Very Large Vocabulary," *Proc. IEEE ICASSP'95*, pp. 57–60, 1995.

[12] Y. Gao, H.-W. Hon, Z. Lin, and G. Loudon, "Tangerine: A Large Vocabulary Mandarin Dictation System," *Proc. IEEE ICASSP'95*, pp. 77–80, 1995.

[13] J.-S. Shyu, J.-F. Wang, and C.-H. Wu, "A Robust and Huge Vocabulary Mandarin Speech Recognition System with a Friendly Human-Interface Design," *Proceedings of 1994 Global Cooperative Software Development Conference*, pp. 45–55, 1994.

[14] J.-F. Wang, C.-H. Wu, and J.-Y. Lee, "Mandarin Syllable Recognition System with Learning Ability Based on Neural Network Model," *Computer Processing of Chinese & Oriental Languages*, Vol. 4, Nos. 2&3, pp. 124–141, July 1989.

[15] R.-C. Shyu, J.-F. Wang, C.-H. Wu, M.-Y. Chen, and J.-Y. Lee, "A Robust Connected Mandarin Digit Recognizer Based on Bayesian Template," *Computer Processing of Chinese & Oriental Languages*, Vol. 7, Supplement, pp. 45–60, Aug. 1993.

[16] C.-H. Wu, J.-F. Wang, and W.-H. Wu, "A Shunting Multi-layer Perceptron Network for Confusing/Composite Pattern Recognition," *Pattern Recognition*, Vol. 24, No. 11, pp. 1093–1103, Nov. 1991.

[17] R. P. Lippmann, "An Introduction to Computing with Neural Nets," *IEEE ASSP Magazine*, Vol. 4, No. 2, pp. 4–22, 1987.

[18] M. A. Franzini and K. F. Lee, "Connectionist Viterbi Training: A New Hybrid Method for Continuous Speech Recognition," *Proc. IEEE ICASSP'90*, 1990.

[19] G. Zavaliagkos, Y. Zhao, R. Schwartz, and J. Makhoul, "A Hybrid Segmental Neural Net/Hidden Markov Model System for Continuous Speech Recognition," *IEEE Trans. Speech and Audio Proces.*, Vol. 2, No. 1, pp. 151–160, Jan. 1994.

[20] G. Rigoll, "Maximum Mutual Information Neural Networks for Hybrid Connectionist-HMM Speech Recognition Systems," *IEEE Trans. Speech and Audio Proces.*, Vol. 2, No. 1, pp. 175–184, Jan. 1994.

[21] C. Dugast, L. Devillers, and X. Aubert, "Combining TDNN and HMM in a Hybrid System for Improved Continuous-Speech Recognition," *IEEE Trans. Speech and Audio Proces.*, Vol. 2, No. 1, pp. 217–223, Jan. 1994.

[22] H. Bourlard and C. J. Wellekens, "Speech Dynamics and Recurrent Neural Networks," *Proc. IEEE ICASSP'89*, pp. 37–40, 1989.

[23] J. Tebelskis and A. Waibel, "Large Vocabulary Recognition by Linked Predictive Neural Networks," *Proc. IEEE ICASSP'90*, 1990.

[24] E. McDermott et al., "Shift-invariant Multi-category Phoneme Recognition Using Kohonen's LVQ2," *Proc. IEEE ICASSP'89*, pp. 81–84, 1989.

[25] C.-H. Wu, J.-F. Wang, C.-C. Haung, and J.-Y. Lee, "Speaker Independent Recognition of Isolated Words Using Concatenated Neural Networks," *International Journal of Pattern Recognition and Artificial Intelligence*, Vol. 5, No. 5, pp. 693–714, Dec. 1991.

[26] L. R. Rabiner, M. Cheng, A. E. Rosenberg, and C. A. McGonegal, "A Comparative Performance Study of Several Pitch Detection Algorithms," *IEEE Trans. Acoust., Speech, Signal Processing*, Vol. ASSP-24, pp. 399–418, Oct. 1976.

[27] R. Zelinski and F. Class, "A Segmentation Algorithm for Connected Word Recognition Based on Estimation Principles," *IEEE Trans. Acoust., Speech, Signal Processing*, Vol. ASSP-31, pp. 818–827, 1983.

[28] T. Svendsen and F. K. Soong, "On the Automatic Segmentation of Speech Signals," *Proc. IEEE ICASSP'87*, pp. 77–80, 1987.

[29] R. Andre-Obrecht, "A New Statistical Approach for the Automatic Segmentation of Continuous Speech Signals," *IEEE Trans. ASSP*, Vol. ASSP-36, pp. 29–40, 1988.

[30] H. Sakoe, "Two level DP-matching—A Dynamic Programming Based Pattern Matching Algorithm for Connected Word Recognition," *IEEE Trans. Acoust., Speech, Signal Processing*, Vol. ASSP-27, pp. 588–596, Dec. 1979.

[31] C. S. Myers and L. R. Rabiner, "A Level Building Dynamic Time Warping Algorithm for Connected Word Recognition," *IEEE Trans. ASSP*, Vol. ASSP-32, pp. 263–271, 1984.

[32] H. Ney, "The Use of One-stage Dynamic Programming Algorithm for Connected Word Recognition," *IEEE Trans. Acoust., Speech, Signal Processing*, Vol. ASSP-32, pp. 263–271, Apr. 1984.

[33] L.-S. Lee, C.-Y. Tseng, H.-Y. Gu, F.-H. Liu, C.-H. Chang, Y.-H. Lin, Y.-M. Lee, S.-L. Tu, S.-H. Hsieh, and C.-H. Chen, "Golden Mandarin (I)—A Real-time Mandarin Speech Dictation Machine for Chinese Language with Very Large Vocabulary," *IEEE Trans. Speech and Audio Processing*, Vol. 1, No. 2, pp. 158–179, 1993.

[34] E.-F. Huang and H.-C. Wang, "An Efficient Algorithm for Syllable Hypothesization in Continuous Mardarin Speech Recognition," *IEEE. Trans. Speech and Audio Proces.*, Vol. 2, No. 3, pp. 446–448, July 1994.

[35] E.-F. Huang, H.-C. Wang, and F.K. Soong, "A Fast Algorithm for Large Vocabulary Keyword Spotting Application," *IEEE. Trans. Speech and Audio Proces.*, Vol. 2, No. 3, pp. 449–452, July 1994.

[36] L. R. Rabiner, J. G. Wilpon, and B.-H. Juang, "A Segmental K-means Training Procedure for Connected Word Recognition," *AT&T Technical Journal*, Vol. 65, No. 3, pp. 21–31, 1986.

[37] R. C. Rose, B.-H. Juang, and C.-H. Lee, "A Training Procedure for Verifying String Hypotheses in Continuous Speech Recognition," *Proc. ICASSP'95*, pp. 281–284, 1995.

[38] J. G. Wilpon, D. M. DeMarco, and R. P. Mikkilineni, "Isolated Word Recognition Over the DDD Telephone Network—Results of Two Extensive Field Studies," *Proc. ICASSP88*, pp. 55–57, 1988.

[39] J. G. Wilpon, L. R. Rabiner, C.-H. Lee, and E. R. Goldman, "Automatic Recognition of Keywords in Unconstrained Speech Using Hidden Markov Models," *IEEE Trans. on ASSP*, Vol. 38, No. 11, pp. 1870–1878, 1990.

[40] B. Chigier, "Rejection and Keyword Spotting Algorithms for a Directory Assistance City Name Recognition Application," *Proc. ICASSP'92*, pp. 93–96, 1992.

[41] H. Tsuboi and Y. Takebayashi, "A Real-time Task-oriented Speech Understanding System Using Keyword Spotting," *Proc. ICASSP'92*, pp. 197–200, 1992.

[42] B.-H. Juang, L. R. Rabiner, and J. G. Wilpon, "On the Use of Bandpass Liftering in Speech Recognition," *IEEE Trans. ASSP*, Vol. ASSP-35, No. 7, pp. 947–953, July 1987.

[43] *Guoyurbao Tzdian* (Mandarin Chinese Daily Dictionary), R. He, ed., Taipei, Taiwan, Guoyurbao, 1976.

[44] L. S. Lee et al., "A Mandarin Dictation Machine Based upon a Hierarchical Recognition Approach and Chinese Natural Language Analysis," *IEEE Trans. Patt. Anal. Mach. Intell.*, Vol. 12, pp. 1417–1419, July 1990.

Chapter 16

HANDWRITTEN RECOGNITION FOR THE MULTIMEDIA HUMAN–MACHINE INTERFACE

Hsin-Chia Fu, Mou-Yen Chen, and Cheng-Chin Chiang

Abstract

The main characteristic of a multimedia information system is its ability to process not only data but also images (both still and motion), graphics, and voice. As such, multimedia information systems are facing challenges to handle various new data types and their interconversions. For some people in the West, and most people in the East, handwriting is still the most convenient and friendly way of communicating with computers. Current technology and future trends of converting handwritings to multimedia data types are presented in this chapter. We first introduce major recognition techniques for English, numeric, and Chinese handwriting. We then present three multilinguistic prototype systems for both on- and off-line handwritten recognition and demonstrate the techniques being used. Finally, we discuss extension of character recognition to image understanding for future multimedia or digital library applications.

16.1 INTRODUCTION

In recent years, we have witnessed a significant increase in the electronic management of information. In particular, many types of media, such as image and sound, that were traditionally processed in analog forms are now processed in digital forms. This advancement brings tremendous opportunities and challenges to information system designers to better meet information users' needs to manipulate multimedia information in a natural and effective manner. Multimedia information systems (MMIS) allow the creation, processing, storage, management, retrieval, transfer, and presentation of multimedia information for diverse applications. MMIS achieves its synergism in many different fields, including databases, digital signals processing, image processing, optical communication, mass storage, artificial intelligence, new paradigms for programming languages, text processing, and multimedia authoring. However, a great deal more remains to be done so that multimedia systems can fully utilize the inputs from the traditional information media, especially printed materials such as pictures and books. Thus, it would be desirable to have computers that recognize natural inputs, such as handwritings, printed texts, drawings, and gestures. Therefore, developing an intelligent I/O interface for natural interaction between human and machine is an essential technology for multimedia systems. In this chapter, we focus on the discussion of handwritten recognition technologies for multimedia systems.

16.1.1   Motivation and Applications of Handwritten Recognition to Multimedia Systems

Most multimedia information systems require that the systems be capable of supporting a wide range of services: multimedia databases, multimedia document structures, real-time conferencing, user-friendly human interfaces, multimedia mailing, and editing functions. The handling of multimedia documents consists of the editing and display of texts, graphics, images, and handwriting. Currently, the keyboard and the mouse are still the dominant input devices for personal computer-based multimedia systems. However, in preparing a first draft and concentrating on content creation, pencil and paper are often superior to keyboard entry. Handwritten recognition allows handwritten characters (words) and hand-drawing line figures to be combined with the advantages of modern hypermedia authoring tools. Recently, the personal digital assistant (PDA) has become popular in mobile computing. Thus, computer system developers have already proposed the next-generation PDA, packaged as small as a pocket calculator, to incorporate both computing and communication functions. Since a pen-based computer system utilizes an input panel to replace the keyboard, one can therefore input characters as well as symbols by writing on the panel with a stylus.

It may be possible to build a multimedia document system by extracting figure and text information from an existing traditional medium, such as books and handwritings. Usually, by using advanced image compression techniques, image data can be stored very efficiently in a magnetic or optical medium. However, by using image processing and handwritten/printed character recognition techniques, a computer may automatically extract text from image data for indexing, searching, and other purposes. By incorporating character recognition with a text-to-speech technology, converting handwritings directly to voice will be an interesting multimedia application. In addition, the handwritten/printed character recognition technique can be combined with artificial intelligence techniques to become an intelligent document editing and recognition tool.

16.1.2   Current Status and Related Problems in Handwritten Recognition

Generally speaking, handwriting recognition techniques can be categorized as on-line and off-line approaches. For the on-line approach, a computer receives trajectory coordinates by sampling the writing trace from a pen-based panel or a tablet. Thus, the recognition process is performed right after a character is written. For the off-line approach, the whole text image is scanned into a computer and is stored in digital image format. In general, the off-line recognition approach requires more image preprocessing and more character layout features than the on-line recognition approach does. Therefore, off-line character recognition processes are usually more difficult than on-line approaches. Nevertheless, both on-line and off-line recognition techniques have their unique technical problems. Among these problems, wide variation in personal handwriting is a major issue. The variation on personal writing style makes extraction of stable features difficult, thus degrading the character recognition performance. Besides, languages like Chinese and Kanji have large character sets. The large character set of a language usually causes degradation in recognition accuracy and speed. In addition, problems like connected or touching characters and symbols make the segmentation of a string of handwritten characters and symbols extremely difficult. Therefore, document analysis and recognition becomes an interesting and fascinating research topic in the field of intelligent information processing.

16.2 TECHNIQUES FOR HANDWRITTEN RECOGNITION

The machine recognition of characters has been a topic of intense research since the 1960s. The objects of interest vary from machine-printed text to handwritten, on-line writing to off-line manuscript, alphanumericals to characters of a particular language. During the last decade, more and more commercial products have come of age. Recognition of machine-printed text, in particular, plays a major role in current commercial applications of data processing. On the other hand, owing to the enormous number of variations involved, handwritten recognition applications still require more work before they can reach comparable performance by a human. In this section, we present an overview of recent advances of both on-line and off-line handwritten recognition techniques. Considering the different characteristics of Western and oriental languages, we will describe the techniques for developing an off-line handwritten recognition system in two parts: one for alphanumerical characters, and the other for Chinese characters.

16.2.1 Overview of Handwritten Recognition

The Role of a Handwritten Word Recognition System. Usually, people communicate with each other by talking and writing. The corresponding media could be voice, handwriting, or both. For the past two decades, people have started ''talking'' to machines in several different ways. Among them, handwriting is still one of the most natural and friendly input media. As a human–machine interface, a handwritten recognition mechanism attempts to understand human handwritings. Figure 16.1 illustrates the interface between human writing and handwritten recognition. At the human writing side, the ''writer'' translates the language into written text, which may include ''noises.'' In the handwritten word recognition (HWR) side, the machine tries to recover the linguistic word from the noisy word image.

An HWR system can always perform a stand-alone task (e.g., recognition of a single word). However, in many circumstances, word recognition alone is not the final goal. Often, other functions need to be performed following the recognition task. In an automatic mail-sorting system, for example, a decision may be made only after combining all the recognition results from different address parts: ZIP codes, state names, city names, street names, and so on. Even a general document recognition system would combine recognition hypotheses of individual words with grammar analysis, word-to-word transition statistics, and the like, rather than merely recognize the words separately. Thus, pre- and postprocessing modules are often included in the HWR system. The detailed techniques of these modules will be discussed later in this chapter. In HWR, the input to the system is assumed to be an isolated word image with an associated lexicon. The objective is to order the lexicon entries so that the word inscribed by the original writer is as close to the top of the lexicon as possible. Figure 16.2 depicts the role of an HWR system.

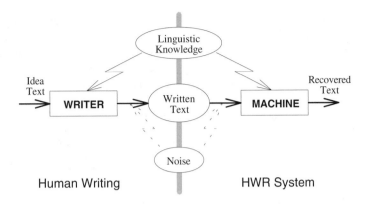

Figure 16.1 The writer writes words based on his or her linguistic knowledge. The writing may include noises (e.g., misspelling, writing styles). An HWR system seeks to uncover the true words from the noisy word image by removing (or reducing) the uncertainties using slant correction, dictionary matching, and so on.

16.2.1.1 *Types*

On-line and Off-line. In on-line handwritten recognition, the machine recognizes the writing while the user writes. Off-line handwritten recognition, in contrast, is performed after the writing is completed [70]. Considering the different types of recognition methods, on-line recognition has some advantages over off-line recognition, such as temporal information, interactivity, and adaptation. Generally, the on-line recognition system is suitable for interactive applications, and the off-line system is useful in batched data input applications.

Language Issues. There are great differences between English and Chinese. For instance, Chinese is not an alphabetical-type language. Taking modern Chinese language as

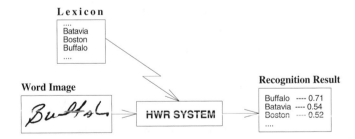

Figure 16.2 The functions of an HWR system are associating a word image with its most matched lexicon and ordering the lexicon entries, so that the word scripted by the original writer is as close to the top of the lexicon as possible.

an example, we find that there are more than 5000 commonly used characters and at least 40,000 commonly used words. A word may consist of one or several characters. Moreover, a Chinese character looks like a complicated connected graph. Thus, it might be easier to segment Chinese characters than English characters in cursive script. These distinct characteristics lead to different methodologies in the recognition of these two languages, while the basic recognition component might be similar. We will discuss the recognition techniques of these two languages in the following two sections.

Components. For general text recognition in a multimedia information system, the objective is to ''understand'' a document. This application may involve two major fields of technology: document analysis and recognition. To understand a document, we need to identify and analyze the desired text blocks first, and then to recognize characters in the text block. The recognition task as shown in Fig. 16.3 is a combination of character recognition and its corresponding pre- and postprocessing. Preprocessing includes line separation, character segmentation, noise removal, image enhancement, and character size normalization. Postprocessing usually indicates the use of a language model to enhance recognition accuracy. Figure 16.4 illustrates a brief roadmap of text recognition techniques. Each component will be discussed in depth later as it is applied to the recognition systems.

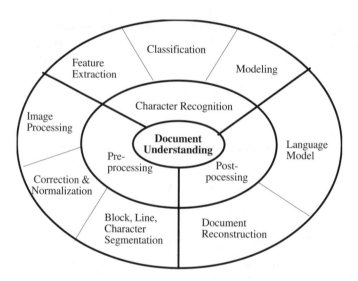

Figure 16.3   The techniques used in document understanding can be partitioned in three phases: preprocessing, recognition, and postprocessing. The preprocessing phase includes any process that is required in obtaining good object images for recognition. During the recognition phase, the pixel information is actually translated into text. The recognized text is then proofread and reorganized in the postprocessing phase to reconstruct the original document.

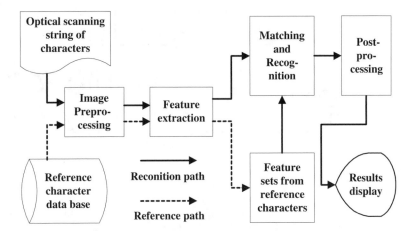

Figure 16.4   The processing flow diagram of handwritten recognition.

16.2.2   Handwritten English and Numerical Character Recognition

16.2.2.1   Handwritten Word Recognition Methodologies

According to writing styles, handwritten words can be divided into two categories: cursive script and hand-printed characters. In practice, however, it is difficult to draw a clear distinction between them. A combination of these two forms can frequently be seen. Based on the nature of writing styles and degree of difficulty in segmentation processes, Tappert [68] has defined the following five stages in handwritten word recognition:

- Stage 1: Boxed discrete characters
- Stage 2: Spaced discrete characters
- Stage 3: Run-on discretely written characters
- Stage 4: Pure cursive scriptwriting
- Stage 5: Mixed cursive, discrete, and run-on discrete

Figure 16.5 illustrates several examples [12] of these stages.

Hand-printed character recognition (e.g., stages 1, 2, and 3) is simpler due to the absence or near absence of the segmentation problem and fewer variations at the character level. There has been fairly extensive research on this topic. (For an overview and bibliography, see [30,47,62,64,75].) Note that the numerical characters appear only in stages 1, 2, and 3. Thus, the recognition of numerical strings is similar to the recognition of English words in these three stages except that English has fewer classes of characters. The strategies for

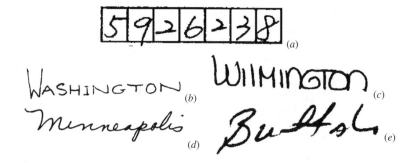

Figure 16.5   Different types of handwriting: (*a*) Stage 1: boxed discrete numerical characters (*5926238*); (*b*) Stage 2: spaced discrete characters (*WASHINGTON*); (*c*) Stage 3: run-on discretely written characters (*WIlMINGTON*); (*d*) Stage 4: pure cursive script
(*Minneapolis*); (*e*) Stage 5: mixed cursive, discrete, and run-on
discrete (*BuffALo*).

cursive script recognition (stage 4) can be roughly classified into three categories. In the
first category, the word is segmented into several characters, and the character recognition
techniques are applied to each segment [10]. We shall call this the *character-based* word
recognizer. In the second category, the *wholistic approach*, whole words are recognized
without any segmentation process. In this approach, the global shape is analyzed to hypoth-
esize the words it may signify. The third category, the *hybrid method*, is the compromise
solution between the first two schemes. A loose segmentation to find a number of potential
segmentation points in the pre-segmentation procedure is performed first. By using information provided from lexica, final segmentation and wordlength are determined later in the
recognition stage.

Character-based Word Recognition. Character segmentation, character recognition,
and contextual postprocessing are three major components of this method. Commonly used
methods in character segmentation include analyses of connected components, projection
profiles, and contours [20]. Although the segmentation decision can be further assisted
by the pitch or character-size estimation, heuristic rules are often used to locate the best
segmentation points. This method depends heavily on the accuracy of the segmentation
points found. However, a sufficiently accurate segmentation technique is not yet available.
It is conceivable that such a technique may involve the interaction of character segmentation
and character recognition.

Wholistic Word Recognition. Motivated by discoveries in psychological studies of
human reading, several word-shape analysis methods have been proposed [21,34,59]. The
string of selected features found in a word is used to discriminate the words in the lexicon.
The advantage of this approach is that errors in character segmentation can be avoided.
However, this is not a practical approach in the case of a large lexicon if each word is to be

considered as a distinct class. Also, this method is likely to be very sensitive to the styles of different writers.

Hybrid Methods. Similar to the character-based method, a segmentation procedure is applied to the word image first in this method. However, the difference is that each segment found here is not necessary to be a character. Instead, a special matching procedure is used to identify the actual character boundaries later when the recognition takes place. Elastic matching and hidden Markov models have been proposed as the techniques for this purpose [6,12,13].

16.2.2.2 Handwritten Recognition Techniques

Preprocessing. A general document may consist of different image types such as text, diagrams, and photographs. Before the text can be processed, it is necessary to identify the text regions in the document. The identified text regions are then further segmented into individual words or characters for recognition at word or character levels. Thus, text segmentation is a crucial technique for document preprocessing.

The scanned image usually contains unwanted noise that presents an obstacle to good recognition results. Several image processing techniques are frequently used for image correction and normalization. They are boundary smoothing (filling holes and breaks in line segments), noise removal (e.g., removing isolated dots), and normalization of stroke width, character size, and the like.

Feature Extraction. To represent each pattern by a more compact form, a mathematical model with a finite number of parameters, that is, a feature vector, is desirable. Many different moment features such as geometric, Legendre, and Zernike moments [71] are widely considered for binary document images. The moments are mathematical transforms of the original signals with more compact information representation capacity. In essence, these moments form a spectral representation of the original signals. Unfortunately, the moments are very sensitive to noise. Any spurious dot, stroke, ligature, or the like, is considered as part of the shape by the moment generation algorithm.

As a result, many recognition algorithms rely on heuristic features. It must be clearly understood, however, what specific information these heuristic features should capture. The features that capture topological and geometrical shape information, both globally and locally, are most desired. In this structural approach, a detection algorithm, which is often designed by intuition, is required to precisely detect certain perceptual entities such as holes, arcs, crossings, and endpoints. Examples can be found in references [2,35,53]. The second type of important features are predefined combinations of pixel values. The features that capture the spatial distribution of black pixels (assuming that white pixel represents the background) are also very important [18,63]. Furthermore, features related to positional information of the segment vis-à-vis others are also desired. A good mix of these features is expected to work well [12].

Classification. The most commonly used classifiers include nearest-neighbor, Bayesian, and polynomial discriminant classifiers. These are referred to as statistical classifiers.

Good reviews of these classical approaches can be found in [17,19,49]. Also, various neural networks, especially the multilayer perceptrons (MLP), have been used in handwritten recognition recently [41]. In addition, hidden Markov models (HMM) have been used in handwritten recognition as well. Chen et al. [12] propose a morphology-based segmentation algorithm to divide a word image into a sequence of segments. From the segmentation results, which depend on the variation in writing styles, the segmentation statistics are computed. These segmentation statistics are then used as a component in computing the probabilities of an HMM-type stochastic network. In this method, the state has a more general connotation; that is, it could signify a whole character, a partial character, or joint characters. Thus, a handwritten character can be converted into a graph where the nodes reflect changes in direction (e.g., using Freeman chain code). Then, the HMM method applies a stochastic model on the graph representations of handwritten characters to build a transition probability matrix. In a word-based recognizer, the Markov matrix is trained for each word of a dictionary. During the recognition, the graph representation of the input strokes of a character (or the input characters of a word) is compared to the Markov matrix according to the transition probabilities for each node which yield the matching score between the input image and the reference word. Some basic concepts of the HMM for handwriting recognition are briefly introduced, as follows.

Hidden Markov Models. An HMM is a doubly stochastic process with an underlined Markov process that is not observable (the states are hidden), but can only be observed through another set of stochastic processes that are produced by the Markov process (the observations are probabilistic functions of the states) [54]. Let's assume that a sequence of observation

$$O = \{o_1, \ldots, o_T\} \tag{1}$$

is produced by a Markov state sequence

$$Q = \{q_1, \ldots, q_T\} \tag{2}$$

where each observation o_t is from the set of M observation symbols

$$V = \{v_k; 1 \le k \le M\} \tag{3}$$

and each state q_t is from the set of N states

$$S = \{s_i; 1 \le i \le N\} \tag{4}$$

Thus, an HMM can be characterized by

$$
\begin{aligned}
&\Pi = \{\pi_i\}, \text{ where } \pi_i = P(q_1 = s_i) \text{ is the initial state probability}\\
&A = \{a_{ij}\}, \text{ where } a_{ij} = P(q_{t+1} = s_j \mid q_t = s_i) \text{ is the state transition probability}\\
&\Gamma = \{\gamma_j\}, \text{ where } \gamma_j = P(q_T = s_j) \text{ is the last state probability}\\
&B = \{b_j(k)\}, \text{ where } b_j(k) = P(o_t = v_k \mid q_t = s_j) \text{ is the symbol probability}
\end{aligned}
\tag{5}
$$

and they satisfy the probability constraints

$$\sum_{i=1}^{N} \pi_i = 1; \quad \sum_{j=1}^{N} a_{ij} = 1 \ \forall \ i;$$

$$\sum_{j=1}^{N} \gamma_j = 1; \quad \sum_{k=1}^{M} b_j(k) = 1 \ \forall \ j \tag{6}$$

Please note that the last state probability Γ is included in this definition. In a Markov state sequence, the last state probability models the different probable final states as the initial state probability does for the initial states. This kind of definition makes the HMM more robust for many general real-world applications [12], although it does not appear in much of the HMM-related literature. The HMM will be denoted by a compact notation $\lambda = \{\Pi, A, \Gamma, B\}$. With these definitions, the sequence of events of an HMM is generated as

- Initialization
  —Choose an initial state $q_1 = s_i$ according to the initial state probability π_i, for $i = 1, \ldots, N$.
  —Choose $o_1 = v_k$ according to the observation probability in state s_i (i.e., $b_i(k)$).
- Recursion
  For $t = 2, \ldots, T - 1$,
  —Choose the new state $q_t = s_j$ according to the state transition probability from state $s_i = q_{t-1}$ (i.e., a_{ij}, for $j = 1, \ldots, N$).
  —Choose $o_t = v_k$ according to the observation probability in state s_j (i.e., $b_j(k)$).
- Termination
  —Choose a last state $q_T = s_j$ according to the state transition probability a_{ij} from state $s_i = q_{T-1}$, and last state probability γ_j, for $j = 1, \ldots, N$.
  —Choose $o_t = v_k$ according to the observation probability in state s_j (i.e., $b_j(k)$).

In a first-order HMM, there are two assumptions. The first one is the *Markovian assumption*. The joint probability $P(Q)$ of a sequence of states $Q = \{q_1, \ldots, q_T\}$ can be defined as

$$P(Q) = P(q_1, \ldots, q_T)$$

$$= P(q_1)P(q_2 \mid q_1)P(q_3 \mid q_2, q_1) \cdots P(q_T \mid q_{T-1}, \ldots, q_1) \tag{7}$$

If the states are statistically independent, Eq. (7) is reduced to the product of the individual probabilities $P(q_t)$. Suppose that the occurrences of the states are not independent but depend only on their immediate preceding states; that is,

$$P(q_t \mid q_{t-1}, \ldots, q_1) = P(q_t \mid q_{t-1}) \tag{8}$$

then we have a first-order Markov chain as

$$P(Q) = P(q_1)P(q_2 \mid q_1)P(q_3 \mid q_2) \cdots P(q_T \mid q_{T-1}) \qquad (9)$$

Similarly, nth order Markov chains can be defined if we assume that q_t depends only on n immediate preceding states. The assumption that a given state q_t depends only on certain preceding states is often reasonable if we are dealing with a sequential signal. The second assumption is the *output-independence assumption*:

$$P(o_t \mid o_1, \ldots, o_{t-1}, q_1, \ldots, q_t) = P(o_t \mid q_t) \qquad (10)$$

Eq. (10) states that a particular output observation emitted at time t depends only on the state occurring at that time (q_t) and is statistically independent of the past. Although these assumptions are somewhat restrictive, they reduce the complexity of model parameters significantly.

Classification by Hidden Markov Models. In the handwriting recognition, there are two ways of building hidden Markov models (HMMs): model discriminant HMMs and path discriminant HMMs. In model discriminant HMM, one or more HMMs can be built for each class of characters. On the other hand, in path discriminant HMM, only one model is built for all classes of characters, and different paths are used to distinguish one class from the others. Detailed discussion on applications of HMMs in handwritten word recognition can be found in [12,13].

Although our discussion has focused on off-line handwritten recognition, there are many techniques common to both on-line and off-line recognition. For example, segmentation strategies, shape analysis, and classification techniques are useful for both cases.

Postprocessing and Language Models. In the postprocess stage, handwritten recognition accuracy can be further improved by applying the context-sensitive language model. For example, as shown in Fig. 16.6, the recognizer output may be: ''Tne mem loves in Japen.'' Note that the correct characters were one of the three top-scoring candidates, although they may have different measures of confidence. By making different combinations of the top-scoring characters, the postprocessor then associates these possible words with a word in a dictionary according to the matching scoring and language grammar rules. The related techniques for postprocessing may include the probabilistic model [5], string correction algorithm [31], and hypothesis generation and testing [6,34].

16.2.3 Handwritten Chinese Character Recognition

It is well known that Chinese characters (including Japanese Kanji) are unique and different from those of Western languages such as English, in that they are nonalphabetic and have quite complicated stroke structures. Such properties make Chinese character recognition by computer particularly difficult and challenging.

Early work on machine recognition of handwritten Chinese character (HCC) research was originated in Japan—over 25 years ago [52,84]. Since then, hundreds of papers have appeared on this topic, which assumes both scientific and commercial importance.

The man lives in Japan.

First:	Tne	mem	loves	i n	J a p e n.
Second:	h	an	i		e a
Third:			a		o o
Result:	The	man	l i ves	i n	J a p a n.

Figure 16.6 Example of context-sensitive postprocessing.

Because of the large character set[1] in the Chinese language, until 1988 Shyu et al. built a prototype recognition system for the 5401 printed Chinese characters (PCC) and successfully demonstrated the system with a recognition rate of 95.6% [57]. Four years later (1992), the first commercial PCC recognition machine, based on a 386 personal computer, was announced, which is capable of recognizing four types (Kai, Ming, Black, and Sung) of 5401 characters, with an accuracy of 95% at a speed of seven characters per second. Thus, machine recognition of Chinese characters is by no means a pure research topic. Nevertheless, the machine recognition of HCC is still considered to be a very difficult problem owing to the following aspects:

1. Large number of characters set
2. Complexity of character structures
3. Wide variation in personal handwriting
4. Many similar characters

16.2.3.1 Handwritten Chinese Character Recognition Techniques

As depicted in Fig. 16.4, general techniques for handwritten text recognition include: (1) image preprocessing, (2) feature extraction, (3) character recognition, and (4) postprocessing.

Image Preprocessing. Image preprocessing of a HCC recognition system is very similar to that of English character recognition system, as described in previous sections. In addition to boundary smoothing, noise removing, and space normalization, stroke thinning is required in most of the HCC recognition system. The objective of the thinning process is to obtain the skeleton of a character with only a pixel in width and, ideally, to achieve a noise-insensitive skeleton without excessive erosion on the structural features. Figure 16.7 depicts a series of preprocessing results on some Chinese characters.

---

[1] There are more than 40,000 Chinese words, and 5401 characters are used frequently in daily life.

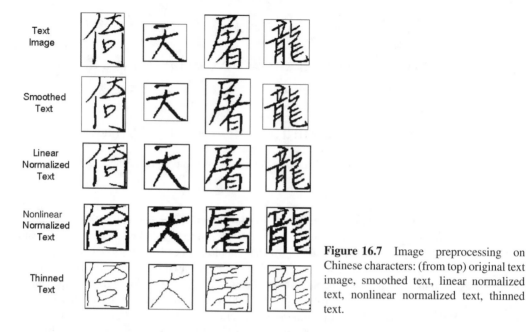

Text Image

Smoothed Text

Linear Normalized Text

Nonlinear Normalized Text

Thinned Text

Figure 16.7 Image preprocessing on Chinese characters: (from top) original text image, smoothed text, linear normalized text, nonlinear normalized text, thinned text.

Feature Extraction and Character Recognition. The character recognition methods can be generally classified as three types: (1) structural methods, (2) statistical methods, and (3) hybrid methods, which are a combination of the two previous methods. The structural method basically contains two processes: (a) decomposing a Chinese character into a set of structural primitives, such as lines, curves, and closed loops, and then (b) matching these primitives with the reference characters. The best matched reference character is considered to be the recognition result. The statistical methods use a set of characteristic measurements, which are usually called global features, to identify characters by their corresponding feature spaces.

Coarse Classification and Candidate Selection. Since the number of frequently used Chinese characters is quite large, a coarse classification (or clustering) is desirable in order to provide a reduced recognition domain for the fine-grained classification (i.e., character recognition). By having a small working domain, not only the overall recognition speed and recognition rate can be improved greatly, but also the training of the fine-grained classifiers can be much easier and faster. Two approaches have been proposed for this purpose: (1) coarse classification and (2) candidate selection.

The concept of the coarse classification is to partition the whole character set into several smaller subsets according to some feature primitives. Then, based on the same feature primitive, an unknown character can be classified into one of the subsets. The candidate selection method uses primitive or simple features and some fast recognition processes to select a number of candidates for an unknown character in a short time. Details of these methods are found in [25,37].

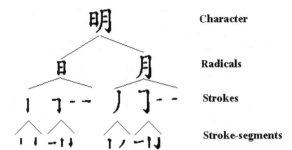

Figure 16.8 A Chinese character can be hierarchically decomposed into segment, stroke, and radical layers.

Structural Features and Character Recognition. From a hierarchical point of view, the composition of a Chinese character can be partitioned in three layers, as shown in Fig. 16.8. They are stroke-segment, stroke, and radical layers. Thus, structural-type recognition of a Chinese character can be classified into segment, stroke, and radical-based recognition [11,16].

From a syntactic point of view, radicals and strokes of a Chinese character can be represented by a 2-D graph, as depicted in Fig. 16.9.

Chen and Lieh [11] proposed two-layer attribute graphs to represent Chinese characters by using radicals and strokes as primitives, and their relative locations and orientations as relations. In the first layer, the primitives are the character radicals, and the relations are their relative locations. In the second layer, the primitives are the strokes of radicals, while the relation between them are their relative orientations. The relaxation matching techniques are used in the learning stage to synthesize different attribute graphs into a two-layer random graph. The relaxation matching method is also applied at the recognition stage to match the attribute graph of an input character with the random graph of each reference character. A similarity measure, based on whether or not the attribute graph is a possible outcome of the random graph, is used for recognition. Recognition tests were carried out on a set of 14 Chinese numerals, that is, 0~9, ten, hundred, thousand, and ten thousands. During the learning stage, about 1000 samples were used to construct the random graph mask by using relaxing matching. The test data set consists of 651 samples outside from the

Figure 16.9 A Chinese character in (*a*) can be hierarchically decomposed and represented as a 2-D graph in (*b*).

(*a*)   (*b*)

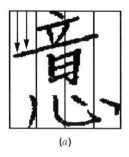

(*a*)

(*b*)

Figure 16.10 Extracting the CCT and BSPN features of a Chinese character.

learning samples. The testing performance was reported to be 96.31%, 2.77%, and 0.92% for recognition, rejection, and substitution rates, respectively.

Although structural-type recognition seems a natural approach for the handwritten Chinese characters, so far no test performance and evaluation result has been reported for the large character set (5401 characters). Based on our observation, the difficulties are as follows.

1. Stroke and radical features are unstable or too sensitive to noisy character images.
2. Fully automated feature extraction on the large character set is not matured yet.
3. Relaxation matching techniques are too computationally intensive to be implemented on a large character set.

Statistical Features and Character Recognition. Using statistical features for various pattern recognitions has been very successful for a long time. Since a character can be best represented by a 2-D image pattern, many statistical pattern recognition techniques can be and have been applied in this type of character recognition. Since pixel distribution features can be easily extracted from a character, these features have been widely used for this purpose. For example in [25], features such as *crossing count* (CCT), *belt shape pixel number* (BSPN), and *stroke orientation feature* (STKO) were used in statistical Chinese character recognition. As shown in Fig. 16.10, features such as CCT, and BSPN represent the stroke complexity and pixel density of a character image, respectively. The STKO feature vectors can be constructed by dividing the character image into n^2 square areas and counting the segment number in four quantized directions. The preprocessing and STKO feature extraction of a Chinese character are depicted in Fig. 16.11.

It is well known that the Bayes decision rule can be implemented as an optimal data classifier. By using these statistical features, the Bayes rule can help match a character image to a reference character with minimal classification error. In [25], Fu and Chiang applied a Bayesian decision-based neural network to implement a statistical character recognition system on a personal computer. A successful recognition rate of 86.54% on the 5401 frequently used character set has been reported. In addition, Fu and Chiang also noted many similar characters among the first 10 most possible candidate characters. Therefore, they [26] proposed a similar character-recognizing neural network (SCRNN), which has brought the recognition rate up to 91~94%.

(a.1) text image   (a.2) smoothed image   (a.3) thinned image

(*a*) Text image and preprocessed image

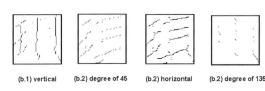

(b.1) vertical   (b.2) degree of 45   (b.2) horizontal   (b.2) degree of 135

Figure 16.11 Preprocessing and STKO feature extraction of a Chinese character.

(*b*) Stroke of four direction

Since the statistical HCC recognition is the only recognition method so far that has been implemented on the large (5401) character set, we would like to present this method in some detail.

Suppose there are M categories $\omega_1, \ldots, \omega_M$ in the feature space, the Bayes decision rule classifies input patterns based on their posterior probabilities: Input $x = [x_1, x_2, \ldots, x_D]^T$ is classified to category ω_i if $P(\omega_i \mid x) > P(\omega_j \mid x)$, for all $j \neq i$. Suppose the likelihood density of input pattern x given category ω_i is a D-dimensional Gaussian distribution, $(p(x \mid \omega_i) \equiv N(\mu_i, \Sigma_i))$. The posterior probability $P(\omega_i \mid x)$ by Bayes rule is

$$P(\omega_i \mid x) = \frac{P(\omega_i)p(x \mid \omega_i)}{p(x)},$$

where $P(\omega_i)$ is the prior probability of category ω_i ($\sum_{i=1}^{M} P(\omega_i) = 1$), and $p(x) = \sum_{i=1}^{M} P(\omega_i)p(x \mid \omega_i)$.

The category likelihood function $p(x \mid \omega_i)$ can be extended to the mixture of Gaussian distributions. Define $p(x \mid \omega_i, \Theta_{r_i})$ to be one of the Gaussian distributions that comprise $p(x \mid \omega_i)$ ($p(x \mid \omega_i, \Theta_{r_i}) \equiv N(\mu_{r_i}, \Sigma_{r_i})$),

$$p(x \mid \omega_i) = \sum_{r_i=1}^{R_i} P(\Theta_{r_i} \mid \omega_i)p(x \mid \omega_i, \Theta_{r_i})$$

where Θ_{r_i} represents the rth cluster in category ω_i. $P(\Theta_{r_i} \mid \omega_i)$ denotes the prior probability of cluster r, when input character patterns are from category ω_i. By definition, $\sum_{r_i=1}^{R_i} P(\Theta_{r_i} \mid \omega_i)=1$. The discriminant function of each category ω_i can be defined as the following log-likelihood function:

$$\phi(\boldsymbol{x}, \omega_i) = \log p(\boldsymbol{x} \mid \omega_i)$$

$$= \log \left[\sum_{r_i} P(\Theta_{r_i} \mid \omega_i) p(\boldsymbol{x} \mid \omega_i, \Theta_{r_i}) \right] \tag{11}$$

In most general formulations, the basis function of a cluster should be able to approximate the Gaussian distribution with full rank covariance matrix. However, for those applications that deal with high-dimension data but a finite number of training patterns, the training performance and storage space discourage such matrix modeling. A natural simplifying assumption is to assume uncorrelated features of unequal importance. That is, suppose that $p(\boldsymbol{x} \mid \omega_i, \Theta_{r_i})$ is a D-dimensional Gaussian distribution with uncorrelated features,

$$p(\boldsymbol{x} \mid \omega_i, \Theta_{r_i}) = \frac{1}{(2\pi)^{D/2} \prod_d^D \sigma_{r_i d}} \exp\left(-\frac{1}{2} \sum_{d=1}^{D} \frac{(x_d - \mu_{r_i d})^2}{\sigma_{r_i d}^2} \right) \tag{12}$$

where $\mu_{r_i} = [\mu_{r_i 1}, \mu_{r_i 2}, \cdots, \mu_{r_i D}]^T$ is the mean vector, and diagonal matrix $\Sigma_{r_i} = \text{diag}[\sigma_{r_i 1}^2, \sigma_{r_i 2}^2, \cdots, \sigma_{r_i D}^2]$ is the covariance matrix. To approximate the density function in Eq. (12), the elliptic basis functions (EBF's) can be applied to serve as the cluster basis function

$$\psi(\boldsymbol{x}, \omega_i, \Theta_{r_i}) = -\frac{1}{2} \sum_{d=1}^{D} \alpha_{r_i d}(x_d - \mu_{r_i d})^2 + \theta_{r_i} \tag{13}$$

where

$$\theta_{r_i} = -\frac{D}{2} \ln 2\pi - \sum_{d=1}^{D} \ln \alpha_{r_i d}.$$

After passing an exponential function, $\exp\{\psi(\boldsymbol{x}, \omega_i, \Theta_{r_i})\}$ can be viewed as the same Gaussian distribution, as described in Eq. (12), except for a minor notational change: $1/\alpha_{r_i d} = \sigma_{r_i d}^2$.

Recently, Lin et al. [45] proposed a probabilistic Decision-Based Neural Network (PDBNN) for the implementation of the Bayesian decision rule. As shown in Fig. 16.12, for a K-category recognition problem, a PDBNN character recognizer consists of K different subnets. The training scheme for PDBNN contains the following two phases. The *Locally Unsupervised* (LU) phase for the PDBNN can adopt several unsupervised learning schemes (e.g., VQ, k-means, EM, ...). As for the *Globally Supervised* (GS) learning, the *reinforced* and *antireinforced* learning is applied to *all* the clusters of the global winner and the supposed (i.e., the correct) winner with a weighting distribution proportional to the degree of possible involvement (measured by the likelihood) by each cluster.

Postprocessing and Language Models. When the handwritten characters are a string of context-related text characters, we can apply their embedded contextual information to improve the recognition accuracy. When a character recognition module (either a statistical or a structural recognition module) generates a set of candidate characters for an unknown input character, the contextual information with the related language model may be applied

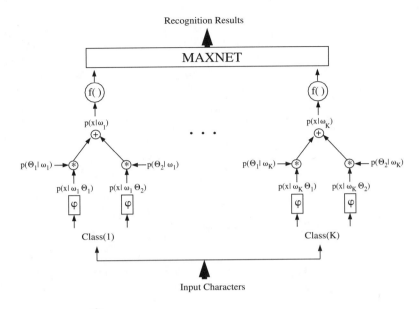

Figure 16.12 Schematic diagram of a k-class PDBNN character recognizer.

to select the appropriate character for each candidate to correct possible recognition error or to confirm some uncertain recognition results. Lee and Chien [42] proposed a *bi*-gram Markov language model for postprocessing. They used the language model based on POS (part-of-speech), which includes 30 POS to represent the various character groups or classes. They claimed that this approach could correct recognition error significantly when the previous recognition rate was not high enough. Instead of using the *bi*-gram language model to improve recognition rate, Wang, Shiau, and Suen [78] proposed *n*-gram-based linguistic decoder for postprocessing. The system overview of the linguistic decoder is illustrated in Fig. 16.13. After the text recognition processing, the linguistic decoder is first applied to detect the most misrecognized characters, and then the *n*-gram model is used to determine the most probable character in order to replace the misrecognized character. This linguistic decoder and the *n*-gram model can improve the recognition rate from 3 to 5% of the overall performance.

16.2.4 On-Line Handwritten Recognition

Even before the advent of the first computer, the keyboard was an interactive device for typewriters. However, typing characters or editing text files for patternlike characters (e.g., Chinese and Kanji) from a keyboard still is formidable and unpleasant work for most nonprofessional computer users. Accordingly, inputting characters or editing text files by writing or drawing on a tablet seems a natural and convenient approach. Therefore, develop-

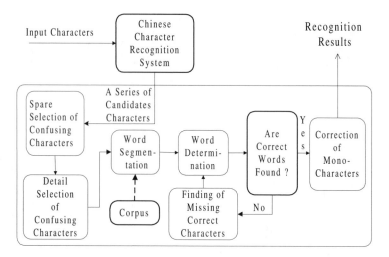

Figure 16.13   System overview of the linguistic decoder.

ing reliable on-line character recognition techniques has always been a promising research topic. On-line handwritten recognition means that the machine recognizes the writing as it is being written. In this section, some basic techniques and methods of on-line handwritten recognition are introduced. The popular input device is an electromagnetic tablet with a stylus pen, which typically has a resolution of 200 points/inch and a sampling rate of 100 points per second. The trace of the handwriting or line drawing is captured as a sequence of coordinate points of the pen-down and pen-up activities. In general, on-line recognition should be fast enough to keep up with the writing speed. Average writing rates are 1.5∼2.5 characters per second for English alphanumerics and 0.2∼2.5 characters per second for Chinese [70]. Compared with off-line recognition, on-line handwritten recognition has the following advantages:

- **Temporal information**: Temporal or dynamic information on the writing can be captured by on-line devices. This information consists of the number of strokes, the order of strokes, the direction and speed of each stroke, and so on.
- **Interactivity**: In an editing application, for example, inputting a symbol by the user can cue the system to make appropriate changes in its display. Also, the user can immediately correct recognition errors.
- **Adaptation**: When a user sees that certain characters are not accurately recognized for a few times, the user can alter his or her inscription to improve recognition. On the other hand, the recognizer can also adapt to the writer by storing samples of characters for subsequent recognition. There is potential of adaptation for both writer to machine and machine to writer.

On-line handwritten recognition of English, Chinese, and Japanese are quite different from each other. Basically, there are two styles of handwriting: hand-printed characters and cursive script. Chinese characters consist of many more strokes than English characters. A modern Japanese document usually contains Hiragana, Katakana, Kanji, and some English alphanumerics. Therefore, Japanese handwritten recognition represents a typical mixture or multilinguistic character recognition process. With regard to the irregularity of on-line handwriting, there are two types of variation: the static and dynamic. The static types of variation concern the varying on character size or shape. The dynamic variations are related to the changing of stroke number and order in a character trace. These types of variation make the extracting of stable character features extremely difficult, as to the machine recognition of handwriting. In addition, similar character pairs (e.g., 2-Z, U-V, C-L, a-d, and n-h) are not easily distinguished without context-sensitive postprocessing.

In general, on-line handwritten recognition can be partitioned into three stages [70]: *preprocessing, recognition*, and *postprocessing*. In the preprocessing stage, the sampled x-y coordinates of pen-down and pen-up can be used to reconstruct input character images. However, in the English scriptwriting, several characters of a word are scripted continuously. Segmenting the connected characters can be a difficult task. Spatial segmentation [24,39,46] has been proposed to check for a two-dimensional separation of writing units. Fox and Tappert [24] combine spatial, temporal, and some other information in a writing trace to achieve better word segmentation. Some recently announced commercial systems have restricted the handwritten characters within a predefined box, so that the character segmentation problem can be alleviated. Since the recognition of cursive scriptwriting by itself seems a difficult task, techniques that integrate the segmentation and recognition procedures are proposed. In other words, the word-base recognition is proposed. By recognizing as many characters as possible in a word at first, the combined method can identify proper character segmenting points in a word. In addition to the character segmentation, some other problems need to be solved, such as noise reduction and character size normalization. Many noise reduction methods [1,3,4,8,69,79] have been proposed to eliminate redundant or noisy signals in the input to improve the recognition accuracy. The character normalization process [1,7,8,9] aims to reduce the recognition degradation owing to the variation of character size, shape, and so on.

On the recognition stage, the segmented character or word images are recognized or identified with a reference character. Usually, on-line handwriting features, such as Fourier descriptors [1,27] and stroke codes [33,38,83], represent the static and dynamic properties of an input character or word. During the past decade, one of the most popular approaches for speech and pattern recognition has been the hidden Markov model (HMM) [54]. The HMM approach performs extremely well for on-line cursive handwritten recognition. By converting the sampled coordinates of the on-line written characters into a graph, the HMM model can be applied to classify the input characters accordingly. For detailed descriptions of HMM classification methods, readers can refer to Section 16.2.2.

In addition to the HMM, there are many other alternatives to design the recognizer for on-line handwriting. To name a few, Dynamic Programming (DP) [55,72,73], string matching, relaxation, elastic matching [36], and neural networks are preferred techniques.

For languages with large character sets, such as Chinese, the matching between the input features and the precompiled templates of all the possible reference characters could be a long time period of computing process. To speed up the matching process, many candidate selection algorithms [73] have been proposed and developed. The basic concept of the candidate selection is to use simple features and fast algorithms to rule out, at very high speed, the less possible candidates. After the candidate selection stage, the number of candidates for slow but precise recognition process is greatly reduced; thus, the overall recognition time can be significantly reduced. To further improve the character recognition rate, the recognition stage is usually followed by a postprocess stage. The postprocessing for on-line handwriting is similar to that of off-line recognition. Readers may refer to previous sections for English and Chinese context-sensitive language models.

The hand-held computer, the Personal Digital Assistant (PDA), provides people with an efficient way of managing personal databases as well as communicating with large network databases. High-performance on-line handwriting has become more demanding than ever before. Future developments in computer hardware will greatly improve the speed of computation. In the software development area, more sophisticated handwritten analysis and recognition algorithms will lead to greater understanding of more natural and unconstrained handwritings.

16.2.5 Source of Information on Handwritten Recognition

After more than 30 years, handwritten recognition research remains as active as ever. Numerous papers, technical reports, patents, and products have resulted from intensive research and development effort. For instance, a large number of papers are published in the proceedings of the *International Conference on Pattern Recognition* (ICPR), the *International Workshop on Frontiers in Handwritten Recognition* (IWFHR), the *International Conference on Document Analysis and Recognition* (ICDAR), and the *International Conference on Chinese Computing* (ICCC). Most of these papers are quite short, however. More complete descriptions of methods and experiments appear in *IEEE-PAMI*, *Journal of Pattern Recognition*, *Computer Vision*, *Graphics and Image Processing*, *International Journal of Pattern Recognition and Artificial Intelligence*, and *Computer Processing of Chinese and Oriental Languages*.

A comprehensive set of references to recent research and developments in *handwritten recognition* can be found in two special issues of the *International Journal of Pattern Recognition and Artificial Intelligence* (Vols. 1 and 2, 1991) and *Proceedings of IEEE* (July 1992). These two issues describe not only the state of the art but also, in many cases, ongoing research efforts. A historical overview of a field is the first step in introducing readers to a new area; in this regard, especially see the paper "Historical Review of the OCR Research and Development" by S. Mori, C. Y. Suen, and K. Yamamota [48]. This paper covers a very wide time span, starting with the predigital computer era and ending with the current commercial machines. On cursive word recognition, J.-C. Simon of the University of Paris describes his method in [60], which was based on the separation of the smooth part (axis) and loops, crossings, dots, and other special forms (tarsi) of a word. For the neural networks approach to this field, Sukhan Lee and Jack C.-J. Pan [43] have reported that an off-line, unconstrained, handwritten numeral recognition can be improved by transforming a two-dimensional (2-D) spatial representation of a numeral into a three-dimensional (3-D) spatiotemporal representation. Their radial-basis competitive and cooperative neural networks can achieve up to a 97% recognition rate on the handwritten zip code numerals acquired by the U.S. Postal Service. The paper by A. J. Filipski and R. Flandrena [22] of the GTX Corporation covers the automatic conversion of engineering drawings into CAD form. The conversion process covers not only character recognition but also detection of line structures (vectorization). As far as on-line alphanumeric character recognition is concerned, Tappert et al. [70] wrote an excellent survey in 1990.

It is well known that characters based on oriental languages are unique and different from those of Western alphabetic characters. Nagy wrote an excellent retrospective survey paper [50] for the Chinese recognition. In this paper, the author attempted to assess the overall status in the field and to place the problems of Chinese recognition in perspective compared with other areas of optical character recognition. For a general and technical description of the Kanji OCR, the reader can refer to [82]. A comprehensive set of references and surveys of activities in China can be found in [67,81]. Cheng and Hsu [15] wrote a survey paper on recent research activities and achievements on Chinese OCR in Taiwan. T. Wakahara, H. Murase, and K. Odaka of Nippon Telephone and Telegraph described a method [76] for on-line handwritten recognition. The paper covered Chinese character (Kanji) recognition as well as the recognition of line figures such as flowcharts.

To search for the most updated activities, achievements as well as demonstrations on handwritten recognition, the World Wide Web (WWW) seems an excellent medium for the researcher and in fact for everyone interested. For instance, the following is a listing of the search on one of the database servers (`www.yahoo.com`), according to the keywords: *Science/Computer Science/Handwritten Recognition.*

- **CEDAR** (`http://www.cedar.buffalo.edu`)
- **CENPARMI** (`http://www.cenparmi.concordia.ca`)
- **Handwritten Recognition Conferences**
  (`http://www.nici.kun.nl`)
- **Handwritten Recognition Home Page**
  (`http://hcslx1.essex.ac.uk`)
  This page provides pointers to research groups around the world working in the areas of both on-line and off-line handwritten recognition.

Another Internet site (pointer) for document image understanding and OCR is located at (`http://documents.cfar.umd.edu/`). At the time of writing (May 1996), the website contained the following information:[2]

- Server information
- Conference and special issue information
- Job information
- Mailing lists and news groups
- Publications on-line
- Bibliographies on-line

---

[2]This WWW page was maintained by Chris Vance (cvance@cfar.umd.edu) and David Doermann (doermann@cfar.umd.edu).

- Contributed source code
- Data sets and standards information
- Public domain OCR Resources
- Commercial resources
- Document understanding research groups
- Related topic and application home pages
- Utilities and Internet resources

16.2.5.1 Data Sets for Handwritten Recognition

The recognition rate, which has been considered primarily as a measurement for performance of the handwritten recognition, depends heavily on the variability, layout, context, and quality of the images. So far, we have not seen a predictive model for handwritten recognition evaluation because we do not have a mathematically tractable model for general digitized handwritten documents. We do not know how to measure quality accurately enough to predict performance on new data. Therefore, repeatable and statistically valid comparison experiments are essential for further progress.

Over the years, the U.S. Postal Research Office has released increasingly larger handwritten character sets[3] lifted from envelope address blocks. The National Institute of Standards and Technology announced a CD-ROM sample set [28,80] with more than 800,000 alphanumeric character images from 3600 writers. On-line handwritten recognition addresses the problem of recognizing handwriting from data collected with a sensitive pad that provides discretized pen trajectory information. At the initiative of Technical Committee 11 of the International Association for Pattern Recognition (IAPR), the UNIPEN project was started to stimulate research and development in on-line handwritten recognition (e.g., for pen computers and pen communicators). UNIPEN provides a platform of data exchange at the Linguistic Data Consortium (LDC) and is under the control of the U.S. National Institute of Standards and Technologies (NIST). The benchmark[4] is concerned with writer independent recognition of sentences, isolated words, and isolated characters of any writing style (hand-printed or cursive). Although UNIPEN, in the future, will provide data for various alphabets, the current benchmark is limited to letters and symbols from an English computer keyboard.

The database for Chinese handwritten recognition research in Taiwan was created by CCL of ITRI [74] in 1988. The CCL/HCCR1 database contains more than 200 samples of 5401 frequently used Chinese characters. The samples were collected from 2600 people, including junior high school and college students as well as employees of ERSO/ITRI. In

---

[3]This data set is available on CD-ROM through the CEDAR office: UB Commons, 520 Lee Entrance-Suite 202, Amherst, New York 14228-2567, USA.

[4]Readers interested in the UNIPEN benchmark can contact the LDC at Linguistic Data Consortium, Room 441, Williams Hall, University of Pennsylvania, Philadelphia, PA 19104-6305, USA. The general UNIPEN documentation is located at ``ftp.cis.upenn.edu'' in the ``pub/UNIPEN-pub/documents'' directory.

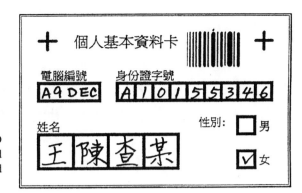

Figure 16.14 An exemplar personal ID registration form, which contains printed and handwritten numerals, English and Chinese characters.

Japan, ETL-8 (160 sets of 950 hand-printed educational characters) and ETL-9 (200 sets of 3036 hand-printed characters by 4000 authors) tapes prepared by the Electrotechnical Laboratory have fostered comparative classification experiments.

16.3 HANDWRITTEN RECOGNITION SYSTEMS

This section presents an overview of three examples of handwritten recognition machines. These machines illustrate the diversity of approaches that have been used in designing multilingual (especially for English and Chinese) handwritten recognition systems. The **FR1000** was designed by the OCR group at CCL of ITRI in Taiwan. **NeuroScan II** was designed by the research staff members of the Neural Network Laboratory in National Chiao-Tung University. The **Pen Power OLCCR Systems** is a commercial product manufactured by the Pen Power Technologies Inc., in Taiwan. These examples were chosen because of our personal familiarity with their designs and because they exemplify the concepts presented in previous sections.

16.3.1 CCL FR1000 Form Processing System

In 1994, the Computer and Communication Research Laboratories (CCL) in Taiwan announced its first multilinguistic OCR system, FR1000 [58]. The FR1000 is a general-form reading system that can recognize both machine-printed and handwritten characters of numerals, English and Chinese. An exemplar personal ID registration form is shown in Fig. 16.14. From a system point of view, FR1000 consists of a scanning unit, a form learning unit, a form recognition unit, and an editing unit. There are two phases in the operation of FR1000: training and recognition. The purpose of the training phase is to define the geometric and logical information of the forms. Using this predefined information, the FR1000 knows where to extract important information from the forms during the recognition phase.

The details of these steps, as shown in Fig. 16.15, are as follows:

- **Image scanning**: By using a full-page scanner, the paper forms are scanned into digital images, which are then processed for form training or recognition. During

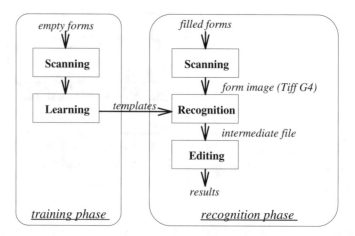

Figure 16.15   There are two phases in the operation of FR1000: training and recognition. The purpose of the training phase is to learn the geometric and logical information of the forms. During the recognition phase, based on the learned form information, the FR100 knows where and how to extract the needed information on the forms.

recognition, the dropout features of the scanner delete form lines out of the documents for better image compression and character recognition performance.

- **Form learning**: For each ready-for-recognition form, we have defined:

   1. Fiducial marks: These marks are used to calculate the distortion of shift and rotation made by the scanner.

   2. Fields: The attribute and location of each field are defined.

   3. Characters: The type and character set are specified for each character in each field.

   4. Rules: The intrafield rules define the constraint for a particular field while the interfield rules express the relation between fields.

- **Form recognition**: Referring to the template that contains learning results, FR1000 extracts each character from the fields and then sends them to the corresponding recognition engine. Finally, the learned rules are applied to the recognition results for data verification. Figure 16.16 shows the block diagram of the form recognition engine.

The FR1000 could be applied to many applications, such as tax form reader, fax order, fax routing, application form processing, and time sheet management. Moreover, an automatic form processing scheme, which combines FR1000 with the document image management and Internet distribution, was proposed in [14]. The functional block diagram is shown in Fig. 16.17.

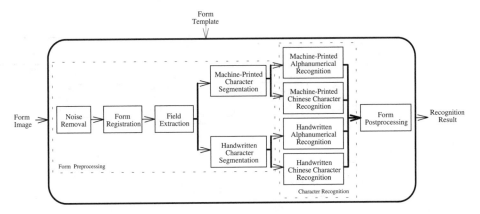

Figure 16.16   The FR1000 recognition kernel is composed of form pre-processing, character recognition, and form postprocessing modules.

16.3.1.1   *Performance Analysis on FR 1000*

In October 1994, FR1000 was tested using 10,000 tax forms from the Data Processing Center of the Ministry of Finance, ROC (Republic of China). For comparison purposes, only fields of alphanumeric characters were read. Table 16.1 shows that the FR1000 prototype did a better job compared to a commercial product XP80 from REI (Recognition Equipment Incorporation). Note that this result does not imply that FR1000 is always better since the test samples were written by Chinese people and the FR1000 was actually designed for them. However, we could say that the FR1000 is a practical solution for handwritten data processing. The performance indices in Table 16.1 are described and commented on as follows. On the form processing, the system rejects a form (sheet) if the rejection rate of the form exceeds the predefined threshold. A rejected form will be rescanned or handled manually. Hence, the form correction rate indicates the percentage of forms processing, which can be fully automated by machines. With regard to character recognition and rejection, a rejected character needs to be recovered by manually editing. Thus, a desirable form recognition scheme needs to have a lowest character recognition error rate (no greater than the human recognition/editing error, at least) and an acceptable character rejection rate. The editing speed is measured on the number of forms (sheets) to be manually edited per minute. Usually, the speed of manually editing heavily depends on the design of user interface and the processing flow. Another system performance index for a form processing system is the editing keystroke ratio, which reflects the combined performance measure on the design of recognition engine and the user interface. A better recognition engine and a graphical user interface usually reduce the number of keystrokes during the editing or correcting processes. In general, the higher correction rate and the lower form rejection rate indicate better overall system performance.

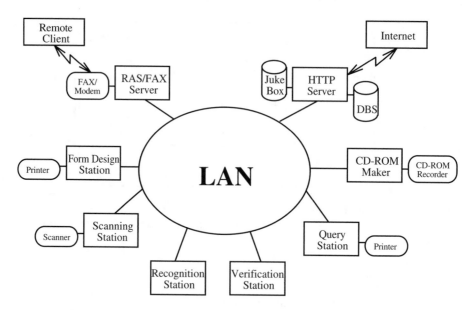

Figure 16.17   The functional block diagram of the FR1000 system on LAN and Internet environment.

Table 16.1   Performance Comparison Between FR1000 and XP80 of REI

Performance Indices	FR1000	XP80
Form Rejection Rate($F_R/F_0\%$)	1	28
Form Correction Rate($F_c/F_0\%$)	47	29
Character Rejection Rate($C_R/C_0\%$)	4.4	2.21
Character Error Rate($C_e/C_0\%$)	0.47	1.31
Editing Speed (sheet/min)	28	8
Editing Key Stroke Ratio($E_s/E_0\%$)	9.97	30

F_R: no. of rejected forms in a batch job, F_0: total no. of forms processed, F_c: no. of forms that can be fully automated processing without human interference, C_r: no. of rejected characters in a form (sheet), C_0: total no. of characters in a form (sheet), C_e: no. of misclassified characters in a form (sheet), E_s: no. of key strokes required to edit a form, E_0: no. of key strokes needed to type the whole characters in a form.

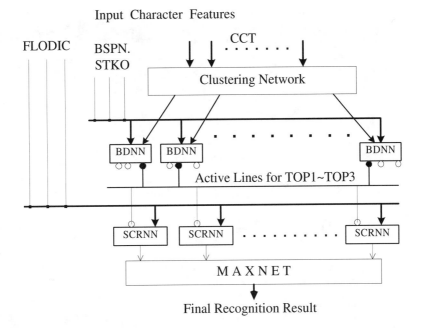

Figure 16.18   The multistage recognition architecture in NeuroScan II.

16.3.2   NeuroScan II: A Handwritten Chinese Character Recognizer

The NeuroScan II was built at National Chiao-Tung University during 1994–1995 using the Bayesian decision-based neural networks [25]. It contains an optical scanner and a MS Windows-based character recognition software. Considering both speed and recognition accuracy, we decided to implement a multistage recognition system, which contained (1) a clustering network, (2) a fine-grained character recognizer, and (3) a similar character recognizer. The overall system diagram is depicted in Fig. 16.18.

16.3.2.1   Multistage Classifier Architecture

NeuroScan II was designed to recognize at least 5401 frequently used handwritten Chinese characters. On the consideration of recognition accuracy and speed, we decided to include a coarse classification (or clustering) to reduce the candidate domain size of the fine-grained classification (i.e., the character recognition). By having a small working domain, not only can the overall recognition speed and recognition accuracy be greatly improved, but also the training of the fine-grained classifiers can be much easier and faster. The first clustering stage is implemented as a k-means coarse classifier to partition the 5401 characters into 60 smaller clusters. Then, the second stage is implemented according to Bayesian decision-based neural networks [25]. An unknown character is first assigned to

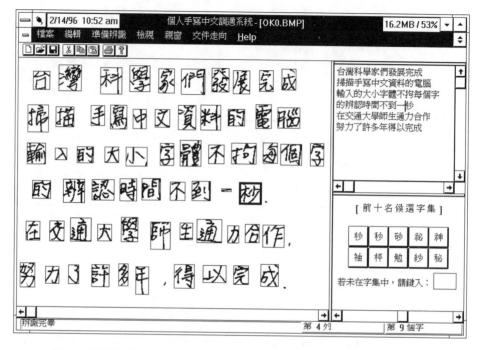

Figure 16.19   The user interface and a recognition snapshot of NeuroScan II.

one of the 60 clusters. According to the output confidence score from each of the Bayesian decision neural networks, the top three reference candidates (TOP3) are selected. Suppose there is a large difference in the confidence score between the first two candidates, then the TOP1 character will be considered as the recognition result without any further recognition process. Otherwise, these three candidates are sent to the similar character recognizer (*SCRNN*) [26] to find the most matched reference character.

16.3.2.2 *Performance Analysis of NeuroScan II*

The training and testing of this multistage classifier were conducted on a Pentium-90 based personal computer. The training data set for the NeuroScan II are the first 50 odd-numbered samples from the CCL/HCCR1 database, while the testing data set are the first fifty even-numbered samples. Figure 16.19 depicts the user interface and a snapshot of recognition results from NeuroScan II.

Testing results of the fine-grained recognition stage and the final similar character recognizer are listed in Table 16.2. By attaching the similar character recognition stage, the recognition accuracy can be improved by 3~4%. On average, the recognition speed is 0.278 second per character on a Pentium-90 based personal computer.

Table 16.2   Experimental Results of the NeuroScan II

Test type	Top 1	Top 2	Top 3
2nd stage recog.	86.68%	91.76%	93.60%
Final recog.#1	90.12%	93.49%	94.75%
Final recog.#2	94.11%	97.01%	97.67%

Final recognition results were measured in two ways: #1 was measured without any rejection, and #2 was measured with 6.7% of rejection rate.

16.3.3 Pen Power OLCCR Systems

Due to the huge marketing potentials of on-line Chinese character recognition (OLCCR) systems, a number of companies in Taiwan have been developing pen-based recognition systems for years. The Pen Power OLCCR System is one of the popular products among them.

The hardware of Pen Power OLCCR system consists of a tablet and a stylus. Figure 16.20 shows the system configuration of the Pen Power OLCCR system. The software can be partitioned into two parts. The first is the DOSPEN, which is a resident on-line recognition engine running under Microsoft DOS. By using the DOSPEN, a user can input and edit characters by writing on the tablet. The second part of the software is WINPEN, which runs under the Windows 3.1 (or above) and Windows 95. WINPEN is functionally the same as DOSPEN, but it is much more user friendly.

The Pen Power recognition engine can recognize up to 13,053 Chinese characters used in Taiwan, as well as 6763 simplified Chinese characters used in Mainland China. In addition, English characters, numerals, punctuation, and Mandarin phonetic symbols

Figure 16.20   Configuration of the Pen Power OLCCR system.

are also recognizable. Two other prominent features in this system are user adaptation and on-line character segmentation functions. The user adaptation function enables the system to gradually improve its recognition capability by adapting the system to the user's writing style. Since the character segmentation and recognition processes are performed in parallel, the system response time becomes much faster than the traditional word-by-word on-line recognition systems. Pen Power claimed that the recognition speed is 10 characters per second on a 486-33 personal computer, and the memory requirement for the recognition engine is only about 20K bytes. Recently, Pen Power OLCCR system has been extended to recognize Kanji for Japanese users and Hangul for Korean users.

16.4 FUTURE TRENDS AND CONCLUSIONS

This chapter provides a survey of current handwritten recognition technologies. First, we presented an overview on machine recognition of handwriting for the multimedia human–machine interface. We focused on image preprocessing, feature extraction, and recognition aspects of the handwritten English and Chinese character recognition problems, using information drawn from on-line and off-line devices. Furthermore, we introduced three handwritten recognition systems to illustrate the diversity of approaches for multilingual human–machine interface design. As the state of art, researchers are trying to integrate on-line handwritten recognition, gesture recognition, facial expression recognition, and speech recognition in order to construct a natural and friendly multimedia interface for computer users. We believe it is time to apply these technologies to a multimedia computer for various real-world applications, to name a few, business card organizers, newspaper and magazine organizers, personal digital assistants (PDAs), automated check processing, postal address reading systems, and geographic information systems.

Given the recent interest in multimedia systems, information retrieval from a mixture of text and image databases has attracted the attention of researchers across several disciplines. Advances in scanning, networking, compression, and video technology, as well as the proliferation of multimedia computers, have led to the generation of large on-line collections of texts, images, and videos. These collections have created a need for new methods to locate specific texts, images, or video clips. For example, the interaction of textual and photographic information in an integrated text/image database environment is being explored at the Center of Excellence for Document Analysis and Recognition (CEDAR) [61], SUNY, Buffalo. The idea is to develop a computational model for *understanding* pictures based on its accompanying descriptive text. Furthermore, researchers at IBM Almaden research center have proposed the Query by Image Content (QBIC) project [23], which studies methods to extend and complement text-based retrievals by querying and retrieving images and videos by text content. A mature multimedia retrieving system should allow users to query on large text, image, and video databases based on example images, user-sketched characters and drawings, and color and texture patterns. We hope the ideas presented here will be useful to readers interested in current developments and to practicing engineers interested in developing their information systems. It is hoped that this work will further stimulate research in this exciting and commercially important field.

Acknowledgments

We thank Professor S. Y. Kung, Dr. S. H. Lin, and Dr. H. T. Pao for their helpful suggestions regarding the probabilistic DBNN and statistical pattern recognition methods. Our sincere appreciation goes to Professors T. S. Yum, Jean J. J. Shann, and many other anonymous reviewers for their critical and constructive suggestion on many drafts of this chapter. We also thank students L. J. Shen, S. C. Chuang, W. H. Su, and Y. Y. Xu in the Neural Network Laboratory of National Chiao-Tung University for preparing diagrams.

References

[1] H. Arakawa, "On-line Recognition of Handwritten Characters—Alphanumerics, Hiragana, Katakana, Kanji," *Pattern Recognition*, Vol. 16, No. 1, pp. 9–16, 1983.

[2] H. S. Baird, "Feature Identification for Hybrid Structural/Statistical Pattern Classification," *Computer Vision, Graphics, and Image Processing*, Vol. 42, pp. 318–333, 1988.

[3] M. I. Bernstein, "A Method for Recognizing Handprinted Characters in Real-time," in L. N. Kanal, ed., *Pattern Recognition*, Washington, DC: Tompson, 1968, pp. 109–114.

[4] B. Blesser, "Multistage Digital Filtering Utilizing Several Criteria," U.S. Patent 4 375 081, Feb. 1983.

[5] R. Bozinovic and S. N. Srihari, "A String Correction Algorithm for Cursive Script Recognition," *IEEE Trans. Pattern Anal. Machine Intell.,* Vol. PAMI-4, pp. 655–663, Nov. 1982.

[6] R. M. Bozinovic and S. N. Srihari, "Off-line Cursive Word Recognition," *IEEE Trans. Pattern Anal. Machine Intell.*, Vol. 11, pp. 68–83, Jan. 1989.

[7] M. K. Brown and S. Ganapathy, "Cursive Script Recognition," *Proc. Int. Conf. Cybern. and Soc.,* pp.47–51, 1980.

[8] M. K. Brown and S. Ganapathy, "Preprocessing Techniques for Cursive Script Word Recognition," *Pattern Recognition,* Vol. 16, pp. 447–458, 1983.

[9] D. J. Burr, "Designing a Handwriting Reader," *IEEE Trans. Pattern Anal. Machine Intell.,* Vol. PAMI-5, pp. 554–559, 1983.

[10] R. G. Casey and G. Nagy, "Recursive Segmentation and Classification of Composite Characters," *Proc. Int. Conf. Pattern Recog.*, pp. 1023–1025, 1982.

[11] L. H. Chen and J. R. Lieh, "Handwritten Character Recognition Using a 2-layer Random Graph Model by Relation Matching," *Pattern Recognition*, Vol. 23, pp. 1189–1205, 1990.

[12] M.-Y. Chen, A. Kundu, and J. Zhou, "Off-line Handwritten Word Recognition Using a Hidden Markov Type Stochastic Network," *IEEE Trans. Pattern Anal. Machine Intell.*, Vol. 16, pp. 481–496, May 1994.

[13] M.-Y. Chen, A. Kundu, and S. N. Srihari, "Variable Duration Hidden Markov Model and Morphological Segmentation for Handwritten Word Recognition," *IEEE Trans. Image Processing*, Vol. 4, pp. 1675–1688, Dec. 1995.

[14] M.-Y. Chen, Y.-S. Lin, I.-S. Shyu, L.-T. Tu, W.-W. Lin, and Y.-H. Chou, "Internet Applications Using Form Reader," *CCL Technical Journal*, Vol. 45, pp. 70–78, Dec. 1995.

[15] F. H. Cheng and W. H. Hsu, " Research on Chinese OCR in Taiwan," *Int. J. of Pattern Recognition and Artificial Intelligence*, Vol. 5, No. 1 & 2 (1991), pp. 139–164.

[16] S. L. Chou and W. H. Tsai, "Recognition Handwritten Chinese Character by Stroke-segment Matching Using an Iteration Scheme," *Int. J. Pattern Recognition Artificial Intelligence*, Vol. 5, pp. 175–197, 1991.

[17] P. A. Devijver and J. Kittler, *Pattern Recognition: A Statistical Approach*, Englewood Cliffs, NJ: Prentice-Hall, 1982.

[18] W. Doster, "Contextual Post-processing System for Corporation with a Multiple-choice Character Recognition System," *IEEE Trans. Computers*, Vol. 26, pp. 1090–1101, Nov. 1977.

[19] R. O. Duda and P. E. Hart, *Pattern Classification and Scene Analysis*, New York: Wiley-Interscience, 1973.

[20] D. G. Elliman and I. T. Lancaster, "A Review of Segmentation and Contextual Analysis Techniques for Text Recognition," *Pattern Recognition J.*, Vol. 23, pp. 337–346, 1990.

[21] R. Farag, "Word Level Recognition of Cursive Script," *IEEE Trans. Computer*, Vol. C–28, No. 2, pp. 172–175, 1979.

[22] A. J. Filipski and R. Flandrena, "Automated Conversion of Engineering Drawings to CAD Form," *Proceedings of IEEE*, Vol. 80, No. 7, pp. 1195–1209, July 1992.

[23] M. Flicker, H. Sawhney, W. Niblack, J. Ashley, Q. Huang, B. Dom, M. Gorkani, J. Hafner, D. Lee, D. Petkovic, D. Steele, and P. Yanker, "Query by Image and Video Content: The QBIC System," *IEEE Computer*, Vol. 28, No. 9, pp. 23–32, 1995.

[24] A. S. Fox and C. C. Tappert, "On-line External Word Segmentation for Handwriting Recognition," in *Proc. 3rd Int. Symp. Handwriting Comput. Appl.*, July 1987.

[25] H. C. Fu and K. P. Chiang, "Recognition of Handwritten Chinese Characters by Multi-stage Neural Network Classifiers," *Proc. of 1995 IEEE Int. Conf. Neural Networks*, Perth, Australia.

[26] H. C. Fu and J. M. Chen, "Recognition of Handwriting Similar Chinese Characters by Neural Networks," *Proc. of the 6th IEEE Workshop on Neural Networks for Signal Processing*, Kyoto, Japan, Sept. 1996.

[27] H. Fujisaki, S. Nagai, and N. Hidaka, "On-line Recognition of Handwritten Numerals," *Annual Rep.*, Eng. Res. Inst., Faculty Eng., Univ. of Tokyo, Japan, Vol. 30, pp. 103–110, Aug. 1971.

[28] M. D. Garris and R. A. Wilkinson, "Handwritten Segmented Characters Database," Technical Report Special Database 3, **HWSC**, National Institute of Standards and Technology, Feb. 1992.

[29] M. D. Garris, J. L. Blue, G. T. Candels, D. L. Dimmick, J. Geist, P. J. Grother, S. A. Kamet, and C. L. Wilson, "NIST Form-Based Handprint Recognition System," Technical Report **NISTTR 5469**, National Institute of Standards and Technology, July 1994.

[30] V. K. Govindan and A. P. Shivaprasad, "Character Recognition—A Review," *Pattern Recognition J.*, Vol. 23, No. 7, pp. 671–683, 1990.

[31] P. A. V. Hall and G. R. Dowling, "Approximate String Matching," *Comput. Surveys*, Vol. 12, pp. 381–402, 1980.

[32] S. Hanaki and T. Yamazaki, "On-line Recognition of Handprinted Kanji Characters," *Pattern Recognition*, Vol. 12, pp. 421–429, 1980.

[33] R. Hing-Hua, "A Practical Recognition System for Inputting Handwritten Chinese Characters On-line," *Proc. 1988 Int. Conf. Comput. Processing of Chinese and Oriental Languages,* 1988, pp. 62–64.

[34] J. J. Hull and S. N. Srihari, "A Computational Approach to Word Shape Recognition: Hypothesis Generation and Testing," *Proc. IEEE Conf. Computer Vision and Pattern Recognition*, pp. 156–161, 1986.

[35] S. Kahan, T. Pavlidis, and H. S. Baird, "On the Recognition of Printed Characters of Any Font and Size," *IEEE Trans. Pattern Anal. Machine Intell.*, Vol. 9, pp. 274–288, Mar. 1987.

[36] J. B. Kruskai, "An Overview of Sequence Comparison: Time Warps, String Edits, and Macromolecules," *SIAM Rev.,* Vol. 25, pp. 201–237.

[37] T. Kumamoto, K. Toraichi, T. Horiuchiz, K. Yamamota, and H. Yamada, "On Speeding Candidate Selection in Handprinted Chinese Character Recognition," *Pattern Recognition*, Vol. 24, pp.793–799, 1991.

[38] H.-W. Kuo, J.-C. Lee, and T.-C. Kuo, "IOLCR, An On-line Chinese Character Recognition System," *Proc. 1988 Int. Conf. Comput. Processing of Chinese and Oriental Languages,* 1988, pp. 108–112.

[39] J. M. Kurtzberg and C. C. Tappert, "Segmentation Procedure for Handwritten Symbols and Words," *IBM Tech. Disclosure Bull.,* Vol. 25, pp. 3848–3852, 1982.

[40] Y. C. Lai, C. C. Chiang, and S. S. Yu, "Hybrid Learning Vector Quantization and Its Application to Handwritten Chinese Character Recognition," *Proc. Third National Workshop on Character Recognition*, Dec. 1993, Hsinchu, Taiwan.

[41] Y. Le Cun, B. Boser, J. S. Denker, D. Henderson, R. R. Howard, W. Hubbard, and L. D. Jackel, "Handwritten Zip Code Recognition with Multilayer Networks," *Proc. 10th Int. Conf. Pattern Recognition*, 1990, pp. 35–40.

[42] H. J. Lee and C. H. C. Chien, "A Markov Language Model in Handwritten Chinese Text Recognition," *Proc. 2nd Int. Conf. Document Analysis and Recognition*, Tsukuba, Japan, pp. 72–75, 1993.

[43] Sukhan Lee and Jack Chien-Jan Pan, "Unconstrained Handwritten Numeral Recognition Based on Radial Basis Competitive and Cooperative Networks with Spatiotemporal Feature Representation," *IEEE Trans. Neural Networks,* Vol. 7, No. 2, pp. 455–474, Mar. 1996.

[44] M. Y. Lin and W. H. Tsai, "A New Approach to On-line Chinese Character Recognition by Sentence Contextual Information Using the Relaxation Technique," *Proc. 1988 Int. Conf. Computer Processing of Chinese and Oriental Languages*, Toronto, Canada, pp. 131–134, 1988.

[45] S.-H. Lin, S.-Y. Kung, and L.-J. Lin, "Face Recognition/Detection by Probabilistic Decision-Based Neural Network," *IEEE Trans. Neural Networks*, Vol. 8, No. 1, pp. 114–132, 1997.

[46] E. Mandler, "Advanced Preprocessing Technique for On-line Script Recognition of Nonconnected Symbols," *Proc. 3rd Int. Symp. Handwriting Comput. Appl.,* July 1987, pp. 64–66.

[47] J. Mantas, "An Overview of Character Recognition Methodologies," *Pattern Recognition J.*, Vol. 19, No. 6, pp. 425–430, 1986.

[48] S. Mori, C. Y. Suen, and K. Yamamoto, "Historical Review of OCR Research and Development," *Proceedings of IEEE*, Vol. 80, No. 7, pp. 1029–1058, July, 1992.

[49] G. Nagy, "Optical Character Recognition," *Handbook of Statistics*, P. R. Krishnaiah and L. N. Kanal, eds., pp. 621–649, North Holland, 1982.

[50] G. Nagy, "Chinese Character Recognition: A Twenty-five Year Retrospective," *Proc. 12th Int. Conf. Pattern Recognition*, pp. 163–167, 1988.

[51] K. Odaka, H. Arakawa, and I. Masuda, "On-line Recognition of Handwritten Characters by Approximating Each Stroke with Several Points," *IEEE Tran. Sys. Man Cyber.*, Vol. SMC-12, pp. 898–903, 1982.

[52] H. Ogawa and Y. Tezuka, "Recognition of Handwritten Chinese Characters by Means of Hierarchical Representation," *Proc. Int. Comput. Symp.*, Taipei, Vol. 1, pp. 411–420, 1975.

[53] T. Pavlidis, "A Vectorizer and Feature Extractor for Document Recognition," *Computer Vision, Graphics, and Image Processing*, Vol. 35, pp. 111–127, 1986.

[54] L. Rabiner, "A Tutorial on Hidden Markov Model and Selected Applications in Speech Recognition," *IEEE Proceedings*, Vol. 77, No. 2, pp. 257–286, 1989.

[55] V. I. Rybak and G. I. Fursin, "Recognition of Handwritten Symbols in the Process of Writing," *Kibernetika*, Vol. 2, pp. 104–112, Mar. 1972.

[56] S. L. Shiaw, J. W. Chen, A. J. Hsieh, and S. J. Kung, "On-line Handwritten Chinese Character Recognition by String Matching," in *Proc. 1988 Int. Conf. Computer Processing of Chinese and Oriental Languages*, Toronto, Canada, pp. 76–80, 1988.

[57] I.-S. Shyu, L.-T. Tu, M.-Y. Chen, K.-H. Chou, and W.-W. Lin, "Design of a Decision Tree and Its Application to Large-Set Printed Chinese Character Recognition," *Proc. Int. Conf. Comp. Processing of Chinese & Oriental Lang.*, Toronto, Canada, 1988, pp. 126–130.

[58] I.-S. Shyu, M.-Y. Chen, W.-W. Lin, L.-T. Tu, K.-H. Chou, and Y.-H. Chou, "The FR1000 Form Reading System," *CCL Technical Journal*, Vol. 35, pp. 62–70, Dec. 1994.

[59] J.-C. Simon, "Handwriting Recognition as an Application of Regularities and Singularities in Line Picture," *Proc. Int. Workshop Frontiers in Handwriting Recognition* (Montreal, Canada), pp. 23–36, Apr. 1990.

[60] J.-C. Simon, "Off-line Cursive Word Recognition," *Proceedings of IEEE*, Vol. 80, No. 7, pp. 1150–1161, July 1992.

[61] R. K. Srihari, "Automatic Indexing and Content-Based Retrieval of Captioned Images," *IEEE Computer*, Vol. 28, No. 9, 1995, pp. 49–56.

[62] S. N. Srihari, eds., *Computer Text Recognition and Error Correction*, Silver Spring, MD: IEEE Computer Society Press, 1984.

[63] F. W. Stentiford, "Automatic Feature Design for Optical Character Recognition," *IEEE Trans. Pattern Anal. Machine Intell.*, Vol. 7, pp. 349–355, May 1985.

[64] C. Y. Suen, M. Berthod, and S. Mori, "Automatic Recognition of Handprinted Character—The State of the Art," *IEEE Proceedings*, Vol. 68, pp. 469–487, Apr. 1980.

[65] C. Y. Suen, "Computer Recognition of Kanji Characters," in *Proc. of 1983 Conference on Text Processing with a Large Character Set*, Chinese Language Computer Society, pp. 429–435.

[66] C. Y. Suen, "Character Recognition by Computer and Applications," in *Handbook of Pattern Recognition and Image Processing*, T. Y. Young and K. S. Fu, eds., New York, Academic Press, pp. 569–586.

[67] Ju-Wei Tai, "Some Research Achievement on Chinese Character Recognition in China" *Int. J. of Pattern Recognition and Artificial Intelligence*, Vol. 5, No. 1 & 2, pp. 199–206, 1991.

[68] C. C. Tappert, "Adaptive On-line Handwriting Recognition," *Proc. 8th Int. Conf. Pattern Recognition*, Montreal, Canada, pp. 1004–1007, July–Aug. 1984.

[69] C. C. Tappert, "Speed, Accuracy, Flexibility Trade-offs in On-line Character Recognition," IBM Res. Rep. RC13228, Oct. 1987.

[70] C. C. Tappert, C. Y. Suen, and T. Wakahara, "The State of the Art in On-line Handwriting Recognition," *IEEE Trans. Pattern Anal. Machine Intell.*, pp. 787–808, Vol. 12, No. 8, Aug. 1990.

[71] C.-H. Teh and R. T. Chin, "On Image Analysis by the Methods of Moments," *IEEE Trans. Pattern Anal. Machine Intell.*, Vol. 10, pp. 496–513, July 1988.

[72] W. H. Tsai and S. S. Yu, "Attributed String Matching with Merging for Shape Recognition," *IEEE Trans. Pattern Anal. Machine Intell.*, Vol. PAMI-7, pp. 453–462, 1985.

[73] Y. T. Tsay and W. H. Tsai, "Model-guided Attributed String Matching by Split-and-Merge for Shape Recognition," *International J. Pattern Recognition and Artificial Intelligence*, Vol. 3, No. 2, pp. 159–179, 1989.

[74] L. T. Tu, Y. S. Lin, C. P. Yeh, I. S. Shyu, J. L. Wang, K. H. Joe, and W.-W. Lin, "Recognition of Handprinted Chinese Characters by Feature Matching," *Proc. of 1991 First National Workshop on Character Recognition*, Taipei, ROC, 1991, pp. 166–175.

[75] J. R. Ullmann, "Advances Character Recognition," *Applications of Pattern Recognition*, K.-S. Fu, eds., ch. 9, Roca Baton, FL: CRC Press, 1986.

[76] T. Wakahara, H. Murase, and K. Odaka, "On-line Handwriting Recognition," *Proceedings of IEEE*, Vol. 80, No. 7, pp. 1181–1194, July 1992.

[77] T. Wakahara and M. Umeda, "On-line Cursive Script Recognition Using Stroke Linkage Rules," *Proc. 8th Int. Conf. Pattern Recognition*, pp. 1065–1068, 1984.

[78] J. F. Wang, H. S. Shiau, and H. M. Suen, "A Linguistic Decoder for Postprocessing of Chinese Character Recognition," *Proc. 4th Int. Workshop on Frontiers in Handwriting Recognition*, Taipei, Taiwan, Dec. 7–9, pp. 402–409, 1994.

[79] J. R. Ward, "Method and Apparatus for Removing Noise at the Ends of a Stroke," U.S. Patent 4 534 060, Aug. 1985.

[80] C. L Wilson and M. D. Garris, "Handprinted Character Database," Technical Report Special Database 1, **HWDB**, National Institute of Standards and Technology, Apr. 1990.

[81] L. D. Wu and J. W. Tai, "Some Advances of Pattern Recognition in China," *Proc. 8th Int. Conf. Pattern Recognition*, 1984, pp. 134–143.

[82] K. Yamamoto, H. Yamada, and T. Saito, ''Current State of Recognition Method for Japanese Characters and Database for Research of Handprinted Character Recognition,'' *Proc. Int. Workshop Frontiers in Handwriting Recognition* (Xhateau de Bonas, France), pp. 81–89, Sept. 1991.

[83] E. F. Yhap and E. C. Greanias, ''An On-line Chinese Character Recognition System,'' *IBM J. Research and Development*, Vol. 25, No. 3, pp. 187–195, 1981.

[84] M. Yoshida and M. Eden, ''Handwritten Chinese Character Recognition by A-b-s Method,'' *Proc. 1st Int. Joint Conf. Pattern Recognition*, Nov. 1973, pp. 197–204.

Chapter 17

HARDWARE DESIGN FOR 3-D GRAPHICS

Chein-Wei Jen and Bor-Sung Liang

Abstract

Three-dimensional graphics has played an important role in multimedia systems and virtual reality systems. Since its applications emerge rapidly from technical areas to nontechnical areas, state-of-the-art 3-D graphics hardware design focuses not only on high performance and quality, but also on low cost and system integration. In this chapter, we discuss the methodology and bottlenecks in hardware design. The techniques for high- performance 3-D graphics synthesis and various considerations are discussed, especially parallelism and advanced memory I/O architecture. Then, some existing architectures for various design considerations are illustrated. Because most programmers rely on application program interfaces (APIs) to develop applications on hardware, the API becomes important and affects the 3-D hardware design in integrated system.

17.1 INTRODUCTION

Over the past 20 years, computer graphics has become the primary means of communication between people for a variety of applications. CAD, medical imaging, and visualization in scientific research are some major applications. Until the early 1990s, applications of 3-D graphics emerged rapidly from technical to nontechnical areas. For example, multimedia products have become important. The use of graphics for animation is exploding as a key technology in the entertainment area. On the other hand, virtual reality is finding a significant role in entertainment and video games. All these applications are based on low-cost, real-time 3-D graphics systems.

In integrated multimedia systems, visual display has been developed and applied in three major areas: video, image processing, and computer graphics [1]. Unlike video and image processing applications which handle existing signals, computer graphics synthesizes images. Two-dimensional graphics is a widespread technique for visualizing data and concepts, especially in interactive applications. On the other hand, 3-D computer graphics is a larger and more interesting branch of computer graphics. It utilizes a 3-D model and specified lighting techniques to generate photorealistic scenes on output devices.

Users keep asking for 3-D graphics systems of higher performance and lower cost. Semiconductor technology makes this feasible. VLSI technology has enabled the development of graphics processors and is pushing 3-D graphics with the quality of workstation class into personal computers.

17.1.1   Goal of the 3-D Graphics Processor

Real-time Rendering. We can classify various 3-D applications by the demands of response time:

1. *Real-time applications:* Several to dozens of frames are rendered per second, typically 1/24 or 1/30 frames per second.
2. *Interactive applications:* The response time to render a frame is less than one second or several seconds.
3. *Batch applications:* The response time to render a frame is more than dozens of seconds.

Due to the prevalent multimedia and virtual reality applications, more and more, computer graphics has been asking for real-time rendering. Nevertheless, huge computation load, data traversal, and memory bandwidth problems have made it a big challenge to implement 3-D graphics functions on a general-purpose processor. Hence, it is natural to develop specific hardware for the sake of speed.

Image Quality. Three-dimensional graphics has been widely applied in various fields, from the high-end CAD to the low-end entertainment, and there are different demands of image complexity and quality. With the advance of computer performance, the desired image quality is elevated. This implies that the complexity of each frame is higher, and some algorithms, like texture mapping, can be applied for more realism. Therefore, the computation complexity, information storage, and communication burden also increase.

Low Cost. In the past 20 years, many hardware implementations have been proposed to accelerate 3-D graphics synthesis, but they are too expensive for most customers. Hence, applications of 3-D graphics in those systems are always developed for academic research, CAD/CAE, scientific visualization, medical image, and simulation, but seldom for entertainment and consumer production purposes. Since the multimedia and virtual reality systems have become increasingly popular, even in consumer electronics, low cost is a large consideration for designers when they are designing a hardware to accelerate 3-D graphics. With the progress of the semiconductor industry, specified processors have been developed for 3-D graphics; the processors, being mass produced, can reduce the price.

System Integration. Today multimedia systems are playing an important role in consumer electronics. A multimedia system integrates text, graphics, video, image, and audio signals. In order to handle various types of signals in real time and maintain synchronization, multimedia systems must be able to deal with a huge amount of operations in a short period of time. Therefore, different processors are implemented to enhance performance in various parts of a multimedia system. The 3-D graphics processor is one of them and needs to communicate with the other processors. Accordingly, some hardware implementations have to be compatible with most popular frame buffer display system in order to enhance 3-D graphics performance. Instead of designing an extremely different architecture from the existing display architecture, the 3-D graphics processor can be easily integrated into multimedia systems, but this constraint gives 3-D graphics architects a big burden. Figure 17.1 shows an integrated multimedia display system on PC.

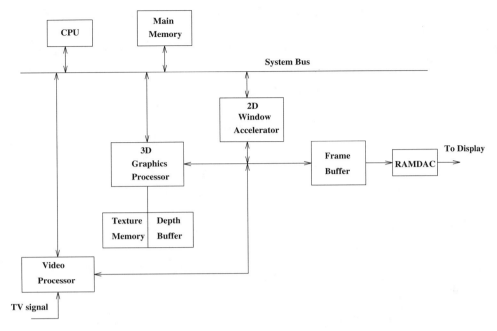

Figure 17.1   The integrated multimedia display system on PC.

On the other hand, to achieve compatibility and system integration, architects have to consider not only hardware design but also software development. The well-defined and powerful software interfaces are good guidelines for 3-D graphics processor architects to implement host interface and memory control. Because the application and software interface (API) is an enabling technology to spreading 3-D graphics processors, we will explain it in this chapter.

17.1.2 Methods for Rendering 3-D Graphics

The Whirlwind project at MIT in the early 1950s is generally said to mark the beginning of computer graphics [2]. At first, the output device was a vector display, and thus the 3-D graphics was based on wireframes. But computer graphics was not widely applied until the 1970s when display memory became cheaper. Due to affordable larger memory for frame buffer, bit-mapped raster scan displays became feasible on workstations and personal computers. With their brilliantly colored, filled-in graphics and reasonable price, raster scan displays emerged as the dominant technology, while the old vector displays began to disappear.

The raster scan displays with frame buffer memories have become the most popular architecture for state-of-the-art computer rendering systems. Almost all the computer graphics algorithms have been developed to be implemented based on its attributes. To show an image stored in frame buffer on the CRT (Cathode Ray Tube), an electronic beam sweeps the image plane, from left to right and from top to bottom, to form the visible 2-D image pixel by pixel. Some frame buffers are used to keep all pixel information in linear order.

In this chapter, we focus on the hardware design for 3-D graphics synthesis and rendering, and discuss some basic terms in 3-D graphics rendering.

17.1.2.1 Rendering Directions

Because light is reversible, there are two logical directions to render 3-D object models into 2-D images: object order and image order [3]. We can classify the two methods by tracing the light: object order means tracing light from the objects to the viewer, while image order means tracing light from the viewer to the objects. The pseudo-codes of the algorithms are as follows:

1. **Object order:**
       for each *primitives P* **do**
           for each *pixel q within P* **do**
               update frame buffer based on color and visibility of P at q

2. **Image order:**
       for each *pixel q* **do**
           for each *primitive P covering q* **do**
               compute P's contribution to q, outputting q when finished

In these two algorithms, the primitive P is the 3-D/2-D object model in the database, and the pixel q is a pixel on the raster scan display.

Besides object order and image order, yet another lighting technique is utilized in radiosity. This technique treats light as a kind of radiating energy, not as a sort of beam with direction. Rather than starting from the objects and the light sources, it models the intensity of light, leaving each point in the environment as a function of the light leaving all other points [4]. Because the view direction is not predefined in lighting, this technique is neither object order nor image order.

17.1.2.2 Illumination Models

The Illumination model calculates color values of pixels by the geometric information of objects and the properties of light sources. There are two kinds of illumination models:

1. *Local illumination model:* Local illumination models simulate how a single ray of light is scattered after being reflected from an object. Only interaction between a point on the illuminated surface and the light source is considered. No global illumination or illumination reaches the point under consideration through an indirect path, although sometimes the model takes into account directless ambient light. For light sources, only the properties of directionality and intensity are considered. About reflection and transparency, which have not been considered in the local illuminate model, the texture mapping or other algorithm is utilized to generate these effects in 3-D graphics.

2. *Global illumination model:* Global illumination models take into account the indirect path illumination because the local illumination model only treats the lighting operations locally and lacks the capacity of reflection and transparency. The global illumination model can be applied in two ways: one is an extension of the local illumination model and considers the indirect paths for light tracing; the other one treats light as energy.

17.1.2.3 Three Methods for Rendering

Considering different rendering directions and illumination models, common methods of rendering 3-D graphics can be classified into three major sorts in general:

Primitive shading:	Object order,	local illumination
Ray tracing :	Image order,	global illumination
Radiosity :		global illumination

The primitive shading method is a cost-effective solution for today's volume-level 3-D graphics hardware. This method decomposes all objects into lots of 3-D primitives, and then treats 3-D primitives as an extension of 2-D primitives. Therefore, it is easier to integrate the hardware implementation of this method into existing multimedia architecture. To synthesize 3-D graphics, objects are described by 3-D models and decomposed into many primitives. This method applies the local illumination model on each primitive individually to calculate color values, transfers 3-D coordinates into 2-D coordinates referred to eyepoint, tests whether or not primitives are hidden, and then writes primitives into the frame buffer.

The ray tracing method follows the light from specified eyepoint through each pixel on the screen into object space. The ray is tested against each object in the database. Then, the model information on the intersection of ray and objects is used to calculate the intensity of the pixel on the screen. To consider shadows, reflection, refraction, and transparency, the light from the indirect path is traced to form the recursive tree of rays at each pixel to find the pixel value [5]. The ray tracing handles the indirect light well to generate reflection and the transparency effect, but the ray/surface-intersection calculation proves to be a bottleneck.

The radiosity method was first developed in radiative heat transfer and was introduced in the context of image synthesis in 1984 [4]. This method treats light as energy, and the results are generated after converging all radiating light calculations. Unlike the case in the primitive shading and ray tracing methods, the color values are not generated by tracing light between eyepoint and objects. In this method, the object models are decomposed into many surface patches, and all patches affect each other by energy radiosity, like emission and diffuse reflection. Then, the results of patches are evaluated from a matrix formulation. This method can generate high-quality photorealism, but as a tradeoff it involves a huge amount of computation.

Because all surfaces are assumed to exhibit diffuse reflection and emission in the radiosity method, the nondiffuse reflecting surfaces cannot be easily generated in this method. Hence, a hybrid method which incorporates ray tracing and radiosity for better photorealism, like [6], has been developed.

To sum up these rendering methods, the radiosity method can synthesize high-quality, realistic 3-D images, especially the diffusion effect in inner rooms, but it demands heavy computation. When the 3-D models are decomposed into more patches for more photo-realism, the complexity of matrix formulation increases immensely. Hence, the radiosity and hybrid methods are always applied on batch applications for high-quality 3-D image synthesis, especially for publishing.

On the other hand, there is less computation in the ray tracing method than in the radiosity method. The advantage of the ray tracing method is the image quality when rendering reflective and transparent objects, but its disadvantage is its heavy burden in necessitating ray/surface-intersection calculation, especially in hardware implementation. To calculate pixel values, each pixel on display starts a ray tracing and checks any possible intersection with all 3-D object models. Hence, huge amounts of comparison and model database access limit the speed of rendering, and those database access operations are irregular and difficult to accelerate by hardware. Despite the disadvantages of this method, ray tracing is still the most popular rendering method in some applications in which 3-D objects are described by CSG (Constructive Solid Geometry) or voxel. Therefore, some hardware architectures are proposed to accelerate volume rendering [7] and CSG rendering applications, such as scientific visualization, medical image synthesis, and some specific CAD/CAM graphics.

Among those methods, the primitive shading method generates poor quality in photo-realism, but image quality can be moderately improved by use of some tricky techniques such as texture mapping for reflection and alpha blending for transparency. Because the primitive shading method applies local illumination models for lighting and handles each primitive individually, this method provides rich parallelism. The operations are regular, and the data have the property of spatial locality. Therefore, it is easy to speed up 3-D graphics by including acceleration hardware in the existing multimedia system. Hence, many 3-D accelerating architectures have proposed use of the primitive shading method for real-time 3-D graphics rendering, with acceptable image quality in multimedia systems.

From the viewpoint of the overall system in most popular multimedia, response time is very important in real-time interactive applications, as are cost, image quality, and system integration. To compare those rendering methods, the method based on primitive shading can be realized in low-cost 3-D hardware, and achieve high rendering throughput for real-time applications. But there is often a trade-off between image quality and performance. On the other hand, the rendering methods based on ray tracing and radiosity are often hard to be realized on low-cost real-time 3-D hardware, due to the complex computation for indirect paths in global illumination model. But these two methods can generate high image quality. Rather than very high image quality, many multimedia system designers emphasize real-time performance, especially in the mass-production systems. Hence, we will focus on the hardware implementations that are based on the primitive shading method in multimedia systems.

17.1.2.4 *Shading Schemes for the Primitive Shading Method*

In most popular primitive shading methods, all 3-D objects are decomposed into mesh models, and then mesh models are further decomposed into primitives for independent shading. For shading, several shading schemes can be used to apply lighting on primitives according to different demands of realism. Generally speaking, the more lighting operations inside primitives the better shading quality and more computations.

Flat Shading. Because of the complexity of calculation in lighting, the quickest shading scheme for primitives is flat shading [8], which is also known as faceted shading or constant shading. It just applies lighting once to calculate the color value on each primitive, and then it shades all primitives with the same color. Though quick, this scheme produces only poor quality. Therefore, it is implemented only on low-end applications, such as entertainment and games.

Gouraud Shading. Gouraud shading [9], also called smooth shading, intensity interpolation shading, or color interpolation shading, calculates the color values at each vertex of a primitive according to the local illumination model. Then it calculates the color values inside the primitives by interpolation. The main disadvantage of Gouraud shading is that it cannot show the highlight effect inside a primitive.

Phong Shading. Phong shading [10] can overcome some of the drawbacks of Gouraud shading. In particular, the highlight can be shown in the middle of a polygon. The vertex normal vectors, rather than the vertex color value, are interpolated. For each pixel inside the polygon, the color values are calculated by interpolated normal vectors according to the local illumination model. Figure 17.2 shows three shading schemes and pseudocodes on a point P inside a triangle.

17.1.2.5 The Phong Local Illumination Model

The most popular local illumination model for applying lighting on primitive shading is the Phong illumination model proposed in 1975 [10]. This model simulates reflected light in terms of a diffuse and specular component, and calculates the illumination according to the light source position and view position. The intensity at a point on a surface is taken to be the linear combination of these three components: diffuse, specular, and ambient terms. The reflection model is as follows [11]:

$$I = I_a \times K_a + [I_i \times K_d(\mathbf{L} \cdot \mathbf{N}) + I_i \times K_s(\mathbf{H} \cdot \mathbf{N})^n] \tag{1}$$

where

I_a = intensity of the ambient light

I_i = intensity of the light source

$\mathbf{L}$ = the unit vector from pixel to the light source

$\mathbf{N}$ = the normal vector of the pixel

$\mathbf{H} = \frac{(\mathbf{L}+\mathbf{V})}{2} = \mathbf{V}$ is the vector from the pixel to the viewer

n = gloss to the model highlight

K_a, K_d, K_s = coefficients to model the characteristic of the material

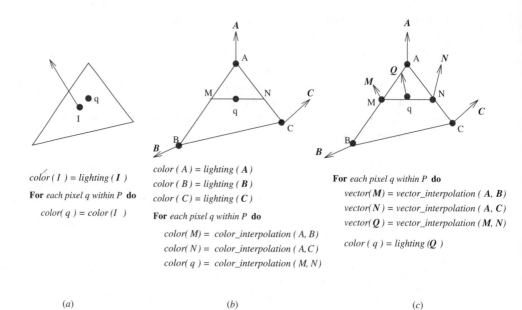

$color\,(\,I\,) = lighting\,(\,I\,)$

For *each pixel q within P* **do**

   $color(\,q\,) = color\,(I\,)$

$color\,(\,A\,) = lighting\,(\,A\,)$
$color\,(\,B\,) = lighting\,(\,B\,)$
$color\,(\,C\,) = lighting\,(\,C\,)$

For *each pixel q within P* **do**

   $color(\,M\,) = \; color\_interpolation\,(\,A,\,B\,)$
   $color(\,N\,) = \; color\_interpolation\,(\,A,\,C\,)$
   $color(\,q\,) = \; color\_interpolation\,(\,M,\,N\,)$

For *each pixel q within P* **do**

   $vector(\boldsymbol{M}) = vector\_interpolation\,(\,\boldsymbol{A},\,\boldsymbol{B}\,)$
   $vector(\boldsymbol{N}) = vector\_interpolation\,(\,\boldsymbol{A},\,\boldsymbol{C}\,)$
   $vector(\boldsymbol{Q}) = vector\_interpolation\,(\,\boldsymbol{M},\,\boldsymbol{N}\,)$

   $color\,(\,q\,) = lighting\,(\boldsymbol{Q}\,)$

(*a*)   (*b*)   (*c*)

Figure 17.2   Three shading schemes and pseudocodes: (*a*) Flat shading;
(*b*) Gouraud shading; (*c*) Phong shading.

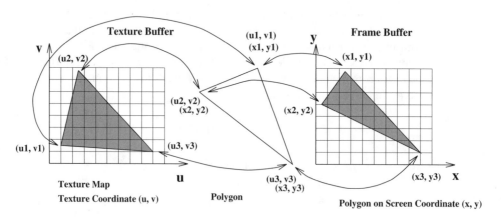

Figure 17.3   The scheme of texture mapping [13].

17.1.2.6 Texture Mapping

Texture mapping, pioneered by Catmull [12], is a popular rendering technique for increasing photorealism. It allows textures to be represented as digital images and be mapped across surfaces in a 3-D scene, and it provides a simple method for adding realistic detail to computer-generated imagery. The texture image is called a texture map, and its individual elements are often call texels. In Fig. 17.3, we show the process that performs the texture mapping from pixel to the surface and then to the texture map [13].

In the add-on scheme of texture mapping, some techniques are applied on this scheme for photorealism; examples of these techniques are anti-aliased texture mapping, and perspective texture mapping for reflection [14].

17.2 3-D GRAPHICS HARDWARE ARCHITECTURE

17.2.1 Standard 3-D Graphics Rendering Pipeline

To accelerate 3-D graphics, the most popular method in hardware design is the primitive shading method. Here we discuss the most popular 3-D graphics rendering pipeline, which is shown in Fig. 17.4 [11].

17.2.1.1 Function Blocks in Pipeline

In Fig. 17.4, the standard rendering pipeline is divided by different coordinate systems. All objects are modeled and stored individually in a model database; therefore, the model description of each object refers to its own local coordinates, called local coordinate space. A 3-D scene is made up of several 3-D objects inside a virtual 3-D world that is spanned by uniform 3-D coordinates, which is called world coordinate space. To synthesize a desired 3-D graphics, the concerned objects in this 3-D scene are fetched from a model database and placed in the virtual 3-D world according to the programmer's instruction. Thus, each concerned object must convert its own local coordinates into the uniform world coordinates. This transformation is called modeling transformation. Then, just like a camera that takes

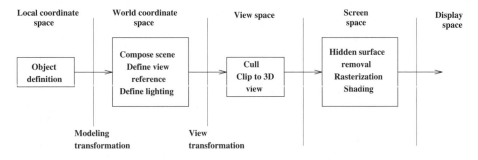

Figure 17.4 The scheme of the standard 3-D graphics rendering pipeline [11].

a photo in the real 3-D world, a viewpoint is necessary to generate an image for this virtual 3-D world. The view coordinate space is defined with respect to the viewpoint, and all objects in the virtual 3-D world are transferred into this coordinate system. This operation is called view transformation.

After the view transformation, all objects are presented by view space. Due to the resolution limit of raster scan display, the continuous view coordinates must be converted into the X-Y screen coordinates with depth value, called the 3-D screen space.

After the hidden surface removal and other per-pixel operations, the frame buffer keeps the result image and then outputs to the display.

The function units that handle standard pipeline operations usually are divided into two parts: geometric subsystem and raster subsystem. As illustrated in Fig. 17.4, in local coordinate space, world coordinate space, and view space, the spaces are spanned by continuous geometric coordinates in three dimensions, and the precision of coordinate is important for lots of space transformations. Hence, the coordinate values are always presented in floating-point numbers. The unit that handles functions in those three coordinates space is usually called the geometric subsystem, and the processor that implements this subsystem is called the geometric engine.

17.2.1.2 The Geometric Subsystem

The detail of a geometric subsystem with its several stages is shown in Fig. 17.5. There are two coordinate transformations which are 4 x 4 matrices operations. The visualization test identifies and rejects the primitives, which are wholly outside the view volume to avoid invalid operations. Partially inside primitives are clipped to fit the view volume at the clipping stage. The perspective divide stage divides the view space coordinates by a constant w and then uses the 3-D screen coordinates mapping to map the coordinates into X-Y screen coordinates for future operations in the raster subsystem. The lighting module only exists in those geometric subsystems where the Gouraud shading is applied.

17.2.1.3 The Raster Subsystem

On the other hand, because of the discrete nature of screen coordinates space, the coordinates are presented by integers after being transformed into the screen space. Moreover, these descriptions of object-oriented primitives should be decomposed and rasterized

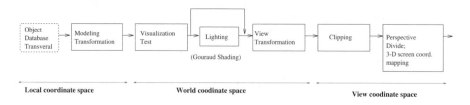

Figure 17.5 Detail of the geometric subsystem [11].

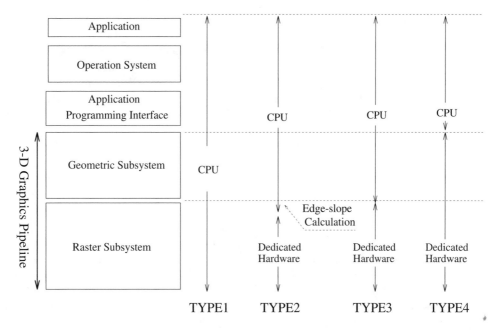

Figure 17.6 Different schemes for hardware implementation on 3-D graphics pipeline.

into pixel-oriented information for further processing. Therefore, the unit performing the rasterization in integer coordinates is called a raster subsystem, and the 3-D graphics processor implementing this subsystem is called a raster engine. Since most operations inside the raster subsystem are massive and regular, this subsystem is suitable for acceleration by specific hardware with parallelism.

17.2.1.4 Hardware Implementations for the Standard 3-D Graphics Pipeline

To implement the standard 3-D graphics pipeline, there are many different schemes for hardware implementation, as shown in Fig. 17.6. Type 1 is not a hardware implementation, and all operations of 3-D graphics are executed totally by software. On the other hand, type 2 and type 3 realize the hardware implementation of the raster subsystem. In type 2, the software must handle the edge-slope calculations to initiate rasterization works. Type 4 is the total hardware solution on the 3-D graphics pipeline.

17.2.2 The Bottlenecks of 3-D Graphics Rendering

As mentioned by Molnar and Fuchs [3], if a system has sufficient frame buffer memory, a suitable CRT display, and enough computation time, it can generate and display scenes of virtually unlimited complexity and realism. In this situation, all rasterization work is done by the CPU with large memory for temporary storage, and we allow long computation time for calculation. It is suitable for batch applications. But some 3-D applications need higher performance on 3-D rendering. Like multimedia systems, real-time response and low cost are the major considerations of system design. Different hardware architectures are suitable for different 3-D applications. On the other hand, many designers have tried to design specific hardware for 3-D graphics, but have encountered three barriers: floating-point operations, fixed-point operations, and memory bandwidth problems.

17.2.2.1 Floating-point Operations

The coordinate systems in a standard pipeline are generally represented by floating-point numbers. Therefore, the floating-point operations of coordinate transformations are main computation demands in the geometric subsystem.

Both modeling and view transformations are needed for each vertex of primitives. They are 4 x 4 matrices operations, and the multiply-accumulation is the main operation for transformation. Then, the clipping units clip these primitives, which are partially inside the view volume. For lighting, the local illumination model, like the Phong illumination model, is applied on the primitives. Operations such as addition, multiplication, vector inner product, and power operations are needed. The complexity of lighting is always a burden for speeding up the systems.

17.2.2.2 Fixed-point Operations

Most operations in raster subsystems are fixed-point operations. To convert primitives, dozens to hundreds of pixels are generated after rasterization, and the raster subsystem must process all pixel information. Hence, the number of fixed-point operations depends on the number and average size of primitives.

17.2.2.3 Memory Bandwidth

To implement raster subsystem, one of the major differences between the CPU and graphics processor is the additional memory interfaces. Because of the huge amount of 3-D graphics data transfer, the memory bandwidth problem is always a serious bottleneck of the graphics system.

Three major types of memory interfaces have memory bandwidth problems: the frame buffer, depth buffer, and texture buffer. The bandwidth problem will become worse if we want to speed up the fixed- and floating-point operations by some advanced technique such as parallelism and pipeline. Especially in a single-chip 3-D graphics processor, owing to cost considerations, pin count numbers always limit the width of data bus.

Frame Buffer. With higher resolution, more color depth, and higher screen refresh rate for better display quality, a large frame buffer size is needed. It implies that more memory bandwidth will be occupied by the continuously display refreshing, because the frame buffer stores the color value for every pixel on screen, and it will send the whole

Table 17.1 The Display Bandwidth Requirements
of Some Display Modes

Resolution	Color bits (bits per pixel)	Frame buffer size (bytes per frame)	Refresh rate (frames per second)	Display bandwidth (M bytes per sec)
640 x 480	4	150 K	35.5	5.2
640 x 480	16	600 K	35.5	20.8
640 x 480	24	900 K	35.5	31.2
640 x 480	24	900 K	70	61.52
800 x 600	24	1406 K	70	96.1
1024 x 768	24	2304 K	70	157.5
1280 x 1024	24	3840 K	72	270
1600 x 1200	24	5625 K	72	395.5

frame information to display in each refresh cycle. For example, in a display screen with 1024 x 768 x 24 bits in a refresh rate of 60 Hz in noninterlaced format, the required memory bandwidth is:

$$3 \text{ (bytes/pixel)} \times 1024 \text{ (pixels/line)} \times 768 \text{ (lines/frame)} \times 60 \text{ (frames/sec)} = 135 \text{ M (bytes/sec)}$$

The display bandwidth requirements of some general display modes are listed in Table 17.1. In the earlier discussion, we haven't considered in the necessary memory bandwidth burden of 3-D graphics specific algorithms, so the real bandwidth requirement is much larger. In general, the sustained output rate of the 3-D graphics rendering is up to several or tens of mega pixels per second.

Depth Buffer. In most popular depth-buffer algorithms for hidden surface removal, we need to offer the depth value storage (typically 16, 24, or 32 bits per pixel). After the pixel value is generated from the rasterization unit, one read or read-modified-write cycle is needed to determine whether the pixel value can be written into the frame buffer. Therefore, in practice the desired memory bandwidth in the depth buffer will be larger than the bandwidth in the frame buffer.

Texture Buffer. The texture buffer is a memory block that stores information for the texture map. Generally, texture maps are much smaller than the display size; hence, the memory capacity of the texture buffer is also smaller. We can afford to implement it by faster but more expensive memory. However, if we share the memory with the depth buffer or frame buffer for a low-cost solution, it will lower the performance of memory access. Since texel coordinates are different from pixel coordinates in regard to the depth buffer and frame buffer, the shared memory will lose the locality of accessing. Moreover, for anti-aliased texture mapping, some implementations use the mip-mapped texture mapping [15], even trilinear interpolation for texels. In such conditions, 2, 4, even 8, texels are needed to calculate the bilinear or trilinear color value for each pixel, and the overall bandwidth of texture buffer is enlarged.

17.2.3   Techniques for 3-D Graphics Hardware

The most efficient way to improve the performance of 3-D graphics is through use of special-purpose hardware. However, before the engineers develop the hardware architecture, some important issues should be discussed. Since the CPU with sufficient memory can handle any rendering jobs by software, can hardware be better than the CPU in improving 3-D graphics synthesis? Three-dimensional graphics hardware have many different design goals, including performance, rendering quality, configurablility and ease of integration into the multimedia system. On the other hand, some designers just want to improve some features in the graphics pipeline and reduce the burden on the CPU.

To overcome bottlenecks in floating-point operations, fixed-point operations and memory bandwidth, lots of methods were proposed. Those methods can be classified into two major sorts: the first sort of methods make use of parallelism to improve computation-bound problems; the others try to improve memory bandwidth bottlenecks by advanced memory technology.

17.2.3.1   Parallelism

With huge but regular calculations in 3-D graphics synthesis, parallelism is a good strategy for improving performance. Parallelism can be realized through the architectural design or through graphics information.

Parallelism in Architectural Design.   The following parallel architectural designs are always realized in the graphics system; these designs refer to the techniques of advanced CPU and parallel processing architectural design.

(a) *Pipelining:* Pipelining is a widespread technique used to enhance the throughput of data processing. In dedicated pipeline design, the pipeline is always divided by the 3-D functions, and each stage is related to different operations. In general, there are two levels of pipelining in 3-D graphics rendering. The first level is pipelined in coarse grain. The rendering jobs are divided by the different coordinates when data processing, such as the standard 3-D graphics rendering pipeline in Fig. 17.4. The second level is pipelined in fine grain. The overall processing path is further divided into small individual operations units, such as the pipeline in the graphics core of GLINT 300SX of 3DLabs [16].

On the other hand, some designs enhance the ability of the CPU or DSP to handle 3-D operations or to implement an embedded RISC core in dedicated hardware design. The hardware provides the mathematical operations, and the software program handles the desired 3-D functions. These designs may be slower than the design with dedicated pipeline in the same clock rate, but are more flexible in the realization of various algorithms, such as the Intel i860 RISC processor [17].

(b) *Multiprocessors:* By considering the parallelism in 3-D graphics processing, multiple processing elements (PEs) are utilized to process parallel information. Many structures implement multiprocessors. The SIMD (single-instruction multiple data stream) is a good structure for graphics subsystems because of the rich homogeneous parallelism in 3-D graphics data. Choice of the algorithms for PEs is important, and the memory architecture should be designed to support the multiprocessor; hence, 3-D data processing can be much improved. However, the structure with heavy parallelism causes a load-balance problem. The highly parallel SIMD approach always suffers from the low utilization of PEs [3,18]; because all PEs work in lock step, they cannot retarget to other tasks.

Besides, given the cost of communication and synchronization, the multiple-instruction multiple data stream (MIMD) structure can be applied in the coarse grain of parallelism. Especially in 3-D animation, the rendering jobs of frames are often independent and can be handled by a cluster of networked workstations [19].

(c) *VLIW structure:* In order to optimize the function units inside the processor, the Very Long Instruction Word (VLIW) structure utilizes the long-length instruction format with different fields directly mapped to the control signals of function units. Because of encoding parallelism in the long instruction, its instruction decoding is easy. The main advantage of the VILW structure is its simplicity in hardware control [20], even in handling heterogeneous PEs for various operations in parallel. Compared with the CPU with its 3-D ability or embedded RISC design, the VLIW structure can be further optimized for performance in general. Because of the special instruction format and the optimized data path for some desired algorithms, the VLIW structure often loses compatibility and some flexibility in the realization of various algorithms. Moreover, the performance of the VLIW structure depends heavily on software optimization, such as trace-scheduling compiling. In TGPx4 of Fujitsu, the VLIW structure is utilized for geometric operations [21].

(d) *Superscalar:* In the superscalar structure, multiple data processing paths are provided inside the processor. This structure utilizes instruction-level parallelism to speed up operations, but there are various dependencies between instructions. Thus, in order to avoid possible mistakes caused by dependencies and to improve performance, its decoder and control hardware are very complex. In fact, because the rendering jobs are often regular and the operations are predictable after the algorithm has been decided, the instructions can be prearranged to avoid dependence. In order to improve performance, the SIMD and VLIW structure can optimize their data paths for regular and predictable processing and do not need complex control. Thus, if the designer focus is on performance, the SIMD and VLIW structures are more suitable than the superscalar structure in 3-D hardware design. If flexibility of algorithm is more important, the designer may use the design of the CPU with 3-D ability or embedded RISC. The superscalar structure can be utilized inside these designs. Because there are many excellent existing superscalar CPUs, the burden of hardware design will cause the designer to use a superscalar CPU that is already on the market rather than design a new one.

(e) *Systolic array:* In the postprocessing of rendering pipeline, the data of each pixel often relate to the data of nearby pixels. In addition, the pixel-level operations lead to the parallelism in fine grain. Because of the regular operations, parallelism, and locality of data dependence in 3-D graphics rendering, some designers realize the 3-D hardware through systolic array. SAGE of IBM and HSSP of Matsushita, for example, implement the 1-D systolic array for shading and hidden surface removal [22,23]. The systolic array can provide very high rendering performance, but expensive hardware cost and lack of flexibility are its major drawbacks. Key issues in systolic array design are synchronization, stable data I/O, and control hardware. In order to fulfill the design issues of systolic array, the consideration for hardware dominates the choice of rendering algorithm, and the operations almost cannot be configured.

In various designs for parallelism in 3-D hardware architecture, the way to realize rendering algorithm is an important issue. The flexibility for algorithm is the advantage of software implementation, while the implementation by dedicated hardware can process 3-D rendering in high performance for some desired algorithms.

The algorithm realization in the CPU with 3-D ability and the embedded RISC is often software implementation, and the parallelism is often in the instruction level. The VLIW structure can also treat the algorithm as software, but its data path can be further optimized for performance in general. Hence, the VLIW structure does not realize algorithm through either pure hardware or pure software. The dedicated hardware implementations for algorithm make use of various forms of parallelism in 3-D graphics data, and most of them focus on data flow, such as SIMD and systolic array.

The pipeline structure is widely utilized in various 3-D hardware designs. The MIMD structure can be found on the workstation clusters for rendering 3-D animation. Figure 17.7 roughly classifies the methods for 3-D hardware design with parallelism.

Parallelism in Graphics Data. In 3-D hardware, the rendering hardware transfers the 3-D object model into a 2-D image. Because there is potential for parallelism in each level, the hardware architecture can be designed with parallelism.

As shown in Fig. 17.8, there are two different hierarchical structures in 3-D graphics data. In the front processing of the rendering pipeline, the graphics data are object-oriented, and the hierarchical structure is shown in Fig. 17.8(a). Except for the lighting attribute and some global information, object-oriented data are described in wireframe models in general, and models can be decomposed into several primitives. The object-oriented primitives are often described in several points or vertices in 3-D coordinates. On the other hand, the graphics data are pixel-oriented in the postprocessing of the rendering pipeline, as shown in Fig. 17.8(b). Each frame is a 2-D image made up of a group of primitives, such as a polygon, line, and points. Different from the object-oriented primitives, the pixel-oriented primitives are illustrated by a group of pixels on a 2-D image plain. They may overlay or be overlaid by each other.

The primitives are the common terms between object-oriented and pixel-oriented hierarchy structures. Rasterization is the way to convert the object-oriented primitives into the pixel-oriented primitives. Hence, the processing before rasterization is called the geometric subsystem, and the object-oriented hierarchy structure is utilized for the data format. The other processing is called the raster subsystem, and the pixel-oriented hierarchy structure is utilized for data format.

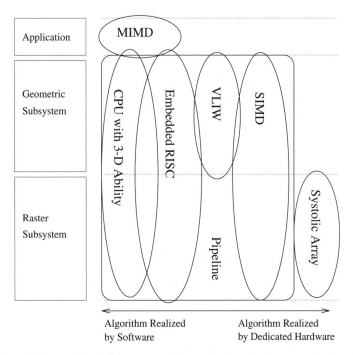

Figure 17.7   Architectural designs with parallelism for 3-D graphics hardware.

The two hierarchical structures encompass several levels of parallelism. Those levels are as follows.

(a) *Parallelism in multiframes:* This parallelism appears in rendering multiple frames, like the 3-D animation. This level of parallelism involves two kinds of hierarchical structures. It exists only between many frames, but not in one frame. There is very little dependency in rendering between frames, and this parallelism can be realized by the multiprocessor structure, such as the MIMD. In some designs, each processor can store the common information and final result in its own private memory, so real-time communication is not necessary. Hence, distributed computation on networked computers is a solution for this parallelism. It is an example for rendering each frame in 3-D animation on networked workstations [19].

(b) *Parallelism in multiprimitives:* In both hierarchical structures, several primitives can be rendered in parallel. The designers can duplicate the rendering pipelines, and each individual pipeline handles different primitives. Thus, the SIMD or MIMD structure is a good solution here. In object-oriented hierarchical structures, designers can provide the necessary computation hardware to realize this parallelism. In the pixel-oriented hierarchical structure, there is an "overlay problem" in pixel-oriented primitives. Since the pixel-oriented primitives may be partially overlaid, a depth comparison between

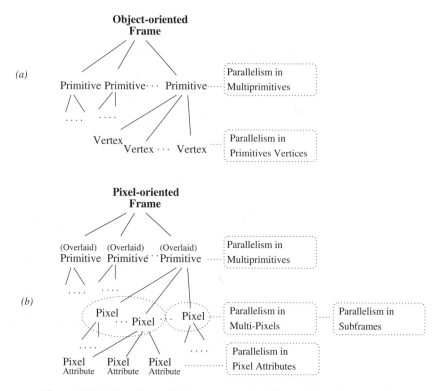

Figure 17.8   Two hierarchical structures for 3-D graphics data: (*a*) object-oriented, (*b*) pixel-oriented.

each primitive is necessary. That is, there is less parallelism between multiprimitives in the pixel-oriented hierarchical structure. The GSP-NVS system in Schlumberger Palo Alto Research has utilized another way to effect this parallelism. It makes use of a group of triangle processors in a serial to decide each pixel's value [24].

(c) *Parallelism in primitives vertices:* In the object-oriented hierarchy structure, 3-D primitives are always described by vertices or points in 3-D coordinates. Most operations in the geometric subsystem are linear transformations between different coordinate spaces. Because of the homogeneous operations on all the vertices, there is parallelism in primitive vertices. The coordinate transformations are usually 4 x 4 matrices linear transformations; hence, many multiplication and addition operations are demanded here. In general, realizing parallelism in primitive vertices is a computation-bound problem. Some systems make use of this parallelism to handle operations in parallel; examples are the pipelining in SPC1500 [25] and floating-point processors in Leo graphics system of Sun [26].

(d) *Parallelism in multipixels:* In the pixel-oriented hierarchical structure, a frame is made up of a group of individual pixels, and each pixel has its own x-y coordinate. Hence, parallelism exists between pixels. The number of pixels in a frame ranges from 64K (resolution: 320 x 200) to several million (resolution 1280 x 1024 or 1600 x 1200). This parallelism is very massive; hence, communication and load-balance problems are important issues. Some designs for this parallelism follow the SIMD structure but often suffer from low hardware utilization. On the other hand, because of massive parallelism, locality, and regular operations, the systolic structure can be suitably applied in this level of parallelism.

(e) *Parallelism in subframes:* In order to avoid the drawbacks of massive parallelism in pixels, designers divide each frame into subframes. Essentially, the parallelism in subframes is an extension of the parallelism in multipixels, and both of them appear in the same hierarchy in the pixel-oriented hierarchical structure, as shown in Fig. 17.8(*b*). Because each pixel has its own coordinate, each subframe is a group of pixels related to coordinates, and it is often in the shape of a scanline, block, interleaved pixel plane, and so on. The data in different subframes are processed by different processors, and then the results are gathered to generate the whole image. The multiprocessor structure is always used to effect this parallelism. The Pixel planes of the University of North Carolina utilized pixel processors to implement massive parallelism [27,28]. Another good example is the footprint processor in GS1000 of Stellar, with 4 x 4 block interleave in the frame [18].

(f) *Parallelism in pixel attributes:* Between the attributes in each pixel, there is still parallelism. The typical attributes are the color values R, G, B, the screen coordinates x, y, z, the texture coordinates s, t, and so on. The SIMD structure is often utilized for this parallelism. In some designs that use the DDA structure to generate results, the incremental interpolators are the major PEs which handle pixel attributes in parallel, such as the image chip of the University of Sussex [29] and the edge processors in the scan conversion subsystem of SGI 4D/240 GTX [30].

17.2.3.2 *Advance Memory I/O Architecture*

As mentioned earlier, the memory bandwidth poses a big challenge for 3-D graphics systems. To improve the memory I/O, there are two candidate methods: one that focuses on the memory I/O structure design, and the other that focuses on the high-bandwidth memory technologies.

Memory I/O Structure. The hierarchical memory structure is the most popular method used to improve memory bandwidth by architectural design. This structure is called the virtual-buffer technique when it is implemented in the frame buffer [31]. It renders primitives into a temporary buffer, and it uses the temporary buffer repeatedly to construct a piece of the whole image at a time. The virtual-buffer technique can improve performance only when the temporary buffer is smaller but faster than the frame buffer memory, and when the data transfer between two memories is fast enough not to become a bottleneck. There are several distinct ways to realize the virtual-buffer technique:

(a) *Sweep algorithm:* To raster a whole image, the mapped area of the temporal buffer sweeps the entire area of the frame buffer once. For each operation on different mapped areas, the temporal buffer is cleared and there is no mutual affection which is stored in

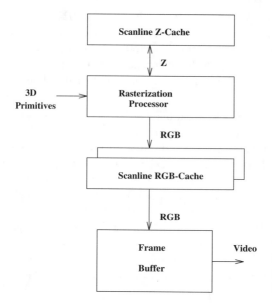

Figure 17.9 The virtual-buffer techniques with scanline RGB temporal buffer [31].

the temporary buffers between mapped areas. The temporary buffer can be a scanline, a band, or a block, and its goal is to assist with the sweep operation. The algorithm is based on the parallelism of pixel-level. Figure 17.9 presents an example of the virtual-buffer technique with scanline RGB temporal buffer [31].

(b) *Pixel cache:* The cache is a fast memory block mapping to the frame buffer and realized by a fast memory with general cache control. It works well for the locality of most rasterization algorithms.

Due to the penalty of data transfer, however, there are limitations when improving the performance by memory I/O structure. Because there is an average size of primitives, some research shows that improvement by the pixel cache is inefficient if the cache size is beyond the average size of the primitives [31].

(c) *Interleave:* The interleaved memory bank is a typical frame buffer designed to improve memory bandwidth. Some designers use this structure in the VRAM frame buffer, because the scanout pixel rate exceeds the data rate of the VRAM serial port in high resolution. A high-speed off-chip shift register is utilized and loads the multiple banks of VRAMs in parallel, and then it shifts out serially for display. Sometimes the shift register is used in conjunction with the lookup table and digital-to-analog converters, as shown in Fig. 17.10 [32].

(d) *Double buffer:* The double-buffered system is another way to solve memory problems. It duplicates the frame buffer memory. When the pixel data are sent out from one frame buffer, the input pixel data are able to be written into another frame buffer. Hence, this structure can make the single-port RAM work like the two-port RAM. Although it utilizes double memory size, the double-buffered system is widespread, especially in 3-D real-time animation rasterization.

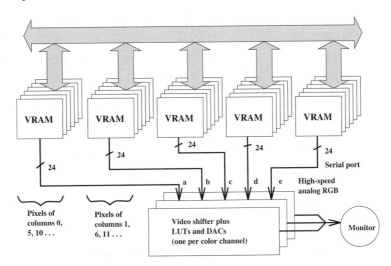

Figure 17.10   The interleaved five-way memory bank structure for frame buffer [32].

Memory Technology. With the advance of semiconductor technology, a lot of research began to focus on large-capacity, high-density, high-speed memory design. However, with the large-bandwidth demand of multimedia systems, more memory designs for higher bandwidth appeared. Some special RAMs are designed to meet the new applications. The following are the memory techniques designed for 3-D graphics and image applications.

(a) *Faster memory access:* Some acceleration techniques are applied in RAM, and they drive the faster memory access for various applications, like pipeline, page mode, burst mode, synchronization, and EDO (Extended data-out) mode RAM [33]. The 2ns cycle, 4ns access pipelined CMOS ECL SRAM of IBM [34] is an example.

(b) *Dual port:* The display pixel scan-out is very regular and serial but wastes too many memory bandwidths. The best way to solve this problem is to design a dedicated individual port for scan-out and keep the random access port for the processor to read/write this RAM. Examples are VRAM, which was first introduced by TI Corporation in 1983 [35], and WRAM, launched by Samsung Corporation.

(c) *Logic-in-memory:* As the DRAM processor grows to the gigabit scale, embedded logic in DRAM has become a trend for higher performance. With logic embedded, the RAM has the capability of not only storing data but also doing logic operations on each bit or bit groups. This structure is also called logic-embedded-memory. For general purposes, the CDRAM of Mitsubishi embeds the SRAM and cache logic into the DRAM chip [36,37], and the RDRAM of Rambus Inc. utilizes the logic-in-memory in its design to improve the performance of the memory access [33]. On the other hand, for special 3-D graphics accelerations, Stanford University implements the SLAM structure to improve the polygon filling operation in each scanline [38]. 3D-RAM of Mitsubishi

[39] and FBRAM of Sun [40] integrate the alpha-blending and depth buffer logic with DRAM on-chip.

(d) *Memory-in-logic:* Compared with logic-embedded-memory, there is another way to implement memory on logic VLSI processes: namely, memory-in-logic, or memory-embedded-logic. Generally, most processors need internal memory or registers. Owing to cost considerations, few register files are embedded in a processor. Because of the large buffer size in 3-D graphics, it is not feasible to include all buffers in one chip. However, this structure can still be utilized, providing the data processing is interleaved into many subframes and the size of each distribute buffer is small enough. For systolic array, the design of distributed buffers for each PE can improve the communication problem, and each PE only needs to hold one pixel data. Hence, some systolic array design uses memory-in-logic to store the distributed frame buffer information in each cell; examples are SAGE of IBM [22] and the HSSP system [23].

17.2.3.3   Other Considerations for Hardware Design

All the designs described here are high-performance designs, and most of them are designed following the standard 3-D graphics pipeline by the primitives shading method. However, for different applications, there are various hardware design considerations: photorealism, applications, and configurability.

The Consideration of Photorealism.   The rendering result of primitives shading always looks like plastic objects. To increase photorealism in primitive shading, some patch works have been developed, such as alpha blending for transparency [41], the various texture mappings for surface attributes [12], and shadow generating.

For higher quality of lighting photorealism, different rendering methods, such as ray tracing and radiosity, are utilized for 3-D graphics synthesis. The ray tracing method often supports recursive shading processing. The hardware needed to implement ray tracing is often based on intersection processing, because most operations in ray tracing are intersection determinations [42]. In most applications, this architecture is always utilized for volume rendering, scientific visualization [7], medical image generation [43], and 3-D model visualization [44]. On the other hand, the radiosity method can achieve a high-level realism, especially when generating the indoor scene with diffused light. Some hardware architectures for radiosity are discussed in [45].

The Consideration of Applications.   For greater acceptance, many 3-D graphics hardware designs follow the de facto standards. For hardware integration, there are some de facto standards on the hardware interface, like the host interface, bus structure, and memory interface. To make use of hardware designs in miscellaneous applications, the interfacing logic must follow these standards. Besides, the modular flexibility in hardware architecture is another consideration for 3-D graphics processors. An example is the chip module of GVIP serial processors for 3-D graphics and multimedia applications [46].

On the other hand, considering applications and software development, a 3-D hardware should also be designed to support and accelerate de facto standard 3-D graphics APIs, like OpenGL, Direct 3-D, and PHIGS+. The issues of APIs are discussed later in Section 17.4.

The Consideration of Configurablility. In architecture design, architecture has to be configurable. Hence, the 3-D hardware can become more scalable for future demand. This consideration always leads to a problem: the hardware design should follow the data flow or control flow design. For data flow design, the 3-D hardware may be realized by the specific dedicated function pipeline. For control flow design, the rendering algorithm is realized by software. It is possible to implement hardware by the embedded RISC core in system. Generally, the data flow gets good performance in regular information processing but lacks configurability. The control flow design, especially the embedded RISC core, is often full of flexibility. But with the high image quality demand, performance will decrease quickly when program complexity increases.

17.3 3-D GRAPHICS PROCESSORS

As we explained in the last section, there are many elegant designs for high-performance 3-D graphics synthesis. In this section, we discuss some hardware designs for 3-D graphics and focus on system integration and low-cost strategies, because there will be a large demand on those designs in multimedia applications.

17.3.1 Geometric Subsystem

17.3.1.1 Pipelined Design for Geometric Subsystem

The S-MOS SPC1500 is an example of fully pipelined hardware used to improve geometric operations and compliant with OpenGL and PHIGS+ [25]. This chip utilizes the concurrency in 3-D primitives models to accelerate 3-D graphics synthesis. It is based on the consideration of API compatibility for OpenGL and PHIGS+, configurablility by upgradable microcode, and image quality by floating-point operations.

The main purpose of this chip is to accelerate the view transformation, lighting, and clipping operations, and then to convert the primitives information to screen coordinate for further operations in the graphics subsystem. Figure 17.11 shows the block diagram of SPC1500.

The main programmable and fully pipelined processor core in SPC1500 is called the SRIN (Super Raster Initialization eNgine) and is controlled by the microcode stored in memory. To process the floating-point geometric coordinates, there are ALU and multiply-accumulators with floating point and integer ability, divide and inverse root computation hardware, and multiport and single-port register files. The microcode execution in SPIN is controlled by the SPIN microsequencer; the microcodes can be fetched from the internal uCode ROM or uCode RAM. The uCode ROM contains basic operations programs for geometric accelerating; the uCode RAM can be downloaded from external microcode programs for new functions. The DMA Controller and Command Queue can perform DMA transactions for fetching command, parameters, data, and microcodes from the external bus. The IOU is the system bus interface and is synchronous with the system bus. Because

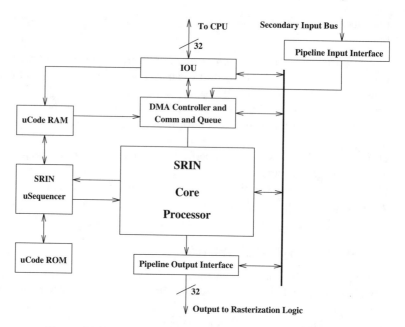

Figure 17.11   The block diagram of SPC1500 architecture [25].

the SPC1500 internal registers are mapped to the external system bus, the registers inside this chip can be programmed through this interface. After processing, the pipeline output interface buffers the result and handshakes with the external rasterization logic.

This geometric processor is a microcode-upgradable coprocessor design, and the instructions are optimized for transformation and lighting. With programmable microcode store, it has the capacity for microcode upgrade. However, users still find it difficult to generate desired microcodes.

17.3.1.2   VLIW Design for Geometric
Subsystem

The Fujitsu geometric processor TGPx4 is a floating-point DSP design based on VLIW structure for geometric subsystem. This chip utilizes the parallelism in primitive vertices to accelerate the processing. Its considerations include API compatibility, configurability by external VLIW instruction, and image quality by floating-point operations.

It uses the 64-bit horizontal format, with four-paralleled operation LIW (Long Instruction Word) structure, as shown in Fig. 17.12 [21]. The execution units are MUL, ALU, shifter, and ROM stored with approximate values of $\frac{1}{X}$, $X^{\frac{-1}{2}}$ and log X. The main purpose of the LIW structure is to minimize the overhead of multiply and add calculation in matrix transform. It consists of six main internal units: execution, control, instruction RAM, address, data RAM, and data I/O. There are two internal 32-bit data buses for con-

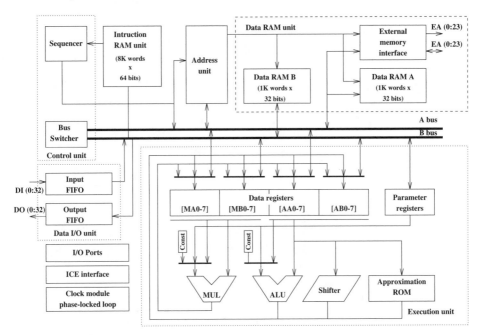

Figure 17.12   The block diagram of TGPx4 architecture [21].

currency data transfer. TGPx4 can perform coordinate transformations, clipping, lighting, and screen projection. In addition, it can generate delta calculations to support the DDA (Digital Differential Analyzer) initialization in the raster subsystem.

Since no additional memory interface is necessary in geometric subsystem data processing, the major portion of geometric processor architecture is specified by the floating-point computation unit with special register and data flow design to support metric transforms and lighting. Hence, the design of geometric processor always takes advantage of the technologies of CPU design.

17.3.2 Raster Subsystem

17.3.2.1 Pipelined Design for the Raster Subsystem

For raster subsystem design, the 3DLabs GLINT 300SX is an example for pipeline hardware design in a single chip [16]. This chip utilizes the parallelism in multiprimitives to accelerate 3-D graphics synthesis. It is based on the consideration of API compatibility for OpenGL and window-dependent APIs, system integration by additional multimedia function design, and image quality by anti-aliasing.

In the 3-D graphics core for this chip, the standard graphics pipeline is implemented by hardware, as shown in Fig. 17.13, and the lines between stages represent the internal buses.

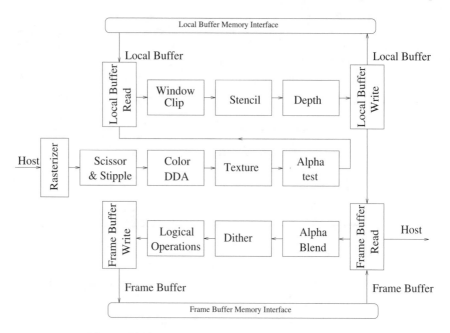

Figure 17.13   The graphics core of GLINT 300SX [16].

Therefore, this chip also provides important insights into the standard graphics pipeline technique for rasterization.

For the smoothly pipelined rasterization, the 3-D graphics core is a data flow design and is divided into pipeline units for API compatibility. It implements the pixel-level operations of the OpenGL specification. There are two memory interface units: local buffer interface and frame buffer interface. The local buffer is implemented by DRAM, while the frame buffer, by VRAM to avoid the large-display scan-out memory bandwidth.

Like the standard pipeline, the internal data size is enlarged after the rasterization in the Rasterizer unit, because the primitive-description commands are decomposed into many pixel-mapping operations to the frame buffer. The generated pixels with associated information for further processing are called fragments, which are tagged with x-y coordinates in the frame buffer. This fragment goes through all pipeline units, but any unit may be bypassed if it is not required by the application.

To speed up rasterization, the basic primitives in the Rasterizer unit are screen-aligned trapezoids, which are characterized by top and bottom edges parallel to the X-axis. If the length of top or bottom edge degenerates into a point, it is a screen-aligned triangle. Any polygon can be decomposed into screen-aligned trapezoids or triangles. There are two directions for rasterization: one is along the edge that is not parallel to the X-axis, and the other is along the scanline. Anti-aliasing is implemented by 4 x 4 or 8 x 8 subpixel point sampling.

To shade polygons, the GLINT 300SX can do the flat shading and Gouraud shading. The interpolation operations for Gouraud shading and depth value are implemented by DDA (Digital Differential Analyzer), but the setup division operations of DDA are done by the host CPU so that the setup cost may be a bottleneck when rendering large collections of small polygons. All the operations inside this processor are integer operations, and the slope values of DDA are represented by fixed point with fractional parts, for example, 2's complement the 16-bit integer and 16-bit fraction format.

The Texture unit implements the filter operations in order to execute different application modes in OpenGL [47], which helps to interpolate texel values and blend the pixel value after shading with texel value. However, texel coordinate interpolation and texel extraction are performed by the host CPU. Therefore, the GLINT 300SX does not fully support texture mapping by hardware. Memory accessing is necessary for texel extraction, and there exists a performance barrier here when applying texture mapping in this system.

The GLINT 300SX utilizes the depth buffer algorithm for hidden surface removal. All depth data per pixel are stored in local buffer with a graphics identification number, and stencil information, because all of those data are the additional information related to the pixels on display, while the color values are stored in the frame buffer. The local buffer values are fetched per fragment, and the value will be updated and written into local buffer again only if it passes the test. If the test is successfully passed, the fragment will write color values into frame buffer memory after alpha-blending and logic operations. The dithering is a processing step to degenerate the color bits for the small frame buffer or low-cost display system. The host output is an auxiliary output to feed back the status of graphics pipeline.

The GLINT 300SX overall system architecture is developed under the consideration of system integration, as shown in Fig. 17.14. The host interface is designed to be compatible with the industry standard PCI (Peripheral Component Interconnect) local bus interface, and the frame buffer interface incorporates the shared buffer design to share the frame buffer with other graphics devices, like the 2-D graphics accelerator. Additional DMA controller and local/frame buffer bypass units to support direct data transfer between the main memory and the two buffer memory blocks. The internal timing generator is included for synchronization.

GLINT 300SX is compatible with *de facto* standard APIs, such as OpenGL. Generally, designs of APIs tend to offer more flexibility and configurability for programmers, making complete API function a hung burden in hardware design, especially in pipelined design. Hence, specific software drivers are common solutions to provide compatibility in today's 3-D graphics processors. The driver receives the API function calls and then converts them into a group of control signals for 3-D graphics processor. The performances of software drivers also can affect the overall throughput.

17.3.2.2 Pipelined Design for the Raster Subsystem with Three Memory Interfaces

Different considerations arise in implementing the three kinds of buffers. In the low-end 3-D processors for entertainment, some designs utilize only one memory buffer to store all the data, but this method makes performance low. For an integrated system with

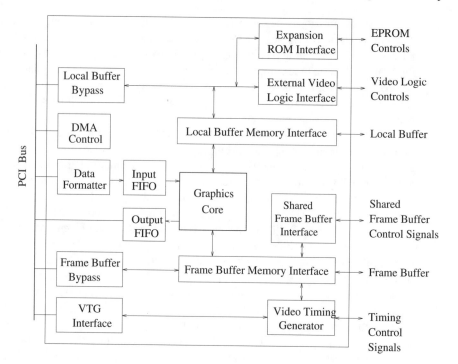

Figure 17.14 The GLINT 300SX architecture [16].

multimedia functions, the dual-port RAM is a good choice for the frame buffer, because of the second serial port for display to reduce the memory bandwidth burden of screen refreshing. For higher precision in hidden surface removal, more bits of depth are needed, but this requirement also increases the depth buffer memory bandwidth. Moreover, the desired memory bandwidth of the depth buffer is larger than the frame buffer in general. In the texture buffer, due to different coordinates, memory sharing with the frame buffer or local buffer will decrease performance due to the destruction of locality. Table 17.2 lists memory access in three memory buffers per pixel.

Thus, for best memory performance, three independent memory interfaces are desired in some designs for the raster subsystem, especially the 3-D processor with complex rendering features. A design for the 3-D graphics raster subsystem with three memory interfaces is shown in Fig. 17.15 [48].

This design focuses on the performance of memory bandwidth. The dual-port RAM is utilized in the frame buffer, whereas the high-performance RAM is utilized in the texture buffer for real-time high-quality, anti-aliased texture mapping. Since the texture buffer is not as large as the frame and depth buffers, use of high-performance RAM in a low-cost system is still affordable. The moderate priced RAM is utilized for the depth buffer, and the RAM with burst mode and read-modify-write cycle is better.

The u-v texture coordinates are linear mapped from x-y screen coordinates. Hence two pixels in the neighborhood in x-y screen coordinates possibly diverge in u-v texture

Table 17.2 The Memory Accessing in Three Memory
Buffers per Pixel in Rasterization

	Read	Write	Read-Modify-Write	R/W Unit	Coordinates
Frame Buffer	$(1)^a$	1	—	Color value	geometric X-Y
Depth Buffer	—	—	1	Depth value	geometric X-Y
Texture Buffer	1,2 $4,8^b$	—	—	Texel Color value	texture coordinates U-V

[a] We assume the dual-port RAM is utilized for frame buffer. But read is needed if the alpha-blending function or the logic operation is enabled, and the successive read and write operations can be replaced by the read-modify-write operation.

[b] It depends on the algorithm of anti-aliasing texture mapping.

coordinates. Even common 3-D rendering procedures often generate pixels with spatial locality in x-y coordinates, but the locality cannot benefit memory access for texture buffer. Besides, some special texture algorithms need to access texture maps with different resolutions, such as mip-map texture mapping. Hence, although sequential locality is generated

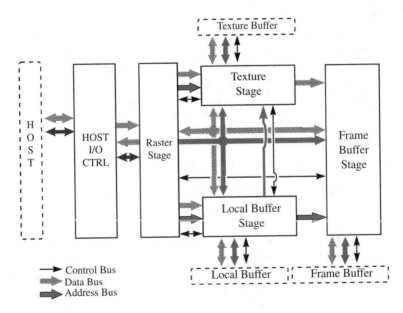

Figure 17.15   The NCTU raster engine core design.

by rasterization in screen coordinates, the locality is violated in texture coordinates after linear transformation. Therefore, even pixels appear in successive screen coordinates, the texture coordinates may not be in the neighborhood.

Under this consideration, the rasterization pipeline is divided into four stages, and each stage is equipped with its own state machine. The main duty of the state machine in each stage is to communicate with each other and handle the operations of that stage when running 3-D graphics pipeline functions. The controller and the data path in the rasterization stage are optimized for the heavy work of converting primitives into fragments. There are memory interfaces in the other three stages, so the three stages must handle functions on memories. Because each stage can access its own buffer independently, memory access can be optimized for various needs.

17.3.2.3 Logic-in-Memory Design for the Raster Subsystem

For logic-in-memory design, the Pixel Planes is a good example. The Pixel Planes 4 is a SIMD raster subsystem and provides a separate processor for every pixel in the display. Each SIMD pixel processor is a 1-bit ALU with a small amount of memory [27]. This design utilizes fine grain and massive parallelism to make use of concurrency in the subframe buffer to accelerate the 3-D graphics synthesis. High performance is the most important goal in this design. For the structure much different from the standard 3-D graphics pipeline, the specified algorithm is necessary. As described in [49], the global algorithm can generate values from the basic form: $F(x, y) = Ax + By + C$ for every pixel (x,y) in parallel. The structure of Pixel Planes 4 is shown in Fig. 17.16.

There is a limitation in this SIMD with massive parallelism structure. Development of Pixel Planes 5 was reported in [28]. The SIMD with massive parallel homogeneous PEs architecture leads to large amounts of hardware and to poor utilization. Pixel Planes 5 has solved this problem by screen-space subdivision. It utilizes the parallelism in subframes. Pixel Planes 5 makes use of this parallelism at two levels. First, the screen (frame) space is divided into blocks with 128 x 128 pixels, and then four sets of operators with 128 x 128 logic-in-memory pixel processors, called Renderers, are used. When rendering 3-D graphics, the four Renderers process different blocks on screen and move to the next unoperated block when any Renderer finishes its work in the current block. Hence, the Renderers are floating and not dedicated to a fixed area of the screen. The Renderers, frame buffer, and graphics processors for the geometric subsystem are linked on the ring network. The block diagrams of Pixel Planes 5 are shown in Fig. 17.17.

17.3.2.4 Logic-in-Memory Design for Raster Subsystem Memory

The 3D-RAM of Mitsubishi Corporation is an embedded logic design on the DRAM process supporting the memory access of the 3-D graphics raster system [39]. It implements depth comparison and alpha blending in memory. Therefore, if only depth comparison and alpha blending are the per-fragment operations that need local buffer and frame buffer memory access, the 3D-RAM can directly realize the back-end of the 3-D raster subsystem. The block diagram and connection of the 3D-RAM are shown in Fig. 17.18.

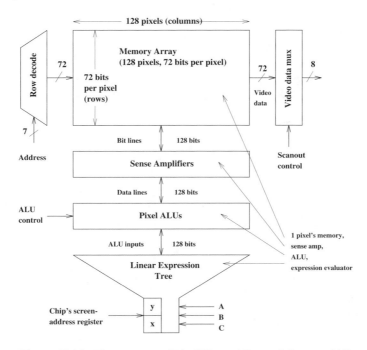

Figure 17.16   The structure of Pixel Planes 4 Raster Subsystem [49].

Besides the memory bandwidth bottleneck, the read-modify-write specific of depth buffer and alpha-blending algorithms always makes the pipeline design challenged. Without the read-modify-write support from memory, those operations will cause two miss times compared to write only. In 3D-RAM, all those operations are finished by the memory-embedding pixel ALU. Hence, the 3-D raster subsystem only needs to transfer depth and color values, and the output port of 3D-RAM can do the scan-out operations for RAMDAC to display. With 10Mb DRAM and SRAM cache inside, this design works well to associate with the raster subsystem.

17.3.3 The Overall Graphics System

17.3.3.1 Multiprocessing Design for the Overall Graphics System

The SGI 4D/240 GTX is a good example of overall architecture utilizing various concurrencies on different levels, as shown in Fig. 17.19 [30,50].

In this architecture, the overall system is divided into four subsystems. The definition of the raster subsystem that we used earlier is now divided into three parts: the scan conversion subsystem, the raster subsystem (for frame buffer operations), and the display subsystem.

In the geometric subsystem, use is made of the pipeline structure and five geometric engines for dedicated operations like transformation and lighting. It also makes use of parallelism in primitive vertices.

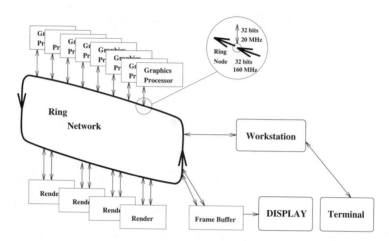

Figure 17.17   The structure of Pixel Planes 5 Raster Subsystem [28].

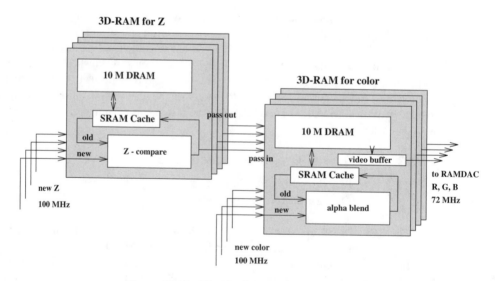

Figure 17.18   The block diagram of 3D-RAM [39].

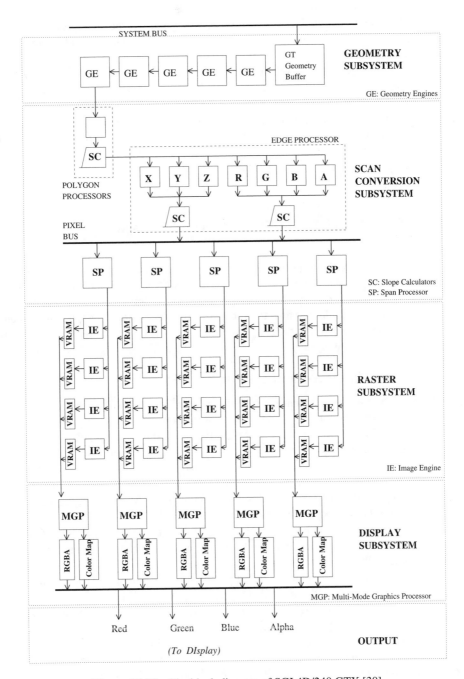

Figure 17.19   The block diagram of SGI 4D/240 GTX [30].

In the scan conversion subsystem, the parallelism in pixel attributes is utilized for edge processors to handle DDA slope divisions in parallel. The span processors are responsible for one-fifth of the columns of the display screen. The parallelism in subframes and multiprimitives is used for this purpose.

In the raster subsystem, each image engine with its own VRAM block handles one-fourth the area of a span processor, that is, one-twentieth of a screen by interleave. This structure is also based on the parallelism in subframes.

The multimode graphics processors in the display subsystem generate the RGB signals and transfer them into the multiplexer, and then display on screen after digital-to-analog conversion. The multiplexer here is similar to the five-way memory bank structure for frame buffer, which is shown in Fig. 17.10.

17.4 THE 3-D GRAPHICS APPLICATION PROGRAM INTERFACE

A graphics application program interface (API) is an interface for applications and programs running on a system with a graphics subsystem (software implementation or partial hardware support). It should provide some means to assess the desired functionality of the subsystem. Because the API defines how to execute the functions called by applications and programs, hardware design for multimedia system must now refer to the API structure for the highly integrated overall system.

17.4.1 Window-independent 3-D API

The window-independent 3-D interfaces are developed under the demand of 3-D graphics standards on various window systems and operation system platforms; examples are the PHIGS (Programmer's Hierarchical Interactive Graphics System), which is ANSI/ISO standard, and OpenGL (Open Graphics Library). In general, the windows-independent software interfaces define a common principle and structure guideline that can be realized on existed systems, but the real bottom-layer structures to implement the functions are window-dependent. For examples, the PEXlib and GLX are the implemetations of PHIGS and OpenGL on the x windows system.

To design a window-independent software interface, the architecture designers must consider not only performance and compatibility, but also transparency and portability. We can take OpenGL as an example.

OpenGL is a graphics standard proposed by the OpenGL ARB (Architecture Review Board), and its block diagram is shown in Fig. 17.20 [47]. The GL (Graphics Library) of Silicon Graphics Inc. is its pioneering product. This interface consists of a set of several hundred procedures and functions that allow a programmer to specify the objects and operations involved in producing high-quality graphical images, specifically color images of three-dimensional objects. To serve various applications on different platforms and even across the platforms, it is an API with specification of window system independence, client-server architecture, network transparency and device independence.

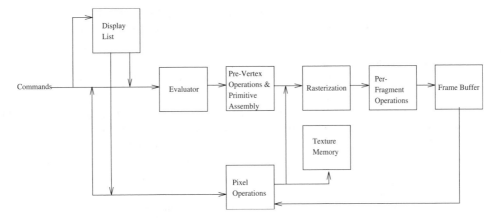

Figure 17.20 The high-level block diagram of OpenGL [47].

It is a rendering-only software interface, and it can be incorporated into any window system or even nonwindow system. In developing OpenGL, some important considerations are described by Segal and Akeley [51]:

(a) *Performance:* In an API, performance is first subject to be challenged because it is the base for application development, and there are different demands of response time, especially in real-time and interactive applications. Because there is always a tradeoff between image quality and rendering speed, the API design should provide the switch to turn on or off the complex rendering functions for interactive applications.

(b) *Orthogonality:* Many functions may be enabled and disabled in API depending on the applications, but each function should be independent when turned on or off. Switching any single feature should not affect an undefined state. The API with orthogonality can reduce the error and makes the system stable.

(c) *Completeness:* In general, the API should access all significant functionality of the graphics subsystem, but there is no uniform graphics subsystem in various computer systems. To design a window-independent API, the designers should consider the feature completeness for different applications. On the other hand, implementation of API in the specific system should consider the API's completeness. Since the specialized graphics hardware is part of the graphics subsystem, the hardware design always refers to API specification and realizes a major subset of API functions.

(d) *Interoperability:* Because the network environment trend and some 3-D graphics rendering can be accelerated by a cluster of computers via network, the client-server architecture is an elegant design for API. The API with client-server ability rules the notations to communication and how the client issues commands and the server executes them. Because of the network delay, tight coupling between client and server is impractical. Hence, there should be a feedback feature.

(e) *Extensibility:* With the advances in computer systems, extensibility is always one important factor in deciding the lifetime of a standard. Orthogonality system design is always more extensible.

(f) *Acceptance:* The API is not useful unless the programmers use it in variety applications. Hence, the API design should refer to the state-of-the-art display structure.

After examining design considerations for an API, we find that some goals of API design and hardware implementation meet halfway. Although the hardware cannot realize all parts of API, the orthogonality makes sure that the hardware accelerates some functions without affecting others. The interface between the host CPU and specific hardware is easy because of loose coupling under the interoperability strategy. The specific 3-D hardware can accelerate the API performance, but lack of completeness and extensibility must be patched by software. Therefore, the lower level of window-dependent API is needed to handle the complete set of function calls and hardware control.

In the network environment, there is another trend for image transfer, including synthesized 3-D graphics. For example, the Virtual Reality Modeling Language (VRML) describes the 3-D primitive for the virtual reality environment as an extentsion of World Wide Web (WWW) on the Internet, and the browser (WWW client) interprets the VRML description and generates 3-D VR environment image locally [52]. In addition, some research has been done on the 3-D graphics synthesizing both client and server, but the server does more rasterization and appends the detail of synthesized image via network to client display to improve the image quality without network burden [53]. Hence, those client-server interfaces on network for 3-D graphics can be developed as higher level platform which is independent of existing API.

17.4.2 Window-dependent 3-D API

The 3-D graphics applications emerge rapidly after the de facto standard appears in popular operating systems and window platforms. Because the application developers can add the 3-D functions based on standard API, demand for 3-D performance and image quality will increase. Using the hardware processor to accelerate the 3-D graphics will be a trend in the future.

On the workstations, the X window is the most popular window platform. The OpenGL and PHIG extension to the X window are GLX and PEXlib, and both of them are in the 3-D graphics library to support programming. With powerful rasterization and modeling ability, the library is suitable for CAD and high-level applications.

On the other hand, the demand for 3-D graphics in personal computers is increasing. In MS Windows, 3-D ability has been supported by some patchwork from some game APIs such as BRender, RenderMorphics, and RenderWare. Since Windows NT, Microsoft has announced OpenGL support and included the 3-D API into Windows 95 graphics architecture. The Windows 95 graphics architecture is shown in Fig. 17.21 [54].

The Reality Lab and OpenGL are both 3-D graphics API directly supported by Windows 95. Although two APIs are designed with different considerations, both can be implemented by lower API named Direct3D, which is polygon- and vertex-based API and can give developers easy access to the features of the 3-D hardware.

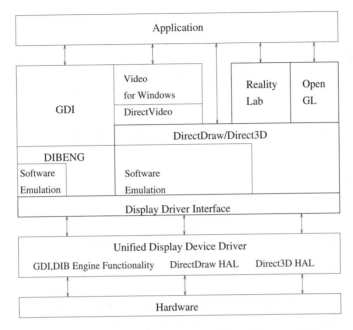

Figure 17.21   The Windows 95 graphics architecture [54].

Apple Computer has introduced the QuickDraw 3D as part of its foundation for 3-D graphics [55], and has also provided a standard cross-platform 3-D API, a set of 3-D interface standards, a consistent file format, and a developer's toolkit. The cross-platform API is machine-independent, whereas the standard developer API includes a complete set of 3-D geometry, shading, and rendering architecture, a device and acceleration manager, and a common approach to the 3-D point device.

17.5 SUMMARY

In this chapter we provide an overview of the hardware design for 3-D computer graphics. Given the trend toward multimedia system integration, we discuss the goals for state-of-the-art 3-D graphics processor design. Performance, image quality, low cost, and system integration are important design issues for 3-D hardware. We show the basic methods for rasterization and describe how fixed-point, floating-point computation and memory bandwidth affect the performance. Then we explain and classify some elegant design methods and various considerations, and also detail the relationship between hardware designs and software APIs.

In the future, the 3-D graphics hardware design will not be a closed system. It must share system resources with other subsystems in a multimedia architecture. Due to the trend of networked computation and Internet, the future system will be integrated via networks. Therefore, the protocol between systems will be developed referring to the API standard.

Acknowledgments

We thank Tian-Sheuan Chang and Jinn-Wang Yeh for their discussion of memory and parallelism; Chein-Liang Chen, K. C. Chen in Winbond, Raj Singh, and Joyce Evans in 3DLabs for providing materials; and Chih-Ching Chen and Ching-Chao Yang for their help in information gathering, and thank Sheng-Jyh Wang for many useful suggestions.

References

[1] Jon Peddie, "Multimedia & Graphics Controllers," New York: McGraw-Hill, 1994.

[2] Carl Machover, "Four Decades of Computer Graphics," *IEEE CG&A*, Nov. 1994.

[3] Steven Molnar and Henry Fuchs, "Advance Raster Graphics Architecture," *Computer Graphics: Principles and Practice,* 2nd ed, Reading, MA: Addison-Wesley, 1990.

[4] C. M. Goral, K. E. Torrance, and D. P. Greenberg, "Modeling the Interaction of Light Between Diffuse Surface," *Computer Graphics,* Vol. 18, pp. 213–222, 1984.

[5] T. Whitted, "An Improved Illumination Model for Shaded Display," *Communications of ACM,* Vol. 23, No. 6, pp. 343–349, 1980.

[6] J. R. Wallace, M. F., Cohen, and D. P. Greenberg, "A Two-pass Solution to the Rendering Equation: A Synthesis of Ray Tracing and Radiosity Method," *Computer Graphics,* Vol. 21, No. 4, pp. 311–320, 1987.

[7] J. Hesser et al., "Three Architectures for Volume Rendering," *EUROGRAPHICS '95,* Vol. 14, No. 3, pp. C–111 to C–122, 1995.

[8] W. J. Bouknight, "A Procedure for Generation of Three-dimensional Half-toned Computer Graphics Presentations," *Comm. of ACM,* Vol. 13, pp. 527–536, 1970.

[9] H. Gouraud, "Continuous Shading of Curved Surfaces," *IEEE Trans. on Computers,* Vol. C–20, No. 6, pp. 623–629, June 1971.

[10] B-T. Phong, "Illumination for Computer Generated Pictures," *Communication of the ACM,* Vol. 18, No. 6, pp. 311–317, June 1975.

[11] A. Watt, *Fundamentals of Three-Dimensional Computer Graphics,* 2nd ed., Reading, MA: Addison-Wesley, 1993.

[12] Catmull, E., *A Subdivision Algorithm for Computer Display of Curved Surface,* Ph.D. Thesis, Report UTEC-CSc-74-133, Computer Science Department, University of Utah, Salt Lake City, UT, Dec. 1974.

[13] J. Foley, A. van Dam, S. Feiner, and J. Hughes, *Computer Graphics: Principles and Practice,* 2nd ed., Reading, MA: Addison-Wesley, 1990.

[14] J. F. Blinn and M. E. Newell, "Texture and Reflection in Computer Generated Images," *Communication of ACM,* Vol. 19, No. 10, pp. 542–547, Oct. 1976.

[15] D. R. Williams, "Pyramidal Parametrics," *Computer Graphics*, Vol. 17, No. 3, 1983.

[16] 3D Labs Inc., *GLINT 300SX*^{TM} *Hardware Reference Manual Version 1.6,* Oct. 1994.

[17] J. Grimes, L. Kohn, and R. Bharadhwaj, "The Intel i860 64-bit Processor: A General-purpose CPU with 3D Graphics Capabilities," *IEEE CG&A,* Vol. 9, No. 4, pp. 85–94, July 1989.

[18] B. Apgar, B. Bersack, and A. Mammem, "A Display System for the *Stellar*^{TM} Graphics Supercomputer Model GS1000TM," *Computer Graphics,* pp. 255–262, Vol. 22, No. 4, Aug. 1988.

[19] Franklin Crow, "3D Image Synthesis on the Connection Machine," *Parallel Processing for Computer Vision and Display,* Reading, MA: Addison-Wesley, 1989.

[20] K. Hwang, *Advanced Computer Architecture—Parallelism, Scalability, Programmability,* New York: McGraw-Hill, 1993.

[21] M. Awaga, T. Ohtsuka, H. Yoshizawa, and S. Sasaki, "3D Graphics Processor Chip Set," *IEEE Micro,* Vol. 15, No. 6, pp. 37–45, Dec. 1995.

[22] N. Gharacholoo et al, "Subnanosecond Pixel Rendering with Million Transistor Chips," *Computer Graphics,* pp. 41–49, Vol. 22, No. 4, Aug. 1988.

[23] T. Nishizawa et al., "A Hidden Surface and Shading Processor (HSSP) with a Systolic Architecture," *IEEE J. Solid-State Circuits,* Vol. 23, No. 5, pp. 1236–1240, Oct. 1988.

[24] M. Deering, M. Winner, B. Schediwy, C. Duff, and N. Hunt, "The Triangle Processor and Normal Vector Shader: A VLSI System for High Performance Graphics," *Computer Graphics,* Vol. 22, pp. 21–30, Aug. 1988.

[25] S-MOS Systems, Inc., *Data Sheet: Graphics Grometry Processor—SPC1500POB,* San Jose, CA, Dec. 1994.

[26] M. F. Deering and S. R. Nelson, "Leo: A System for Cost Effective 3D Shaded Graphics," *Computer Graphics,* pp. 101–108, 1993.

[27] J. Eyles et al., "Pixel-Planes 4: A Summary," *Advances in Computer Graphics Hardware II,* Eurographics Seminars, pp. 183–208, 1988.

[28] H. Fuchs et al., "Pixel-planes 5: A Heterogeneous Multiprocessor Graphics System Using Processor-enhanced Memories," *Computer Graphics,* Vol. 23, pp. 79–88, July 1989.

[29] G. J. Dunnett, M. White, P. F. Lister, and R. L. Crimsdale, "The Image Chip for High Performance 3d Rendering," *IEEE Computer Graphics and Applications,* pp. 41–52, Nov. 1992.

[30] K. Akeley and T. Jermoluk, "High-Performance Polygon Rendering," *Computer Graphics,* Vol. 22, pp. 239–246, Aug. 1988.

[31] N. Gharacholoo, S. Gupta, R. Sproull, and I. Sutherland, "A Characterization of Ten Rasterization Techniques," *Computer Graphics,* pp. 355–368, Vol. 23, No. 3, July 1989.

[32] Brooktree Corp., *Product Databook 1988,* Brooktree Corp., San Diego, CA, 1987.

[33] F. Jones, "A New Era of Fast Dynamic RAMs," *IEEE Spectrum,* pp. 43–49, Oct. 1992.

[34] T. Chappell et al., "A 2ns Cycle, 4ns Access 512kb CMOS ECL SRAM," *IEEE Int'l Solid-State Circuit Conf.,* pp. 50–51, 1991.

[35] R. Pinkham, M. Novak, and K. Guttag, "Video RAM Excels at Fast Graphics," *Electronics Design,* Vol. 37, No. 17, pp. 161–182, Aug. 18, 1983.

[36] Dosaka, K. et al, "A 100-MHz, 4-Mb Cache DRAM with Fast Copyback Scheme," *IEEE J. Solid-State Circuits,* pp. 1534–1539, Nov. 1992.

[37] M. Kumanoya, T. Ogawa, and K. Inoue, "Advances in DRAM Interfaces," *IEEE Micro,* Vol. 15, No. 6, pp. 30–36, Dec. 1995.

[38] S. Demetrescu, "High Speed Image Rasterization Using Scan Line Access Memories," *Proc. of Chapel Hill Conf. on VLSI,* 1985, pp. 221–243, May 1985.

[39] K. Inoue et al., "A 10Mb 3D Frame Buffer Memory with Z-Compare and Alpha-Blend Units," *IEEE Int'l Solid-State Circuit Conf.,* 1995.

[40] M. Deering, S. Schlapp, and M. Lavelle, "FBRAM: A New Form of Memory Optimized for 3D Graphics," *Computer Graphics,* July 1994.

[41] T. Porter and T. Duff, "Compositing Digital Images," *Computer Graphics,* Vol. 18, pp. 253–259, 1984.

[42] H. Niimi et al., "A Parallel Processor System for 3 Dimensional Color Graphics," *Proc. of SIGGRAPH '84,* pp. 67–76, 1984.

[43] A. R. Borges and A. M. B. Ferrari de Almeida, "A Multimicroprocessor Architecture for Image Reconstruction in CT," *Parallel Processing for Computer Vision and Display,* Reading, MA: Addison-Wesley, 1989.

[44] G. Kedem and J. L. Ellis, "The Ray-Casting Machine," *Parallel Processing for Computer Vision and Display,* Reading, MA: Addison-Wesley, 1989.

[45] M. F. Cohen, "Radiosity," *State of the Art in Computer Graphics: Visualization and Modeling,* pp. 59–90, Berlin: Springer-Verlag, 1991.

[46] Ikedo, T., "A Scalable High-performance Graphics Processor: GVIP," *The Visual Computer,* pp. 121–133, Berlin: Springer-Verlag, 1995.

[47] OpenGL Architecture Review Board, *OpenGL Reference Manual, The Official Reference Document for OpenGL, Release 1,* Reading, MA: Addison Wesley, 1992.

[48] Bor-Sung Liang, *The Hardware Design for Rasterization with Antialiasing in 3-D Graphics Processor,* Master's Thesis, Directed by Chein-Wei Jen, National Chiao Tung University, Taiwan, R.O.C., 1996.

[49] H. Fuchs et al., "Fast Spheres, Shadows, Textures, Transparencies, and Image Enhancements in Pixel-Planes," *SIGGRAPH 85,* pp. 111–120, 1985.

[50] K. Akeley et al., "Superworkstation the Silicon Graphics 4D/240GTX Super-workstation," *IEEE CG&A,* pp. 71–83, July 1989.

[51] Mark Segal and Kurt Akeley, *The Design of OpenGL Graphics Interface,* Silicon Graphics Computer Systems, Mountain View, CA, 1994.

[52] D. Raggett, *Extending WWW to Support Platform Independent Virtual Reality,* The VRML Forum, http://vrml.wired.com/concepts/raggett.html, 1995.

[53] M. Levoy, "Polygon-Assisted JPEG and MPEG Compression of Synthetic Image," *Computer Graphics Annual Conference Series,* pp. 21–28, 1995.

[54] Microsoft Corp., *The Windows 95 Graphics Architecture,* http://www.microsoft.com/windows/support/graphics.htm, Sep. 1995.

[55] Apple Computer, Inc., *QuickDraw 3D: Apple's Foundation for 3D Graphics,* http://product.info.apple.com/qd3d/AboutQuickDraw3D.HTML, Oct. 1995.

Chapter 18

VIRTUAL WORLDS AS FUZZY DYNAMICAL SYSTEMS

Julie A. Dickerson and Bart Kosko

Abstract

Fuzzy cognitive maps (FCMs) can structure virtual worlds that change with time. A FCM links causal events, actors, values, goals, and trends in a fuzzy feedback dynamical system. A fuzzy rule defines a fuzzy patch in the input-output state-space of a system. It links commonsense knowledge with state-space geometry. A FCM connects the fuzzy rules or causal flow paths that relate events. It can guide actors in a virtual world as the actors move through a web of cause and effect and react to events and to other actors. Experts draw FCM causal pictures of the virtual world. Complex FCMs can give virtual worlds with ''new'' or chaotic equilibrium behavior. Simple FCMs give virtual worlds with periodic behavior. They map input states to limit-cycle equilibria. A FCM limit cycle repeats a sequence of events or a chain of actions and responses. Limit cycles can control the steady-state rhythms and patterns in a virtual world. In nested FCMs each causal concept can control its own FCM or fuzzy function approximator. Appendix A shows how an additive fuzzy system can uniformly approximate any continuous (or bounded measurable) function on a compact domain to any degree of accuracy. This gives levels of fuzzy systems that can choose goals and causal webs as well as move objects and guide actors in the webs. FCM matrices sum to give a combined FCM virtual world for any number of knowledge sources. Adaptive FCMs change their fuzzy causal web as causal patterns change and as actors act and experts state their causal knowledge. Neural learning laws change the causal rules and the limit cycles. Actors learn new patterns and reinforce old ones. In complex FCMs the user can choose the dynamical structure of the virtual world from a spectrum that ranges from mildly to wildly nonlinear. We use an adaptive FCM to model an undersea virtual world of dolphins, fish, and sharks.

18.1 FUZZY VIRTUAL WORLDS

What is a virtual world? It is what changes in a ''virtual reality'' [1] or ''cyberspace'' [2]. A virtual world links humans and computers in a causal medium that can trick the mind or senses.

At the broadest level, a virtual world is a dynamical system. It changes with time as the user or an actor moves through it. In the simplest case, only the user moves in the virtual world. In general, both the user and the virtual world change and they change each other.

Change in a virtual world is causal. Actors cause events to happen as they move in a virtual world. They add new patterns of cause and effect and respond to old ones. In turn, the virtual world acts on the actors or on their physical or social environments. The virtual world changes their behavior and can change its own web of cause of effect. This feedback causality between actors and their virtual world makes up a complex dynamical system that can model events, actors, actions, and data as they unfold in time.

567

Virtual worlds are fuzzy as well as fedback. Events occur and concepts hold only to some degree. Events cause one another to some degree. In this sense virtual worlds are fuzzy causal worlds. They are fuzzy dynamical systems. A fuzzy rule defines a fuzzy patch in the input-output state-space of a system and links commonsense knowledge with state-space geometry. An additive fuzzy system approximates a function by covering its graph with fuzzy patches in the input-output state space and averaging patches that overlap.

How do we model the fuzzy feedback causality? One way is to write down the differential equations that show how the virtual "flux" or "fluid" changes in time. This gives an exact model. The Navier-Stokes equations [3] used in weather models give a fluid model of how actors move in a type of virtual world. They can show how clouds or tornadoes form and dissolve in a changing atmosphere or how an airplane flies through pockets of turbulence. The inverse kinematic equations of robotics [4] show how an actor moves through or grasps in a virtual joint space. The coupled differential equations of blood glucose and insulin [5] cast the patient as a diabetic actor awash in a virtual world of sugar and hormones. Such math models are hard to find, hard to solve, and hard to run in real time. They paint too fine a picture of the virtual world.

Fuzzy cognitive maps (FCMs) can model the virtual world in large fuzzy chunks. They model the causal web as a fuzzy directed graph [6,7]. The nodes and edges show how causal concepts affect one another to some degree in the fuzzy dynamical system. The "size" of the nodes gives the chunk size. In a virtual world the concept nodes can stand for events, actions, values, moods, goals, or trends. The causal edges state fuzzy rules or causal flows between concepts. In a predator-prey world survival threat increases prey runaway. The fuzzy rule states how much one node grows or falls as some other node grows or falls.

Experts draw the FCMs as causal pictures. They do not state equations. They state concept nodes and link them to other nodes. The FCM system turns each picture into a matrix of fuzzy rule weights. The system weights and adds the FCM matrices to combine any number of causal pictures. More FCMs tend to sum to a better picture of the causal web with rich tangles of feedback and fuzzy edges even if each expert gives binary (present or absent) edges. This makes it easy to add or delete actors or to change the background of a virtual world or to combine virtual worlds that are disjoint or overlap. We can also let a FCM node control its own FCM to give a nested FCM in a hierarchy of virtual worlds. The node FCM can model the complex nonlinearities between the node's input and output. It can drive the motions, sounds, actions, or goals of a virtual actor.

The FCM itself acts as a nonlinear dynamical system. Like a neural net it maps inputs to output equilibrium states. Each input digs a path through the virtual state space. In simple FCMs, the path ends in a fixed point or limit cycle. In more complex FCMs the path may end in an aperiodic or "chaotic" attractor. These fixed points and attractors represent *meta-rules* of the form "If input, then attractor or fixed point." The rules are stored in the cube itself.

18.2 ADDITIVE FUZZY SYSTEMS

A fuzzy system approximates a function by covering its graph with fuzzy patches and averaging patches that overlap. The approximation improves as the fuzzy patches grow in number and shrink in size. Figure 18.1 shows how fuzzy patches in the input-output

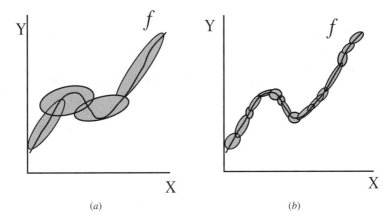

Figure 18.1 (*a*) Four large fuzzy patches cover part of the graph of the unknown function $f : X \rightarrow Y$. Fewer patches can decrease computation but decrease approximation accuracy. (*b*) More smaller fuzzy patches better cover f but at greater computational cost. Each fuzzy rule defines a patch in the product space $X \times Y$. A large but finite number of fuzzy rules or precise rules can cover the graph with arbitrary accuracy. Optimal rules cover extreme.

product space $X \times Y$ cover the real function $f : X \rightarrow Y$. In Fig. 18.1*a*, a few large patches approximate f. In Fig. 18.1*b*, several smaller patches better approximate f. The approximation improves as we add more small patches, but storage and complexity costs increase. This section gives the algebraic details of the fuzzy approximation.

An additive fuzzy system adds the then-parts of fired if-then rules. Other fuzzy systems combine the then-part sets with pairwise maxima. A fuzzy system has rules of the form, "If input conditions hold, then output conditions hold," or "If X is **A**, then Y is **B**" for fuzzy sets **A** and **B**. Each fuzzy rule defines a fuzzy patch or a Cartesian product $\mathbf{A} \times \mathbf{B}$ as

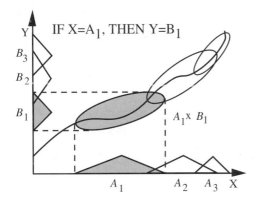

Figure 18.2 The fuzzy rule patch "If X is fuzzy set A_1, then Y is fuzzy set B_1" is the fuzzy Cartesian product $A_1 \times B_1$ in the input-output product space $X \times Y$.

shown in Fig. 18.2. The fuzzy system covers the graph of a function with fuzzy patches and averages patches that overlap. Uncertain fuzzy sets give a large patch or fuzzy rule. Small or more certain fuzzy sets give small patches.

Additive fuzzy systems fire all rules in parallel and average the scaled output sets B'_j to get the output fuzzy set $\mathbf{B}$ as in Fig. 18.3. Correlation product inference scales each output set B_j by the degree $m_{A_j}(x)$ (or $a_j(x)$) that the rule "IF A_j, THEN B_j" fires. Most rules fire to degree 0. Defuzzification of $\mathbf{B}$ gives a number or a control signal output. Centroidal defuzzification with correlation product inference [8] gives the output value y_k at time k:

$$y_k = F(x_k) = \frac{\int y m_{\mathbf{B}}(y)dy}{\int m_{\mathbf{B}}(y)dy}$$

$$= \frac{\sum_{j=1}^{m} Volume\,(B'_j)Centroid(B'_j)}{\sum_{j=1}^{m} Volume(B'_j)} \tag{1}$$

$$= \frac{\sum_{j=1}^{m} c_{y_j} V_j m_{A_j}(x_k)}{\sum_{j=1}^{m} V_j m_{A_j}(x_k)}$$

V_j is the volume of the jth output set B_j. We can always normalize the finite volumes V_j to unity to keep some rules from dominating others. c_{y_j} is the centroid of the jth output set. Fit value $m_{A_j}(x_k)$ scales the output set B_j. m is the number of output fuzzy sets. In practice $\mathbf{A}$ is connected; it need not be. But then we could view the rule "If X is $\mathbf{A}$, then Y is $\mathbf{A}$ " as two or more rules of the form "If X is $\mathbf{A}$, then Y is $\mathbf{B}_1$ " and "If X is $\mathbf{A}$, then Y is $\mathbf{B}_2$ " where $\mathbf{B}_1$ and $\mathbf{B}_2$ are two of the disjoint components of $\mathbf{A}$. So assume $\mathbf{B}$ is connected. Then the rule patch $\mathbf{A} \times \mathbf{B}$ is connected and a patch proper.

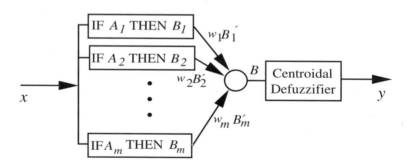

Figure 18.3 Additive fuzzy system architecture. The input x_k acts as a delta pulse (or unit bit vector) and fires each rule to some degree. The system adds the scaled output fuzzy sets. The centroid of this combined set gives the output value y_k. The system computes the conditional expectation value $E[Y|X = x_k]$.

The additive fuzzy system computes the conditional expectation $E[Y|X = x]$ if we *view* fuzzy sets as random sets [9,10]—if the curve $m_A : [0, 1] \rightarrow X$ is a locus of two-point conditional densities. Then $m_A(x)$ is the probability of **A** given that X takes on x or $m_A(x) = p(x \in A \mid X = x)$ and $m_A(x) = p(x \notin A \mid X = x)$. The conditional mean $E[Y|X]$ is the mean-squared optimal estimate of Y given the information known about X—given the information in the random or fuzzy subsets **A** of X.

In Appendix A we show that a fuzzy system can approximate any continuous real function defined on a compact (closed and bounded in R^n domain) and that even a bivalent expert system can uniformly approximate a bounded measurable function. The fuzzy systems have a feedforward architecture that resembles the feedforward multilayer neural systems used to approximate functions [11]. The uniform approximation of continuous functions allows us to replace each continuous fuzzy set with a finite discretization or a point in a unit hypercube [8] of high dimension.

Combining the scaled or ''fired'' consequent fuzzy sets $B'_1, \ldots, B'_m$ in Fig. 18.3 with pairwise maximum gives the envelope of the fuzzy sets and tends toward the uniform distribution. Max combination ignores overlap in the fuzzy sets B_j. Sum combination adds overlap to the peakedness of **B**. When the input changes slightly the additive output **B** changes slightly. The max-combined output may ignore small input changes since for large sets of rules most change occurs in the overlap regions of the fuzzy sets B'_j. Here overlap problem arises since the centroid tends to stay the same for small changes in input. But the centroid smoothly tracks changes in the fuzzy-set sum (1).

We now formally derive the *standard* additive model (SAM) in (1) that we shall use in this chapter and show how an additive fuzzy system acts as a conditional mean. A general additive fuzzy system is a map $F : R^n \rightarrow R^p$. Both in practice and in uniform approximation proofs, we restrict the domain to a compact subset $U \subset R^n$ but we need not. Watkins [12] has proved that an additive fuzzy system with just two rules can exactly *represent* any bounded function $f : R \rightarrow R$ even if f is not continuous. In this case the domain is the entire real line.

The additive fuzzy system stores m fuzzy patches $A_j \times B_j$ or rules of the form ''*If X is A_j, then Y is B_j.*'' Here $A_j \subset R^n$ and $B_j \subset R^p$ multivalued or ''fuzzy'' sets with set functions $a_j : R^n \rightarrow [0, 1]$ and $b_j : R^p \rightarrow [0, 1]$. We also use the membership notation $m_{A_j}(x)$ and $m_{B_j}(y)$ in this chapter for the set functions. For the following derivation we use the *fit* (fuzzy unit) notation a_j and b_j for simplicity.

In practice we define the then-part set A_j by its n coordinate-projection sets $A_j^1, \ldots, A_j^n$ and thus $A_j = A_j^1 \times A_j^2 \times \ldots \times A_j^n$. How we define this fuzzy Cartesian product dictates the conjunctive (or *t*-norm) form of how we factor the joint set function a_j into its coordinate set functions $a_j^1, \ldots, a_j^n$. Minimum combination is the most popular form

$$a_j(x) = a_j^1(x_1) \wedge a_j^1(x_2) \wedge a_j^2(x_2) \wedge \ldots \wedge a_j^n(x_n) \tag{2}$$

for input vector $x = (x_1, \ldots, x_n)$. Product combination

$$a_j(x) = \prod_{i=1}^{n} a_j^i(x_i) \tag{3}$$

can simplify the analysis and computation of additive systems with Gaussian [13] or radial-basis [14] set functions of the form

$$a_j^i(x_i) = s_i^j \, \exp\left[-\frac{1}{2}\left(\frac{x_i - \bar{x}_i^j}{\sigma_i^j}\right)^2 \right] \tag{4}$$

for scaling constant $0 < s_i^j \le 1$. The choice of combination operator does not affect the structure of the standard model (1).

The first step to show the conditional-mean property is to view each scalar fuzzy set a_j^i as a random set [10]. Then $a_j^i(x_i)$ is not the degree to which $x_i \in A_j^i$ but the conditional probability $p(x_i \in A_j^i \mid X_i = x_i)$. In the same way, the complement fit value $1 - a_j^i(x_i)$ is just the dual conditional probability: $p(x_i \notin A_j^i \mid X_i = x_i)$. So A_j^i is not a locus of membership degrees but a locus of two-point conditional densities.

The next step is the additive step. The m fit values $a_j^i(x_i)$ "fire" the then-part sets B_j to give the "inferred" sets B_j'. Again the result combines $a_j^i(x_i)$ and B_j in some conjunctive (*t*-norm) way, and again it depends on how we define the Cartesian patch $A_j \times B_j$. Here min is less popular than product. The min "clip" discards all information in B_j above the fit height $a_j^i(x_i)$ and can thus change the centroid of B_j if B_j is not symmetric. Product combination or *correlation product decoding* [8] keeps all relative information in B_j and does not change its centroid:

$$B_j' = a_j^i(x)B_j \tag{5}$$

We use (5) as a default for a SAM. We can also view the inferred sets B_j' as random sets. An additive model [8] then sums these inferred sets to produce the final output set B:

$$B = \sum_{j=1}^m B_j' \tag{6}$$

Each rule can have a weight w_j that scales B_j' in (6). Learning can change these weights, or we can use them to model frequency or "usuality" rule weights. Here we take them as unity: $w_j = 1$.

The only constraint on B or b is that it have a finite integral or *volume*:

$$0 < V = \int b(y)\, dy < \infty \tag{7}$$

This means that each input x fires at least one rule to nonzero degree. Then B/V is a probability density function. Indeed it is a conditional probability since it depends on the fuzzy variable X taking on the input value x (the ratio of a joint to a marginal):

$$\frac{B}{V} = p(Y|X = x) \tag{8}$$

Note this does not require that we view the if-part sets as probability density functions. They are not. Each is a locus of continuum-many two-point conditional densities. Formally the system accepts input x_0 as a delta pulse to produce the m fit values:

$$a_j(x_0) = \int \delta(x - x_0) \, a_j(x) \, dx \tag{9}$$

Then the additive system output $F(x)$ equals the centroid of B:

$$F(x) = \frac{\int yb(x, y)dy}{\int b(x, y)dy} \tag{10}$$

$$= \int yp(Y|X = x)dy \tag{11}$$

$$= E[Y|X = x] \tag{12}$$

What holds for one realization of a random vector holds for them all. Hence, $F = E[Y \mid X]$ as claimed. The SAM model (1) then computes the global conditional mean value $E[Y \mid X = x]$ as a convex sum of local conditional means in (26).

We now assume that the additive fuzzy system maps real vectors into scalars $F : R^n \to R$. Then we put the additive assumption (6) in the centroidal output (10) to get the standard form of an additive model [8] we use in this chapter:

$$F(x) = \frac{\int_{-\infty}^{\infty} y \sum\limits_{j=1}^{m} b'_j(y)dy}{\int_{-\infty}^{\infty} \sum\limits_{j=1}^{m} b'_j(y)dy} \tag{13}$$

$$= \frac{\sum\limits_{j=1}^{m} \int_{-\infty}^{\infty} y a_j(x) b_j(y)dy}{\sum\limits_{j=1}^{m} \int_{-\infty}^{\infty} a_j(x) b_j(y)dy} \tag{14}$$

$$= \frac{\sum\limits_{j=1}^{m} a_j(x) V_j \frac{\int_{-\infty}^{\infty} y b_j(y)dy}{V_j}}{\sum\limits_{j=1}^{m} a_j(x) V_j} \tag{15}$$

$$= \frac{\sum\limits_{j=1}^{m} a_j(x) V_j c_j}{\sum\limits_{j=1}^{m} a_j(x) V_j} \tag{16}$$

for then-part set volumes

$$V_j = \int_{-\infty}^{\infty} b_j(y)\,dy \tag{17}$$

and then-part set centroids

$$c_j = \frac{\int_{-\infty}^{\infty} y b_j(y)\,dy}{\int_{-\infty}^{\infty} b_j(y)\,dy}. \tag{18}$$

The model in (16) is the standard additive model or SAM and the same as (1). It holds for $F : R^n \rightarrow R^p$ as well.

The standard model (16) reduces to the Gaussian additive model of Wang and Mendel [13]:

$$F(x) = \frac{\sum\limits_{j=1}^{m} \bar{z}^j (\prod\limits_{i=1}^{n} \mu_{A_i^j}(x_i))}{\sum\limits_{j=1}^{m} (\prod\limits_{i=1}^{n} \mu_{A_i^j}(x_i))} \tag{19}$$

for the Gaussian if-part set in (4) and Gaussian then-part sets with these identifications:

$$y = z \tag{20}$$

$$a_j(x) = \prod_{i=1}^{n} a_j^i(x_i) \tag{21}$$

$$= \prod_{i=1}^{n} \mu_{A_i^j}(x_i) \tag{22}$$

$$V_j = 1 \tag{23}$$

$$c_j = \bar{z}^j \tag{24}$$

The choice of product combination (2) gives (21) and (22). The unity volume follows in (23) since Wang and Mendel integrate their m then-part Gaussian sets over all of R (and thus use the scaling constant in (4) to account for the input truncation to a compact set). (24) follows because the mode of a Gaussian set equals its centroid and Wang and Mendel use the mode definition, "the point in R at which $\mu_{B_j}(z)$ achieves its maximum value." They used the Stone-Weierstrass Theorem to prove that additive Gaussian systems with all-product combination in (19) are uniform approximators of continuous maps on compact sets. This nonconstructive result is a special case of the uniform approximation theorem for all additive systems. We review this general theorem and its constructive proof in Appendix A. It holds as well for Gaussian sets with min combination (2) of if-part fit values or min clipping of then-part sets B_j.

Next, observe that taking the centroid of the additive B in (6) leads to a set of convex coefficients:

$$F(x) = \frac{\sum\limits_{j=1}^{m} a_j(x) \ V_j \ c_j}{\sum\limits_{j=1}^{m} a_j(x) \ V_j} \tag{25}$$

$$= \sum\limits_{j=1}^{m} p_j(x) \ c_j \tag{26}$$

for the m convex coefficients (or m terms of a discrete probability density)

$$p_j(x) = \frac{a_j(x) \ V_j}{\sum\limits_{k=1}^{m} a_k(x) \ V_k} \tag{27}$$

Wang and Mendel [13] refer to the convex sum of centroids (26) in the Gaussian case as a "fuzzy basis function expansion" even though the "basis functions" $p_j(x)$ in (27) are not orthogonal.

Feedforward fuzzy systems suffer exponential rule explosion as the number of inputs increases. Optimal rules [15] and function representation [16] offer two ways to deal with this "curse of dimensionality." Appendix B shows how supervised learning can tune the parameters of an additive fuzzy system. FCMs allow a fuzzy system to approximate nonlinear dynamical systems with a fixed number of rules [17].

18.3 FUZZY COGNITIVE MAPS

Fuzzy cognitive maps (FCMs) are fuzzy signed digraphs with feedback [6,7]. An FCM is an additive fuzzy system with feedback. Nodes stand for fuzzy sets or events that occur to some degree. The nodes are causal concepts. They can model events, actions, values, goals, or lumped-parameter processes.

Directed edges stand for fuzzy rules or the partial causal flow between the concepts. The sign (+ or -) of an edge stands for causal increase or decrease. The positive edge rule in Figure 18.4a states that a survival threat increases runaway. It is a positive causal connection. The runaway response grows or falls as the threat grows or falls. The negative edge rule in Figure 18.4b states that running away from a predator decreases the survival threat. It is a negative causal connection. The survival threat grows the less the prey runs away and falls the more the prey runs away. The two rules in Figure 18.4c define a minimal feedback loop in the FCM causal web.

A FCM with n nodes has n^2 edges. The nodes $C_i(t)$ are fuzzy sets and so take values in [0, 1]. So a FCM state is the *fit* (fuzzy unit) vector $\mathbf{C}(t) = (C_1(t), \dots, C_n(t))$ and thus a

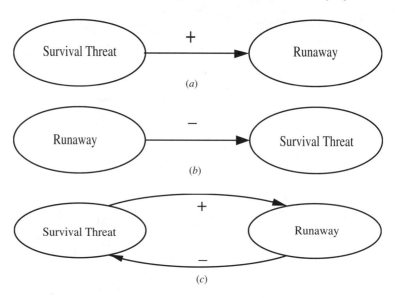

Figure 18.4   Directed edges stand for fuzzy rules or the partial causal flow
between the concepts. The sign (+ or -) of an edge stands for
causal increase or decrease. (*a*) A positive edge rule states that
a survival threat increases runaway. (*b*) A negative edge rule
states that running away from a predator decreases the survival
threat. (*c*) Two rules define a minimal feedback loop in the FCM
causal web.

point in the fuzzy hypercube $I^n = [0, 1]^n$. A FCM inference is a path or point sequence in
I^n. It is a fuzzy process or indexed family of fuzzy sets $\mathbf{C}(t)$. The FCM can only "forward
chain" [18] to answer what-if questions. Nonlinearities do not permit reverse causality.
FCMs cannot "backward chain" to answer why questions.

The FCM nonlinear dynamical system acts as a neural network. For each input state
$\mathbf{C}(0)$ it digs a trajectory in I^n that ends in an equilibrium attractor $\mathbf{A}$. The FCM quickly
converges or "settles down" to a fixed point, limit cycle, limit torus, or chaotic attractor
in the fuzzy cube. Figure 18.5 shows three attractors or meta-rules for a 2-D dynamical
FCM.

The output equilibrium is the answer to a causal what-if question: What if $\mathbf{C}(0)$ happens? In this sense each FCM stores a set of global rules of the form "If $\mathbf{C}(0)$, then
equilibrium attractor $\mathbf{A}$."

The size of the attractor regions in the fuzzy cube governs the number of these global
rules or "hidden patterns" [7]. All points in the attractor region map to the attractor. A
FCM with a global fixed point has only one global rule. All input balls "roll" down its
"well." FCMs can have large and small attractor regions in the fuzzy cube. The attractor

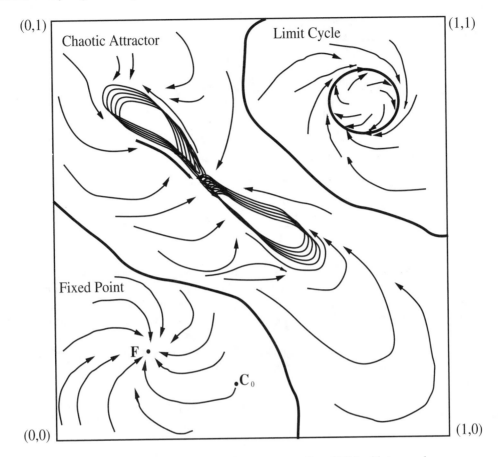

Figure 18.5 The unit square is the state space for a FCM with two nodes. The system has at most four fuzzy edge rules. In this case, it has three fuzzy meta-rules of the form "If input state vector **C** then attractor **A**." The state C_0 converges to a fixed point **F**.

types can vary in complex FCMs with highly nonlinear concepts and edges. Then one input state may lead to chaos and a more distant input state may end in a fixed point or limit cycle.

18.3.1 Simple FCMs

Simple FCMs have bivalent nodes and trivalent edges. Concept values C_i take values in $\{0,1\}$. Causal edges take values in $\{-1,0,1\}$. So for a concept each simple FCM state vector is one of the 2^n vertices of the fuzzy cube I^n. The FCM trajectory hops from vertex to vertex. I^n ends in a fixed point or limit cycle at the first repeated vector.

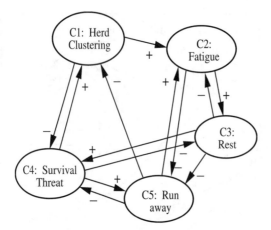

Figure 18.6   Simple FCM with five concept nodes. Edges show directed causal flow between nodes.

We can draw simple FCMs from articles, editorials, or surveys. Most persons can state the sign of causal flow between nodes. The hard part is to state its degree or magnitude. We can average expert responses [7,19] as in Eq. (30) or use neural systems to learn fuzzy edge weights from data. The expert responses can initialize the causal learning or modify it as a type of forcing function.

Figure 18.6 shows a simple FCM with five concept nodes. The connection or edge matrix $\mathbf{E}$ lists the causal links between nodes:

$$\mathbf{E} = \begin{array}{c} \\ C_1 \\ C_2 \\ C_3 \\ C_4 \\ C_5 \end{array} \begin{array}{ccccc} C_1 & C_2 & C_3 & C_4 & C_1 \\ \hline 0 & 1 & 0 & -1 & 0 \\ 0 & 0 & 1 & 0 & -1 \\ 0 & -1 & 0 & 1 & -1 \\ 1 & 0 & -1 & 0 & 1 \\ -1 & 1 & 0 & -1 & 0 \end{array}$$

The ith row lists the connection strength of the edges e_{ik} directed out from causal concept C_i. The ith column lists the edges e_{ki} directed into C_i. C_i causally increases C_k if $e_{ik} > 0$, decreases C_k if $e_{ik} < 0$, and has no effect if $e_{ik} = 0$. The causal concept C_4 causally increases concepts C_1 and C_5. It decreases C_3. Concepts C_1 and C_5 decrease C_4. Concept C_3 increases C_4.

18.3.2 FCM Recall

FCMs recall as the FCM dynamical system equilibrates. Simple FCM inference thresholds a matrix-vector multiplication [7,20]. State vectors $\mathbf{C}_n$ cycle through the FCM adjacency matrix $\mathbf{E} : C_1 \rightarrow \mathbf{E} \rightarrow C_2 \rightarrow \mathbf{E} \rightarrow C_3 \rightarrow \dots$. The system nonlinearly transforms the weighted input to each node C_i

$$C_i\,(t_{n+1}) = S \left[\sum_{k=1}^{N} e_{ki}\,(t_n)\,C_k\,(t_n) \right] \tag{28}$$

Here $S(x)$ is a bounded signal function. For simple FCMs the sigmoid function

$$S(y) = \frac{1}{1 + e^{-c(y-T)}} \tag{29}$$

with large $c > 0$ approximates a binary threshold function.

Simple threshold FCMs quickly converge to stable limit cycles or fixed points [7,20]. These limit cycles show "hidden patterns" in the causal web of the FCM. The FCM in Fig. 18.6 give a three-step limit cycle when input state $\mathbf{C}_1 = [0\ \ 0\ \ 0\ \ 1\ \ 0]$ fires the FCM network. Equation (28) and binary thresholding give the four-step limit cycle $\mathbf{C}_1 \rightarrow \mathbf{C}_2 \rightarrow \mathbf{C}_3 \rightarrow \mathbf{C}_4 \rightarrow \mathbf{C}_1$.

$$\mathbf{C}_1 = [0\ 0\ 0\ 1]$$

$$\mathbf{C}_1\mathbf{E} = [1\ 0\ -1\ 0\ 1] \rightarrow \mathbf{C}_2 = [1\ 0\ 0\ 0]$$

$$\mathbf{C}_2\mathbf{E} = [-1\ 2\ 0\ -2\ 0] \rightarrow \mathbf{C}_3 = [0\ 1\ 0\ 0\ 0]$$

$$\mathbf{C}_3\mathbf{E} = [0\ 0\ 1\ 0\ -1] \rightarrow \mathbf{C}_4 = [0\ 0\ 1\ 0\ 0]$$

$$\mathbf{C}_4\mathbf{E} = [0\ -1\ 0\ 1\ -1] \rightarrow \mathbf{C}_1 = [0\ 0\ 0\ 1\ 0]$$

In a virtual world the limit cycle might make in order wake up, go to work, come home, then wake up again. Some complex actions such as walking break down into simple cycles of movement [21].

Each node in a simple FCM turns actions or goals on and off. Each node can control its own FCM, fuzzy control system, goal-directed animation system, force feedback, or other input-output map. The FCM can control the temporal associations or timing cycles that structure virtual worlds. These patterns establish the rhythm of the world. "Grandmother" nodes can control the time spent on each step in a FCM "avalanche" [22]. This can change the update rate and thus the timing for the network [22].

18.3.3 Augmented FCMs

FCM matrices additively combine to form new FCMs [6]. This allows combination of FCMs for different actors or environments in the virtual world. The new (augmented) FCM includes the union of the causal concepts for all the actors and the environment in the virtual world. If a FCM does not include a concept, then those rows and columns are all zero. The sum of the augmented (zero-padded) FCM matrices for each actor forms the virtual world:

$$\mathbf{F} = \sum_{i=1}^{n} w_i \mathbf{F}_i \tag{30}$$

The w_i are positive weights for the ith FCM $\mathbf{F}_i$. The weights state the relative value of each FCM in the virtual world and can weight any subgraph of the FCM. Figure 18.7a shows

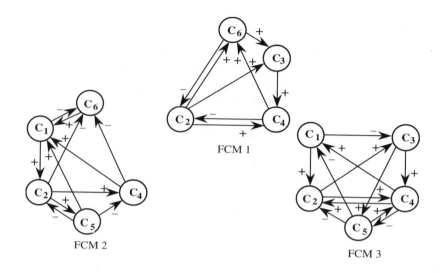

(a)

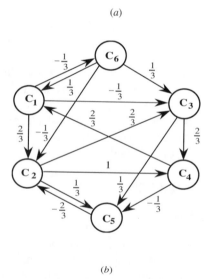

(b)

Figure 18.7   FCMs combine additively. (a) Three bivalent FCMs. (b) Augmented FCM. The augmented FCM takes the union of the causal concepts of the smaller FCMs and sums the augmented connection matrices as shown in (31).

three simple FCMs. Equation (30) combines these FCMs to give the new simple FCM in Fig. 18.7*b* that has fuzzy or multivalued edges:

$$\mathbf{F} = \frac{1}{3}(\mathbf{F}_1 + \mathbf{F}_2 + \mathbf{F}_3) = \frac{1}{3} \cdot \begin{bmatrix} 0 & 2 & -1 & 0 & 0 & -1 \\ 0 & 0 & 2 & 3 & 1 & 0 \\ 0 & 0 & 0 & 2 & 1 & 0 \\ 2 & 0 & 0 & 0 & -1 & 0 \\ 0 & -2 & 0 & 0 & 0 & 0 \\ 1 & -1 & 1 & 0 & 0 & 0 \end{bmatrix} \tag{31}$$

The FCM sum (30) helps knowledge acquisition. Any number of experts can describe their FCM virtual world views and (30) will weight and combine them [19]. The additive structure of combined FCMs also permits a Delphi [32] or questionnaire approach to knowledge acquisition. In contrast an AI expert system [18] is a binary tree with graph search. Two or more trees need not combine to a tree. Combined FCMs tend to have feedback or closed loops and that precludes graph search with forward or backward "chaining." The strong law of large numbers [7] ensures that the knowledge estimate $\mathbf{F}$ in (30) improves with the expert sample size n if we view the experts as independent (unique) random knowledge sources with finite variance (bounded uncertainty) and identical distribution (same problem-domain focus). The sample FCM converges to the unknown population FCM as the number of experts grows.

The FCM sum (30) can lead to new limit cycles that are not found in the individual summed FCMs. The limit cycles in the FCMs shown in Figure 18.7*a* are given below. FCM 1 has the fixed point (001101) and the three-step limit cycles:

$$(000100) \rightarrow (000001) \rightarrow (001000) \rightarrow (000100)$$

$$(000101) \rightarrow (001001) \rightarrow (001100) \rightarrow (000101)$$

FCM 2 has a three-step limit cycle:

$$(010000) \rightarrow (000110) \rightarrow (100000) \rightarrow (010000)$$

FCM 3 has one fixed point: (110100). The combined FCM has no fixed points and one four-step limit cycle:

$$(100100) \rightarrow (110000) \rightarrow (011110) \rightarrow (101110) \rightarrow (100100).$$

This limit cycle is distinct from the limit cycles of each of the summed FCMs.

18.3.4 Nested FCMs

FCMs can bring goals and intentions to virtual worlds as they define dynamic physical and social environments. This can give the "common representation" needed for a virtual world [23]. The FCM can combine simple actions to model "intelligent" behavior [21,24]. Each node in turn can control its own simple FCM in a *nested* FCM. Complex actions such as walking emerge from networks of simple reflexes. Nested simple FCMs can mimic this process as a net of finite state machines with binary limit cycles.

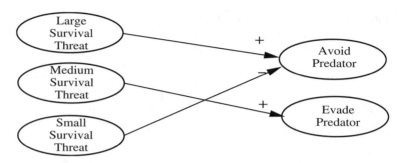

Figure 18.8   Subconcepts map to other concepts. This gives a more varied
response.

The output of a simple FCM is a binary limit cycle that describes actions or goals
[7]. This holds even if the binary concept nodes change state asynchronously. Each output
turns a function on or off as in a robotic neural net [21]. This output can control smaller
FCMs or fuzzy control systems. These systems can drive visual, auditory, or tactile outputs
of the virtual world. The FCM can control the temporal associations or timing cycles that
structure virtual worlds. The FCM state vector drives the motion of each character as in a
frame in a cartoon. Simple equations of motion can move each actor between the states.

FCM nesting extends to any number of fuzzy sets for the inputs. A concept can divide
into smaller fuzzy sets or subconcepts. The edges or rules link the sets. This leads to a
discrete multivalued output for each node. Enough nodes allow this system to approximate
any continuous function [11] for signal functions of the form (29). The subconcepts Q_{ij}
partition the fuzzy concept C_j

$$C_j = \bigcup_{i=1}^{N_j} Q_{ij} \tag{32}$$

Figure 18.8 shows the concept of a SURVIVAL THREAT divided into subconcepts. Each
subconcept is the degree of threat.

The FCM edges or rules map one subconcept to another. These subconcept mappings
form a fuzzy system or set of fuzzy if-then rules that map inputs to outputs. Each mapping
is a fuzzy rule or state-space patch that links fuzzy sets. The patches cover the graph of
some function in the input-output state space. The fuzzy system then averages the patches
that overlap to give an approximation of a continuous function [9]. Figure 18.8 shows how
subconcepts can map to different responses in the FCM. This gives a more varied response
to changes in the virtual world.

18.4   VIRTUAL UNDERSEA WORLD

Figure 18.9 shows a simple FCM for a virtual dolphin. It lists a causal web of goals and
actions in the life of a dolphin [25]. The connection matrix $\mathbf{E}_D$ states these causal relations
in numbers:

$$\mathbf{E}_D = \begin{array}{c c} & \begin{array}{c c c c c c c c c c} D_1 & D_2 & D_3 & D_4 & D_5 & D_6 & D_7 & D_8 & D_9 & D_{10} \end{array} \\ \begin{array}{c} D_1 \\ D_2 \\ D_3 \\ D_4 \\ D_5 \\ D_6 \\ D_7 \\ D_8 \\ D_9 \\ D_{10} \end{array} & \left[\begin{array}{c c c c c c c c c c} 0 & -1 & -1 & 0 & 0 & 1 & 0 & 0 & 0 & 0 \\ 0 & 0 & 0 & 0 & 1 & 0 & 0 & 0 & 0 & 0 \\ 0 & 0 & 0 & 1 & 1 & -1 & -1 & 0 & 0 & -1 \\ 1 & 0 & -1 & 0 & 0 & -1 & -1 & 0 & 0 & -1 \\ 0 & 0 & 1 & 0 & 0 & 0 & 0 & 0 & -1 & 0 \\ 0 & 0 & 0 & 0 & -1 & 0 & 1 & 0 & 0 & 0 \\ 0 & 0 & 0 & 0 & 0 & 0 & 0 & 1 & 0 & 0 \\ -1 & 1 & -1 & 0 & 1 & 0 & -1 & 0 & 0 & 0 \\ 0 & 0 & 0 & 0 & 1 & -1 & -1 & -1 & 0 & 1 \\ -1 & -1 & 1 & 0 & -1 & -1 & -1 & -1 & -1 & 0 \end{array} \right] \end{array}$$

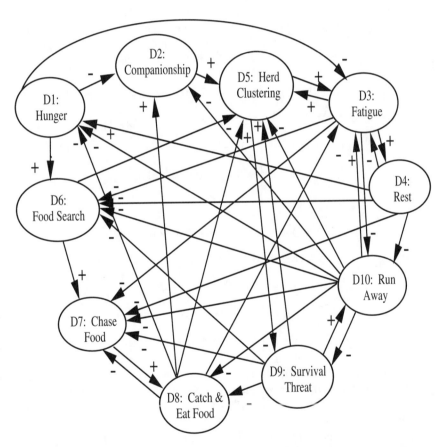

Figure 18.9 Trivalent fuzzy cognitive map for the control of a dolphin actor in a fuzzy virtual world. The rules or edges connect causal concepts in a signed connection matrix.

The ith row lists the connection strength of the edges e_{ik} directed out from causal concept D_i, and the ith column lists the edges e_{ki} directed into D_i. Row 9 shows how the concept SURVIVAL THREAT changes the other concepts. Column 9 shows the concepts that change SURVIVAL THREAT.

We can model the effect of a survival threat on the dolphin FCM as a sustained input to D_9. This means $D_9 = 1$ for all time t_k. C_0 is the initial input state of the dolphin FCM:

$$C_0 = [\ 0\ 0\ 0\ 0\ 0\ 0\ 0\ 0\ 1\ 0]$$

Then

$$C_0 E_D = [0\ 0\ 0\ 0\ 1\ -1\ -1\ -1\ 0\ 1] \rightarrow C_1 = [0\ 0\ 0\ 0\ 1\ 0\ 0\ 0\ 1\ 1]$$

The arrow stands for a threshold operation with $1/2$ as the threshold value. C_1 keeps D9 on since we want to study the effect of a sustained threat. C_1 shows that when threatened the dolphins cluster in a herd and flee the threat. The negative rules in the ninth row of E_D show that a threat to survival turns off other actions. The FCM converges to the limit cycle $C_1 \rightarrow C_2 \rightarrow C_3 \rightarrow C_4 \rightarrow C_5 \rightarrow C_1 \ldots$ if the threat lasts:

$$C_1 E_D = \begin{bmatrix} -1 & -1 & 2 & 0 & 0 & -2 & -2 & -2 & -2 & 1 \end{bmatrix} \rightarrow$$

$$C_2 = \begin{bmatrix} 0 & 0 & 1 & 0 & 0 & 0 & 0 & 0 & 1 & 1 \end{bmatrix},$$

$$C_2 E_D = \begin{bmatrix} -1 & -1 & 1 & 1 & 1 & -3 & -3 & -2 & -1 & 0 \end{bmatrix} \rightarrow$$

$$C_3 = \begin{bmatrix} 0 & 0 & 1 & 1 & 1 & 0 & 0 & 0 & 1 & 0 \end{bmatrix},$$

$$C_3 E_D = \begin{bmatrix} 1 & 0 & 0 & 1 & 2 & -3 & -3 & -1 & -1 & -1 \end{bmatrix} \rightarrow$$

$$C_4 = \begin{bmatrix} 1 & 0 & 0 & 1 & 1 & 0 & 0 & 0 & 1 & 0 \end{bmatrix},$$

$$C_4 E_D = \begin{bmatrix} 1 & -1 & -1 & 0 & 1 & -1 & -2 & -1 & -1 & 0 \end{bmatrix} \rightarrow$$

$$C_5 = \begin{bmatrix} 1 & 0 & 0 & 0 & 1 & 0 & 0 & 0 & 1 & 0 \end{bmatrix},$$

$$C_5 E_D = \begin{bmatrix} 0 & -1 & 0 & 0 & 1 & 0 & -1 & -1 & -1 & 1 \end{bmatrix} \rightarrow$$

$$C_1 = \begin{bmatrix} 0 & 0 & 0 & 0 & 1 & 0 & 0 & 0 & 1 & 1 \end{bmatrix}.$$

Flight causes fatigue (C_2). The dolphin herd stops and rests, staying close together (C_3). All the activity causes hunger (C_4, C_5). If the threat persists, they again try to flee (C_1). A threat supresses hunger. This limit cycle shows a "hidden" global pattern in the causal virtual world.

The FCM converges to the new limit cycle $C_6 \rightarrow C_7 \rightarrow C_8 \rightarrow C_9 \rightarrow C_{10} \rightarrow C_{11} \rightarrow C_{12} \rightarrow C_{13} \rightarrow C_6 \rightarrow \ldots$ when the shark gives up the chase or eats a dolphin and the threat ends ($D_9 = 0$):

$$C_6 = \begin{bmatrix} 0 & 0 & 1 & 1 & 1 & 0 & 0 & 0 & 0 & 0 \end{bmatrix},$$

$$C_7 E_D = \begin{bmatrix} 1 & 0 & 0 & 1 & 1 & -2 & -2 & 0 & -1 & -2 \end{bmatrix} \rightarrow$$

$$C_7 = \begin{bmatrix} 1 & 0 & 0 & 1 & 1 & 0 & 0 & 0 & 0 & 0 \end{bmatrix},$$

$$C_8 E_D = \begin{bmatrix} 1 & -1 & -1 & 0 & 0 & 0 & -1 & 0 & -1 & -1 \end{bmatrix} \rightarrow$$

$$C_8 = \begin{bmatrix} 1 & 0 & 0 & 0 & 0 & 0 & 0 & 0 & 0 & 0 \end{bmatrix},$$

$$C_9 E_D = \begin{bmatrix} 0 & -1 & -1 & 0 & 0 & 1 & 1 & 0 & 0 & 0 \end{bmatrix} \rightarrow$$

$$C_9 = \begin{bmatrix} 0 & 0 & 0 & 0 & 0 & 1 & 0 & 0 & 0 & 0 \end{bmatrix},$$

$$C_{10} E_D = \begin{bmatrix} 0 & 0 & 0 & 0 & -1 & 0 & 1 & 0 & 0 & 0 \end{bmatrix} \rightarrow$$

$$C_{10} = \begin{bmatrix} 0 & 0 & 0 & 0 & 0 & 0 & 1 & 0 & 0 & 0 \end{bmatrix},$$

$$C_{11} E_D = \begin{bmatrix} 0 & 0 & 0 & 0 & 0 & 0 & 0 & 1 & 0 & 0 \end{bmatrix} \rightarrow$$

$$C_{11} = \begin{bmatrix} 0 & 0 & 0 & 0 & 0 & 0 & 0 & 1 & 0 & 0 \end{bmatrix},$$

$$C_{12} E_D = \begin{bmatrix} -1 & 1 & -1 & 0 & 1 & 0 & 0 & 0 & 0 & 0 \end{bmatrix} \rightarrow$$

$$C_{12} = \begin{bmatrix} 0 & 1 & 0 & 0 & 1 & 0 & 0 & 0 & 0 & 0 \end{bmatrix},$$

$$C_{13} E_D = \begin{bmatrix} 0 & 0 & 1 & 0 & 1 & 0 & 0 & 0 & -1 & 0 \end{bmatrix} \rightarrow$$

$$C_{13} = \begin{bmatrix} 0 & 0 & 1 & 0 & 1 & 0 & 0 & 0 & 0 & 0 \end{bmatrix},$$

$$C_{14} E_D = \begin{bmatrix} 0 & 0 & 1 & 1 & 1 & -1 & -1 & 0 & -1 & -1 \end{bmatrix} \rightarrow$$

$$C_6 = \begin{bmatrix} 0 & 0 & 1 & 1 & 1 & 0 & 0 & 0 & 0 & 0 \end{bmatrix}.$$

The dolphin herd rests from the previous chase (C_6, C_7). Then they begin a hunt of their own (C_9, C_{10}). They eat (C_{11}), and then they socialize and rest (C_{12}, C_{13}, C_6). This makes them hungry and the feeding cycle repeats.

18.4.1 Augmented Virtual World

Figure 18.10 shows an augmented FCM for an undersea virtual world. It combines fish school, shark, and dolphin herd FCMs with: $F = F_{\text{fish}} + F_{\text{shark}} + F_{\text{dolphin}}$. The new links among these FCMs are those of predator and prey where the larger eats the smaller. The actors chase, flee, and eat one another. A hungry shark chases the dolphins, and that leads to the limit cycle (C_1, C_2, C_3, C_4) above. Augmenting the FCM matrices gives a large but sparse FCM since the actors respond to each other in few ways. Figure 18.11 (page 588) shows the connection matrix for the augmented FCM in Fig. 18.10. The augmented FCM moves the actors in the virtual world. The binary output states of this

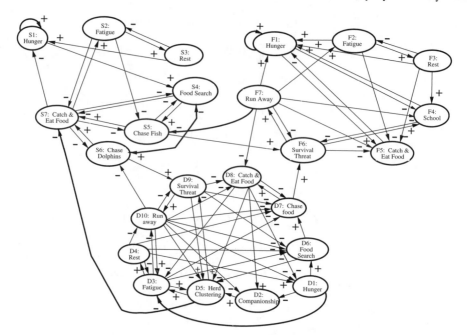

Figure 18.10   Augmented FCM for different actors in a virtual world. The actors interact through linked common causal concepts such as chasing food and avoiding a threat.

FCM move the actors. Each FCM state maps to equations or function approximations for movement.

We used a simple update equation for position:

$$p\,(t_{n+1}) \;=\; p\,(t_n) + (t_{n+1} - t_n) \cdot v\,(t_n) \tag{33}$$

The velocity $v(t)$ does not change at time step Δt. The FCM finds the direction and magnitude of movement. The magnitude of the velocity depends on the FCM state. If the FCM state is "run away" then the velocity is FAST. If the FCM state is "rest" then the velocity is SLOW. The prey choose the direction that maximizes the distance from the predator. The predator chases the prey. When a predator searches for food it swims at random [26]. Each state moves the actors through the sea.

The FCM in Fig. 18.10 encodes limit cycles between the actors. For example if we start with a hungry shark and set the causal link between concept S4: FOOD SEARCH and S6: CHASE DOLPHINS equal to zero to look at shark interactions with the fish school then the first state C_1 is

$$C_1 = [0\ 0\ 0\ 0\ 0\ 0\ 0\ 0\ 0\ 1\ 0\ 0\ 0\ 0\ 0\ 0\ 0\ 0\ 0\ 0\ 0\ 0\ 0\ 0]$$

This vector gives a seven-step limit cycle after four transition steps:

$C_1 E_A$ = [0 0 0 0 0 0 0 0 0 0 1 0 0 1 0 0 0 0 0 0 0 0 0 0] →

 C_2 = [0 0 0 0 0 0 0 0 0 0 1 0 0 1 0 0 0 0 0 0 0 0 0 0],

$C_2 E_A$ = [0 0 0 0 0 0 0 0 0 0 1 0 0 1 1 0 −1 0 0 0 0 0 0 0] →

 C_3 = [0 0 0 0 0 0 0 0 0 0 1 0 0 1 1 0 0 0 0 0 0 0 0 0],

$C_3 E_A$ = [0 0 0 0 0 0 0 0 0 1 0 0 0 1 0 0 0 0 0 0 0 1 0] →

 C_4 = [0 0 0 0 0 0 0 0 0 0 1 0 0 0 1 0 0 0 0 0 0 0 1 0],

$C_4 E_A$ = [0 0 0 0 0 0 0 0 0 0 1 0 0 0 0 0 1 0 0 0 1 −1 1 1] →

 C_5 = [0 0 0 0 0 0 0 0 0 0 1 0 0 0 0 0 1 0 0 0 1 0 1 1],

$C_5 E_A$ = [0 0 0 0 0 0 0 −1 0 0 0 1 0 0 −2 −1 0 2 1 0 0 −2 −2 1] →

 C_6 = [0 0 0 0 0 0 0 0 0 0 0 1 0 0 0 0 0 1 1 0 0 0 0 1],

$C_6 E_A$ = [0 0 0 0 0 0 0 −1 0 0 0 0 1 0 −2 0 −1 3 1 1 −2 −1 −1 0] →

 C_7 = [0 0 0 0 0 0 0 0 0 0 0 0 1 0 0 0 0 1 1 1 0 0 0 0],

$C_7 E_A$ = [0 0 0 0 0 0 0 0 0 1 −1 0 0 0 0 0 3 −1 1 0 −1 0 0] →

 C_8 = [0 0 0 0 0 0 0 0 0 0 1 0 0 0 0 0 0 1 0 1 0 0 0 0],

$C_8 E_A$ = [0 0 0 0 0 0 0 0 0 0 1 0 0 1 0 0 0 2 −1 0 0 0 0 0] →

 C_9 = [0 0 0 0 0 0 0 0 0 0 1 0 0 1 0 0 0 1 0 0 0 0 0 0],

$C_9 E_A$ = [0 0 0 0 0 0 0 0 0 0 1 0 0 1 1 0 −1 1 0 0 −1 1 0 0] →

 C_{10} = [0 0 0 0 0 0 0 0 0 0 1 0 0 1 1 0 0 1 0 0 0 1 0 0],

$C_{10} E_A$ = [0 0 0 0 0 0 0 0 0 0 1 0 0 0 1 0 0 0 0 0 −1 1 1 0] →

$\phantom{C_{10} E_A =}$ C_{11} = [0 0 0 0 0 0 0 0 0 0 1 0 0 0 1 0 0 0 0 0 0 1 1 0],

$C_{11} E_A$ = [0 0 0 0 0 0 0 0 0 0 1 0 0 0 0 0 1 −1 0 0 1 −1 1 1] →

$\phantom{C_{11} E_A =}$ C_5 = [0 0 0 0 0 0 0 0 0 0 1 0 0 0 0 0 1 0 0 0 1 0 1 1].

In this limit cycle a shark searches for food (C_1, C_2, C_3). The shark finds some fish (C_4), chases the fish (C_5), and then eats some of the fish (C_6). To avoid the shark most fish run away and then regroup as a school (C_5, C_6, C_7). Then the fish rest and eat while the shark rests (C_8, C_9). In time the shark gets hungry again and searches for fish (C_{10}, C_{11}).

The result is a complex dance among the actors as they move in a 2-D ocean. Figure 18.12 shows these movements. The forcing function is a hungry shark $(C_{11} = 1)$. The

| | \multicolumn{10}{c}{Dolphin} | \multicolumn{7}{c}{Shark} | \multicolumn{7}{c}{Fish} |
	D_1	D_2	D_3	D_4	D_5	D_6	D_7	D_8	D_9	D_{10}	S_1	S_2	S_3	S_4	S_5	S_6	S_7	F_1	F_2	F_3	F_4	F_5	F_6	F_7
D_1	0	−1	−1	0	0	1	0	0	0	0	0	0	0	0	0	0	0	0	0	0	0	0	0	0
D_2	0	0	0	0	1	0	0	0	0	0	0	0	0	0	0	0	0	0	0	0	0	0	0	0
D_3	0	0	0	1	1	−1	−1	0	0	−1	0	0	0	0	0	0	0	0	0	0	0	0	0	0
D_4	1	0	−1	0	0	−1	−1	0	0	−1	0	0	0	0	0	0	0	0	0	0	0	0	0	0
D_5	0	0	1	0	0	0	0	0	−1	0	0	0	0	0	0	−1	0	0	0	0	0	0	0	0
D_6	0	0	0	0	−1	0	1	0	0	0	0	0	0	0	0	0	0	0	0	0	0	0	0	0
D_7	0	0	0	0	0	0	0	1	0	0	0	0	0	0	0	0	0	0	0	0	0	0	1	0
D_8	−1	1	−1	0	1	0	−1	0	0	0	0	0	0	0	0	0	0	0	0	0	0	0	0	0
D_9	0	0	0	0	1	−1	−1	−1	0	1	0	0	0	0	0	0	0	0	0	0	0	0	0	0
D_{10}	−1	−1	1	0	−1	−1	−1	−1	−1	−1	0	0	0	0	0	−1	0	0	0	0	0	0	0	0
S_1	0	0	0	0	0	0	0	0	0	0	1	0	0	1	0	0	0	0	0	0	0	0	0	0
S_2	0	0	0	0	0	0	0	0	0	0	0	0	1	0	−1	0	−1	0	0	0	0	0	0	0
S_3	0	0	0	0	0	0	0	0	0	0	1	−1	0	0	0	0	0	0	0	0	0	0	0	0
S_4	0	0	0	0	0	0	0	0	0	0	0	0	0	0	1	1	−1	0	0	0	0	0	0	0
S_5	0	0	0	0	0	0	0	0	0	0	0	0	0	−1	0	0	1	0	0	0	0	0	1	0
S_6	0	0	0	0	0	0	0	0	1	0	0	0	0	−1	0	0	1	0	0	0	0	0	0	0
S_7	0	0	0	0	0	0	0	0	0	0	−1	1	0	−1	−1	−1	0	0	0	0	0	0	0	0
F_1	0	0	0	0	0	0	0	0	0	0	0	0	0	0	0	0	0	1	0	0	−1	1	0	0
F_2	0	0	0	0	0	0	0	0	0	0	0	0	0	0	0	0	0	1	0	1	0	−1	0	0
F_3	0	0	0	0	0	0	0	0	0	0	0	0	0	0	0	0	0	1	−1	0	1	−1	0	0
F_4	0	0	0	0	0	0	0	0	0	0	0	0	0	0	0	0	0	1	0	0	0	0	−1	0
F_5	0	0	0	0	0	0	0	0	0	0	0	0	0	0	0	0	0	−1	0	0	0	0	0	0
F_6	0	0	0	0	0	0	0	0	0	0	0	0	0	0	0	0	0	0	0	0	1	−1	0	1
F_7	0	0	0	0	0	0	−1	0	0	0	0	0	0	0	−1	0	0	1	1	0	−1	−1	−1	0

Figure 18.11 Augmented FCM connection matrix for the dolphin herd, fish school, and shark. Figure 18.10 shows the nodes and edges. The lines show the FCMs of the actors. The sparse region outside the lines shows the interaction space of the FCMs.

shark encounters the dolphins who cluster and then flee the shark. The shark chases but cannot keep up. The shark still searches for food and finds the fish. It catches a fish and then rests with its hunger sated. Meanwhile the hungry dolphins search for food and eat more fish. Each actor responds to the actions of the other.

18.4.2 Nested FCMs for Fish Schools

In a simple FCM, the threat response concepts link as a rule: SURVIVAL THREAT implies RUN AWAY. Fish change their behavior as the degree of threat changes. This rule does not model the effects of different threats. For that we need a nested FCM or a fuzzy function approximator that links the threat degree to different responses. The size of the threat is a function of the size, speed, and attack angle of the predator [27]. A small threat

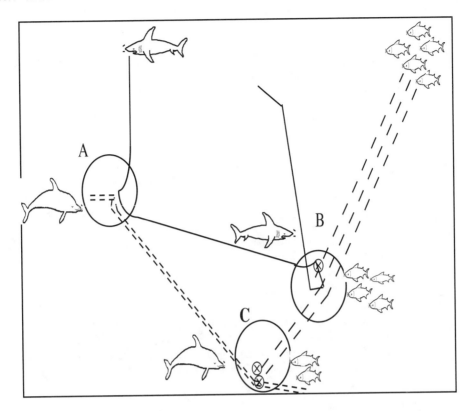

Figure 18.12 FCMs control the virtual world. The augmented FCM controls the actions of the actors. In event A, the hungry shark forces the dolphin herd to run away. Each dashed line stands for a dolphin swim path. In event B, the shark finds the fish and eats some. Each dashed line stands for the path of a fish in the school. The cross shows the shark eating a fish. In event C, the fish run into the dolphins and suffer more losses. The solid lines are the dolphin paths. The dashes are the fish swim paths. The cross shows a dolphin eating a fish.

leads to avoidance behavior. Figure 18.13a shows how fish avoid a predator. The fish move in direction α to maximize their distance from the predator [28]:

$$\cot \alpha \;=\; \cot \alpha_m \;+\; \frac{V_p}{V_f \,\sin \alpha_m} \tag{34}$$

V_p and V_f are the velocities of the predator and the fish. α_m is the angle that minimizes the time in terms of the predator's sighting angle γ_p:

$$\tan \alpha_m = - \cot \gamma_p \tag{35}$$

A large threat causes the fish to evade the predator. The fish try to maximize the minimum distance from the predator D_p [28]:

$$D_p^2 = \left[(X_o - V_p\,t) + V_f\,t\cos\alpha \right]^2 + \left(V_f\,t\sin\alpha \right)^2 \tag{36}$$

X_0 is the initial distance between predator and prey. α is the escape angle of the prey. V_p and V_f are the velocities of the predator and the fish. Figure 18.13*b* shows how fish evade a predator. A fuzzy system can approximate these responses using hand-picked rules or a neural-fuzzy learning [29]. These threat responses cause the "fountain effect" and the "burst effect" in fish schools [27] as each fish tries to increase its chances of survival. The fountain effect occurs when a predator moves towards a fish school and the school splits and flows around the predator. The school re-forms behind the predator. In the burst effect, the school expands in the form of a sphere to evade the predator.

A small survival threat may be a slow-moving predator that either has not seen or decided to attack the fish. A large survival threat may be a fast predator such as a barracuda or shark that swims toward the center of the school. If we insert this new sub-FCM into the Fish FCM in Fig. 18.10 we get the FCM in Fig. 18.14. Different limit cycles appear for different degrees of threat. For a small threat (F_6), the fish avoid the predator (F_9) as they move out of the line-of-sight of the predator. Large threats (F_7) cause the fish to scatter quickly to evade the predator F_8. This leads to fatigue and rest $(F_2$ and $F_3)$.

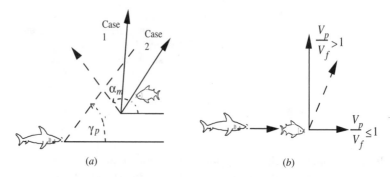

(a)   (b)

Figure 18.13   Fish change their behavior as the degree of threat changes. (*a*) The fish minimize time within the sighting angle of the predator. Case 1 shows the angle of escape when the fish swim faster. Case 2 shows the desired angle when the predator swims faster. (*b*) The fish maximize the distance between themselves and the predator to evade the predator. The fish swim straight ahead when the fish swim faster than the predator. The fish swim away at an angle if the predator swims faster.

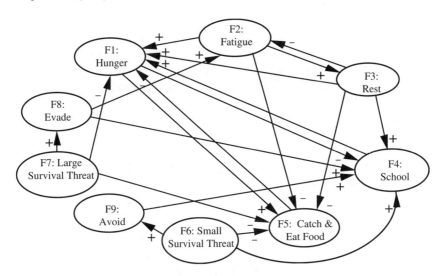

Figure 18.14   Example of a nested FCM. The concept of a survival threat divides into two subconcepts that each map to a different survival tactic.

18.5 ADAPTIVE FUZZY COGNITIVE MAPS

An adaptive FCM changes its causal web in time. The causal web learns from data. The causal edges or rules change in sign and magnitude. The additive scheme is a type of causal learning since it changes the FCM edge strengths. In general, an edge e_{ij} changes with some first-order learning law:

$$\dot{e}_{ij} \;=\; f_{ij}\,(E,C) \;+\; g_{ij}\,(t) \tag{37}$$

Here g_{ij} is a forcing function. Data fire the concept nodes and in time this leaves a causal pattern in the edge. Causal learning is local in f_{ij}. It depends on just its own value and on the node signals that it connects:

$$\dot{e}_{ij} \;=\; f_{ij}\left(e_{ij}, C_i, C_j, \dot{C}_i, \dot{C}_j\right) \;+\; g_{ij}\,(t) \tag{38}$$

Correlation or Hebbian learning can encode some limit cycles in the FCMs or temporal associative memories (TAMs) [7]. It adds pairwise correlation matrices in (37). This method can only store a few patterns. Differential Hebbian learning encodes changes in a concept in Eq. (38). Both types of learning are local and light in computation.

To encode binary limit cycles in connection matrix **E**, the TAM method sums the weighted correlation matrices between successive states [7]. To encode the limit cycle $C_1 \rightarrow C_2 \rightarrow C_3 \rightarrow C_1$, we first convert each binary state C_i into a bipolar state vector X_i by replacing each 0 with a -1. Then **E** is the weighted sum

$$\mathbf{E} = q_1\mathbf{X}_1^T\mathbf{X}_2 + q_2\mathbf{X}_2^T\mathbf{X}_3 + \ldots + q_{n-1}\mathbf{X}_{n-1}^T\mathbf{X}_n + q_n\mathbf{X}_n^T\mathbf{X}_1 \tag{39}$$

The length of the limit cycle should be less than the number of concepts. Else crosstalk can occur. Proper weighting of each correlation matrix pair can improve the encoding [30] and thus increase the FCM storage capacity. Correlation learning is a form of the unsupervised signal Hebbian learning law in neural networks [8]:

$$\dot{e}_{ij} = -e_{ij} + C_i(x_i)C_j(x_j) \tag{40}$$

A virtual world can encode an event sequence with (39) or (40). A simple chase cycle might be $\mathbf{C}_1 \rightarrow \mathbf{C}_2 \rightarrow \mathbf{C}_3$:

$$\mathbf{C}_1 = [1\ 0\ 1\ 0\ 0\ 0\ 0\ 0\ 0\ 1]$$

$$\mathbf{C}_2 = [1\ 0\ 1\ 1\ 1\ 0\ 0\ 0\ 1\ 0]$$

$$\mathbf{C}_3 = [1\ 0\ 0\ 0\ 1\ 0\ 0\ 0\ 1\ 1]$$

Then (39) gives the FCM connection matrix $\mathbf{E}$ when $q_i = 1$ for all i:

	D_1	D_2	D_3	D_4	D_5	D_6	D_7	D_8	D_9	D_{10}
D_1	3	−3	1	−1	1	−3	−3	−3	1	1
D_2	−3	3	−1	1	−1	3	3	3	−1	−1
D_3	1	−1	−1	1	3	−1	−1	−1	3	−1
D_4	−1	1	−3	−1	1	1	1	1	1	1
D_5	1	−1	−1	−3	−1	−1	−1	−1	−1	3
D_6	−3	3	−1	1	−1	3	3	3	−1	−1
D_7	−3	3	−1	1	−1	3	3	3	−1	−1
D_8	−3	3	−1	1	−1	3	3	3	−1	−1
D_9	1	−1	−1	3	−1	−1	−1	−1	−1	3
D_{10}	1	−1	3	1	−1	−1	−1	−1	−1	−1

$$\mathbf{E} =$$

Then

$$\mathbf{C}_1\mathbf{E} = [5\ -5\ 3\ 1\ 3\ -5\ -5\ -5\ 3\ -1] \rightarrow \mathbf{C}_2 = [1\ 0\ 1\ 1\ 1\ 0\ 0\ 0\ 1\ 0]$$

$$\mathbf{C}_2\mathbf{E} = [5\ -5\ -5\ -7\ 3\ -5\ -5\ -5\ 3\ 7] \rightarrow \mathbf{C}_3 = [1\ 0\ 0\ 0\ 1\ 0\ 0\ 0\ 1\ 1]$$

$$\mathbf{C}_3\mathbf{E} = [6\ -6\ 2\ -6\ -2\ -6\ -6\ -6\ -2\ 6] \rightarrow \mathbf{C}_1 = [1\ 0\ 1\ 0\ 0\ 0\ 0\ 0\ 0\ 1]$$

Correlation encoding treats negative and zero causal edges the same. It can encode "spurious" causal implications between concepts such as $e_{6,2} = 3$. This means searching for food causes a desire to socialize. Correlation encoding is a poor model of inferred causality. It says two concepts cause each other if they are on at the same time. Differential Hebbian learning encodes causal changes to avoid spurious causality. The concepts must move in the same or opposite directions to infer a causal link. They must come on and turn off at the same time or one must come on as the other turns off. Just being on does not lead to a new causal link. The patterns of turning on or off must correlate positively or negatively.

The differential Hebbian learning law [7] correlates concept changes or velocities:

$$\dot{e}_{ij} = -e_{ij} + \dot{C}_i(x_i)\dot{C}_j(x_j) \tag{41}$$

So $\dot{C}_i(x_i)\dot{C}_j(x_j) > 0$ iff concepts C_i and C_j move in the same direction. $\dot{C}_i(x_i)\dot{C}_j(x_j) < 0$ iff concepts C_i and C_j move in opposite directions. In this sense (41) learns patterns of causal change. The first-order structure of (41) implies that $e_{ij}(t)$ is an exponentially weighted average of paired (or lagged) changes. The most recent changes have the most weight. The *discrete* change $\Delta C_i(t) = C_i(t) - C_i(t-1)$ lies in $\{-1,0,1\}$. The discrete differential Hebbian learning can take the form

$$e_{ij}(t+1) = \begin{cases} e_{ij}(t) + c_t\left[\Delta C_i(x_i)\,\Delta C_j(x_j) - e_{ij}(t)\right] \\ \qquad\qquad\qquad\qquad\qquad\qquad if \quad \Delta C_i(x_i) \neq 0 \\ e_{ij}(t) \\ \qquad\qquad\qquad\qquad\qquad\qquad if \quad \Delta C_i(x_i) = 0 \end{cases} \tag{42}$$

Here c_t is a learning coefficient that decreases in time [20]. The sequence of learning coefficients $\{c_t\}$ should decrease slowly [8] in the sense of

$$\sum_{t=1}^{\infty} c_t = \infty$$

but not too slowly in the sense that

$$\sum_{t=1}^{\infty} c_t^2 < \infty$$

In practice $c_t \approx \frac{1}{t}$. $\Delta C_i \Delta C_j > 0$ iff concepts C_i and C_j move in the same direction. $\Delta C_i \Delta C_j < 0$ iff concepts C_i and C_j move in opposite directions. **E** changes only if a concept changes. The changed edge slowly "forgets" the old causal changes in favor of the new ones. This causal law can learn higher-order causal relations if it correlates multiple-cause changes with effect changes.

We used differential Hebbian learning to encode a feeding sequence and a chase sequence in a FCM. The concepts in the ith row learn only when $\Delta C_i(x_i)$ equals 1 or -1. We used

$$c_t(t_k) = 0.1\left[1 - \frac{t_k}{1.1N}\right]$$

The training data came from the rest, eat, play, and chase sequences in Section 18.4. This gave the $\mathbf{E}_D$:

	D_1	D_2	D_3	D_4	D_5	D_6	D_7	D_8	D_9	D_{10}
D_1	-0.25	0.00	0.00	-0.24	-0.24	0.76	-0.51	0.00	0.00	0.00
D_2	0.00	-0.49	0.49	-0.51	0.00	0.00	0.00	0.00	0.00	0.00
D_3	-0.26	0.00	-0.25	1.00	0.75	0.00	0.00	0.00	0.00	0.00
D_4	1.00	0.00	-0.25	-0.25	-0.25	-0.50	0.00	0.00	0.00	0.00
D_5	0.51	-0.16	0.49	-0.34	-0.51	-0.33	0.00	0.00	0.00	-0.16
D_6	0.00	0.00	0.00	0.00	0.00	-0.49	1.00	-0.51	0.00	0.00
D_7	0.00	-0.51	0.00	0.00	-0.51	0.00	-0.49	1.00	0.00	0.00
D_8	0.00	1.00	-0.33	0.00	0.67	0.00	0.00	-0.67	0.00	0.00
D_9	0.00	0.00	-1.00	0.00	1.00	0.00	0.00	0.00	0.00	1.00
D_{10}	0.00	0.00	1.00	-0.51	-1.00	0.00	0.00	0.00	0.00	-0.49

This learned edge matrix $\mathbf{E}_D$ resembles the FCM matrix in Fig. 18.9. The causal links it lacks between $\mathbf{D}_10$ and $(\mathbf{D}_6,\mathbf{D}_7,\mathbf{D}_8)$ were not in the training set. The diagonal links terms for self-inhibition of each concept. This occurs since each concept is on for one cycle before the matrix transitions to the next state. The hunger input $\mathbf{CL}_0 = [\ 1\ 0\ 0\ 0\ 0\ 0\ 0\ 0\ 0\ 0]$ with a threshold of 0.51 now leads to the limit cycle:

$$\mathbf{CL}_0\mathbf{E}_D = [-0.25\ 0.00\ 0.00\ -0.24\ -0.24\ 0.76\ -0.51\ 0.00\ 0.00\ 0.00] \rightarrow$$
$$\mathbf{CL}_1 = [0\ 0\ 0\ 0\ 0\ 1\ 0\ 0\ 0\ 0],$$

$$\mathbf{CL}_1\mathbf{E}_D = [0.00\ 0.00\ 0.00\ 0.00\ 0.00\ -0.49\ 1.00\ -0.51\ 0.00\ 0.00] \rightarrow$$
$$\mathbf{CL}_2 = [0\ 0\ 0\ 0\ 0\ 0\ 1\ 0\ 0\ 0],$$

$$\mathbf{CL}_2\mathbf{E}_D = [0.00\ -0.51\ 0.00\ 0.00\ -0.51\ 0.00\ -0.49\ 1.00\ 0.00\ 0.00] \rightarrow$$
$$\mathbf{CL}_3 = [0\ 0\ 0\ 0\ 0\ 0\ 0\ 1\ 0\ 0],$$

$$\mathbf{CL}_3\mathbf{E}_D = [0.00\ 1.00\ -0.33\ 0.00\ 0.67\ 0.00\ 0.00\ -0.67\ 0.00\ 0.00] \rightarrow$$
$$\mathbf{CL}_4 = [0\ 1\ 0\ 0\ 1\ 0\ 0\ 0\ 0\ 0],$$

$$\mathbf{CL}_4\mathbf{E}_D = [0.51\ -0.65\ 0.98\ -0.85\ -0.51\ -0.33\ 0.00\ 0.00\ 0.00\ -0.16] \rightarrow$$
$$\mathbf{CL}_5 = [0\ 0\ 1\ 0\ 0\ 0\ 0\ 0\ 0\ 0],$$

$$\mathbf{CL}_5\mathbf{E}_D = [-0.26\ 0.00\ -0.25\ 1.00\ 0.75\ 0.00\ 0.00\ 0.00\ 0.00\ 0.00] \rightarrow$$
$$\mathbf{CL}_6 = [0\ 0\ 0\ 1\ 1\ 0\ 0\ 0\ 0\ 0],$$

$$\mathbf{CL}_6\mathbf{E}_D = [1.51\ -0.16\ 0.25\ -0.59\ -0.76\ -0.83\ 0.00\ 0.00\ 0.00\ -0.16] \rightarrow$$
$$\mathbf{CL}_1 = [1\ 0\ 0\ 0\ 0\ 0\ 0\ 0\ 0\ 0],$$

Figure 18.15a shows the hand-designed limit cycle from the previous section. Figure 18.15b shows the limit cycle from FCM found with differential Hebbian learning. The DHL limit cycle is one step shorter. Both FCMs have just one limit cycle and the null fixed point in the space of 2^{10} binary state vectors. The value of $\mathbf{E}_{D5}$ does not change over two intervals. The learning law in (42) learns only if there is a change in the node.

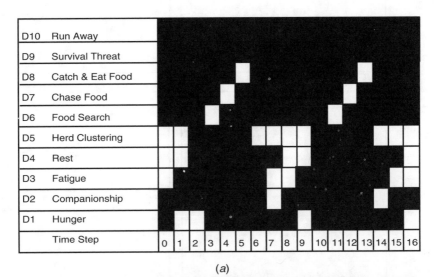

(a)

(b)

Figure 18.15   Limit cycle comparison between the hand-designed system and
the FCM found with differential Hebbian learning. Each col-
umn is a binary state vector. (a) Rest, feed, play, rest limit cycle
for the FCM in Figure 18.9. (b) Limit cycle for the FCM found
with (42).

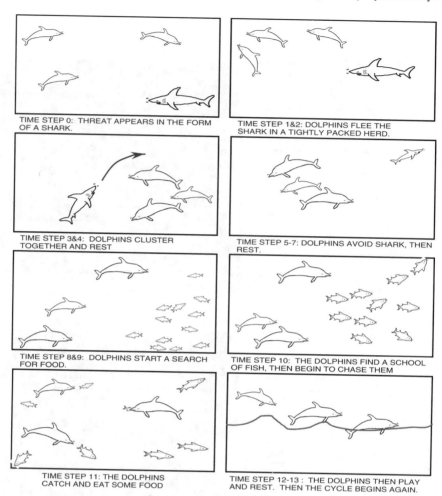

Figure 18.16   The FCM output states can guide a cartoon of the virtual world. This cartoon shows the dolphin chase, rest, eat sequence described in Section 18.3. The cartoon animates the FCM dynamics as the system trajectory moves through the FCM state space.

18.6 CONCLUSIONS

Fuzzy cognitive maps can model the causal web of a virtual world. The FCM can control its local and global nonlinear behavior. The local fuzzy rules or edges and the fuzzy concepts they connect model the causal links within and between events. The global FCM nonlinear dynamics give the virtual world an ''arrow of time.'' A user can change these dynamics at will and thus change the causal processes in the virtual world. FCMs let experts and users choose a causal web by drawing causal pictures instead of by stating equations.

FCMs can also help visualize data. They show how variables relate to one another in the causal web. The FCM output states can guide a cartoon of the virtual world as shown in Figure 18.16. This cartoon shows the dolphin chase, rest, eat sequence described earlier. The cartoon animates the FCM dynamics as the system trajectory moves through the FCM state space. This can apply to models in economics, medicine, history, and politics [31] where the social and causal web can change in complex ways that may arise from changing the sign or magnitude of a single FCM causal rule or edge.

The additive structure of combined FCMs permits a Delphi [32] or questionnaire approach to knowledge acquisition. These new causal webs can change an adaptive FCM that learns its causal web as neural-like learning laws process time-series data. Experts can add their FCM matrices to the adaptive FCM to initialize or guide the learning. Such a causal web can learn the user's values and action habits and perhaps can test them or train them.

More complex FCMs have more complex dynamics and can model more complex virtual worlds. Each concept node can fire on its own time scale and fire in its own nonlinear way. The causal edge flows or rules can have their own time scales too and may increase or decrease the causal flow through them in nonlinear ways. This behavior does not fit in a simple FCM with threshold concepts and constant edge weights.

A FCM can model these complex virtual worlds if it uses more nonlinear math to change its nodes and edges. The price paid may be a chaotic virtual world with unknown equilibrium behavior. Some users may want this to add novelty to their virtual world or to make it more exciting. A user might choose a virtual world that is mildly nonlinear and has periodic equilibria. At the other extreme the user might choose a virtual world that is so wildly nonlinear it has only aperiodic equilibria. Think of a virtual game of tennis or racquetball where the gravitational potential changes at will or at random.

Fuzziness and nonlinearity are design parameters for a virtual world. They may give a better model of a real process. Or they may simply offer more entertainment choices.

References

[1] M. Krueger, *Artificial Reality II*, 2nd ed., Reading, MA: Addison-Wesley, 1991.

[2] W. Gibson, *Neuromancer*, New York: Ace Books, 1984.

[3] R. A. Brown, *Fluid Mechanics of the Atmosphere*, New York: Academic Press, 1991.

[4] J. J. Craig, *Introduction to Robotics*, Reading, MA: Addison-Wesley, 1986.

[5] E. Ackerman, L. Gatewood, J. Rosevear, and G. Molnar, ''Blood Glucose Regulation and Diabetes,'' in *Concepts and Models of Biomathematics*, F. Heinmets, ed., New York: Marcel Dekker, 1969.

[6] B. Kosko, ''Fuzzy Cognitive Maps,'' *International Journal Man-Machine Studies*, Vol. 24, No. 1, pp. 65–75, 1986.

[7] B. Kosko, ''Hidden Patterns in Combined and Adaptive Knowledge Networks,'' *International Journal of Approximate Reasoning*, Vol. 2, pp. 337–393, 1988.

[8] B. Kosko, *Neural Networks and Fuzzy Systems*, Englewood Cliffs, NJ: Prentice Hall, 1992.

[9] B. Kosko, "Fuzzy Systems as Universal Approximators," *IEEE Transactions on Computers*, Vol. 43, No. 11, Nov., pp. 1329–1333, Nov. 1994.

[10] H. T. Nguyen, "On Random Sets and Belief Functions," *Journal of Mathematical Analysis and Applications*, Vol. 65, No. 1–2, pp. 531–542, 1978.

[11] K. Hornik, M. Stinchcombe and H. White, "Multilayer Feedforward Networks Are Universal Approximators," *Neural Networks*, Vol. 2, No. 5, pp. 359–366, 1989.

[12] F. A. Watkins, "Fuzzy Engineering," Ph.D. Thesis, University of California at Irvine, 1994.

[13] L. Wang and J. M. Mendel, "Fuzzy Basis Functions, Universal Approximation, and Orthogonal Least-Squares Learning," *IEEE Transactions on Neural Networks*, Vol. 3, No. 5, pp. 807–814, Sept. 1992.

[14] D. F. Specht, "A General Regression Neural Network," *IEEE Transactions on Neural Networks*, Vol. 2, No. 6, pp. 569–576, Nov. 1991.

[15] B. Kosko, "Optimal Fuzzy Rules Cover Extrema," *International Journal of Intelligent Systems*, Vol. 10, No. 2, pp. 249–255, 1995.

[16] F. A. Watkins, "The Representation Problem for Additive Fuzzy Systems," *Proceedings of the 1995 IEEE International Conference on Fuzzy Systems (IEEE FUZZ-95)*, Vol. I, pp. 117–122, 1995.

[17] J. A. Dickerson and B. Kosko, "Virtual Worlds as Fuzzy Cognitive Maps," *Presence*, Vol. 3, No. 2, pp. 173–189, Spring, 1994.

[18] P. H. Winston, *Artificial Intelligence*, 2nd ed. Reading, MA: Addison-Wesley, 1984.

[19] W. R. Taber and M. Siegel, "Estimation of Expert Weights with Fuzzy Cognitive Maps," *Proceedings of the 1st IEEE International Conference on Neural Networks (ICNN-87)*, San Diego, Vol. II, pp. 319–325, 1987.

[20] B. Kosko, "Bidirectional Associative Memories," *IEEE Transactions Systems, Man, and Cybernetics*, Vol. 18, No. 1, pp. 49–60, 1988.

[21] R. A. Brooks, "A Robot That Walks: Emergent Behaviors from a Carefully Evolved Network," *Neural Computation*, Vol. 1, No. 2, pp. 253–262, 1989.

[22] S. Grossberg, *Studies of Mind and Brain*, Boston: Reidel, 1982.

[23] N. I. Badler, B. L. Webber, J. Kalita and J. Esakov, "Animation from Instructions," in *Making Them Move: Mechanics, Control, and Animation of Articulated Figures*, N. I. Badler, B. A. Barsky and D. Zeltzer, eds., San Mateo, CA: Morgan Kaufmann, pp. 51–98, 1991.

[24] J. H. Connell, *Minimalist Mobile Robotics: A Colony-style Architecture for an Artificial Creature*, New York: Academic Press, Harcourt Brace Jovanovich, 1990.

[25] S. H. Shane, "Comparison of Bottlenose Dolphin Behavior in Texas and Florida, with a Critique of Methods for Studying Dolphin Behavior," in *The Bottlenose Dolphin*, S. Leatherwood and R. R. Reeves, eds., New York: Academic Press, pp. 541–558, 1990.

[26] B. O. Koopman, *Search and Screening*, New York: Pergamon Press, 1980.

[27] B. L. Partridge, "The Structure and Function of Fish Schools," *Scientific American*, Vol. 246, No. 6, pp. 114–123, 1982.

[28] D. Weihs and W. P. W., "Optimal Avoidance and Evasion Tactics in Predator–Prey Interactions," *Journal of Theoretical Biology*, Vol. 106, No. 2, pp. 189–206, 1984.

[29] J. A. Dickerson, "Fuzzy Function Approximation with Ellipsoidal Rules," *Ph.D. Thesis*, University of Southern California, 1993.

[30] Y. F. Wang, J. B. Cruz, and J. H. Mulligan, "Guaranteed Recall of All Training Pairs for Bidirectional Associative Memory," *IEEE Transactions on Neural Networks*, Vol. 2, No. 6, pp. 559–567, 1991.

[31] W. R. Taber, "Knowledge Processing with Fuzzy Cognitive Maps," *Expert Systems with Applications*, Vol. 2, No. 1, pp. 83–87, 1991.

[32] J. P. Martino, *Technological Forecasting for Decisionmaking*, New York: American Elsevier, 1972.

[33] J. A. Dickerson and B. Kosko, "Fuzzy Function Approximation with Supervised Ellipsoidal Learning," *Proceedings of the World Conference on Neural Networks (WCNN '93)*, Portland, OR, Vol. II, pp. 9–17, 1993.

[34] J. A. Dickerson and B. Kosko, "Fuzzy Function Learning with Covariance Ellipsoids," *Proceedings of the IEEE International Conference on Neural Networks (IEEE ICNN-93)*, San Francisco, pp. 1162–1167, 1993.

[35] J. A. Dickerson and B. Kosko, "Fuzzy Function Approximation with Ellipsoidal Rules," *IEEE Transactions on Systems, Man, and Cybernetics*, Part B, Vol. 26, No. 4, pp. 542–560.

[36] B. Kosko, "Stochastic Competitive Learning," *IEEE Transactions on Neural Networks*, Vol. 2, No. 5, pp. 522–529, 1991.

[37] H. M. Kim and B. Kosko, "Fuzzy Prediction and Filtering in Impulsive Noise," *Fuzzy Sets and Systems*, Vol. 77, No. 1, pp. 15–33, 1996.

Appendix A: Proof of the Fuzzy Approximation Theorem

Fuzzy Approximation Theorem An additive fuzzy system uniformly approximates $f: X \to Y$ if X is compact and f is continuous.

Proof: Pick any small constant $\epsilon > 0$. We must show that $|F(x) - f(x)| < \epsilon$ for all $x \in X$. X is a compact subset of R_n. $F(x)$ is the centroidal output (1) of the additive fuzzy system F. Continuity of f on compact X gives uniform continuity. So there is a fixed distance δ such that, for all x and z in X, $|f(x) - f(z)| < \epsilon/4$ if $|x - z| < \delta$. (Replace δ by δ/n for any L^p space with $p > 1$.) We can construct a set of open cubes $M_1, \cdots, M_m$ that cover X and that have ordered overlap in their n coordinates so that each cube corner lies at the midpoint c_j of its neighbors M_j. Pick symmetric output fuzzy sets B_j centered on $f(c_j)$. So the centroid of B_j is $f(c_j)$.

Pick $u \in X$. Then by construction u lies in at most 2^j overlapping open cubes M_j. Pick any w in the same set of cubes. If $u \in M_j$ and $w \in M_k$, then for all $v \in M_j \cap M_k$: $|u - v| < \delta$ and $|v - w| < \delta$. Uniform continuity implies that $|f(u) - f(w)| \leq |f(u) - f(v)| + |f(v) - f(w)| < \frac{\epsilon}{2}$. So for cube centers c_j and c_k, $|f(c_j) - f(c_k)| < \frac{\epsilon}{2}$.

Pick $x \in X$. Then x too lies in at most 2^j open cubes with centers c_j and $|f(c_j) - f(x)| < \frac{\epsilon}{2}$. Along the kth coordinate of the range space R^p, the kth component of the additive system centroid $F(x)$ lies on or between the kth components of the centroids of the B_j sets. So, since $|f(c_j) - f(c_k)| < \frac{\epsilon}{2}$ for all $f(c_j)$, $|F(x) - f(c_j)| < \frac{\epsilon}{2}$. Then

$$|F(x) - f(x)| \leq |F(x) - f(c_j)| + |f(c_j) - f(x)| < \frac{\epsilon}{2} + \frac{\epsilon}{2} = \epsilon$$

Q.E.D.

Appendix B: Learning in SAMs: Unsupervised Clustering and Supervised Gradient Descent

A fuzzy system learns if and only if its rule patches move or change shape in the input-output product space $X \times Y$. Learning can change the centers or widths of triangle or trapezoidal sets. These changing sets then change the shape or position of the Cartesian rule patches built out of them. The mean-value theorem and the calculus of variations show [15] that optimal lone rules cover the extrema or bumps of the approximand. Good learning schemes [33,34,35] tend to quickly move rules patches to these bumps and then move extra rule patches between them as the rule budget allows. Hybrid schemes use unsupervised clustering to learn the first set of fuzzy rule patches in position and number and to initialize gradient descent in supervised learning.

Learning changes system parameters with data. Unsupervised learning amounts to blind clustering in the system product space $X \times Y$ to learn and tune the m fuzzy rules or the sets that compose them. Then k quantization vectors $q_j \in X \times Y$ move in the product space to filter or approximate the stream of incoming data pairs $(x(t), y(t))$ or the concatenated data points $z(t) = [x(t)|y(t)]^T$. The simplest form of such *product space clustering* [8] centers a rule patch at each data point and thus puts $k = m$. In general, both the data and the quantizing vectors greatly outnumber the rules and so $k >> m$.

A natural way to grow and tune rules is to identify a rule patch with the uncertainty ellipsoid [33,34,35] that forms around each quantizing vector q_j from the inverse of its positive definite covariance matrix K_j. Then sparse or noisy data grow a patch larger and gives a less certain rule than do denser or less noisy data. Unsupervised competitive learning [8] can learn these ellipsoidal rules in three steps:

$$\|z(t) - q_j(t)\| = \min(\|z(t) - q_1(t)\|, \ldots, \|z(t) - q_k(t)\|) \tag{B.1}$$

$$q_i(t+1) = \begin{cases} q_j(t) + \mu_t[z(t) - q_j(t)] & \text{if } i = j \\ q_i(t) & \text{if } i \neq j \end{cases} \tag{B.2}$$

$$K_i(t+1) = \begin{cases} K_j(t) + v_t[(z(t) - q_j(t))^T(z(t) - q_j(t)) - K_j(t)] & \text{if } i = j \\ K_i(t) & \text{if } i \neq j \end{cases} \tag{B.3}$$

for the Euclidean norm $\|z\|^2 = z_1^2 + \cdots + z_{n+p}^2$.

The first step (B.1) is the competitive step [36]. It picks the nearest quantizing vector q_j to the incoming data vector $z(t)$ and ignores the rest. Some schemes may count nearby vectors as lying in the winning subset. We used just one winner per datum. This correlation matching approximates the competitive dynamics of nonlinear neural networks. The second step updates the winning quantization or ''synaptic'' vector and drives it toward the centroid of the sampled data pattern class [36]. The third step updates the covariance matrix of the winning quantization vector. We initialize the quantization vector with sample data $(q_i(0) = z(i))$ to avoid skewed groupings and to initialize the covariance matrix with small positive numbers on its diagonal to keep it positive definite. Projection schemes [33,34,35] can then convert the ellipsoids into fuzzy sets along each coordinate of the input-output space. Other schemes can use the unfactored joint set function directly [37]. Supervised learning can also tune the eigenvalue parameters of the rule ellipsoids.

The sequences of learning coefficients $\{\mu_t\}$ and $\{v_t\}$ should decrease slowly [8] in the sense of $\sum_{t=1}^{\infty} \mu_t = \infty$ but not too slowly in the sense of $\sum_{t=1}^{\infty} \mu_t^2 < \infty$. In practice, $\mu_t \approx \frac{1}{t}$. The covariance coefficients obey a like constraint as in our choice of $v_t = 0.2[1 - \frac{t}{1.2N}]$ where N is the total number of data points. The supervised learning schemes below also use a similar sequence of decreasing learning coefficients.

Supervised learning changes SAM parameters with error data. The error at each time t is the desired system output minus the actual SAM output: $\varepsilon_t = d_t - F(x_t)$. Unsupervised learning uses the blind data point $z(t)$ instead of the desired or labeled value d_t. The teacher or supervisor supervises the learning process by giving the desired value d_t at each training time t. Most supervised learning schemes perform stochastic gradient descent on the squared error and do so through iterated use of the chain rule of differential calculus.

Supervised gradient descent can learn or tune SAM systems [34,35] by changing the rule weights w_j in (B.4), the then-part volumes V_j, the then-part centroids c_j, or parameters of the if-part set functions a_j. The rule weight w_j enters the ratio form of the general SAM system

$$F(x) = \frac{\sum_{j=1}^{m} w_j \, a_j(x) \, V_j \, c_j}{\sum_{j=1}^{m} w_j \, a_j(x) \, V_j} \tag{B.4}$$

in the same way as does the then-part volume V_j in the SAM Theorem. Both cancel from (B.4) if they have the same value—if $w_1 = \cdots = w_m > 0$ or if $V_1 = \cdots = V_m > 0$. So both have the same learning law if we replace the nonzero weight w_j with the nonzero volume V_j [35]:

$$w_j(t+1) = w_j(t) - \mu_t \frac{\partial E_t}{\partial w_j} \tag{B.5}$$

$$= w_j(t) - \mu_t \frac{\partial E_t}{\partial F} \frac{\partial F}{\partial w_j} \tag{B.6}$$

$$= w_j(t) + \mu_t \, \varepsilon_t \frac{p_j(x_t)}{w_j(t)} [c_j - F(x_t)] \tag{B.7}$$

for instantaneous squared error $E_t = \frac{1}{2}(d_t - F(x_t))^2$ with desired-minus-actual error $\varepsilon_t = d_t - F(x_t)$. We include the rule weights here for completeness. Our fuzzy systems were unweighted and thus used $w_1 = \cdots = w_m > 0$. The volumes then change in the same way if they are independent of the weights (which they may not be in some ellipsoidal learning schemes):

$$V_j(t+1) = V_j(t) - \mu_t \frac{\partial E_t}{\partial V_j} \tag{B.8}$$

$$= V_j(t) + \mu_t \varepsilon_t \frac{p_j(x_t)}{V_j(t)} [c_j - F(x_t)] \tag{B.9}$$

The learning law (B.7) follows since $\frac{\partial E_t}{\partial F} = -\varepsilon$ and since

$$\frac{\partial F}{\partial w_j} = \frac{a_j(x) \, V_j \, c_j \sum\limits_{i=1}^{m} w_i \, a_i(x) \, V_i - a_j(x) \, V_j \sum\limits_{i=1}^{m} w_i \, a_i(x) \, V_i \, c_i}{\left(\sum\limits_{i=1}^{m} w_i \, a_i(x) \, V_i \right)^2} \tag{B.10}$$

$$= \frac{w_j \, a_j(x) \, V_j}{w_j \sum\limits_{i=1}^{m} w_i \, a_i(x) \, V_i} \left[\frac{c_j \sum\limits_{i=1}^{m} w_i \, a_i(x) \, V_i}{\sum\limits_{i=1}^{m} w_i \, a_i(x) \, V_i} - \frac{\sum\limits_{i=1}^{m} w_i \, a_i(x) \, V_i \, c_i}{\sum\limits_{i=1}^{m} w_i \, a_i(x) \, V_i} \right] \tag{B.11}$$

$$= \frac{p_j(x)}{w_j} [c_j - F(x)] \tag{B.12}$$

from the SAM Theorem.

The centroid c_j in the SAM Theorem has the simplest learning law:

$$c_j(t+1) = c_j(t) - \mu_t \frac{\partial E_t}{\partial F} \frac{\partial F}{\partial c_j} \tag{B.13}$$

$$= c_j(t) + \mu_t \varepsilon_t \, p_j(x_t) \tag{B.14}$$

So the terms w_j, V_j, and c_j do not change when $p_j \approx 0$ and thus when the jth if-part set barely fires: $a_j(x_t) \approx 0$.

Tuning the if-part sets involves more computation since the update law contains an extra partial derivative. Suppose that the if-part set function a_j is a function of l parameters: $a_j = a_j(m_j^1, \ldots, m_j^l)$. Then we can update each parameter with

$$m_j^k(t+1) = m_j^k(t) - \mu_t \frac{\partial E_t}{\partial F} \frac{\partial F}{\partial a_j} \frac{\partial a_j}{\partial m_j^k} \tag{B.15}$$

$$= m_j^k(t) + \mu_t \, \varepsilon_t \, \frac{p_j(x_t)}{a_j(x_t)}[c_j - F(x_t)]\frac{\partial a_j}{\partial m_j^k} \tag{B.16}$$

Exponential if-part set functions can reduce the learning complexity. They have the form $a_j = e^{f_j(m_j^1,\ldots,m_j^l)}$ and obey $\frac{\partial a_j}{\partial m_j^k} = a_j \frac{\partial f_j(m_j^1,\ldots,m_j^l)}{\partial m_j^k}$. Then the parameter update (B.16) simplifies to

$$m_j^k(t+1) = m_j^k(t) + \mu_t \, \varepsilon_t \, p_j(x_t)[c_j - F(x_t)]\frac{\partial f_j}{\partial m_j^k} \tag{B.17}$$

This can arise for independent exponential or Gaussian sets $a_j(x) = \prod_{i=1}^{n} \exp\{f_j^i(x_i)\} = \exp\{\sum_{i=1}^{n} f_j^i(x_i)\} = \exp\{f_j(x)\}$. The exponential set function

$$a_j(x) = \exp\{\sum_{i=1}^{n} u_j^i(v_j^i - x_i)\} \tag{B.18}$$

has partial derivatives $\frac{\partial f_j}{\partial u_j^k} = v_j^k - x_k(t)$ and $\frac{\partial f_j}{\partial v_j^k} = u_j^k$.

The Gaussian set function

$$a_j(x) = \exp\{-\frac{1}{2}\sum_{i=1}^{n}(\frac{x_i - m_j^i}{\sigma_j^i})^2\} \tag{B.19}$$

has mean partial derivative $\frac{\partial f_j}{\partial m_j^k} = \frac{x_k - m_j^k}{(\sigma_j^k)^2}$ and variance partial derivative $\frac{\partial f_j}{\partial \sigma_j^k} = \frac{(x_k - m_j^k)^2}{(\sigma_j^k)^3}$.
Such Gaussian set functions reduce the SAM model to Specht's [14] radial basis function network. We can use the smooth update law (B.17) to update non-differentiable triangles or trapezoids or other sets by viewing their centers and widths as the Gaussian means and variances.

Chapter 19

MULTIMEDIA VISUAL
TELEPHONE SYSTEM

Liang-Gee Chen and Chung-Wei Ku

Abstract

This chapter concentrates on multimedia visual telephone systems. The related standards, such as ISO MPEG-4 and ITU-T H.324, are explored briefly, and the goal of these standards is explained, respectively. The basic function of an H.324 terminal for multimedia communications is described, and related standards for a video and speech codec are covered. The differences between H.261 and H.263, which serves as the video standard for H.324, are pointed out, and the new advanced coding modes for H.263 are described. Both objective and subjective results are provided to show the excellent performance of the H.263 coding method. Finally, future developments of the multimedia visual telephone systems are also discussed.

19.1 INTRODUCTION

From simple telephone communications to advanced virtual reality applications, multimedia will enter our daily life. What is multimedia? Generally speaking, a multimedia system supports a large variety of information, which includes text, audio, image, video, or other signals for human sense. The basic motivation of multimedia is to support a vivid interface for humans to understand, analyze, or interact with computers and other users. The influence of this evolution encompasses the area of education, entertainment, consumer electronics, or even sociology. The focus of this chapter is the impact of multimedia communications, especially the video coding technology for visual telephony application.

19.1.1 Why Multimedia Communication?

We communicate with other people every day. It may be about business, ordinary gossip, or private appointment via telephones, FAX, or cordless terminals. Since the basic purpose of "communication" is to exchange messages with other individuals, the interface and the way to present this information are very important in terms of both efficiency and convenience. In order to give a complete presentation to others, a multimedia interface for such a purpose is required. For example, we discuss with others in a business conference, we would like to show our slides, product videotapes, or even 3-D demonstrations, in addition to the original speech and gesture presentations. In order to satisfy many kinds of interactions, multimedia communications over networks become an emergent solution. Try to imagine how much can be saved by using this approach: traveling cost, paper materials, printing equipment, and delivery expenses. On the other hand, the way for us to interact/present the information might be changed. Many difficulties due to distance will be conquered by the power of networks.

multimedia.eps

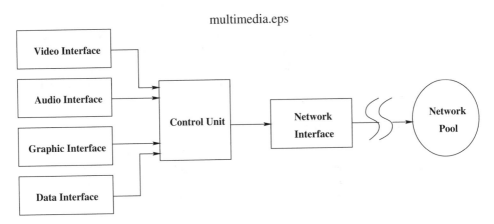

Figure 19.1   Basic block diagram of a multimedia communication system.

Since the way for us to receive messages is bounded by our sensory system, some basic requirements for a multimedia communication system are described and displayed in Fig. 19.1. In order to achieve long-distance communications, a network interface is necessary. This network may be the Integrated Services Digital Network (ISDN), the General Switched Telephone Network (GSTN), or a wireless network. In addition, to achieve satisfactory interaction with others, video and audio interfaces are necessary for a basic face-to-face virtual environment. Due to the requirements of other multimedia demonstrations, communications of data, or graphics, such as white board, are also included but not necessary. However, it is believed that the portion of this information will grow rapidly for multimedia communications. Because of the network's limited bandwidth, compression of this information becomes inevitable. Compared to other types of information, the bandwidth and speed requirements of video are the highest; therefore, video coding becomes the crucial part of this system. In fact, one of the most impressive developments in the recent history of digital video compression has occurred in the standard area. In the last six years, a spectrum of standards in digital video coding have been developed for different applications. These standards include the ISO/IEC Joint Picture Coding Expert Group (JPEG) [1] for still images; the ITU-T (CCITT before) H.261 [2] for coding videophone/videoconferencing pictures over ISDN; the ISO/IEC Motion Picture Coding Expert Group Phase 1 standard (MPEG-1) [3] for coding full-motion video with VHS quality; the ISO/IEC MPEG-2 international standard [4] at various quality levels for different applications; and the North America HDTV standard from the "Grand Alliance" companies [5].

All of these digital video coding standards have been developed for video communications at relatively higher bit rates. For example, MPEG-1 addresses entertainment applications in which about 1.5 Mbps is typically needed for a reasonable quality. H.320 (with H.261 video codec) deals with video conferencing applications with ISDN connection where the bandwidth is $p \times 64$ Kbps. Currently, however, the largest existing communication infrastructure is based on the General Switched Telephone Network (GSTN). As a result, it is desirable to define an audiovisual standard that can use the state-of-the-art modem technology, that is, V.34 modem, over the existing GSTN. Moreover, the trend of future communication is toward mobility, which will add to design difficulties even more. Based on these motivations, MPEG-4 and H.263 video coding standards started from the point of very low bit-rate video coding for the communication of multimedia over a bandwidth-limited channel.

19.1.2 The MPEG-4 Standard

As early as May 1991, the ISO Moving Picture Expert Group (MPEG) raised the issue of an audiovisual standard targeted at the bit rate of 4.8–64 Kbps, for limited channel bandwidth and limited storage capacity. These efforts were approved in July 1993 with the MPEG-4 nickname and the title ''Very Low Bit-Rate Coding of Moving Pictures and Associated Audio'' [6]. To avoid building an expensive high-speed network, it seems to be more cost-effective to transmit information via current GSTN. Basically, the MPEG-4 standard was originated by the ISO/SG15/WG11 to provide a generic coding for very low bit-rate below 64 Kbps, mainly by the United States. In addition to the need of infrastructure, it was felt that a breakthrough in video compression technology might occur by 1997. Such a huge advance in the compression ratio may require a fundamentally different methodology from the existing waveform-based coding scheme. Therefore, very low bit-rate video coding has become a hot topic and attracted the attention of many researchers at that time. Until July 1994, however, there was still no significant evidence that such a revolution had been achieved within the MPEG-4 schedule. In light of this situation, a change of direction was proposed to focus on new or improved functionalities that are not addressed by other existing and emerging standards. This new direction and vision materialized in the 1994 meeting in New Jersey, and was incorporated into the MPEG-4 Proposal Package Description (PPD) in the Singapore WG11 meeting in November 1994.

Currently, MPEG-4 is still under development, but its goal focuses on supporting new ways (especially content-based) for communications, access, and manipulation of digital audiovisual data. MPEG-4 would like to provide a flexible framework and an open set of tools supporting a range of both novel and conventional functionalities. Because of the tendency towards integration of video services and the increasing importance of multimedia services, a demand has also arisen for new functionalities of the coding algorithm. With the vision that a new class of applications is emerging from the enlarging intersection of telecommunication, TV/film entertainment, and the computer industry, MPEG-4 will try to provide an audiovisual coding standard that will allow interactivity, high compression, universal accessibility, a high degree of flexibility, and extensibility. In order to meet the above trends, eight new or improved functionalities, which are not supported by existing standards, are defined as follows:

1. Content-based manipulation and bit-stream editing.
2. Content-based multimedia data access tools.
3. Content-based scalability.
4. Coding of multiple concurrent data streams.
5. Hybrid natural and synthetic data coding.

6. Improved coding efficiency.

7. Improved temporal access at very low bit rates.

8. Robustness in error-prone environments.

At the present time, MPEG-4 is structured in terms of syntax, tools, algorithms, and profiles. MPEG-4 might be a quite large superset of many intelligent coding methods, including one set for visual telephone which is covered by the ITU-T H.263 standard. Since this chapter focuses on the multimedia visual telephone, more details about MPEG-4 can be found in other chapters.

19.1.3 H.263: Video Coding Standard for the Visual Telephone System

The ITU-T efforts concerning the multimedia visual telephone system can be subdivided into a near-term and a long-term activity. The goal of the near-term effort was to develop a complete set of recommendations for a very low bit-rate audiovisual terminal by 1995. One motivation for this standard, H.324, was the actual need for interoperability between GSTN-videophones. However, the goal for the near term is a low bit-rate multimedia platform, which is also suitable for mobile channels. The goal of the long-term activity is to develop new audio and video coding algorithms with more advanced innovations by 1998. The quality of the coded video is a key issue to judge the performance of the very low bit-rate visual telephony. Currently, the objective for the near term is significantly better quality compared with H.261, and it is indeed achieved and defined in H.263. However, the coding algorithm for the near term is based on existing technologies with little modifications. For the long-term solution, the objective should be considerably better than the near term. The new algorithm that will improve the coding quality greatly is expected to be available in 1998.

The near-term standard of H.263 is an adaptation and improvement of existing standards. The important issue for the near term involves picture format, overhead, and reduction of block artifacts. Basically, the coding quality of H.263 is much better than that of H.261 depending on the content of the video scene and the coding parameters. However, the overhead for H.263 is negligible if the minimal requirement is implemented. H.263 includes several negotiations that will increase its complexity, but also enhance the coding performance. More attention should be paid to the relation between the near-term and long-term standards. Even when the long-term standard replaces the near-term one, the near-term standard might be a fallback mode for the long-term standard. In addition to the new techniques, such as shape coding or affine motion compensation, the traditional DCT and block-based motion compensation will still be used in the long-term standard for picture initialization and model failure areas. Besides, the picture formats must be compatible for both standards.

The goal of the long-term standard is to achieve significant progress in coding efficiency compared with the near-term standard. New coding concepts, such as a good source model, is expected to produce an improvement in quality. Similar to what happened in speech coding, the progress of video coding can be briefly described in Table 19.1. The new coding methods based on advanced source models, such as knowledge-based coding, object-based coding, 3-D model-based coding, and 3-D structure extraction coding, can be found in the

Table 19.1 Different Source Models Based on Video
Coding Methods

Stage	Source model	Coded element	Coding techniques
1	Pixel	Color of pixels	PCM
2	Statistically dependent pixels	Color or block of pixels	Predictive or transform coding
3	Translated blocks	Color of blocks or motion vectors	Motion-compensated DCT coding
4	Moving structure	Affine parameters or shape and motion	Fractal, color/texture coding
5	Moving unknown objects	Shape, motion, and color of objects	Analysis/synthesis coding
6	Moving known objects	Shape, motion, and color of known objects	Knowledge-based coding
7	Facial expression	Action units	Semantic coding

literature [9]. The methods listed in the table are ordered according to the complexity of coding models. Obviously, going downward in Table 19.1, more restriction about video content is assumed, but more coding gain is obtained. However, due to the limitation of current computer technologies and understanding of video content, the feasibility of those advanced model-based video coding methods is still under exploration. Since H.263 is part of a set of recommendations for a very low bit-rate audiovisual terminal, the long-term standard will be developed in joint cooperation with MPEG-4.

19.2 SYSTEM CONFIGURATION FOR THE MULTIMEDIA VISUAL TELEPHONE

In this section, only the near-term standard is discussed. Basically, the goal of the near term is merely focused on the audiovisual terminal over GSTN or wireless channels. However, more considerations are included for future multimedia progress and the compatibility of heterogeneous networks. In addition, the proposed standard gives backward compatibility with H.320 which is designed for video conferencing over ISDN. Furthermore, the V.34 modem or even a mobile interface such as IS-54, IS-96, or GSM are also available because of the layered coder.

19.2.1 Overview of the System

The overall multimedia visual telephone system is described in the ITU-T H.324 standard. The proposed terminal may carry real-time voice, data, and video, or any combination. In fact, the visual telephone might be just one of the applications. H.324 terminals

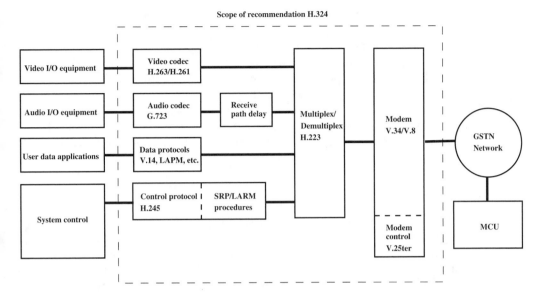

Figure 19.2 Block diagram for the H.324 multimedia system.

may be integrated into personal computers or implemented in stand-alone devices such as videophones. Support of the media type is optional; however, the ability to use a specified common mode for the given media is required for the purpose of interworking. In fact, the compatibility of H.324 and H.320 terminals is quite high.

The block diagram of the H.324 terminal is shown in Fig. 19.2. The video codec is based on H.263, and the speech codec is defined in the G.723 standard. In addition, control of the system is covered in H.245. All the coded elements are multiplexed according to the rules in H.223 into a single bit stream for the V.34 modem, which modulates the digital data for the analog GSTN channel. In fact, several standards are related to the audiovisual telephone:

1. ITU-T Recommendation H.324: "Terminal for low bit-rate multimedia communication," Nov. 1995.

2. ITU-T Recommendation H.263: "Video coding for lot bit-rate communication," Nov. 1995.

3. ITU-T Recommendation G.723: "Dual rate speech coder for multimedia communications transmission at 5.3 & 6.3 Kbps," Nov. 1995.

4. ITU-T Recommendation H.223: "Multiplexing protocol for low bit-rate multimedia communications," Nov. 1995.

5. ITU-T Recommendation H.245: "Control protocol for multimedia communication," Nov. 1995.

T.120 is used for data interface; the V.8 procedure is employed to start and stop data transmission.

H.324 makes use of the logical channel signaling procedures of H.245, in which the content of each logical channel is described when the channel is open. Since the transmission is limited to the ability of the decoder, procedures are provided for expressing the abilities of receiver and transmitter. Because the protocols of H.245 are also planned for use by Recommendation H.310 for ATM networks, and Recommendation H.323 for nonguaranteed bandwidth LANs, interworking with these systems should be straightforward. H.324 terminals may be used in multipoint configurations through MCUs and may interwork with H.320 terminals on the ISDN, as well as with terminals on wireless networks.

19.2.2   H.263: Video Codec

The most computationally expensive part of the H.324 terminal concerns the H.263 video codec. It is an optimized version of the combination of H.261 and MPEG-1 in order to achieve more advanced schemes. The target bit rate for this near-term video coding standard is up to 64 Kbps, but for GSTN videophone the maximum video bit rate will be about 20 Kbps since other bandwidth must be reserved for speech, data, control, or others via the 28.8 Kbps V.34 modem. Target networks are the GSTN and mobile networks. A generalized form of the source coder can be shown as Fig. 19.3. It is almost the same as H.261 or MPEG. The main elements are prediction (motion estimation), block transform (discrete cosine transform), and quantization. More details about the improved negotiations and the differences between H.261 and H.263 will be discussed in the next section.

One of the important issues in H.263 is the picture format. Selection of picture format for H.263 was based on subjective picture quality, interworking with H.320/H.261, and feasibility for future needs. Finally, five picture formats were adopted for H.263: sub-QCIF (128×96), QCIF (176×144), CIF (352×288), 4 CIF (704×576), and 16 CIF (1408×1152). All the picture formats have the same aspect ratio as CIF, similar to H.261. According to the content of H.263, an H.263 decoder must accept and decode sub-QCIF bit streams. QCIF-type decoders may upsample the sub-QCIF picture but are allowed to display QCIF pictures with black borders. Decoders must also accept and decode QCIF format bit streams. The sub-QCIF-type decoder may downsample the QCIF picture but is allowed to display only parts of the QCIF pictures. In this way, the cost of the codec can be saved, and the interworking with H.261 is guaranteed.

During the development of the H.263 algorithm, the Test Model for the Near-term (TMN) plays an important role. TMN-5 [20] described an encoder implementation of H.263, so that all the H.263 codecs can achieve exactly the same results or generate new proposals on a fair basis. Similar to H.261, H.263 is built on a hybrid DPCM/DCT video coding method. Both H.261 and H.263 use block-based motion compensation, DCT, variable-length coding, scalar quantization, and the macroblock (MB) structure. Although there are many similarities between H.261 and H.263, especially the global procedure of source coding, four additional negotiations are appended to H.263 for performance enhancement. Furthermore, details of the coding algorithm are also quite different from those of H.261. The next section will explain them more clearly.

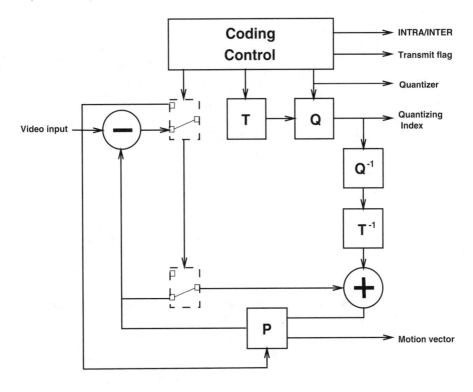

T: Discrete cosine transform

Q: Scalar quantization

P: Picture memory with motion compensation

Figure 19.3 Outline block diagram of the H.263 source coder.

Another important consideration is error resilience. Since H.263 will be used for communication channels under a noisy environment, the immunity of noise and recovery from channel errors are the major concerns. A critical aspect of this issue is that in GSTN or mobile channels network errors appear in burst. Burst errors imply that the single-bit-error correction code, BCH (Boss Chandhuri–Hocquenghem) Code, which is used for H.261, will not be appropriate for H.263. Therefore, resynchronization of the picture structure (such as Group-of-Blocks, GOB) will be quite important, but long delay may be introduced. However, in terms of cost and efficiency, H.263 has only one start code at the beginning of the picture because the retransmission of a new picture might be frequent for most cases. The resilience strategies for decoders are also important. In addition to error resilience, error concealment might be another important issue. Whereas using temporal or spatial correlation is popular and it gives relatively good performance, finding a cost-effective design is still under intensive research.

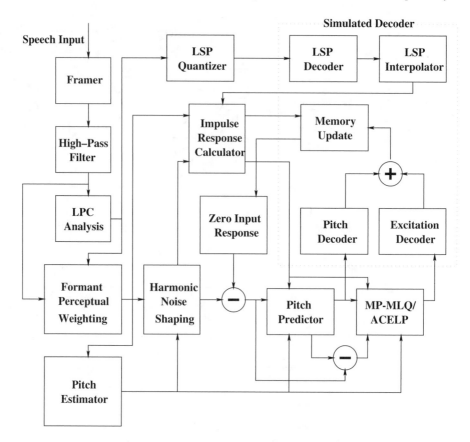

Figure 19.4   Block diagram of the G.723 speech coder.

19.2.3   G.723: Speech Codec

The speech codec for H.324 is defined in G.723. In fact, the standard is now named G.723.1 in order to avoid any confusion with the obsolete ITU standard. It is based on a codeword excitation linear prediction styled codec architecture. That is, speech data are LPC coded at first. The excitation signal is divided into periodic/nonperiodic parts. The pitch of the periodic part is estimated and coded. The nonperiodic component for excitation is approximated in two ways: for the high bit-rate mode, multipulse maximum likelihood quantization (MP-MLQ) excitation is used; and for the low bit-rate mode, an algebraic codebook excitation (ACELP) is used. The block diagram of the speech encoder is shown in Fig. 19.4.

As can be seen, the procedure for speech coding is also a little complex. However, compared with video encoding, speech codec, in terms of implementation, does not cause the bottleneck partly because of its relatively low sampling rate requirements. Since a coding process of the speech part is usually finished before that of the corresponding video part, a delay path is appended to the speech codec, as shown in Fig. 19.2 for the purpose of lip synchronization, which makes the user feel the speech and the movement of lips matched. Since the algorithms of speech coding are covered in other chapters, we do not include the details of the speech codec.

19.3 VIDEO CODING ALGORITHMS FOR THE SYSTEM

We have roughly explained the algorithms about H.263. Since it is the most time-consuming part of the whole system, more details will be provided, especially the difference from H.261 and the negotiations.

19.3.1 H.263 vs. H.261

Although H.263 is indeed an extension of H.261 with some MPEG-like optimization, their primary goals are different. First, target bit rates: the bit rate of H.261 is $p \times 64$ Kbps, while H.263 focuses on a bit rate below 64 Kbps. The reason of the bit rate difference is due to different transmission media. H.261 is used for ISDN, but H.263 is designed for GSTN or a mobile channel via the V.34 modem. Second, the picture formats they use are not the same. H.261 operates on CIF or QCIF pictures, but H.263 supports three other formats, which include sub-QCIF, 4CIF, and 16CIF. It is designed for later heterogeneous media communications. In order to obtain a better coding gain, some other differences are as follows:

1. Half-pixel motion prediction
   The resolution of motion vectors for H.263 is within half-pixel accuracy, which is similar to the definition in MPEG. According to some simulation results from [15], half-pixel accuracy allows significant improvement for conversation applications.

2. Unrestricted motion vector mode
   The motion vectors for H.263 would be able to point a position outside the real frame. It is one of the optional negotiations and will be explained in later subsections.

3. 8×8 block with motion vectors
   Traditionally, motion estimation uses blocks with size 16×16 (macroblock), and the block size for DCT is 8×8 (block) in standards. However, motion vectors for 8×8 blocks are possible in the advanced prediction mode, which is discussed in Section 19.3.4.

4. Syntax-based Arithmetic coding (SAC)
   This is another negotiation for H.263. The Huffman coding-based, variable-length codec might be replaced by Arithmetic coding. A later subsection explains it more clearly.

5. Different Group-of-Block (GOB) structure in H.263
   For H.263, each GOB contains one macroblock row for the purpose of error resilience.

6. No still picture mode
   JPEG can be used for still pictures in H.324.

7. No BCH marker
   Because the error detection/correction in H.261 is not suitable for H.263, it is removed from H.263.

8. Different form of macroblock (MB) addressing
   H.263 has less overhead and different VLC tables at the macroblock level.

9. Different VLC tables at block level
   The quantized coefficients are coded with a 3D VLC (run, level, last coefficient) instead of a 2D VLC (run, level) with the end-of-block (EOB) marker for a higher efficiency.

10. Filter in the loop
    H.261 utilizes a spatial loop-filter in the feedback loop to eliminate the block effect due to block-based motion estimation. However, since the accuracy of the motion estimation for H.263 is half-pixel and overlapped motion compensation is applied to luminance components, they introduce some low-pass filtering effect and the loop filter is removed for H.263.

11. DPCM of motion vectors
    The motion vectors are DPCM coded traditionally. However, the predictor for H.263 is the median of the motion vectors from three previously coded blocks. Such a more precise prediction makes the DPCM (Differential Pulse Code Modulation) coding more efficient.

Generally, most of these differences try to eliminate the overhead of the bit stream for H.263 since they may occupy a large portion of data, especially for very low bit-rate applications. The half-pixel accuracy of the motion vectors is similar to that in MPEG; the way to interpolate the nonexisting pixels is shown in Fig. 19.5. In fact, even if all the optional coding modes for H.263 are turned off, the performance of H.263 is still much

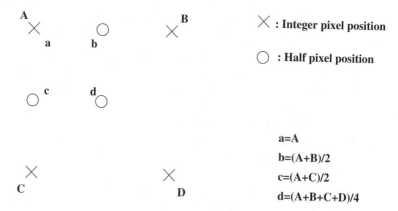

Figure 19.5   Bilinear interpolation for half-pixel positions.

better than H.261 owing to the motion vectors with half-pixel accuracy. In the following subsections, the four negotiations for H.263 are explained, respectively.

19.3.2 Unrestricted Motion Vectors Mode

In traditional standards, the motion vectors are restricted, so that all pixels are required from the previous image inside the frame. As a result, many complete macroblocks at the border of the picture will have a suboptimal prediction. However, for H.263, if the unrestricted motion vector mode is enabled, the motion vector coded can point to a position outside the actual frame region. In addition, the maximal range of motion vectors is extended from the original [-16,15.5] to [-31.5,31.5]. That is, for the current block located in the boundary regions, the range of its motion vector is still from -31.5 to 31.5. The pixels located in the extended region in the referenced frame are assigned values to the nearest existing pixel on the boundary of the original frame. The idea is explained in Fig. 19.6; for a pixel with value $Rumv(x, y)$ in the new extended frame, its pixel value is related to the pixel with value $R(x', y')$ by the following relationship (the following is for QCIF format):

$$Rumv(x, y) = R(x', y'), \tag{1}$$

where $x' = 0, x < 0$
$x' = 175, x > 175$
$x' = x$, others

Similarly,

where $y' = 0, y < 0$
$y' = 143, x > 143$
$y' = y$, others

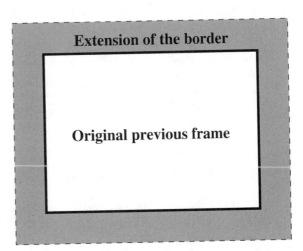

Figure 19.6 Extension of the searching range for the unrestricted motion vector mode.

The unrestricted motion vector mode is useful when the moving objects are entering or moving around the frame border. Consequently, a better prediction candidate can be found in the extended border, especially for small-motion vectors where most pixels of the current macroblock still reference the pixels inside the previous frame. For example, the camera movement might cause such a situation. An important issue is that for a small-image format such as sub-QCIF or QCIF, up to 50% of all the macroblocks are located at the border region. All the definitions of the unrestricted motion vector mode are described in Annex D, document of H.263 [11].

19.3.3 Syntax-based Arithmetic Coding Mode

In the optional Syntax-based Arithmetic Coding (SAC) mode for H.263, the corresponding variable-length coding/decoding process is Arithmetic coded rather than with the previous Huffman coding. To make our explanation clear, first we briefly discuss the Huffman coding and Arithmetic coding methods.

19.3.3.1 Huffman Coding

According to Shannon's theory, the entropy of a source S is defined as

$$H(S) = \sum_i p_i \log_2 \frac{1}{p_i} \qquad (2)$$

where p_i denotes the probability that symbol s_i from S will occur. From the information theory, if the symbols are distinct, then the average number of bits needed to encode them is always bounded by its entropy. For Huffman coding, the probability of each symbol is assumed to be known in advance. To show the coding procedures, Fig. 19.7 gives an example. Here the characters 's', 'l', 'i', 'd', 'e', 'r', and '?' will be transmitted or stored, and their occurrence frequencies are also available. Therefore, the Huffman tree can be constructed by merging the two symbols with the least probabilities; the new symbol owns the probability as the sum of the merged two symbols. After that, if we assign the left branch with a '1' and the right branch with a '0', the Huffman codeword for each symbol is constructed. Basically, the wordlength of each codeword is dependent on the probability of the symbol; for more frequently appearing symbols, shorter wordlengths are assigned, and vice versa. The decoding of the Huffman code is similar to template matching by finding the exact codeword from the bit stream. The restriction of the Huffman code is that at least one bit must be used for one symbol. Therefore, some improved methods are developed, such as Arithmetic coding.

19.3.3.2 Arithmetic Coding

In the theory of Arithmetic coding, a single codeword is assigned to a half-open subinterval in the interval [0,1) according to the ratio of its probability. The same example for Huffman coding is used here for comparison. The coding process of Arithmetic coding can be described as follows.

Symbol	Probability	Codeword
s	0.02	11111
l	0.15	110
i	0.04	11110
d	0.08	1110
e	0.3	10
r	0.25	01
?	0.16	00

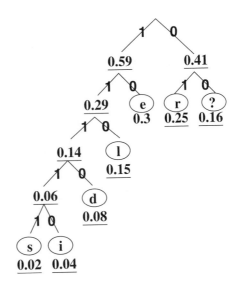

Figure 19.7   An example of Huffman codeword construction.

1. For the first input symbol, assign its subintervals $subinterval_l$ and $subinterval_h$ to P_l and P_h.

2. Let $Range = P_h - P_l$, for each subsequent input, $P_l = P_l + Range \times subinterval_l$, $P_h = P_l + Range \times subinterval_h$.

3. Continue the above process.

According to the coding process of Arithmetic coding, we always obtain a subinterval when a new input is given. If we would like to transmit the data and restart the process for later input, any number within the final subinterval is valid for encoding. The decoding process is similar to the encoding process; the transmitted number is checked to find which subinterval it falls in, and the range is updated in a way similar to encoder. More details can be found in [19]. Since Arithmetic coding utilizes the fractional parts of the binary representation, the limitation of a single bit for a single symbol is removed.

For this mode, Arithmetic coding might be enabled to replace the Huffman coding for all variable-length coding. For more details about the operations for H.263, interested readers can check Annex E in the H.263 documentation [11].

19.3.4 Advanced Prediction Mode

This optional mode includes overlapped block motion compensation and the possibility of four motion vectors for a macroblock instead of the original single-motion vector. In this mode, the unrestricted motion vector mode will be automatically enabled. Therefore, the maximal range of the motion vectors is also [-31.5,31.5]. This option leads to a significant

Symbol	Probability	Subinterval
s	0.02	[0.98,1.00)
l	0.15	[0.83,0.98)
i	0.04	[0.79,0.83)
d	0.08	[0.71,0.79)
e	0.3	[0.41,0.71)
r	0.25	[0.16,0.41)
?	0.16	[0.00,0.16)

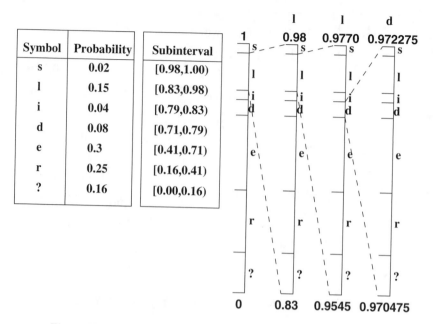

Figure 19.8   Arithmetic coding: an example of the coding process.

objective gain in terms of PSNR; besides, the block artifact is alleviated since the block size for motion compensation is reduced to 8 × 8 for better objective quality. We will introduce the above two functions, respectively, in the following.

19.3.4.1 Four Motion Vectors per Macroblock

This additional coding mode is enabled on a macroblock basis. In this mode, the one/four vectors decision is indicated in the macroblock header. If four motion vectors are used, each of the motion vectors is used for all pixels in one of the luminance blocks in the macroblock. Half-pixel accuracy is found by the bilinear interpolation, as described earlier. The motion vectors for the chrominance blocks are derived by summing up the four motion vectors for the luminance and then dividing this sum by eight; the component values of the resulting sixteenth resolution vectors are rounded to the nearest half-pixel positions. In addition, since the unrestricted motion vector mode will be enabled automatically in this mode, the maximal range of the motion vectors is also extended to [-31.5,31.5].

The DPCM prediction for H.263 is the median of three candidate motion vectors in the neighborhood. However, since the motion vectors are changed on a block basis, the prediction must be modified to fit the real situation. As displayed in Fig. 19.9, the candidate predictors must be redefined so that a better prediction can be obtained. The redefinition for boundary situation is also made in a similar way for original 16 × 16 macroblocks.

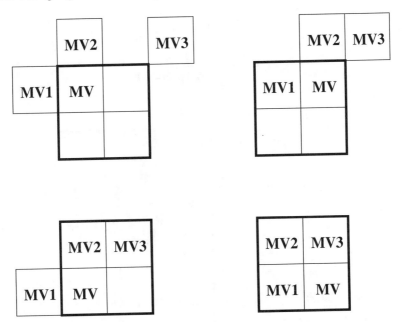

Figure 19.9   The redefinition of the candidate predictors for each of the luminance blocks in a macroblock.

Finally, the decision of when to use one/four motion vectors is open to users for the H.263 standard. In some proposed models, the comparison of the total mean absolute error (MAE) is utilized as the criterion for this decision.

19.3.4.2 Overlapped Motion Compensation for Luminance Blocks

Overlapped block motion compensation is an advanced scheme in which the current frame of a sequence is predicted by motion-compensated overlapping blocks from the reference frame, each weighted by a smoothing window. The main purpose of this mode is to prevent an irregular and nonmeaningful motion field due to smaller block size. Therefore, the function of this mode can be considered as a low-passed scheme of the prediction frame. In H.263, this mode is executed on a 8×8 block basis for the luminance signal only. Each pixel in an 8×8 luminance is a weighted sum of three prediction values, divided by eight (with rounding). In order to obtain the three prediction values, three motion vectors are used: the motion vector of the current luminance block, and two out of the four "remote" vectors:

- The motion vector of the block at the left or right side of the current luminance block
- The motion vector of the block above or below the current luminance block

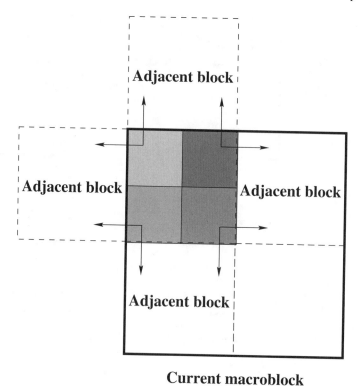

Current macroblock

Figure 19.10   The physical meaning of the overlapped motion compensation.

Remote motion vectors from other GOBs are used in the same way as remote motion vectors inside the current GOB. Figure 19.10 explains this idea more clearly. For example, for the luminance 4 × 4 block on the left-up corner of the current block, the used three motion vectors are: the motion vector of the current macroblock or block (which depends on one/four motion vector), the motion vector of the upper block, and the motion vector of the block at the left side.

The resulting motion vectors are then used to form the actual prediction, which is the weighted sum of the three referenced luminance values. The weight is dependent on the location of the luminance pixel; for the upper half of the block, the motion vector corresponding to the block above the current block is used, while for the lower half of the block the motion vector corresponding to the block below the current block is used, as Fig. 19.12 shows. Similarly, for the left half of the block, the motion vector corresponding to the block at the left side of the current block is used, while for the right half of the block the motion vector corresponding to the block at the right side of the current block is used, as Fig. 19.13 shows.

All the weighting matrices are illustrated in Figs. 19.11, 19.12, and 19.13. If one of the surrounding blocks is not coded or is coded in INTRA mode, the corresponding

4	5	5	5	5	5	5	4
5	5	5	5	5	5	5	5
5	5	6	6	6	6	5	5
5	5	6	6	6	6	5	5
5	5	6	6	6	6	5	5
5	5	6	6	6	6	5	5
5	5	5	5	5	5	5	5
4	5	5	5	5	5	5	4

Figure 19.11 Weighting values for prediction with motion vector of current luminance block.

2	2	2	2	2	2	2	2
1	1	2	2	2	2	1	1
1	1	1	1	1	1	1	1
1	1	1	1	1	1	1	1
1	1	1	1	1	1	1	1
1	1	1	1	1	1	1	1
1	1	2	2	2	2	1	1
2	2	2	2	2	2	2	2

Figure 19.12 Weighting values for prediction with motion vectors of the luminance block on top or bottom of current luminance block.

2	1	1	1	1	1	1	2
2	2	1	1	1	1	2	2
2	2	1	1	1	1	2	2
2	2	1	1	1	1	2	2
2	2	1	1	1	1	2	2
2	2	1	1	1	1	2	2
2	2	1	1	1	1	2	2
2	1	1	1	1	1	1	2

Figure 19.13 Weighting values for prediction with motion vector of the luminance blocks to the left or right of current luminance block.

remote motion vector is set to zero. If the current block is at the border of the picture and a surrounding block is therefore not presented, the corresponding remote motion vector is replaced by the motion vector of the current block. Observing the distribution of the weights in Figs. 19.11, 19.12, and 19.13, we see that the influence of the remote motion vectors is reduced as the position gets closer to the center of the current 8×8 block. However, at the border regions, a smooth transition between the boundary of the block is achieved due to the increasing influence of the remote motion vectors. As a result, the block artifacts will be reduced for better visible quality. Annex F in the H.263 document explains this negotiation.

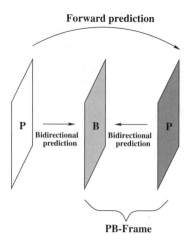

Figure 19.14 Prediction in PB-frames mode.

19.3.5 PB-frames Mode

PB-frames mode, as its name describes, consists of two pictures in which one is similar to the P-frame in MPEG and the other is similar to the B-frame. The main benefit of the PB-frames mode is to increase the frame rate with just a little overhead of the coded data. The P-picture is predicted from the last decoded P-picture , and the B-picture is predicted both from the last decoded P-picture and the P-picture currently being decoded. This last picture is named as a B-picture since parts of the frames might be bidirectionally predicted similar to a B-frame in the MPEG standard. The prediction procedure is displayed in Fig. 19.14.

The prediction of a B-macroblock in a PB-frame, for both luminance and chrominance blocks, is performed on a 8×8 block basis. Therefore, there are a total of 12 blocks per macroblock in a PB-frame instead of the original 6. At first, the motion vector for each block belonging to the P-picture is transmitted and then followed by the blocks of the B-picture; from the motion vector, MV, of each P-block, a backward motion vector MV_B and a forward motion vector MV_F for the related B-block are derived by the following equations:

$$MV_F = (TR_B \times MV)/TR_D + MV_D$$

$$MV_B = [(TR_B - TR_D) \times MV]/TR_D, if \ MV_D = 0$$

$$MV_B = MV_F - MV, if \ MV_D \neq 0$$

where TR_D is the increment of temporal reference tag from the last picture header and TR_B is the temporal reference tag for B-pictures. We can imagine the above equation, assuming the movement of the objects is linear. Therefore, both of the forward and backward motion vectors are generated from the ratio of the time difference between the last P-picture and the currently decoded P-picture. The motion vector MV of the current P-picture is used to

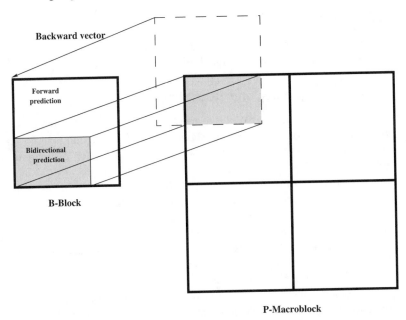

Figure 19.15 Forward and bidirectional prediction for a B-block.

generate the above two vectors. However, since the movement might be nonlinear, another delta vector MV_D can be utilized to enhance the quality of forward vector, but the backward vector is still derived from the linear assumption. For chrominance blocks, the forward and backward vectors are generated by summing the vectors of luminance blocks and then divided by 8.

If we named the P-macroblock which is decoded as PR, the prediction of the B-block has two modes that are used for different parts of the block:

- For pixels where the backward vector MV_B points inside PR, use bidirectional prediction. This is obtained as the average of the forward prediction using MV_F relative to the previous decoded picture, and the backward prediction using MV_B relative to PR. The average is calculated by dividing the sum of the two predictions by two.
- For all other pixels, forward prediction using MV_F relative to the previous decoded picture is used.

Figure 19.15 indicates which part of a block is predicted bidirectionally (shaded part of the B-block) and which part with forward prediction only (rest of the B-block).

This mode is described in Annex G in H.263. If both the advanced prediction mode and the PB-frames mode are enabled, overlapping motion compensation is used for P-frames but not for B-frames.

19.4 PERFORMANCE EVALUATION

In this section, we present a brief evaluation of H.263. Some of the results are from [17], and computer software can be found in [20] and [21].

19.4.1 Complexity and Bottleneck

According to the profile of the software supported by [20], the most time-consuming part belongs to motion estimation. About 60% of the computational power is allocated for this part. It should be emphasized that full-searched motion estimation algorithm is applied in TMN-5. For the advanced prediction mode, the overhead complexity for motion estimation is almost doubled intuitively. However, it strongly relies on the way of implementation. For example, in TMN-5, only a small refinement search is executed to find the four motion vectors MV_1 to MV_4. For overlapped motion compensation, a weighted sum of three prediction values must be generated to obtain the final values of the pixels. Since the multiplication of the weight must be done for all the pixels, the overhead will be quite high. In addition, this operation is also necessary for the decoder, so that the complexity of decoder increases at the same time.

Another mode that might influence the complexity is the PB-frames mode. A full-searched motion estimation is finished for the P-frames, and usually a small search range is used to generate the delta vector for the B-frames. In fact, a searching range for B-frames is also a tradeoff between complexity and performance; however, since the improvement of B-frames by full search is not significant, the exhaustive method seems to be unnecessary. Therefore, the complexity will increase if the doubled frame rate is expected. However, the reduced complexity due to this mode is a benefit under the same frame rate requirement. On the other hand, delay will be another important issue because of the interactive property. Under the same frame rate specification as the input signal, if the PB-frames mode is turned on, delay will be prolonged; the encoder must wait an extra frame for the P-picture and then encode the B-picture, and the decoder must decode the later P-picture first and then decode the former B-picture. Since two frames must be stored on the frame buffer for the encoding/decoding of the B-pictures, the total delay will be as much as six frames or larger. In addition, the required memory for the codec increases, too. However, if this mode is used to double the frame rate, no additional delay is introduced.

The other two modes, syntax-based Arithmetic coding and unrestricted motion vector modes, will not increase the complexity too much. Since most of the computational power for the encoder is used for motion estimation, the increased complexity for these two modes sometimes becomes negligible.

19.4.2 Bit Rate vs. PSNR

The performance of the H.263 (TMN-5) is summarized in Tables 19.2 and 19.3. The frame rate of the test sequences is fixed at 12.5 Hz, and the fixed quantization step is also listed in the tables. Table 19.2 is the result without any advanced modes for H.263. However, the performance still outperforms H.261 by a significant margin; the bit rate for H.261 is generally above 128 Kbps for an acceptable quality. In Table 19.3, the performance with all the options is shown. Obviously, these optional modes enhance the performance for all

Table 19.2 Performance of H.263 (TMN-5) Without Any Negotiations

Sequence Name	Quantization Step	Bit Rate (Kbit/s)	PSNR (dB) P-frame
Forman	20	26.68	28.85
Carphone	16	22.18	30.92
Claire	7	27.15	38.64
Mother-daughter	13	30.94	31.68
Susie	14	22.24	32.86
Miss America	7	24.46	38.87

Table 19.3 Performance of H.263 (TMN-5) With All the Negotiations

Sequence Name	Quantization Step	Bit Rate (Kbit/s)	PSNR (dB) P/B-frame
Forman	20	22.26	29.17/28.68
Carphone	16	19.44	31.06/30.63
Claire	7	19.87	38.70/38.12
Mother-daughter	13	19.65	31.72/31.34
Susie	14	18.12	33.07/32.66
Miss America	7	16.75	39.00/38.45

the sequences, especially for those sequences with simple content and movement, such as *Miss America* and *Claire*.

To observe the effect of each mode, interested readers can check the detail comparisons in [17]. Generally, most of the improvement is due to the advanced prediction mode; about 1 to 2 dB in PSNR depending on the sequences is enhanced. The improvement from the unrestricted motion vector mode and syntax-based Arithmetic coding is not significant; usually, less than 1 dB can be expected. The PB-frames mode generally introduces an obvious loss of image quality; however, since the frame rate is increased, a smoother temporal motion can be expected for better subjective feelings.

19.4.3 Subjective Tests

In this subsection, the sequence "*Miss America*" is selected to demonstrate the subjective results of the H.263 standard. For more information, please check [20]. In order to illustrate the effect of motion estimation, frames 80 and 81 are shown in Fig. 19.16. The H.263 reconstructed frames 80 and 81 are also displayed in Fig. 19.17. There is a large

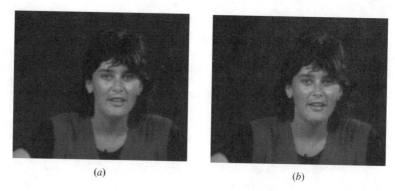

Figure 19.16   Original "Miss America": (a) frame 80, (b) frame 81.

Figure 19.17   H.263 (TMN-5) reconstructed "Miss America": (a) frame 80, (b) frame 81.

horizontal movement between these two frames. From the H.263 reconstructed frames, no obvious blocking exists due to the advanced motion prediction. However, the pictures seem to be blurred by a low-pass filter, and the sharpness of the edges is degraded. In fact, some edge-enhancement works are under development; interested readers can check the work in [20].

19.5   CONCLUSIONS

This chapter presents an overview of multimedia visual telephone systems. The basic components of such systems are video, audio, and network interfaces. The roles of ISO MPEG-4 and ITU-T H.263 are described; more attention is given to the details of ITU-T H.263 near-term scheme/goal. The long-term H.263 will cooperate with the MPEG-4 standard to develop a more advanced technology for multimedia communications. On the other hand, the MPEG-4 standard will pay more attention to the functionalities that are not addressed by the current standards.

For an H.324 terminal, the specified functions of a video codec and a speech codec are defined in H.263 and G.723, respectively. Moreover, H.245 deals with the control issue, and H.223 defines the multiplexing protocol. The V.34 modem is the default interface for GSTN, and the H.26P/M might be a potential standard for mobile channels. For a visual telephone system, important issues such as picture format, error resilience, and delay are discussed. The differences between H.261 and H.263 are explained. In addition, four optional modes are explored in more detail, and the tradeoffs between complexity and performance are shown. Generally, H.263 outperforms H.261 in terms of both subjective and objective qualities, which are achieved with a little extra complexity.

As software and hardware technologies evolve rapidly, the telephone, computer, television, network terminal, or even the personal digital assistance (PDA) will become integrated into the Global Information Infrastructure (GII). With this powerful network structure, worldwide communications will no longer be just a dream. In order to meet the needs of the human sensory system, multimedia presentations of the messages will make communications more efficient and convenient. The development of all the standards mentioned here does not mark the end of technical exploration; on the contrary, we believe it is just a beginning leading to more versatile approaches. New topics such as model-based video coding, applications of speech recognition, virtual reality (VR), or the recently developed World Wide Web (WWW) were all developed quite rapidly and have given us more space to think about the future of multimedia communications. In addition, with modern VLSI technology, the implementation of a multimedia visual telephone system will be low-powered and more efficient, and have transparant user interface. Lots of questions can be asked at any time; how to solve all these problems should be the goal of the engineers, researchers, and even all the laypeople in the world.

References

[1] ISO/IEC 10918-1, "JPEG Still Image4 Coding Standard," 1990.

[2] CCITT Study Group XV, "Draft Revision of Recommendation H.261—Video Codec for Audio Visual Services at p×64 Kbps," *Temporary Document 5-E*, July 1990.

[3] ISO/IEC JTC1/SC29/WG11 MPEG 93, *Coding of Moving Pictures and Associated Audio*, 1993.

[4] ISO/IEC JTC1/SC29/WG11/602 Recmmendation H.262, *Generic Coding of Moving Pictures and Associated Audio, Committee Draft*, 1993.

[5] *Grand Alliance HDTV System Specification, Version 2.0*, Dec. 1994.

[6] ISO/IEC JTC1/SC29/WG11 MPEG 92/699, *Project Description for Very Low Bitrate A/V Coding*, 5, 1992.

[7] Dept. of Electronic Systems Engineering, University of Essex, U.K., *International Workshop on Coding Technique for Very Low Bit-rate Video*, 1994.

[8] Y.-Q. Zhang, "Very Low Bit Rate Video Coding Standards," *Proceedings of Visual Communications and Image Processing*, Vol. 2501, part 2, pp. 1016–1023, May 1995.

[9] H. Li, A. Lundmark, and R. Forchheimer, "Image Sequence Coding at Very Low Bit-rate: A Review," *IEEE Trans. Image Processing*, Vol. 3, No. 5, pp. 589–609, Sept. 1994.

[10] ITU-T Study Group 15, Q2/15. "Draft ITU-T Recommendation H.324—Terminal for Low Bit-rate Multimedia Communication," Nov. 1995.

[11] ITU-T Study Group 15, Q2/15, "Draft ITU-T Recommendation H.263—Video Coding for Low Bit-rate Communication," Nov. 1995.

[12] ITU-T Study Group 15, Q2/15, "Draft ITU-T Recommendation G.723—Dual Rate Speech Coder for Multimedia Communications Transmitting at 5.3 & 6.3 Kbps," Oct. 1995.

[13] ITU-T Study Group 15, Q2/15, "Draft ITU-T Recommendation H.223—Multiplexing Protocol for Low Bit-rate Multimedia Communication," Nov. 1995.

[14] ITU-T Study Group 15, Q2/15, "Draft ITU-T Recommendation H.245—Control Protocol for Multimedia Communication," Nov. 1995.

[15] B. Girod, "Motion-compensating Prediction with Fractional-pel Accuracy," *IEEE Trans. Communications*, Vol. 41, No. 4, pp. 604–612, Apr. 1993.

[16] K. Rijkse, "ITU Standardisation of Very Low Bitrate Video Coding Algorithms," *Signal Processing: Image Communication*, No. 7, pp. 553–565, Nov. 1995.

[17] B. Girod, E. Steinbach, and N. Färber, "Comparison of the H.263 and H.261 Video Compression Standards," *First International Symposium on Photonics Technologies and Systems for Voice, Video, and Data Communication, Pennsylvania*, Oct. 1995.

[18] V. Bhaskaran and K. Konstantinides, *Image and Video Compression Standards: Algorithms and Architectures*, Boston: Kluwer Academic Publishers, 1995.

[19] I. Witten, R. Neal, and J. Cleary, "Arithmetic Coding for Data Compression," *Comm. ACM*, Vol. 30, No. 6, pp. 520–540, June 1987.

[20] TMN—Test Model for H.263, Version 1.6a Telenor Research, 1995 (Internet: http://www.nta.no/brukere/DVC/).

[21] H.261 software codec, Portable Video Research Group, Stanford (Internet: ftp://havefun.stanford.edu/pub/p64/).

ADVANCED TECHNIQUES IN AUDIOVISUAL INTERACTION

Tsuhan Chen and Ram Rao

Abstract

In this chapter, we present state-of-the-art technologies in the research of audiovisual interaction for multimedia applications. We show the interaction between audio and video in multimedia communications, especially for person-to-person conversational environment. Topics covered in this chapter include audiovisual bimodality in speech production and perception, automatic lipreading, face animation, and lip synchronization. We present useful tools for image analysis and synthesis that enable these technologies. A new research trend that we discuss is utilization of audiovisual interaction in joint audio-video processing of talking-head sequences. We show that the marriage of speech analysis and image processing opens up numerous new applications.

20.1 INTRODUCTION

What do we mean by *multimedia*? To many people, the word "multimedia" simply means the presentation of a combination of various forms of media: text, speech, audio, music, images, graphics, and video. What is often overlooked, however, is the interaction among these different forms of information. In this chapter, we address an important aspect of such interaction: the interaction between audio and video. Particularly in multimedia applications that involve person-to-person conversation, including video telephony and video conferencing, the interaction between acoustical information and visual information becomes very significant. We will show that joint audio-video processing provides major improvement compared to the situation where audio and video are processed independently.

20.1.1 Audiovisual Interaction

The interaction between audio and visual information has been an interesting, yet mysterious, research topic for many years. A simple example of audiovisual interaction is the well-known fact that the perceptual quality of a video clip can be significantly enhanced if it is associated with high-quality sound. For human speech perception, audiovisual interaction is even more prominent. In the "McGurk effect" [31], it was shown that human perception of acoustic speech can be affected by the visual cues of lip movements. For example, a video clip in which the speaker's mouth is saying /ga/ but the audio is dubbed with the sound /ba/, is often perceived as /da/. Similarly, the combination of visual /ga/ and acoustical /pa/ is perceived as /ta/, and the mouthed /da/ and acoustic /ma/ is frequently identified as /na/. There also exists the "reverse McGurk effect"; that is, the results of lipreading are affected by the dubbed audio speech [14]. In addition to artificially chosen consonant–

vowel syllables as mentioned above, the existence of both the McGurk effect and the reverse McGurk effect in *natural* speech has also been proven by a series of experiments [12].

Another example of audiovisual interaction is human lipreading [2]. A person skilled in lipreading is able to infer the meaning of spoken sentences by looking at the configuration and variation of the visible articulators of the speaker, such as the tongue, lips, and teeth, together with clues from the context. Lipreading is widely used by the hearing-impaired for speech communication. People who are not hearing-impaired also utilize lipreading to some extent [51], especially when the auditory environment is not good (e.g., with background noise). For example, sounds such as /p/ and /t/ that are acoustically similar but visually different can be distinguished by lipreading.

20.1.2 Bimodal Speech Production and Perception

One reason why audiovisual interaction is important is that human speech is bimodal, that is, auditory and visual, in both production and perception. Human speech is produced by the vibration (or absence of vibration in the case of voiceless sounds) of the vocal cord and the configuration of the vocal tract. The vocal tract is composed of articulatory organs including the pharynx, the nasal cavity, the tongue, teeth, velum, and lips. Using these articulatory organs, together with the muscles that generate facial expressions, a speaker produces speech. Among the articulatory organs, lips, teeth and the tongue are visible. Thus, an observer listens to the acoustic speech and looks at visible articulatory organs and facial expressions to perceive speech.

20.1.3 Phonemes and Visemes

The basic unit of acoustic speech is called the phoneme. In American English, the ARPABET table consisting of 48 phonemes is commonly used [39]. Similarly, in the visual domain, the basic unit of mouth movements is called the viseme. A viseme therefore is the smallest visibly distinguishable unit of speech. For example, /p/, /b/, and /m/ all represented by a closed mouth shape belong to one viseme. Similarly, /f/ and /v/ both belong to the same viseme that represents a mouth of which the upper teeth are touching the lower lip. Figure 20.1 shows a number of visemes. Strictly speaking, a viseme can be a sequence of mouth images, so the *movement* of the mouth is involved. For example, the viseme /ow/ represents the movement of the mouth from a position close to /o/ to a position close to /w/. In Fig. 20.1, we show a few visemes, each of which can actually be represented by a still image. Unlike phonemes, so far there is no standard viseme table that is commonly used by researchers [16].

Both in the acoustic domain and in the visual modality, most of the vowels are distinguishable [13]. However, this is not true for consonants. For example, in the acoustic domain, the sounds /p/, /t/, /k/ are very similar. When people spell words on the phone, expressions such as "B as in boy," or "D as in David," are often used to clarify acoustic confusion. Interestingly, the confusion sets in the auditory modality are usually distinguishable in the visual modality. One good example is the sounds /p/ and /k/. In the visual modality, it's commonly agreed that the visemes for English consonants can be grouped into nine distinct groups as follows: [13]

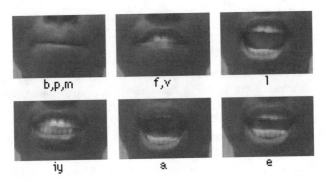

Figure 20.1   Example visemes.

1: f, v   6: w

2: th, dh   7: r

3: s, z   8: g, k, n, t, d, y

4: sh, zh   9: l

5: p, b, m

The bimodality of speech makes it clear that audiovisual interaction is a very important issue in personal communication applications. The research and development of multimedia communication systems should account for this interaction. In this chapter, we address a number of areas related to audiovisual interaction, such as automatic lipreading, speech-driven talking heads, and lip synchronization. In particular, we discuss a new trend in video coding research: joint audio-video coding. Given that mouth movements are very difficult to code because of the mouth's rapid, complex, and nonrigid motion (so conventional block-based motion-compensation methods fail), we will explain how having extra help from the acoustic signal can enable us to code the mouth movements more efficiently.

In Section 20.2, we discuss work related to conversion between acoustic and visual speech, which includes automatic lipreading and facial animation. In Section 20.3, we discuss issues related to lip synchronization, such as dubbing in movie productions and improving lip synchronization for videoconferencing applications. Image analysis and synthesis tools commonly used in the field of audiovisual speech research are summarized in Section 20.4. In Section 20.5, we describe a new trend in multimedia information processing, that is, joint audio-video processing. In Section 20.6, we conclude this chapter by outlining other multimedia applications that will benefit from the marriage of speech analysis and image processing.

20.2   MEDIA CONVERSION: AUDITORY AND VISUAL SPEECH

In this section, we discuss the conversion between audio and visual speech. Topics include automatic lipreading and speech-driven face animation.

20.2.1 From Visual to Audio: Automatic Lipreading

Recently, researchers have been using image analysis techniques to track lip movements and hence to automate lipreading [5,16]. One example tracking algorithm is proposed in [40]. It uses a variant of deformable templates called state-embedded deformable templates, with which the lips are modeled as a pair of parabolas. Details of this algorithm are discussed in Section 20.4.3.

Furthermore, automatic lipreading has been used to enhance the results of acoustic speech recognition [36,37]. This is feasible because sounds such as /p/ and /t/ that are acoustically similar can easily be distinguished using automatic lipreading techniques. In [49], a system formed by combining an acoustic speech recognizer and an automatic lipreader with a fuzzy logic is demonstrated to give better performance in audiovisual speech recognition than recognition using either subsystem alone.

Researchers have also tried to convert mouth images into acoustic speech directly. In [33], a system called "image input microphone" is built to take the mouth image as input, analyze the lip features such as mouth width and height, and derive the corresponding vocal-tract transfer function that is used to synthesize the output audio speech waveform. This system is useful as a speaking-aid for people whose vocal cords have been injured. It can also be used as an input device to a computer. Compared to an acoustic microphone, the image input microphone has the advantage that it is not affected by acoustic noise and therefore is more appropriate for noisy environment.

20.2.2 From Audio to Visual: Speech-Driven Face Animation

Researchers have also tried to produce visual speech from auditory speech, that is, to generate speech-driven talking heads [25,27,32,55,56]. The major applications of this technique include human-computer interfaces, computer-aided instruction, cartoon animation, video games, and multimedia telephony for the hearing-impaired.

Two approaches to generating talking-head images are the flipbook method [18] and the wireframe model (2-D or 3-D) [54]. In [32], a 3-D wireframe facial model was used to synthesize the facial expressions, particularly the lip motion. The lip parameters used therein form an eight-dimensional vector that includes the position of the upper lip, the position of the chin, and so on. These parameters can be derived by either text or speech input. In the case of text input, a sequence of the eight-dimensional feature vectors is manually extracted for each phoneme. The input text is then analyzed into a sequence of phonemes, and the corresponding lip feature vectors are used to drive the facial model to produce the lip motion. In the case of speech input, the lip feature points are driven by a classifier that derives lip parameters from the input acoustic speech. The input speech is first converted into linear prediction coefficients (LPC) cepstrum [39]. During the training of the classifier, the acoustic features (i.e., LPC cepstra) in the training data are classified into groups using vector quantization. For each acoustic group, the corresponding lip feature vectors are grouped together and the centroid is computed. In the classifying phase, the LPC cepstrum of the input speech is classified, and the corresponding lip-feature centroid is produced by the classifier, which in turn drives the facial wireframe model. In this work, facial features other than lip movements, such as eyebrows and eyelids, were controlled randomly to make the facial motion look more realistic.

In [56], a 3-D wireframe similar to that in [32] was used to synthesize talking faces to be used as human-computer interfaces. To derive the lip movements from the speech signal, hidden Markov model (HMM) techniques [39] that are widely used for speech recognition are extended to find the speech-to-viseme mapping. The acoustic speech is LPC-analyzed and VQ-classified into 64 groups. The mouth shape is parameterized using height and width, and classified into 16 groups using VQ. The 16×16 transition probabilities (transition from one mouth shape to another) and the 16×64 observation probabilities for a given mouth shape producing a particular sound are estimated from the training data to form the HMM. During the recognition phase, the speech waveform is first LPC analyzed and vector quantized. Given the HMM, the Viterbi algorithm [39] is then used to find the most probable sequence of mouth shapes. Finally, the sequences of mouth shapes are fed to the facial model to create the mouth movements.

A recent work with focus on a multimedia telephone for the hearing-impaired is presented in [25]. In this work, the conversion from speech to lip movements is performed by a number of time-delayed neural networks (TDNN). An important feature of this work, compared to previous results in literature, is as follows. To find the lip features, it considers not only the current audio segment, but also the previous and future audio segments. The purpose is to incorporate the coarticulation effect in speech production, that is, the fact that the mouth shape for a particular sound is dependent on the previous sound and the following sound.

20.3 LIP SYNCHRONIZATION

Lip synchronization—that is, the synchronization between lip movements and the associated acoustic signal—is an important issue in movie production, videotelephony, and video conferencing. There are essentially two possible approaches to lip synchronization: one is to warp the audio to match the video, and the other is to warp the video to match the audio. In this section, we summarize state-of-the-art techniques that achieve lip synchronization.

20.3.1 Automatic Dialog Synchronization

In movie production, the dialog is usually recorded in a studio to replace the dialog recorded while filming a scene, because the latter has poor quality due to background noises. To ensure lip synchronization, a system known as Wordfit [3] was designed to time-warp the studio dialog to match the original recording. First, both the studio audio and the original recording are analyzed by a spectrum analyzer. The results are then input to a processor to find the best ''time-warping path'' that is required to modify the time scale of the studio audio to align the original recording. According to this time warping path, the studio audio is edited pitch-synchronously—that is, a period of sound segment is cut out or repeated. Thus, the studio dialog can be made in synchronization with the original lip movement.

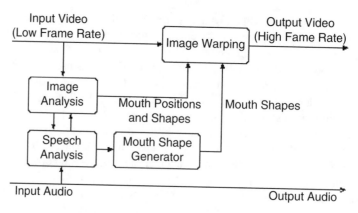

Figure 20.2   Speech-assisted frame-rate conversion.

20.3.2   Speech-Assisted Video Processing

Instead of warping the audio, one can time-warp the video. Furthermore, one can warp the image of the speaker to make the lip movement fit the studio dialog. We will discuss these aspects in the following application.

Due to limited bandwidth or storage space, a video coder typically does not encode all incoming frames. Instead, it skips some frames without coding them, which results in a lower frame rate at the decoder. Frame skipping introduces artifacts such as jerky motion and loss of lip synchronization in talking-head video. Therefore, interpolation at the decoder is required to increase the frame rate to reconstruct lip synchronization. Notice that in this case, it is impossible to achieve lip synchronization simply by warping the audio, because visual information is completely lost due to the low frame rate. To solve this problem, we can extract information from the speech signal and apply image processing to the mouth image to achieve lip synchronization. We call this speech-assisted frame-rate conversion [7,8]. This postprocessing approach has two advantages: it is compatible with existing coding standards, and it requires no side information to be sent from the encoder to the decoder. Therefore, we can combine it with standard video coding techniques to improve both image quality and lip synchronization.

Figure 20.2 shows the block diagram of speech-assisted frame-rate conversion. In this system, image analysis [7,9,17,40] is applied to the input video frames to locate the vertices of the mouth model shown in Fig. 20.3. Meanwhile, the audio signal is analyzed to produce a sequence of phonemes. The mouth shape generator then generates a sequence of corresponding mouth shapes that are missing in the low frame-rate video. Controlled by the output of the mouth shape generator, an image-warping technique [57] is then applied to the input frames in order to modify the mouth shape to produce new frames that are to be inserted. Hence, lip synchronization is achieved in the high frame-rate output video.

Note the interaction between image analysis and speech analysis in Fig. 20.2. The results of image analysis are used to improve the accuracy of speech recognition, as in automatic lipreading. On the other hand, speech information is used to improve the image

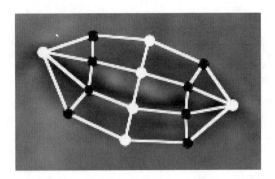

Figure 20.3   The mouth model.

analysis. For example, we can decide whether the mouth is open or closed by speech analysis and then apply different algorithms to locate the lip points.

Mouth closures, for example, during /p/, /b/, /m/ and silence, are important perceptual cues for lip synchronization. Therefore, the lip synchronization is good as long as speech analysis and image analysis together detect these closures correctly, and image synthesis renders mouth closures precisely.

20.3.2.1 Example Results

We apply speech-assisted frame-rate conversion to the "Mom" sequence in which she is saying "...told me...". The result is shown in Fig. 20.4. The frame on the left (corresponding to "...old") and the frame on the right (corresponding to "...e") are existing frames in the low frame-rate sequence. The middle one is obtained by interpolation. Note that a closed mouth shape is rendered for /m/, which would not be possible without speech information.

In addition to the low frame rate, another issue that causes loss of lip synchronization in video conferencing is that the transmission delay for video is typically longer than the audio delay. Although we can delay the audio to match the video, this increases the overall delay, and hence is not desirable in interactive two-way communication. The speech-assisted video

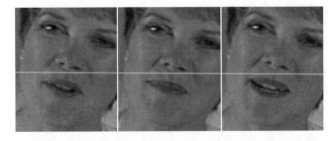

Figure 20.4   Result of speech-assisted interpolation.

processing technique can solve this problem. By warping the mouth image of the speaker to be synchronized with the audio, effectively we decrease the overall delay.

20.3.3 Dubbing of Films and Language Translation

One main issue in dubbed foreign films is the loss of lip synchronization. Also, in cartoon animation, one main task is to animate the lip synchronization of the cartoon characters. To facilitate these tasks, we can analyze the speech or image of the dubber, and then modify the dubbee's mouth accordingly. The same technique can also be combined with language translation to create an automatic audiovisual dubbing system, in which the mouth motion is made synchronous with the translated speech. In some applications where the transcript is available, for example, close caption, text-based language translation can also be used.

20.4 IMAGE ANALYSIS AND SYNTHESIS TECHNIQUES

In this section, we present some techniques for facial image analysis and synthesis. These are useful tools for research in audiovisual interaction. We also discuss in detail an image analysis system for lip tracking [40,42].

20.4.1 Image Analysis: Lipreading

Any system that seeks to exploit audiovisual interaction must, at some point, analyze both the audio and video signals. The acoustic analysis has been well-studied for many decades. Researchers have developed a number of ways to parameterize speech, depending on the application. For example, linear-predictive coefficients or line-spectral pairs are often used for coding purposes, and filterbank outputs or cepstral coefficients are used for recognition purposes.

The question then arises as to how one can "measure" the visual signal. Unlike the speech signal which is essentially one-dimensional, the visual input is three-dimensional, with two spatial and one temporal dimension. A visual analysis system must convert this sequence of images into a meaningful parameter set to be used by the application. In this section, we first define the tasks that a visual analysis system must perform. We also discuss some of the conditions to which the analysis system must be invariant. Then, we examine which image processing algorithms provide information that can be used by the analysis system. Finally, we outline some of the existing methods to perform visual analysis.

20.4.1.1 Problem Definition

First, we must define the problems that need to be solved by the visual analysis system. One problem is that of finding a mouth in an image [24,44]. This problem is beyond the scope of this chapter. A problem that is more pertinent to our discussion is that of tracking and parameterizing the *shape* of the mouth throughout the video sequence. The parameter extraction may employ either a classification strategy where the input image is classified to one of several possible types, or it may actually parameterize the shape of the mouth by fitting a model to the mouth, or measuring dimensions such as the width and height of the mouth.

One goal of the tracking and extraction routines is to be invariant to many different conditions. Consider attempting to vector quantize an input mouth image to one of several classes using an L_1 norm. This would seem to be a reasonable idea, but it would suffer from many problems. First, it would not be translation invariant. Shifts in the input image would lead to high distortion. It would also be susceptible to changes in rotation and scale. Furthermore, lighting variations and differing skin colors could offer problems. Finally, deformations of mouth shapes could lead to mistaken results. There is no reason to believe that an image of a quarter-open mouth would be quantized to an image of a closed mouth instead of an open mouth. This quantization system could be improved by adding levels of complexity. A more complex distance measure can be used instead of an L_1 norm to add invariance to lighting conditions and skin color. Translation effects can be compensated by evaluating the metric with many shifted versions of the input image. Rotation and scale invariance can be increased by adding clusters whose centroids represent mouths that have been rotated or increased in size. This example shows how a relatively simple quantization scheme becomes fairly complex when attempting to account for all the varying conditions that might be encountered by the visual analysis routine.

20.4.1.2 *Extraction of Information by Image Processing*

In the previous example, the image analysis routine used only the intensity information in the mouth image. Many other information sources can be obtained by applying image processing operations on the original image or video source. These other information sources may be better suited for a particular application, or for certain analysis methods. Here is a synopsis of the advantages and disadvantages of some of these information sources:

Intensity. Pixel intensity is the most logical information source to use in an analysis system. Problems arise, however, in developing an analysis system based on intensity which is invariant to the conditions mentioned earlier. Nonetheless, for simple systems, a grid of intensities has often been used as input to either a vector quantizer or a neural network.

Color. Color is an extremely useful information source when it is available. It adds an extra layer of complexity because the system needs to deal with three times as much raw data as grayscale images. The fact that a person's face, lips, teeth, tongue, and mouth opening are all different colors would suggest that much information is to be obtained from color. Analysis systems have tried to use color information in two ways. One method is to divide the RGB (Red-Green-Blue) cube into regions and decide which regions of the cube belong to which facial feature based on color histograms [20,46]. The other method involves modeling the probability distribution of pixel colors by a Gaussian mixture density for each feature [40].

Edge Strength. Another logical choice is to use information obtained by applying an edge detector on the input image. The resulting edge image can then be analyzed, and edges can be joined and labeled. A problem arises because different mouth configurations

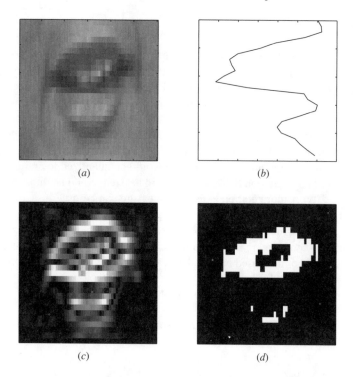

Figure 20.5 Pertaining to image analysis.

have different types of edges. For example, if the teeth or tongue is showing, there will be associated edges. It is also possible that expected edges may not be visible. Take, for instance, the frame from the Miss America sequence shown in Fig. 20.5a, and the associated edge image in Fig. 20.5b. Most models of the mouth look for four edges: two associated with the upper lip and two with the lower lip. In the Miss America sequence, however, only one edge is associated with the upper lip because the transition between the upper lip and the mouth opening is weak. Furthermore, an edge is generated by the shadow of the lower lip, and multiple edges are generated by the teeth. This would provide erroneous information for a system that blindly attempts to label edges.

Thresholding. A simple, efficient front end might choose to threshold the input image at a specific level as shown in Fig. 20.5c. If the threshold is chosen properly, one may isolate the mouth opening since, in general, the opening will contain pixels that are much darker than the rest of the image. This will result in an image that contains a connected blob of pixels. The height, width, and area of the blob will provide information related to the height, width, and area of the mouth opening. The obvious problem in this method is the choice of threshold. This threshold would be adversely affected by changes in lighting conditions and skin color.

Principal Components. Some work has been done on recognizing facial features based on principal component analysis [47,52]. This involves generating a set of "eigen-images'' for the entire space of mouth images, and then using this as a basis for any input image. Any input image can be transformed into a vector of weights where the input image will be a sum of weighted eigen-images. This vector of weights may be suitable for classification purposes.

Vertical and Horizontal Projections. A very simple, yet effective, method for finding features of the mouth is to sum the input image along the rows to form a horizontal projection, or along the columns to form a vertical projection. The peaks and valleys in these projections will correspond to different features. For example, the minimum in the horizontal projection of the input image will likely occur at the row that passes through the middle of the mouth as shown in Fig. 20.5d. The vertical and horizontal projections of the edge images can also provide much useful information. If the input image only contains the mouth, then the first peak in the horizontal projection will pass through the top of the upper lip. If the input image contains an area larger than the mouth, projections of image slices, or simply cross sections, may be used. Therefore, a few of the slices will contain the mouth. These projection operations, however, assume that there is little or no rotation of the mouth.

Morphological Operations. The morphological peaks and valleys [29] of images also provide useful information. Since the opening of the mouth is darker than the rest of the image, it would be part of a valley, and the lips and teeth would be part of the peaks.

Motion and Optical Flow. Motion vectors associated with regions near the lips and the optical flow through these regions can also be used by an analysis subsystem [28,30]. If there is no translational motion, then the motion in the regions surrounding the mouth are physically linked to motions that are allowed by the muscles controlling the mouth. This means, for instance, that the lower lip will predominantly have vertical motion because it is controlled by the jaw. In fact, the facial action coding system (FACS) [15] has derived a set of possible lip movements that can result from different muscle actions. Some analysis systems try to link the observed motion or optical flow with realistic movements to determine the action that has taken place.

Fourier Analysis. Although Fourier coefficients wouldn't normally seem to be useful, they may provide some shift invariance to the analysis system. This results from the well-known Fourier property that shifts in one domain lead to multiplication by complex exponentials in the other domain. Therefore, if an analysis system used magnitudes of Fourier coefficients as an input to a neural network, it might add some shift invariance.

20.4.1.3 Analysis Systems

The visual analysis systems can be divided into two major classes: those that classify the input image into one of several categories, and those that measure parameters or dimensions from the input image.

Vector quantization and neural networks are standard methods for classifying input images into several classes. As input, one could use intensity images, Fourier transform coefficients, binary images obtained by thresholding, and many of the other processed versions of the images noted earlier. As already mentioned, vector quantization of the gray level image may not be invariant to many of the conditions normally faced by analysis systems.

This matter has been addressed by Brunelli and Poggio [6]. Their system normalizes for scale and rotation based on the position of the eyes and the interocular distance. They use a normalized cross-correlation coefficient:

$$C_N(y) = \frac{<I_T T> - <I_T><T>}{\sigma(I_T)\sigma(T)} \tag{1}$$

where I_T is the patch of the image I which must be matched to template, T. $<>$ is the average operator, and $I_T T$ represents a pixel-by-pixel product between the image patch and template. Finally, σ is the standard deviation over the area being matched. This metric provides better resilience to intensity variations than an L_1 norm or L_2 norm.

A more difficult problem is obtaining parameters or dimensions that have some physical significance. For instance, we might wish to measure the height between the lips or the width between the corners of the mouth. An even more ambitious task would be to construct a model for the lips and find the parameters of the model that provide the closest match between the model and the image.

A system used by Petajan [35] in his visual speech recognition experiments took input images and applied a set threshold. The binary images were then analyzed, and parameters such as the area of the mouth opening, height, width, and perimeter length were all extracted. These parameters provided an adequate representation of the shape of the mouth and were successfully used in speech recognition experiments.

An analysis system designed by Prasad et al. [38] used the vertical and horizontal projections of both intensity and edge images to locate points of interest on the mouth. The distances between these points were successfully used in speech recognition applications.

Much of the recent work in visual analysis has centered around deformable models. Both deformable templates and snakes fit into this category. The basic idea is that an energy function that relates a parameterized model to an image is formed. This energy function is minimized using any standard optimization technique, and the resulting parameter set is said to be optimal.

Snakes [21] allow one to parameterize a closed contour. The simplest snakes have energy functions that are sums of internal energy forces and external energy forces. The internal energy acts to keep the contour smooth, while the external energy acts to attract the snake to key features in the image such as edges. When the total energy is minimized, the optimal snake location can be found. Researchers have also introduced more complexity into the system by adding surface learning [4] and flexible appearance models [23]. These techniques seek to constrain the position of snake nodes to a smaller subspace which is constructed through eigenvector decomposition. At the end of each minimization stage, the resulting snake parameters are projected onto the smaller subspace of "eigen-lips" to constrain the shape of the snake to those that are acceptable.

Deformable templates [58] provide both a parameterized model and an energy function. The model may be simple, such as modeling the outer contour of the mouth by two intersecting parabolas. More complex models can also be built. For example, the original mouth-open template given by Yuille et al. consists of five parabolas, as shown in Fig. 20.6 where two are for the upper edge of the upper lip and the other three are for the lower edge of the upper lip, and upper and lower edges of the lower lip. Each of these models has

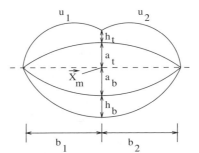

Figure 20.6 Deformable template after Yuille et al.

different numbers of parameters. The simplest two parabola models may be specified by four parameters, while a complex mouth model may contain more than 10 parameters.

The energy function associated with deformable templates relates the template to the image. For instance, part of the energy function may accumulate the negative edge strength along the contour of the template. Therefore, this term will attract the contours of the template to the edges in the image. Energy terms relating to peak potentials, valley potentials, and intensity are also common. The energy function may also have terms that bias the template to keep parameters within reasonable limits. For instance, an energy term might be added to keep the top edge of the lower lip below the lower edge of the upper lip. These energy functions are often derived through both intuition and trial and error. Once an acceptable energy function is defined, an optimization algorithm is used to find the best-fit template for each image. Many researchers have used deformable templates to achieve excellent results in speech recognition. Extensions that apply deformable templates on image sequences have also been studied [50], and one suggestion [22] has been to incorporate Kalman filtering techniques into deformable templates. These extensions attempt to exploit the correlation between adjacent video frames and to add continuity to the extracted parameter sets.

20.4.2 Image Synthesis: Facial Animation

Two approaches to generating talking-head images are the flipbook method and the wireframe model (2-D or 3-D). Both methods attempt to solve the same problem, but they tackle the problem in different ways.

In the flipbook approach, a number of mouth images of a person, called key frames, are captured and stored. Each image represents a particular mouth shape. Then, according to speech, the corresponding mouth images are "flipped" one by one to the display to form an animation. This method typically generates jerky motion during the key frame transition, when the number of key frames is limited. Morphing and image warping can be used to create some intermediate frames to make the transition look smoother [19]. Image warping is a process whereby one image is distorted, through the use of geometric transformations, to look like another image. Image morphing is useful for producing realistic intermediate images between video frames. To accomplish this, correspondences are made between points in video frame i and video frame $i + 1$. These correspondences provide a blueprint for distorting the first image into the second. Using this blueprint, we can warp the first image forward by half a frame. The second image can be warped backward by half a frame

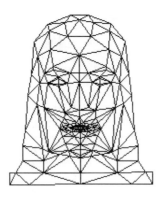

Figure 20.7   The   wireframe   model "Candide."

by reversing this blueprint. The two intermediate images are then averaged to produce the morphed intermediate frame.

Wireframe methods use more sophisticated computer graphics techniques to achieve realism. A wireframe is composed of a large number of triangular patches that model the shape of the face. One of the early facial models was developed by Parke [34]. Figure 20.7 shows a more recent facial model called "Candide" developed at Linköping University [45]. A fully 3-D model would contain vertices that correspond to points throughout the head, and would allow synthesis of facial images with arbitrary orientations. However, since most animation is primarily concerned with the face, and not the back of the head, models are often developed only for a frontal view of the face. For a limited set of orientations, these models work well, but as the rotations become large, the images give the appearance of hollow opera masks. These vertices in these wireframe models can be deformed to synthesize new expressions. For example, vertices in a neutral model can be repositioned to form a facial model that is smiling. In order to synthesize various facial expressions, the facial action coding system (FACS) [15] is often used to generate the required trajectories of the vertices.

These wireframe models, by themselves, give only a structural representation of the face. To generate natural-looking synthetic faces, these wireframe models must be combined with lighting models that specify how to map the shape and position of the wireframe into intensity when the wireframe is projected onto a 2-D image. It is possible to use algorithms such as Gouraud shading to synthesize artificial looking faces. For more realism, texture mapping is necessary. Texture mapping is an algorithm that maps points on a 2-D image onto patches of a wireframe. The texture from the original image helps create realistic synthetic images.

In essence, there is a duality between the two approaches we have outlined. When images are synthesized using key frames, images are known at fixed intervals, and models are used to aid in the warping process. When wireframes are used, the models are manipulated into realistic positions; then the images are texture mapped onto the models. The morphing process is less computationally intensive, but it requires more data (images at key frames). The wireframe approach is more computationally intensive, but it also leads to a more

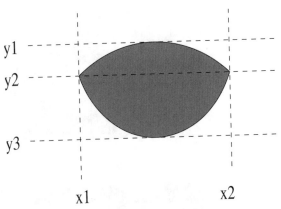

Figure 20.8 Template. $\lambda = [x1, x2, y1, y2, y3]$.

flexible animation system. Only one image is needed for texture mapping purpose; then arbitrarily oriented images can be synthesized with the model.

20.4.3 An Example Lip-Tracking System

Here we will examine one image analysis system in detail. This system, state-embedded deformable templates, is a variant of deformable templates, which exploits statistical differences in color to track the shape of the lips through successive video frames [40]. A few assumptions are made concerning the structure of the input images. First, it is assumed that the image can be divided into foreground (pixels within the outer contour of the lips) and background (pixels that are part of the face) regions. Next, it is assumed that the shape of the foreground can be modeled by two parabolas as shown in Fig. 20.8. This is the template, and it is completely specified by the parameter, λ, which is five-dimensional ($\lambda = [x1, x2, y1, y2, y3]$). When the value of λ changes, the shape and position of the template change. This template is used to divide the image into foreground and background regions. Finally, we assume that there are distinct probability density functions (pdf) which govern the distribution of pixel colors in the foreground and background. Since the lips and face have different colors, the assumption is valid.

If we have estimates for the foreground (pixels within the lips) pdf and background (pixels of the face) pdf, we can evaluate the joint probability of all pixels in the image. This joint probability is given by

$$P[I|\lambda] = \prod_{(x,y)\epsilon fg} b_{fg}(I(x,y)) \prod_{(x,y)\epsilon bg} b_{bg}(I(x,y)) \tag{2}$$

where $P[I|\lambda]$ is the joint probability, $I(x,y)$ is the 3-D pixel value at location (x,y), and b_{fg} and b_{bg} are the foreground and background pdf's, respectively. Notice the dependence on λ: if λ is changed, different pixels become part of the foreground and background, thus changing the joint probability value. Our visual analysis system uses a maximization algorithm to find the parameter λ, which maximizes the joint probability of the pixels in the image.

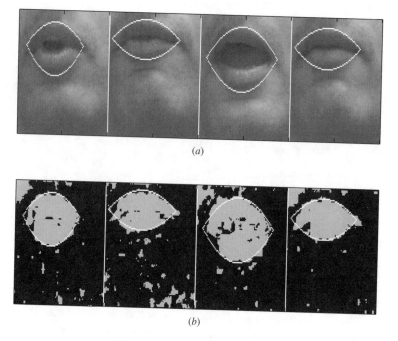

(a)

(b)

Figure 20.9 Tracking results.

20.4.3.1 Real-Time Implementation

A real-time implementation of our system functions as follows [42]. First, the subject aligns his mouth with a pair of parabolas pre-drawn on the screen. When a button is pressed, the parameters of the pdf's for the foreground and background are estimated. We model the foreground and background pdf's as Gaussian mixtures with two Gaussians per mixture. At least two mixtures are needed because one would expect different statistical characteristics for pixels in the lips and for those in the mouth opening. Therefore, a unimodal distribution would not suffice.

The analysis system tracks the shape and position of the mouth through successive video frames. For each new frame, our system must compute the following quantity for every pixel:

$$P(x, y) = \log[b_{bg}(I(x, y))] - \log[b_{fg}(I(x, y))] \tag{3}$$

Since evaluating this quantity is an intensive task, a lookup table is used to store all the possible values of the log likelihood quantity. This lookup table is filled once the pdf's are trained in the initial frame. Therefore, converting an input image into one log likelihood image only involves indexing into the lookup table.

Once we have the log likelihood image, we can find the template parameter λ, which maximizes the quantity in Eq. (2). This is equivalent to minimizing:

$$f(\lambda) = \sum_{(x,y)\epsilon fg} P(x, y) \tag{4}$$

This minimization of $f(\lambda)$ is done using a log search. Our parameter, λ, is five-dimensional, so given an initial value, we find the new minimum by perturbing the first dimension ± 8 pixels, evaluating $f(\lambda)$ at these points and choosing the minimum location. Then we perturb the second dimension and find the new minimum, all the way down the line. When all five dimensions are finished, we reduce the step size to 4, then to 2, then to 1. This method is similar to the logarithmic search used in block matching algorithms.

Sample results from our mouth tracking algorithm are shown in Fig. 20.9. The bottom image shows points for which $P(x, y) < 0$. This corresponds to points that are more likely to be part of the foreground.

20.5 JOINT AUDIO-VIDEO PROCESSING

For the coding of talking-head sequences, audio-coding researchers and video-coding researchers have been working independently so far. Even the perceptual quality evaluation of audio coding and video coding has often been separate. With audiovisual interaction considered, it is clear that at the very least, bimodal perceptual quality tests should be examined while evaluating video or audio coding standards [1,53]. In this section, we present some recent work in joint audio-video processing. A new research trend is joint audio-video coding [26,41,48]. We will explain how the coding of talking-head video is facilitated by taking into account the associated speech information.

20.5.1 Cross-Modal Predictive Coding

Predictive coding of video has traditionally used information from previous video frames to help construct an estimate of the current frame. The difference between the original and estimated signal can then be transmitted to allow the receiver to reconstruct the original video frame. This method has proven extremely useful for removing the temporal redundancy in video. Similarly, we can explore methods that remove cross-modal redundancy. The basic premise is that information in the acoustic signal can be used to help predict what the video signal should look like. If the audio indicated that a vowel is being said, one could predict that the person's mouth is open. Similarly, if the audio indicated that a /p/, /b/, or /m/ were being spoken, one could predict that the person's mouth is closed. Since the acoustic data are also transmitted, the receiver is able to reconstruct the video with little side information. Some sample data are shown in Fig. 20.10. This graph shows that similar sounds have similar lip shapes. Notice that all the AXR sounds are clustered in the middle, the AA sounds in the upper middle, the IH sounds in the right, and the closed mouth sounds (e.g., /p/, /b/, and /m/) in the lower left.

The cross-modal predictive coding process is shown in Fig. 20.11. In this coding system, an acoustic to visual predictor estimates a visual parameter set, such as mouth height and width, given the acoustic data. The video analysis routine measures the actual parameter set from the image. The measured parameter set is compared with the

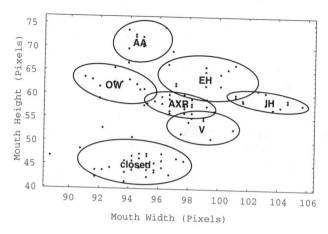

Figure 20.10   Clustering of various sounds (in ARPABET representation) in the visual parameter space.

parameter set estimated from the acoustics, and the encoder decides what information must be sent based on rate-distortion criteria. Therefore, if the acoustic data lead to a good prediction, no data have to be sent. If the prediction is slightly off, an error signal can be sent. If the prediction is completely wrong, the measured parameter set can be sent directly. The system in Fig. 20.11 also provides a coding scheme that is scalable to a wide range of bit rates. When the bit rate is high enough, the mouth parameters can be transmitted. At a very low bit rate, nothing needs to be transmitted except the audio signal.

20.5.1.1 Acoustic to Visual Mapping

The most important part of cross-modal predictive coding is a reliable acoustic to visual conversion system. In [41], a classification/mapping strategy as shown in Fig. 20.12 was

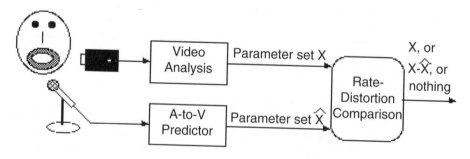

Figure 20.11   Cross-modal predictive coding.

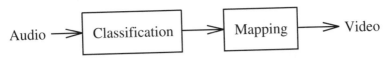

Figure 20.12 Classification-based conversion strategy.

used. This strategy breaks the conversion from acoustics to video into a two-step process. First, the acoustics are classified into one of a number of groups. Then the visual centroid corresponding to the group is output. Each member of a particular acoustic class is mapped to the same visual output.

A method based on joint clustering of the audiovisual features has also been developed [43]. The probability distribution of the joint audiovisual vectors was modeled using Gaussian mixtures. With this parametric model for the joint probability of audio and video, it is possible to analytically derive the optimal estimate of the video given the audio. Consider estimating a single visual parameter, v, given the acoustic vector $\mathbf{a}$, where a Gaussian mixture density, $f_{av}(\mathbf{a}, v)$, with K mixtures governs the joint distribution of $\mathbf{a}$, v:

$$f_{av}(\mathbf{a}, v) = \sum_{i=1}^{K} c_i \mathcal{N}(\mu_i, \mathbf{R}_i) \tag{5}$$

c_i is the mixture weight, and $\mathcal{N}(\mu_i, \mathbf{R}_i)$ is a Gaussian density with mean, μ_i, and correlation matrix, $\mathbf{R}_i$. The optimal estimate of v given $\mathbf{a}$ is then given by

$$\hat{v} = E[v|\mathbf{a}] = \int v \frac{f_{av}(\mathbf{a}, v)}{f_a(\mathbf{a})} dv \tag{6}$$

A simple illustration of prediction based on mixtures is shown in Fig. 20.13. Here a mixture with two components models the distribution of the two-dimensional data. The 1-σ, 2-σ, and 3-σ curves for each component are plotted as elliptical contours. The dotted staircase plot shows the optimal y value for each x using a classification-based strategy with five classes. The solid line shows the optimal y value for each x using a mixture-based approach. One obvious advantage of the mixture-based approach is the more accurate estimation. Another advantage is the continuity of the estimate. For example, consider an input that is oscillating between 4 and 6. The output would jitter between the two reconstruction levels if a classification-based approach was used. The mixture-based approach would lead to smooth variations.

20.5.1.2 *Example Results*

The experiment we performed consisted of gathering audiovisual data while the subject repeatedly cycled through four different vowel sounds. We trained two different systems to predict the video from the audio. The first involved a classification/mapping strategy. The acoustic training data were used to train a vector quantizer with eight classes, and for each

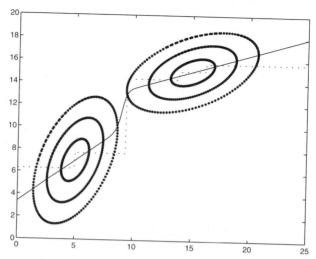

Figure 20.13 Synthetic example using two-dimensional data with two mixture components with optimal prediction functions (dotted–classification, solid–mixture modeling). Ellipses show equiprobable contours.

class, the centroid of the corresponding visual data was used as the reconstruction value for all data in that class. The second strategy involved training a Gaussian mixture on the joint audiovisual data.

Shown in Fig. 20.14 (top) is the result of predicting the lip height from the acoustics using the optimal prediction strategy for a Gaussian mixture strategy. The solid line is the original signal, and the dotted line is the estimate. The noise is filtered out by median filtering. As Fig. 20.14 shows, this estimate performs well in tracking peaks and valleys in the original waveform. This is compared with the classification/mapping strategy in Fig. 20.14 (bottom). The classification strategy results in the averaging of visual centroids, which makes it difficult to reproduce peaks and valleys in the visual signal.

20.5.2 Speech-Assisted Motion Compensation

For motion-compensated predictive coding, the prediction error is typically large around the mouth area, because the mouth is the most active area in a talking head video sequence. Its relatively small dimensions also create problems for block-based motion estimation. With speech information, it has been shown that a better prediction of the mouth can be obtained [7,10,26].

20.5.3 Bimodal Person Authentication/ Identification

Speech recognition has been used for speaker verification and identification. This can be combined with face recognition for better accuracy. Furthermore, the voice and lip

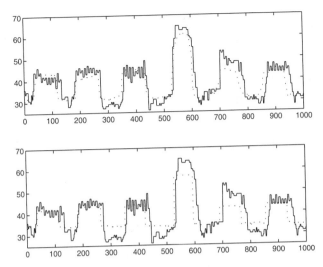

Figure 20.14 Comparison of reconstruction using optimal prediction using Gaussian mixtures (top), and classification/mapping (bottom).

movements can be used jointly for even more secure person authentication/identification [11].

20.6 CONCLUSIONS

Although we live in a world of multimedia where we have audiovisual media and audiovisual transmission in everyday life, so far speech researchers and image researchers have been working independently. Once we break down the boundary between speech research and image research, we can invent a large number of new techniques and applications. In addition to the techniques we described in this chapter, the marriage of speech processing and image processing can be useful in several other directions, a number of which are outlined as follows:

1. *Bit-rate allocation for audiovisual coding:* The interaction between audio and video goes beyond the issue of lip synchronization. For example, the bit-rate allocation between audio and video remains an important issue for audiovisual communications.

2. *Perception-based frame-skipping:* A typical video coder skips frames without coding them to save bits. The decision on which frames to skip is based on the available bit rate. For better lip synchronization, frame-skipping should be controlled by the perceptual importance of mouth shapes and the ease of speech-assisted interpolation at the decoder. For example, the encoder can avoid skipping frames that are crucial for lip synchronization, for example, frames that contain mouth closures.

3. *Removal of redundancy in videotapes:* In educational tapes that include talks and lectures, there is much redundancy such as unnecessary pauses or hesitation or disfluency

due to repeated words and self-correction. If these can be removed based on the results of speech detection/recognition, the storage can be reduced, the viewing time can be shortened, and the fluency can be improved. In particular, we can design an activity detector that evaluates the activity in both the audio and video channels, and clip out those portions in which the activity is low.

4. *Interaction between speech and expression:* We can try to extract expressions, for example, happiness or sadness, from speech and generating corresponding facial images. We can exploit the interaction between speech and face images further. For example, people tend to blink their eyes at the end of a sentence, raise their brow when they raise the pitch of their voice, open their mouth wider when they raise their volume, and so on.

References

[1] Bellcore, "Experimental Combined Audio/video Subjective Test Method," ITU-T Study Group 12, SGC/12-01, Feb. 1994.

[2] K. W. Berger, *Speechreading: Principles and Methods*, pp. 73–107, Baltimore: National Educational Press, 1972.

[3] P. J. Bloom, "High-quality Digital Audio in the Entertainment Industry: An Overview of Achievements and Challenges," *IEEE ASSP Magazine*, pp. 2–25, Oct. 1985.

[4] C. Bregler and Y. Konig, " 'Eigenlips' for Robust Speech Recognition," *ICASSP 94, Australia*, 1994.

[5] N. N. Brooke, and Q. Summerfield, "Analysis, Synthesis, and Perception of Visible Articulatory Movements," *Journal of Phonetics*, Vol. 11, pp. 63–76, 1983.

[6] R. Brunelli and T. Poggio, "Face Recognition: Features versus Templates," *IEEE Transactions on PAMI*, Vol. 15, No. 10, pp. 1042–1052, Oct. 1993.

[7] T. Chen, H. P. Graf, and K. Wang, "Speech-assisted Video Processing: Interpolation and Low-bitrate Coding," *28th Annual Asilomar Conference on Signals, Systems, and Computers*, Pacific Grove, CA, pp. 975–979, Oct. 1994.

[8] T. Chen, H. P. Graf, and K. Wang, "Lip-synchronization Using Speech-assisted Video Processing," *IEEE Signal Processing Letters*, Vol. 2, No. 4, pp. 57–59, Apr. 1995.

[9] T. Chen, H. P. Graf, H. Chen, W. Chou, B. Haskell, E. Petajan, and Y. Wang, "Lip Synchronization in Talking Head Video Utilizing Speech Information," *SPIE VCIP*, Taipei, Taiwan, May 1995.

[10] T. Chen and R. Rao, "Audio-visual Interaction in Multimedia: From Lip Synchronization to Joint Audio-video Coding," *IEEE Circuits and Devices Magazine*, Nov. 1995.

[11] M. R. Civanlar and T. Chen, "Joint Use of Audio and Video for Authentication," to be presented at the *Ninth IEEE IMDSP Workshop*, Belize, Mar. 1996.

[12] D. J. Dekle, C. A. Fowler, and M. G. Funnell, "Audiovisual Integration in Perception of Real Words," *Perception and Psychophysics*, Vol. 51, No. 4, pp. 355–362, 1992.

[13] B. Dodd and R. Campbell, *Hearing by Eye: The Psychology of Lipreading*, Hillsdale, NJ: Lawrence Erlbaum Associates.

[14] R. D. Easton and M. Basala, "Perceptual Dominance During Lipreading," *Perception and Psychophysics*, Vol. 32, pp. 562–570, 1982.

[15] P. Ekman and W. Friesen, *The Facial Action Coding System,* San Francisco: Consulting Psychologists Press, 1978.

[16] A. J. Goldschen, *Continuous Automatic Speech Recognition by Lipreading*, Ph.D. Dissertation, George Washington University, Sept. 1993.

[17] H. P. Graf, T. Chen, E. D. Petajan, and E. Cosatto, "Locating Faces and Facial Parts," Intl. Workshop on Automatic Face- and Gesture-Recognition, Zurich, Switzerland, June 1995.

[18] P. Griffin and H. Noot, "FERSA-Lip-Synchronous Animation," Lecture Notes in Computer Science, V. 1024, pp. 528–529, 1995.

[19] L. Hughes and T. Chen, "Morphing Images to Generate Talking Head Sequence," Technical Memorandum, AT&T Bell Laboratories, Aug. 1995.

[20] H. Hunke, "Locating and Tracking of Human Faces with Neural Networks," Technical Report CMU-CS-94-155, Carnegie Mellon University, Aug. 1994.

[21] M. Kass, A. Witkin, and D. Terzopoulos, "Snakes: Active Contour Models," *Proc. Int'l Conf. on Computer Vision*, pp. 259–268, London, 1987.

[22] C. Kervrann and F. Heitz, "Robust Tracking of Stochastic Deformable Models in Long Image Sequences," *ICIP 94*, pp. 88–92, Austin, TX, 1994.

[23] A. Lanitis, C. Taylor, and T. Cootes, "Automatic Tracking, Coding and Reconstruction of Human Faces, Using Flexible Appearance Models," *Electronic Letters*, Vol. 30, No. 19, pp. 1587–1588, Sept. 1994.

[24] F. Lavagetto and S. Curinga, "Object-oriented Scene Modeling for Interpersonal Video Communication at Very-low Bit-rate," *Signal Processing: Image Communication*, Vol. 6, No. 5, pp. 379–395, 1994.

[25] F. Lavagetto, "Converting Speech into Lip Movements: A Multimedia Telephone for Hard of Hearing People," *IEEE Trans. on Rehabilitation Engineering*, Vol. 3, No. 1, pp. 1–14, Mar. 1995.

[26] F. Lavagetto, "Speech-assisted Motion Compensation in Videophone Communications," *Symp. on Multimedia Communication and Video Coding*, New York, Oct. 1995.

[27] A. Lippman, "Semantic Bandwidth Compression: Speechmaker," *Picture Coding Symp.*, June 1981.

[28] M. Mak and W. Allen, "A Lip-tracking System Based on Morphological Processing and Block Matching Techniques," *Signal Processing: Image Communication*, Vol. 6, No. 4, pp. 335–348, Aug. 1994.

[29] P. Maragos and R. Schafer, "Morphological Systems for Multidimensional Signal Processing," *Proceedings of the IEEE*, Vol. 78, No. 4, pp. 690–709, Apr. 1990.

[30] K. Mase and A. Pentland, "Automatic Lipreading by Optical-flow Analysis," *Systems and Computers in Japan*, Vol. 22, No. 6, pp. 67–75, 1991.

[31] H. McGurk and J. MacDonald, "Hearing Lips and Seeing Voices," *Nature*, Vol. 164, pp. 746–748, Dec. 1976.

[32] S. Morishima, K. Aizawa, and H. Harashima, "An Intelligent Facial Image Coding Driven by Speech and Phoneme," *Proc. IEEE ICASSP*, p. 1795, Glasgow, Scotland, 1989.

[33] K. Otani and T. Hasegawa, "The Image Input Microphone—A New Nonacoustic Speech Communication System by Media Conversion from Oral Motion Images to Speech," *IEEE Journal on Selected Areas in Communications*, Vol. 13, No. 1, pp. 42–48, Jan. 1995.

[34] F. I. Parke, "Parameterised Models for Facial Animation," *IEEE Computer Graphics and Applications*, Vol. 12, pp. 61–68, Nov. 1982.

[35] E. D. Petajan, "Automatic Lipreading to Enhance Speech Recognition," Ph.D. thesis, University of Illinois at Urbana-Champaign, 1984.

[36] E. D. Petajan, "Automatic Lipreading to Enhance Speech Recognition," *IEEE Global Telecommunications Conference*, pp. 265–272, Atlanta, GA, Nov. 1984.

[37] E. D. Petajan, B. Bischoff, D. Bodoff, and N. M. Brooke, "An Improved Automatic Lipreading System to Enhance Speech Recognition," *CHI 88*, pp. 19–25, 1988.

[38] K. Prasad, D. Stork, and G. Wolff, "Preprocessing Video Images for Neural Learning of Lipreading," Tech. Report CRC-TR-9326, Ricoh California Research Center, Sept. 1993.

[39] L. R. Rabiner and B. H. Juang, *Fundamentals of Speech Recognition*, Englewood Cliffs, NJ: Prentice Hall, 1993.

[40] R. Rao and R. Mersereau, "On Merging Hidden Markov Models with Deformable Templates," *ICIP 95*, Washington, DC, 1995.

[41] R. Rao and T. Chen, "Cross-Modal Predictive Coding," *Symp. on Multimedia Communication and Video Coding*, New York, Oct. 1995.

[42] R. Rao, T. Chen, R. M. Mersereau, and R. Andersson, "Towards a Real-time Model Based Coding System," *IEEE IMDSP Workshop*, Belize, Mar. 1996.

[43] R. Rao and T. Chen, "Exploiting Audio-visual Correlation in Coding of Talking Head Sequences," *Picture Coding Symposium*, Melbourne, Australia, Mar. 1996.

[44] M. Reinders, P. Beek, B. Sankur, and J. van der Lubbe, "Facial Feature Localization and Adaptation of a Generic Face Model for Model-based Coding," *Signal Processing: Image Communication*, Vol. 7, No. 1, pp. 57–74, Mar. 1995.

[45] M. Rydfalk, "CANDIDE: A Parameterized Face," Report LiTH-ISY-I-0866, Linköping University, Oct. 1987.

[46] H. Sako, M. Whitehouse, A. Smith, A., and A. Sutherland, "Real-time Facial Feature Tracking Based on Matching Techniques and Its Application," *Proceedings 12th IAPR Conf. on Pattern Recognition*, pp. 320–324, 1994.

[47] D. Shah, S. Marshall, and W. Welsh, "Principal Component Coding of Mouth Sequences, *ICASSP 93*, Minneapolis, MN, pp. 373–376, 1993.

[48] D. Shah and S. Marshall, "Multi-modality Coding System for Videophone Application," *WIASIC '94*, Berlin, Germany, Oct. 1994.

[49] P. L. Silsbee and A. C. Bovik, "Medium-vocabulary Audio-visual Speech Recognition," NATO-ASI BUBION, 1993.

[50] P. Silsbee, "Motion in Deformable Templates," ICIP 94, pp. 323–327, Austin, TX, 1994.

[51] Q. Summerfield, "Lipreading and Audio-visual Speech Perception," *Phil. Trans. R. Soc. Lond.*, B., pp. 71–78, 1992.

[52] M. Turk, and A. Pentland, "Face Recognition Using Eigenfaces," *Proceedings of IEEE CVPR*, pp. 586–591, June 1991.

[53] S. Voran and S. Wolf, "Proposed Framework for Subjective Audiovisual Testing," ANSI Working Group T1A1.5, T1A1.5/93-151, Nov. 1993.

[54] K. Waters and T. M. Levergood, "DECface: An Automatic Lip-synchronization Algorithm for Synthetic Faces," Technical Report, DEC Cambridge Research Lab, Sept. 1993.

[55] W. J. Welsh, A. D. Simons, R. A. Hutchinson, and S. Searby, "A Speech-driven 'Talking-head' in Real Time," *Picture Coding Symp.*, pp. 7.6-1–7.6-2, 1990.

[56] W. J. Welsh, A. D. Simons, R. A. Hutchinson, and S. Searby, "Synthetic Face Generation for Enhancing a User Interface," *Proc. Image Com Conf.*, pp. 177–182, Bordeaux, Nov. 1990.

[57] G. Wolberg, *Digital Image Warping*, IEEE Computer Society Press, Los Alamitos, CA, 1990.

[58] A. Yuille, P. Hallinan, and D. Cohen, "Feature Extraction from Faces Using Deformable Templates," *International Journal of Computer Vision*, Vol. 8, No. 2, pp. 99–111, 1992.

INDEX

ABOUT THE EDITORS

Bing Sheu is a member of the Electrical Engineering Department at the University of Southern California. He is Chair of Colloquium Series and Publications in Integrated Media Systems Center (IMSC) and NSF Engineering Research Center in the multimedia field. He has published more than 180 papers in international scientific and technical journals and conferences, and is coauthor of the book *Neural Information Processing and VLSI* (1995) from Kluwer Academic Publishers, and coeditor of *Microsystems Technology for Multimedia Applications* (1995) from IEEE Press. He was Technical Program Chair of the 1996 IEEE ICNN Conference and Technical Program Chair of the 1997 International Conference on Computer Design. He is Editor-in-Chief of *IEEE Transactions on VLSI Systems*, 1997–1999, and Guest Editor of the *Multimedia Special Issue* (June 1997) in the IEEE T-CSVT Journal. Dr. Sheu was elected a Fellow of IEEE in 1996.

Mohammed Ismail is a professor in the Electrical Engineering Department at Ohio State University. Previously, he held several positions in both industry and academia and served as a corporate consultant to nearly 20 companies in the United States and abroad. Dr. Ismail has authored many publications in silicon circuit design and signal processing, and has been awarded several patents in the area of analog integrated circuits. He co-edited and coauthored several books including *Analog VLSI Signal and Information Processing* (1994) from McGraw-Hill. He is Editor-in-Chief of *Journal of Analog ICs and Signal Processing* from Kluwer Academic Publishers. Dr. Ismail was the recipient of the 1984 IEEE Outstanding Teacher Award, the 1985 NSF Presidential Young Investigator Award, the 1993 OSU Lumley Research Award, and the 1992/1993 SRC Inventor Recognition Awards. Dr. Ismail was elected a Fellow of IEEE in 1997.

Assistant Editors

Michelle Y. Wang received the B.S.E.E. and M.S.E.E. degrees from Tsinghua University in Beijing, China, in 1992 and 1994, respectively. Since August 1995, she has been a researcher at the VLSI Multimedia Laboratory in the Integrated Media Systems Center (IMSC), an NSF/Engineering Research Center at the University of Southern California. Ms. Wang assisted the instruction of two graduate-level courses in multimedia systems and technology in 1995–1996. Her research interests are image and signal processing, low-power VLSI system design, and intelligent microsystems.

Richard H. Tsai received the B.S.E.E. and M.S.E.E. degrees from National Taiwan University in Taipei, Taiwan, in 1990 and 1992, respectively. Since August 1994, he has been a researcher at the VLSI Multimedia Laboratory in the Integrated Media Systems Center (IMSC), an NSF/Engineering Research Center at the University of Southern California. Mr. Tsai taught an electronics laboratory course in the Fall of 1996. His research interests include multimedia, neural networks, and mixed-signal VLSI system design.